DEDICATION

To Cathy Dow-Royer
JMR

To my mother, Leah Radler Brochstein,
and the memory of my father, Saul D. Feldman
RSF

EDUCATIONAL PSYCHOLOGY

APPLICATIONS AND THEORY

EDUCATIONAL PSYCHOLOGY

APPLICATIONS AND THEORY

James M. Royer
University of Massachusetts

Robert S. Feldman
University of Massachusetts

Alfred A. Knopf, Inc. New York

First Edition
987654321

Copyright © 1984 by Alfred A. Knopf, Inc.

Library of Congress Cataloging in Publication Data

Royer, James M., 1941–
    Educational psychology.
    Bibliography: p.
    Includes index.
    1. Educational psychology.   I. Feldman, Robert S.
(Robert Stephen), 1947–   . II. Title.
LB1051.R689   1983   370.15   83-19642
ISBN 0-394-32380-7

Manufactured in the United States of America

Cover photograph: © Dan McCoy/Rainbow

PREFACE
To the Instructor

In most educational psychology textbooks, there is little relationship between the educational techniques and methodologies discussed within the book and the way the book itself functions as an educational tool. In this text, however, we have indeed practiced what we have preached.

In writing the text, we were guided by the philosophy that theory, research, and practice in educational psychology are inextricably intertwined, and that a thorough understanding of each is required before a student can be considered to have mastered the field. Therefore, every chapter presents theoretical explanations of phenomena relevant to education, examples of research that supports or disproves such theories, and practical applications of the theories and research findings.

The book contains a number of features that distinguish it from most introductory educational psychology texts.

- It covers the breadth of the field in an eclectic manner, instead of following the dictates of one theoretical orientation. Rather, the strengths and weaknesses of different positions are presented in a way that is representative of current thinking in the field of educational psychology.
- The field of educational psychology is covered more broadly and with more comprehensiveness than is typical of an introductory text. We focus not only on instructional processes, but also on schools and education as they relate to society and culture.
- We have tried to present material in a clear, direct, and engaging style, but without glossing over inconsistencies that are the product of an evolving science.
- We have given careful attention to appropriate examples and analogies and provided a logical sequencing of materials.
- This book embodies good science. The content is up-to-date, and the material is representative of the state-of-the-art in educational psychology.
- The book is geared not just to potential teachers, but to anyone with a broad interest in education. We feel that the discipline of educational psychology has relevance both for teachers *and* for students, so both perspectives are taken into account in this text. Thus, the practical examples that we present are drawn from across the educational spectrum, ranging from preschool to college, and even to education involving the elderly.
- Although the book is formally a "first edition," it is far from a first draft. We have used earlier drafts of the manuscript with many students, and we have received detailed and in-depth feedback, which we have incorporated into subsequent revisions. We feel confident, then, that this is a book that does what we intended it to do.
- Each chapter in the text contains a number of special features, including the following:

Chapter interview. At the start of each chapter is an interview with an educator—someone with experience in the real-world aspects of the topics to be covered in the chapter.

Chapter overview. The overview presents the major topics of each chapter, organizing in advance the material to follow.

Highlights. Each chapter has a number of inserted boxes that focus on material of special interest.

Summary. The major topics of each chapter are reiterated concisely in a summary at the end of the chapter.

Further readings and applications. Each chapter closes with a list of annotated references that provide information of both a theoretical and applied nature.

- The ancillary materials—student *Study Guide* and *Instructor's Manual*—are among the best that are available for *any* text on the market today. The text, the *Study Guide*, and the *Instructor's Manual* form a versatile integrated package that may be employed in courses using a traditional, mastery-based, or Personalized System of Instruction (PSI) organization. The *Study Guide* includes objectives, goals, extensive self-tests, and chapter summaries. The *Instructor's Manual* includes chapter outlines, goals and objectives, discussion questions, field exercises, additional readings, lists of films and other audiovisual aids, and a very large test-item book in which the items are keyed to particular goals and objectives.

A great deal of thought and effort has gone into this textbook to make it an effective and interesting introduction to educational psychology. We hope you and your students will learn from it and, in the process, enjoy it.

PREFACE
To the Student

If you are reading this preface, it is likely that you have been assigned this textbook by your instructor as part of an educational psychology course. Although you are thus part of a captive audience, we hope you will feel, by the time you finish using this text, that you would have freely chosen it yourself. For we have written this book with *you*, the reader, in mind.

We have tried to make this book interesting, informative, and, ultimately, useful to all of you. This is not an easy goal to achieve, since people who enroll in educational psychology classes are a diverse lot. Many of you plan to be teachers, but quite a few do not. Moreover, the future teachers among you want to work with students of all different ages, from nursery-school age to adulthood.

Because of the different backgrounds and interests of our readers, we have employed a wide range of examples to illustrate important points. We have also tried to make all the discussions in this text reflect our belief that the field of educational psychology has direct relevance not only for teachers, but for *students* as well—and all of us play the role of student throughout our lives.

We have taken the task of writing an interesting, as well as informative and useful, book, very seriously. We have written in an informal, easy-going style so that you will want to keep reading. We have included features such as interviews with practicing educators in order to emphasize that the theories and research we discuss invariably have practical applications as well and that the teaching techniques actually used in the classroom have all grown out of theory and research. We also have field-tested earlier drafts of the text in our own educational psychology classes, and then listened to the feedback that we received in order to improve the text. Finally, we have followed the principles that we discuss in the text which have been demonstrated to enhance learning, and try to exemplify a good deal of what has been found to constitute effective teaching.

We hope you enjoy reading this book. More important, we hope you are attracted to the field of educational psychology. It has a great deal to offer.

ACKNOWLEDGMENTS

This book could not have been written without the help and encouragement of many people. We can start with Professor Harry Schumer (who also reviewed the manuscript for us) and Beth Sulzer-Azaroff, our colleagues in the educational psychology field at the University of Massachusetts, who provided a consistent, supportive, and amiable atmosphere. Our students were also crucial in maintaining our enthusiasm and excitement; these include Doug Lynch, Andy Theiss, Bucky Chesley, Cliff Konold, Jack Bates (also a reviewer), Liz Shea, John White, Chris Fox, Ben Handen, and Ronnie Salestsky.

We are also grateful to the educators whom we interviewed and featured at the start of each chapter. They gave generously of their time, and their comments supply a unique flavor for the text.

The staff at Alfred A. Knopf was extraordinarily competent and supportive. Among the people who helped us at various stages were Judith Rothman, Leslie Carr, Susan Israel, Chris Rogers, Steve Boillot, Heidi Udell, Barry Fetterolf, and Seibert Adams. We're grateful to them and proud to be Alfred A. Knopf authors.

To our intelligent, perceptive, and hard-working secretaries, Jean Glenowicz, Kate Cleary, Anne Peterson, and Alta May Miller, our gratitude is enormous.

We were graced with thoughtful, responsible reviewers. The following people read portions or all of the manuscript:

Ethel B. Albinski, *Pennsylvania State University*
Thomas Andre, *Iowa State University*
John K. Bengston, *University of Florida*
Jeffrey L. Derevensky, *McGill University*
Ron Hambleton, *University of Massachusetts*
Robert L. Hohn, *University of Kansas*
Pat Jones, *San Francisco State University*
Philip Langer, *University of Colorado*
Kathryn W. Linden, *Purdue University*
John T. Lloyd, *Washington State University*
Hubert Lovett, *Mississippi State University*
Joel Levin, *University of Wisconsin*
Martin L. Maehr, *University of Illinois*
Ann J. Pace, *University of Delaware*
Thomas S. Parish, *Kansas State University*
Walter T. Petty, *State University of New York at Buffalo*
Royce R. Ronning, *University of Nebraska*
Alan G. Slemon, *The University of Western Ontario*
Sigmund Tobias, *City University of New York*
R. Keith Van Wagenen, *Arizona State University*
Harold Wilson, *Central Missouri State University*
David C. Yang, *Louisiana State University*

The Royer half of the authorship wants to acknowledge the love and support provided by his parents, Marge and Robert Doty, and the spiritual and intellectual sustenance provided over the years by the charter members of the Gray Beard Loon Society, Don, Ray and Tom. I also want to thank Richard C. Anderson, who taught me what excellence in this business is all about. Finally, thanks to my wife, Cathy Dow-Royer, who makes it all worthwhile.

Finally, the Feldman half of the authorship wants to acknowledge the support of various generations of his family. My parents, Leah Radler Brochstein and the late Saul D. Feldman, provided inestimable contributions to this project, and I am grateful for their love and support. My children, Jonathan, Joshua, and Sarah Feldman, contribute delight, pleasure, and a new perspective on life every day. Finally, thanks go to my wife, Katherine Vorwerk, who is supportive in every way and the joy of my life.

We welcome comments and suggestions on this book. Please send them to us at the Department of Psychology, University of Massachusetts, and we will try to incorporate them into the next edition of *Educational Psychology: Appplications and Theory*.

James M. Royer
Robert S. Feldman

Amherst, Massachusetts

CONTENTS

CHAPTER 10:
Understanding and Judging Others: Attitudes, Expectations, and Person Perception 325

CHAPTER 11:
Communication Processes in the Classroom 357

CHAPTER 12:
The Cultural Context of Education 391

PART IV:
SCHOOLS AND
TEACHERS

EDUCATIONAL PSYCHOLOGY

APPLICATIONS AND THEORY

I

INTRODUCTION: INDIVIDUAL DEVELOPMENT

1

WHAT IS EDUCATIONAL PSYCHOLOGY?

CHAPTER OVERVIEW

One of the concerns frequently raised by students in educational psychology courses is that the material is not relevant to classroom teaching. We have tried to write a book that is relevant to classroom teaching, and our interviews with teachers have contributed a great deal to that effort. As we traveled around the country, speaking to teachers in widely differing schools and settings, we found many instances of educational psychology translated into practice. An interview with a teacher, like the one presented below, introduces each chapter in the book.

Verla Taylor teaches fourth grade in the Kyrene Elementary School District in Tempe, Arizona. She grew up in the Phoenix, Arizona, area, and after graduating from high school, she enrolled in Arizona State University, where she graduated with a B.A. degree in elementary education. She also has an M.A. degree in counseling education from Arizona State. In her ten years of teaching, Ms. Taylor has taught first grade, Head Start classes, and a mixed fourth- and fifth-grade class. Currently she is teaching fourth grade.

Ms. Taylor comes from a very large family where, as she says, "education was highly valued." She also says that for as long as she can remember, she wanted to be a teacher. The interview began with a question about the factors that contribute to quality education. What makes the difference between a good school and a bad school?

A.   Four factors contribute to quality education. First, the types of goals set will determine a "good" school from a "bad" school and are the foundation of quality education, high student aspiration, and achievement. Second, parental involvement and support of these goals are definitely important. A personal commitment is also needed from every staff and faculty member involved. Third, quality education is prevalent in schools with good student-teacher rapport. Finally, well-trained teachers are a key factor in quality education.

Q.   What would the ideal teacher training program look like from your point of view?

A.   I haven't really thought about this, but I would say it should involve formal book learning interwoven with working with students. When I say working with students, I mean working with students under the direct supervision of a master teacher. The problem with training programs when I went through formal training was that there was too much time lag between the book learning part and the practical part. By the time I got into the classroom, I had forgotten many of the principles I learned in class. I needed a program where I could learn and apply immediately, with no lag in between.

Q.   If you were asked to address a group of prospective teachers about the most important things involved in being a successful teacher, what would you tell them?

A.   There are several things involved in being a successful teacher. First, one has to have a true love for this profession. A prospective teacher needs to be patient, sensitive to the needs of students, and well prepared to teach. Teachers must be prepared mentally and physically to fulfill a number of roles: sometimes they are teachers, sometimes they are counselors, sometimes they are moms and dads, sometimes they are social workers. Finally, formal training in the theory and principles of child development, and actual classroom experience are essential.

Q.   Has knowledge of the theory and principles of child development been of any use to you?

A.   Yes, cognitive development, social development, emotional development, these are all things that are important to a teacher. A teacher has to understand the total child, and to understand that children are at different developmental points. It is imperative that teachers try to understand how all of the different aspects of development are interwoven to make up the total child.

Q.   Do you have to have both book learning and experience to understand development, or can you rely solely on your own personal observations and experiences?

A.   I found I needed both. I first became aware of the principles of development through books, but the books were not really meaningful to me until I gained some experience.

Q.   How about the area of special students? Most classrooms today contain some students who differ from the norm in physical characteristics and in learning abilities. Do teachers need training in how to work with these students?

A.   Having students with disabilities in a classroom makes the teacher's job more difficult—particularly for those teachers who do not have any background in this area. Personally, it doesn't bother me because my first job was working with students with a wide range of disabilities.

Q.   What do you do with behavioral problems in your classroom?

A.   That's like asking me, "What do I do with flat tires?" I fix them! But I can't just deal with the visible problem. I have to look at the total child and try to understand the cause of the problem. I've had problems with a child that surfaced because the child was hungry. Another child who seemed to be very hostile really needed a friend. Each child is different, but I try to approach every problem by understanding where a child has been, where he [she] is, and where he [she] is going.

Q.   When you are teaching, do you first develop mastery of basic material and then move on to more complicated material, or do you use some other approach?

A.   It depends on what I am trying to teach. In a subject like mathematics, for example, there are principles that build on top of one another like stacking blocks. One needs to give students a good strong foundation in an area like that. In other areas though, like social studies, it is not so clear what principles follow what. In areas like social studies, I draw a great deal on things that are happening around the world.

Q.   What do you do when you run into a problem with getting kids to understand difficult concepts?

A.   The things that are difficult for kids to learn are the things that they can't see; things that they have not experienced. To help children understand these foreign concepts, it is necessary for them to experience the things that you're trying to teach. The teacher must be very sensitive to the child's understanding. Sometimes teachers think they're teaching when all they are really doing is a lot of talking. Teaching is a two-way process: teacher-give, student-take; student-give, teacher-take. When the teacher gets the signal that the student isn't understanding, it's time to try something new or use a different approach.

Q.   Are signals always something that a student says?

A.   No. Sometimes it's the way a child looks, or the way he [she] sits. You have to look out for all kinds of signals.

Q.   Does a teacher have to know anything about the social, cultural, and ethnic backgrounds that students come from?

A. It's very important. I'm convinced that different backgrounds add to differences in children. My teaching philosophy is that one needs to understand the total child. If you don't know anything about the child's background and values, how can you know the child? I previously mentioned that I try to understand where a child is, his [her] present functioning ability, where he has been, his experiences, and where he [she] is going, his goals. Knowing something about the social, cultural, and ethnic factors is very important in understanding the total child.

Q. How important is it for a teacher to know something about educational testing?

A. I think it's very important, but sometimes I think we do too much testing. Diagnostic and placement testing are very important, but I've seen elementary students who I'm convinced are "burned-out" on testing. When I test, it's really important for me to know what I am measuring, and why I am measuring it. If I do this, I am less likely to become involved in testing for testing's sake.

Q. Does testing ever provide you with important feedback about how you are doing as a teacher?

A. Sure it does. You need a certain amount of it. You need a tool to measure student growth. You need to know how you are doing as a teacher, and testing is one way of getting the necessary feedback.

Q. Where do you get ideas for trying out new things when you are teaching?

A. Everywhere! I read. I'm always searching for new ideas. I borrow techniques from other teachers. If a technique works, I keep it; if it doesn't, I get rid of it. I am constantly searching for new ways of doing things.

Q. What closing comments would you like to pass on to future teachers?

A. I think that teaching is probably the most important and challenging career there is. A doctor takes care of your body, and a dentist takes care of your teeth. But a teacher, in many ways, takes care of the total child. I'm a teacher, a social worker, a mother, a psychologist, and a friend. I do something different every day, and I'm constantly learning and trying out new things to help my students learn. Unfortunately, I don't think teachers get the credit they deserve. Teachers are not baby-sitters—as some people seem to think. We are a great profession, and we deserve to be treated as one.

EDUCATIONAL PSYCHOLOGY DEFINED

Educational psychology is a scientific discipline that is concerned with producing general knowledge about how the educational process affects students. This knowledge takes several forms. It can be in the form of broad general principles that are useful in understanding how and why the educational process works as it does. Examples of knowledge in this form are the principles of cognitive development, the principles governing overt behavior, or generalizations about how ethnicity and social class interact with particular educational approaches.

At another level, knowledge of educational psychology can take the form of steps that can be used to produce certain educational outcomes. For example, later in this book, techniques are described for reducing the frequency of undesirable behavior in the classroom or for developing sound instructional sequences.

Another form that knowledge of educational psychology takes is "state-of-the-art" information about frequently researched topics. Knowledge in this form is not well enough established to be used as a principle or a rule. But it can be an important source of ideas about how to solve particular educational problems, and it can contribute to understanding of an event or a situation.

Areas of Educational Psychology

In the interview with Verla Taylor, a number of topics pertinent to educational psychology were raised. Such topics as child development, classroom discipline, learning, social and cultural influences in education, and educational measurement are covered, to some extent, in almost all educational psychology courses. What varies considerably from course to course, however, is the way these topics are organized. In this book the focus is on the principles of development and the relationship of instruction to development, on learning and instruction, on social factors in education, and on schools and teachers.

Development

Part I of this book is devoted to an examination of individual development. The behavior of any individual is a joint product of inherited characteristics on the one hand and learning and experience on the other. Consequently, the child's passage through a series of cognitive, social, and emotional stages, outlined in Chapter 2, is a function both of the genetically determined unfolding of a *maturational sequence* and of learned behaviors acquired through particular experiences. As indicated in the interview that began this chapter, it is very important that teachers gain some familiarity with developmental principles and with the implications of those principles for educational practice.

One application of the study of individual development to educational practice is designing educational *treatments* that meet the specific needs of individual students—a topic dealt with in Chapter 3. Classroom teachers are acutely aware that an enormous range of abilities is present in any given classroom, and in recent years, there has been considerable interest among researchers in devising educational approaches suited to the individual capabilities of students. A second application is designing individualized programs for students having unique problems or abilities. Children with emotional,

maturational sequence the series of developmental changes due principally to the appearance of inherited characteristics with the passage of time

treatments patterns of actions or manipulations of the environment in order to achieve a goal

physical, or cognitive problems, who once would have been segregated from "normal" children, have in recent years been integrated into regular classrooms. At the same time there has been an upsurge of interest in what to do with gifted children. Teachers are virtually certain to encounter unusual children of one kind or the other (probably both), and the teacher who is totally unprepared to work with these children is in for some trying experiences. Chapter 4 is concerned with the special student.

Learning and instruction

Part II of this text is concerned with learning. To a considerable extent, learning is what the educational process is all about, and it certainly is the most intensively researched topic in educational psychology. While Chapter 5 provides a general overview, Chapters 6–8 describe how three separate views of the learning process can be translated into educational practice. The first view to be considered is operant learning theory—a theory ideally suited to approaching classroom problems that involve observable behaviors. Step-by-step guidelines for translating operant learning theory into techniques of classroom management are presented in Chapter 6.

Providing positive feedback about a student's work is one key to successful teaching. (© Elizabeth Crews/Stock, Boston)

Associative learning theory, the second perspective on learning, is dealt with in Chapter 7. It provides an excellent framework for approaching classroom problems that involve the learning of basic information. The chapter outlines step-by-step procedures for developing instructional materials within the framework of associative learning theory.

Cognitive learning theory, the third perspective from which learning can be viewed is described in Chapter 8. Cognitive approaches provide valuable insights into the question of understanding, and the chapter provides guidelines for presenting instruction in such a way that it will be understood.

Social factors in education

In addition to behavioral differences attributable to inherited characteristics and individual experiences, students also differ as a function of their membership in social and cultural groups. Moreover, the differences associated with membership in these groups frequently have relevance for educational practice. Taken as a group, children from upper-class homes differ in a number of ways from middle-class children. Likewise, lower-class children differ from upper- and middle-class children.

Looking at another dimension, black children differ from white children, and children from Hispanic homes differ, on the whole, from children in the other two groups. Such differences—produced by experiences common to particular social-class, ethnic, or cultural groups—have a substantial impact on the educational process. A good many classrooms include children who vary considerably in terms of their attitude toward education, the value they set on school performance, the kind of classroom material they find relevant and interesting, and even the language they speak at home. The teacher who treats all children the same cannot hope to accomplish what might be accomplished. Part III of the book is concerned with these social and cultural differences and with ways of changing educational practice to accommodate the differences.

School and teachers

Part IV, the final section of the book is concerned with aspects of the school setting that influence the effectiveness of education, including such factors as class size and physical environment. It discusses strategies that teachers can use to enhance the quality of education.

One of the central concerns of any teacher is student motivation, and this is the first topic considered in the last section (i.e., in Chapter 13). A student who is highly motivated to learn can gain something from the worst of teachers; a student who could care less about learning is unlikely to benefit from the best of teachers. One aspect of being an excellent teacher is knowing how to motivate students. In fact, one definition of a good teacher is one who strives for, and attains, excellence by instilling in children a desire for excellence, and by presenting instruction so that it can be efficiently and meaningfully learned.

Chapter 14 deals with aspects of a school other than the quality of the

Good teaching is a mix of techniques, learned through experience, and principles, learned from scientific investigation. (© Elizabeth Crews)

teaching that can influence educational outcomes: the way a classroom is arranged, the number of students in a class, the number of students in the school, the amount of time spent in direct instruction.

Educational measurement is discussed in Chapter 15. Teachers spend far more time in developing, administering, scoring, and interpreting educational tests than may be generally realized. Testing can be overdone, but it is also an essential component of quality education. Measurement provides teachers with placement and *diagnostic information* that is useful in designing educational experiences for individual students; it provides both teachers and students with objective feedback on their performance; and it can provide information that is useful when making decisions about admission to special programs and about whether students have mastered specific educational material.

*diagnostic information
data that identify the cause or nature of a condition*

THE ROLE OF EDUCATIONAL PSYCHOLOGISTS IN HISTORICAL PERSPECTIVE

Educational psychology as a discipline has undergone a number of changes during its history in the United States. Psychology itself was first recognized as a scientific discipline in the late 1800s. The early founders of American psychology such as G. Stanley Hall and William James were very concerned with applying psychological principles to educational practice. For a number of years, Hall had taught what was called "child study" to prospective teachers, and in 1899 James published a book entitled *Talks to Teachers* that summarized what he felt psychology had to offer education.

The Educational Psychologist as Translator of Research

The early conceptualization of an educational psychologist was as a translator of psychological knowledge into educational practice. For example, the lead editorial in the first issue of the *Journal of Educational Psychology*, published in 1910, described future educational psychologists as middlemen who would mediate between the science of psychology and the art of teaching (Grinder, 1978). This view placed the educational psychologist in the role of one who provides service to the educational community. This service role can be contrasted to the role pf psychologists, who were seen as basic scientists generating the knowledge that the educational psychologist translated into practice. This view was maintained through midcentury—as is illustrated by a report prepared in 1948 for the American Psychological Association by a group of educational psychologists, who described the educational psychologist as "functioning as a scientist among teachers of education and acting, both in psychology and education, as an intermediary between pure research and its application" (Grinder, 1978, p. 287).

The Educational Psychologist as Generator of Knowledge

At the same time that the role of educational psychologist as translator of basic psychological science was developing, another, different view of the role of the educational psychologist was emerging. This role can be traced back to Edward L. Thorndike, who was a giant in early American psychology (Grinder, 1978; Feldhusen, 1978). Thorndike was a prodigious researcher who moved easily between very basic research on the learning process and applied research on problems in educational practice. Thorndike's active example, and his writings on the subject, suggested that the role of the educational psychologist was not merely to mediate between researchers and teachers but, in addition, to be an active generator of original and generalizable knowledge. This research role for educational psychologists exists for at least two reasons. First, basic psychological knowledge can rarely be translated directly into educational practice. Frequently, there has to be intermediate research that examines the feasibility of translating basic knowledge into practice. And second, very worthwhile research questions can emerge from the educational context itself; therefore, not all of the research findings to be put into practice need have their origin in the basic psychologist's laboratory.

The Roles Assumed by Today's Educational Psychologists

Educational psychologists today are active in both of the roles described (see, for example, Feldhusen, DiVesta, Thornburg, Levin, and Ringness, 1976). Educational psychologists serving the function of translators of knowledge into practice are active in schools, in universities and colleges, in research institutions, in government, and in industry. Many large school districts employ educational psychologists to direct in-house research and evaluation efforts, to evaluate and make recommendations about curriculum materials and instructional procedures, and to advise teachers about approaches to educational problems. Educational psychologists in universities and colleges who are in the role of translators of knowledge are typically involved in teacher preparation programs. They keep a close watch on new findings in the research literature and incorporate those findings into teacher training programs. Other educational psychologists in the translator's role work in research institutions, in government, or in industry. There their role might be to lend their expertise to such activities as the development of curriculum materials or training procedures, the evaluation of instructional approaches, the selection of individuals to fill certain positions, or the formulation of answers to specific questions.

Educational psychologists who generate original knowledge can also be found in a number of settings. As might be expected, most educational psychologists in this role are to be found in large universities that emphasize original research. However, they can also be found in research institutions that obtain either contracts or grants to conduct basic research, and in private firms that are paid to perform research.

Many educational psychologists assume only one of the roles described. But there are also a good many who move back and forth between the roles during their careers, and even some who assume both roles simultaneously. Educational psychologists in universities, for example, frequently are heavily involved in research while at the same time being involved in teacher training and teacher in-service programs.

THE METHODS OF EDUCATIONAL PSYCHOLOGY

The goal of educational psychology is to produce knowledge that can be used to understand, predict, and control the way in which education affects an individual. To achieve this goal, educational psychologists and other researchers use a variety of research methods, each of which brings with it several advantages and disadvantages. Some research methods operate with great precision, yielding conclusions about which there would be little disagreement. But frequently this precision is obtained at the expense of being able to generalize beyond the particular subjects used in the study. For example, research findings may be applicable only to students with certain characteristics, or only to a relatively narrrow range of educational settings. At the other extreme are research methods that have considerable generality; but they involve a great deal of imprecision, which results in conclusions that are tentative at best. The advantages and limitations of each research method must be recognized and a method chosen that most directly addresses the research question of concern, yields the greatest generality, and provides the firmest conclusions.

The Case Study Method

The *case study method* involves the intensive study of a single individual or, in some cases, a group of individuals. The purpose of a case study is to acquire as much information as possible about the person or persons being studied. This information is obtained either in the form of a *case history*—consisting of memories, historical records, and other sources of information—or in the form of *longitudinal records*—data obtained by observing an individual or group of individuals over a long period of time, as is described in the accompanying box.

In educational settings, the case study method is most likely to be used by a school psychologist who is attempting to deal with a specific problem displayed by a specific student. For example, a school psychologist working with a student who has severe behavior problems might collect information about the student's home life, previous educational history, aptitudes and interests (as measured by psychological tests), and attitudes, emotions, and goals (through interviews and counseling sessions). All of this material can then be used to devise a treatment program for the student.

Strengths and weaknesses of the case study method

Case studies provide important and useful information about the individual or individuals being studied. In addition, they occasionally provide insights that are useful in understanding the behavior of individuals other than those under study. For example, Sigmund Freud used the case study method as a source of data and hypotheses while developing his revolutionary theory of human behavior. However, use of the case study method to *generalize* beyond the individual being studied is the exception rather than the rule. Saying that scientific information is generalized means that information collected in one situation is assumed to be applicable to other situations. Usually, the knowledge gained from the case study method cannot be confidently applied to another individual or another group. For instance, we may learn via a case study that

case history information such as memoirs or historical records that is collected for the investigation of an individual or group

longitudinal records data obtained by observing individuals or groups over a long period of time

Lewis Terman's Longitudinal Study of Genius

In 1921, Lewis Terman began a longitudinal study of genius that continues to this day, over twenty years after Terman's death. Terman identified 1,528 youngsters (857 boys and 671 girls) from the state of California who had scored 140 or above on the Stanford-Binet intelligence test. The youngsters ranged in age from 3 to 19 years, and in IQ from 140 to 200; and they came from a wide variety of backgrounds. Follow-up studies of the group were conducted in 1927, 1936, 1939, 1945, 1950, 1955, and 1960. Future studies will examine the children and grandchildren of members of the original groups.

During the years the study has been under way, data have been collected on subsequent school history, job attainment and job progress, salary, physical and psychiatric history, marriage, children, police record (if any), and distinctions and awards attained. The following are some of the findings from the study:

- Contrary to the stereotype of the "puny" and "crazy" genius, Terman's subjects were taller than, and physically and mentally healthier than, the average person.
- As a group, Terman's subjects had remarkable educational careers. Over half of them went on to graduate school, and approximately 16 percent of the group completed a Ph.D. or other doctoral degree.
- The group published over 2,000 scientific and technical papers, 60 books and monographs, 33 novels, 375 short stories and plays, and over 300 essays, critiques, sketches, and articles on a variety of subjects.
- Not all of the individuals in the group were successful. Approximately 15 percent of the original sample were "failures by the usual standards extant in our society" (Matarazzo, 1972, p. 183). This group included individuals who had not finished high school, who earned incomes well below the national average, who had committed suicide, who were alcoholics or homosexuals, or who had spent considerable time under psychiatric care; and it included three individuals who had police records.

The Terman study has provided a wealth of information about genius as measured by intelligence tests. It is obvious that having a high IQ is related to success in later life. But it is equally obvious that this relationship is not causal in nature. Some individuals having high measured intelligence do not succeed in later life, and a good many individuals who *do not* have a high IQ succeed just as well as those who do (Matarazzo, 1972).

a particular child learns best when taught in a particular way. But that does not mean that another child will learn equally well with the method. As an example, some students make remarkable progress if allowed to work independently and at their own pace. Other students learn best in group instructional situations. This means that a finding about method of instruction cannot be generalized to all students.

In addition to having limited generalizability, the case study has another important limitation: a cause-effect relationship cannot be established using the method. Cause-effect relationships are the basic building blocks of science, and it is important to understand what they are. When one event is said to cause another, the assertion is being made that the second will happen because the first has occurred. So, for example, one can say that drinking a sufficient quantity of alcohol *causes* the state called intoxication, or as another example, that the presence of active tuberculous bacilli in the lungs causes the disease state called tuberculosis.

generalize to derive or induce a common principle from particulars

Education isn't restricted to the young. It continues throughout our lives. (© Bettye Lane/Photo Researchers)

An Observational Study of Early Elementary Education

Project Follow-Through was a very large-scale research effort conducted for an 11-year period, beginning in the late 1960s, that was designed to develop effective early educational approaches for children from disadvantaged backgrounds. Part of the research effort was an observational study of classroom settings and activities. The study, which was directed by Dr. Jane Stallings, a psychologist at Stanford Research Institute, involved observing a total of 136 first-grade classrooms and 137 third-grade classrooms for 15 hours spread over 3 days (this amounts to a total of about 4,100 hours of observations).

The observers used three instruments in their observations. The first instrument recorded aspects of the physical environment, including such features as materials available to the students and the seating arrangements in the classrooms. The second instrument recorded the grouping of the children (e.g., large-group versus small-group instruction), the way the teaching staff were distributed in the classrooms, and the type and duration of teaching activity being conducted (e.g., math instruction, reading instruction, etc.). The last instrument recorded the nature of the interactions that occurred between adults and children. This included recording the person who initiated the interaction (student, teacher, aide), the nature of the interaction (e.g., question, direction, etc.), the person to whom the communication was directed (teacher, student, aide), and several other aspects of classroom interactions. The following are some of the more important findings from the study (Stallings, 1976):

It is necessary to distinguish cause-effect relationships from correlational relationships. For many years, it was thought that intelligence declined with age after one reached adulthood. The evidence for this conclusion seemed fairly clear-cut: when the intelligence of randomly selected groups of 20-year-olds, 30-year-olds, 40-year-olds, 50-year-olds, and 60-year-olds was measured, a slight but steady decline in intelligence from the youngest group to the oldest group was apparent—hence the conclusion that advancing age *causes* a decline in intelligence. It turns out though that the advancing age/intelligence relationship is correlational rather than causational. A number of years ago, investigators noted that randomly selected older groups have had less formal education than randomly selected younger groups. For instance, a fairly large

- The more time that was spent on instruction in reading and math, the better the performance.
- Classrooms in which the teacher frequently asked questions and gave immediate positive feedback for correct answers performed higher in reading measures than classrooms where these conditions were less frequent.
- Students in classrooms where teachers delivered frequent praise for good performance tended to do better in mathematics than students in classrooms where praise was less frequent.
- Students in classrooms where a wide variety of materials were present, where many different activities were available to students, and where flexible scheduling of curriculum activities was practiced tended to perform better on measures of nonverbal problem solving than did students in less flexible classrooms.
- Absenteeism was lower in classrooms where students and teachers frequently laughed and smiled.
- Absenteeism was higher in classrooms where the predominant instructional style was large-group instruction.
- Absenteeism was higher in classrooms where punishment was a common classroom practice.

Note that all of the findings are stated in terms of *relationships* between a classroom characteristic and an educational outcome. Thus a relationship between the factors is demonstrated, but no claim is made that one factor *causes* another.

proportion of 60-year-olds have not graduated from high school. In contrast, the proportion of 20-year-olds who have not graduated from high school is much smaller. Having noted this, researchers conducted studies in which groups varying in age were matched on educational level. The result was no difference in intelligence between the groups. That is, intelligence did not decline with age. This means that advancing age merely happened to be accidentally correlated with level of education, the factor that actually caused the decline (Baltes and Schaie, 1974).

All sciences—including educational psychology—strive to establish cause-effect relationships between events. The case study method does not allow the establishment of cause-effect relationships because too many events are varying simultaneously. The individual under study is experiencing many events at the same time and it cannot be said with certainty that any *one* of the events is causing particular behavior to occur. It can only be said that the occurrence of one or more of the events is *related* to (or correlated with) the subsequent behavior. In contrast, the experimental method, which is examined in a later section, provides a means of determining *which* of several simultaneously occurring events is responsible for producing subsequent behavior.

The Naturalistic-Observation Method

naturalistic observation a method of studying subjects that consists of observing their behavior in a natural setting without intrusions by the researcher

One of the most popular methods of study among cultural anthropologists (scientists who specialize in the study of primitive human groups) is the *naturalistic-observation method.* A scientist using this method to study a primitive Indian tribe would actually live with the tribe for an extended period of time. During this time, the scientist would carefully record events as they occur naturally in the everyday life of the tribe. Scientists studying animals have used a similar technique with considerable success. Years ago, scientists who were interested in the behavior of chimpanzees studied them in their laboratories, or they would observe the animals in zoos or circuses. From these observations, there emerged a picture of the chimpanzee as a rather passive, generally sweet-tempered vegetarian who was never more happy than when munching on lettuce, bananas, or grapes. This picture changed radically, however, when a young scientist by the name of Jane Goodall went to live with chimpanzees in their natural, wild habitat. Dr. Goodall found that many of the things thought to be true about chimpanzee behavior were quite wrong. For example, she found that chimpanzees were clever, efficient hunters who stalked, killed, and ate with great relish rodents and smaller primates.

Educational psychologists also make use of the naturalistic-observation method. Researchers may sit in classrooms, join study groups, observe playground activities, or watch children through one-way mirrors. While observing children, the researchers carefully record the occurrences of specific behaviors.

Strengths and weaknesses of the naturalistic-observation method

The naturalistic-observation method is an excellent source of information about what actually happens in classrooms. The method also provides data that can be a rich source for the generation of hypotheses. In addition, if the method is used on a very large scale—as was the case in the example presented in the box entitled "An Observational Study of Early Elementary Education," which appears later in this chapter—the data can be used to draw tentative conclusions about how particular classroom activities affect student learning or student behavior. But it is important to recognize that cause-effect relationships cannot be established using the naturalistic-observation method. Here again there is the problem of too many things happening at once. Given all of the things happening at once in a classroom (we cannot even record all of them), it is impossible to say with certainty that any one thing produced a learning or behavioral outcome.

The Test and Survey Method

The *test and survey method* of research is designed to provide information about the characteristics, attitudes, or beliefs of selected groups. Students are probably most familiar with the test part of this method, having taken hundreds of tests during their educational careers. The most common use for tests is to evaluate learning. Teacher-made tests are used for this purpose. Teachers give examinations to determine how much students have learned. The scores on these tests are then used as informative feedback to the student, and to the teacher, indicating how well they have performed, in addition to providing a means for determining students' grades.

Another kind of test used for the purpose of evaluation is the *standardized achievement test*. Standardized achievement tests are tests that have gone through a long developmental process and have been tried out with thousands of students. Such tests generally provide a score which indicates where that score stands relative to the score of all other students who have taken the test (e.g., the student scored at the 80th percentile), or they provide a score that indicates the extent to which certain educational content has been mastered. The example of the test and survey method presented in the accompanying box illustrates the use of tests to compare educational achievement over a number of age levels.

standardized tests   tests that yield scores that may be interpreted with reference to representative norms

A second use for educational tests is to predict future performance. A great many readers of this book will recently have taken the Scholastic Aptitude Test (SAT) or the American College Test (ACT). The SAT and ACT are tests used to predict how well a student will perform if he or she attends college. Admission officials at colleges and universities use scores from the SAT or ACT, along with information from other sources, to determine which students should be granted the limited number of admission slots available.

Another example of a test used for the purpose of prediction is the intelligence test, or IQ test. The appropriate educational use of IQ tests is to assist educators in making decisions about the placement, curriculum, and rate of progress of individual students. Although in recent years IQ tests have become the source of considerable controversy, they continue to be used quite frequently to assist in decision making.

Survey research is closely related to testing procedures. Generally, survey research entails asking individuals their opinions or beliefs about a particular topic. The results of survey research are commonly reported in newspapers or on television in the form of a Gallup or Harris poll. In educational situations survey techniques are frequently used to gather such information as the

Determining the Nation's Educational Progress

When the U.S. Office of Education was founded in 1867, it was charged with determining the nation's progress in education. That charge was largely ignored, however, for the next 100 years. This situation was remedied in 1969, when an organization titled the National Assessment of Educational Progress (NAEP) was founded (*NAEP Information Yearbook,* 1974). NAEP was given the task of charting the educational progress of four age groups: 9-year-olds, 13-year-olds, 17-year-olds, and adults ranging in age from 26 to 35 years. These progress reports were to reflect accurately the performance of groups at the above ages and also to reflect such variables as sex, geographic region, level of parental education, size and type of community, and race of student. NAEP reported a summary of the skills mastered by 9-, 13-, and 17-year-olds. The results of the summary are presented in the table in this box.

Skills Mastered by 9-, 13-, and 17-Year-Old Students

	Percentage Mastering Skill		
	0–32	33–67	68–100
9-year-olds			
Can tell time			×
Can add two-digit numbers			×
Can tell the difference between odd and even			×
Can name the President and generally know how he is chosen			×
Can read and comprehend literal facts in simple, brief stories			×
Can write without making punctuation or word choice errors			×
Can subtract three- and four-digit numbers	×		
Can do multiplication and division or understand fractions	×		
Know that the head of a state is called a governor	×		
Can understand detailed instructions	×		
Can organize and elaborate ideas in writing	×		

attitudes of children toward a particular textbook or curriculum, the beliefs of parents about what should be taught in schools, and the opinions of students about the effectiveness of their teachers.

Skills Mastered by 9-, 13-, and 17-Year-Old Students

	Percentage Mastering Skill		

13-year-olds

Can add, subtract, multiply, and divide whole numbers			X
Can make change			X
Know the functions of the major parts of the body			X
Know how to use basic reference materials			X
Can manipulate algebraic expressions		X	
Understand basic nutrition		X	
Understand specific facts about the earth		X	
Can read and understand detailed instructions		X	
Can organize and elaborate on ideas in writing	X		
Understand the structure and function of the legislative branch of government	X		
Understand the basic principles of economics	X		

17-year-olds

Can add, subtract, multiply, and divide whole numbers and decimals			X
Can multiply fractions			X
Can calculate a simple average			X
Can solve word problems requiring multiplication			X
Know the names of particles that make up an atom			X
Can read and understand short straightforward materials such as newspaper ads and telephone calls			X
Know about human reproduction		X	
Can convert decimals to common fractions		X	
Can add fractions		X	
Can make inferences after reading a long paragraph		X	
Can calculate the area of a square given its perimeter	X		
Can simplify algebraic expressions	X		
Can convert Fahrenheit to Centigrade [Celsius] given the conversion formula	X		
Know the function of the legislative branch of government	X		
Have discussed aptitude test results with anyone who could advise them about career plans	X		

(NAEP Newsletter, 1977)

Strengths and weaknesses of the test and survey method

The test and survey method is an extremely important research method for the educational psychologist, as well as being a valuable tool for the classroom teacher. Using this method, researchers can acquire, relatively inexpensively, vast quantities of information about the characteristics, opinions, and attitudes of students. Moreover, if the testing and surveying is done with care and skill, the results can be generalized to virtually any student group—or, for that matter, to the entire population of American students.

Although the test and survey method is a very valuable research tool, it has the same limitation as the other research methods thus far examined. It may reveal *what* students have learned and *what* their attitudes and beliefs are, but it cannot reveal *why*. That is, it cannot establish what specific event caused learning to take place or caused an attitude or opinion to be formed. In short, the test and survey method can establish that things are related, but it cannot establish that one thing caused another.

The Experimental Method

The *experimental method* is, in a sense, what science is all about. Without the experimental method, science as we know it would not exist. The reason is that through use of the experimental method it can be established beyond a reasonable doubt that *one event caused another*—which in turn allows one to predict and control the nature of the events in question. Consider the tuberculosis example. Prior to determining, via the experimental method, that the presence of tuberculous bacilli in the lungs causes tuberculosis, medical scientists, and people in general, had all sorts of ideas about what caused the disease. Night air, damp air, evil vapors—all sorts of things were advanced as the causative agent. Interestingly enough, some of these things were related to the occurrence of tuberculosis. Tuberculosis occurs more frequently, for example, in cool damp climates than in hot dry climates. But this has nothing to do with the direct cause of tuberculosis. It was only when the causative relationship between the bacillus and the disease was established that doctors could predict who might contract the disease, and could control its effects and spread through medication.

Educational psychologists, like other scientists, use the experimental method to discover cause-effect relationships so that they will be able to predict and control events occurring within educational settings. The experimental method is conceptually very simple: one event is systematically varied while all other events are controlled. If observed behavior differs, it can then be safely said that the varying event caused the difference in behavior.

Let's consider some examples—beginning with a study that is *not* an experiment. Suppose a team of researchers wanted to test the idea that watching the television program "Sesame Street" improves reading perform-ance. Imagine that they tested this idea (called a *hypothesis*) by having a group of twenty-five first graders watch "Sesame Street" on a daily basis, and they compared reading performance at the beginning and end of the school year. The results of this imaginary study as depicted in Table 1-1 indicate that the students read well below first-grade level at the beginning of the school year

Table 1-1 Imaginary Data from Sesame Street Study

	Tested Reading in September: Average Grade-Level Score	Treatment	Tested Reading in June: Average Grade-Level Score
25 first graders	.4*	Watch "Sesame Street" daily	1.7

*A score of 1.0 would mean that the student was reading at the same level as the average beginning first grader.

and well above first-grade level at the end of the school year. The question is, would the researchers be justified in saying that watching "Sesame Street" caused the improvement in reading level? ABSOLUTELY NOT! The truth of the matter is that they would not really know what had caused the improvement, and they would have no way of finding out. Consider some of the other reasons performance might have improved:

1. Reading levels might have improved because the reading teacher did a good job. In that case the teacher, not "Sesame Street," will have taught the children to read.
2. Parents might have taught the children to read at home.
3. The children were older in June than they were in September. Older children naturally perform better on tests than younger children.
4. When the children took the tests in September, they had never taken tests before. Since then they have had lots of practice, and their improved performance might be due to their increased understanding of how to take tests.

These are just some of the alternative explanations that could be generated to explain the improvement in reading. All of the explanations (including the effect of watching "Sesame Street") would be plausible; but given the type of study conducted, there would be no way to choose among them.

Now let's consider an example that *is* an *experiment*. Suppose a team of researchers started with fifty first graders and randomly assigned them to two groups. (Random assignment means that any individual has an equal chance of being in either group. The researchers might, for example, flip a coin with each individual: heads they go to Group 1, tails to Group 2.)

Before the results of this hypothetical experiment are examined, the logic behind it should be analyzed. When researchers randomly assign students to groups, they are setting up a situation in which both the experimental group and the control group will be equally affected by extraneous *variables*. If teachers do a good job, both groups will benefit from it. The children whose parents teach them to read are as likely to be in the control group as in the experimental group. Getting older cannot be an explanation for differences

variables changing conditions that may affect the outcome of an experiment

Table 1-2   Imaginary Data from Sesame Street Study with Control Group

	Tested Reading in September: Average Grade-Level Score	Treatment	Tested Reading in June: Average Grade-Level Score
Group 1 (experimental)	.4	Watch "Sesame Street" daily	1.7
Group 2 (control)	.5	Watch cartoons daily while experimental group is watching "Sesame Street"	1.2

between the groups because it applies to both groups. Likewise, increased understanding of how to take tests cannot account for differences between the groups because the groups will have had an equal opportunity to acquire such understanding. These examples do not exhaust the possibilities. If the experiment has been properly set up, all explanations for differences between the experimental and control groups should be easy to discredit except the one the research team is interested in: the experimental group watches "Sesame Street," the control group does not. Thus any difference between the groups can be safely attributed to watching "Sesame Street." That is, if the experimental group scores higher than the control group, we can say that watching "Sesame Street" caused the higher performance.

The results of this hypothetical experiment as given in Table 1-2 indicate that watching "Sesame Street" did produce an improvement in reading performance. Children who watched "Sesame Street" increased their reading performance by an average of 1.3 grade equivalent units. In comparison, children who did not watch "Sesame Street" improved by only .7 grade equivalent units.

Strengths and weaknesses of the experimental method

As indicated earlier, experiments allow scientists to establish that one event causes another. But the experimental method has an important limitation: the only thing that can be said with certainty is that one event causes another *under the conditions of the original experiment*. This is the issue of *generalizability*. When a finding is obtained in experimental research, the results can be generalized only to similar populations exposed to similar treatments in settings similar to the original experimental setting. If the situation to which one wants to generalize differs considerably from the conditions of the original research, the findings may or may not hold true for the new situation. As an example, consider again the tuberculous bacilli. Suppose it is ascertained that individuals who live in England when exposed to tuberculous bacilli will usually contract the disease. Can this finding be safely generalized to Eskimos living in the Arctic? The answer is no. The Arctic may be as inhospitable to

generalizability the validity of results or treatments from an original experiment when applied to different populations or situations

tuberculous bacilli as it is to humans accustomed to warmer climates. The Eskimos may or may not get the disease. Nor can we safely generalize the finding to all individuals living in a cool, damp climate. Some individuals appear to be genetically predisposed to contract such respiratory ailments as tuberculosis, whereas others seem to be genetically resistant. Thus the finding can be confidently generalized only to individuals, situations, and settings that are similar to those originally investigated.

Limitations on the generalizability of experimental results is a problem in educational psychology research. In order to obtain the controls necessary to establish firm cause-effect relationships, it is frequently necessary to conduct research under laboratory conditions. This means that the results cannot be generalized with certainty to real-world classrooms. Type of student presents a similar problem. If the research was conducted with white middle-class children in the fifth grade, that is the only type of group to which the results can be confidently generalized.

Research that is not limited by generalization problems is exorbitantly expensive. As an instance, the U.S. Office of Education in the 1970s completed an experiment on the best means of conducting early elementary education with students from disadvantaged populations (one aspect of this study is described in the box on pp. 16–17). This experiment, called Project Follow-Through, took eleven years to complete and involved thousands of children across the entire United States. The research budget alone for this experiment was over $100 million! Research on this scale can be generalized; but obviously such generalizability is acquired at considerable expense.

The limitations on generalization of educational psychology experimental research is a problem, but it is not a problem that cripples the science. The reason is that even though the results of an experiment cannot be generalized with certainty to a new situation, those results still provide a very strong hypothesis as to what will happen in the new situation. Moreover, it is frequently the case that a conclusion about the causal relationship between educational events is supported not by a single experimental study but by a number of studies, each conducted under somewhat different circumstances. With each additional study that finds similar results, the likelihood of the results holding in a new situation increases. Thus even though educational psychologists are rarely in a position to generalize with certainty, they are in a position to say that given one set of circumstances or events, there is a strong probability that certain events will occur.

SUMMARY

Educational psychology is a scientific discipline that is concerned with producing general knowledge about how the educational process affects students. This knowledge takes several forms. It can be in the form of broad general principles that are useful in understanding how and why the educational process works as it does; it can be in the form of steps that can be followed when attempting to produce a particular outcome; or it can be in the form of "state-of-the-art" information that might suggest solutions or approaches to certain problems.

In this text, educational psychology is divided into four areas of study: development, learning, social and cultural factors, and schools and teachers. The area of development includes an examination of the principles of child development and how these principles interact with the educational process, as well as a study of individual differences (including special students) and the manner in which these differences relate to education. An analysis of learning and of how learning principles can be translated into educational practice is also presented.

The area of learning and instruction includes the study of basic theories and principles of learning and the methods of translating the theories and principles into educational practice. This translation process provides approaches to problems ranging from observable student behaviors to difficulties in understanding.

The area of society and culture examines such topics as the way in which student membership in socioeconomic groups, racial groups, and ethnic groups can influence the educational process. Teachers need to be sensitive to these factors and adjust their educational practices accordingly.

The final section of the book is concerned with factors within the school setting that can influence the effectiveness of a school. It examines such topics as motivation, classroom activities, the physical arrangement of the classroom and the school, and educational measurement.

Educational psychologists have historically assumed two roles when practicing their discipline. The first role is as one who translates psychological knowledge into educational practice. This role views the educational psychologist as a middleman who mediates between the science of psychology and the art of teaching. The second role is as an active researcher generating original knowledge. Both of these roles are being carried out by modern-day educational psychologists.

Educational psychologists and other researchers use a variety of research methods, each of which has advantages and disadvantages. The case study method entails the intensive study of an individual or a group of individuals. Advantages of the case study method are that important and useful information about an individual can be acquired, and the method sometimes provides insights that are useful in understanding the behavior of individuals other than those under study. The disadvantages of the case study method are that the findings usually cannot be generalized beyond the group being studied, and cause-effect relationships cannot be established. A cause-effect relationship is one in which the researcher can confidently say that the occurrence of one event caused the occurrence of a second event. Cause-effect relationships can be contrasted with correlational relationships, in which two events merely occur together but one event does not cause the other.

A second method used by educational researchers is the naturalistic-observation method. This method, when used in an educational context, entails having researchers observe and record the behavior of children in educational settings. The advantages of the naturalistic-observation method are that it provides a wealth of descriptive information about what actually happens in classrooms; it is a rich source of hypotheses for future research and, when conducted on a large scale, can be used to draw tentative conclusions about how classroom activities influence student learning or student behavior. The disadvantage of the method is that it cannot be used to establish cause-effect relationships.

A third method is the test and survey method. It involves administering tests or surveys to selected groups in order to collect information about their characteristics, attitudes, or beliefs. The advantage of the test and survey method is that considerable amounts of generalizable information (assuming the method was used appropriately) can be gathered. The disadvantage of the method is that cause-effect relationships cannot be established.

The final method considered was the experimental method, which involves systematically varying one event while controlling for the effect of all other events. The advantage of the experimental method is that it does allow the researcher to establish cause-effect relationships. The disadvantage of the experimental method is that it frequently yields results that are limited in generalizability.

FOR FURTHER STUDY AND APPLICATION

Feldhusen, J. F., DiVesta, F. J., Thornburg, H. D., Levin, J. R., and Ringness, T. A. Careers in educational psychology. *Educational Psychologist*, 1976, *12*, 83–90.   Describes the job activities of educational psychologists in universities, research firms, government, and industrial settings.

Grinder, R. E. What 200 years tells us about professional priorities in educational psychology. *Educational Psychologist*, 1978, *12*, 284–289.   Provides a useful overview of the historical development of educational psychology.

Campbell, D. T., and Stanley, J. C. *Experimental and quasi-experimental designs for research*. Chicago: Rand McNally, 1966.   The classic presentation of the logic of educational research.

2

COGNITIVE, SOCIAL, AND PHYSICAL GROWTH

CHAPTER OVERVIEW

In this chapter, some of the changes that occur during the course of an individual's life are examined. Defined formally, the field of study examining growth and change is *developmental psychology*. The importance of understanding development lies in the fact that an individual's performance on school tasks is a direct function of the level of development the individual has reached. Five major types of development relevant to education are examined: cognitive, linguistic, social, moral, and physical. The focus of interest is not merely age-related changes but the processes that underlie such changes.

When Marcia McBeath received her B.A. degree in teacher education from the University of Illinois in 1973, one of the last places in which she ever anticipated teaching was a one-room school. Yet confronted—like many newly graduated teachers—with a scarcity of job opportunities, she found a position at the McAuley School in McAuley, Illinois. Today, she considers herself lucky to have taken the job.

Located about 35 miles west of Chicago, the McAuley School is something unusual in an educational world intent on adopting the latest, most progressive fad. Based on the traditional system of educating small, multi-aged groups simultaneously, McAuley is one of the last one-room schools in Illinois—or in the entire country, for that matter. The interview began with a question about the size and organization of the school.

A.   We have a total of eighteen students in the school, with three teachers. There is a preschool/kindergarten teacher, who works with five children. Then we have a primary group, which is composed of first, second, and third grades. Finally we have an intermediate group, made up of fourth, fifth, and sixth grades.

Q.   Do those three groups meet simultaneously?

A.   Yes. The preschool/kindergarten teacher teaches her group all morning long—they go home at noon. The primary group and the intermediate group are taught by myself and another teacher. She teaches science and social studies, and I do reading and math. So we take turns. When I have the primary group, she teaches the intermediate group, and vice versa.

Q.   Is there an age spread across the three grades within the primary and intermediate groups?

A.   Yes. There are four first graders, one second grader, and three third graders in the primary group; and two fourth graders, a fifth grader, and two sixth graders in the intermediate group.

Q.   How do you teach such diverse groups simultaneously? Not only do they differ in age, but I assume they also vary in ability. Is it hard to keep things straight?

A.   I'm able to do it because the groups are so small. If they were much larger I don't think it would be workable. But look at it this way: In a regular classroom you might have three or four reading groups representing different levels of ability. That's basically what I have, except they're different levels *and* ages as well. Take, for instance, a skills lesson. I'll gear it to one group, say the first graders, and I'll expect a certain level of performance from them. But then I will expect something more of the second and third graders at the same time. What this means is that I really need to know with a great degree of precision what level each student is at.

Q.   How do the kids get along with one another? Do they interact, or is there a lot of age segregation, as in a traditional school?

A.   There isn't very much age segregation at all. For one thing, because it's such a small school, the children wouldn't have anyone to talk to if they segregated themselves by age. But basically they interact with one another because they enjoy it. It's really interesting to see them at play. Everybody has recess together; one day a child might be involved with children from a younger age group, another day with children from an older age group. Sometimes the sixth graders play with the kindergarten students.

Q.   That sounds great. Do you think this helps their social and cognitive development?

A.   I really think it's helpful to older students to keep being reminded what younger kids are like. I think it helps them realize how far they've come. In addition, I encourage tutoring—with the older children teaching the younger ones, and sometimes vice versa. I think tutoring is very helpful to the development of both the younger and the older children.

Q.   Are there any drawbacks to the fact that this is such a small school?

A.   Yes. It may be that we're just too small. The students don't get the experience of meeting a lot of people; it's a very small, sheltered group. But I do think the pluses outweigh the minuses.

Q.   If you had a child of your own and had the choice of sending him or her to a more traditional school or to a one-room school, which would you choose?

A.   That's hard. I'm prejudiced. I know we really have a good program going, so I would probably send my child to our school. They get so much more individual attention here. When the kids come back in September, I don't spend a month thinking, "Oh, what does this child know?" We just pick right up where we left off. I feel that since I understand the children better, I am able to present a better program for them.

Q.   One last question: What makes a good teacher, in your estimation?

A.   Basically, I think it boils down to understanding children and being able to work with their needs. I don't really think it matters what style you have. Regardless of whether you are very traditional or are nontraditional, if you are open and try to be warm and honest with the children and work with them from the level they're at, you are going to be a good teacher.

Marcia McBeath's emphasis on understanding children and working with them at their own level is probably crucial to the considerable success she has experienced at the McAuley School. There is an enormous difference in abilities involved in a span of kindergarten through sixth grade—not just in quantitative terms but in the way children of different ages think *qualitatively*. By the end of the chapter, it should be apparent just how complicated Ms. McBeath's job (or any teacher's, for that matter) is in dealing with such diversity.

COGNITIVE DEVELOPMENT

It would seem reasonable to assume that by the time a student reaches kindergarten, he or she has a fairly clear understanding of such basic concepts as size and quantity. Surprisingly, though, research on how children's under-

cognitive development development of the mental processes of perceiving and conceiving, of knowing and comprehending

standing of the world changes as a function of age and experience—known as children's *cognitive development*—shows that this is not the case at all. Children's thinking undergoes rather drastic qualitative and quantitative changes as they increase in age so that at a particular age a child may be completely unable to grasp a concept that adults take for granted and that older children master easily. Children's success in school is affected by the sensitivity of teachers to their stage of cognitive development. This chapter, which deals with human growth and development, begins with a description of cognitive development and how it is related to educational performance.

Piaget's Theory

It is unlikely that any theory of cognitive development currently has an impact as great as that propounded by the Swiss psychologist Jean Piaget. A remarkably prolific author (he wrote over 230 books and papers, beginning at the age of 10!), Piaget suggested that cognitive development proceeds in an orderly and systematic fashion through a series of four separate stages. Like other kinds of developmental theories that are based on stages, Piaget's theory has the following characteristics:

1. The stages are *universal*, which means that all people are expected to pass eventually through all stages.
2. The order in which the stages are passed through is *fixed* and *invariant*. All individuals go through all of the stages, and they do so in the same order. Thus a person could neither skip a stage completely, nor could he or she pass through the stages in any order other than the one specified by the theory. Moreover, the stages are *irreversible:* once an individual enters a higher stage, functioning does not permanently regress to that of an earlier one.

qualitative describing the basic nature or property that characterizes a particular state or object

3. The stages are *qualitatively* different from one another. Therefore, not only are there *quantitative* changes as a person moves from a lower stage into a higher one (such as the ability to remember longer sets of numbers), but there are qualitative changes as well (such as being able to manipulate numbers in a more sophisticated way).

quantitative describing a particular state in terms of amount or relative degrees of its characteristics

It is obvious that Piaget's theory, along with other stage theories, is primarily meant to explain behavior in terms of people in general and is not designed to explain individual differences. But there are two important ways in which stage theories do approach the problem of how individuals differ (Lerner, 1976). First, it is recognized that there are differences in the *rate* at which people progress through the stages. Second, not all people are necessarily assumed to reach the highest stages of development. That is, some people may stop at a lower stage than others eventually reach.

Table 2-1   Summary of Piaget's Stages

Approximate Age Range	Stage	Major Characteristics
Birth–2 years	Sensorimotor	Development of object permanence; little or no symbolic representation; development of motor skills
2–7 years	Preoperational	Development of language and symbolic thinking; egocentric thinking
7–12 years	Concrete operations	Development of conservation; mastery of concept of reversibility
12–adulthood	Formal operations	Logical thinking; abstract thinking

It is also important to note that although one way of looking at stages is in terms of children's *limitations* at a given point, each stage actually represents a rather large increase in ability over earlier performance. Thus behaviors in each stage should be viewed as a set of important new capabilities providing opportunities for the use of particular kinds of teaching strategies.

Keeping in mind the preceding description of how stage theories operate, let us examine each of the four stages that Piaget (1970) has suggested. (These stages are summarized in Table 2-1.)

Stage 1: The sensorimotor stage

The infant is in the *sensorimotor stage* from birth until the age of 18–24 months. At first, the child's behavior is limited primarily to *instinctual reflexes;* and throughout the stage the infant has little or no competence in representing the world through images, language, or other sorts of symbols. What this means, in effect, is that the infant has no awareness of objects (or people) who are not immediately in view; when objects are removed from sight, they simply cease to exist for the child. One of the hallmarks of development that occurs toward the end of the sensorimotor stage is the realization of *object permanence,* in which the child becomes aware that objects continue to exist even if they are out of sight.

What evidence is there for the belief that infants lack object permanence? While researchers cannot of course question the infant directly, evidence for the lack of object permanence can be found in experiments in which a toy is hidden from an infant's view. Until about 9 months of age, children make no attempt to locate or search for the toy. And it is still a few more months before they clearly demonstrate awareness of object permanence. Thus, children must, in the course of the sensorimotor stage, develop the ability to represent objects internally (Bremner, 1978).

instinctual activity innate patterns of behavior fulfilling certain basic functions for an organism

concept of object permanence the awareness that objects continue to exist even if they are out of sight

Stage 2: The preoperational stage

If the major development of the sensorimotor stage is acquisition of the concept of object permanence, the most noteworthy characteristic of the preoperational stage is the development of language. The *preoperational stage* begins at about 18–24 months and continues through the age of 6 years. During this period, children develop internal representational systems that allow them to use language to describe people, feelings, and occurrences. Moreover, they also start to play symbolically. For instance, a child may use a stick to imitate her father sweeping the floor, or she may pretend that a cereal box is a truck.

During the preoperational stage, the child's way of thinking is still qualitatively quite different from that of the adult. For instance, the child displays *egocentric thought,* in which the world is viewed entirely from the individual's own perspective. The possibility that others may have a different perspective is neither considered nor understood. A child in this stage of development may look at a bookcase filled with books and, when asked what bedtime story she wants to have read to her, say "That one," without pointing or otherwise indicating the particular book. The child does not realize that the image of a specific book in her head is not necessarily shared by others.

Children in the preoperational stage lack an understanding of the *principle of conservation*—the knowledge that one aspect of a stimulus can remain unchanged even though other aspects have changed. This lack of understanding is a consequence of children's egocentric mode of thought; they are not able to consider two different aspects of a *stimulus* or situation simultaneously (Lerner, 1976). As a result, they are not able to understand that the quantity, volume, or height of a given object does not change when its shape or configuration is changed. When a change in shape occurs, children in this stage think that all other aspects of the stimulus must also vary concurrently.

There are a number of ways of determining if children have an understanding of conservation, some of which are illustrated in Figure 2-1. For instance, in one frequently used method, children are shown two identical tall glasses. The experimenter pours a liquid into the first glass, and the child is asked to fill the second glass to exactly the same level as the first. When the child is satisfied that the two glasses contain an equal amount, the experimenter asks the child to pour the liquid from one of the tall glasses into a shorter but wider third glass, where, of course, the level of the liquid appears much lower. The experimenter then asks the crucial question: Which glass has more liquid, the tall one or the short one?

To an adult, the answer is clear—there is no difference in the amounts of liquid in the two glasses. The liquid in the short glass has simply undergone an irrelevant transformation in terms of shape. To the child who has not achieved conservation, however, the transformation in appearance means that there has also been a transformation in amount. Thus the child will say that the tall glass has more liquid. Even more surprising, if the liquid from the short glass is poured back into the tall one, the child will say that the amounts

egocentric thought children's thinking in which the world is viewed entirely from an individual's own perspective

principle of conservation the idea that one aspect of a stimulus can remain unchanged even though other aspects have changed

stimulus any object, event, or energy change either outside of or within the individual that excites a response

FIGURE 2-1   Some Simple Tests for Conservation

1. Conservation of substance

A   B

The experimenter presents
two identical plasticene
balls. The subject admits
that they have equal amounts
of plasticene.

One of the balls is deformed.
The subject is asked whether
they still contain equal amounts.

2. Conservation of length

A   B

Two sticks are aligned in front
of the subject. He admits their
equality.

One of the sticks is moved to
the right. The subject is asked
whether they are still the
same length.

3. Conservation of number

A · · · · ·   B
· · · · ·

Two rows of counters are placed
in one-to-one correspondence.
Subject admits their equality.

One of the rows is elongated
(or contracted). Subject is asked
whether each row still has the
same number.

4. Conservation of liquids

A   B

Two beakers are filled to the
same level with water. The
subject sees that they are equal.

The liquid of one container is
poured into a tall tube (or a flat
dish). The subject is asked whether
each contains the same amount.

5. Conservation of area

A.   B

The subject and the experimenter
each have identical sheets of
cardboard. Wooden blocks are
placed on these in identical
positions. The subject is asked
whether each cardboard has the
same amount of space remaining.

The experimenter scatters the blocks
on one of the cardboards. The
subject is asked the same question.

(Lefrançois, 1973, p. 305)

are again equal. There is no puzzlement or hesitancy in the response; to the child, it seems perfectly reasonable that there should be more liquid when it is in the taller glass than when it is in the shorter one.

In another, similarly surprising example of young children's inability to conserve, the experimenter shows a child two balls of clay that are of equal size. If one of the balls of clay is then rolled out into a sausage shape, the child who has not yet learned to conserve will say that the sausage shape has more clay than the ball. In this example, the child has not learned that transformation of shape has no effect on mass.

As is evident from these examples, ideas about physical reality that seem clear and obvious to adults can be completely misunderstood by children during the preoperational period. Toward the end of this stage, however, children do begin to understand the principle of conservation, and by the time they enter the third stage, they have pretty well mastered the concept. Nevertheless, there are still instances in which the child's understanding is incomplete; conservation is not totally mastered until some time after the start of the third stage.

Stage 3: The concrete operations stage

reversibility refers to the idea that a sequence of events can be undone by reversing an earlier action

The *concrete operations stage* begins at about age 6, and it continues until about age 11 or 12. Probably the major sort of understanding that is developed during this stage is that of reversibility. *Reversibility* refers to the idea that some changes can be undone by reversing an earlier action. For instance, individuals in the concrete operational stage are able to understand that when one of two equal-size balls of clay is rolled into a sausage shape, the ball can be returned to its original size by reversing the action. Indeed, at this stage it is not necessary to see the action reversed; children can reverse the sequence in their heads and come to the proper conclusion. Thus a child is able to understand events, and draw conclusions about their consequences, without actually viewing the events.

Although children in the concrete operations stage have begun to think logically, there is still one major limitation to the quality of their thought: they are bound to concrete, physical reality; they cannot understand hypothetical situations. This means that a curriculum which emphasizes the literal and stresses the development of concrete skills is most apt to be successful; subjects requiring abstract thought—such as philosophy or the theoretical sciences— are less likely to be understood by the child in this stage.

Stage 4: The formal operations stage

Around the age of 12, children generally enter the *formal operations stage*, which is characterized by the ability to think in a formal, logical manner. When presented with a problem, the individual will use logical techniques to try to determine the solution.

One excellent example of how thinking matures in the formal operations stage is illustrated by what is known as the "pendulum problem" (Piaget and Inhelder, 1958). Children are shown an object hanging from a string, and they are instructed on how to vary the length of the string and weight of the object, how to drop the pendulum from different heights, and how to push it with different amounts of force. The question the child is asked is, What determines how fast the pendulum swings? (The answer is that the length of the string is the determining factor.)

Prior to the formal operations stage, subjects try to solve the problem in a very haphazard manner. Preoperational children are not able to put together a logical or rational plan to test the various factors. For instance, they may push a short pendulum with a heavy weight and then compare its speed with that of a long pendulum pushed with a light weight. Since length of string *and* weight are both being varied, it is impossible to know which—if either—is responsible for the speed at which the pendulum swings. Children in the concrete operational stage are a bit more logical in their approach. But they still do not carry out true experiments—in which all but one factor is held constant and that factor is then systematically varied. Moreover, even when children in the concrete operational stage are able to carry out the experiments in a reasonably systematic way, they frequently make errors in interpreting the meaning of the results.

In contrast, children in the formal operations stage not only design appropriate kinds of experiments; they are also accurate in their observation of the results and are able to draw appropriate conclusions from those results. Thus individuals in the formal operations stage think much as adults do. Although quantitative growth in cognitive abilities continues during this stage, Piaget suggests that little in the way of *qualitative* change occurs. It should be noted, however, that even in adulthood, people do not always approach problems in a formal, logical manner and sometimes fall back temporarily to earlier modes of thought.

In essence, Piaget's theory suggests that the nature of children's thinking changes in four distinct ways as the child matures. In each successive stage, the child's understanding of the world becomes more complete and sophisticated.

Assimilation and accommodation

Thus far the major differences that distinguish the cognitive abilities of individuals in each of the four stages of development have been outlined; but no explanation has yet been given for *how* an individual moves from one stage to another. The basic mechanism that leads to cognitive advancement, according to Piaget, is comprised of two complementary processes, assimilation and accommodation.

Assimilation refers to the process whereby an individual understands an experience in terms of his or her present stage of cognitive development and way of thinking. Thus when an environmental event or stimulus is perceived and understood in accordance with existing patterns of thought, assimilation has occurred. Piaget has suggested that assimilation is analogous to chewing food to make it digestible: the food is shaped and molded into a form that is usable to the body. Similarly, assimilating a thought or idea consists of molding it into a form that will make it comprehensible, that is, congruent with existing

assimilation the process by which an individual understands an experience in terms of his or her present stage of cognitive development

frameworks of thought. For example, a young child on encountering his first butterfly may call it a "bird"; he has assimilated the stimulus (butterfly) to his existing patterns of thought regarding flying creatures.

accommodation the process of changing one's existing ways of thinking as a response to encountering a new event or stimulus

differentiation the process of noting differences between two or more observations

The converse process to assimilation is accommodation. *Accommodation* refers to changes that occur in existing ways of thinking as a response to encountering new events or stimuli. When previously existing cognitive structures are altered to fit or match novel experiences, accommodation has occurred. For example, the characteristics that differentiate butterflies from birds will eventually become apparent to the child, and he will modify his thought patterns—i.e., accommodate his way of thinking—to take into account the new stimulus. That is, his thinking will have accommodated the *differentiation* between birds and butterflies.

Piaget suggests that assimilation and accommodation are balanced against each other to form an equilibrium. Therefore, there is no automatic, unvarying progression from one stage to another. Rather, cognitive development is the result of the interplay between the individual's attempts to deal with novel stimuli by assimilating them to his or her existing cognitive framework or by accommodating them into modified modes of thought.

Implications for teaching

Very direct implications for educational practice can be drawn from Piaget's theory, although Piaget himself did not make them explicit. The following are a few of those implications (Ginsburg and Opper, 1969):

1. There is a substantial difference between the thinking of children and adults—not just *quantitatively* but qualitatively as well. Children bring a unique perspective to problems. For instance, the preoperational child who does not conserve believes completely that the amount of liquid varies in quantity according to the container into which it has been poured. No amount of cajoling or reassuring will make him or her think otherwise. Thus teachers must understand how children think at a particular age and work from there—not try to change the way of thinking that is characteristic of a given stage. On the other hand, people do not always use their cognitive skills to the fullest. Thus, teachers should encourage students to use consistently the highest levels of cognitive development they have attained.

2. A second important proposition that can be derived from Piaget concerns the role of concrete activities. For the child, thought patterns are developed by acting upon the world—touching objects, turning them, playing with them. In this fashion, assimilation and accommodation are promoted. Thus a teacher should not just impart knowledge verbally, by teaching and lecturing in the traditional way, but should encourage the manipulation of objects as an intrinsic part of the child's educational experience.

Life-Span Development: Learning in Later Life

While Piaget and other major cognitive theorists have been concerned primarily with changes in cognitive ability during the first two decades of life, other theorists have been examining what occurs at the other end of the spectrum—in old age. At the same time, a number of educational programs for the aged have been developed, the most successful being the Elder Hostel program.

Education programs for the elderly were slow to develop, partly because of a widespread feeling that cognitive abilities in the elderly generally decline with age. However, most of the recent evidence suggests that while there is some loss in abilities that require speed and those that involve the conceptualization and manipulation of arrangements of objects, little if any decline occurs in verbal abilities or the capacity to store information. Moreover, the decline that does occur can be attributed to diseases that are frequently present in the elderly—such as problems with circulation and blood pressure—and not to aging per se (Schaie and Parham, 1977).

The Elder Hostel program is designed to offer a week-long program in which elders stay in dormitories on college campuses and attend up to three courses. The program began in 1975 with classes at five New England colleges, and in 4 years had expanded to 235 colleges and universities (Knowlton, 1980). The median age of participants is 68 years.

Perhaps the most important change that has occurred in relation to the education of the elderly is one of attitude. Rather than considering education of the adult—and particularly the elderly adult—in terms of either remediation of a deficit or as a luxury, education is seen today as part of an evolutionary, developmental process that is important in all stages of life.

3. An important implication of Piaget's theory is that for material to be accommodated into new cognitive frameworks, it must be sufficiently similar to what is already known but at the same time different enough so that accommodation can occur. Material that is too dissimilar from existing thought patterns cannot be accommodated, and no learning will result. Only when the material is of moderate novelty will cognitive growth in the form of accommodation occur. Of course, this fact demands that the teacher know a good deal about each specific child's cognitive level in order to be able to provide suitable materials. It also suggests that children need to have curriculum materials prepared for them individually.

4. The egocentric thought patterns of the young child tend to prevent the development of an objective view of reality. According to Piaget, one of the ways in which such egocentrism is reduced is through social interaction. By playing and talking with others, children learn that not everyone sees the world in the same way they do, and this realization facilitates the development of a more objective and accurate way of looking at the world. Thus social interaction should not be looked upon as a frivolous adjunct to a child's "real" education; rather, it ought to be considered an intrinsic part of schooling.

Alternative Conceptions: Learning Theory Approaches

Not everyone agrees with Piaget's views on cognitive development. Although there is widespread acknowledgement that cognitive development does proceed generally according to the sequence described by Piaget, the mechanism by which development occurs is hypothesized very differently by learning theorists. To them, the notion that cognitive development proceeds in universal stages is simply wrong. Instead, they suggest, children's thinking is a reflection of what they have learned and been taught. Learning theorists would say that if there are universals in cognitive development, they can be explained by similar cultural and teaching practices, which have led to common learning. Thus cognitive changes are viewed not as unfolding automatically, in a universal and orderly fashion, but rather as a result of learning.

Learning theory approaches are discussed in detail in subsequent chapters, but their basic view is straightforward. Learning theorists feel that cognitive abilities in the separate stages differ not so much qualitatively as quantitatively. Their underlying assumption is that a child enters the world essentially as a "blank slate" (or *tabula rasa*, to use the term coined by the English philosopher John Locke), and that through experience with the world, cognitive abilities are increased. Indeed, to the learning theorist, it is primarily a child's behavior and performance that are important; such hypothetical notions as "thought patterns," "assimilation," and "accommodation" are not of much interest.

Implications of learning theory approaches for teaching
For the teacher, the learning theory view of cognitive development reinforces the commonsensical notion that learning takes place in incremental steps. It suggests that the most effective technique for presenting new material is to begin teaching at the level of the student's existing knowledge and gradually add new material. Learning theory approaches, in contrast to Piagetian theory, also imply that the way the teacher presents material should not depend on the nature of the subject matter; that teaching success comes most readily from the use of basic principles of learning. (These principles are presented in Chapters 4–8.)

Alternative Conceptions: Bruner's Theory

Another alternative to Piagetian theory is the approach taken by Jerome Bruner (1966), who has focused on specific aspects of the way in which the nature of children's thinking is modified with age. Bruner's interest is concentrated on how children *represent* knowledge internally. He suggests that the child's understanding of the world takes one of three forms: enactive representation, iconic representation, and symbolic representation.

Enactive representation is found in very young children. In this mode, understanding is represented through *motor activities* and actions. For example, children may be able to catch a ball but be unable to describe verbally how they do it. Still, the fact that the child repeatedly catches the ball implies that he or she has an understanding of catching—but on a motoric level. (Adults may also represent knowledge enactively at times; when it comes to hitting a backhand in tennis, for example, people may not be able to articulate very well what they are doing yet they may be able to do it quite proficiently.)

The second mode is known as *iconic representation,* which is understanding by means of perceptual images. Emerging after enactive representation, iconic representation is predominant during the years just prior to kindergarten and in the first few years of elementary schooling. According to Bruner, children at these ages view the world largely in perceptual terms. This fact provides an explanation of why young children have difficulty on conservation tasks: they tend to understand things primarily on a perceptual basis, and when solving problems they tend to be disproportionately influenced by what they see.

Finally, older children develop the capacity for *symbolic representation.* The symbols employed are those of language. Language provides a means by which the child is able to move beyond perceptual cues and begin to understand complex and abstract phenomena in the world.

It should be noted that Bruner's ideas suggest that all three forms of representation—enactive, iconic, and symbolic—remain functional throughout an individual's lifetime once they have emerged. This view contrasts with those of Piaget, who suggests that earlier, less sophisticated forms of thinking are largely lost as the child moves from one stage of development to another.

Implications of Bruner's theory for teaching

The fact that at various ages a particular form of representation is dominant suggests that teachers should gear instruction to the mode of representation currently prevailing in the child. For instance, very young children should be taught through action. When teaching a young child how to throw a ball, the hand and arm should be actually guided into the proper position; verbal instruction alone is unlikely to succeed. For children who tend to favor iconic representation, instruction can employ pictures and diagrams. Finally, when language skills emerge and symbolic representation is possible, abstract subjects, in which enactive and iconic modes of presentation are not appropriate,

representation an image or idea formed by the mind that takes the place of previous experience

motor activities physical actions generated by muscular responses

enactive representation the representation of understanding through motor activities and actions

iconic representation the representation of understanding through perceptual images

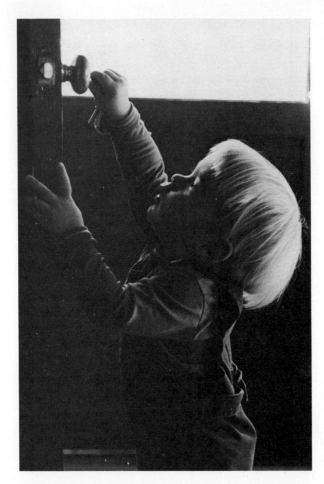

Young children's think-
ing about the world is
derived from touching,
manipulating, and play-
ing with concrete ob-
jects.   (©   Elizabeth
Crews)

may be taught. Bruner also points out that particular kinds of subjects may be taught most effectively through specific modes of presentation. For instance, map-reading skills are best taught using iconic techniques, whereas philosophy demands the employment of curriculum materials that use symbolic representation.

LANGUAGE DEVELOPMENT

Central to the development of cognitive abilities is increasing sophistication in the use of language. Indeed, many psychologists argue that the major distinction between humans and primates is the capacity for complicated and complex communication via linguistic channels. This section describes the way in which language develops and the mechanisms that lead to its acquisition.

Early Speech

The precursor of language is *babbling*, which emerges around the age of 3 to 6 months. Earlier vocalizations consist of crying, cooing, and screaming—none of which much resembles human speech. By 6 months of age, however, children begin to make sounds that are akin to speech. In fact, the sounds they utter are ones that are found in all languages, not just the one to which they are exposed. Thus the babbling of babies in these early months is identical across all cultures.

By the time the child is 9 or 10 months old, however, the babbling becomes more specific to the particular language of the baby's environment. Sounds found in the language are repeated; those not in the language are simply dropped, and they rarely reappear without specific training. At this point in development, it is a short step to the actual production of distinguishable words. In English, first words generally begin with an easily pronounceable consonant—*b*, *d*, *m*, *p*, or *t*—and the proverbial "mama" and "dada' are, in fact, the typical first words. It should be noted, too, that the child's comprehension generally precedes his or her production of speech. Thus children can understand considerably more than they are capable of saying during these early stages of language production. They can be receptive to language before their verbal expressivity indicates that they are, in fact, comprehending what is being said to them.

Finally, real language begins to be acquired after the age of 1 year. The child begins by constructing two-word combinations that are rudimentary sentences, and the number of words and the complexity of the sentences produced increase rather dramatically. For instance, at 24 months, the average child has a vocabulary of more than fifty words, but 6 months later, the vocabulary consists of several hundred words, and sentences of three to five words are commonplace.

Theories of children's grammar

Although the number and complexity of verbal utterances undergo important increases, even more significant are the changes in the manner in which the child uses language. One school of thought holds that children's speech is not just an imperfect version of adult speech but a special form of language in and of itself. The language has a set of systematic rules—a grammar—that is unique to childhood. Its structure has little relationship to that of adult speech and is eventually replaced (Braine, 1963).

One such view of children's language, expressed in the *pivot grammar theories*, postulates that the two-word sentences used by young children are made up of two elements: pivot words and open words. *Pivot words* are few in number but are used frequently. They are combined with other words (open words) to make two-word sentences. Examples of pivot words are "my," "see," and "all gone" in the sentences "my mommy," "see dog," and "all gone shoe." The pivot words are always used in the same position in the two-word sentences; typically they come at the beginning. Children are theorized to have different pivot words but to use those words consistently as pivots. *Open words* are more numerous and are used much more frequently than pivots. While pivots almost never occur alone, open words are frequently used by themselves. For instance, "my mommy" could be replaced by just "mommy" (use of open word alone), but the child would be unlikely to use the pivot "my" alone. The pivot grammar theories assume that this sort of grammatical structure is unique to childhood.

More recent attempts to understand children's grammar have rejected the view that the structure of children's language differs from that of adults. Theories of pivot grammar, in particular, have come under fire. For one thing, they ignore the meaning of two-word sentences. For example, the child using the phrase "mommy sock" has one meaning when pointing to his mother's sock and quite a different meaning when indicating that his mother is putting his sock on (Bloom, 1970). In addition, it appears that not all children use pivot grammar (Bloom, 1970; Bowerman, 1973). Thus the pivot grammar point of view does not seem to provide an adequate representation of children's grammatical capabilities.

An alternative conception of young children's grammar has been suggested by some theoreticians (Bloom, 1970; Schlesinger, 1971). They argue that children's use of grammar is more complex than is suggested by the pivot grammar school of thought—that it is in fact a simplified form of adult grammar. Thus rather than there being essential qualitative differences in children's grammar, the differences are primarily quantitative. Still, it is not known for sure just which view of children's grammar is correct, and it will take further careful study to determine the process by which children learn adult grammar.

Telegraphic Speech

telegraphic speech children's speech in which words that are not central to the message being conveyed are dropped

Psychologists and linguists are more confident in describing the surface appearance of children's speech (as opposed to its underlying rules). A form of speech that is particularly prevalent in young children is known as *telegraphic speech*, in which words that are not central to the message being conveyed are dropped. The words that are omitted are the words that adults might drop if they were sending a telegram—hence the term. Articles ("the," "a") are typically dropped, as are word endings such as "-ed" or "-s." Interestingly, telegraphic speech is a phenomenon that is found in children speaking many different languages (Slobin, 1973).

Telegraphic speech occurs even when children are asked to make direct imitations of adult speech. Some examples of such attempts are shown in Table 2-2. Note that as children increase in age, the degree of telegraphic speech declines.

Table 2-2 Children's Imitation of Sentences Showing Decline of Telegraphic Speech

	Eve, 25½ Months	Adam, 28½ Months	Helen, 30 Months	Ian, 31½ Months	Jimmy, 32 Months	June, 35½ Months
I showed you the book.	I show book.	(I show) book.	C	I show you the book.	C	Show you the book.
I am very tall.	(My) tall.	I (very) tall.	I very tall.	I'm very tall.	Very tall.	I very tall.
It goes in a big box.	Big box.	Big box.	In big box.	It goes in the box.	C	C
I am drawing a dog.	Drawing dog.	I draw dog.	I drawing dog.	Dog.	C	C
I will read the book.	Read book.	I will read book.	I read the book.	I read the book.	C	C
I can see a cow.	See cow.	I want see cow.	C	Cow.	C	C
I will not do that again.	Do—again.	I will that again.	I do that.	I again.	C	C

C = correct imitation
(Brown and Fraser, 1963)

Later Language Development

Once children have moved beyond the two-word sentence, language ability continues to increase rapidly. Children 3 years of age are able to make plurals by adding the letter "s" to nouns, and they can use past tense constructions by adding "-ed" to verbs.

One researcher has suggested that there are a number of principles to which children seem to adhere when producing speech. These principles appear to be universal, as they are similar across many diverse languages, and they guide both the learning and the production of language. For instance, children seem to pay more attention to suffixes than they do to prefixes or prepositions (Slobin, 1973). Because of this, it is easier for them to learn how to use suffixes.

The principles involved in children's attempts to use language are of two sorts. One principle is the child's feeling that language ought to be logical and consistent. For instance, children seem to feel that exceptions to rules should be avoided (e.g., plurals should *always* have an "s" at the end). The other principle governs how children attend to the language of others—they think that they ought to pay particular attention to the ends of words, as well as to the order of words. These principles are sound; however they do not result in perfect language performance because the English language is so full of illogical exceptions. The result of the use of these principles is that linguistic structures that are congruent with the operating principles are learned earlier than are those structures that do not conform to the principles (Clark and Clark, 1977).

Most of the major grammatical structure that a child acquires is in place by about the age of 5. However, there are still problems that must be overcome. For instance, one study by Noam Chomsky (1969) compared 5- and 9-year-olds in their ability to understand the question, "Is the doll easy or hard to see?" when the doll was blindfolded. The younger children tended to have difficulty with the question, and when they were asked to make the doll easier to see, they tried to take off its blindfold. In contrast, the 9-year-olds had no difficulty in understanding the question; they made the doll hard to see by holding their hands over their eyes. Thus children may not understand language in the same way that adults do until well into middle childhood.

Explaining Language Acquisition

Up to now the discussion has been primarily descriptive: we have traced how children's use of language changes as they grow older. But what are the mechanisms involved in children's acquisition of language? There are two major approaches to this question, one of which is based on learning theory principles, the other on innate theories.

Learning theory views

When a child first uses the word "dada" on seeing her father walk into the room, the father's likely reaction is to smile, express delight, and touch or hug the child. A learning theorist viewing the scene would say that the child is receiving strong reinforcement for her use of "dada," and that her appropriate use of the word will therefore tend to increase, just as would any behavior that is praised.

The *learning theory view*, espoused by B. F. Skinner (1957), suggests that children first learn speech by being praised for making sounds that approximate adult language. Because of the rewards involved in making speechlike sounds, the child produces them with greater frequency and with greater accuracy. Over time, these successive approximations become more akin to adult speech, the ultimate result being that the child acquires a vocabulary.

Learning the grammar of a language is a more complex process and is not as easily explained by learning theory. If children were consistently praised *only* when they used correct grammar, then a learning explanation would be viable. However, research has shown that this is not the case. For instance, Brown (1973) has shown that parents respond to "Why the dog won't eat?" as readily as they do to the correct "Why won't the dog eat?" Parents can easily understand the ungrammatical sentence, and they are not apt to correct it. This being the case, it is difficult to view learning theory as the sole explanation for how grammar is acquired.

The innate view

An alternative explanation is the *innate view* of language acquisition, which suggests that innate mechanisms play a major role in learning a language. Proposed by Noam Chomsky (1968), this theory suggests that humans are born with an innate competence in language due to a neural system in the brain known as a *language acquisition device*. Although the specific overt form of spoken language will differ according to the culture in which a child is raised, the underlying structure of all languages shares some similarities, according to this view. Not only does the language acquisition device permit the understanding of the structure of the language, it also provides individuals with strategies and hypotheses for learning the unique characteristics of the specific language to which they are exposed.

This innate theory also entails problems, however, and it has been subjected to strong criticism. For instance, there is no unequivocal evidence for the existence of universals in underlying linguistic structure, which would be necessary if a language acquisition device were innate. Thus it is not clear whether the learning approach or the innate approach provides the better explanation. Indeed, it seems likely that neither theory, by itself, is adequate to explain the complexities involved in language acquisition.

language acquisition device a neural system suggested by Chomsky to account for innate competence in language

Promoting Language Acquisition

It is difficult to suggest what specific actions a teacher should take to promote the linguistic capabilities of students, since so much learning of language appears to take place on an almost spontaneous level at a very young age. But our knowledge of language acquisition does permit a number of suggestions.

First, exposure to language seems to be the key to the appropriate development of language in children. The greater the opportunity to hear a language, correctly spoken, the more likely that children will be able to learn it themselves. Second, it does not seem necessary to correct children's usage constantly. Particularly with young children, it is more important to respond to their language attempts per se, rather than to ignore the message and concentrate on the poor grammar.

It is also helpful for the teacher to expand on what the child says, by using words different from the ones the child has chosen. For instance, if a child begins a conversation talking about a fire truck, the teacher can respond by discussing various qualities of the truck (big, red, long) or things the truck could do (rush, pump water, park). This strategy helps build the child's vocabulary, as well as teaching the child precision in choosing appropriate words.

Finally, it is important for the teacher to realize that words do not always have the same meaning for children as they do for adults. For instance, Piaget's work on cognitive development has shown that the words "more," "less," and "some" mean very different things according to the age of the child. To a child below the age of 4 or 5, such terms refer only to things that can be seen. In

Exposure to correctly spoken language is a cornerstone of appropriate language development in children. (© Elizabeth Crews)

contrast, older children understand that the terms can be used in the abstract as well. Thus, a 4-year-old is able to say that ten candies are more than five only if the candies are physically present; but an 8-year-old would know that ten candies are more than five without any candies being present—he would have counted the difference in his head. The 4-year-old and the 8-year-old would reach the same conclusion, but their reasoning would be quite different. Hence, the teacher needs to keep in mind the level of capabilities and skills of the individual student and to be aware that children can use terms they do not fully understand or appreciate and may miscomprehend questions and directions because of linguistic difficulties.

SOCIAL DEVELOPMENT

In the same way that children grow in cognitive and linguistic competence, they also develop socially. They learn how to get along with their peers, and their understanding of social relationships increases.

The Development of Peer Interactional Patterns

Interaction between children can be seen as early as 6 months of age. However, there are marked differences in infant sociability, with some children appearing more "popular" than others. How is popularity among infants measured? One way is to count the number of times an infant is approached or avoided (Lee, 1973). Infants seem to avoid the aggressive child as well as the child who does not respond to their own initiations or interactions. Popular children are those who respond positively when an approach is made toward them.

There seems to be a clear pattern of development in the nature of children's peer interactions, starting in the first year. At first, infants spend most of their time attending to toys and objects rather than to each other. For instance, two children may play with two trucks, right next to each other, yet not engage in any form of social interaction for relatively long periods of time. In a later stage, children actively try to modify each other's behavior. One of the two children with the trucks, for example, might tell the other child that he should pretend to have an ice cream truck, and the other child may start to make pretend deliveries. In the next stage, which occurs in the second year of life, children become involved in exchanging roles during play. One child may chase another; then they reverse roles, so that the one initially chased becomes the chaser (Mueller and Lucas, 1975).

As children get older, their social interactions become increasingly formalized, as well as more frequent. One study (Wright, 1967) found that as the amount of contact with adults decreased with age, there was a marked increase in peer contacts. Until the age of 8 or 9, children's contacts with one another

Development of Sex Differences

There can be little argument on the point that boys are different from girls. But aside from the obvious physiological differences, are there differences that lead males and females to perform differently in school?

The best evidence seems to indicate a possible affirmative answer. According to Maccoby and Jacklin (1974), among the more established differences are the following:

- Females have greater verbal ability than males, particularly after age 11. They score higher on tests of analogies, reading comprehension, and spelling than do boys.
- Males have better mathematical and visual-spatial ability than females. Boys tend to master quantitative concepts more readily than do girls, although this difference does not appear until about age 12 or 13. Likewise, the visual-spatial differences begin at adolescence and continue through adulthood.
- Males are more physically and verbally aggressive than females. This difference is apparent from the age at which social play starts— around 2 years.

It should be noted, however, that in all these cases the differences are not great; there are far larger differences among individuals *within* a sex than *between* the sexes.

Although the sex differences we have cited seem fairly well established, the reason for them is not. The topic of sex differences is a very controversial one, and there are many competing theories. Basically, they boil down to two sorts of explanations: biological and cultural. The biological theories suggest that sex differences are caused by such physiological factors as hormones and brain structure. For instance, scientists are currently studying the fascinating hypothesis that the brains of the male and female may be

are fairly informal, and the groups that do exist generally have no fixed membership or rules. However, at about 10 or 11 years of age, children begin to show growing conformity to their peer group, and this results in greater group organization. It also leads to the ostracism of nonmembers (Hartup, 1970). In addition, there is a shift toward the development of close relationships between particular same-sex friends at about this time.

During adolescence, peer interaction takes on new forms. For example, one

differently organized (Gelman, 1981), and that this could lead to differences in behavior.

Cultural theories, while not denying the possibility of biological differences, suggest that the major reason for male-female differences lies in the differential treatment the sexes receive from society. The argument goes like this: Because boys are *expected* to be aggressive, they are given toy guns to play with, and this leads to the expected aggression. Likewise, because girls are *expected* to be nurturant, they are given dolls to play with, and this leads to the nurturant behavior that is expected. Thus society's view of what behavior is appropriate for a boy or girl brings about that behavior.

How are these expectations regarding appropriate sex-role behavior transmitted? One way has been through children's books. One analysis of the contents of prize-winning picturebooks showed that the boys were portrayed as being active, leading and rescuing others, while the girls were shown as being passive, following and serving others. There was a range of occupations for male adults, whereas females were shown only as wives and mothers (Weitzman, Eifler, Hokada, and Ross, 1972). Analyses of children's textbooks have confirmed the pattern, although more recent textbook authors have made conscious efforts to avoid implying that some behaviors are more appropriate for one sex than for the other.

There are a number of strategies a classroom teacher can employ to avoid promoting the idea that certain behavior is appropriate for one sex and not the other. Teachers should avoid treating males and females differently. The findings on sex differences in academic abilities are not sufficiently unequivocal or strong to warrant holding different performance expectations for members of a given sex, especially since many of the differences that have been found do not seem to emerge until the secondary school years. In addition, children should be encouraged not to deprecate activities that are untraditional for their sex. Finally, teachers should remember that the example that they themselves present to their students is crucial. Teachers are powerful role models, and teachers' nonsexist behavior is sure to be observed by their students.

classic study (Dunphy, 1963) found that there is a general pattern to the development of social interaction. When adolescence begins, males and females are generally in same-sex groups. A gradual shift to integrated, male-female groups then occurs and is followed by a transition period, in which some individuals pair off as couples but are still associated closely with the group. Eventually, in late adolescence, the group begins to disintegrate, as primary interest shifts to male-female couples.

In sum, individuals' relationships with their peers evolve as they grow older. A teacher should be sensitive to the important role that peers play in children's lives and indeed should actively promote positive social interaction among students. Just as there are cognitive benefits to be gained from social interaction (by promoting the decline of egocentrism), there are social benefits in the form of increased understanding and sensitivity toward others from the development of strong, positive relationships with peers.

Erikson's Theory of Psychosocial Development

Erik Erikson, a clinical psychologist, has provided one of the more comprehensive theories of social and personality development (Erikson, 1963). Employing a stage approach, Erikson argues that individuals move through a series of eight stages (summarized in Table 2-3), each having a characteristic pattern of social interaction. Erikson suggests that these stages occur through an "epigenetic principle," in which various aspects of personality evolve and

Table 2-3   Erikson's Eight Stages of Psychosocial Development

Stage Name	Approximate Age	Major Characteristics
1. Trust vs. mistrust	Birth–1½ yrs.	Feelings of trust from environmental support; or fear and concern
2. Autonomy vs. shame	1½–3 yrs.	Independence if exploration is encouraged; or self-doubt and shame
3. Initiative vs. guilt	3–6 yrs.	Identification of self as male or female; or guilt because of actions and thoughts
4. Industry vs. inferiority	6–12 yrs.	Development of sense of competence; or lack of mastery feelings
5. Identity vs. role diffusion	12–18 yrs.	Awareness of uniqueness of self; or inability to identify appropriate role
6. Intimacy vs. isolation	18–30 yrs.	Development of loving, sexual relationships; or fear of relationship with others
7. Generativity vs. stagnation	30–60 yrs.	Sense of contribution to continuity of life; or trivialization of one's activities
8. Ego integrity vs. despair	60–death	Sense of unity of life's accomplishments; or regret over lost opportunities

appear at particular times in an individual's development. One of the unique features of this theory is that it is a life-span approach; it covers modifications in social and personality functioning from birth to old age.

Each of Erikson's stages is presented as a dichotomy, identifying the major positive and negative consequences of the stage. The first two stages, trust versus mistrust and autonomy versus shame, correspond to the periods of infancy and toddlerhood, respectively. In the *trust versus mistrust* stage, infants develop feelings of trust if their interactions with the world are generally positive, mistrust if they experience a lack of warmth and care. From about 1½ to 3 years of age, children are said to be in the *autonomy versus shame* period. Here, children develop independence and autonomy if their attempts at exploration and freedom are supported, or they feel shame and unhappiness if too restricted and protected.

At about 3 years of age, children enter the next stage, labeled *initiative versus guilt*. During this stage children develop a sense of their identity as male or female and learn to identify with same-sex models. The next stage, *industry versus inferiority*, occurs during the elementary school years, from about 6 to 12 years of age. The feelings of industriousness and mastery that can emerge during this period are related to the tremendous increases in competence levels that can occur. The child can learn the joy of carrying out activities for their intrinsic rewards rather than doing things just to win some external benefit. On the other hand, the child who experiences failure and lack of encouragement in this period is apt to develop feelings of guilt over his or her incompetence.

Schooling plays a particularly important role during the industry versus inferiority stage of development. Instruction that is geared to optimizing a child's sense of success and competence can lead to positive academic development, as well as enhancing future motivation to learn. On the other hand, teaching that is restrictive and harsh, and leads children to feel they have failed, is apt to destroy their sense of mastery and industriousness, and lead to passive and apathetic pupils.

From about 12 to 18 years, the period of adolescence, one of the more dramatic stages of psychosocial growth, occurs—the *identity versus role diffusion* stage. This is the time in which individuals may experience an identity crisis. The major thrust of this crisis is adolescents' attempts to determine what is unique and individualistic about themselves; they try, basically, to discover who they are, what skills they have, and for what roles they are best suited. Coming at a time of major physical changes, as well as of important changes in the rules society requires them to follow, it is often a difficult period. Erikson suggests that the task of defining "self" is the major undertaking of this stage.

The identity versus role diffusion stage has special relevance for the teacher. Students may be undergoing considerable personal stress, and their search for appropriate roles can lead them to unusual and extreme choices of behaviors. Teachers should bear in mind the source of these behavioral changes and attempt to provide constructive methods of facilitating the choices that adolescents must make as they move into adulthood.

The last three stages of social and personality development, according to Erikson, are *intimacy versus isolation* (ages 18–30), *generativity versus stagnation* (ages 30–60 years), and *ego integrity versus despair* (age 60 years to death). Although these later years have less relevance for teaching, development is assumed to continue throughout the life span, and each period brings its own set of possibilities for growth. Erikson's greatest contribution, perhaps, is that he saw psychosocial growth as being possible at all stages of life and realized that social and personality issues pose a continuing challenge to individuals as they move through their lives.

MORAL DEVELOPMENT

The development of a sense of morality constitutes one of the major accomplishments of human growth, but it requires mastery of a set of concepts that are quite complex. Consider, for example, the following two stories:

> A little boy who is called John is in his room. He is called to dinner. He goes into the dining room, but behind the door there was a chair with a tray with 15 cups on it. John couldn't have known that there was all this behind the door. He goes in, the door knocks against the tray, bang go the 15 cups and they all get broken!

> Once there was a little boy whose name was Henry. One day when his mother was out he tried to get some jam out of the cupboard. He climbed up on a chair and stretched out his arm. But the jam was too high and he couldn't reach it to have any. But while he was trying to get it he knocked over a cup. The cup fell down and it broke. (Piaget, 1932, p. 122)

If asked to decide who is the "naughtier" of the two—John, who broke fifteen cups, or Henry, who broke just one—most adults would probably say Henry, given that he was doing something his mother had probably warned him against. More specifically, John's *intent* was quite benign, while Henry's was not so innocent.

However, most 6- and 7-year-olds, on hearing the stories, would insist that John is the naughtier. The reason? To children of that age, intent is secondary to the *amount of damage* that is done. Piaget, who wrote the above two scenarios to investigate children's moral development, suggests that the important difference between younger and older children is that younger children have an *objective* sense of morality, in which amount of damage is the important concept. In contrast, children aged about 8 years or older have a *subjective* view of right and wrong, in which intent is the basis for judgment. They take into account the reasoning behind the action; even if an action results in a poor outcome, it is still considered more appropriate behavior than an action with a positive outcome that is motivated by selfish intentions.

Another way in which young children differ from older children and adults in their concept of morality concerns the idea of *imminent justice*. To a young child, deviation from a rule or moral standard is expected to result in some form of punishment. For example, a child who steals candy from another child then later trips and hurts his arm may view the two incidents as linked to one another. The fall may be seen as punishment for the transgression. Children above the age of 7 or 8, however, begin to realize that they can break rules without necessarily being punished. They view the world more realistically and begin to realize that rules are arbitrary social contracts that are open to questioning and subject to change.

Kohlberg's Theory

Lawrence Kohlberg, a Harvard psychologist, has extended and refined Piaget's analysis of moral development. He suggests that there are six stages of

As they develop, children realize that rules are "social contracts" that can be negotiated and are open to questioning. (© Mark Godfrey/Archive)

development relating to the moral judgments (although not necessarily behaviors) of a person. Although there is no direct relationship between age and stage level, the stages are assumed to be in a fixed order. Many individuals do not reach the highest levels of moral development, according to Kohlberg.

The six stages of development are divided into three levels of moral orientation (Kohlberg, 1976):

LEVEL 1: PRECONVENTIONAL MORALITY: At this level, the concrete interests of the individual are considered.

Stage 1: Obedience and punishment orientation: In this stage, people stick to rules in order to avoid punishment, and there is obedience for its own sake.

Stage 2: Naive, hedonistic, and instrumental orientation: In this stage, the individual follows rules only for his or her own benefit. Obedience occurs because of rewards that are anticipated.

LEVEL 2: CONVENTIONAL MORALITY: At this level, the individual approaches moral problems as a member of society.

Stage 3: "Good boy" morality: Individuals in this stage show an interest in maintaining the respect of others and doing what is expected of them.

Stage 4: Authority and social order morality: People at this stage conform to society's rules and consider that "right" is what society defines as right.

LEVEL 3: POSTCONVENTIONAL MORALITY: At this level, moral principles are seen as broader than the precepts of any individual society.

Stage 5: Morality of contract, individual rights, and democratically accepted law: People in this stage do what is right because of a sense of obligation to laws that are agreed upon within society. They perceive that laws, as part of an implicit social contract, can be modified or changed.

Stage 6: Morality of individual principles and conscience: In this final stage, an individual follows laws that are seen as they are based on universal ethical principles. Laws that violate the principles are disobeyed. Stage 6 individuals feel that equality of human rights and respect for human beings as individuals are the most basic universal principles.

To determine what stage of moral development an individual has reached, Kohlberg devised a series of scenarios involving a moral dilemma and asked children how they would resolve the problem. The following is one such dilemma:

> In Europe, a woman is near death from a special kind of cancer. There is one drug that the doctors think might save her. It is a form of radium that a druggist in the same town has recently discovered. The drug is expensive to make, but the druggist is charging ten times what the drug cost him to make. He paid $200 for the radium and is charging $2,000 for a small dose of the drug. The sick woman's husband, Heinz, goes to everyone he knows to borrow the money, but he can get together only about $1,000, which is half of what it costs. He tells the druggist that his wife is dying and asks him to sell the drug cheaper or let him pay later. The druggist says, "No, I discovered the drug and I'm going to make money from it." Heinz is desperate and considers breaking into the man's store to steal the drug for his wife.

The person is then asked whether Heinz should steal the drug, under what circumstances it would or would not be permissible to steal, and other questions designed to assess the person's stage of moral reasoning. For instance, a person at the preconventional level would focus on the question of whether Heinz would be punished for stealing, while a person at the postconventional level would be concerned with whether breaking the law in this case would be morally justified to save an innocent life.

Most adults in the United States never reach the postconventional stages of moral development, although there is wide variability. Indeed, Kohlberg (1963) has found that children as young as 13 years of age make responses indicative of Stage 6 morality. Figure 2-2 suggests the age progression in the use of various levels of reasoning.

FIGURE 2-2   The Use of Six Types of Moral Judgments at Four Ages

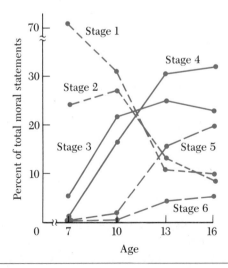

(Kohlberg, 1963)

Cheating in School

The impetus for much of the work on moral education comes from a classic study on cheating in school carried out by Hugh Hartshorne and Mark May in 1928. In a series of pioneering studies, these psychologists investigated dishonesty in grade school age children. They devised thirty-three different situations with which to measure three different types of dishonesty: cheating, lying, and stealing.

The results of the investigation were unexpected. There was little evidence that a child could be said to be generally "honest" or, for that matter, generally dishonest. Hartshorne and May found that dishonesty, instead of being a generalized personality trait, was highly influenced by situational factors. A person who was honest in one situation could not be counted on to be honest in another. Similarly, dishonesty in one situation did not necessarily mean that the person would be dishonest in other situations.

More recent work tends to confirm that the characteristics of the situation in which individuals find themselves have a significant effect on the degree of honesty displayed. The following are among the more important situational factors:

- *Group codes.* If the classmates around an individual tend to be honest and support honesty in general, it is more likely that that

The Acquisition of Morality

Both Kohlberg and Piaget suggest that moral development is related to the individual's level of cognitive functioning. In order to understand the complexities of the higher levels of morality, one must have sufficient cognitive maturity. Particularly important is the ability to take the role of others—that is, the ability to understand that others may not share one's own intentions and feelings (Selman, 1974). With the child's growing awareness that others do not necessarily share the same perspective comes increasing differentiation of the personality of others. This increase in role-taking skills allows the child to begin to understand the subtleties involved in making moral judgments and decisions. Consistent with this view is evidence showing that children who do not have much opportunity for social interaction with peers (which increases role-taking skills) are not as advanced in their moral development as children raised in less restrictive environments. Moreover, children with greater levels

individual will be honest than in a situation in which the group is relatively dishonest. People tend to reflect, at least partially, the views about cheating of the people around them. Moreover, some research has indicated quite clearly that viewing a model behaving dishonestly can lead to increased dishonesty (Burton, 1976). (The evidence is less clear, however, in demonstrating that honest models can increase honest behavior.)

- *Size of risks of discovery and punishments.* Not unexpectedly, the greater the risk of discovery involved in dishonest behavior, the less likely it is that cheating will occur. However, the relationship between magnitude of potential punishment and incidence of cheating is less clear. Some studies have demonstrated a direct relationship, others have not. The degree of risk seems to be the more crucial factor.

- *Certainty of discipline.* Children are less apt to behave dishonestly if they know they will be punished for transgressions. Knowing that certain behaviors are acceptable (such as working together on a particular homework assignment) but others are not (sharing answers on a test), and knowing that punishment is sure to be incurred for the dishonest behavior, is more apt to promote honesty than is the situation in which punishment is only an ambiguous possibility. Thus teachers should be clear in delineating what behavior is acceptable and what unacceptable—and punish dishonest behavior.

of participation in social activities tend to have higher levels of moral judgment (Keasey, 1971).

Other theorists interested in the development of morality have emphasized the importance of child-rearing practices. For instance, some writers stress that a child learns morality through a process of *identification* with a parent (Sears, Maccoby, and Lewin, 1957). When a child identifies with a parent, he or she adopts the rules and social morality of the parent. The basic motivation is to win the love and respect of the parent and avoid punishment for any supposed deviation. Ultimately, the child internalizes adult moral standards and behaves appropriately even when there is no authority figure present.

*identification
the conscious
or unconscious
adoption of
values held by
a significant
person*

Learning theorists tend to reject the concept of identification. They say that rather than trying to pattern themselves after an adult figure, and incidentally picking up the adult's moral standards, children learn morality through a direct teaching process. Parents provide their children with specific rules and regulations, and children are rewarded for obeying those rules and punished for violating or ignoring them. Additionally, children learn through imitation of adult models whom they observe being rewarded for appropriate behavior (Bandura, Ross, and Ross, 1961). Evidence for this position comes from a study in which children who viewed an adult being rewarded for moral judgments that were either higher or lower than their own level tended to move subsequently toward the model's level (Bandura and MacDonald, 1963).

Promoting Moral Development

When schools were first organized in the United States, one of the primary motivations was to provide children with a "moral" education. As will be seen in subsequent chapters, schools still function as a major transmitter of the society's values. However, until recently, there were few efforts to formalize the teaching of morals and values and make it part of the curriculum.

Part of the reason for this lack of formal attention was the concern—still evident today—that to teach morality was to usurp the rights and responsibilities of parents. But another reason was that there were few well-developed approaches that could be used by classroom teachers. This latter reason is no longer valid, however. At least two techniques have now been used quite successfully in schools to promote moral education. One, known as values clarification, teaches students to become aware of their own and others' values. The second method, based on Kohlberg's theory of moral development, involves the discussion of moral reasoning in relation to moral dilemmas.

Values clarification
In this approach, the goal of the teacher is to encourage examination of the students' values (Raths, Harmin, and Simon, 1966). Rather than espousing any particular set of values and morals, the teacher attempts to make students aware of what their values are, whether their values differ from those of others, and how values are formed. Indeed, there is a conscious effort to avoid promoting any particular type of value.

An example of a specific technique that has been used to clarify students' values is known as the "Either-or Forced Choice" (Simon, Howe, and Kirschenbaum, 1972). The teacher provides an either-or question for the students that is indicative of two opposing underlying values, such as "do you identify more with a Volkswagen or a Cadillac?" The students are forced to choose one side or the other, and then to explain their reasons. This kind of exercise can bring students a great deal of insight into their own underlying value structure.

Values clarification techniques are not without their detractors, however. Opponents argue that although value clarification creates awareness of values, it does not help to resolve value conflict; it does not say what is right or wrong. Rather, it is just a framework for the examination of values. What is missing, according to critics, is the deliberate teaching of basic principles and standards that are morally right. To remedy this deficit, another technique for promoting moral development has been suggested, one based on Kohlberg's model of moral growth.

Moral reasoning—education based on Kohlberg's theory

Rather than concentrating on promoting students' discovery of the definition of their own existing values, educators working in the Kohlbergian framework attempt to teach moral *reasoning*, in order to raise the level of moral development at which the student functions (Hersh, Paolitto, and Reimer, 1979).

The procedure is based on the notion that the crucial mechanism for stimulating moral growth is promoting students' perspective and role-taking skills. As in values clarification, students are taught to see the many sides an issue has, but they also learn about the various perspectives that can be brought to bear on the issue. In addition, they are guided to higher levels of moral reasoning by the creation of conflict between their current level of reasoning and higher levels. The conflict leads to the creation of moral thinking of greater complexity, and eventually to movement to new, higher stages of thought.

Is moral education effective?

There are no data to show that children who are taught values clarification or moral reasoning are more moral than those who do not receive such teaching. However, it seems reasonable to suppose that such students would be sensitive to the subtleties involved in moral reasoning and ultimately might, in fact, act in a more moral fashion. It could also be argued that teaching morals and values can enhance students' thinking in general.

But caution should be exercised. Teachers should be aware that examining specific moral judgments means venturing into a sensitive area. For example, the question of whether or not abortion should be legalized does not lend itself to clear-cut, noncontroversial moral instruction. Teachers should be careful in their choice of topical material. The teacher's role should be that of facilitator, clarifier, and presenter of alternative views in examining moral issues—not that of preacher for a particular viewpoint.

PHYSICAL DEVELOPMENT

The least subtle of the changes that take place in the developing child are transformations of a physical nature. Beginning life as awkward, immobile beings, children improve immensely in coordination and dexterity as they mature. But many of the effects of these rapid physical changes are less obvious, and as will become clear, physical development is related to school performance in a number of ways. Two aspects of physical development are examined: growth and motoric development.

Growth

Changes in height and weight constitute the most overt form of physical development. At the typical age of first schooling—around 5 years—children average about 42 inches in height and 37 pounds in weight. By the time they reach adolescence, they have grown a further 2 feet and have just about doubled their weight. Growth continues even more rapidly during adolescence, when height can increase by as much as 3 inches in the course of a year.

What determines the physical growth patterns of children? The greatest influence is undoubtedly genetic: children with tall parents tend to be taller, on average, than those with short parents. But other factors also play a role in affecting growth. For example, the nutritional content of a child's diet is likely to influence both the rate of growth and the ultimate size of a child. Moreover, children who are malnourished are likely to be lethargic and relatively uninterested in their environment, and they are not able to participate in intellectual and physical activities in the same way that better-nourished children are.

Other factors affecting children's growth relate to the amount of rest and quality of care a child receives, and the amount of illness he or she sustains during childhood (Strommen, McKinney, and Fitzgerald, 1977). It is also the case that there are profound individual differences among children in the rate of development and level of growth attained. Thus within the same classroom— that is, among children who are generally the same chronological age—there can be considerable variation in size and physical maturity. This phenomenon is particularly true in junior high schools, where children are entering the period of puberty. Indeed, even the age range at which puberty can start is wide: girls considered normal can begin menstruating any time between the ages of 9 and 15 (the average age being about 12 years).

Physical growth is important to the teacher for at least two reasons. First, it is associated with general physical and athletic ability—lags in growth being related to below average physical skills. Second, the level of growth of an individual affects the way the child's peers interact with him or her. Children who are notably above or below the size and growth norms for a given age can be subject to teasing and other forms of humiliation from their peers, and this in turn may affect the child's self-esteem and level of classroom functioning. Likewise, problems can occur when physical and cognitive growth patterns do not correspond. All in all, then, physical growth can have a significant effect on performance in school.

Motoric Development

The ability to coordinate muscles in complex activities is known as muscular or motor behavior. Such diverse behaviors as the grasping of a toy by an infant,

Motoric and physical development are enhanced through participation in games like "double Dutch" jump rope. (© Hazel Hankin 1981)

the hitting of a baseball by a young child, or the playing of a Beethoven sonata by an adolescent are all examples of motor skills. Because many of the most fundamental scholastic tasks (including writing) require motoric ability, an awareness of motoric development is essential for teachers.

Physical strength is one index of motoric skill that shows a clear and regular rise over the school years. There is also a clear difference between males and females. When measured by the typical technique of determining grip strength (which seems to correlate with other forms of strength), boys tend to outperform girls by about 2 pounds, during the elementary school years, and this superiority increases during adolescence (Jones, 1960). Because strength is related to success in so many physical activities, it is of importance to children and their social functioning.

Another motoric skill that shows increases with age is response time. The successful use of motor skills requires that a complex series of muscular activities be initiated in a coordinated sequence, and thus the appropriate timing of responses is essential. The improvements in response time that occur allow children to perform such tasks as catching a ball more easily with increasing age (Cratty and Martin, 1969). Improvements in response time are also accompanied by increases in what is known as response inhibition, which is the ability to *avoid* responding to stimuli. Response inhibition is important because it allows children to avoid making a first, frequently erroneous, response and gives them a chance to examine alternative choices (White, 1965).

Motor abilities typically increase with age, although there are wide individual differences. Research has also shown that the degree of skill in motoric areas has a considerable effect on children's social standing and self-concept. For instance, there is a positive relationship between ratings of social competence and physical coordination (Sheppard and Willoughby, 1975). However, the importance of motor skills seems greater for boys than for girls, particularly in the preadolescent years. By midadolescence, motor ability declines in importance for males as well, which suggests that other attributes come to play a greater role in gaining status.

Implications for Teaching

Teachers have somewhat less control over physical growth and development than they do over many other aspects of their students' performance, since such factors as height and weight are determined largely by genetic factors. However, teachers can play a role by encouraging children to develop their physical potential and by teaching them motoric and sports skills. In addition, teachers should bear in mind that participation in physical activities and sports is a significant part of social interaction for both girls and boys.

SUMMARY

The topic of human development is concerned with the growth and changes that occur in individuals as they age. Developmental processes are important for the teacher in that they directly affect the ability of a student to perform a particular task in school.

Cognitive development refers to the way in which a child's understanding of the world changes as a function of age and experience. Piaget's theory of cognitive development has been the most influential. A stage theory, it suggests that children pass through four stages in a universal order, and that the stages are qualitatively different from one another. The four stages are: (1) sensorimotor, (2) preoperational, (3) concrete operations, and (4) formal operations. According to Piaget, cognitive growth occurs through the processes of assimilation and accommodation. While assimilation molds the understanding of a new stimulus to previous thinking patterns, accommodation changes thinking patterns to fit the new stimulus.

A number of practical implications have been drawn from Piaget's theory. These include taking the child's perspective into account, encouraging the manipulation of objects, being aware of the child's specific cognitive level, and promoting social interaction.

Learning theory approaches to cognitive development take an alternative view to Piaget's theory. These approaches suggest that thinking is a reflection solely of what people have learned and been taught. The concept of universal stages has been rejected by learning theorists. Bruner's approach to cognitive development focuses on modes of representation. He suggests that knowledge can be represented in enactive, iconic, and symbolic modes.

Children's language development begins with babbling and proceeds to the use of real words after the age of 1 year, with expansion of capabilities being very rapid. Not only do the number of words increase, but the quality of the grammar improves. Telegraphic speech, in which words not central to a message are dropped, occurs in children's first sentences. But by the age of 5, most major grammatical structures have been acquired.

There are two major views to explain language acquisition. Learning theory approaches suggest that language is learned through a series of rewards for making sounds that are linguistically appropriate. Innate theories suggest that humans are born with an innate competence in language due to a neural system in the brain, known as the language acquisition device, which permits understanding of the structure of language.

Social development occurs as the nature of children's peer interactions changes. Interactions with peers increase with age and become more frequent and more formalized. Through interaction, children become increasingly sensitive to and understanding of others. Erikson's theory of psychosocial development suggests that individuals move through a series of eight stages. These stages describe the dominant patterns of positive or negative outcomes of social interaction and personality development. The theory is life-span in nature, covering social and personality development from birth to death.

Kohlberg's theory traces moral development as it changes from an objective view to a subjective one. He designates three major stages of moral development: (1) preconventional morality, in which rules are followed to avoid punishment or receive rewards; (2) conventional morality, in which the primary concern is to maintain the respect of society and conform to its norms; and (3) postconventional morality, in which moral behavior occurs because of a sense of obligation toward and respect for human beings.

Cognitive approaches to the acquisition of moral development view the phenomenon as resulting from child-rearing practices and internalization of the parent's morality, which follows from identification. Learning theorists suggest that morals are learned through teaching—from parents and, more directly, from schools. Approaches to promoting moral development include values clarification techniques and teaching moral reasoning via Kohlberg's theory.

Physical development occurs very obviously as the child ages. Height and weight increase, with large individual differences being seen within the same chronological level. Motor development also occurs with age, particularly in terms of strength, response time, and response inhibition. Physical development is important because it is related to skill in such academic tasks as writing; it also affects the way in which individuals are perceived by their peers.

FOR FURTHER STUDY AND APPLICATION

Wadsworth, B. J. *Piaget for the classroom teacher.* New York: Longman, 1978.

Ginsburg, H., and Opper, S. *Piaget's theory of intellectual development: An introduction.* Englewood Cliffs, N.J.: Prentice-Hall, 1969.   Two eminently readable guides to Piaget's theory of cognitive development. Both of these books provide direct applications for teachers interested in using Piaget in the classroom.

Dale, P. S. *Language development: Structure and function.* (2nd ed.) New York: Holt, Rinehart and Winston, 1976.   Gives a theoretical exposition of the major current approaches to language development and use.

Lickona, T. *Moral development and behavior.* New York: Holt, Rinehart and Winston, 1976.   A series of readings on how individuals develop morally and the kinds of educational practices that promote moral development.

Simon, J. B., Howe, L. W., and Kirschenbaum, H. *Values clarification: A handbook of practical strategies for teachers and students.* New York: Hart, 1972.   Provides teachers with a practical guide to using values clarification techniques in the classroom.

3

INDIVIDUAL DIFFERENCES AND INSTRUCTIONAL APPROACHES

CHAPTER OVERVIEW

One essential characteristic of good teaching is that it be responsive to the individual needs of students. Virginia Plott's class illustrates this point. There are simply too many differences between the students for a teacher to be able to teach all of them the same thing at the same time. Quality teaching entails being sensitive to individual differences, and knowing what to do when you find them.

In general, educators have responded in two ways to individual differences in students. The first way is to attempt to *minimize the differences—by grouping together* students having certain characteristics. For example, one might form one class out of students who are very fast learners, and another out of very slow learners. In theory, this would allow a teacher to present the same material in the same way to an entire class. The second kind of response to individual differences is to *change the nature or content of the instruction,* or both, to accommodate individual differences. Both of these approaches are discussed in this chapter.

One individual difference that every teacher thinks about at least occasionally is pupil intelligence. The chapter briefly reviews the history of intelligence theory and measurement and describes several responses to the charge that current IQ tests are biased against certain minority groups. It also considers the issue of whether intelligence is determined by heredity or by environment, and it discusses research dealing with the ways in which students with differing degrees of general and specialized abilities respond to different kinds of instruction.

A second individual difference that has been of considerable interest to educators is creativity. The chapter reviews some views of creativity, discusses what teachers can do to encourage creativity, and describes several models that can be used to develop materials and activities designed to enhance creativity.

The final section of the chapter is concerned with such student traits as personality attributes and anxiety level. Research is reviewed that indicates that students with certain personality traits often respond best to particular kinds of instructional approaches.

Virginia Plott teaches first grade at Astoria Park Elementary School in Tallahassee, Florida. Ms. Plott grew up and went through school in Pennsylvania. She attended Harrisburg Community College and Pennsylvania State University before transferring to Florida State University in Tallahassee, where she received a B.A. in education. She also has an M.A. degree in reading and language arts from Florida State. Tallahassee, Florida, is a community of 90,000 people located in the north-central part of the state. Ms. Plott has been teaching at Astoria Park School for 9 years. Astoria Park has about 700 students, distributed from kindergarten to fifth grade. The school itself was built during the period when "open" classrooms were in vogue, and it consists of large, open areas divided by bookshelves and tables. However, children are assigned to a particular class, and most of their work is done in a designated area.

Florida is one of several states in the country that has passed a law that will eventually award high school diplomas only on attainment of certain "minimal educational competencies" as demonstrated by a test administered statewide. In an attempt to identify and aid at an early age children who may have difficulty attaining these competencies, the state has mandated the development of what is called the Primary Education Program (PREP). At the time the following interview took place, the program was in its first year, and several aspects of individualized teaching that Ms. Plott describes are in response to PREP. The interview began with a request for a little background information about the students at Astoria Park School.

A.   Most of the children in the school are from middle- and lower-middle-class backgrounds. I'd say our racial mix is about 70 percent white and 30 percent black.

Q. Is there any attempt to group the children into classes in any way? By ability, for example.

A. No. In fact they try to make sure that the classes are heterogeneous, with each teacher having a mix of high, low, and average children, and a mix of black and white children.

Q. Are the children tested when they first come into the school?

A. This year was the first year we had a lot of testing, and it was because of the PREP program. There was physical screening as well as academic testing. We assessed hearing and vision and measured height and weight, and we thoroughly checked children for any physical, motor coordination, or medical problems. Then we used readiness tests to divide the children into three groups: a remedial group, a developmental group, and an enrichment group. The remedial children are well below where an entering first grader should be. The developmental children are average; they're where they are supposed to be at the beginning of grade one. The enriched children are advanced; they come to you already with a lot of skills.

Q. What happens after the children have been divided into the groups?

A. This was the first year of the program, and the focus was mostly on the remedial group. Next year we'll work with the developmental and enrichment children. With the remedial children, we wrote an individual educational prescription (IEP) for each child in each area in which the child did not score high enough on the readiness tests. So I had children who had IEP's in the math area, some in reading, and some in both. I had some children who had IEP's written up for their gross motor skills. The physical education teacher worked with them in a class that emphasized gross or fine motor skills.

Q. After you have the IEP's, what happens?

A. I develop special materials to meet the children's needs in whatever areas they're weak in. I continue to test a lot to prove that the children are improving in skills, and I keep records to indicate when I change from one level to the next, what materials I used to get them to the next level, and what test I used to evaluate improvement.

Q. You have all three levels of children in your classroom at the same time, right?

A. Yes.

Q. What do you do with developmental and enrichment children?

A. I select materials at the appropriate levels. But actually it's more than that. You have incredible differences among first-grade children. Some children come to first grade reading, some come ready to read but are nonreaders, and still others come needing a lot of work with kindergarten, or readiness, concepts. You also have differences in writing skills. Some children know how to hold a pencil, others don't. Some children have had a lot of experience with crayons and pencils, others have had limited experience, at least until they entered kindergarten. I try to give everybody what they need, so if a child needs to have a big space to draw or write with a crayon, I give him or her a huge piece of paper. In my class there are always ten things going on at once. When kids progress, I just change whatever they're doing to meet their needs. But all through the year, I have to keep up with the children and keep them moving along. I try to meet everybody's needs no matter what those needs may be.

Talking with an experienced teacher like Virginia Plott reveals the amazing degree to which individual differences influence instructional decisions. This is especially true at the lower elementary grade levels, where, as Ms. Plott has indicated, children enter the classroom with widely varying skills, abilities, and experiences. But it is also true at the higher grade levels, where attention to individual differences can significantly affect a student's response to schooling.

Some aspects of individualizing instruction can be acquired only by experience. Teachers must learn how to respond to children who have never handled a pencil, they must learn what materials to use when a child passes from one skill level to the next, and they must learn how to maintain order in a classroom where ten things may be going on simultaneously. There are no general rules to pass along here; teachers must learn these things through experience.

However, there is information that can help prepare the new teacher to acquire experiential knowledge, and this chapter seeks to impart such information.

ADAPTING TEACHING TO INDIVIDUAL DIFFERENCES

Teachers who change their teaching to accommodate to the capabilities of particular students (or groups of students) are doing one of two things. Either they are varying the rate or amount of the instruction given, or they are varying the nature or content of the instruction given.

Varying the Rate or Amount of Instruction

One response to individual differences is to group together in one class all students who display certain characteristics. Essentially the same instruction can then be given to every student in the class. Tracking systems are an example of this type of approach. In a *tracking system,* students are divided into groups on the basis of their judged learning abilities. Students who are judged to be fast learners are assigned to the "fast track," medium learners to the "middle track," and slow learners to the "slow track." The instruction each track receives is then varied to accord with the judged abilities of the students. Students in the fast track receive more instruction at a faster pace than do students in the middle and slow tracks.

The decision regarding how much instruction a student will receive, or the rate at which the instruction will be given, is usually dependent on test scores, such as those derived from standardized achievement or ability tests, and on teacher evaluations. If a student does not perform well on standardized tests and is also judged a slow learner by the teacher, the student is a likely candidate for a slower track. Alternatively, students who both perform well on tests and are judged by their teachers to be fast learners are likely to be selected for the faster track.

Tracking—the strategy of varying the rate or amount of instruction for entire classes of students—has come under a good deal of research scrutiny, and such research is examined in greater detail later in this chapter and in subsequent

Every student is an individual and needs individual consideration and attention. (© George Bellerose/Stock, Boston)

chapters. But for now it can be said that, with several notable exceptions, procedures for varying the rate or amount of instruction when applied to entire classes of students have the potential for doing more harm than good.

As a point of comparison, recall the system for dividing students into remedial, developmental, and enriched groups described by Virginia Plott. This system obviously had the potential to be used as the basis for a tracking system, but it was not. Students at each level were systematically intermingled in each classroom. As a result, individualization had to occur by varying the nature or content of the instruction within the classroom.

Varying the Nature or Content of Instruction

A second way that instruction can be adapted to individual characteristics is by varying its nature or content. In addition to having different intellectual capabilities, people differ in their preferred style of learning. Some can learn quite effectively by listening to a teacher or lecturer talk. Others find it difficult to learn by listening and find that they must read material before it can be learned. Some students can read a description of a process or activity and master it without ever engaging in the process or activity itself. Other students find they must go through a "hands-on" experience before they can learn the task.

Such differences in preferred learning style do not represent discrepancies in a global aptitude for learning that would justify sorting people into fast- or slow-learner categories. Yet they may produce different learning outcomes depending on the instructional procedure used. The teacher who is sensitive to individual differences can adapt instructional techniques to conform both to the capabilities and to the preferred learning style of each student. If done successfully, this tailoring of instruction to fit the pupil can produce the dual benefit of making the instructional process more effective and producing a positive motivational outlook in the student.

General glimpses of this approach were given in Virginia Plott's interview. The children in her class were doing a wide variety of things, all of which had as their goal the individualization of instruction to fit the needs of the pupils.

Having considered the two general techniques for adapting instruction to individual differences, let us now turn to a discussion of specific individual differences, and the manner in which instruction can be altered to accommodate those differences.

INTELLIGENCE

Of all the human capabilities studied by psychologists, probably none is more popularized and controversial than intelligence. Virtually everyone shares a general sense of what intelligence is. The controversy comes in, however, when an attempt is made to move beyond a commonsensical idea of intelligence

Annehurst School: A Response to Individual Differences

Annehurst School in Westerville, Ohio, is one of the few schools in the United States that has a completely individualized curriculum. The heart of the approach is the Annehurst Curriculum Classification System (ACCS), which relates twelve student characteristics to specific curriculum materials. The student characteristics are age, previous experience, intelligence, motivation, emotion/personality, creativity, sociability, verbal expression, auditory perception, visual perception, motor perception, and interest in particular topics.

Over the years, the staff of the Annehurst School has classified thousands of pieces of curriculum material in terms of their appropriateness for students of differing abilities, interests, and needs. As a system, ACCS is designed to "bring students and curriculum materials together in precise ways to help each learner achieve objectives that the teacher has identified as being especially appropriate" (Frymier, 1980, p. 683).

A good deal of research has been completed on the ACCS approach, and this research has been summarized as supporting the basic theory on which the system is based (Frymier, 1980). In addition, the approach is being adopted by other schools around the United States, and it is being described as a system that is truly responsive to the needs and capabilities of individual students.

to a precisely defined capability that is measurable and can be used in important educational and career decisions. To facilitate understanding of the way in which psychologists define and measure intelligence, a brief history of the theory and measurement of intelligence is called for.

Intelligence Theory and Intelligence Measurement

Galton

Sir Francis Galton (1822–1911) was one of the first psychologists to attempt to define intelligence in a manner precise enough to lead to measurement procedures. The prevailing theory of the mind during Galton's time was that it consisted of ideas that in turn were formed from "basic sensations." Since intelligence was thought to consist of the ability to construct and manipulate ideas, Galton thought that a reasonable approach to measuring intelligence would be to measure sensitivity to basic sensations, the presumed building blocks of ideas. Accordingly, Galton measured the "keenness of sight," "breathing power," "reaction time," and "strength of pull" of thousands of subjects in the 1870s and 1880s (Fancher, 1979). Much to Galton's dismay, however, the data he collected on these various measures did not conform to his ideas of intelligence. Individuals whom he judged to be highly intelligent frequently did not score well on his tests. Alternatively, people whose intelligence he considered unremarkable often did very well. Galton eventually abandoned his attempt to define and measure intelligence, but his place in the history of psychology is assured.

Binet

The next major development occurred in France. The Paris school system at the turn of the century was faced with a problem of fairly serious dimensions: a significant number of children enrolled in the Paris schools were not benefiting from regular instruction. Unfortunately, these children—many of whom we would now think of as retarded—were frequently not identified early enough to shift them to special classes. The minister of instruction in Paris approached psychologist Alfred Binet with the problem of devising a technique for the early identification of students who might benefit from instruction outside of the regular classroom.

Binet tackled his task in a thoroughly pragmatic manner. His years of observation of school-aged children had provided him with some initial ideas on the kinds of tasks and test items that would discriminate between successful and unsuccessful learners. He launched into a trial-and-error process, in which items and tasks were administered to students who had been previously identified by teachers as being either "bright" or "dull." Tasks that the bright students completed correctly and the dull students failed to complete correctly were retained in the test. Tasks that did not discriminate between the two groups were discarded. The end result of this process was the development of a test that reliably distinguished students who had previously been identified as fast or slow learners.

Binet published his test, which he called the Metrical Scale of Intelligence, in 1905. The test subsequently crossed the Atlantic, and its adaptation by Lewis Terman at Stanford University was published as the Stanford-Binet Intelligence Scale in 1916. The Stanford-Binet, which was the first test to use IQ as the unit of intelligence, is still one of the bench marks against which all other tests of intelligence are compared.

Binet's pioneering efforts in intelligence testing left three important legacies. The first was his pragmatic approach to the construction of a viable intelligence test. Unlike Galton, Binet did not have theoretical preconceptions about what intelligence was. Instead, he adopted a trial-and-error approach to psychological measurement that continues to serve as the predominant approach to test construction to this day.

The second legacy of Binet was his novel strategy of *defining intelligence as the thing that his test measured.* This atheoretical stance on defining intelligence has been adopted by many modern psychologists, and it is particularly popular among test developers who respect the widespread utility of intelligence tests but are wary of theoretical disputes (Hopkins and Stanley, 1981).

Binet's third legacy was his tying together of intelligence and school success. In effect, Binet's procedure for constructing an intelligence test ensured that intelligence—defined as performance on the test—and school success were virtually one and the same thing. This situation continues today.

> These Binet tests, and in effect all their descendants [current intelligence tests], had their origin in the educational setting of the Paris schools of 1900, and the various modifications and refinements they have undergone since then have been implicitly shaped by the educational traditions of Europe and North America. The content and methods of instruction represented in this tradition, it should be remembered, are a rather narrow and select sample of all the various forms of human learning and of the ways of imparting knowledge and skills. (Jensen, 1969, p. 7)

The connection between education and intelligence testing is an important one to keep in mind. Intelligence tests are fairly good indicators of the degree to which individuals possess attributes that contribute to successful school performance. They are not particularly good indicators of a vast number of other attributes that are largely unrelated to academic learning.

Modern approaches to measurement and theory

A number of perspectives contribute to present-day intelligence testing and theory. In 1939, David Wechsler published a test known as the Wechsler Adult Intelligence Scale (WAIS). This test was scaled down in 1949 and published as the Wechsler Intelligence Scale for Children (WISC). The WAIS was revised in 1955 and again in 1980, becoming the WAIS-R; and the WISC in 1974, becoming the WISC-R. The WISC-R is the most widely used individual intelligence test for children ranging in age from 6 to 16 (Hopkins and Stanley, 1981).

Wechsler's intelligence tests are in the Binet tradition, in that they are not based on a formal theory of intelligence. Instead, the emphasis is on developing tests that identify students with particular patterns of abilities.

A modern view of intelligence that is much more theoretical in nature has been proposed by J. P. Guilford (1967, 1968). Guilford examined human performance on a wide variety of cognitive tasks, and by grouping together those tasks that seemed related to one another, he developed a structure of intellect (SI) model. The model, which is presented in Figure 3-1, proposes that there are three dimensions to intellectual functioning. The first relates to the type of content of a test item or task: content may be figural, symbolic, semantic, or behavioral. The second dimension relates to the type of mental operation required by the task's content: the operation may be evaluation, convergent thinking, divergent thinking, memory, or cognition. The final dimension is the "product" of the mental operation when exposed to a particular content: products may be units of information, classes of units, relations among units, systems of information, transformations, or implications.

FIGURE 3-1   Guilford's Model of the Three Faces of Intelligence

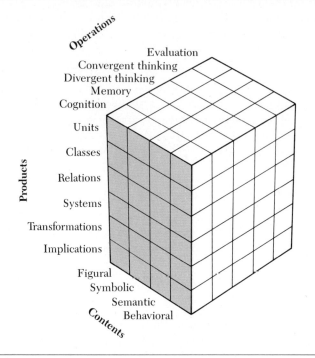

(Guilford, 1967)

As Figure 3-1 illustrates, Guilford's SI model postulates 120 (4 contents × 5 operations × 6 products) separate mental abilities. The model has been criticized for having more theoretical than practical interest (e.g., Mehrens and Lehman, 1975), but it remains one of the more impressive efforts to analyze the psychology of intelligence.

A more recent approach to the analysis of intelligence involves an attempt to define intelligence in terms of the information-processing capabilities that are assumed to underlie mental activity (e.g., Hunt, 1978; Sternberg, 1977). These theories are based on the assumption that the human cognitive system consists of structural entities (such as short-term memory capacity) and processing operations (such as speed of decision making) that can vary from individual to individual. Hence if one had a measure of an individual's structural characteristics and his or her processing capabilities, one would have an excellent description of the individual's intellectual capabilities. *Information-processing theories* are so new that little information has so far been gathered regarding their validity. However, they appear very promising, and as will be seen in the chapter on cognitive learning (Chapter 8), they seem to be consistent with recent theoretical developments in the area of human learning and memory.

information processing the progression of stimuli through a cognitive system in a relatively systematic manner

Is Intelligence Determined by Heredity or by Environment?

One of the most controversial questions regarding intelligence is whether it is determined by genetic inheritance or by environmental experience. The question is a highly controversial one because if intelligence is seen as being largely determined by genetics, the implication is that it is largely fixed at birth and that very little can be done to alter it. Alternatively, if intelligence is seen as environmentally determined, the implication is that it can be changed by altering the environmental conditions—for example by modifying the school system. The greatest source of controversy is the suggestion—put forward by several psychologists—that racial differences in measured IQ may be attributable to genetic differences among racial groups (e.g., Jensen, 1969).

Before this question is considered in depth, it should be made clear that the debate involves only intelligence as measured by an intelligence test. There is no scientific evidence one way or the other regarding the inheritance of intelligence as measured by any other criteria.

Each of us is an individual because of our genetic endowment and our own unique set of experiences. (© Phyllis Stoffman 1982/Woodfin Camp & Assoc.)

Heritability of IQ

Some psychologists have claimed that intelligence has a heritability of .75 or higher (e.g., Jensen, 1969); others have claimed a heritability factor that is considerably lower (e.g., Scarr-Salapatek, 1971).

heritability
the extent to
which a trait is
determined by
genetics

    Heritability—a term that refers to the extent to which a trait is determined by genetics—is expressed in terms of a number, called a *heritability index* or quotient, that ranges in value between 0 and 1. A value of 0 indicates that no part of the variability in the trait has been determined by genetics; that all of the variability is attributable to variations in the environment. Conversely, a heritability index of 1 means that all of the variability in the trait is accounted for by genetic variation; that environment has had no influence whatsoever. The heritability index of .75 suggested by Jensen proposes that 75 percent of the variability in intelligence test scores is attributable to genetic influences, leaving only 25 percent to be accounted for by environment.

The meaning of heritability

As an example of what heritability means, consider the following imaginary experiment. Suppose that you went to a local seed store and picked up 10 kernels of corn of one type, 10 of another, etc., until you had 100 kernels— that is, ten sets of kernels, each set having different genetic characteristics. Suppose you then took the 100 kernels home and planted them in a nutrient-filled trough in a greenhouse. All of the kernels would be bathed in the same nutrient solution, and as nearly as possible all would be exposed to exactly the same environmental circumstances. If after three months you measured the height of each stalk of corn and found systematic differences in height among the various types of corn, the variation would *have* to be attributed to genetics. The heritability index for the height of the corn would be 1—the reason being that the genetic factor had been allowed to vary while all of the seeds had been exposed to exactly the same environment.

    The converse of this experiment would be one that allowed the environment to vary while the genetic factor remained unvaried. Imagine that 100 kernels of corn, all of the same genetic type, were planted in ten troughs, each containing a different percentage of nitrogen. Since all the seeds had exactly the same genetic characteristics, any variations in the height of the stalks three months after planting would have to be attributed to environment. Thus the heritability index would be 0.

    Unfortunately (or perhaps fortunately), events controlling the development of human beings cannot be controlled to the same extent as those controlling the development of corn. Consequently, estimating the heritability of a human trait—such as performance on an intelligence test—is much more problematic. Nevertheless, the data of concern in the heredity/environment debate come from studies that are conceptually very similar to the imaginary experiments just described.

Human studies

Identical twins have exactly the same genetic make-up. One important piece of information in the heredity/environment debate involves how closely identical twins resemble one another in intelligence when they are reared apart—as when they are adopted by different families. Note that this situation conceptually mirrors the second imaginary experiment, in which genetic variation was controlled and the environment was allowed to differ. If twins reared in very different environments turn out to have a very similar IQ, it would be strong evidence for the genetic position. Alternatively, if they turned out to have a very different IQ, that would be strong evidence for the environmental position.

A second kind of study, one that is conceptually very similar to the first imaginary experiment, involves comparing the IQ of unrelated individuals who have been reared in the same household—as in the case of unrelated children adopted by the same family. If the children turned out to be very different in IQ, it would be evidence for the genetic position (see the accompanying box).

Identical twins raised together have the same genetic make-up and virtually the same environmental experiences. (© George W. Gardner)

Is IQ Determined by Heredity or by Environment?—Two Views

Heredity

In 1969, University of California educational psychologist Arthur Jensen published a very scholarly but explosive article which maintained that 75 percent of the variability in IQ scores can be accounted for by heredity. The principal evidence that Jensen offered in support of his position is presented in the following table.

Correlations for IQ Between Related and Unrelated Individuals: Obtained and Theoretical Values

Correlations Between	Number of Studies	Obtained Median Correlation	Theoretical Value
Unrelated persons			
Children reared apart	4	.01	.00
Foster parent and child	3	.20	.00
Children reared together	5	.24	.00
Related persons			
Second cousins	1	.16	.063
First cousins	3	.26	.125
Uncle/aunt and nephew/niece	1	.34	.215
Siblings reared apart	33	.47	.50
Siblings reared together	36	.55	.50
Fraternal twins, different sex	9	.49	.50
Fraternal twins, same sex	11	.56	.50
Identical twins, reared apart	4	.75	1.0
Identical twins, reared together	14	.87	1.0
Grandparent and grandchild	3	.27	.25
Parent (as adult) and child	13	.50	.50
Parent (as child) and child	1	.56	.50

(Jensen, 1969)

The theoretical values are those obtained by assuming that IQ is determined solely by heredity. For instance, unrelated individuals do not share any genes, hence the theoretical value of their correlation in IQ scores is 0. Siblings, fraternal twins, and a parent and child share 50 percent of their genes, thereby providing a theoretical value of .50.

Jensen emphasized several features of the data presented in the table. First, he pointed to the general correspondence between the predicted values and the theoretical values. Although the fit is certainly not exact, there is a clear pattern of correspondence. Second, he pointed to the critically important values for unrelated children reared together, and for identical twins reared apart. The data for the unrelated children reared together suggest that 24 percent of the variability in IQ scores is determined by environmental factors, leaving 76 percent of the variability to be determined by heredity. The data for the identical twins reared apart suggest that 75 percent of the variability in IQ scores is determined by heredity, leaving 25 percent to be accounted for by environmental factors. Jensen concluded that the remarkable correspondence between the two ways of estimating the heritability of IQ could not be attributed to chance, and that 75 percent represented the best estimate of how much of the variability in IQ scores was determined by genetic factors.

Other scholars have interpreted Jensen's data differently. First, they point out that environmental similarity is likely to increase at the same rate as genetic similarity. That is, the environment shared by first cousins is likely to be more similar than the environment shared by second cousins, and the environment shared by siblings is certain to be more similar than the environment shared by first cousins. Because increasing genetic similarity is accompanied by increasing environmental similarity, it cannot be determined whether the increase in the relationship of IQ scores as a function of increasing kinship is attributable to environment or to heredity.

Jensen's interpretation of the identical twins reared apart data has also been challenged. Kamin (1974), for example, has argued that the majority of cases making up the instances of twins being reared apart do not really involve different environments. As an instance, he cites the case of a pair of twins adopted by different sets of relatives on the death of their parents. The children lived next door to one another, played together daily, and attended the same school. Kamin's argument is that this case and others do not really involve differing environments.

As a final point of criticism environmentalists frequently argue that the focus on correlations masks the impact of environment on IQ. They suggest that instead of focusing on correlations, researchers should focus on changes in average IQ as a function of changing environment. This suggestion provides a lead-in to the research of Sandra Scarr-Salapatek.

Environment

Sandra Scarr-Salapatek has contributed two studies to the heredity/environment IQ debate. In the first study, Scarr-Salapatek (1971) culled through a list of the 250,000 children enrolled in the Philadelphia public school system and identified over 3,000 twins. After classifying the twins by race, socioeconomic status, and same or opposite sex, she correlated their IQs.

Box continues on next page

She found that the genetic model provided a reasonable fit to the actual data with both black and white twin pairs from upper- and middle-class families. However, there was little support for a strong genetic model when the black and white twin pairs were from lower-class families. Scarr-Salapatek suggested that this finding raised serious doubts about universally applying a strong genetic explanation to variations in IQ scores.

Scarr-Salapatek's second study (Scarr-Salapatek and Weinberg, 1975) examined the IQs of 321 children from 101 highly educated white families that had adopted black children. Of these 321 children, 145 were natural and 176 adopted. Of the 176 adopted children, 130 were black and 46 were either white, Asian, or American Indian. The essential details of the study are presented in the accompanying table.

Sandra Scarr-Salapatek and Richard Weinberg point to the increase in the scores of the black children over national or regional averages as evidence for an environmental influence on IQ and school achievement. Moreover, they point out that those children (both black and white) who were adopted early, thereby lengthening their exposure to an advantageous environment, had even higher IQs than those adopted later. These researchers conclude: "Our work does not rule out genetic contributions to intelligence, but it does demonstrate that a massive environmental change can increase black IQ scores to an above-average level. Social factors, such as age at placement and the adoptive family's characteristics, play a strong role in accounting for this increase" (Scarr-Salapatek and Weinberg, 1975, p. 8).

Critics searching for evidence that supports genetic influence on IQ could emphasize several aspects of the Scarr-Salapatek–Weinberg adoption study. First, they might point out that black adopted children with two black natural parents had an average IQ of 97, whereas black adopted children with one black natural parent and one white natural parent had an average IQ of 109. The authors dealt with this point by stressing that the black children with two black parents had been adopted at a later age (average

The evidence regarding the extent to which intelligence test performance is determined by genetics is not definitive at this point. The bulk of the studies that at first glance appear to offer support for one position or the other turn out, on closer analysis, to be subject to interpretations that favor the opposite view. The most that can be said at this point is that the question is still an open one. The intensity of the debate has lessened from the high point that it reached in the early and mid 1970s. It is safe to say, however, that the question will be around for some time to come.

Average IQs for Family Members in Homes Having Natural and Adopted Children

	Number	Average Scores	Expected Scores Based on National or Regional Averages
IQs of parents			
Father	101	121	100
Mother	101	118	100
IQs of adopted children			
Black	130	106	90
White	25	111	100
Other	21	100	?
IQs of natural children	144	117	100
IQs of early adopted children			
Black	99	110	90
White	9	117	100
Other	only 3 cases		—
Reading and math achievement test scores for adopted black children	130	55th percentile	15th percentile*

*Average for black children in the Minneapolis-St. Paul area where study was conducted. (Scarr-Salapatek and Weinberg, 1975)

age at adoption = 32 months) than had the black adopted children with a mixed natural parentage (average age at adoption = 9 months). More difficult to counter, however, is the observation that, regardless of adoption age, white adopted children scored better on tests than did black adopted children.

Assessing Intelligence in Different Cultural Groups

Members of cultural and social minority groups typically score lower on standardized intelligence tests than do members of the white majority group. The most frequently cited reason for this difference is that traditional intelligence tests measure attributes that are valued and taught in the dominant white culture. This situation places members of minority cultures at a disadvantage when they take the tests.

Culture-fair intelligence tests

One response to the charge of cultural bias has been an attempt to develop what are known as "culture-fair" tests of intelligence. The idea behind the culture-fair intelligence test is to ensure that no single cultural group has an unfair advantage on the test, and hence to avoid the emergence of any marked differences in performance among different cultural groups.

Several culture-fair tests have been developed, and most share the common characteristic of measuring nonverbal performance. Examples include Raymond Cattell's Culture-Fair Intelligence Tests, Raven's Progressive Matrices, and the Leiter International Performance Scale. Unfortunately, the performance of majority and minority groups on these tests has turned out to be not very different from the performance on tests charged with being culturally biased. Majority groups have typically scored higher on the tests than have minority groups (Jensen, 1969; Popham, 1981).

SOMPA: An alternative approach

A second approach has been developed by sociologist Jane Mercer (Mercer and Lewis, 1978). Mercer has developed an assessment technique called the System of Multi-Pluralistic Assessment (SOMPA). SOMPA can be used with children aged 5 to 11 and consists of two components: a Parent Interview and a set of Student Assessment Materials. The Parent Interview is an interview schedule that collects sociocultural information about such factors as the size and structure of the family, the socioeconomic status of the family, and the extent of the family's urban acculturation. In addition, the interview collects such personal information as the child's health history, his or her family role, his or her community role, his or her peer relations, his or her nonacademic roles in school, and his or her earner/consumer and self-maintenance roles. The student assessment includes several physical dexterity tasks, the *Bender Visual Motor Gestalt Test*, the Wechsler Intelligence Scale for Children, measurement of height and weight, and assessment of visual and auditory acuity.

SOMPA is designed to measure what Mercer and Lewis (1978) have called, *estimated learning potential*—defined as an estimate of what a child can learn from his or her environment in comparison with children who have had similar opportunities and encouragement. In essence, then, SOMPA attempts to compare a child's performance with that of other children who have had very similar environmental experiences.

SOMPA is such a new assessment technique that very little evaluational research has accumulated. It is a very promising technique, however, and as one reviewer has commented, it may "offer a reasonable solution to the issues of cultural bias in testing" (Nuttall, 1979).

Intelligence and Teaching

Earlier in this chapter, it was indicated that educators can respond to individual student differences in two ways: they can alter the rate or amount of instruction being presented, or they can change the nature of the instruction. Both of these procedures have been used in response to differing levels of intelligence.

Varying the rate or amount of instruction

One common response to differing intelligence and achievement levels is to form *ability groups*. A good many school systems, for example, divide children into fast-, moderate-, and slow-learner groups. The assignment of a student to a particular group rarely occurs solely as a function of his or her score on an IQ test. More commonly, assignment is based on a combination of prior academic record, teacher recommendation, and test performance.

Major reviews of research on ability grouping (e.g., Ekstrom, 1959; Findley and Bryan, 1971) indicate that while there is virtually no evidence that grouping produces positive effects, there is suggestive evidence of possible negative effects. This topic is reviewed in greater detail in Chapter 10, but the following extract summarizes the available evidence:

> Briefly, we find that ability grouping shows no consistent positive value for helping students generally, or particular groups of students, to learn better. Taking all studies into account, the balance of findings is chiefly of no strong effect either favorable or unfavorable. Among studies showing significant effects, the slight preponderance of evidence showing the practice favorable to the learning of high ability students is more than offset by evidence of unfavorable effects on the learning of average and low ability groups, particularly the latter. There is no appreciable difference in these effects at elementary and secondary school levels. Finally, those instances of special benefit under ability grouping have generally involved substantial modification of materials and methods, which may well be the influential factors wholly apart from grouping. (Findley and Bryan, 1971, p. 54)

The exception to the generalization contained in the extract is with groups at the extreme ends of the spectrum. As will be seen in the chapter on exceptional children (Chapter 4), there may at times be some advantage to instructing children with very exceptional abilities outside of the regular classroom.

Varying the nature or content of instruction

General ability as measured by intelligence tests has also figured prominently in research on various instructional methods. In general, this research has focused on the question of whether there is an educational advantage associated with assigning a student with one ability level to instructional method A, and a student with a different ability level to instructional method B. One heavily researched area involves the presentation of instruction in either a highly programmed or a relatively unconstrained manner.

Ability levels and instructional programming

In a massive study of individual differences in ability and instructional methods, Lee Cronbach and Richard Snow (1977) suggest that knowledge of students' general ability (e.g., performance on an IQ test) might be used in a beneficial

Aptitude-Treatment Interactions

One of the most highly researched areas in educational psychology in recent years involves the search for aptitude-treatment interactions. The basic idea in this research is that not all students are equally responsive to the same instructional method. Aptitude-treatment interaction research involves trying to answer the question of which students will be maximally responsive to which instructional methods.

A study by George Domino (1971) provides a good example of aptitude-treatment interaction research. Domino isolated two groups of college students: one (called the Ac group) that scored high on the achievement-via-conformity *and* low on the achievement-via-independence subscales of the California Personality Inventory, and one (called the Ai group) that scored high on the achievement-via-independence *and* low on the achievement-via-conformity subscales. These two groups of students were then systematically assigned to four different sections of an introductory psychology course taught by the same instructor. The instructor taught two sections of the course in a "conforming" manner and two sections in an "independent" manner. In the conforming sections, great emphasis was put on factual knowledge, lectures, and close parallels between material presented in class and in the textbook. In the independent sections, emphasis was placed on ideas rather than facts, and upon active participation of the students in the learning process. All of the students received the same textbook assignments and took the same examinations. Neither the students nor the instructor were aware that students had been assigned to the four sections of the course in such a way that one of the independent sections consisted entirely of Ai students and the other entirely of Ac students. Similarly, one of the conforming sections consisted entirely of Ac students and the other entirely of Ai students. At the end of the semester, all of the students rated both the instructor (see graph A) and the course (see graph B) on a 7-point scale, in which 7 was an excellent rating and 1 a very poor rating. The students' results on the final exam are shown in graph C.

As can be seen in the graphs, there was a striking advantage for student attitudes toward the instructor and the course, as well as for student performance when there was a match between the student's learning style

fashion to expose them to procedures that vary in their degree of instructional programming or instructional control.

An example of a highly controlled instructional procedure is programmed instruction. In one style of programmed instruction, called *linear programming,*

Student Evaluation of Teacher Effectiveness

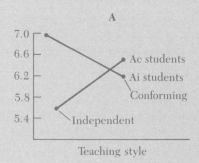

A

Student Evaluation of Course

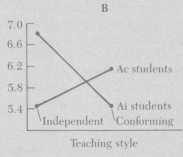

B

Student Performance on Final Exam

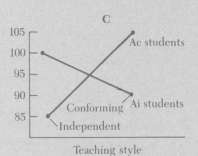

C

(Domino, 1971)

and the style in which the course was taught. Domino's study provides a classic instance of an aptitude-treatment interaction, and it illustrates the potential practical implications of this research area. For example, an administrator wanting to maximize learning and promote positive attitudes to instruction might administer the California Personality Inventory to incoming students and then assign them—on the basis of their scores on this inventory—to classes given in the appropriate teaching style.

students read a short instructional segment and then respond to a question regarding what they have read (Markle, 1966). The steps taken by the student through the material are generally a series of small ones, and the student's progress is methodical and controlled.

intrinsic programming an instructional program that uses branches after each question so that students can be shunted to different sequences depending on how they answer

Offering greater flexibility is a programming style called *intrinsic* or *branching programming* (Markle, 1966). In branching programming, students can be shunted to different instructional segments, depending on how they have answered a particular question: Students who provide answers that indicate thorough mastery of the content can be guided to an accelerated instructional sequence. Conversely, students who give answers indicating they are having trouble can be directed to a sequence of remedial instruction.

Another technique involving a fairly controlled instructional approach is called mastery learning (e.g., Block, 1971). *Mastery learning* is an instructional procedure that involves establishing learning goals and then allowing students to achieve those goals at their own rate. The procedure is controlled, in that the specific goals to be mastered and the means of attaining those goals are generally the same for each student.

mastery learning an instructional procedure that involves setting goals students may achieve at their own rates

At the opposite end of the continuum are instructional procedures that allow students considerable freedom in deciding what they are going to learn, how they are going to learn it, and when they are going to learn it. The most prominent and extreme example of this type of approach is the Summerhill School, founded and written about by the noted English educator A. S. Neill (1960). Neill advocated leaving virtually all educational decisions to the students themselves; in fact at Summerhill, teachers served primarily as resource persons; they performed as teachers only when asked by students to do so.

Cronbach and Snow (1977) found a general tendency for lower-ability students to do better when they were exposed to instruction that was on the controlled end of the continuum. They still did not perform as well as high-ability students, but the differences between the two groups tended to be reduced by controlled instructional programming. Conversely, low-ability students tended to be handicapped when much of the organization and interpretation of the instruction was left to the students. In contrast, high-ability students did better in more loosely controlled instructional settings. In the words of Cronbach and Snow: "Highs profit from the opportunity to process the information in their own way" (1977, p. 500).

aptitude-treatment interactions programs that adapt instructional treatments to individual differences in student aptitudes

The outcomes reported by Cronbach and Snow (1977), in which high-ability students had a tendency to do better with loosely controlled instructional procedures whereas low-ability students tended to do better with more tightly controlled instructional procedures, are an example of what educational psychologists call an *aptitude-treatment interaction* (see the accompanying box on pp. 88–89). Cronbach and Snow's survey of the research literature suggests that in some cases both high- and low-ability students might profit from being assigned to instructional procedures that vary appropriately in the amount of control they exert over the students' activities.

Special Abilities and Mode of Instruction

General assessment procedures such as IQ tests generally provide an overall score and several subscales relating to more specialized abilities. For example, many intelligence tests provide subscales for verbal and nonverbal IQ; others provide scores for verbal performance and quantitative performance. More specialized tests provide an assessment of more specialized abilities. For example, the Illinois Test of Psycholinguistic Abilities (ITPA) is an instrument that assesses the general language competence of children aged 2 to 10 years. It provides specialized subscales on auditory reception, visual reception, visual sequential memory, auditory association, auditory sequential memory, visual association, visual closure, verbal expression, grammatic closure, manual expression, auditory closure, and sound blending (Buros, 1974).

The testing of specialized abilities has frequently been suggested as being an excellent means for selecting appropriate educational treatments. As an instance, students who score high on the auditory reception subscale of the ITPA might, in theory, benefit maximally from a technique emphasizing the auditory presentation of instruction. Likewise, students scoring high in visual reception might benefit maximally from an instructional approach emphasizing the visual presentation of material.

Unfortunately, Cronbach and Snow (1977) found little evidence that specialized ability scores provide a viable means of choosing beneficial educational approaches. The research studies they surveyed sometimes found an advantage for students assigned to an instructional procedure because of specialized aptitude score, but more often there was no evidence of a beneficial effect.

CREATIVITY

Creativity has attracted a considerable amount of interest from both researchers and educators. Researchers are interested in creativity because it may be a basic attribute of the individual, similar to intelligence and temperament. Educators have been interested in creativity as a trait that can perhaps be developed or enhanced through educational experience.

Differing Views of Creativity

Over the years a number of views of creativity have been developed. These views have generally evolved from already established theoretical positions, and each emphasizes a somewhat different aspect of the global concept of creativity (Bloomberg, 1973).

The psychoanalytic view
Sigmund Freud viewed creativity as the behavioral consequence of the release of sexual or aggressive energies into culturally approved behaviors (Bloomberg, 1973). Interestingly enough, Freud (1934a, 1934b) suggested a theoretical linkage between creativity and *psychopathology*. Both resulted from the release of energy derived from instinctual drives; the difference was that creativity

psychopathology disordered mental or behavioral functioning

involved energy released into socially acceptable behavior, whereas psycho-pathology involved energy channeled into unacceptable behaviors. Support for this type of interpretation was acquired in a study by MacKinnon (1965), who found that architects judged to be highly creative also displayed fewer neurotic tendencies that architects judged to be lower in creativity.

Freud's theory of creativity is consistent with his pessimistic view of human nature. Creativity is merely the by-product of the individual's attempt to deal with the dark and instinctual human drives in a socially acceptable manner. In contrast, the humanistic theory of creativity is based on a more optimistic view of human nature.

The humanistic view

The humanistic theory of creativity differs from the psychoanalytic in that it begins with a positive view of human nature. It postulates that every human being is born with considerable potential for creative expression; the only question is whether or not that potential will be *actualized* (allowed to develop). Carl Rogers (1964), for example, has suggested that creative potential is blocked

Many classrooms are set up so that each student can have learning experiences tailored to his or her individual needs. (© Elizabeth Crews)

by the development of defense mechanisms, which are in turn developed in response to a threatening and inhibiting societal environment. In effect, these defense mechanisms prevent individuals from becoming themselves, thereby preventing creativity from reaching its full potential.

Notice that the humanistic view is similar to the psychoanalytic in that both depict people in conflict with society. The basic difference is that the psychoanalytic view suggests that this conflict is the source of creativity, whereas the humanistic view sees the conflict as being a barrier to creativity.

Rogers (1964) and other humanistic writers (e.g., Holt, 1964, 1967; Maslow, 1968) have suggested that the creative potential inherent in each individual can develop fully only in an environment free from pressures for conformity or of stern evaluation. This suggestion has, in turn, led to educational recommendations that emphasize acceptance of individual expression and de-emphasize negative evaluations of individual accomplishment.

The environmental view

The two views just discussed suggest that creativity is inherent within the individual—either as the channeling of an instinctual drive or as an expression of a natural human quality. In contrast, the environmentalists view creativity as an acquired characteristic—one that is learned for the most part from certain advantageous experiences. Paul Torrance (1961), for example, has suggested that creativity can be increased by encouraging naturally occurring creative behaviors and by training individuals to be creative. This position led Torrance to suggest that teachers could enhance the creativity of their students by such actions as respecting unusual questions and unusual ideas, demonstrating that children's ideas have value, providing opportunities for self-initiated learning, and allowing children to engage in nonevaluated activity (Torrance, 1961).

Torrance's recommendations are derived from a series of longitudinal studies (Torrance, 1959, 1961) that isolated factors in nature, in society, and in schools that were related to creative behavior. These ranged from such factors as home and parental care, educational level of parents, and premature attempts to eliminate child fantasy, to such factors as the use of teaching approaches that would reward creative thinking and help students to value their own ideas.

The factorial view

Earlier in this chapter, Guilford's structure of intellect (SI) model was discussed in relation to intelligence. The SI model has also been the basis for a theory of creativity (Guilford, 1965). Refer back to the SI model presented in Figure 3-1. Creativity can be thought of as consisting of some subset of the 120 independent factors illustrated in the model.

The Guilford model has been criticized for not being descriptive of creative behavior in the real world (Hilgard, 1959), and because individuals judged to be creative by some external criteria do not always perform creatively on the tests derived from Guilford's SI model (Golann, 1957, 1963). However, the model has received support from a major study of creativity in adolescents which suggested that intelligence and creativity were separable attributes. Jacob Getzels and Philip Jackson (1962) used Guilford's tests to identify a group of high-IQ (average IQ = 150), low-creativity adolescents, and a group of lower-IQ (average IQ = 127), high-creativity adolescents. (It should be pointed out that use of the terms "high" and "low" for the two groups was purely relative, in that the groups were above the average of the general population in both creativity and intelligence.)

Getzels and Jackson (1962) found some striking differences between their two groups of adolescents. The high-creativity, lower-IQ group was not especially interested in possessing qualities pleasing to others, whereas the high-IQ, low-creativity group desired those qualities. Moreover, in projective tests and biographical themes, the high-creativity group was more humorous and playful than the high-IQ group, and the high-creativity group indicated more fanciful and original career plans than the high-IQ group. These differences are in contrast to the finding that the groups did not differ on tests of academic achievement.

One of the most interesting findings of the Getzels and Jackson study, from an educational viewpoint, was that teachers indicated they preferred having members of the high-IQ group in their classes more than they did members of the high-creativity group. This finding is consistent with the frequently expressed opinion that highly creative students are much more troublesome to teachers than are highly intelligent students.

The Enhancement of Creativity

Ways of enhancing creativity in the classroom include such strategies as providing a nonthreatening atmosphere that allows unusual ideas to be expressed, rewarding children for coming up with creative ideas or products, and providing opportunities for self-initiated learning. Carol Callahan's (1978) review of educational techniques for developing creativity contains these teacher ideas, and many others culled from a survey of the pertinent literature.

Having teachers behave in an appropriate manner is one avenue to enhancing student creativity. A second is developing instructional materials designed to enhance creativity. Paul Torrance (1978) has reviewed a number of models that can be used as the basis for generating instructional materials and activities. One, the Creative Problem Solving Model (Parnes, Noller, and Biondi, 1977), is based on the idea that creativity can be enhanced by training students to approach problem solving in a disciplined manner that entails defining a problem, obtaining necessary information, producing alternatives, and enhancing group skills.

A second model, the Lateral Thinking Model, was developed in England by Edward de Bono (1974). De Bono's approach makes heavy use of drawing and is based on attempts to encourage lateral (as contrasted to logical) thinking, different points of view, "out of boundary" thinking, and data processing by the right hemisphere of the brain.

A third model reviewed by Torrance is the sociodramatic model that he himself developed (Torrance, 1975), which involves defining a problem and then developing a psychodrama around it. This process entails developing a consequence or collision associated with the problem, casting key characters, involving the audience in the production, acting out the conflict, and cutting the action at various points in time to analyze the situation from the perspective of trying to resolve the conflict.

PERSONALITY TRAITS

In addition to varying in ability, students also vary in *personality* characteristics. Some students are introverted, others extroverted. Some are aggressive and assertive, others retiring and shy. Many of these traits have been examined in a search for aptitudes that could be used to select students for individualized instructional programs. Most, however, have not been found helpful in the selection process. The exceptions to this generalization are the traits of achievement-via-conformity/independence, and achievement relative to level of anxiety.

personality the dynamic organization of all the traits that determine an individual's unique adjustment to his or her environment

Personality Traits and Mode of Instruction

The box on page 89, entitled "Aptitude-Treatment Interactions," reported an instance where a personality trait had been used as a means of selecting an optimal instructional approach. Domino's (1971) finding was that college students scoring high on the achievement-via-conformity subscale of the California Personality Inventory benefited maximally from a highly structured course, whereas students scoring high on the achievement-via-independence subscale benefited maximally from a course emphasizing independent learning.

Similar results have been found using anxiety as a personality trait. Fred Dowaliby and Harry Schumer (1973) reported a study in which college students took an introductory psychology course that was taught in either a "teacher-centered" or a "student-centered" style. The teacher-centered course emphasized lectures and note taking, questions held to the end of class, and little student participation in learning activities. The student-centered course encouraged student questions, and students were actively involved in class demonstrations and activities. Students who were high in anxiety tended to do poorly in the student-centered class and well in the teacher-centered class. The opposite pattern held for students who were low in anxiety; they did well in the student-centered class and poorly in the teacher-centered class. Domino (1974) has replicated these results in a college-level literature course.

Another research area has examined the question of whether students having certain personality traits do better when they take classes from teachers having complementary traits. These studies, like those examining the relationship between specialized abilities and differing modes of instruction, have not found

Is Learning Style a Personality Trait Important to Education?

An idea that has captured the imagination of educators in recent years is that students differ in a personality trait called learning style. Learning style was the topic of a 1980 publication of the National Association of Secondary School Principals: *Student Learning Styles: Diagnosing and Prescribing Programs.*

One of the most thoroughly developed systems of translating learning styles into educational practice is one that has been developed by Rita Dunn, Kenneth Dunn, and Gary Price. The system begins by having each student answer the 104 true-false questions contained in *The Learning Style Inventory* (Dunn, Dunn, and Price, 1979a). This inventory assesses a student's opinion about how his or her learning is influenced by such factors as sound, light, temperature, the time of day, the need for food or beverages, and the presence of other learners; whether learning occurs best in the presence or absence of adults; and whether the student prefers to learn with or without the aid of tactile and kinesthetic teaching aids.

After the student's learning style has been established, the teacher is referred to the *Learning Style Inventory Manual* (Dunn, Dunn, and Price, 1979b), which contains recommendations about how to set up an educational environment that meshes with the student's learning style. For example, the following is the recommendation for a student who has been judged to be "teacher-motivated":

> *Establish den area near teacher; praise often; incorporate reporting to teacher into prescription; include in small-group instructional techniques when teacher is involved. (Dunn, Dunn, and Price, 1979b, p. 5)*

The effectiveness of the Dunn, Dunn, and Price approach to incorporating learning styles into educational practice has yet to be proven (see Davidman, 1981, for a critique), but the system is a good example of attempts being made by educators to individualize instructional approaches.

any consistent pattern indicating that students with certain personality traits respond better when taking classes from teachers having corresponding personality traits (Cronbach and Snow, 1977).

The research on personality traits and instructional procedures indicates that there can be some benefit to altering the nature of instruction in response to certain student characteristics. Students who are constructively motivated or low in anxiety tend to respond better to teaching that places part of the responsibility for learning on their shoulders. Students who are higher in anxiety or more conformity-oriented tend to respond better to more directive teaching styles.

INDIVIDUAL DIFFERENCES AND THE TEACHER

This chapter has focused on research findings about altering instruction to accommodate individual differences. However, the research that has been completed thus far barely scratches the surface of a fascinating and important topic. The teacher who is sensitive to individual differences and willing to change instructional approaches to suit differing abilities can take the matter much further.

When looking at the relationship between student characteristics and instructional approaches, researchers commonly look at only a very small number of characteristics at a time. Keeping track of more than five characteristics in a given study, for example, would severely tax the abilities of most research teams. This means that research can identify positive relationships between student characteristics and instructional styles only when those relationships are simple and direct. More complicated relationships, involving several characteristics interacting with one another, are seldom the focus of formal experiments.

Teachers, however, do not have this limitation. Most teachers interact with a relatively small number of students over a long period of time. They get to know those students very well. Moreover, observant teachers know a great deal about the individual characteristics of their students. This knowledge, when joined with a willingness to try out new instructional approaches, can greatly enhance a teacher's effectiveness. Instructional approaches can be selected to fit the needs of the individual student. As mentioned earlier, when this process of adapting instruction to the needs of the individual student is done well, it has the dual benefit of enhancing both learning and student attitudes.

One important aspect of individualizing instruction is record keeping. In the interview that began this chapter, Virginia Plott described the extensive records she keeps on the children in her class. These records are invaluable as a basis for shaping instructional decisions. Records that document a child's responsiveness to differing instructional approaches allow the teacher to make informed choices about future instructional approaches. The teacher can then operate as a practitioner/scientist rather than as someone who proceeds strictly on a trial-and-error basis.

SUMMARY

Adapting instruction to individual differences can enhance a student's learning and it can enhance the student's attitude toward school. When teachers adapt instruction to individual differences they do one of two things: (1) they change the amount of instruction or the rate at which the instruction is presented, or (2) they change the nature of the instruction. Grouping students according to their aptitudes so as to be able to adapt the rate or amount of instruction to the students' needs has the potential of doing more harm than good. However, altering the nature of instruction in response to individual differences can have positive effects.

Intelligence, one of the more educationally important individual differences, was first scientifically investigated by Sir Francis Galton. Galton attempted to measure intelligence by measuring sensitivity to basic sensations, the presumed "building blocks" of ideas, which in turn were thought to make up the contents of the mind. Galton's approach to defining and measuring intelligence did not work, and the task of developing the first usable intelligence test fell to French psychologist Alfred Binet.

Binet's test, which was developed in response to problems being experienced in the Paris school system, contributed three lasting ideas to the science of intelligence. First, Binet's pragmatic approach to test development is still a popular one. Second, his definition of intelligence as being the thing that his test measured is still widely accepted by psychologists. And third, his tying together of intelligence and school success is a connection that is still very much with us.

Modern approaches to intelligence theory and measurement include (1) Wechsler's adult and children's intelligence scales (the WAIS and WISC, respectively), which are in the Binet tradition; (2) Guilford's structure of intellect (SI) model, which says that human intellect consists of 120 factors: 4 contents (figural, symbolic, semantic, and behavioral) × 5 operations (evaluation, convergent thinking, divergent thinking, memory, and cognition) × 6 products (units, classes, relations, systems, transformations, and implications); and (3) information-processing theories, which divide intellectual functioning into structural entities and cognitive processes.

The extent to which intelligence is determined by heredity is indexed by a heritability quotient—a number that ranges in value from 0 to 1. If the quotient is 0, it means that all of the variability in intelligence is determined by environment; if the quotient is 1, it means that all of the variability is determined by heredity; if the quotient is .5, it means that heredity and environment are equally important in determining intelligence. Several researchers have claimed that the actual heritability quotient for intelligence is .75 or higher; others claim it is much lower. At this point in time it is impossible to tell which of these claims is more accurate.

Minority groups frequently perform worse on intelligence tests than do members of the majority group. One possible reason is that the tests assess values and information that is strongly identified with the majority group. Two responses to this possibility are culture-fair intelligence tests and Mercer's System of Multi-Pluralistic Assessment (SOMPA).

Intelligence has been found to be a useful characteristic for differentially assigning students to different instructional procedures. In particular, research has shown that high-ability students seem to benefit maximally from instructional approaches emphasizing student contributions to learning, whereas lower-ability students have been found to benefit more from more highly controlled approaches to instruction. Little evidence has been found to indicate that more specialized abilities can be used to select optimal instructional practices.

Creativity has been viewed from several perspectives. The psychoanalytic view suggests that creativity is the result of channeling sexual and aggressive energy into socially acceptable behavior. The humanistic view suggests that creativity is a natural human potential whose expression can be blocked by a restrictive and judgmental environment. The environmental view maintains that creativity is a trait that can be learned if the environmental circumstances are right. The factorial view, derived from Guilford's SI model, postulates that creativity consists of a number of separable intellectual factors.

Personality traits have also been found useful in selecting instructional approaches. Students who score high on an achievement-via-independence scale do better in classrooms emphasizing independent learning. Those who score high on an achievement-via-conformity scale do better in more constrained classrooms. Students who exhibit high levels of anxiety seem to do best in classrooms where the teacher assumes the major part of the instructional responsibilities. Students exhibiting lower levels of anxiety tend to do better in more student-centered classrooms.

FOR FURTHER STUDY AND APPLICATION

Sperry, L. (Ed.). *Learning performance and individual differences*. Glenview, Ill.: Scott, Foresman, 1972.

Gagné, R. M. (Ed.). *Learning and individual differences*. Columbus, Ohio: Merrill, 1967.   Two early but classic presentations of the theory and research supporting the individualization of instruction.

Cronbach, L. J., and Snow, R. E. *Aptitudes and instructional methods.* New York: Irvington Publishers, 1977.   A highly technical but exhaustive survey of the research on aptitude-treatment interactions.

Eysenck, H. J., and Kamin, L. *The intelligence controversy.* New York: Wiley, 1981.   A direct confrontation between one psychologist who believes intelligence is primarily genetic in origin and another who believes it is primarily environmental in origin.

Bloomberg, M. (Ed.). *Creativity: Theory and research.* New Haven, Conn.: College and University Press, 1973.   An excellent overview of the theory of and research on creativity.

Callahan, C. M. *Developing creativity in the gifted and talented.* Reston, Va.: Council for Exceptional Children, 1978.

Torrance, E. P. Five models for constructing creativity instructional materials. *Creative Child and Adult Quarterly,* 1978, 3, 8–14.

4

THE EXCEPTIONAL STUDENT

CHAPTER OVERVIEW

Exceptional students, who formerly might have been called "abnormal" and been relegated to segregated classes, are now an integral part of the American educational system. Because of changes in the law, exceptional students with handicaps must be "mainstreamed" into regular classes to the fullest extent possible. This chapter discusses the rationale for the law, the kinds of procedures involved in mainstreaming, and the research indicating the success of the method. Material on the specific forms that special needs can take—including specific learning disabilities, mental retardation, sensory impairments, speech impairments, and emotional disturbance—is then presented. Finally, the discussion turns to one type of exceptional student that is just beginning to be recognized as having special needs: the gifted student.

On a quiet, shaded street, across from an old town common in Amherst, Massachusetts, Sheila Crimmins teaches in the Fort River Elementary School. Trained originally at the University of Massachusetts as a regular education teacher, for the past 6 years she has been involved in preschool programs for exceptional children. She is presently instructing what she calls an integrated preschool class. The interview that follows took place amidst the toys and paraphernalia typical of any preschool classroom, one summer morning. The interview began with a question about the meaning of the term "integrated preschool."

A.   Our program is integrated in that the class is made up of about half special needs and half regular needs children. It is not what is traditionally known as a mainstreamed class, because in such cases the classroom primarily has a regular education program, with a relatively small percentage of special needs children. In our class, we have seven special needs students and eight regular needs students—all three and four years old.

Q.   How many hours a week do you meet?

A.   We meet for three hours a day throughout the school year.

Q.   What is the range of special needs represented in your class?

A.   We've had a very wide range. We have had a paraplegic, a child with visual impairment, and a child who has severe emotional disturbances. Right now we have a child with a very rare genetic syndrome that makes him unable to walk because of a muscular problem. And what happens frequently with children with locomotive problems is that although their basic cognitive ability may not be impaired, their access to the world and opportunity to act upon objects is so limited that they show delays in cognitive skills, which need to be helped.

Q.   How do you view your role as a teacher in this program?

A.   I see this program in many ways as a regular nursery school. I see my role as a teacher, and the role of people who work with me, as having to be the eyes, the ears, the ego, the control—the whatever we have to be—to help the special needs children to participate in activities. It's very different from traditional special education, in which the focus used to be on deficits. You did an assessment and found out where the weaknesses were, and then you spent 9 months teaching to those weaknesses. In the meantime, the children fell behind in the areas in which they weren't being taught. To me, the focus of traditional remedial education is, in a sense, to deny disability and expect that the special needs children will then be the *same* as the non–special needs children. I don't believe this. I don't think that everyone's ever going to be the *same*. But people do have the same *rights*. That's why I feel that mainstreaming is a cultural issue, not an educational one. We have no more right to exclude handicapped people from our culture than we do to exclude black people. The children's schools are their culture, so that mainstreaming is really a civil rights issue.

Q.   I agree with what you are saying. But let me bring up a critical point that I've heard others make: By mainstreaming, you're short-changing regular needs children—you're not providing the kind of quality education that you could for the regular needs children. What would be your response to that?

A.   First of all, I would disagree that one has to give so much attention to the special needs children that the other children are neglected. I don't think that's true. I do think that in order to mainstream successfully the teachers need a tremendous amount of support. In fact, I think that teachers in general need more support—even if you take the special needs children out of the classroom. Teaching has become an almost overwhelming sort of activity. In this school, for example, we have lots of children who are in regular education who need, and get, an incredible amount of support. So even among the regular needs children, everybody doesn't get equal teacher attention. But if there is sufficient support personnel, everyone can benefit and do well.

Q.   What kind of help do you have in your classroom?

A.   We have a half-time speech pathologist, an assistant teacher who is there full-time, and a physical therapist one day a week.

Q.   That's a tremendous amount of support, isn't it?

A.   Yes. But we need that support in order to provide individualized educational programs for the children.

Q.   Do the support personnel get in each other's way?

A.   No, but it takes a lot of coordination. Organizing the child's time is a major undertaking. In fact, a good deal of teacher time is spent in meetings to arrange the child's activities. Another thing we do is try to integrate a child's specialized therapy into the regular classroom activities. For instance, we had a child who was unable to walk when he started school, and one of our goals was to get him to move while standing and holding on to something. One of the things we did was to place a large guinea pig cage on the floor. Pretty soon he was "cruising" around the cage. It was very stimulating for him, and it was part of his therapy that didn't require him to be out of the classroom. We try to do this kind of thing regularly.

Q.   What happens after the special needs children leave your classroom?

A.   It depends on the severity of the handicap. Some will always be behind, but others can catch up. We try to determine the year of high school graduation so that each child always has a specified peer group. The children may never, for instance, read as well as the others, but at least they have a group to which they belong. And they will always spend a considerable amount of time with their peer group in school. What actually happens is that the peers develop a tremendous amount of concern and interest in the progress of the special needs children.

Q.   How does this interest and acceptance evolve?

A.   In my class—and remember that we're talking about three- and four-year-olds—there seem to be three stages. At first, the children act like "mother hens." They're very solicitous and treat the special needs children as kind of curious babies. The next stage is almost one of denial—where they act as if *nothing* were the matter with the special needs child, that he or she has *no* limitations. The third stage is a realistic, educated, accepting view of the handicapped child. Eventually, they develop a tremendous amount of sophistication and understanding.

As is evident from the interview, Ms. Crimmins's class is exciting and innovative, and it is representative of the best of current approaches to educating exceptional students. It is also an example of the dramatic changes that have occurred in removing special needs students from more restrictive environments and integrating them into the mainstream of the American educational system, changes that are discussed in this chapter.

STUDENTS WITH SPECIAL NEEDS

The typical classroom contains children who vary drastically along many different dimensions, and teachers expect that not all children will learn at the same rate and in the same way. However, occasionally children are found whose skills and abilities differ markedly from the average. How best to educate such children—known as *students with special needs*—is one of the major concerns of educators today.

A decade ago, this issue would not have been of great importance to the average teacher, and little space would have been devoted in an educational psychology text to children with special needs, particularly the handicapped. After all, children with handicaps would rarely have been seen by the average teacher; they would have been under the supervision of special education teachers and not in regular classrooms.

least restrictive environment the educational environment required by law for children with special needs; it often means they are integrated into regular classrooms

However, over the past decade there has been a dramatic change, largely mandated by state and federal laws. In 1975, Congress passed Public Law 94-142, the Education for All Handicapped Children Act. The intent of the law—an intent that has to a large degree been put into effect—is to place handicapped children in the *least restrictive environment*. In practice, this means that children with special needs must be integrated into regular classrooms and regular activities to the greatest extent possible, as long as doing so is educationally beneficial. Thus children are to be isolated from the regular classroom only for those subjects that are specifically affected by their handicaps; for all other subjects, they are to be taught with nonhandicapped children in the regular classroom. However, children with severe handicaps can still legally be educated entirely separately, depending on the severity of their condition. This educational approach to special education, which was

In mainstreaming, children with handicaps are integrated into regular classrooms to the greatest extent possible. (© David S. Strickler/The Picture Cube)

designed to end as far as possible the segregation of handicapped youngsters, has come to be known as *mainstreaming*. Children with special needs are kept in the mainstream of the educational system and are provided with a broad range of educational alternatives.

Problems with Traditional Approaches to Special Education

What were the disadvantages of traditional special education that led to such an upheaval? The need for change was made clear in an influential paper by Lloyd Dunn in 1968. In the paper, he argued that there were four major reasons for abandoning the tradition of segregating handicapped children for purposes of schooling. First, any separate tracking system is likely to be inferior if it is meant to service some minority group. For instance, the best equipment and resources are likely to be diverted for majority group usage—in this case, nonhandicapped populations. Second, Dunn suggested that there are no data to support the efficacy of special classes for handicapped students. Research that has examined such factors as academic achievement, self-concept, social adjustment, and personality has generally failed to discern any advantages for special needs children placed in special education, as opposed to regular, classes. Thus, it could be argued that the effort and cost of providing special classes is unwarranted.

A third argument against the use of totally segregated special education classes involved the issue of labeling students—as "mentally retarded," "handi-

How Congress Does—and Does Not—Use Educational Psychology Research to Pass Laws: The Case of P.L. 94-142

It would be reasonable to assume that Congress passes its laws on the basis of the latest and best in scientific research data and evidence. But even a cursory examination of how P.L. 94-142, the Education for All Handicapped Children Act, was passed indicates that this is not the case.

It appears that the major reason that P.L. 94-142 was made into law had little to do with the weight of research evidence. Indeed, if the availability of research was the sole criterion for passing the law, it is likely the bill would never have made it off the floor of the House and Senate. Because in 1975, the year the bill was passed, there was *no* unequivocal empirical evidence to indicate that mainstreaming is superior to traditional forms of educating special needs children. There were logical arguments that could be made in favor of mainstreaming (and these are discussed in the body of this chapter), but there were no definitive research studies to support it.

The passage of the law, then, was based on the logical—if unproven— proposition that segregated classes for handicapped children were inherently unfair, just as segregated classes for blacks had been judged inequitable by the Supreme Court 20 years earlier. (Incidentally, in that landmark case, too, social science research carried little weight; the decision was made primarily on the basis that segregation was inherently cruel and unfair to black children, as a matter of law.) In the case of P.L. 94-142, a great deal of pressure was also placed on Congress by parents and teachers of special needs children to pass the law.

In sum, a law that makes extraordinarily large changes in the educational system of almost all public schools in the United States was passed on the basis of very little supportive evidence. The law made logical sense, but no one really knew when it was passed what its effects would be.

capped," "special," etc. There is a good deal of evidence that labeling students can lead to the development of a set of negative expectations regarding their capabilities, which in turn can lead others to behave in ways that actually cause these expectations to be fulfilled. Moreover, being thus labeled can lead to a decrease in peer acceptance and self-concept. For instance, one study found that subjects presented with an example of behavior supposedly carried out by a student labeled "mentally retarded" rated the behavior significantly less positively than when the behavior was carried out by a student who was not so labeled and was thus assumed to be "normal" (Cook and Wollersheim, 1976).

Perhaps the most compelling argument suggested in Dunn's 1968 paper concerned the availability of new and improved teaching techniques. For example, individualized curriculum methods, in which the teacher provides special material geared to the level of each student, were becoming more common. Moreover, many teachers were adopting programmed learning based on *operant learning principles*. With instruction already becoming more individualized for all children, handicapped children could more easily be integrated into regular classrooms.

operant learning principles educational philosophy based on conditioning in which a subject learns to respond to a stimulus based on rewards for previous responses to it

Another educational advance also weighed in favor of the end of segregation for special needs children: the greater use of nontraditional structural arrangements in the classroom. For example, many schools had abandoned the traditional system of carefully ordered rows of desks in self-contained classrooms and had begun to adopt more open arrangements, in which many classes met simultaneously in large, open spaces. In addition, schools had begun to use team teaching more frequently, and elementary teachers increasingly were specializing in particular subject areas. Such innovations all pointed toward greater ease in the integration of handicapped children into more regular situations.

Finally, schools had increased the number of ancillary support staff that were involved in the educational process. The use of teacher aides, guidance counselors, learning specialists, resource room personnel, and psychologists had become commonplace in many schools. The relative abundance of support personnel could free up the classroom teacher to provide more specialized and individualized attention, thus making the mainstreaming of handicapped students more feasible.

Dunn (1968) thus presented a number of arguments clearly in favor of mainstreaming. But there was one other reason for abandoning the tradition of enrolling handicapped children in segregated special education classes. Because special needs students must ultimately function in a normal environment, greater experience with their peers could be expected to enhance their integration into society, as well as positively to affect their learning. Mainstreaming therefore provided a mechanism to equalize the opportunities available to all children—the goal of much of American education.

What Is Involved in Mainstreaming?

There are a number of factors involved in the implementation of a mainstreaming program (Birch, 1974). Each exceptional child is assigned to a regular classroom, which employs special instructional techniques for the special needs child. An attempt is made to keep the student within the regular classroom at least half of each day, even if the child requires outside instruction by special education experts. The regular and special education teachers jointly develop assignments and lessons. All this requires, of course, that the regular classroom teacher

Mainstreaming: It Works Here

The Madison School in Santa Monica, California, has developed a mainstreaming program that serves as a model of the virtues of mainstreaming
(Hewett and Forness, 1974). When a special needs student first enters the
school, he or she is immediately placed in a regular class for 2 weeks. This
initial assignment allows the student to feel a part of a class, as well as
giving teachers and the student's peers an opportunity to become acquainted
with the student. It also helps the teacher to learn the student's strengths
and weaknesses. If the child's handicaps are so severe that he or she cannot
be placed initially in a regular classroom, the student is simply kept out of
school for this 2-week period.

All handicapped students are eventually assigned to a "resource room"
program. The resource rooms—actually a series of three adjacent classrooms—are called Pre-Academic I, Pre-Academic II, and Academic I. A
student who cannot be placed in a regular classroom is initially assigned to
Pre-Academic I for training in areas in which he or she is particularly weak.
However, it is possible for the student to be moved into Pre-Academic II
or Academic I for some activities. The eventual goal is to have the child
join the class in Academic I, which is modeled after a regular classroom
with twelve students. All three units are designed to interface with the
instruction that the student can receive in his or her regular classroom.
Even when the student is attending one of the resource rooms, his or her
seat and placement in the regular class are always maintained.

Of course the Madison School has had to commit tremendous resources
to the program. The three resource units are staffed by two teachers and
two teacher aides, in addition to various personnel who provide occasional
support. In addition, the units take up the space of two regular classrooms.

One of the greatest feats of the program is the development of a high
degree of coordination between the regular and special education teachers.
It is the flexibility with which a student can be assigned—and reassigned—
to the resource rooms and regular classroom that optimizes the student's
chances for academic success. The coordination and flexibility also allow for
maximum academic and social contact between the special needs student
and his or her peer group, which is, after all, what mainstreaming is all
about.

have a broad knowledge of handicapping factors in order to be maximally
effective with the special needs student.

Obviously, mainstreaming handicapped children into a regular classroom
situation is a complicated matter, but many programs have been quite

successful—see, for example, the accompanying box. However, teachers should be aware that implementation of mainstreaming requires not only knowledge of many handicapping conditions but also a great deal of sensitivity to the psychological requirements of both the handicapped and the nonhandicapped.

Who Educates the Special Needs Student?

Although this chapter describes a variety of special needs that are likely to be encountered in the average classroom, it cannot provide more than an overview. Educating special needs children is a complex undertaking, and no one regular classroom teacher can be expected to deal effectively with every type of problem that may arise. Fortunately, along with the implementation of mainstreaming has come the development of support teams in school settings. Beginning with the special education teacher, there are a number of specialists who may play an active role in educating the special needs child (Turnbull and Schulz, 1979).

Resource teachers
The resource teacher, who has a degree in special education, is used to supplement the instruction given in regular classes. The special needs students meet with the resource teacher for part of each day, alone or in small groups, either in the regular class or in a special resource room. Because both the resource teacher and the regular classroom teacher have responsibility for teaching the special needs child, there must be a great deal of coordination between the two. In some school systems, the resource teacher specializes in a particular type of special needs, but in others he or she caters to a wide variety of special needs.

School psychologists
Trained psychologists provide diagnostic testing and evaluation services, and they help to make decisions regarding the placement, and the degree of mainstreaming, that is appropriate for each special needs student. In addition, they help to devise individualized programs of instruction.

Therapists
Therapists are specialists who work with special needs students on an individual basis to improve skills or functioning in a particular area. For instance, students with speech impairments might work with a speech therapist; those with emotional problems might work with a therapist who specializes in working with the emotionally disturbed.

Paraprofessionals, aides, and community volunteers
Services for special needs children can be provided not just by specialized experts but also by paraprofessionals, aides, and community volunteers who come into the classroom for specified periods of time each week and help the

teacher in the normal classroom activities. The aid provided by these people can play an important role in the handicapped child's education, by allowing for more individualized attention to the student.

Special education teachers in self-contained classrooms

Some students are so severely handicapped that they cannot be mainstreamed into regular classrooms. In such cases, the children are typically assigned to a self-contained classroom made up entirely of special needs children. With a degree in special education, a teacher in this setting must have the capability of dealing simultaneously with a very diverse set of handicaps in their students.

Individualized Education Programs

It would be relatively easy for a student to get lost in a crowd of providers of special services unless very careful attention were given to the planning of the educational program. To ensure that proper planning is carried out, P.L. 94-142 specifically requires that each special needs student be provided with an individualized education program, in writing, which is updated each year. The program must be specific and include the following information (Torres, 1977, pp. 52–53):

psychomotor skills abilities that require strength, coordination, and dexterity as a result of thought processes

1. A statement of the student's present level of educational achievement in areas such as academic achievement, social adaptation, prevocational skills, *psychomotor skills,* and self-help skills.
2. A statement of annual goals that describes the educational performance to be achieved by the end of the school year under the child's individualized education program.
3. A statement of short-term instructional objectives, which must be measurable intermediate steps between the present level of educational performance and the annual goals.
4. A statement of specific educational services needed by the child, including a description of all special education and related services that are needed to meet the unique needs of the child, also including the type of physical education program in which the child will participate.
5. The date when these services will be initiated and terminated.
6. A description of the extent to which the child will participate in regular education programs.
7. Objective criteria, evaluation procedures, and schedules for determining, on at least an annual basis, whether the short term instructional objectives are being achieved.

The program is devised each year by a committee made up of the child's teachers, the parents or guardians, an expert in special education who is going to supervise the child's education, and where possible, the child. An example is shown in Figure 4-1. Note how detailed and explicit the plan is, and how it sets very precise goals.

FIGURE 4-1   Excerpt from an Individualized Educational Plan for a Girl Mainstreamed in a Public School

STUDENT PROFILE

R. is a 6-year-old girl whose primary diagnosis is severe retardation and who exhibits many behavior patterns characteristic of autism. She does not seek out interactions with peers or adults, and she engages in a variety of self-stimulatory behaviors during unstructured time. R. is currently functioning at approximately the 11-month level in most areas. She is able to walk with the aid of a walker and can stand unsupported for brief periods. She has no functional speech but frequently babbles to herself, and she indicates her wants with a whole-hand point. R. is currently learning to perform simple tasks, to establish eye contact with an adult upon request, and to reduce her self-stimulatory behaviors.

Type	Setting	Location	Personnel	Projected date service will begin	Hours
Language Self-care Social Academic Motor	Individual	Pine Haven School	M. Smith	9/13/82	15 hours/ week

Current level	General student-centered goal	Teaching approach
Self-care: R. has no dressing, toileting, or grooming skills. She can eat finger foods independently, and can drink from a cup and eat with a spoon with physical guidance.	R. will improve her eating skills and acquire some basic components of dressing and grooming skills.	Strategies used will include shaping, fading, chaining, prompting, reinforcement, modeling, and interruption of inappropriate behaviors. All tasks should be broken down into small steps leading to the terminal goal. Reinforcers will include edibles, milk, toys, and praise. R. will work individually with a teacher, and should be faded back gradually into a classroom setting.
Academic: R. is currently learning to perform simple tasks upon command (e.g., put blocks in a container), to sit quietly, and to look at the instructor when asked (learning readiness skills).	R. will improve her learning readiness and imitation skills, as well as her ability to follow simple directives and perform simple tasks.	

(Table continues)

Current level	General student-centered goal
Language: R. has no functional language, and very little imitation of sounds. She uses a whole-hand point to indicate her wants.	R. will learn to imitate sounds and to use appropriate signs or gestures to indicate her needs.
Social: R. will not interact with peers or adults. She engages in self-stimulatory behaviors most of the time.	R. will increase her interactions with others, and decrease her self-stimulatory behaviors.
Motor: R. has poor motor skills. She can walk with the aid of a walker and can stand unassisted for a few seconds. She has an accurate pincer grasp, and can imitate a few motor movements (e.g., clapping hands).	R. will improve both her gross and fine motor skills.

Goal	Objective	Specific student-centered objectives	Quarter in which goal will be addressed			
			1	2	3	4
1.	A.	R. will use a spoon to scoop food from a bowl and place it in her mouth 90 percent of the time for ten consecutive sessions.	√	√	√	√
	B.	R. will drink liquids from a cup without spilling 80 percent of the time for ten consecutive sessions.	√	√	√	√
	C.	R. will use a napkin to wipe her hands and mouth after eating, 80 percent of the time for ten consecutive sessions.				
	D.	R. will complete 80 percent of a hair-brushing chain for five consecutive sessions.				
2.	A.	R. will establish eye contact with an adult, within 5 seconds of being asked, 90 percent of the time for three consecutive sessions.	√			
	B.	R. will turn and look at a person who calls her name, within 5 seconds, 90 percent of the time for five consecutive sessions.	√			
	C.	R. will put ten blocks into a container, when asked, 90 percent of the time for three consecutive sessions.	√			

Goal	Objec-tive	Specific student-centered objectives	Quarter in which goal will be addressed			
			1	2	3	4
	D.	R. will stack ten rings on a pole, when asked, 80 percent of the time for three consecutive sessions.				
	E.	R. will place her hands in her lap when asked, 90 percent of the time for five consecutive sessions.				
3.	A.	R. will imitate three different vocalizations, within 5 seconds of being asked, 80 percent of the time for five consecutive sessions.				
	B.	R. will learn to sign appropriately for food, drink, yes, and no, 80 percent of the time for five consecutive sessions.				
4.	A.	R. will learn to push a toy car to the instructor and receive it back at least five times for five consecutive sessions.				
	B.	R. will learn to shake hands with an adult, when asked, 80 percent of the time for five consecutive sessions.				
5.	A.	R. will imitate three different motor actions (e.g., clap hands, wave, nod head), within 5 seconds of being asked, 80 percent of the time for five consecutive sessions.				
	B.	R. will stand unassisted for at least 15 seconds, 80 percent of the time for ten consecutive sessions.				
	C.	R. will take at least ten steps unassisted for ten consecutive school days.				
	D.	R. will turn the pages of a book singly, at least five pages, 80 percent of the time for five consecutive sessions.				

Does Mainstreaming Work?

Of course, the fundamental question that must be answered is how well mainstreaming works in practice. Unfortunately, there are no clear and easy answers to this question. One reason for this is primarily methodological: it is difficult to set up controlled experiments that can really show whether mainstreaming is effective, because appropriate comparison groups are generally not available. For instance, in order to say that a mainstreaming program is working, it needs to be compared with one in which students are *not* mainstreamed. In addition, both sets of students (mainstreamed and nonmainstreamed) need to be comparable in terms of handicaps, intelligence, geographic area, socioeconomic status, and a host of other variables. Because the methodological requirements are so stringent, it is hard to carry out research in this area.

The other reason that easy answers as to whether mainstreaming works are difficult to provide is that there is such great diversity among the various programs. Mainstreaming in one school may mean simply placing all special needs students in regular classrooms that they never leave. In another it may mean following the elaborate program described in the box, "Mainstreaming: It Works Here," in which there is great variability in the amount of time students spend in the regular classroom. Therefore, before it can be stated unequivocally whether or not mainstreaming works, the critical characteristics of the term must be identified.

For the classroom teacher, the best strategy probably is to be less concerned with whether experimental data and research support the concept of mainstreaming than with the reality that mainstreaming is now a fact of life in American public schools. What this means is that teachers must be prepared to deal with students with a wide range of handicaps and special needs. The remainder of this chapter discusses the major types of handicaps that a teacher is likely to encounter in the course of a teaching career: children with specific learning disabilities, children who are mentally retarded, children with visual, auditory, or speech problems, and children who are emotionally disturbed.

SPECIFIC EDUCATIONAL NEEDS

Who Is Exceptional?

It seems at first almost ridiculously simple to determine who is normal and who has a special need. We all know of children who are mentally retarded, have obvious physical defects, or have severe behavior problems. However, coming up with a precise, scientific definition of what is meant by the terms "handicap" or "special need" is not at all simple.

The problem of identifying students with special needs can be approached by considering the various ways in which clinical psychologists have thought about the concept of abnormality (Offer and Sabshin, 1974). The first way of looking at abnormality or a handicapping condition is as a *deviation from the average*. This is a statistical definition: in order to find out what is abnormal, one finds the most common behavior within a group and calls that normal; then anything that deviates from the norm is considered abnormal. While this at first seems a sensible approach, on closer examination there are difficulties. In the case of intelligence, such a definition would suggest that people who score well *above* the average on IQ tests are as abnormal as those who score well *below* the norm. Similarly, extremely creative people would be considered abnormal by such an approach. Thus the deviation-from-the-average technique is useful in identifying people who are *different*, but not necessarily abnormal.

Another approach to abnormality is to consider behaviors to be abnormal if they *deviate* too much *from some hypothetical ideal*. Thus if acceptable social behavior is thought of as the ideal, the extent to which an individual deviates from the ideal would determine how abnormal his or her behavior is. In reality, this is another kind of statistical approach—one that is even less precise and in many ways less helpful than the deviation-from-the-average definition. Since all people are less than perfect and more or less removed from an ideal state, it is nearly impossible to determine who is normal enough not to require special assistance.

The definition of abnormality that seems to be the most useful concerns itself with a student's *adjustment*. In this approach, the criterion is the individual's relative success in adjusting to the academic demands of the typical classroom, in relating socially to his or her peers, in not disrupting the class. Although this definition is not precise, it is quite useful in identifying students who are in need of special attention, training, and educating; and it is this definition that is adopted in the discussion that follows of students with particular types of special needs.

adjustment achieving a mental and behavioral balance between one's own personal needs and the demands of other individuals and society

Specific Learning Disabilities

Probably the most subtle and elusive, yet nonetheless real, handicaps are those that are subsumed under the heading *specific learning disability* (SLD). In P.L. 94-142, children thus disabled are defined as follows:

> Those children who have a disorder in one or more of the basic psychological processes involved in understanding or in using language, spoken or written, which disorder may manifest itself in imperfect ability to listen, think, speak, read, write, spell, or do mathematical calculations. Such disorders include such conditions as perceptual handicaps, brain injury, minimal brain dysfunction, dyslexia, and developmental aphasia. Such term does not include children who have learning problems which are primarily the result of visual, hearing, or motor handicaps, of mental retardation, of emotional disturbance, or environmental, cultural, or economic disadvantage.

The child with a specific learning disability, then, is typically of normal intelligence and shows no overt, primary sort of handicap such as a visual or auditory impairment or severe emotional disturbance.

As may be seen from this definition, the term "specific learning disability" is very broad, and the condition is quite difficult to identify in practice. One factor that does distinguish the child with a specific learning disability is his or her poor performance in one or more subject areas, when that performance is strikingly at odds with what would be expected from the child's IQ score (Adamson, 1979). Frequently, there is also an abnormally high level of activity, referred to as hyperactivity. It is generally thought that specific learning disabilities are found in between 5 and 10 percent of all children, which makes it the most common behavioral problem (Wender and Eisenberg, 1974). For some reason, it is three or four times more prevalent in boys than in girls.

There are two ways in which specific learning disabilities may have an impact on school learning. The first is indirect: Because the child with SLD is frequently hyperactive, he or she is easily distracted and, therefore, has difficulty sitting in a classroom and paying attention to the teacher and to class activities. It is also quite hard for such a child to learn new material, since application to a single task for any length of time is sometimes a physical impossibility.

The second way in which specific learning disabilities affect school learning is more direct. Certain basic cognitive skills may be impaired—such as the coordination of perception and movement, facility in spatial relations, being able to relate information from the various sense organs, and having sufficient memory capacity (Elkind and Weiner, 1978). Because such skills are so basic, the child with SLD has great difficulty in keeping up with his or her classmates and, consequently, may fall behind. Usually, however, the problem is specific to a particular subject area. It is rare for an individual to suffer all of the problems listed above.

By far the most prevalent form of specific learning disability is a reading impairment commonly known as *dyslexia*. Children classified as dyslexic often have perceptual and cognitive impairments that lead them to reverse words (reading "ton" instead of "not") or to confuse letters that are similar in shape ("b" instead of "d"). Because reading is so basic to success in school, children with dyslexia are often prevented from doing well in subjects in which they have no disability at all. Moreover, there is potential psychological damage as well. When dyslexic children suffer consistent failure, their self-concept may be lowered. The situation is made more difficult by the fact that parents, teachers, and the children themselves are often unable to identify the problem as due to a learning disability and instead attribute the child's lack of success to laziness or low motivation. Because the child's difficulties are subtle, and restricted to just a few subject areas, and because the child otherwise displays normal and sometimes even above average intelligence, observers frequently fail to show the sympathy that they would to a more overtly handicapped child.

On the other hand, many nondyslexic children make the kinds of mistakes associated with dyslexia at one time or another during their school history. In most cases of simple reversals, for instance, correction can be made through the use of systematic and consistent procedures on the part of the teacher. Teachers should not automatically assume that a child's reading errors are indicative of dyslexia.

Teaching the child with a specific learning disability

Because the SLD child's problems can be so heterogeneous, it is difficult to provide one set of teaching approaches that will fit all cases. For example, many educators dealing with SLD students view perceptual and motor handicaps as the major source of school difficulties. This suggests that SLD children should receive special training to improve their motor coordination, and practice with the identification of numbers, letters, and shapes. But for some students the primary problem relates to the use of language, and such children require special training in speaking and listening. In cases of hyperactivity, drugs are sometimes prescribed as an adjunct to other treatments.

The most important point to bear in mind is that no one treatment is effective for all SLD children. Children who are suspected of having some sort of SLD should be referred to specialists for thorough diagnostic assessment. Once the source of the problem has been identified, a specialized program of treatment, which involves both the classroom teacher and various specialists, can be worked out.

Mental Retardation

> Jonny never liked school. In first grade he managed to get along, but frequently had to be prodded into going to school. His teacher reported that he was the slowest child in the group. He was not particularly troublesome, but he had difficulty in learning any of the things the other children seemed to learn easily. He usually stayed by himself and had to be urged to participate in group activities. He seemed listless and fatigued. When he did show some interest, it soon waned. At times he would doze off in the classroom. It was suspected that there was something wrong physically, but a medical examination was entirely negative, and it was finally concluded that he was "lazy." However, he did show considerable drive and continued interest when he was engaged in "making things" in school (Hutt and Gibby, 1979, pp. 4–5).

What was the source of Jonny's difficulties? An IQ test revealed that he fell into the intelligence range generally regarded as mentally retarded; he scored 63 on the test.

Between 1 and 3 percent of the school-aged population have been identified as having some degree of mental retardation (Masland, Sarason, and Gladwyn, 1958). However, there is wide variation among those labeled mentally retarded—due in part to the inclusiveness of the definition suggested by the American Association on Mental Deficiency. The association states that *mental retardation* exists when there is "significantly subaverage general intellectual functioning existing concurrently with deficits in adaptive behavior" (Grossman, 1973). This means that people classified as mentally retarded can range from those who can be trained to work and function with little special attention to those who are virtually untrainable and do not develop speech or such basic motor skills as walking or even crawling.

The vast majority of the mentally retarded have relatively low levels of retardation and are classified as being *mildly retarded.* Individuals whose IQ score ranges between 55 and 69 fall into this category, and they constitute 89 percent of all the mentally retarded. Typically, their retardation is not even identified before they reach school, although their early development is often slower than the norm. Once they enter elementary school, their retardation and their need for special training usually become apparent. With appropriate training, these students can reach a third- to sixth-grade educational level; and although they cannot carry out complex intellectual tasks, they are able to hold jobs and function quite successfully and independently.

At higher levels of mental retardation, the intellectual limitations of the individual become more apparent. Persons whose IQ scores range between 40 and 54 are known as *moderately retarded,* and they make up about 6 percent of all retarded individuals. Their retardation is evident early in their lives; they are slow to develop language skills, and their motor development is also affected. Regular schooling is not effective in training these children to acquire academic skills, because generally they are unable to progress beyond the second-grade level. However, they are capable of being trained in occupational and social skills, and they can learn to travel independently to familiar places. Typically, they require moderate levels of supervision.

At the highest levels of retardation, the ability of the individual to function normally is severely limited. *Severe retardation* (with an IQ range of 25 to 39) and *profound retardation* (with an IQ of below 25) results in an inability to function independently. Usually there is little or no speech, poor motor control, and an inability to be toilet trained. Most frequently, such individuals require institutionalization, as they are incapable of caring for themselves. It is likely that in earlier times most severely and profoundly retarded individuals died at birth; but medical advances have permitted many to survive into adulthood. The life expectancy of those with this degree of retardation is still generally short, however.

Causes of mental retardation

In about 25 percent to 35 percent of all cases of mental retardation there is a known biological cause, the most frequent being *Down's syndrome*—which was once called Mongolism because of the Oriental appearance of the facial features of those afflicted with the disorder. The condition is caused by the presence of an extra chromosome, and its frequency increases quite dramatically with increasing age of the mother. Birth complications are another biological cause of mental retardation; for instance, an inadequate supply of oxygen to the brain at birth can cause retardation.

Most cases of mental retardation are classified as *familial retardation;* there is no known biological cause, but there is a family history of retardation (Jensen, 1970). There is some controversy as to whether familial retardation is caused by genetic or environmental factors. Those espousing a genetic cause suggest that retarded parents pass on genes that produce the retardation. In contrast,

Down's syndrome a disorder characterized by the presence of an extra chromosome which is a major cause of mental retardation

familial retardation a classification of probable causes of retardation associated with family history of retardation

Some children may require special help to avoid confusing the shapes and directions of letters. (© Meri Houtchens-Kitchens/The Picture Cube)

environmentalists suggest that it is the unenriched environment in which the children of retarded parents find themselves that produces a low IQ score. Lack of intellectual stimulation is thought to be the basic cause of the retardation.

It is, of course, unlikely that either genetic or environmental factors *alone* are the cause of familial retardation. Most researchers would agree that there is an interaction between the two factors, such that the level of functioning is due partly to genetic and partly to environmental causes (Baroff, 1974). For instance, Down's syndrome children generally have significantly higher IQ scores when they are raised in enriched environments than when they are raised in relatively impoverished environments.

Teaching the mentally retarded

There are a number of areas in which the mentally retarded may have specific difficulty, including attention span, memory, learning rates, ability to generalize, and success at conceptualization (Turnbull and Schulz, 1979). With regard to attention span, a retarded child is frequently unable to spend as much time concentrating on a given task as is a regular needs child. This problem not only affects the special needs children themselves, it also tends to disrupt the activities of other children. Thus the teacher must prepare assignments that are sufficiently short to engage the child's attention.

A second problem frequently encountered in retarded children is related to short memory span. Many special needs children simply cannot remember directions, even when they are repeated frequently. Although it may appear that the student is not paying attention, in many cases the problem is caused by memory deficits. A related difficulty concerns the slow learning rate of many retarded children. Even when material is memorized, the learning may be by rote, and the child may not actually understand it. Deficits in learning rate may be reflected early on in a child's school performance, and learning may become progressively slower. Thus the child will fall further and further behind his or her classmates.

The retarded child may also have difficulty in generalizing from the specific to the general, as well as having problems in conceptualization. The conceptualization problem is particularly manifest when *abstract* principles, which require moving from the concrete to the abstract, are involved. For example, forms of mathematics that require abstract thinking can present difficulties for the retarded child.

abstract the symbolic form of stimuli, rather than their real or readily observable material form

A number of specific teaching strategies are quite useful in dealing with retarded children (Turnbull and Schulz, 1979). One technique that has been demonstrated to be successful involves strategies to improve memory. By actively rehearsing material to be memorized, special needs children can increase retention significantly (Butterfield, Wambold, and Belmont, 1973). It is also important for teachers to provide a great deal of practice for retarded children. Tasks must not only be mastered thoroughly, they must be *overlearned*. Overlearning means that the student practices material well beyond the point at which it is first learned; this permits better retention over time.

overlearning practicing material well beyond the point at which it was first learned

Finally, teachers should realize that curriculum goals and objectives should be adjusted for the special needs child. It is not always important to teach very abstract or theoretical material to a retarded child; rather, the emphasis might be on teaching the kind of skills that will best enable the child to manage himself or herself independently in society.

Visual Impairment

One of the problems affecting a student's success in school concerns how well he or she can see. Visual impairment can be thought of in two ways: in a legal sense and in an educational sense. The definition of legal impairment is quite straightforward: *Blindness* is visual acuity of less than 20/200 (i.e., inability to see at 20 feet what a normal person can see at 200 feet) after correction; *partial sightedness* is visual acuity of less than 20/70 after correction. However, visual impairment in an educational sense can occur even when the legal limits are not exceeded. For one thing, ability in distance vision is the sole legal criterion, while most educational tasks require close-up vision. In addition, the legal definition does not consider deficits in the perception of color, depth, and light—all of which could be expected to affect an individual's educational success. A teacher must be aware of these potential difficulties.

Although most visual problems are found early in a child's development, there are cases in which the impairment goes undetected. Frequent eye irritations (sties, redness, or infections), frequent blinking and facial contortions when reading or looking at the blackboard, holding reading material unusually close to the face, difficulty in writing, and frequent headaches, dizziness, or burning eyes are some of the signs that the teacher should watch for. Where one or more of these conditions persist in a child, the teacher should suspect some sort of visual acuity problem and should arrange for the child's eyes to be checked (Kirk, 1972; Gearheart and Weishan, 1976).

Teaching the visually impaired

Because visual impairment is not associated with delays or deficits in cognitive ability, relatively few changes in teaching technique are needed to accommodate the visually impaired student when the problem is not too great. When a student has a severe impairment, there are a number of things a teacher can do to facilitate performance. At the commonsensical level, the teacher should keep the classroom relatively free of obstacles, should provide verbal explanations of work on the blackboard and in films, and should seat the visually impaired child close to the front of the classroom. There is also a variety of specialized equipment that can be employed to aid the visually impaired, including Braille materials, typewriters, and large-print textbooks.

Auditory Impairment

A student with an auditory impairment is at a distinct disadvantage in school—not only in terms of academic work but also in peer interactions that take place through informal conversation. Hearing loss, which affects some 5 percent of the school-aged population, is not simply a matter of not hearing enough. Rather, auditory problems can vary along a number of dimensions, including the frequency, intensity, and age of onset of the loss (Birch, 1974).

In some cases of hearing loss, only a limited range of frequencies, or pitch is affected. For example, the loss may be great at pitches in the normal speech range yet quite minor in some frequencies (such as very high or very low sounds). In addition, a person may require differing levels of amplification at various frequencies. This is why a hearing aid, which amplifies all frequencies equally, is sometimes ineffective.

The age of onset of the hearing loss is another critical factor relating to the success with which a student can adapt to the impairment. If the loss of hearing occurs in infancy, the effects will tend to be much more severe than if it occurs after age 3. The reason relates to the critical role that hearing plays in the development of language. Children who have had little or no exposure to what language sounds like are unable to understand or produce language themselves. However, after a child has learned language, loss of hearing does not seriously affect subsequent linguistic development.

There are a number of ways in which students may indicate previously undiagnosed hearing problems in a classroom (McConnell, 1973; Gearheart and Weishan, 1976). Such behaviors as appearing not to pay attention, turning the head to one side when listening, answering questions inappropriately, lower than typical language ability, and performing better in small groups than in large class settings are all possible indications of hearing difficulties.

Teaching the auditorily impaired

For severe cases of auditory impairment, the major question regarding teaching techniques concerns whether oral or manual communication techniques should be employed. Oral communication methods require that the student communicate through lip reading and speech, without recourse to the use of signs and gestures. In contrast, manual techniques teach the child to use signs or gestures for communication. In one type of manualism, each letter of the alphabet is associated with a particular gesture, and words can be spelled out. In other types of manualism, signs are used to represent whole words and phrases.

The newest approach to teaching the severely hearing impaired is to use "total communication." In this system, both oral and manual techniques are employed. The student is taught to use any or all methods to communicate, depending on what is most facilitative in a given situation. Although some special educators require strictly oral or strictly manual communication from their students, most agree that a combination of techniques works best.

For the classroom teacher, the type of communication an auditorily handicapped student uses has profound implications. Oral communication techniques are considerably easier in mainstreaming situations. On the other hand, regular classroom teachers can learn to use manual signs to facilitate communication with students who have been taught only manualism.

In cases where the use of a hearing aid renders normal speech understandable, manualism may not have to be used. However, the use of a hearing aid still does not make hearing entirely normal. As mentioned earlier, the hearing aid amplifies *all* sounds; thus background noises can drown out conversation. The teacher should be sensitive to this fact and try to seat the partially deaf student in a location that is away from potentially distracting noises. This does not mean, of course, that the student should be isolated from the rest of the class; but various locations should be tried out before assigning the student a permanent seat. Another important point for the teacher to keep in mind is that he or she should orient the face directly toward the hearing impaired student when speaking. It is particularly important to remember this point when writing on the blackboard, when there is a natural tendency to turn away from the class. The teacher should also avoid exaggerated lip and mouth movements, which do not facilitate lip reading and in fact can make it harder for the student. At the same time, speech should not be very rapid.

A problem associated with language difficulties in the hearing impaired relates to the development of abstract thinking. Because the hearing impaired child may have limited exposure to language, abstract concepts that can be explained only through the use of language are often understood at a lower level than concepts that are concrete and can be illustrated visually (Hewett and Forness, 1974). The classroom teacher should be sensitive to such subtleties in the cognitive functioning of the hearing impaired.

Speech Impairment

According to one of the most widely used definitions of *speech impairment,* a person's speech is impaired "when it deviates so far from the speech of other people that it calls attention to itself, interferes with communication, or causes its possessor to be maladjusted" (Van Riper, 1972). Thus if a child's speech sounds impaired, it probably is.

Speech impairment can take a number of forms, including problems with articulation (the substitution, omission, distortion, or addition of sounds), vocal quality (such as unusual pitch or volume), or stuttering. It has been estimated that about 5 percent of school-aged children suffer from a degree of speech impairment sufficient to warrant special attention.

The most common speech impairment is stuttering. Although a great deal of research has been done on the topic, no single cause has yet been identified. *Stuttering* typically takes the form of substantial disruptions in the rhythm and fluency of speech. Although such disfluencies are relatively normal in young children, and occasionally occur in normal adults, chronic stuttering can be a severe problem. Some theories suggest that stuttering has a neurological cause and is related to a disruption in nerve transmission, which causes difficulties in coordinating the muscles used in speech. Other theories suggest that parents who show overconcern or anxiety when their children display even normal speech disfluency during the course of language development may pass such anxiety on to the child, and the child's anxiety then manifests itself in stuttering. However, the precise causes of stuttering have not been identified.

Teaching the speech impaired

A number of suggestions can be made regarding the treatment of students with speech impairments, particularly when the problem is stuttering. For instance, the teacher should try to avoid drawing attention to the stuttering by allowing the student to finish what he or she is saying. It is generally not a good practice to anticipate what the student is trying to say and finish the word for him or her. The teacher should also try to determine the particular circumstances that elicit stuttering and try to reduce their frequency. For instance, if stuttering occurs only in group situations, the child could be assured that the teacher will not ask for oral recitation unless the student volunteers. Such reassurance can reduce some of the pressure on the student (Turnbull and Schulz, 1979).

School Phobia

One emotional disturbance that is particularly relevant to the classroom is known as "school phobia." School phobia is manifested when a child experiences such intense anxiety in school settings that he or she refuses to attend. To avoid school, children with this phobia will often complain about such physical ailments as stomachache, headache, or sore throat—some of which may be quite real. In other cases, the children will complain about an unfair teacher, the poor quality of the school, unfriendly peers, or other ostensible problems that are reasons for not attending. If forced to attend, such children may develop the classic symptoms of severe anxiety: shaking, crying, vomiting, and in general begging to be sent home. In many cases, their behavior is so disruptive that they are in fact allowed to leave school. When they are allowed to go home, their symptoms usually disappear (Elkind and Weiner, 1978; Sperling, 1967).

Although usually real, the physical manifestations of school phobia are not the true problem for school-phobic children. Treating the symptoms, without examining the underlying causes, is usually ineffective. For instance, even when a child is given a new teacher or is placed in a new school, it is likely that after a short period of time he or she will again be complaining and refusing to attend school.

What are the underlying reasons for school phobia? They seem to differ

Emotional Disturbance

Some of the most difficult handicaps to detect and treat with confidence are those relating to the psychological functioning of students. When does a student's rowdiness or unhappiness or frustration move from the range of normal adjustment and become a handicap? There is no universal definition of emotional disturbance, and in fact, the meaning adopted by most authors reflects their own particular theoretical orientation. Thus a psychotherapist might say that an emotional disturbance consists of "impairment of emotional growth during some stage of development with resultant distrust toward self and others and hostility generated from anxiety" (Moustakas, 1955); whereas a behavioral approach might speak of "disorders that consist of inadequate or inappropriate behavior that is learned and can therefore be changed through application of learning procedures" (Dupont, 1969).

Although there is no universal definition, most researchers in the area agree that emotionally disturbed children show significant deviations from age-appropriate emotional reactions and behavior. Hence behavior must be according to the age of onset. In younger children, school phobia can frequently be traced to anxiety over separation from the mother (Beng and McGuire, 1974). When a mother is protective to an extreme and the child is highly dependent, the stage is set for the development of school phobia. The child's anxiety about leaving the mother can be displaced to the reason for the separation—in this case, the school.

In older children, school phobia can be the result of some specific event in school that is anxiety-producing. A student who normally does well in school but, for example, forgets that she has to deliver a report to the class may suffer so much embarrassment and humiliation that she becomes school-phobic. When questioned about why she refuses to attend school, she may not even mention the incident because of the pain involved. Instead, other excuses, or the development of some physical ailment, are substituted.

Treatment of school phobia usually consists of a therapy program that has as its goal the student's understanding of the source of his or her anxiety (Lassers, Nordan, and Bladholm, 1973). Other techniques, based on behavior modification principles, try to desensitize the child to school as a source of anxiety. For instance, the student might first be brought into school for a half-hour, then for a half-day, and eventually for a full day. Overall, treatment is successful in about 90 percent of cases in which the child is 10 years or less in age. Results are not as good with older children, however; treatment is successful in only about 50 percent of cases (Smith, 1970; Weiss and Burke, 1970).

considered in the context of a child's age and his or her peers' typical behavior. One expects 1-year-olds to cry when they are not allowed to touch an attractive toy; one does not expect the same reaction from a 10-year-old. Basically, then, the definition is a statistical one. A child's behavior is compared with some hypothetical average or mean to assess the degree of deviation.

Particularly tricky for the classroom teacher is determining what in fact that average behavior is. One approach to classifying emotional disturbance has been made through the use of teacher ratings. The results of one study (Quay, Morse, and Cutler, 1966) showed that there are three main categories of problems that teachers find troublesome:

1. *Conduct disorder*: Includes such problems as defiance, impertinence, uncooperativeness, irritability, and boisterousness.
2. *Inadequacy-immaturity*: Covers such problems as sluggishness, laziness, lack of interest, preoccupations, dislike for school, and inattentiveness.
3. *Personality problems*: Include "inferiority feelings," "self-consciousness," "lack of confidence," "fearfulness," and "depression."

Unfortunately, these categories are still rather subjective, and many if not all of the behaviors said to be indicative of emotional handicaps can be found in normal children at one time or another. What distinguishes these behaviors in emotionally disturbed children is their frequency and intensity of occurrence. For instance, if a child is consistently self-conscious or preoccupied and does not respond to a variety of attempts on the part of the teacher to alleviate such feelings, then the child is a likely candidate for evaluation by a school psychologist. (It is not recommended that classroom teachers themselves make the decision that a child has an emotional disturbance; it is too easy even for "experts" to make mistakes.)

Treatment of the emotionally handicapped varies a great deal, depending on the nature of the disturbance and what kind of professional is dealing with it. Aid is provided not only by school psychologists; in some cases a *psychiatrist*, social worker, or clinical psychologist may be included in treatment approaches. In most cases, the parents of the emotionally disturbed child will be involved in the treatment program, since part of the child's problems frequently relate to the home situation.

psychiatrist a medical specialist in the investigation and treatment of mental disorders; holds an M.D. degree

Unless the emotional disturbance is severe or it takes the form of consistently aggressive or disruptive behavior, the child is apt to remain in the regular classroom most of the time. It is interesting to note that cases of emotional disturbance in which the child is very withdrawn can *seem* to be less of a problem, since there is less disruption of normal classroom activities. However, a very shy, isolated child may in fact be suffering from a considerably more severe type of emotional disturbance that an outgoing but disruptive peer.

Teaching the emotionally disturbed

The emotionally disturbed student is likely to perform more poorly than his or her nondisturbed classmates. For instance, Bower (1969) found that children with emotional handicaps tended to obtain lower reading and arithmetic standardized test scores than their peers. However, it is not possible to assign causality for the poorer performance to the emotional handicap because it is equally possible that poor performance brought about the disturbance in the first place. For example, poor scholastic performance is frequently associated with low self-concept. Is it the case that doing poorly in school makes children feel negatively about themselves? The answer is probably yes. But it is also possible that having a low self-concept decreases achievement motivation, which in turn leads the student to work less hard and ultimately do poorly in academic work. Both sequences are plausible, and it is difficult to tell which one is actually correct.

Given that emotional disturbances can be either the cause or the result of poor academic performance, it would seem that the best strategy for the classroom teacher would be to act as if both possibilities could be true. Thus not only should the teacher try to help alleviate the emotional disturbance—by cooperating with the school psychologist or other treatment specialists; he or she should also try to improve the student's academic performance—by providing special attention, individualized lesson plans, and motivational boosts.

The Gifted and Talented

The intellectually gifted and talented comprise a unique group among exceptional children. Representing the 2 to 4 percent of the school-aged population who have IQ scores over 130, these students have so much potential that they, no less than students with a very low IQ, warrant special concern.

A list of the adjectives associated with the stereotypic view of the very bright student might include "unsociable," "poorly adjusted," "unhappy," and "neurotic." Yet, there is much evidence to dispel such a picture; in fact, most research suggests that those with superior intelligence tend to be *better* adjusted than the average person.

In recent years, the term "gifted" has been expanded to include the "talented" as well. This definition takes into account the fact that students may be exceptional not just intellectually; they may have special talents in the arts and in such skills as leadership or athletics. There has also been recognition that intelligence is not homogeneous, that a student who has a high overall IQ is not necessarily equally gifted in all subject areas (Stanley, 1980).

Teaching the gifted and talented

While few parents of children who have intellectual or other deficits would hesitate to ask for special programs for their children, many parents of intellectually gifted and talented children do not feel a need for the special education of their children. There is a persistent view that children who are brighter than average ought to be able to "make it on their own." In the words of Bruno Bettelheim, a noted psychologist who holds such an opinion, "I feel that the gifted child . . . is well able to take care of himself. If he isn't, then he isn't gifted" (Maeroff, 1977).

However, such a view is a minority one. Gifted children may have none of the intellectual deficits of other special needs children, but they still require special attention to reach their full potential. Without some form of enrichment, the gifted may become bored and frustrated with assignments that would be appropriate for their nongifted peers. Ultimately, this can result in their intellectual abilities never reaching their full potential, causing a loss not only for the individual but for society as well.

There are two major approaches to teaching the gifted: acceleration and enrichment. *Acceleration* programs allow gifted students to move ahead at their own pace, even if this means skipping to higher grade levels. An alternative approach is *enrichment,* in which the student is kept at the grade level but is enrolled in special programs and given special activities to allow a greater depth of study into a given topic. It should be noted that the acceleration and enrichment approaches are not mutually exclusive; in the words of Julian Stanley, a leading expert on educating the gifted, "Properly conducted acceleration tends to be enriching, and appropriate enrichment is deliberately accelerative" (Stanley, 1980, p. 9).

Acceleration and enrichment programs can both be effective. Most studies have shown that gifted students who begin school much earlier than their age-mates do as well or better than those who begin at the traditional age. And this holds true for nonacademic areas, such as social adjustment, as well as for academic areas. Enrichment programs also permit the gifted to reach their potential, and such programs can be provided by the classroom teacher. For instance, teachers can promote student independence and abstract thinking through the assignment of special projects covering subjects that are relatively abstract, such as philosophy, political science, and mathematics. In addition, students can be encouraged not just to absorb greater amounts of knowledge but to use their unique talents to increase the quality of their thinking.

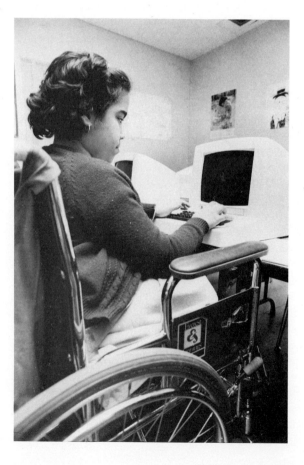

Among the techniques used to facilitate the main-streaming of the physically handicapped are comput-erized learning systems. (© Christina Thomson 1982/ Woodfin Camp & Assoc.)

A FINAL COMMENT

This chapter has merely touched upon the many kinds of exceptional children that may be encountered in educational settings. It is clear that no teacher can expect to be an expert in all of the possible areas of exceptionality; therefore teamwork with any specialists and resource persons that are available is absolutely essential.

As Sheila Crimmins remarked in the interview that began this chapter, teaching can be an almost overwhelming activity. Because, in a sense, *all* students are exceptional, and the goal of the educator ought to be to provide as much individualized instruction as possible to meet the special needs of their students.

SUMMARY

With the passage of P.L. 94-142, Congress mandated dramatic changes in the treatment of special needs students. According to the law, handicapped children must be placed in the least restrictive environment, generally by integrating (or mainstreaming) them into regular classrooms and activities to the fullest extent possible.

The change in the law was brought about for four major reasons: (1) any separate tracking system may produce inequities to minority groups, (2) the research provides little support for the use of segregated special classes, (3) labeling can lead to self-fulfilling prophecies, and (4) teaching innovations in the use of individualization have become more sophisticated.

In practice, mainstreaming involves assigning all special needs children to a regular classroom and providing special services in the regular class as much as possible. It also involves the use of a host of support personnel, including resource teachers, special education teachers, school psychologists, therapists, paraprofessionals, aides, and community volunteers. To guide the student's progress, an individualized education program is devised each year, which outlines detailed plans for the child's instruction.

When discussing special needs children, it is necessary to decide how to identify them. A number of approaches to defining children with special needs have been suggested, including deviation from the average and deviation from some hypothetical ideal. The approach that seems most useful is to examine a student's overall level of adjustment.

One area of special need is that of specific learning disability (SLD), in which the child is of normal intelligence but shows poor performance in a specific subject area. Frequently there is also an abnormally high level of activity, known as hyperactivity. The most common form of specific learning disability is dyslexia, which is displayed as difficulty in reading due to perceptual and cognitive problems.

One of the most obvious special needs relates to mental retardation, which affects from 1 to 3 percent of the school-aged population. Persons with IQ scores below 70 are considered to be retarded and in need of special attention, although there is wide variation among persons identified by this label. Mental retardation is often caused by specific genetic factors, but most cases are known as familial retardation, in which there is no known biological cause but rather a family history of retardation. In teaching the mentally retarded, it is necessary to attend to deficits in attention span, memory, learning rate, ability to generalize, and ability to conceptualize.

Sensory impairments in the form of visual, auditory, and speech deficits constitute another area of special needs. Visual and auditory impairments may go undetected, and it is important for teachers to be aware of the symptoms. Speech impairments are more obvious, as when the child has problems with stuttering, articulation, or unusual vocal quality.

Emotionally disturbed children represent yet another area of special needs. Students with this problem show significant deviations from age-appropriate emotional reactions and behavior, and they do so relatively consistently. They are likely to do poorly in school, although it is hard to tell whether the poor performance is the result or the cause of the emotional disturbance.

The intellectually gifted and talented have their own special needs. Two approaches to the education of this population have been enrichment (the use of special programs) and acceleration (moving students ahead in school at their own pace). Both have proven effective.

FOR FURTHER STUDY AND APPLICATION

Hewett, F. M., and Forness, S. R. *Education of exceptional learners*. Boston: Allyn and Bacon, 1974.

Hutt, M. L., and Gibby, R. G. *The mentally retarded child: Development, training, and education*. (4th ed.) Boston: Allyn and Bacon, 1979.   Both of these books provide a good background for the teacher interested in learning more about the special needs of exceptional children.

Adamson, W. C., and Adamson, K. K. *A handbook for specific learning disabilities*. New York: Gardner Press, 1979.   Provides a current look at different types of specific learning disabilities. Includes information on techniques for conducting and interpreting assessments of children, and discusses various types of therapy.

Turnbull, A. P., and Schulz, J. B. *Mainstreaming handicapped students: A guide for the classroom teacher*. Boston: Allyn and Bacon, 1979. A how-to guide for teachers in mainstreamed classrooms. Excellent for its presentation of concrete techniques for teaching specific subject areas.

Glover, J., and Gary, A. *Mainstreaming exceptional children: How to make it work*. Pacific Grove, Calif.: Boxwood Press, 1976. Another excellent introduction to ways of organizing regular classrooms in which special needs students have been placed.

II

LEARNING AND INSTRUCTION

WHY DOES EDUCATION NEED A PSYCHOLOGY
OF LEARNING?

TYPES OF LEARNING
Imprinting

Habituation

Classical Conditioning

Operant Conditioning

Concept Learning

The Learning of Rules and Principles

THE INTERRELATIONSHIPS AMONG TYPES OF LEARNING
Unpacking Rules and Principles

The Role of Habituation in Concept Learning

Imprinting as the Most Basic Process

LEARNING THEORIES
The Role of Learning Theories

Behavioral Theories of Learning

Cognitive Theories of Learning

WHICH LEARNING THEORY IS RIGHT?

TRANSFORMING LEARNING THEORY
INTO EDUCATIONAL PRACTICE
Three Conditions for Successful Teaching

Using the Three Conditions to Select Approaches
to Educational Problems

Putting Together the Approaches to Problems

SUMMARY
For Further Study and Application

5

LEARNING: AN OVERVIEW

CHAPTER OVERVIEW

Learning is the central focus of the educational process. The purpose of this chapter is to present an overview of the scientific study of learning. The chapter begins by noting that if instruction is to succeed, students must be attentive and motivated to learn, and the information must be presented in such a way that it can be acquired. The scientific study of learning has much to offer in accomplishing these ends.

Learning is a complicated topic that becomes easier to study when it is broken into units. The second and third sections of the chapter break learning into six different types, which have a hierarchical relationship to one another. The section describes the different types of learning and indicates how simpler types of learning serve as the building blocks for more complicated types of learning.

Learning theory organizes the different types of learning, and the facts we know about the types, into coherent patterns. It provides an explanation of how learning occurs and a basis for conducting further research. The fourth section of the chapter reviews five theories of learning. Two of the theories accept the position that learning can best be understood by analyzing the experiences of an organism. Because these theories focus on the behavior of organisms in the presence of particular events, they are classified as behavioral theories. The remaining three theories begin with the assumption that learning can best be understood by analyzing how the mind works. Because these theories focus on internal cognitive events, they are classified as cognitive theories.

In an old and well-established science, there are generally only one or two competing theories that attempt to explain a given phenomenon. Psychology, given its relatively young age as a science, has not yet attained this status. There are numerous competing theories, and at this stage there is no way of deciding which of the theories is correct. This does not, however, severely restrict the applicability of the learning theories to educational problems. In fact, it turns out that behavioral learning theories can be powerful tools for dealing with problems involving observable student behaviors, and for problems involving the mastery of basic information. In addition, cognitive learning theories can provide useful guidelines for approaching problems involving the understanding of higher-level information.

Nancy Bates teaches fifth grade in the Las Vegas public school system. She attended Youngstown State University in Youngstown, Ohio, and graduated with a B.S. degree in elementary education. Her first teaching job was in Youngstown, where she taught sixth-grade reading, English, and social studies for 3 years. She then moved to Granby, Massachusetts, where she taught seventh- and eighth-grade science, reading, social studies, and health for 4 years. The interview began with a question about what a teacher can do to ensure that learning takes place.

A.   First of all, you have to make sure that you have the students' attention. Second, you have to provide them with a reason for why they should learn, you have to motivate them. Once you have those two major things under way you are in a good position to begin the learning process.

Q.   You say, "in a good position to begin the learning process," it sounds as if these things sort of set the stage so that learning can begin.

A.   That's right. I believe in a kind of pyramid approach to learning. Attention and motivation provide the setting for learning basic information. Once you have a base you can build on that. You can use the base, that is, what they know and where they're coming from, to teach other, more complicated things.

Q.   What do you mean exactly when you say you have to have their attention?

A.   Attention is the key ingredient in learning. Without it you haven't got anything. You can't motivate, and you certainly can't teach. By attention, I basically mean being aware of what the teacher is doing and paying attention to what they should be doing.

Q. Is classroom discipline part of attention?

A. Absolutely! Good classroom discipline and good pupil behavior are essential to everything else you try to do as a teacher.

Q. What about motivation? How do you go about motivating students?

A. By explaining to students the reason for learning the material I'm asking them to learn. Frequently, this means touching base with where they are. I always try to relate the material I'm teaching to something they're interested in, or something that's going to be important to them in the future.

Q. Can you give me an example of what you're talking about?

A. Sure. A couple of years ago I was working with an eighth-grade class in reading. I was trying to get them to use context clues to figure out the meaning of words they didn't know. I wasn't having much success with the reading materials I was using, so I went down to the local driver's license office and picked up a bunch of manuals that people read to prepare them to take the driver's license exam. We used the manuals as reading material, and the learning process went much more easily.

The driver's license material worked with eighth graders because that's something that's important to kids that age. With a little thought, most things that we teach in school can be related to where kids are at all ages.

Q. OK, imagine that you've got attention and motivation in good shape, how do you work on the base of your pyramid? How do you teach basic information?

A. There are a lot of ways to do it, but one of the most important is repetition. You do a lot of repeating when you're teaching. But it isn't repeating the same thing the same way every time. Repetition in teaching is changing the technique but repeating the basic information you want to get across.

Q. What do you do when repetition doesn't work? When you repeat and repeat but the kid still doesn't understand?

A. Then you try something else. I get very annoyed when people say that you can't teach a kid a certain subject or a certain concept. It's just a matter of finding the right plug to plug in. You have to find a way to make the information meaningful to that kid. If you can make it meaningful, he'll learn it.

The Nancy Bates interview touches upon a good deal that is important in classroom learning. Students must be attending to instruction if they are to learn from it, and they must be motivated to learn. In addition, the instruction must be presented in such a way that students can acquire the information without undue effort. All of this is probably self-evident. But the real trick is how to accomplish these goals. How does a teacher get students to attend to instruction? What can be done to motivate students? How can information be presented so that it can be learned and understood? Answers to these questions can be approached through a study of the psychology of learning.

In the chapters that follow, the questions of attention, motivation, and understanding, which are central to the educational process, are taken up. However, understanding of the principles that guide approaches to these problems requires an understanding of the basic theories of learning. That is the purpose of this chapter: to provide an overview of the basic science and theory of learning. Subsequent chapters can then proceed to explain how the science and theory can be used to solve real-world educational problems.

WHY DOES EDUCATION NEED A PSYCHOLOGY OF LEARNING?

Why do teachers need to know about the psychology of learning? Even though learning is the central focus of schooling, this does not necessarily mean that teachers should be familiar with the scientific study of learning. For many years prior to the birth of psychology, teachers simply followed their intuition about the best means of teaching children. Why should they attend to a scientific discipline that is based, in large part, on data collected in laboratories under conditions not even remotely resembling those found in classrooms? There are a number of ways to answer this question.

A number of psychologists (e.g., Nelson, 1977) have made a distinction between contextualized and decontextualized knowledge. Contextualized knowledge can be described as a rule or set of rules applicable to a particular situation or setting. Decontextualized knowledge consists of principles applicable to a very broad range of situations and settings. Teachers obviously make extensive use of both of these kinds of knowledge. They derive contextualized rules from observation and personal experience, and they then repeatedly use the rules. For example, if one were to observe a teacher closely over a period of time, one would see numerous examples of stereotypic behavior. That is, given similar situations on different occasions, the teacher would tend to handle them in the same way. Teachers also make extensive use of decontextualized knowledge—knowledge derived from study and research—in their teaching of subject matter content, whether it is mathematics, social studies, or kindergarten they are teaching.

Teachers, then, use both contextualized and decontextualized principles in teaching. The question is, does having decontextualized knowledge about the process of learning itself make a person a better teacher? This is obviously a

Learning Theory: Research and Practice

One example of the way the scientific study of learning has influenced educational practice can be found in the way learning-impaired individuals are now treated. Not so many years ago, the diagnosis "retarded" would result in an individual being locked up in an institution; or if the parents chose to keep the child, he or she would be restricted to the house so that no one would be bothered by the child. This practice was based on the belief that such individuals could not learn. But over the years the situation has changed dramatically, and many people who formerly would have lived their entire lives behind the walls of an institution now lead worthwhile and productive lives. A good part of this change can be attributed to research and practices derived from the scientific study of learning.

In the early part of this century, learning theories focused on the idea that learning could be understood by carefully examining events that happen to an organism, the organism's responses to those events, and the things that happen to the organism following the response. Much of the research designed to explore this idea used animals as subjects, and some of the research was directed at the question of whether animals could learn complex tasks. After much research, and a considerable amount of ingenuity, techniques and principles were developed that allowed rats and other laboratory animals to learn highly complex tasks. Other researchers then began to consider the implications of this research: If laboratory animals could be taught complex behaviors, couldn't the same techniques be used to teach learning-impaired humans worthwhile life skills?

The answer to this question has proven to be affirmative. Many individuals who formerly would have been institutionalized now care for themselves, work, pay taxes, and marry. In short, they are leading useful, productive lives.

question that could be answered by research, but unfortunately, no research on the topic is available. Since empirical data are lacking the issue is pursued here with argument.

A great many teachers have marvelous intuition and insight about the teaching/learning process, and over time they develop personal rules of teaching that prove to be highly effective. But even the very best teachers must on occasion ask themselves if there isn't another way of doing things that would work even better. Where do ideas about how to approach a teaching problem differently come from? If the teacher's only knowledge of the learning process has been derived from personal experience and observation, the pool of potentially good and worthwhile ideas is probably relatively small. The qualifications "good" and "worthwhile" are emphasized, because it is easy to come up with ideas that don't work but much more difficult to produce ideas of real merit. Now consider the situation when teachers have not only personally derived knowledge but also scientifically verified knowledge about the learning process. There is an infinite number of potentially worthwhile ideas that can be generated from knowledge of the principles of learning. Thus teachers can use their scientific knowledge about the learning process, or for that matter, about the various other topics dealt with in this book, to become truly innovative teachers. Without this kind of knowledge, they may be good teachers, but they are not as good as they could be.

This overview of learning begins by dividing it into different types. Such classification simplifies what would otherwise be a very complex task. A second advantage of classification is that it highlights the relationship of the different types of learning to one another and demonstrates how simple types provide the foundation for more complicated types.

TYPES OF LEARNING

At first glance, learning seems a staggeringly complex topic. One's habits, fears, loves, hates, memories—all are learned. Moreover, virtually all organisms have the capacity to learn. Is a rat's learning significantly different from that of a human being? These are all extremely complicated issues. But they seem less complex when, in a classic scientific manner, they are divided into smaller, simpler units. Accordingly, the topic of learning is first divided into units that constitute types of learning.

Imprinting

Imprinting is a type of learning that is strongly guided by instinct. The behavior of newborn ducklings and chicks is the most well-known example of imprinting. In an 1873 edition of a popular magazine, D. A. Spalding wrote that newly hatched chicks followed the first moving object they saw, irrespective of whether that object was a mother hen, a rooster, a duck, or even a human being. Years later, Spalding's observations were the subject of more rigorous scientific scrutiny. Konrad Lorenz (1937) demonstrated that the following response of ducklings was instinctual, whereas the particular object they followed (had imprinted upon them) was learned. Hess (1957) demonstrated that the object that ducklings had imprinted upon them need not even be alive. Hess imprinted ducklings to follow all manner of moving inanimate objects, including a duck decoy, a wooden block, and a yellow metal disc.

In addition to finding that young birds would follow the first moving object they saw, investigators also found that there was a *critical period* for the imprinting process. Hess (1957) found that ducklings would imprint for only about 30 hours after hatching. After this 30-hour period, the birds would no longer imprint. This means that the ducklings were genetically prepared, for a certain time period, to have a moving object imprinted upon them. If a moving object did not appear, the potential for imprinting was lost.

critical period the time in an organism's life in which learning can occur most readily

The concept of imprinting has been a source for important hypotheses. Language acquisition is an example. As noted in the chapter on development (Chapter 2), some scientists have argued that there is an innate component to language acquisition. This hypothesis is suggested by several kinds of evidence, among which are the incredibly rapid rate at which language is acquired and the fact that all children go through stages of using grammatical structures they have never heard before. Moreover, in the few isolated cases of children advancing to adolescence without experiencing language, it has proven to be very difficult to teach them language. In fact, Eric Lenneberg (1967) has suggested that humans who are not exposed to language before the age of 14 or so may be unable to acquire it. These facts have contributed to the hypothesis that language learning has similarities to imprinting. The hypothesis states that the potential for language learning has an inherited base that will be expressed only if the individual is exposed to language during the critical acquisition period.

Habituation

Professor Drone's lecturing style involves entering the classroom, getting settled behind the lectern, and reading his notes in a monotone for 50 minutes. Even the most conscientious students claim they cannot pay attention to his lectures.

The Professor Drone example illustrates a type of learning called habituation. *Habituation* is the decrease in response to a stimulus with repeated presentation of that same stimulus. Virtually all organisms, whether they be single cell protozoan (Applewhite, 1968) or human beings, display a similar pattern of behavior when encountering a novel stimulus. The organism first *orients* to the stimulus. Orientation in higher organisms is a pattern of behavior that involves a change in brain-wave patterns, dilation of the pupils, constriction of surface blood vessels, and head or body movements that move the sense receptors toward the source of the stimulus. When one hears a strange noise at night, or when a changing traffic light interrupts a daydream, one engages in an orienting response. If a novel stimulus is presented repeatedly, the organism no longer orients to it. When the organism ceases attending to a stimulus, we say that the organism has habituated to the stimulus; the organism has learned that a particular stimulus is familiar and deserves no special attention.

habituation decrease in response to a stimulus with repeated presentation of the stimulus

It is apparent that the complementary processes of orientation and habituation have important survival value. Organisms cannot carefully attend to all of the stimulus events in their environment. They need to learn which stimuli are familiar and safe, and which are novel and of potential benefit or danger. Orientation and habituation serve these functions. One orients to unfamiliar events, and one ignores those that are familiar.

One reason that habituation is interesting to the human researcher is that it provides a means of examining learning in preverbal children. Much of what we know about the development of cognitive capacities in infants comes from the study of habituation. For example, children between birth and 8 weeks of age appear to focus on stimuli in an indiscriminate fashion, displaying no more habituation to repeated stimuli than to novel stimuli (Fantz, 1961, 1964; Wetherford and Cohen, 1973). This might be characterized as a period in which the infant is trying out the visual and cognitive machinery necessary for attention and memory (Fishbein, 1976). From the age of 2 months to 1 year, infants show rapid improvement in their rate of habituation, as indicated by a decrease in average looking time in response to stimuli in general, and by an increasing preference for examining novel stimuli in comparison with familiar stimuli (Fantz, 1964; Lewis, Goldberg, and Campbell, 1969). These changes, from 8 weeks onward, may signal the beginning of the child's ability to learn abstract conceptual information.

Classical Conditioning

Ivan Pavlov was a Russian physiologist who won a Nobel prize in 1904 for his brilliant research on the physiology of digestion. Pavlov developed a technique whereby he could collect substances from virtually every part of a live animal's digestive system. Prior to Pavlov, digestive functioning had been studied by examining dead animals, or by examining animals that had recently undergone surgery and, because of poor conditions of hygiene or poor surgical technique, were soon to die. Pavlov's emphasis on aseptic surgical techniques, and his virtuosity as a surgeon, enabled him to prepare permanent openings in an animal's digestive organs, allowing easy collection of digestive substances (Fancher, 1979).

During the course of his research on digestive processes, Pavlov noted that the dogs he was using as research animals would begin to salivate when the caretakers who normally brought food to the animals entered the laboratory. This was most intriguing, since salivation is an automatic, unlearned response made whenever food or some unpleasant (e.g., mild acid) substance enters the mouth. How could it be that the mere sight of a person could elicit a response thought to be completely independent of the learning process? With his usual ingenuity, Pavlov set out to answer this question, and to his mild displeasure, he thereby achieved everlasting psychological fame. (He maintained to his death that he was a physiologist, not a psychologist.)

FIGURE 5-1   Pavlov's Classical Conditioning Apparatus

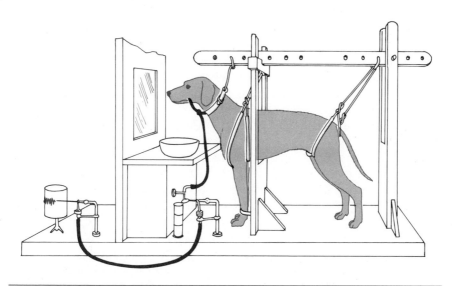

In Pavlov's apparatus for classical conditioning of a dog's salivation, the experimenter sits behind a two-way mirror and controls the presentation of the conditioned stimulus (bell) and the unconditioned stimulus (food). A tube runs from the dog's salivary gland to a vial, where the drops of saliva are collected as a way of measuring the strength of the dog's response.

The procedure for the most famous of Pavlov's experiments is presented in Figure 5.1. The experiment starts out with three elements: (1) meat powder, which Pavlov called the *unconditioned stimulus,* (2) a salivary response, which Pavlov called the *unconditioned response,* and (3) a bell, which Pavlov called the *neutral stimulus.* The term "neutral stimulus" is used because at the outset of the experiment, sounding the bell has no effect on the salivary response; the bell is neutral relative to the response of salivation. Pavlov chose the terms "unconditioned stimulus" and "unconditioned response" because he wanted to make clear that the effect of the meat powder on the salivary response had nothing to do with learning. Meat powder is an unlearned (that is, unconditioned) stimulus, and salivation is an unlearned (therefore unconditioned) response.

The experiment started with the sounding of the bell, followed a fraction of a second later by a puff of meat powder being blown into the dog's mouth. The meat powder elicited salivation. After repeated trials in which the bell was paired with presentation of the meat powder, Pavlov presented a trial in which the bell was sounded, but meat powder was not blown into the dog's mouth. The dog salivated at the sound of the bell. An automatic, unlearned response, which previously had been elicited only by the presentation of food, was now being elicited by a bell!

unconditioned stimulus a stimulus that evokes an unconditioned response without training

unconditioned response the original response evoked by an unconditioned stimulus without training

neutral stimulus a stimulus that has no naturally occurring effect upon the unconditioned response

conditioned
stimulus a
stimulus to
which a new
response be-
comes related
through the
process of con-
ditioning

conditioned re-
sponse the re-
sponse that is
evoked by a
conditioned
stimulus after
conditioning
has occurred

Two more terms now need to be added. The bell, initially called the neutral stimulus, now elicits a salivary response. Because the animal has learned that the bell signals forthcoming food, the bell is therefore now called a *conditioned (learned) stimulus*. The salivary response, which previously was automatically elicited by food, can now be elicited by the bell. Pavlov called the salivation elicited by the bell a *conditioned response*, indicating that it is a learned response rather than an automatic reflex.

Since Pavlov's initial investigations of *classical conditioning*, there have been thousands of other studies examining various aspects of the conditioning process. Classical conditioning has also been suggested as being involved in some forms of human neuroses. Phobias, for example, which are irrational fears of places (e.g., confined spaces) or things (e.g., snakes), are sometimes thought to have their origin in unfortunate experiences that result in a conditioned fear response.

Operant Conditioning

B. F. Skinner, who has been recognized in polls as being one of the best-known psychologists in the world, has spent the past 40 years investigating a form of learning known as operant conditioning.

Operant conditioning, which is essentially the study of learning under conditions of reward and punishment, did not originate with Skinner. Edward Thorndike (1874–1949) is thought to be the first psychologist to study operant conditioning systematically. In his Ph.D. dissertation completed in 1898, Thorndike described how he had placed animals (usually cats) inside a puzzle box that would open, providing escape and food, if the animal performed a specific response—such as turning a latch or pulling a string. Thorndike found that learning appeared to progress on a trial-and-error basis, with the large number of errors in early trials gradually decreasing as the animals grew familiar with the problem (Thorndike, 1898).

B. F. Skinner greatly refined Thorndike's original research and developed a tremendously influential school of psychology that is based on three simple but powerful propositions: (1) behavior that is followed by a reinforcer will increase in frequency; (2) behavior that is followed by punishment will decrease in frequency; (3) behavior that has been reinforced will decline in frequency when no longer reinforced. Using these propositions, Skinner was able to teach animals all manner of things, including teaching pigeons to play table tennis and to guide a missile.

Skinner's most important accomplishment has been his emphasis on the analysis of stimulus events and response events, and the consequences (reward, punishment) that follow stimulus and response events. In short, his emphasis is on observable events *outside* the organism. Moreover, he has argued that speculations about unobservable mental "events" (e.g., thinking, cognition, etc.) retard the development of a science of behavior (Skinner, 1974). Using

FIGURE 5-2   Skinner Box

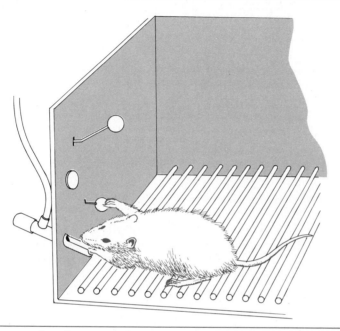

The rat presses a lever because of reinforcement—food pellets—that is delivered through the spout of the feeder. The strength of this learned behavior can be measured as the frequency of lever pressing.

this emphasis on observable events, and the three propositions of learning, Skinner and his followers have advanced the study of operant conditioning into many areas of practical concern. Skinner himself, for example, has written extensively on how the principles of operant conditioning can be directed to educational concerns (e.g., Skinner, 1968). Others have developed techniques, derived from the study of operant conditioning, for treating mentally disturbed patients (Ullmann and Krasner, 1969), for working with juvenile delinquents in prison settings (Cohen and Filipczak, 1971), for assisting the chronically unemployed in finding employment (Schoar, 1976), and for working with patients suffering from severe pain (e.g., Lake, Rainey, and Papsdorf, 1979).

Concept Learning

One of the forms of learning most crucial to human beings, and to the science of educational psychology, is *concept learning*. Formal definitions of what a concept is are cumbersome and confusing, so concepts will be defined by example. Individuals have acquired a concept when they can recognize an example they have never seen before as being an instance of the concept.

Take "dog" as an example. Imagine a visit to someone's home. The proud father asks his young daughter, "Where is the dog?" and the child dutifully points to the family terrier. Can it be said that the child has acquired the concept "dog"? It cannot, because there is nothing to indicate whether the child is associating the word "dog" only with the family terrier or whether she indeed recognizes the terrier as being a member of the general category "dog." For one to determine if the child has truly acquired the concept, one would have to present her with instances of dogs and instances of nondogs (e.g., cats, horses, etc.). Only if the child could accurately classify the instances could she be said to have acquired the concept "dog."

The importance of concept learning becomes obvious if one imagines what it would be like if concepts were not learned. Imagine having to learn the names of the things that you encounter in the same way that you have to learn the names of people. Individual labels (names) are attached to people because it is important to distinguish among them. But it is not, for the most part, important to distinguish among individual chairs, tables, cows, or cars. Think of the difficulty if every time one of these things was encountered one had to rehearse the name of the thing, just as one actively rehearses the names of people one meets. Without conceptual learning, one would not recognize a chair one had never seen as a chair, a dog one had never seen as a dog, or a

Learning through observation is one of the important forms of learning. (© Myron Wood/Photo Researchers)

book one had never seen as a book. With each new thing encountered, one would have to go through the laborious task of attaching a name to the specific entity. Obviously, such a state of affairs would be disastrous.

The importance of concept learning to education should be apparent. Concepts allow one to move beyond things in one's immediate world to things never directly experienced. The ability to learn about foreign lands, forms of governments, the principles underlying internal combustion engines, and abstract mathematical solutions to practical problems—all are based on concept learning. If people could not learn concepts, there would be no such thing as formal education.

The Learning of Rules and Principles

With concepts, rules and principles can be built. A *rule* can be defined as two or more concepts related in a manner indicating a specific application. For example, the saying "*i* before *e* except after *c*" is a rule (unfortunately, one with many exceptions) relating to the spelling of words containing the adjacent letters "i" and "e." For individuals to be able to apply the rule, they must have acquired the concepts making up the rule. That is, they must know what an "i" is, they must know what "before" means, and so on. Another example of a rule as defined above is, "That dog likes to be scratched behind the ears." Again, the rule consists of a statement that expresses specific relationships among several concepts.

A *principle*, as defined here, is two or more concepts or rules expressed in a manner indicating a general application. For example, the statement "Green plants require water to live" expresses a principle that is applicable to the growing of any green plant—whether it be a giant sequoia in the redwood forests of California or an illegal substance growing under artificial light in an attic. The statement "Dogs like to be scratched behind the ears" is a principle because it applies to dogs in general. As was the case with rules, the understanding and utilization of a principle requires an understanding of the concepts making up the principle. Thus in a very real sense, concepts are the building blocks of rules and principles.

Principles can vary enormously in their complexity and applicability. Relatively simple principles of etiquette guide the way in which one eats when dining in a fancy restaurant, at a friend's house, or at the family picnic table. If one were carefully to examine the principles of dining etiquette one would find it possible to reduce or "unpack" the principles into relatively few rules and concepts. In contrast, consider Einstein's famous principle defining the relationship between velocity, mass, and energy, $E = MC^2$. Einstein's principle, if totally unpacked, would undoubtedly contain a staggeringly large number of subsidiary principles, rules, and concepts.

The differing number of subsidiary elements contained in these two examples tells us a great deal about the relative difficulty of "learning" the principles of dining etiquette versus "learning" the principle $E = MC^2$. The word "learning" is in quotation marks because what is meant is not learning in the sense that one can repeat the principle in verbal form but learning in the sense that one truly understands the principle and all its ramifications. The principles of dining etiquette are relatively easy to grasp because they contain few subsidiary rules and concepts, and because the subsidiary elements they do contain are generally elements that have already been mastered. In contrast, $E = MC^2$ contains an enormous number of subsidiary elements, and many of those elements have been mastered by only a relatively small number of professional physicists. One may be able to spout "$E = MC^2$" when asked, "What is Einstein's principle relating mass, energy, and velocity?" But only in a trivial sense can one say that one has learned the principle.

In some ways, the learning of principles is analogous to the construction of an automobile. Automobiles are not constructed by throwing components into a vat and pouring out a completed car. Likewise, principles are not acquired in whole-cloth fashion. Instead, each is built in a piecemeal manner; the separate parts are put together until the whole structure emerges. Cars are built with previously constructed engines, frames, generators, axles, etc. Principles are built with previously acquired concepts, rules, and subsidiary principles. Without all of the components, the car won't run. Likewise, unless the subsidiary elements have been mastered, a principle will not be understood in all of its complexity.

THE INTERRELATIONSHIPS AMONG TYPES OF LEARNING

Unpacking Rules and Principles

Learning is best viewed as a process in which simple types of learning serve as the building blocks for complex types of learning. As an example of this perspective, let's take the principle "Green plants require water to live" and try to *unpack* it to its most elemental level. This principle could be unpacked into a great many subsidiary principles, such as, "House plants require water to live," "Trees require water to live," etc. At least one of these principles could probably be unpacked into a rule. For example, the admonition, "Your Swedish ivy will die if you don't water it." The principle about green plants requiring water also contains a number of concepts. Let's examine the concept "green" in some detail.

The concept "green" is learned through a great deal of associative experience between a physical event (i.e., a particular band of light wavelengths corresponding to the color green) and a verbal label, the word "green." A great deal of this associative experience has undoubtedly occurred under conditions of operant conditioning and, conceivably, even under conditions of classical conditioning. The operant learning aspects are not hard to imagine. Parents or other adults go through a process of pointing to an object, saying its color name, and then either physically or verbally rewarding the child for imitating the name. Or the child points to an object, labels it with an incorrect color name, receives a negative response (perhaps accompanied by a mild form of punishment), and is told the correct label. Classical conditioning could conceivably come into play in a situation where, for example, a mother consistently wears a green apron when feeding an infant. The repeated pairing of the apron color with a pleasant unconditioned stimulus (food) could lead to more rapid discrimination of the color green, relative to other colors. In addition, it could contribute to more rapid learning of the verbal label later on because the color still elicits certain conditioned responses (perhaps this is one explanation for color preferences). These conditioned responses could then serve as additional cues for attaching the appropriate verbal label to the appropriate physical stimulus.

The Role of Habituation in Concept Learning

Concept learning is the process of learning the same response to a number of instances having some set of characteristics in common. At a level lower than verbal, concept learning is the problem of how organisms learn to discriminate among particular features in their environment. For example, how do human beings learn to discriminate the band of light wavelengths that correspond to the color green from those that correspond to other colors. Put another way, how do people know that a house or a car is green when they have never before seen that particular car or house and, therefore, that exact shade of green? They are, in effect, seeing a stimulus they have never seen before. The physics of light waves virtually guarantees that no two surfaces are going to be identical in color. How do they know the color is green? The answer to this question undoubtedly involves the learning process of habituation. It is quite likely that the first few weeks of life are spent "breaking in" the cognitive machinery the child is born with. The child then begins to store perceptual representations in memory, and to organize those representations so that he or she can not only recognize a stimulus that has been seen before but can also recognize a stimulus that is similar to those that have been seen before.

Leslie Cohen (1977) has presented some experimental evidence on how this process works. Cohen presented infants between 18 and 30 weeks old with a series of photographs showing the face of a woman. One group of infants was repeatedly shown the *same* side view of the woman. Another group of infants saw repeated side views of the woman, but in each case, the woman was looking in a different direction. In one photograph, for example, she would be looking to the upper left, in another to the lower right, in a third to the lower left, etc. After repeated exposure to these photographs, both groups of infants were shown two test photographs: one a facing-forward photograph of the familiar woman, and the other a facing-forward photograph of a completely different woman. Thus both photographs, for both groups of infants, were novel. None of the infants had seen either of these photographs before. The results of the experiment indicated that the infants who had repeatedly seen the same side-view picture of the woman displayed the same habituation pattern to both test pictures. They looked as long at the front-facing photograph of the familiar woman as they did at the front-facing new woman. This suggests that the infants did not recognize one face as being familiar and the other as being novel. The habituation times indicate that both pictures were seen as being novel. In contrast to these results, the infants who had seen the differing side views of the woman displayed quite different habituation times to the test pictures of the familiar woman and the novel woman. The infants looked at the familiar woman for much less time than they did at the novel woman. These results indicate that this group of infants recognized the front-facing familiar woman as being familiar, and therefore looked at the photograph for only a short time, whereas the novel woman was recognized as being new, and the infants examined it thoroughly.

Cohen's research suggests that infants acquire a "template" or general representation of a particular stimulus event by repeatedly experiencing that event in differing ways. When sufficient experience has been acquired, the infant has the "concept" of that event and can immediately recognize it as being a familiar event. This is likely to be the way in which people develop the ability to identify the band of light wavelengths corresponding to the color green. As infants, they repeatedly experience colors from the entire spectrum in all manner of shades, brightnesses, and forms. Early on, they orient each time they encounter a color, not recognizing whether the color is novel or familiar. But as experience builds up, they begin to form templates of repeatedly experienced colors and soon begin to habituate to the familiar colors, or to similar colors.

Imprinting as the Most Basic Process

Principle and rule learning, concept learning, instrumental and classical conditioning, and habituation can all be considered as interrelated forms of learning, with the simpler forms serving as building blocks for the more complex forms. It is quite likely that imprinting, or at least a process that has the same critical-period feature as imprinting, serves as the most basic building block in the learning structure. Imprinting is the connective bridge between inherited and learned behavior. Moreover, if the stimulation required to trigger an imprinted behavior does not occur within a critical time period, the opportunity for the expression of the behavior is forever lost. The visual system of mammals has properties similar to these. As an example, A. H. Riesen (1950) raised infant monkeys in the dark for several weeks after birth. Riesen found that even this short period of light deprivation resulted in profound impairment in the perception of patterns. Riesen was also able to show that the impairment was not due to damage to the eye. Rather, it seemed that dark-rearing had somehow reduced the monkeys' ability to learn from their environment. These findings are certainly consistent with the idea that human beings are born with learning machinery that must receive environmental input early if it is to work properly.

LEARNING THEORIES
The Role of Learning Theories

Theories of learning play a crucial role in psychology. Psychologists use learning theories to organize all of the different kinds of learning and all of the results from thousands of research studies into a framework where it is hoped some sense can be made of them. They also use theories of learning to develop predictions for research studies, and then use the results of those studies as a means of evaluating the theories. If the results turn out as predicted, they serve as evidence supporting the theory. If the results turn out differently than predicted, the theory may have to be revised or discarded.

Two early theories of learning

Theories of learning also serve to structure and restructure the way in which psychologists think about learning. As an example, one of the very earliest "theories" of learning suggested that there was a tiny man, called a *homunculus*, sitting inside our skulls. When the little man learned something, he would tell the person whose skull he inhabited what he had learned, and that was the explanation of learning. The problem with this theory came when an explanation was sought of how the little man learns. The answer of ancient learning theorists was similar to the answer given by an American Indian medicine man who believed that the world rested on the back of a turtle. When asked what the turtle rested upon, his answer was, "Another turtle, of course!" Likewise, the explanation of how the homunculus learns is that he has another man inside his skull. Needless to say, there is a never ending question involved in the homunculus theory.

A completely different way of thinking about learning was first expressed with great clarity by the seventeenth-century English philosopher John Locke. In his famous *Essay Concerning Human Understanding*, Locke wrote:

> Let us suppose the mind to be, as we say, white paper, void of all characters, without any ideas; How comes it to be furnished? Whence comes it by that vast store, which the busy and boundless fancy of man has painted on it with an almost endless variety? Whence has it all the materials of reason and knowledge? To this I answer, in one word, from *experience*. In that all our knowledge is founded, and from that it ultimately derives itself. (Quoted in Boring, 1950)

Locke is indicating in this passage that everything of interest about learning can be understood by analyzing experience. If the mind is a *blank slate* that experience writes upon, we need not concern ourselves with the nature of the slate. We need only understand the writing, and that is accomplished by examining experience. Notice that this is a very different position from that taken by the homunculus theory, which said that learning could be completely understood only by examining the nature of the stuff inside the skull. Experience may provide the input, but it's what's going on inside the head that is important in the homunculus theory.

vestigial re-sembling or having the form of some-thing that ex-isted in the past

Interestingly enough, we can see *vestigial* remnants of the homunculus theory and the blank slate theory in the two major classes of modern day learning theories. One major class, the behavioral theories, takes the position that what is learned is identical in some sense to what has been experienced. This class of theories is termed behavioral because the emphasis is on the observable behavior of organisms, and the stimulus events and consequences (e.g., reward, punishment) that accompany the behavior. The other class, cognitive theories, is so called because the emphasis in these theories is on describing the internal workings of the head. The fundamental premise in cognitive theories is that what an organism learns is not the same as what an organism experiences; the structure and content of the mind at any given point in time alter and shape the recording of experiences. Thus from the perspective of cognitive theories, if learning is to be understood, the structure and content of the mind must first be understood.

Behavioral Theories of Learning

stimulus any event that can be perceived by an orga-nism's sense receptors

One important class of learning theories, following the lines initiated by John Locke, suggests that learning can best be understood by examining stimulus events and the behavioral responses that follow those events. This class, *behavioral theories*, can be subdivided into two subcategories: associative learning theory and operant learning theory.

Associative learning theory

Associative learning theory is based on several assumptions about the learning process. Central to these assumptions are the concepts of stimulus and response. A *stimulus* is any event that can be perceived by an organism's sense receptors. A stimulus could be a visual event, a sound, a taste, a smell, a touch, or any combination of these. A *response* is any behavior or behavioral process that is elicited by or accompanies a stimulus. Some responses are unconditioned and do not require learning. Salivation after biting into a steak, or jerking the hand back after one has touched a hot stove, are automatic, innate reflexes. Other responses obviously involve learning. When I hear the question, "What is the greatest number of children a woman has given birth to?" I respond, "Sixty-nine" (an astonishing bit of trivia gleaned from the *Guinness Book of World*

response any behavior or behavioral process that is elicited by or accompanies a stimulus

Many aspects of our environment can be thought of as stimuli. (© Christopher Brown/ Stock, Boston)

Records). I give the response "sixty-nine" to the stimulus question because I have learned to do so.

Another important concept in associative learning theory is *contiguity*. When two events occur together in time, they are said to be contiguous to one another. Thus when I hear (or read) the question about the record for number of children born to a single woman, and I hear (or read) the answer to the question, sixty-nine, the question and the response are contiguous to one another.

contiguity the occurrence of two events close together in time

The central assumption in associative learning theory is that learning involves the formation of associative bonds between stimulus and response events. Associative learning theorists frequently refer to these bonds as *stimulus-response bonds*, or S-R bonds. There are two schools of thought about exactly how stimulus-response bonds are formed. One position (e.g., Guthrie, 1952) says that contiguity is sufficient cause for the formation of S-R bonds. That is, if you hear a particular stimulus event, such as the question, "What is 2 × 5?," and you immediately hear the response, "10," you will form an associative bond between the stimulus event and the response event because they occur together in time.

The second position on how stimulus-response bonds are formed says that some consequence (i.e., reinforcement) must follow the making of a response before an associative bond can be formed. One proponent of the reinforcement view (Hull, 1943) theorized that S-R bonds are formed as a function of the number of reinforced learning events. That is, the more trials on which a stimulus event is accompanied by a response and then is reinforced, the greater the strength of the bond between the stimulus and the response. In contrast, if a stimulus event occurs and a response event occurs, but the events are not followed by reinforcement, no learning occurs.

Apart from this difference about how stimulus-response bonds are formed, most versions of associative learning theory are much the same. They all indicate that learning is the process of forming stimulus-response bonds. In addition, all versions of associative learning theory posit that the correct recall of a learned event is a process in which a stimulus occurring in the environment makes contact with an internal (inside the organism) representation of that stimulus, and since the internal stimulus representation is bonded to the correct response, this leads to correct recall.

threshold the transitional point at which a psychological or physiological effect is first produced

Another assumption shared by all associative learning theories is that bonds form slowly, as a function of either contiguity or reinforcement, and that additional pairings of stimulus and response events result in a "strengthening" of the S-R bond. Moreover, associative learning theories always contain the idea of a recall *"threshold."* This is the idea that the strength of an S-R bond must exceed a certain level before the appropriate response can be recalled on presentation of the stimulus. This can be thought of as being analogous to the starting system in an automobile. If you have ever left your lights on on a foggy or rainy day, you know that turning the key sometimes produces only a click-click noise. But the battery is not totally "dead"—as you would discover if you touched a wire to the poles of the battery. It just doesn't have enough strength to exceed the threshold needed to turn over the engine. Likewise, S-R bonds can be formed and can exist at all levels of strength—some of which fall below a threshold needed for recall and some of which exceed the threshold.

Associative learning theory is classified as a behavioral theory because the bulk of the emphasis in the theory is on an analysis of events external to the organism. Associative learning theorists have focused their attention on stimulus events and response events, and in particular, on the analysis of how different stimulus events and different response events resemble one another. In addition, they have developed principles that describe how S-R bonds are acquired and lost. In Chapter 7, these principles are examined in greater detail, as is the way in which associative learning theory can be applied to educational problems.

Operant learning theory

Operant learning theory is the theory that has evolved to account for operant conditioning. Operant learning theory owes most of its origin to B. F. Skinner, who, as indicated earlier, suggested that learning can be understood in terms of three deceptively simple principles: (1) behavior followed by reinforcement will increase in frequency, (2) behavior followed by punishment will decrease in frequency, and (3) behavior not followed by reinforcement will decrease in frequency.

In order to understand the three principles of operant learning fully, one needs to understand the special meaning given to the terms "reinforcement" and "punishment." In the technical sense used in operant learning theory, a *reinforcer* is any consequence (event, tangible reward, praise, etc.) that follows a behavior and results in an increase in the frequency of that behavior. This is what is known as a *functional* definition of a concept. A reinforcer is defined in terms of the function it performs. The fact that reinforcers are defined functionally means that a given event or thing that is a reinforcer for one person may not be a reinforcer for another. Money can be used as an example. Most people work because they get paid to do so. And, in general, most people would be willing to work harder in a high-paying job than they would in a low-paying job. Thus for most people money serves as a reinforcer. However, money does not serve as a reinforcer for everyone. Some people seek and stay in jobs that they find interesting, rather than choosing jobs on the basis of the amount of salary paid. Others are compulsive workers (workaholics); they work hard at any job, regardless of the rate of pay.

The operant conditioning concept of punishment is the mirror image of that for reinforcement. A *punisher* is defined functionally as any consequence that follows a response and results in a decrease in the frequency of that response. Again, this means that a punisher for one individual or organism may not be a punisher for the next.

At this point the reader might be asking the question, "If some consequences are reinforcers for some people but not others, and if some consequences are punishers for some people but not others, how do psychologists ever determine what are reinforcers and what are punishers?" The answer is, they *observe behavior*. If a consequence results in an increase in the frequency of the behavior it follows, one knows it is a reinforcer. If it results in a decrease in the frequency of the behavior it follows, one knows it is a punisher.

Proponents of operant learning theory take pride in the fact that they are truly "behavioral scientists." That is, they make virtually no assumptions about the content or nature of the mind. Nor, for that matter, do they even speculate about such things. Their theoretical position is that the study of the psychology of learning can proceed quite successfully by attending only to things that can be observed and measured—such as stimuli, responses, rewards, and punishments. Speculation about such intangibles as the structure and content of the mind are, from the perspective of the operant learning theorist, topics best left to philosophers. They are not topics that should be of concern to a research scientist. The application of operant learning theory to educational practice is discussed in Chapter 6.

Social learning theory

A close relative of operant learning theory is *social learning theory*. Social learning theory has been most closely identified with Albert Bandura (e.g., 1977). The theory attempts to explain how people learn from events they see but do not directly experience. Imagine two events as an example. In the first, a teacher explains classroom rules on the first day of class, and the consequences of not following the rules. Two days later, Billy violates the rule of being out of his seat during quiet periods on two successive occasions. The first time he does it, Billy receives a warning; the second time, in accordance with class rules, he loses his recess privileges for the rest of the day. In the second event, imagine the same scenario, except that upon being out of his seat the second time, the teacher merely says, "Billy, I warned you before about being out of your seat; now I don't want it to happen again!" The chances are that children watching Billy in the two situations would learn something different. The children who watched Billy lose his recess privileges for violating the classroom rules would be less likely to violate the rules themselves than would be the children who watched Billy merely receive another warning for his misbehavior. Social learning theory attempts to explain how learning through observation occurs. Moreover, social learning theory attempts to explain observational learning using concepts very similar to those used in operant learning. Of special importance are the details of the event being experienced (observed), the response occurring in conjunction with the observed event, and the consequences following the event.

Bandura's (1977) theory of observational learning consists of four components. The first component is *attentional processes,* which govern the extent to which an observer pays attention to an event being observed. The second component is *retention processes,* which allow for the representation of the observed event within the observer. The third component is *motor reproduction processes,* which allow the observer to reproduce the behavior being observed. The final component is *motivational processes,* including such events as direct external reinforcement for performing a modeled behavior, vicarious reinforcement (reinforcement provided to the model that leads to strengthening of the observer's tendency to perform the behavior), and self-reinforcement. Motivational processes govern the likelihood that the observer will perform the modeled behavior.

Bandura's (1977) theory of social learning extends some of the principles of behavioral learning theory into the realm of observational learning. For example, operant learning theory alone could not explain the behavior of Billy's classmates, because the theory says that an organism must perform a behavior and then itself experience the consequences (reinforcement or punishment) associated with that behavior before learning will occur. Bandura's theoretical concepts, such as vicarious reinforcement, provide an explanation for a good deal of learning that could not be explained by other behavioral learning theories.

Cognitive Theories of Learning

If the theories reviewed in the previous section can be thought of as the offspring of John Locke's blank slate theory, those in this section can be thought of as the offspring of the homunculus theory. The theories are tied together by the idea that a satisfactory account of the learning process can occur only by considering the internal workings of the mind. As will be seen, the different cognitive theories discussed have somewhat different thrusts. Information-processing theories, which are considered first, are primarily concerned with dividing the learning process into different stages of learning—in much the same way as the manufacture of an automobile can be divided into different assembly-line stages. The semantic network theories that are discussed next are primarily concerned with the way information is represented in human memory. These theories have as their premise that an understanding of how information is represented must precede an understanding of how information is learned. The final position discussed is schema theory. Like the semantic network theories, the principal goal of schema theory is to describe how information is represented in memory. However, unlike semantic network theories, which posit a relatively static, fixed memory representation system, schema theory proposes a highly dynamic system that can change considerably with each item of information added to memory.

Information-processing theories

During the early 1960s, psychologists began to use computers to control psychological research and to perform the mathematical calculations involved in analyzing research data. As they became more and more familiar with the internal workings of computers, psychologists began to see human learning and memory as being analogous to the process of computer information processing. As an instance, they began to ask whether the way that humans take in, process, and store information was similar to the way that computers perform these functions. Since computer information processing can be conveniently thought of as a series of separate stages, it was quite natural to begin thinking of human learning in the same terms (e.g., Hunt, 1971).

As an interesting historical coincidence, at about the same time that people were beginning to be thought of as computers, evidence began to appear which indicated that humans did indeed process information in a series of discrete stages. This evidence, when combined with the emerging tendency to think about human learning in computer terms, gave rise to *information-processing theories* of human learning. The research evidence indicated that the human cognitive system contained at least three discrete memory systems. The first system, called the *sensory register*, received input from the sensory receivers (e.g., visual or auditory sensations from the eyes and ears) and stored that input for a brief period of time—ranging from one-quarter of a second for visual sensation to several seconds for auditory sensation. If the information was not passed along for further processing during this brief period, it decayed, leaving no residual trace. If the information was passed along, it entered *short-term memory*, which was a limited-*capacity* memory system capable of storing information not being actively *rehearsed* for approximately 15 seconds or less. Short-term memory is the memory system that comes into play when one looks up a telephone number in the directory, begins to dial the number, and then realizes that it has been forgotten. In addition to the sensory register and

sensory register part of the memory system that stores visual or auditory sensations for less than several seconds

short-term memory a limited-capacity memory system that can store information not being actively rehearsed for up to 15 seconds

capacity the quantity of units that a particular component of the memory system can retain

rehearsal the focusing of attention on information in short-term memory

FIGURE 5-3   An Information-Processing Model of Human Learning

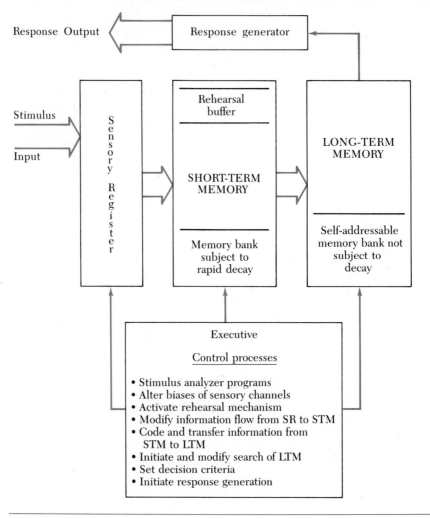

(Adapted from Shiffrin and Atkinson, 1969)

short-term memory, research evidence indicated that there was a third memory system, subsequently called *long-term memory,* which had an unlimited capacity and stored information for long periods of time—perhaps forever. The three memory systems were soon combined into unified models of human information processing, one of the earliest of which (Shiffrin and Atkinson, 1969) is presented in Figure 5.3. The activity of these three systems was controlled by the *executive,* which monitors and governs the flow of information throughout the entire system.

Semantic network theories

The information-processing theories just discussed propose that information flows through three distinct memory stages as it is being processed. Information-processing theories do not, however, contain a description of the *contents* of these memory systems; most particularly, they do not contain a description of the contents of long-term memory. The semantic network theories to be discussed in this section have as their specific purpose the description of the content and workings of long-term memory. The term *semantic network theory* derives from the fact that such theories are concerned only with language-based information. They have little to say, for example, about the nature of memory storage for odors and tactile sensations. In linguistics, semantics is the study of the meaning of language.

It is not obvious that a theory of learning need contain a description of the contents and workings of human memory. In fact, as we have seen, behavioral theorists explicitly believe that cognitive theorizing hinders understanding of the learning process. What has led to such theorizing is research data that seem impossible to understand without speculating about the internal workings of human memory. Consider these examples from John Bransford and Nancy McCarrell (1974) as demonstrations that what you already know influences your understanding of common, everyday English. What do the following sentences mean?

1. The notes were sour because the seam was split.
2. The haystack was important because the cloth ripped.
3. The trip was delayed because the bottle broke.

Chances are you had a great deal of trouble understanding the sentences. But try again, thinking of bagpipes for the first sentence, a parachute for the second sentence, and a ship launching for the third sentence. If you are like most people, you now have an immediate sense of understanding the sentences.

The Bransford and McCarrell sentences demonstrate that comprehension is a process involving both the linguistic messages we are receiving *and* the prior knowledge we have about the topic under discussion. The question then becomes, how does the incoming message make contact with the relevant prior knowledge? The answer to this question obviously requires speculating about the internal workings of memory.

Allan Collins and Elizabeth Loftus (1975) have contributed a semantic network theory that is relevant to the above question. Figure 5.4 contains a schematic representation of a section of human memory surrounding the concept *node* "red." In the diagram, the length of the line between two concept nodes corresponds to the degree of relatedness between concepts. For example, the concept "red" is more closely related to "fire engine" than it is to "sunrises." Examination of the network arrangement proposed by Collins and Loftus also provides an explanation for the difficulty in comprehending the Bransford and McCarrell sentences.

node the point at which subsidiary parts originate, center, or intersect

Imagine presenting a person with the sentence "The notes were sour because the seam was split." The process of comprehending the sentence involves activating the memory nodes for the concepts contained in the sentence and then spreading the activation down the connecting pathways to other concept nodes, and comprehension occurs when there is an intersection of all of the pathways from all of the originally activated concept nodes. If the sentence is presented without the context word "bagpipes," the chances of this intersection occurring are fairly slim. Looking at Figure 5.4, it would be like starting out at the "clouds," "flowers," "street," and "house" concept nodes, and then attempting to find the "red" node where the pathways of those concept nodes intersect. Finding that intersection point would be difficult because of the

FIGURE 5-4   Concept Relatedness

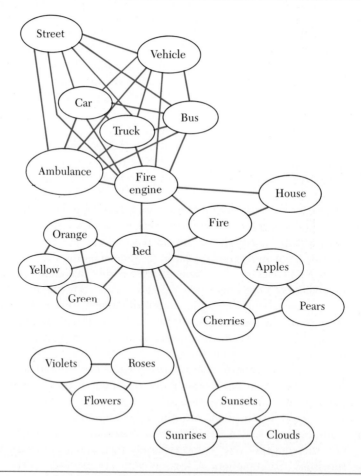

This diagram is a schematic representation of concept relatedness in a stereotypical fragment of human memory (where a short line represents greater relatedness). (After Collins and Loftus)

considerable distance between the originally activated nodes and the intersection nodes, and because in some cases the activation would have to spread through several other concept nodes before arriving at the intersection node. But note how the difficulty diminishes when the *red* node is activated along with the other concept nodes. Activation now spreads outward from the intersection node as well as spreading inward toward the intersection node. This halves the distance that activation has to spread and greatly increases the likelihood that all of the concept nodes will intersect one another. Thus in the Bransford and McCarrell sentence, activating "bagpipe" along with the other concept nodes greatly increases the chances of finding the intersection point, at which comprehension can occur.

Semantic network theories have moved the topic of mind from the area of philosophical speculation to an area of serious scientific investigation. The theories provide explicit accounts of the way in which the linguistic contents of the mind are organized. An additional point of interest about semantic network theories is that they can be programmed on a computer. In fact, several of the theories had their origin as computer programs. Thus one very active area of research on semantic network theories involves attempts to develop computers that will mimic human intellectual behavior.

Schema theory

The previous section was concerned with theories which state that the contents of the mind consist of concept nodes joined together by interconnecting pathways to form networks. Semantic network theories present a rather static, or fixed, sense of human memory. That is, the nodes and their interconnections convey a sense of rigidity—a rigidity that is not likely to change to any great extent in a short period of time. In contrast to semantic network theories, the theories presented in this section convey the sense of a much more dynamic memory system—a memory system that can change, and one that can *generate* information, as contrasted to semantic network theory, which simply deals with the storing of information.

Two kinds of evidence point to the need for a theory of memory representation having dynamic properties. English psychologist Sir Frederick Bartlett conducted a series of studies on memory beginning in 1912 that was published in his famous book on remembering in 1932. Over the years, Bartlett asked his subjects to read a native North American folk tale about two young men who journey down the river to hunt seals and get involved in a battle between warring tribes of ghosts. After reading the story twice, Bartlett had his subjects immediately recall the story and then, at various intervals thereafter, some as long as several years, he asked them to recall the story again.

On the basis of the learning theories discussed thus far, one might predict that memory for Bartlett's story would deteriorate over time, as would be the case, for example, if network pathways decayed because of disuse. This would result in details of the story dropping out of recall. One might also predict that some details would be wrong because subjects chose to guess about a detail when they couldn't remember it. But the results of Bartlett's research were that neither the dropping out of detail nor the fabrication of story elements seemed to characterize his subjects' recall. Instead, recall tended to be affected by preformed interests and tendencies. Moreover, as time passed, the theme and detail of the stories changed more and more toward being consistent with themes and details familiar to the subject. This was not a process of "making up" the story. Rather, the subjects believed they were recalling the story as accurately as they could.

The results of Bartlett's research, which were recently confirmed by Rand Spiro (1977), suggest that memory representations change over time. Let us now consider evidence which suggests that memory is generative (e.g., Wittrock, 1974). The term *generative* here means that memory automatically adds content to what is being learned. Consider the following sets of sentences, which are similar to ones provided by Roger Schank and Robert Abelson (1977):

1. The policeman held up his hand and stopped the car.
2. I went to three drugstores this morning.
3. I had dinner at an Italian restaurant last night. I ordered lasagna, garlic bread, and a glass of red wine. I paid the check with an American Express card. What did I have to eat?

These three sets of sentences all illustrate the extent to which automatic inferencing is a natural part of the comprehension process. In the first sentence, how does one know that the driver of the car voluntarily stopped when the policeman held up his hand, rather than that the policeman physically stopped the car by placing his hand on it? In the second sentence, the interpretation tends to be that the writer was having trouble finding something, therefore he went to three different drugstores looking for it. Why does one automatically draw this inference, rather than simply accepting the information at face value? In the third set of sentences, the automatic response is, "Lasagna, bread, and wine." But if you look at the sentences you will see that they say nothing about anything being *eaten!* Why does one naturally and automatically draw the inference that if people order something in a restaurant, they will also eat it? The answer to the question posed for each of the sets of sentences must be that one's mind generates content and adds it to the content of the message being perceived by the sense receptors.

Schema theory has been proposed as a solution for both the apparent change in memory over time seen in Bartlett's research, and the generative qualities of memory as illustrated by the sample sentences. Bartlett (1932) used the term *schema* (plural *schemata*) to describe the dynamic structural unit that he saw as the basic building block of memory. In Bartlett's view, schemata were "organized patterns" that were in a constant state of change. When new information was acquired, it was integrated into the schema, and this resulted in a change in the schema relative to its former state.

Bartlett had a very vague view of schemata, but the concept has sharpened considerably in recent years. For example, Richard Anderson, a leading proponent of schema theory, views schemata as follows:

> A schema represents generic knowledge; that is, it represents what is believed to be generally true of a class of things, events, or situations. A schema is conceived to contain a *slot* or a place holder for each component. For instance, a Face schema includes slots for a mouth, nose, eyes, and ears. Encoding a particular object is conceived to be a matter of filling the slots in the schema with the features of the object. Part of schematic knowledge is the specification of the constraints on what normally can fill the slots. An object will be recognized as a face only if it has features that qualify as eyes, a mouth, a nose, and so on. To be sure, the constraints on the slots in a Face schema are flexible enough that we can tolerate considerable variation, as in a sketchy drawing in a comic strip, the stylized and transformed representation in a cubist painting, or the exaggerated portrayal in a political cartoon. Nonetheless, there are limits beyond which an object is no longer a face. (Anderson, 1977, pp. 2–3)

Anderson's view, and that of many other modern schema theorists, is that schemata form as a function of repeated experience with a particular kind of event. Take going to a restaurant as an example (see Schank and Abelson, 1977). Over the years, most people acquire considerable experience with restaurants, and they build up a number of things that they know to be true of virtually all restaurants. They know that restaurants are places where one goes to eat; they know that there are people who generally serve the food and clean up afterward; they know that a selection of food is offered; and they know that they have to pay for the food they order. These generically true things that people know about restaurants are what Anderson calls *slots* or *place holders*. The interesting thing is that when one is told something about restaurants, but a value for one of the slots is not filled in, one automatically fills it in oneself on most occasions. The series of sentences about eating in the Italian restaurant serve as an example. One is not told in the sentences what was eaten. Instead, on the basis of one's experience with restaurants, one automatically makes an inference about what was eaten.

Schemata are seen by schema theorists as being profoundly important in virtually all psychological processes. They are thought to play a crucial role in perception, attitudes, emotions, information processing, and memory. In Chapter 8, some of the implications of schema theory for educational practice are examined.

WHICH LEARNING THEORY IS RIGHT?

In the previous section, six different learning theories were reviewed—all of which differed in some detail and several of which held diametrically opposing viewpoints. For instance, operant learning theory holds that a theory of learning should be concerned with only the observables in the learning situation—that is, stimuli, behavioral responses, and response consequences. In contrast, semantic network theory holds that an understanding of the way in which the contents of the mind are represented must precede an understanding of learning. Needless to say, when one has one theory which says that concern with the mind is a waste of time and another which says that mind is all important, one has two theories that are on very different ground. Which of the theories is correct?

In a book filled with important insights, the historian of science Thomas Kuhn (1970) wrote that a characteristic of a mature science, such as physics or chemistry, is that one theoretical point of view—Kuhn uses the term "paradigm"—tends to dominate the thinking of virtually all of the scientists within a discipline. However, immature sciences—those in an early developmental stage—are characterized by the existence of a number of constantly changing, competing theories, none of which is able to reach a position of dominance.

In addition to characterizing the stages of the development of a science, Kuhn has also made some important observations about the "truth" of scientific theories. The romance of science would have it that science is a process of moving ever closer to a state of "truth" about the nature of the universe. New theories replace old theories, the romanticists would say, because the new theories are closer to the truth than are the old theories. That is, they are more correct. But Kuhn argues that nice as this may sound, it bears little resemblance to the way in which science actually progresses. New theories do not replace old theories because the new are more correct than the old. Rather, new theories slowly replace old theories because more and more scientists come to believe in the new theory rather than in the old. Moreover, scientists who continue to believe in the old theory get old and retire from the scientific scene, thereby reducing the number of adherents to the old theory. There are many examples from the history of science that support this view. The modern-day probabilistic theories in physics did not immediately replace the "mechanical" physics of Sir Isaac Newton. Instead, the new view slowly came to be favored over the older theory.

One can learn several things about the correctness of learning theories by examining Kuhn's insights. First, one can note that psychology fits Kuhn's definition of an immature science. There are several competing theories of learning, none of which has assumed a dominant position. Also, the time frame of psychology as a science fits the notion of an immature science. Scientific psychology began in 1879 in Leipzig, Germany, when Wilhelm Wundt founded the first laboratory for the study of psychology. One hundred years is not a very long time span when one considers that such sciences as physics, astronomy, and chemistry have existed for many hundreds of years. Thus psychology has not had the time needed to build the large empirical base that a mature science needs to narrow competing theoretical perspectives.

The psychology of learning is in a stage where one theory cannot be said to be uniformly more useful—in the sense of being consistent with a larger chunk of empirical data—than another. Rather, it is the case that one theory is more useful for analyzing one kind of learning event, whereas another theory is more useful for analyzing another kind of learning event. As an instance, it would be rather nonsensical to approach the problem of how children learn toilet training from the perspective of semantic network theory. However, operant learning theory provides a satisfactory account of the process. In contrast, if one wanted to understand why most individuals can repeat back only about seven random digits they have just heard, whereas they can easily repeat back more than twice that number of words heard in a sentence, one would find that operant learning theory has little to say about the finding, whereas information-processing theory or semantic network theory can provide a convenient explanation. This means that the question of which theory of learning is most correct does not have an answer. The competing theories have different areas of emphasis, and as will be seen, one can use these different areas of emphasis to approach different kinds of educational problems.

TRANSFORMING LEARNING THEORY INTO EDUCATIONAL PRACTICE

Learning theories can provide valuable approaches to educational problems. The first stage in the process of developing an instructional approach involves deciding which learning theory should be used for which problem. In this section, a system for deciding an answer to this question is presented.

Three Conditions for Successful Teaching

1. Students must perform observable behaviors that lead to beneficial learning at a relatively high level, and they must perform observable behaviors that interfere with beneficial learning at a relatively low level.
2. Students must thoroughly master lower-level knowledge that serves as the foundation for the learning of more complex rules and principles.
3. Knowledge and skills must be learned at a deep and significant level.

Let us examine each of these conditions in turn.

Appropriate observable behaviors
The first condition states that appropriate observable behaviors are a necessary first step in the educational process. A student cannot learn from a book if he

or she is not looking at the book. Similarly, a student cannot learn anything from a teacher's discussion if he or she is talking to another student rather than listening to the teacher. Looking at a text is an overt behavior that is consistent with learning from that text. One has no guarantee that students are learning if they are looking at a book, but one can be certain that they are not learning if they are not looking at it. Likewise, one cannot be sure that students will learn something from the teacher if they listen to his or her discussion. But one can be sure that they will not learn anything from the teacher if they are engaged in an overt behavior, such as talking to another student, that blocks learning from the teacher's discussion.

mathemagenic behaviors the term used by Rothkopf to describe behaviors that give birth to learning

Ernst Rothkopf (1970) invented a conceptual system that is directly relevant to this discussion. Rothkopf coined the term, *mathemagenic behaviors*, to describe behaviors that, in Rothkopf's terms, "give birth to learning." Mathemagenic positive behaviors, such as attending to a book or listening to a teacher, are those that lead to relevant learning; whereas mathemagenic negative behaviors, such as staring idly out of the window or gossiping with a classmate, are behaviors that block relevant learning.

Rothkopf (1970) divided positive mathemagenic behaviors into three classes of activities:

> Class I. *Orientation:* Getting students into the vicinity of instructional objects and keeping them there for suitable time periods. In certain institutional settings, this also involves control over activities that may distract or disturb other students.
> Class II. *Object acquisition:* Selecting and procuring appropriate instructional objects. Maintenance and selection of procurement activities.
> Class III. *Translations and processing:* Scanning and systematic eye fixations on the instructional object; translation into internal speech or internal representations; the mental accompaniments of reading; discrimination, segmentation, processing, etc. (Rothkopf, 1970, p. 328)

It is apparent that all of the classes relate to the contents of the first condition presented earlier. If the student does not perform the observable behaviors of being in the vicinity of the instructional material, selecting the appropriate learning device, and attending to the contents of the instruction, then no educationally relevant learning will occur.

Mastery of basic information

The second condition for successful teaching states that important lower-level information must be mastered so that it can serve as the foundation for the learning of more complex information. Nancy Bates made this point; and it was made again earlier in this chapter when it was indicated that complex principles and rules could be mastered only if lower-level principles, rules, and concepts had been mastered. Robert Gagné (1970) has made the same point, using somewhat different terms. Gagné has divided learning into eight varieties, which have a hierarchical relationship with one another (see the accompanying box).

Robert Gagné's Varieties of Learning

Robert Gagné (1970) has suggested that there are eight varieties of learning, which combine to form a hierarchical structure. Gagné's varieties of learning range in order from the most simple to the most complex:

- In *signal learning*, an organism learns to perform an *involuntary* response in the presence of a particular stimulus. This variety of learning is identical to classical conditioning.
- *Stimulus-response learning* involves learning to perform a *voluntary* response in the presence of a stimulus. This variety of learning resembles operant conditioning.
- *Chaining* is a variety of learning that entails stringing stimulus-response units together to form a multiple-unit chain.
- *Verbal associations* are multiple-unit chains that consist of words, rather than of the motor actions that make up chaining.
- *Discrimination learning* involves learning to make a response to a particular stimulus but not to stimuli that may resemble the target stimulus.
- Discrimination learning provides the basis for *concept learning*, which entails learning to classify stimulus situations in terms of such abstracted properties as size, shape, color, function, or animation.
- *Rule learning* involves chaining together two or more concepts in such a way that they form a relation to one another.
- *Problem solving* involves combining previously acquired rules into new, higher-order rules that can then be used in the solution of problems.

As can be seen, Gagné's varieties of learning have many similarities to the types of learning introduced earlier in this chapter. Both classification systems strongly emphasize the idea that complex learning rests on a firm foundation of simpler forms of learning.

Teaching for understanding

The third condition states that students must thoroughly understand the material they are supposed to learn. In this condition, a distinction is being made between information that is learned at a very shallow level, and is therefore only partially understood, and information that is learned at a deep, meaningful level, and is therefore thoroughly understood. Returning to Einstein's formula depicting the relationship between mass, energy, and velocity—$E = MC^2$, most people's knowledge about the formula is so shallow that there isn't a thing in the world they can do with it except recite it. Consider another example: A student in a high school economics class, asked what a household budget is, responds, "A system of allocating income to various expense categories." Can one conclude from that response that the student has a deep understanding of household budgets? Of course not! If one wanted to assess the student's understanding at a deep level, one would provide the student with some raw data and ask him or her to construct a household budget.

Very frequently, the best test of whether someone really understands something involves asking them to use their knowledge in a situation they have not encountered before (Royer and Allen, 1978). This can be contrasted to such typical classroom tasks as asking students to pick a definition of a concept from four multiple-choice alternatives, or asking them to compute the answer to a mathematics problem of a kind they have practiced many times before. Quite frequently, the ability to perform well on such tasks indicates

Most scientific principles are highly complex, involving many subsidiary principles and rules that must be learned thoroughly. (© Van Bucher 1972/Photo Researchers)

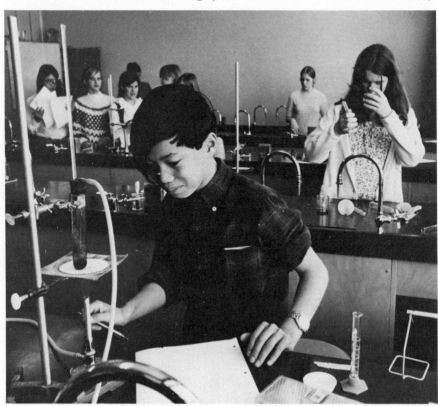

nothing more than the fact that the student has temporarily committed to memory a definition or a formula. Performance on such tasks reveals little about the extent to which the student understands the material.

Using the Three Conditions to Select Approaches to Educational Problems

The three conditions just discussed can be used to select a learning theory based approach to educational problems. The first condition stated that students must perform observable behaviors that are consistent with learning if they are to master important material. Moreover, it said that students must not be performing behaviors that block the learning of important material. The appropriate behaviors and the blocking behaviors cited in the condition are easily observable. One can see when a student is doing things that are consistent with important school learning, and one can see when a student is doing something that may block his or her own learning as well as the learning of other students.

As indicated earlier in this chapter, operant learning theory is a theory that focuses on analysis of the conditions that produce and inhibit overt behavior. As will be seen shortly, educational approaches based on operant learning theory have been very useful in dealing with problems involving observable student behaviors.

The second condition indicated that students must thoroughly master lower-level material before they can master more complex material. Associative learning theory can serve as the basis for approaching problems involving the mastery of basic material, since it can be used to develop techniques for breaking complex knowledge and skills into smaller, more easily learned units. The theory also contains suggestions about how to present material, how to sequence material, and how to arrange review periods so as to maximize learning and retention. These techniques are examined in greater detail in Chapter 7.

The third condition was that students must have learned educational material to a deep and significant level of understanding. The question of what it means to understand is complicated. However, cognitive learning theories do suggest answers. Moreover, these theories contain suggestions as to how to present educational material in a manner that will increase the likelihood that students will attain a thorough understanding of it.

Putting Together the Approaches to Problems

In the previous section, it was indicated that different theories of learning are best suited for approaching different kinds of problems. One mistaken impression that might be derived from the foregoing discussion is that the approaches are used in isolation—that teachers would not be using more than one approach at the same time. But in fact, in the majority of educational settings, teachers would be using several educational approaches at the same time. Some students might be exhibiting behavior problems that would call for the use of operant learning techniques, some students might be experiencing problems in understanding that would call for the use of cognitive learning techniques, and the class as a whole might be covering material that was being presented in accordance with associative learning techniques. In real classroom situations, it frequently happens that a number of educational approaches are being used simultaneously.

SUMMARY

The goal of formal education is for students to learn the material that is presented to them. Attainment of this goal is dependent on students attending to instruction, students being motivated to learn, and the instruction being presented in a manner that allows the students to acquire the information. All of these are problems that can be approached using guidelines provided by the psychology of learning. Knowledge of the psychology of learning can provide approaches that may not occur to a teacher who is solely dependent on his or her own experience.

Learning is a very complicated subject that can be simplified by breaking it into smaller subcategories. These subcategories, called types of learning, range from very simple, primitive forms of learning to highly complex forms of learning attainable only by human beings. The simplest type of learning, imprinting, entails the release of a genetically prepared behavior upon encountering a particular environmental event. An example would be a baby duck following the first moving object it sees. One characteristic of imprinting is that it has a critical period. If the organism does not encounter the relevant event during the critical period, imprinting will not occur.

The next type of learning is habituation—the decrease in response to an event as the event becomes familiar. When one experiences a brand new event one *orients* to the source of the event. With repeated experience of the event, the orienting response decreases, until it is nonexistent. One can then be said to have habituated to the event.

The third type of learning is classical conditioning—the process whereby a neutral stimulus comes to elicit a response over which the organism has no control. This is accomplished by pairing (presenting simultaneously) a neutral stimulus (such as a bell) with an unconditioned stimulus (such as meat powder) for repeated trials. The unconditioned stimulus elicits an unconditioned response (such as salivation) without any learning occurring. That is, meat powder blown into a dog's mouth will automatically elicit salivation. After repeated pairings of the neutral stimulus with the unconditioned stimulus, the neutral stimulus alone will elicit the response. When this happens, the previously neutral stimulus is called a conditioned stimulus (to signify that learning, rather than automatic behavior, is involved), and the response is called a conditioned response (to signify that learning is involved in making the response).

The fourth type of learning is operant conditioning, which occurs when a voluntary response emitted in the presence of a particular stimulus increases in frequency as a function of the response being followed by reinforcement. Operant conditioning also involves techniques for reducing the frequency of a voluntary behavior. Behavior can be reduced in frequency by ceasing to reinforce a previously reinforced behavior (a process called extinction) or by punishing (technically defined as presenting a noxious stimulus) an emitted response.

Concept learning is the next type. Concept learning involves learning to classify together things that have a common attribute or group of attributes. For example, certain things are called chairs because they all share certain physical and functional characteristics. Concept learning is critical to education, since it allows one to think of things in the abstract, rather than having one's thoughts bound by actually experienced events and objects.

Rule and principle learning is the highest-level learning discussed in the chapter. Rules are two or more concepts related in a manner that indicates a specific application. Principles are two or more concepts related in a manner that indicates a general application. This means that any given principle can be decomposed into several rules.

The types of learning discussed in the chapter have a hierarchical relationship to one another. Principles can be broken down into rules, and rules are composed of two or more concepts. Concepts can be acquired through lower-level types of learning, such as operant conditioning, classical conditioning, and habituation. Imprinting may be the most basic type of learning, in that an organism may be born with a genetically "prepared" neural system that "soaks up" environmental experience. If experience is not encountered during a critical-period phase, the organism's learning mechanisms may be seriously damaged.

Learning theories attempt to clarify, organize, and explain the learning process. There are two general classes of learning theories: (1) behavioral theories, which focus their analysis on the stimuli experienced by an organism, the organism's response in the presence of the stimulus situation, and (sometimes) the consequences (e.g., reward, punishment) that follow the response; and (2) cognitive theories, which focus on the internal workings of the mind.

Three behavioral learning theories were described. Operant learning theory, which attempts to explain operant conditioning, suggests that much of learning is governed by three general principles: first, that behavior followed by reinforcement will increase in frequency; second, that behavior followed by punishment will decrease in frequency; and third, that the cessation of reinforcement for a previously reinforced behavior will cause that behavior to decrease in frequency.

The second behavior theory is social learning theory. Social learning theory provides an explanation of how individuals learn from events they see but do not directly experience themselves.

The third behavioral theory is associative learning theory, which suggests that learning involves the formation of associative bonds between stimulus events and response events (referred to as S-R bonds). There are two schools of thought about how S-R bonds are formed: the first says that contiguity is a sufficient condition for the formation of the bonds; the second says that a consequence must follow a response before an associative bond can be formed.

Three types of cognitive theories are discussed in the chapter. The first is information-processing theory, which divides the human cognitive system into a series of stages. In one version of the theory, information passes through a sensory register, short-term memory, and finally into long-term memory during learning. The processing activity that occurs within each of these stages is under the control of the executive, which monitors and controls the entire system.

A second kind of cognitive theory is semantic network theory, which describes the contents of the mind as consisting of many concept nodes joined together by interconnecting pathways. The nodes are heavily interrelated and come to form complex networks of interconnecting concepts. Semantic network theory is useful for explaining facts about memory retrieval and comprehension, and for testing hypotheses about the structure of knowledge in the mind.

The final cognitive theory is schema theory, which suggests that the mind is structured into dynamic schemata. The schemata can change over time and with additional input, and they can generate as well as store information.

At this point it is not possible to decide which learning theory is more nearly correct. All of the theories have particular strengths and weaknesses. However, each theory focuses on a different type of learning event. This fact provides a basis for selecting different learning theories to approach different types of educational problems.

Operant learning theory can provide valuable approaches to problems involving observable student behaviors because the thrust of the theory is toward the principles governing this type of behavior. Associative learning theory can provide valuable approaches to problems involving the mastery of basic information because much of this kind of material can be thought of as involving a kind of stimulus-response learning. Finally, cognitive theory can provide valuable approaches to problems involving the understanding of instructional material because it is concerned with such issues as what it means to comprehend, and why some material is more easily understood than other material.

FOR FURTHER STUDY AND APPLICATION

Hill, W. F. *Learning*. (3rd ed.) New York: Harper & Row, 1977.   A classic presentation of behavioral learning theories.

Wessells, M. G. *Cognitive psychology*. New York: Harper & Row, 1982.   An up-to-date, very readable presentation of recent cognitive theories and research.

Bigge, M. L. *Learning theories for teachers*. (3rd ed.) New York: Harper & Row, 1976.

Kolesnik, W. B. *Learning: Educational applications*. Boston: Allyn & Bacon, 1976.

Snelbecker, G. E. *Learning theory, instructional theory, and psychoeducational design*. New York: McGraw-Hill, 1974.   Three education-oriented presentations of learning; the first two are fairly nontechnical.

6

OPERANT APPROACHES TO INSTRUCTION: CLASSROOM MANAGEMENT

CHAPTER OVERVIEW

The material in this chapter explains how operant learning theory can be translated into approaches to problems involving observable student behaviors. The first part of the first section describes how the frequency of a given behavior can be increased by reinforcing the behavior. A reinforcer is defined as anything that increases the frequency of occurrence of the behavior it follows. Three kinds of reinforcers are described: primary reinforcers, which have inherent reinforcing properties; conditioned reinforcers, which derive their reinforcing properties from being paired with primary reinforcers or with other conditioned reinforcers; and negative reinforcers, which derive their reinforcing properties from releasing the student from an unpleasant situation.

The second part of the first section describes techniques for reducing the frequency of behavior. A behavior can be reduced in frequency in three ways—through a process of extinction, which entails no longer providing reinforcement for a behavior; through a process of denying a student access to reinforcement; or through a process of punishing a student after an undesirable behavior is performed. Punishment must be used with considerable caution, however, because of the many serious side effects that sometimes accompany its use.

The second section details the steps a teacher would take in developing an operant learning theory–based approach to behavioral change. The first step involves identifying the behaviors the teacher wants to change. The second step involves designing a data-recording system and collecting some preliminary data. The third step involves selecting an approach to use, that is, devising a means to increase the frequency of desirable behaviors and decrease the frequency of undesirable behaviors. The fourth step is to communicate the nature of the system to the students and to institute the program. The final step is to evaluate the effects of the program.

The third section of the chapter is concerned with whether students who have been reinforced for desirable behavior will come to expect a reward and will lose their natural interest in learning. This section will review evidence that fears such as the ones mentioned will materialize only when students are rewarded for merely participating in activities. When they are rewarded for the quality of their performance there are no negative consequences of providing rewards.

The final section of the chapter discusses the fact that knowledge of operant learning principles can be a valuable addition to any teacher's "tools of the trade."

Abe Gonzales is dean of boys at Richmond High School in Richmond, California. Richmond, a city with a population of about 79,000, is one of several cities that adjoin one another on the eastern shore of San Francisco Bay. Abe Gonzales grew up in Richmond and graduated from Richmond High School. He attended Chico State University in Chico, California, and graduated with a degree in psychology. He has been teaching and serving as dean at Richmond High for 10 years.

Richmond High School is similar to many urban schools, in that enrollment has been shrinking in recent years—down to 1,200 from a high of 2,000 several years ago. The racial composition of the school is mixed, with blacks making up approximately 50 percent of the student body, Hispanics (largely Mexican) about 15 percent, Asians (many Vietnamese and Cambodians recently) about 7 percent, and the remainder being white. The interview began with a question about what it is like to teach at Richmond High.

A. Richmond High is great! Actually there has been a lot of change in the years that I have been here. When I first came here as a teacher we were on a traditional schedule, where classes followed one another everyday. Then the next year we changed to a modular schedule, similar to college schedules, where classes don't meet every day. The classes met, for example, on Monday, Wednesday, and Friday. But because of the make-up of our school, it was not very successful. We gave the kids free time, and instead of applying it toward studying and using the time wisely, they would just do other things or nothing at all. The schedule suffered for a number of years and just got worse. We finally got a new principal. He's turned things around. He's been here 2 years now, and he was able to see that the scheduling system was really destructive. He changed it, and things have really picked up.

Q.   What kind of schedule are you on now?

A.   We are on a traditional schedule. The students attend classes from 8:30 until 2:55 with an hour for lunch each day. It works much better this way because our kids need a lot of structure. They need a lot of discipline, and I think they appreciate this system more than they did the previous one. Morale in previous years was just terrible. The kids were together all the time, both in and out of class, and they would get on one another's nerves. So we had a lot of discipline problems and vandalism.

Q.   To what extent do you think discipline problems are a major issue for most classroom teachers?

A.   We talked about this a lot when we converted back to the traditional system. I would say that next to attendance, discipline was the major concern expressed by our teachers.

Q.   If you were to talk to a group of beginning teachers about how to maintain discipline in their classrooms, what would you tell them?

A.   Oh gosh! Well, I think you start with the structure of the class first of all. One of the main things is to be organized yourself. This may sound simplistic, but things like a teacher being there on time are important. I know it presents a problem when teachers are changing classes, but many times I have seen teachers get a little lax and start coming in late. Soon the students are coming in late, and you've got the beginning of a problem. But to get back to my point, organization in your own schedule first of all, and then in your class presentations. If you have something going on in your classroom, you're going to keep your students' interest. The real troublemakers are going to try to make trouble no matter what you are trying to teach them because of whatever problems they may have and their need to act out. But I think, basically, if a kid has enough interest to go to a classroom, you can capture his attention with your lessons and then he's going to learn. There's no way of avoiding the minor discipline problems. Somebody makes a remark to someone, something like that. But I think organization in your own life, in your presentations, and to have something going on in your classes are key elements in avoiding discipline problems. Not really presenting an honest lesson is going to lead to problems because the kids can see right through that. They know when you're BS-ing them, it'll show; it is going to cause some problems. Being firm, setting guidelines right from the beginning, letting them know exactly what is expected of them grade-wise—on papers and homework, on tardiness and absenteeism; those kinds of things—and letting them know the consequences.

Teachers, I think, are in a kind of unique situation, in that they cannot afford to have emotional ups and downs. Parents can, but teachers can't. I mean students expect a teacher every day to be a teacher, and it is often very difficult. Most of the time my experience has been that when a teacher slips and allows his emotions to come through in anger or hostility, or maybe some kind of smart remark, then the kids will pick up on that and you'll see it grow. The teachers who have the fewest number of referrals here to me as dean are the ones that are stable. They just don't go up and down very much, and if they do, they keep it pretty much hidden. They provide a steady presentation of material and steady high expectations, and they don't let themselves be put on display. This may sound like they are very much unemotional and mechanical, but I don't mean it like that at all. Our best teachers do show emotion, but it's always controlled to serve a purpose. If they get angry, it's never on a personal basis, it's because they expect things from their students and the students have let them down.

Q.   In other words, the teacher gets angry at a student's behavior, not at the student himself or herself?

A.   Right. The teacher shouldn't let things get on a personal level. The teachers that refer to me most often are the ones that have highs and lows, and oftentimes get into personal confrontations with students. The type of student we have here is for the most part, I think, not what I would categorize as having stable middle-class values and temperament. The students are, I think, insecure in a lot of ways. They have experienced a lot of negativism in their lives; even when they're joking with one another they're frequently putting one another down. They can deal with that on the streets because they are used to it, but when they go into the classroom and they have this happen by a teacher, then it's an explosive situation. They don't tolerate it; it's not within the rules.

Q.   Does it make any difference if the teacher is black or white?

A.   No, it makes no difference. It's the situation. Teachers are expected to maintain at all times when they are in school.

Q.   A few moments ago you talked about setting guidelines and making clear the consequences of not following those guidelines. How does that work?

A.   The best teachers confine consequences to their classrooms. They do everything possible on a personal level to bring a student around to see where he is doing himself harm and what he needs to do to help himself. Other teachers threaten students by saying things like "I'm going to send you to the dean," "I'm going to notify your parents," or "I'm going to flunk you." All this does is antagonize the students and make the situation worse.

Q.   What about providing systematic reinforcement for good behavior? For example, providing systematic encouragement for good work?

A.   It's effective, but it has to be done with the goal in mind of students rewarding themselves for the progress and changes they have gone through. Encouragement from one person to another is effective, but it's not continually effective; especially with our kids. They have their ups and downs, their peaks and valleys, and what works one week or month may not work the next. But what does work consistently is that if you can get the kids to begin having some success and they can see themselves progressing, then they are rewarding themselves. We have a constant battle here with negativism. It is a way of life for students to constantly rank on one another. It's like a pecking order. You may have five or six guys just really on one guy, ranking him from his shoes to his mother to the way he walks, to anything you can imagine. It is hard for a teacher to build and maintain a level of self-esteem in a student because of this. He may feel good about himself in the classroom, but then he has to walk back out and face all kinds of harassment, both from students and from other sources. It may sound like an exaggeration, but it does occur quite a bit. So the teachers have the double battle of raising values, if that can be done—reinforcing the so-called good values—and then battling the influences outside of the classroom. When we win a student—and I say "we" as a school—it's such a great feeling. I mean there is such a conversion in that student—it's unbelievable. He can go from nearly straight F's to straight A's. Most of the successes are not that dramatic though, most are little battles that you win here and there.

The previous chapter ended with discussion of a system for deciding which learning theory approach to apply to a particular educational problem. This chapter describes the specifics of how operant learning theory can guide approaches to problems involving observable behaviors.

The reason that operant learning theory can be particularly valuable when dealing with observable student behaviors is that it is focused on understanding how stimulus events in the environment come to be related to an organism's behavior. Moreover, operant learning theory has a good deal to say about procedures for controlling an organism's behavior. This chapter discusses how procedures derived from operant learning theory can be used by a teacher to bring observable student behaviors under some degree of teacher control. By control, is meant increasing the frequency and duration of behaviors that are consistent with desirable learning, and decreasing the frequency and duration of behaviors that are inconsistent with desirable learning. Also considered are ways to implement the techniques in a program designed to bring observable student behaviors under teacher control.

EDUCATIONAL APPLICATIONS OF OPERANT LEARNING THEORY

Techniques for Increasing the Frequency of Behaviors

Reinforcement

reinforcement the presentation of a stimulus, immediately following a response, that results in an increase or maintenance of the response

Reinforcement is a procedure in which the presentation of an object, or the occurrence of an event, immediately following a behavior results in an increase or maintenance of that behavior. Psychologists typically call an object or event a *stimulus*, and behaviors are called *responses*. Hence reinforcement involves the presentation of a stimulus immediately following a response that results in an increase or maintenance of that response. As an example, when Johnny raises his hand in response to a question, is called upon, and answers the question correctly, and the teacher says "Good, Johnny," the teacher is probably increasing the likelihood that Johnny will raise his hand the next time the teacher asks a question. In this example Johnny's hand raising is the response, and the teacher's verbal praise is the stimulus that serves to increase or maintain the response.

The stimulus that increases or maintains the response is called a *reinforcer*. It is important to remember that reinforcers have no defining features other than their influence on the behavior they follow. This means that a stimulus that is a reinforcer for one person may not be a reinforcer for another. In fact, a stimulus that serves to punish one child may serve as a reinforcer for another. For instance, to an attention-starved child, a teacher's scolding might serve as a reinforcer for misbehavior; but the same scolding might be seen as punishment by a child who receives adequate love and attention at home.

Primary reinforcers

primary reinforcers reinforcers that serve to maintain or perpetuate life

Some stimuli serve as reinforcers for virtually every individual. As a class, these stimuli, called *primary reinforcers*, serve to maintain or perpetuate life. Examples of primary reinforcers are food, water, sex, and warmth.

Primary reinforcers have been used extensively in laboratory research with animals. Much of what we know about operant learning was first discovered in experiments where food, water, or access to sexual partners was provided to animals contingent upon their making a specified response. However, some research has been conducted with humans having severe behavioral deficits, in which primary reinforcers were used. In one study (Meyerson, Kerr, and Michael, 1967) a retarded girl was reported who had not learned to walk at age 9. They were able to teach the child to walk by using a technique that involved edible reinforcers. In another study (Wolf, Risley, and Mees, 1964), a severely disturbed (autistic) child was trained to wear his glasses and to acquire some speech by using food as a reinforcer.

Primary reinforcers have rarely been used, however, in school-based research. This is not because there is anything inherently wrong with using them to encourage the acquisition of desirable behaviors. In fact, teachers frequently make use of primary reinforcers for exactly this purpose. Kindergarten teachers, for example, often make milk-and-cookie breaks contingent upon periods of good behavior. The more likely reason that primary reinforcers are rarely used in research in school settings is that other kinds of reinforcers are available that are more effective, less expensive, and easier to dispense than primary reinforcers.

Conditioned reinforcers

In the previous chapter it was indicated that a conditioned stimulus is a neutral stimulus that has acquired the capability of eliciting a particular response by being paired with an unconditioned stimulus. Conditioned reinforcers work in a similar manner. A *conditioned reinforcer* (also called a secondary reinforcer) is a neutral stimulus—an object or event—that acquires reinforcing properties by being paired with primary reinforcers or with other strong conditioned reinforcers. Infancy is a period when a great many conditioned reinforcers are acquired. As an example, a mother's or father's smiles and words of endearment do not mean anything to a very young infant. However, after many instances in which these stimuli are paired with feeding, warm body contact, and being freed from the discomfort of a wet diaper, the smiles and the words begin to acquire their own reinforcing properties.

conditioned reinforcer a neutral stimulus or event that acquires reinforcing properties by being paired with primary reinforcers

A classic example of a conditioned reinforcer is money. Needless to say, money has no inherent reinforcing properties. But the majority of people are willing to perform all sorts of behaviors, some of which are unpleasant, in order to acquire it. Money has become a reinforcer because individuals have a long history of money being paired initially with primary reinforcers (e.g., candy) and then later with other strong conditioned reinforcers.

Negative reinforcement

As indicated earlier, a reinforcer is any stimulus that increases the frequency of the behavior it followed. Thus reinforcement involves the presentation of a pleasant stimulus. *Negative reinforcement* involves an increase in the frequency of a behavior following the *removal* of an unpleasant stimulus. Consider this classroom instance as an example of negative reinforcement. Sally is out of her seat and talking with a classmate just before recess. The teacher tells Sally she must return to her seat and work quietly on her lesson for 10 minutes or she will not be able to join her classmates for recess. At the end of the 10 minutes during which she has worked quietly, Sally is allowed to go to recess.

negative reinforcement a procedure in which the frequency of behavior increases following the removal of an unpleasant stimulus

All of the characteristics of negative reinforcement can be identified in Sally's situation. She feels bad about staying in the classroom while her classmates are at recess. After she has worked quietly for 10 minutes, the teacher tells her she can go outside, thereby removing the source of the unpleasant feelings and increasing the likelihood that Sally will work quietly in the future.

In general, negative reinforcement should rarely be used systematically in school settings. The reason is that negative reinforcement requires that an unpleasant or aversive stimulus be present so that it can be removed. As will shortly be seen, a danger associated with the presence of aversive stimuli in school is that they can have uncontrollable side effects. Even though the use of negative reinforcement is undesirable, there is little doubt that it receives a great deal of accidental use. When a teacher makes fun of a child in school, he or she is setting up a situation where sometimes the child's only recourse is to escape or avoid the source of unpleasantness. Thus a teacher could be unintentionally rewarding (through negative reinforcement) truancy behavior.

Techniques for Decreasing the Frequency of Behaviors

The use of positive and negative reinforcement are techniques for increasing the frequency of desired behaviors. However, teachers frequently want to *reduce* the frequency of *undesirable* behaviors. Operant learning theory provides three techniques for doing this: extinction, denial of reinforcement, and punishment.

Extinction

The simplest way to reduce the frequency of many behaviors is to stop reinforcing them. The process of ceasing reinforcement of a previously reinforced behavior is called *extinction*.

extinction the disappearance of a previously reinforced behavior due to removal of the reinforcement

Schoolchildren—and adults for that matter—do not behave in a random manner. If any series of repetitive behavior is carefully analyzed one can generally identify one or more reinforcers that are maintaining that behavior. If the reinforcer is withheld, the frequency of the behavior will drop off. As an example, Joe is a sixth grader who jumps up and down, waves his hand, and yells "I know, ask me!" whenever his teacher asks a question. An analysis of Joe's behavior would undoubtedly reveal that his behavior successfully gains the teacher's attention; as often as not, he is called upon to demonstrate his cleverness. This kind of behavior can quickly be reduced if Joe's teacher ignores him when he is yelling and jumping up and down and, instead, calls on someone sitting quietly with hand raised. Before long, Joe will realize that he cannot gain the reinforcement he desires (the teacher's attention) by continuing his show-off behavior, and his behavior will change. In short, Joe's attention-seeking behavior has gone through a process of extinction (it has been extinguished).

Denying access to reinforcers

Another technique for reducing the frequency of undesirable behavior is to deny the misbehaving individual access to reinforcers. One way this is commonly done in schools is through the use of what are called timeout procedures.

Timeout involves removing a child—or in some cases a whole group of children—from a place or milieu where there is access to reinforcers. Common examples of this include such things as sending a child out of the classroom to stand in the hall, sending the child back from the recess yard to the empty classroom, and sending a youngster from the classroom to a study period in the library. Another way to deny access to reinforcers is by changing the nature of the child's environment. For example, the teacher who tells his or her class to put their heads on their desks and sit quietly for 5 minutes, following an outburst of rowdy behavior, is denying the class access to reinforcers by changing the classroom environment.

> *timeout the removal of children from a place where there is access to reinforcers of undesirable behavior*

Timeout and similar techniques have probably been used by teachers to combat undesirable behavior ever since formal teaching began. The techniques are effective in a great many situations, and this probably explains their popularity over the years. Most teachers, however, use such techniques without thinking very much about what they are doing. That is, many teachers tend to assume automatically that an event such as being sent to a hallway or a closet will be unpleasant to a misbehaving child, and that the threat or the fact of being removed from the classroom will serve to alter the youngster's behavior. This assumption rests on a second critical assumption—that the child perceives the classroom he or she is being removed from as a desirable place to be, that is, as a source of reinforcement. However, as the case study presented in the accompanying box illustrates, such assumptions are not always valid.

Punishment

The final technique for reducing the frequency of an undesirable behavior is the use of punishment. *Punishment* can be defined as the presentation of a stimulus that results in a decrease in the frequency of the behavior it follows. Note that punishment, like reinforcement, is functionally defined. One can tell that punishment is being used only by examining behavior after the presentation of the stimulus: punishment will have caused the behavior to decrease in frequency. This is important because punishment is another of the teacher's time-honored tools. In a book published in 1805, Joseph Lancaster, headmaster of an English school, described a "graduated" system for enforcing discipline in the classroom. Lancaster's five-step system began with an oral reprimand from the teacher. The second offense was punishable by having to wear a 4-pound log over the shoulders, and the third offense resulted in the offender's ankles being shackled while he was still wearing the log. Upon a fourth offense, the child was put into a sack and hoisted into the air. The fifth offense resulted in the offender being tied, together with other habitual troublemakers, into an oxen yoke, and made to parade backward around the school (*Boston Globe*, 1981). Given this description, it might come as a surprise to the reader to learn that Lancaster's system was devised as a more lenient alternative to the harsher caning of students that was standard practice in his day.

> *punishment the presentation of a stimulus that results in a decrease in the frequency of the behavior it follows*

When Sending a Child Out of the Classroom Fails

A professor of psychology was consulted by a third-grade teacher who had a very difficult girl in her class. Several times a day the child would fly into a raging tantrum that involved screaming, swearing, and throwing anything she could get her hands on. After trying a variety of approaches without positive results, the teacher began sending the child down to the school psychologist's office whenever a tantrum broke out. Subsequently, the tantrums became more frequent than ever, and both the school psychologist and the school teacher's principal recommended that the child be placed in a classroom for emotionally disturbed children. However, the teacher was very concerned about the long-term negative effects of labeling a child emotionally disturbed, and she wanted to exhaust all possibilities before taking this step. Hence, her visit to the professor of psychology. He agreed to see what he could do.

His initial steps involved two activities. He researched the girl's background and home situation, and he collected data on her classroom behavior. His research on the girl's background indicated that the tantrum behavior had begun near the middle of the girl's year in second grade. Moreover, it was apparent from an examination of the records of both the second-grade teacher and the third-grade teacher that the frequency of the tantrums had steadily increased. Upon looking in on the girl's home life, the professor found that the girl came from a family of six children in which she was the second youngest. The age gap between her and her next oldest sibling was 7 years, and she had a baby brother who was 16 months old.

A detailed record of the girl's classroom behavior was obtained by having an observer sit in the classroom for several hours a day and carefully record the child's behavior. These records indicated that the tantrum behavior was almost always preceded by the class being asked to perform an activity, such as working on spelling or arithmetic problems. A short time after beginning work, the girl would generate a temper tantrum.

After examining the information that had been collected, the professor formulated several hypotheses about the girl's behavior. He suspected that one of the sources of her misbehavior in school was her home situation. She had been the baby of the family for several years, but upon the arrival of her brother, much of the attention that had previously centered on her had shifted to the new baby. In addition, the professor thought that the technique of sending the child to see the school psychologist whenever she had a tantrum tended to encourage the very behavior it was supposed to discourage. He knew that the child had a good rapport with the school psychologist, and he thought that the one-on-one relationship with the psychologist was replacing some of the affection and attention the child had lost at home. He thought that being sent to see the school psychologist was in effect serving to *reinforce* the tantrum behavior. Moreover, since the tantrum behavior had served to alienate both the teacher and her fellow students, the classroom was not a desirable place for the girl to be and she felt no loss when she was sent out.

After considering all of the available information, and formulating hypotheses about the girl's behavior, the professor, in conjunction with the teacher and other relevant school personnel, developed the following program. First, the teacher was instructed to ignore the girl when she went into a tantrum. Second, the teacher was told to try and catch the girl behaving appropriately and to provide encouraging words, smiles, and physical displays of affection when she did so. Third, the other children in the class were told that the girl was going through a difficult period and that she needed their help. They could help by ignoring her when she went into a tantrum, and by being friendly and encouraging when she was behaving nicely. Finally, a male graduate student from one of the professor's psychology classes was seated behind the girl. Whenever she went into a tantrum, the student would put his arms around the girl and prevent her from hurting another student or herself during the tantrum. When the girl quieted down she was released.

Under this program, the child's tantrum behavior stopped entirely within 3 weeks. A child who could very well have ended up in a class for emotionally disturbed children was now indistinguishable from the other children in her classroom.

The above story illustrates several of the techniques that have been discussed to this point. Instructing the teacher and the children to ignore the girl's tantrum behavior involved an attempt to reduce the frequency of the behavior through a process of *extinction*. Instructing the teacher to praise and display affection when the child behaved appropriately was an attempt to increase the frequency of the appropriate behavior through a process of *reinforcement*. And finally, the technique of attempting to alter the child's behavior by removing her from the classroom (a form of timeout) was discontinued. It seems apparent that in this case, at least, timeout had served to reinforce the behavior it was supposed to eliminate.

Punishment can take many forms (© Michael O'Brien/Archive Pictures)

Curiously enough, the United States is behind much of the rest of the world in terms of its continued use of corporal punishment in schools. For example, Poland has banned physical punishment since 1783, the Netherlands since 1850, France since 1887, Finland since 1890, and Sweden since 1958. Moreover, most communist countries, including the Soviet Union, do not allow corporal punishment in the schools. And yet in the United States, forty states specifically allow the use of corporal punishment in schools, and only Massachusetts and New Jersey have state laws prohibiting the use of such punishment (McDaniel, 1980).

One major concern about the use of punishment is the possibility that receiving punishment, and witnessing others receiving it, may contribute to aggressive behavior as an adult (e.g., Bandura, Ross, and Ross, 1961; Freedman, Sears, and Carlsmith, 1978). In addition, there are clear negative side-effects associated with the use of punishment. Moreover, punishment is often counterproductive in its effects (see the accompanying box).

The negative side effects associated with punishment

Much of what psychologists know about the consequences of punishment comes from research using animals. They know that animals can learn to do a variety of things when punished. The three things most relevant to the present discussion are (1) they can learn to escape the punishment, (2) they can learn to perform a response that results in avoiding punishment, and (3) under some conditions, they can subside into a behavioral syndrome known as "learned helplessness." These three consequences of punishment are illustrated by means of various experiments.

Escape Learning.   A researcher places a rat in a cage that has an electric grid on the floor, through which a shock can be delivered. In one corner of the cage is a ladder that leads to an opening in the top of the cage through which the rat can escape. The researcher places the rat in the cage and delivers a shock through the grid every 20 seconds. As might be expected, after several shocks, the rat learns to escape the shock by climbing the ladder and exiting through the opening. Thereafter, whenever the rat is placed in the cage, it immediately exits through the opening, thereby escaping the place where punishment was delivered.

One striking characteristic of escape learning is that it is extraordinarily resistant to extinction. In one experiment, for example, researchers placed a dog in a box divided down the middle by a 3-foot barrier (Solomon and Wynne, 1953). Every 10 seconds a shock would be delivered to the grid on one side of the box, and 10 seconds later a shock would be delivered to the grid on the other side of the box. The dog could escape the shock by leaping repeatedly from one side of the barrier to the other. After receiving only one or two shocks, the dog learned to escape shock by leaping from side to side; and the leaping continued to the point of exhaustion, even though the shock apparatus was turned off after the first few shocks. This extreme resistance to extinction was even more dramatically demonstrated when the dog was returned to the box several days later. The dog immediately began leaping, and again jumped to the point of exhaustion.

Although there is no solid evidence for this, it is likely that the behavior of some schoolchildren is analogous to that displayed by the animals in the above experiments. If a child comes to see school as a place where punishment is delivered, a very natural response is to want to stay away from (escape from) school. One wonders how much habitual truancy and faked illness actually represents behavior designed to escape a punishing environment. If the analogy between escape learning in animals and the behavior of schoolchildren is valid it is a cause for great concern. Particularly since it is known that escape behavior, once learned, is extremely difficult to extinguish.

Avoidance Learning.   The second kind of learning in the presence of punishment involves learning to perform a behavior that results in *avoiding* the punishment. Murray Sidman's (1953a, 1953b) research with white rats can serve as an example of this type of avoidance learning. Sidman used a type of Skinner box that has an electric grid through which a shock can be delivered, and a bar that, when pressed, will delay the onset of the shock. In one experiment, a shock was delivered to the rat every 20 seconds unless the bar was pressed sometime during the interval. If the bar was pressed, the shock

Punishment—How to Turn a Good Classroom into a Bad One

Don Thomas, Wesley Becker, and Marianne Armstrong (1967) have reported a study that illustrates what can happen when punishment is used inappropriately. Thomas and his colleagues had an observer sit in a classroom and record the behavior of ten second-grade children for 2 minutes a day during a morning reading-time session. The observer, who recorded data for 70 days, counted the number of times students were involved in disruptive behavior during the recording interval.

In the first phase of the experiment, labeled "baseline" in the accompanying figure, the teacher was instructed to continue her activities in the normal way. As can be seen in the figure, the level of disruptive behavior was at a low level during this phase. After 10 days, the teacher stopped providing approval for appropriate behavior. This phase of the study continued for 10 days, and as can be seen, the teacher's lack of approval resulted in an *increase* in the rate of disruptive behavior. The third phase was a return to baseline conditions, which resulted in a decline of disruptive behavior to near the original levels. It was followed by a return to the no-approval condition, which again resulted in an increase in the level of disruptive behavior.

During the fifth phase of the study, the teacher tried to catch the children being bad and verbally reprimanded them for their disruptive behavior. In addition, the teacher did not voice approval of appropriate behavior. As a result, the level of disruptive behavior increased to levels approximately four to five times higher than normal. The sixth and seventh phases of the study were a return to the no-approval situation and a return to normal baseline conditions, respectively. As the figure indicates, the levels of disruptive behavior fell systematically during these last two phases.

This study illustrates several important points about the relationship between teacher behavior and student behavior. First, it seems apparent that the teacher's voicing of verbal approval for appropriate behavior is an important factor in reducing the level of disruptive behavior. If students are involved in desirable activities, they cannot simultaneously be doing something they shouldn't be doing. The second important point to emerge

would be delayed for 20 seconds. Thus the rat could avoid the shock entirely by pressing the bar at least once during successive 20-second intervals. Under these conditions, rats very quickly learned to press the bar to avoid the onset of shock.

from the study is that punishment in the form of verbal reprimands does not always result in a decline in the behaviors it is supposed to reduce. In fact, keeping in mind the definition of a reinforcer—as a stimulus that increases the frequency of a response—it would seem that in this study verbal reprimands served to *reinforce* disruptive behavior. The moral of this story is that a teacher should observe carefully what students do in response to the things that he or she is doing. It may turn out that the teacher's behavior is producing an effect opposite to the one intended.

Relationship Between Teacher Behaviors and Student Disruptive Behavior

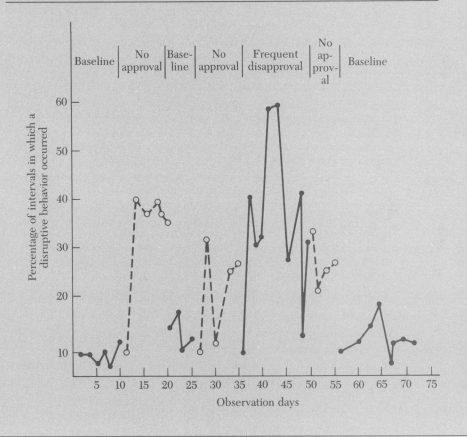

In the experiment just described, the animals stayed in the place where punishment would be delivered (that is, they did not escape), but they learned to perform a response that would result in their avoiding punishment. It is possible to think of some of the behaviors of children in school as responses learned to avoid either actual or perceived punishment. Lying is one example. Children lie about supposedly lost homework, deaths in the family, and misbehavior that they had no part in. Lying is not restricted to young children. College professors have long been aware of the "grandparents disease" that sweeps the nation at regular intervals each year, its onset corresponding with marked predictability to college exam schedules.

Learned Helplessness.   A third kind of learning in the presence of punishment has come to be known as *learned helplessness*. This phenomenon was first investigated by Overmier and Martin Seligman (1967) and by Seligman and Steven Maier (1967). These researchers placed two groups of dogs in a harnesslike apparatus for a period of time and exposed one of the groups to sixty-four unsignaled severe shocks. The next day, both groups of dogs were placed in the previously described barrier box, in which the dogs could escape shock by leaping back and forth over the barrier. The outcome of the experiment was that all of the dogs not shocked on the previous day quickly learned to leap the barrier and escape the shock. However, seven of the eight preshocked dogs never learned to escape the shock. In those cases where punishment had been delivered, the dogs seemed to have lost their capacity for learning. The researchers have described the behavior of these dogs as follows:

> The behavior of the preshocked dogs was bizarre. When they received the first shock in the shuttle-box, they initially looked like the naive dogs: they ran about frantically, howled, defecated, and urinated. However, unlike naive dogs, they soon stopped running around and quietly whimpered until the trial terminated. After a few trials, they seemed to "give up" and passively "accept" the shock. On later trials, these dogs failed to make any escape movements at all. A few dogs would get up and jump the barrier, escaping or avoiding shock; yet surprisingly on the next trial such a dog would go back to taking shock. It did not seem to learn that barrier-jumping produced shock termination. (Seligman, Maier, and Solomon, 1971, p. 355)

Seligman and his associates coined the term "learned helplessness" to describe the behavior of animals exposed to unpredictable and uncontrollable punishment. Learned helplessness has come to be a phenomenon of considerable interest and concern to educational psychologists. Children can easily come to see school as a source of punishment that they cannot avoid or escape, that they cannot even predict. This punishment need not come from the adults in the school. Children themselves can be incredibly cruel to one another, especially to a child who is withdrawn and quiet to begin with, or to one who is physically unattractive or different from the others in some way.

It could be that some of the extreme withdrawal and passivity we see in certain children results from a "learned helplessness" response to what they see as a punishing environment. Moreover, it appears that certain children react in a "helpless" manner to failure experiences; instead of searching for ways to prevent failure, they attribute it to uncontrollable events (e.g., Dweck, 1975; Diener and Dweck, 1978). This response virtually ensures that they will fail on similar tasks in the future.

The use of punishment in school

The research literature on the use of punishment clearly documents potential negative side effects associated with its use. If school is perceived as a source of punishment it is entirely possible that children will learn to either escape or avoid that punishment, or given they cannot escape or avoid the punishment, they may develop the devastating syndrome known as learned helplessness. For this reason, most psychologists would recommend that punishment be used only after every consideration has been given to alternative methods.

To this point, punishment in schools has been discussed as if it consisted primarily of corporal punishment. But in fact the psychological punishment associated with negative comments by teachers or other students represents a far more common, and perhaps more dangerous, form of punishment. Teachers should carefully monitor both their own behavior and the behavior of their pupils to try and prevent damage from this form of punishment.

IMPLEMENTING A BEHAVIOR CHANGE PROGRAM BASED ON OPERANT LEARNING THEORY

Deciding to Implement a Behavior Change Program

The decision to implement a behavior change program should not be lightly made. First, one must decide either that students are not performing behaviors that are consistent with relevant learning, or that they are doing things that block their learning or the learning of other students. Second, if the decision is that observable behaviors are a problem, then one must decide if the implementation of a formal behavior change program is called for. Most problems involving observable behavior can be approached by using common sense, as Abe Gonzales illustrated in his interview. If a child or an entire class is not attending to an instructional activity, they can generally be brought back to attention by a simple verbal statement. Likewise, misbehavior can generally be stopped through a simple request.

It is only when commonsensical approaches do not work that consideration should be given to implementing a systematic behavior change program. Even then, a full-blown program may not be necessary. Certain parts of a procedure may be implemented quite successfully without a complete program being designed and developed.

Step One: Identifying Goals and Target Behaviors

The first step in implementing a behavior change program is to define the goals of the program in behavioral terms and to identify particular behaviors to be targeted for change. As an example, imagine that a sixth-grade teacher has a student in her class who has become a persistent problem. The student bullies and abuses other students in the class, and he is constantly doing things that interfere with his learning and the learning of other students. The teacher's first step would be to identify general behavioral goals for her program.

Sample goals

The program should decrease the frequency of:

> The student's aggressive and abusive behaviors toward other students
> The student's out-of-seat behavior
> Behaviors that disrupt the entire class

The program should increase the frequency of:

> Positive social behaviors toward other students
> Sitting in seat at appropriate times
> Attending to instructional tasks when it is appropriate to do so

Sample target behaviors

Having identified general behavioral goals for the program, the next step is to identify specific target behaviors. *Target behaviors* are behaviors that incorporate the general goal behaviors. For the problem sixth grader, the following target behaviors should decrease in frequency:

Grabbing objects	Making obscene gestures
Hitting	Making obscene noises
Kicking	Whistling loudly
Biting	Getting out of seat
Throwing objects	Running in the class
Spitting at other students	Moving chairs out of position
Yelling out comments	Banging books
Yelling at other students	Tapping pencil
Coughing loudly	Hitting desk with hands

And the following target behaviors should increase in frequency:

> Working with other students in group situations
> Providing assistance to other students
> Receiving help from other students
> Talking quietly with other students
> Raising hand in response to questions
> Sitting quietly and attentively when other students are talking
> Remaining with designated group during group activities
> Studying at designated times
> Working on homework
> Contributing positively to group projects
> Handing in homework on time

Step Two: Designing a Data-Recording System and Recording Preliminary Data

Having established the general behavioral goals and the more specific behaviors that make up those goals, the teacher's next step is to develop a system for recording the occurrence of the targeted behaviors. This system is used to record behaviors both before and after instituting a behavior change program. Collecting information about the occurrence of targeted behaviors prior to instituting any behavior change program is important for several reasons. First, it provides teachers with information they need in order to make an informed choice about the particular techniques they will use to change the occurrence of the targeted behaviors. As an example, one commonly used technique involves reinforcing behavior that one wants to increase in frequency, and ignoring (and thereby, it is hoped, extinguishing) behavior that one wants to decrease in frequency. The success of this approach depends on several factors, one of which is the presence of a minimal level of positive behavior. If the individual who is the target of the change program displays virtually no positive

Some forms of inappropriate behavior are so severe they must be dealt with immediately. (© David S. Strickler/The Picture Cube)

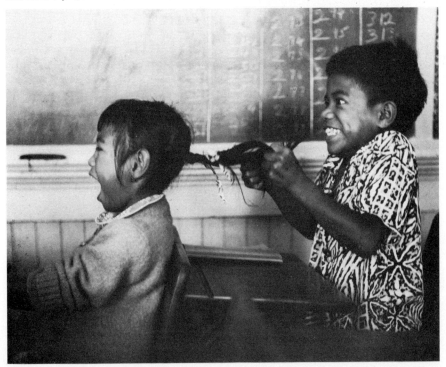

behaviors, then obviously a technique designed to increase the frequency of those behaviors is doomed to failure.

The second reason for collecting information about the occurrence of targeted behaviors prior to instituting a behavior change procedure is to establish a standard of comparison that can be used to assess the effectiveness of the program. For example, imagine that the hypothetical troublemaker described in the previous section was out of his seat when he shouldn't be 50 percent of the time prior to instituting a change procedure. The teacher institutes the procedure and, several weeks later, again checks the frequency of the out-of-seat behavior and finds that it is still at the 50 percent level. The conclusion is inescapable; the procedure is not working and changes will have to be made. Alternatively, if the frequency of out-of-seat behavior shows a drop-off, the teacher has concrete evidence of the effectiveness of her program.

Another purpose of collecting data prior to instituting a behavior change program is that it provides a picture of student behavior that is untainted by the personal reactions of the teacher. Teachers sometimes overreact to particular kinds of student behaviors, and this overreaction tends to color the teacher's view of everything the student does. The data-collection process provides objective information on the frequency and nature of both appropriate and inappropriate behaviors, and this information can help bring teacher perceptions into line with reality. Faced with concrete evidence, teachers sometimes decide that their own perceptions are at fault rather than the student's behavior.

The behavior-recording form

The essential components of any behavior-recording form are (1) a space for the student's name, (2) a space for the dates of the recording period, (3) spaces for listing the specific behaviors to be observed, and (4) spaces for recording each of the targeted behaviors. An example of a recording form filled out with the targeted behaviors identified in the previous section is presented in Figure 6-1.

There are several things to note on this form. First, note that the positive and negative targeted behaviors have been grouped together to facilitate recording. So, for example, all the social behaviors are together, all of the classroom conduct behaviors are together, etc. When observers begin to record the frequency of the targeted behaviors, they will find it much easier to do so if the behaviors are grouped into categories. The second thing that should be noted is the division into days of the week, and then the further division into eight columns per day. The purpose of this division is to allow the recording of data from eight different observation periods each day.

Recording behavioral data

To obtain an accurate picture of the frequency of any targeted behavior it is not necessary to record a student's behavior continuously during each school day. A very accurate picture of the frequency of a behavior can be obtained using sample observation periods at intervals throughout the day. For example,

FIGURE 6-1   Behavior Change Program: Completed Data-Recording Form

Student Name Herman Bonham			Monday	Tuesday	Wednesday	Thursday	Friday
Behavior Category	Positive or Negative	Specific Behaviors	1 2 3 4 5 6 7 8	1 2 3 4 5 6 7 8	1 2 3 4 5 6 7 8	1 2 3 4 5 6 7 8	1 2 3 4 5 6 7 8
Social Behaviors	Negative Social Behaviors	Grabbing objects					
		Kicking					
		Hitting					
		Biting					
		Spitting					
	Positive Social Behaviors	Working with others					
		Providing help					
		Receiving help					
		Talking quietly					
Classroom Conduct	Negative Vocal Disruptions	Yelling comments at teacher					
		Yelling at other students					
		Coughing loudly					
		Making obscene noises					
		Whistling loudly					
	Negative Physical Activity	Out of seat w/o permission					
		Running					
		Jumping					
		Moving chairs					
	Negative Noise with Objects	Banging books					
		Tapping pencil					
		Hitting desk with hands					
	Positive Classroom Conduct	Hand-raising					
		Sitting, listening to student					
		Sitting, listening to teacher					
		Sitting quietly in seat					
		Remaining with group					
Work Habits	Positive Work Habits	Studying					
		Positive group contribution					
		Working on homework					
	Quality and Frequency of Homework	Homework on time					
		Good quality homework					

(Royer and Allan, 1978, p. 42)

using the form in Figure 6-1, the teacher could observe her misbehaving student on eight separate occasions each day. This would be done by watching the student for a certain period of time (say 30 seconds or 1-minute) on eight previously established occasions. If the student was performing one of the targeted behaviors during the observation period, she would place a mark in the appropriate column. These marks could then be transformed into percentages by obtaining a ratio of the number of periods in which the behavior was occurring to the number of observation periods. Thus, for example, if the teacher observed her student on eight occasions during the day, and on two of those occasions he was out of his seat, she would say that for 25 percent of the observation periods, the student was out of his seat.

After designing a data-recording form and deciding on a sampling plan for observing behavior, the teacher would next implement her behavior-recording system for several weeks so as to obtain a stable picture of the extent of the student's positive and negative behavior. If the data-recording form were as detailed as the one presented in Figure 6-1, someone other than the teacher (such as an aide or a teacher trainee) would have to collect the data because of the difficulty of accurately recording behavior and teaching at the same time. However, it is possible to use less complicated forms that a teacher can fill out without being distracted from his or her teaching duties (Royer and Allen, 1978, provide guidelines for doing this).

Step Three: Selecting a Behavior Change Strategy

Data that have been collected during several weeks of preliminary data recording can be easily presented in graphic form. Figure 6-2 presents sample graphs for the hypothetical student discussed in this section. To simplify matters, the graphs combine specific target behaviors and thus provide data on the frequency of categories of behavior. So, for example, it can be seen that during the 2-week observation period, the student was engaged in positive social behaviors of one kind or another for between 10 and 30 percent of the observation periods. In contrast, the student was engaged in negative social behaviors for between 50 and 75 percent of the observation periods.

Having collected and graphed the preliminary data, the teacher is now ready to select a behavior change approach. A behavior change approach typically has two facets: one is to increase the frequency of desirable behaviors; the other is to decrease the frequency of undesirable behaviors.

Increasing desirable behaviors

Earlier in this chapter it was indicated that the frequency of desirable behaviors could be increased by reinforcing them, and that there were three kinds of reinforcement strategies: using primary reinforcers, using secondary reinforcers, or using negative reinforcement.

Both primary reinforcers and negative reinforcement have disadvantages. The problem with primary reinforcers (e.g., food) is that they are frequently expensive and difficult to dispense at the appropriate time. In addition, the most effective primary reinforcers, such as candy, are sometimes detrimental to the child's health. The problem with negative reinforcement is that it requires an aversive situation or event so that reinforcement can be achieved by eliminating the unpleasantness, yet serious consequences are sometimes associated with exposing a child to aversive situations.

In pointing out the disadvantages of using primary reinforcers and negative reinforcement we do not mean to imply they should never be used. There are occasions where either primary reinforcement or negative reinforcement represent the only viable approach to positive behavior change. But, in general, these approaches should be used only after careful consideration of more desirable approaches.

Conditioned reinforcement is the most desirable method of increasing positive behaviors because in many cases it involves the systematic use of *naturally* occurring reinforcers. For example, one of the most commonly used conditioned reinforcers is approval and praise from the teacher, which is

FIGURE 6-2   Behavior Change Program: Baseline Data

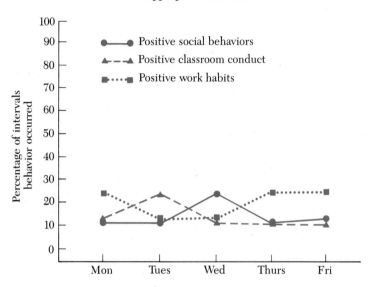

Appropriate Behaviors

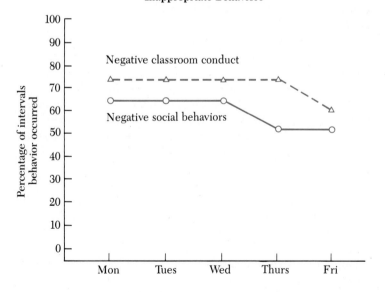

Inappropriate Behaviors

social rein-forcement the use of condi-tioned rein-forcers like smiling that are drawn from social in-teraction

technically known as *social reinforcement*. Another commonly used conditioned reinforcer is grading positively for good performance. Social reinforcement and grading are commonly occurring aspects of virtually every classroom; the only thing that makes them part of a behavior change program is their use in a highly systematic manner. In contrast, such procedures as primary reinforcement and negative reinforcement are not naturally occurring aspects of most classrooms; thus their use is somewhat intrusive upon the everyday activities of the classroom. Moreover, sooner or later procedures such as primary reinforcement and negative reinforcement will have to be discontinued. In contrast, some forms of conditioned reinforcement can remain a part of everyday classroom activities.

Types of Conditioned Reinforcers.   A number of different kinds of conditioned reinforcers can be used in behavior change programs. The most desirable kind is social reinforcement, which is easily dispensed, inexpensive, consistent with humanitarian and social values, and a naturally occurring component in virtually every classroom. Even those behavior change programs that temporarily use some other reinforcement technique strive to move to the use of social reinforcement.

Even though social reinforcement is applicable to a great many behavior change situations, there are occasions when it is not effective. As children get older, for example, they typically become much more sensitive to the approval of their peers, and this lessens the extent to which teacher approval will serve as a reinforcer. Some children, for one reason or another, are never very responsive to social reinforcement delivered by a teacher. In situations where social reinforcement is not effective, a form of conditioned reinforcement known as token reinforcement has been used with considerable success.

token rein-forcement dispensing a token that can later be ex-changed for a desired activity or object fol-lowing positive behavior

Token reinforcement involves dispensing a token, following positive behavior, that can later be exchanged for a desired activity or object. Tokens can take many forms—check marks in a book, stars on a chart, poker chips, or any other item that is easily dispensed and accumulated. Tokens can be exchanged for a great many things and activities; extra recess time, field trips, lunchtime cookies, trips to sporting events, being traffic guard for a week, extra library privileges, records, combs, candy, and classroom parties have all been used in token reward systems.

One distinct advantage of token reinforcement systems is that the exchange rates can be manipulated. As an example, consider a classroom that has a very low rate of a desirable behavior such as quiet study at designated times. In order to achieve a quick increase in the rate of quiet study behavior, a teacher might initially set the exchange rate at a low level. For instance, every 5 minutes of quiet study would earn a token, and ten accumulated tokens could be exchanged for an activity such as a field trip or an extra sports period. As the rate of quiet study behavior increased, the exchange rates could be increased so as to maintain the desirability of the reward. Thus an activity that previously cost ten tokens might now require twenty tokens.

The fact that token systems have been used in a manner analogous to money has led to their being termed "token economies." A *token economy* is a behavior-change procedure in which tokens can be exchanged, at a rate that may fluctuate, for activities or objects desired by students. The accompanying box describes the details of a token economy system used with a group of hard-core adolescent criminals.

Decreasing undesirable behaviors

As mentioned earlier, punishment is not a desirable option for reducing the frequency of inappropriate behavior. However, there are occasions when punishment might be called for. For instance, punishment might be used when the inappropriate behavior is so intense that it represents a physical danger either to the student performing the behavior or to others around him or her. Throwing a heavy object or playing with matches are instances of events that may call for the use of some form of punishment. Even then, however, the preferred form of punishment would be a verbal reprimand rather than corporal punishment.

Another situation that may call for the use of punishment is when the rate of inappropriate behaviors is so high that the student is doing virtually nothing of a positive nature. In this case it may be necessary to attempt to reduce the extraordinarily high rate of inappropriate behavior through punishment so that a suitable procedure for increasing desirable behavior can be introduced.

Extinction and Timeout.
Except for the types of situations just mentioned, punishment is not a good means for reducing undesirable behavior. This leaves extinction and timeout as the more desirable alternatives. Of the two, extinction should be considered first. Extinction, like social reinforcement, has the advantage of fitting into the natural classroom milieu without causing disruption. A teacher can withhold his or her attention from the student who is showing off. And other students can be encouraged to ignore the misbehaving student, whose antics and obscene gestures are designed to elicit gasps and embarrassed titters from peers. These examples of extinction techniques require no special materials or activities. When instituted in a careful manner, extinction techniques can be so unobtrusive that an untrained observer would not even recognize that a behavior change procedure was in operation.

Sometimes it is the case that extinction techniques are ineffective in reducing the frequency of undesirable behaviors. For instance, when a student is unresponsive to a teacher's delivery of social reinforcement, withholding attention for inappropriate behaviors is not likely to reduce the frequency of that behavior. Moreover, with older students it is sometimes difficult to gain student participation in withholding peer approval for antic behavior performed to elicit their attention. In cases such as these, a type of timeout technique may be more effective. If timeout procedures are used, four aspects of timeout use should be considered: (1) Timeout should be used only with manageable students, (2) timeout should be used consistently, (3) timeout should be of

token economy a behavior-change procedure in which tokens can be exchanged at some rate that may fluctuate for activities or objects desired by students

Using a Token Economy with Adolescent Criminals

In a book entitled *A New Learning Environment*, Harold Cohen and James Filipczak (1971) have described a large-scale study using a token economy system. Their study was conducted over a 2-year period with a group of forty-one male adolescents (average age 17) who had been incarcerated for a variety of serious crimes (46 percent for auto theft, 12 percent for robbery, 7 percent for housebreaking, 7 percent for postal violations, 7 percent for petty larceny, 4 percent for assault, 4 percent for homicide, and 13 percent for other assorted felonies). Cohen and Filipczak began with the assumption that the individuals they were working with had a long history of failure experiences in school, and that a positive initial step would be to reverse those experiences. Every student had many instances of truancy and other difficulties on his school record, and all of the students were performing at a seventh-grade level or lower on standardized achievement tests.

The heart of the program was a token economy that awarded points for academic performance. Entering skill levels were established for students in reading, English, science, mathematics, and social studies, and students were provided with self-instructional materials in each of these subject matter areas. Students studied on their own, and when they felt they had mastered the material they took an examination. Points were awarded only if they passed the exam with 90 percent correct.

The points awarded for academic performance functioned rather much like money. They could be used to rent shower stalls, purchase additional furniture for their rooms, use laundry facilities, buy clothing, gain access to a recreation lounge, purchase radios, and buy better food in the cafeteria. In addition, a "bank" was established, in which a student could deposit his points and earn "interest" on the account.

relatively short duration, and (4) the conditions for instituting timeout should be perfectly clear (Sulzer-Azaroff and Mayer, 1977).

Several of these considerations are simply common sense. Timeout will be most effective when students are manageable and not physically resistant to the procedure. If it takes two strong adults to force a student into a timeout room, some other technique needs to be tried (Benoit and Mayer, 1975). It should also be obvious that timeout should be used consistently and that the conditions for instituting the procedure should be clearly communicated. If a student performs an inappropriate behavior and is sent to timeout, and then a second student performs the same behavior but is not sent to timeout, the teacher will very quickly lose his or her credibility and the procedure will

Cohen and Filipczak reported a great deal of data in their book, but the focus here is on just the academic achievement and recidivism data. The accompanying table summarizes the academic performance gains recorded over the 2 years of the program. Though at the beginning of the program, virtually all of the students were performing at the seventh-grade level or lower, by the end of the program, over half of the students were performing at the eighth-grade level or higher.

Recidivism in this case refers to whether an individual who is released from jail ends up in jail again. Follow-ups were conducted on the boys released from the Cohen and Filipczak program and the data were contrasted with those for comparable boys released from another program at about the same time. The boys from the comparison program had a recidivism rate of 55 percent, compared to a rate of 33 percent for boys from the Cohen and Filipczak program. Thus it appears that not only did the program result in considerable academic gain for the participants, it also lowered the likelihood that the students would get into trouble again in the future.

Grade Level Placement at the Beginning and End of the Program

Curriculum Area	Entrance Placement Grade Level				Terminal Achievement Grade Level			
	1–4 # %	5–7 # %	8–10 # %	11–12 # %	1–4 # %	5–7 # %	8–10 # %	11–12 # %
Reading	8 26	13 37	14 37	1 0	1 6	10 28	14 40	11 26
English	35 97	1 3	0 0	0 0	3 8	12 33	9 26	12 33
Science	8 18	28 82	0 0	0 0	5 9	10 29	16 44	5 18
Mathematics	26 75	10 25	0 0	0 0	5 17	3 8	19 50	9 25
Social studies	12 33	24 67	0 0	0 0	2 6	13 36	7 19	14 39

(Cohen and Filipczak, 1971, p. 116)

become ineffective. Likewise, if the conditions for being sent to timeout are not clearly communicated, students may not effectively regulate their own behavior to avoid the consequences of timeout.

The final consideration refers to duration. A number of studies have examined timeout periods of differing duration (e.g., White, Nielsen and Johnson, 1972; Zimmerman and Boydan, 1963; Zimmerman and Ferster, 1963) and have generally found that timeout periods of from 5 to 15 minutes are as effective as those lasting 30 minutes or longer.

Negative Aspects of Timeout.   A number of possible negative consequences associated with using timeout should be considered before the procedure is instituted. The first involves legal considerations. Several cases involving the use of timeout procedures have come to trial in recent years. In general, the decisions have indicated that timeout can be used when its duration is short, when the individual prescribing timeout is qualified to do so, and when data-collection procedures are in use so as to determine if the technique effectively reduces the incidence of objectionable behavior (Sulzer-Azaroff and Mayer, 1977).

Another possible negative aspect of using timeout is the public's reaction to what may be perceived as "solitary confinement." In fact, timeout represents a relatively mild aversive procedure for dealing with persistent undesirable behavior. It is much more mild, for example, than corporal punishment or suspending or expelling a youngster from school. However, the public sometimes reacts to the technique without considering the alternatives. Beth Sulzer-Azaroff and G. Roy Mayer (1977) present several excellent suggestions for representing timeout procedures in a more positive manner to the general public.

Putting procedures together

The previous section described the considerations involved in choosing a technique for increasing the incidence of desirable behaviors and reducing the incidence of undesirable behaviors. Once those techniques have been selected, the next step is to arrange them into a coherent procedure. This would entail determining the frequency with which positive behaviors are to be reinforced and establishing the conditions under which the technique for reducing undesirable behaviors is to be implemented.

In general, reinforcement during the early stages of a behavior change program should be on a fairly "rich" schedule. This means that every effort should be made to "catch the child being good," and to provide reinforcement for that behavior. As the program progresses, and as the rate of positive behavior increases, reinforcement—particularly if it is token or primary reinforcement—can be delivered on a somewhat "leaner" schedule.

The procedure selected to decrease the frequency of undesirable behaviors should be in use at the same time as the reinforcement procedure and should be used consistently with all the targeted behaviors. If the teacher is trying to reduce inappropriate behavior by extinguishing it through withholding attention, but on occasion cannot resist shouting at a student for some particularly outlandish act, then the procedure is virtually certain to fail.

Step Four: Communicating with Students and Instituting the Program

The next step in program implementation is to develop and explain classroom rules to the students and to institute the chosen procedures. Behavior change programs should include full and complete communication with the students for whom the program was designed. A set of classroom rules should specify the behaviors that the teacher considers to be undesirable, and if a technique for reducing undesirable behaviors is involved, the rules should indicate how that technique will be implemented. For example, if an extinction technique involving withholding of attention is being used, the rules should indicate that certain undesirable behaviors will result in the student being ignored. Or as another instance, if timeout is being used, the rules should specify the manner in which timeout will be implemented.

Often, behavior change programs will be directed at an individual student rather than at an entire classroom. In individual cases, behavioral contracts between a student, a teacher, and sometimes even the student's parents can be used to communicate rules of behavior and to specify the consequences of failure to follow those rules. An example of a behavioral contract drawn up for the hypothetical misbehaving student mentioned earlier in this chapter is presented in Figure 6-3.

After the classroom rules and the consequences of failure to follow those rules have been communicated to students, the next step is instituting the chosen procedures. This involves systematically reinforcing behaviors that are

Every teacher's idea of a well-behaved classroom is somewhat different. This picture represents one extreme. (© Tom Bross/Stock, Boston)

FIGURE 6-3   Behavior Change Program: Behavior Contract

Behavior Contract
between
Herman Bonham, you (the teacher),
and Mr. and Mrs. Bonham

The goal of this contract is to reduce the number of times Herman misbehaves and to increase the number of times Herman behaves as he should in the classroom. Herman should not misbehave in the following ways:

Mistreating Others

a. Do not hit, kick, bite, spit at, or throw objects at other students.
b. Do not pick up or grab objects that are not yours without permission.

Since these behaviors are dangerous and someone could be hurt by them, a special punishment will be given if Herman does these things. The first time he does any one of these things, he will receive a warning. The second time he does one of these things, he will be removed from the classroom and left by himself for 10 minutes.

Disrupting the Classroom

a. Do not talk or yell out in the classroom when you are not supposed to.
b. Do not make loud or offensive noises that bother the class or the teacher.
c. Do not leave your seat when you are supposed to be in it.
d. Do not make noises with objects or your hands or feet that bother the teacher or other students.

Rather than doing the above things, Herman should be doing the things below.

Treating Others Well

a. Work with others, provide help to others, and receive help from others.
b. Talk quietly with others when it is appropriate to do so.

Practicing Good Classroom Conduct

a. Raise your hand when you have something to say.
b. Stay in your seat when you are supposed to.
c. Listen when the teacher or someone else is talking.

Practicing Good Work Habits

a. Study in class during study periods.
b. Work on homework when you are supposed to and hand in your homework on time.
c. Be helpful when you are working on projects with others.

Signed: _____   _____
                    Herman Bonham   (the teacher)

_____   _____
              Mr. Bonham   Mrs. Bonham

(Royer and Allan, 1978, pp. 52–53)

desirable and systematically using the procedure designed to decrease behaviors considered undesirable. One critical aspect of instituting a behavior change program is consistency. If the procedure calls for reinforcing appropriate behavior when it occurs, then every effort should be made to catch children being good and to reinforce them for that behavior. Similarly, if the procedure calls for sending a child to a timeout area when a behavior is repeated after an initial warning, then it is critical that this be done. Threats that are not followed through on are virtually guaranteed to provoke the very behavior they were designed to stop.

Another key to a successful behavior change program is to strive constantly for minimally intrusive behavior control procedures. For example, imagine you are working with a group of students who are highly uncooperative and are unresponsive to teacher-delivered social reinforcement. After trying several things, you institute a token economy program accompanied by a timeout procedure. After instituting these procedures, you should strive constantly to get rid of them. For instance, the delivery of tokens should be accompanied by praise and encouragement. The purpose of this is to shift some of the reinforcing properties of tokens to the teacher's social feedback. If successful, the positive behaviors can be maintained by social reinforcement, and the token economy can be faded out. In addition, the timeout procedure can be phased out, as the rate of inappropriate behavior declines and is replaced by positive behavior. Thus the intrusive procedures of token reinforcement and timeout will be replaced by naturally occurring classroom procedures.

Step Five: Evaluating and Altering Ongoing Programs

The final stage in implementing a behavior change program involves evaluation and program alteration. Evaluation is carried out by comparing data records from the program implementation phase with those from the preimplementation (baseline) period. If this comparison reveals changes in accordance with the goals established at the beginning of the program, this would be concrete evidence of the effectiveness of the program. Figure 6-4 presents data on the hypothetical misbehaving student followed in this chapter that indicate program effectiveness.

If the data indicate that behavior has not changed in the direction of program goals, alterations have to be made. For example, if the teacher started out using social reinforcement to increase positive behavior and ignoring inappropriate behavior, and these techniques have proved ineffective, she should institute stronger procedures. She could try a token economy accompanied by a timeout procedure.

The second kind of program alteration involves phasing out a successful behavior change program. In general, phasing out a program involves slowly changing the schedule of reinforcement delivery. For instance, token systems would change from a "rich" schedule to a "lean" schedule and then, ideally, would be eliminated entirely in favor of social reinforcement. Social reinforce-

FIGURE 6-4   Behavior Change Program: Evaluational Data

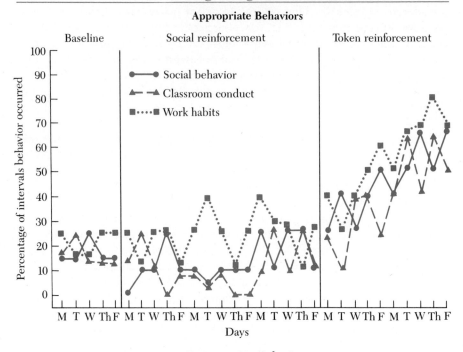

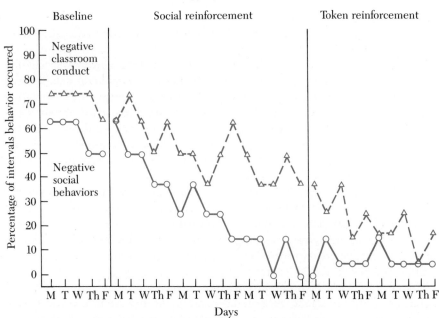

(Royer and Allan, 1978, pp. 61–62)

ment procedures would change from continuous to periodic delivery of reinforcement, and at their final level, would be at a rate that is consistent with good teaching practices. These phasing-out periods should be conducted with a close eye on the data records. If a phasing-out change results in undesirable behavior changes, the phasing-out step is too radical, and a more moderate step should be instituted.

DOES REWARDING POSITIVE BEHAVIOR DESTROY INTRINSIC MOTIVATION?

A persistent concern over the years about behavioral approaches to instruction is that they may reduce a student's desire to acquire learning for it's own sake. Frederick Levine and Geraldine Fasnacht (1974), for example, have written an article entitled "Token rewards may lead to token learning," in which they suggest that children who have been rewarded for school performance may come to expect that reward, and that this approach destroys any intrinsic desire they may have to perform the rewarded behavior. Several other psychologists (e.g., Greene and Lepper, 1974; Lepper and Greene, 1975) have also raised this concern.

A review of the research literature on this topic by John Bates (1979) suggests these concerns are unfounded. Bates indicates that there is no evidence that providing reinforcement for school *performance* lowers intrinsic motivation when reinforcement is given contingent upon the performance of a desirable behavior. An example of performance-contingent reinforcement would be when the targeted behavior is reading quietly, and reinforcement is provided for 10 minutes of quiet reading activity. Bates did, however, find evidence of declining intrinsic motivation when reward is provided for mere participation in an activity. The following account illustrates this point. Imagine that you observe children for several weeks and find that they spend approximately 1½ hours per week reading during free activity periods. You now begin providing reinforcement for going and getting a book during these periods. The reinforcement is provided for simply getting the book, you do not check to see that the children actually read the books. Then, after several weeks, you stop reinforcing the students for getting the books. When you check again several weeks later, you find that the time spent reading during free activity periods has declined to ½ hour per week.

Bates's article clearly points to the dangers associated with rewarding children for merely participating in activities. On the other hand, if reinforcement is provided only for actual performance, and if the intrusive behavior change procedures are phased out in favor of less obvious ones, there appears to be little danger to the intrinsic motivation of students.

OPERANT LEARNING THEORY AND TEACHING

Earlier in this chapter it was indicated that most teaching situations would not call for the full-blown implementation of a behavior change program. Situations calling for the development of recording systems, implementation procedures, and evaluation strategies are the exception rather than the rule. This does not mean, however, that the principles of operant learning theory have little usefulness for the average teacher. A good case could be made for the opposite argument: that knowledge of and the ability to use the principles of operant learning theory is one of the most valuable tools a teacher can possess.

The components of operant learning theory obviously exist in every classroom. Teachers emit behaviors and observe the behavior of their students. Students emit behaviors and observe the behavior of their teachers. Teachers reward and encourage some kinds of student behaviors and discourage other kinds. Students change their behavior in response to the teacher's behaviors. The components are all there; operant learning theory simply explains how the components interact with one another and provides guidelines for using the components in a systematic rather than haphazard manner. This is knowledge that every teacher can put to good use.

SUMMARY

Operant learning theory is a theoretical system that explains how some environmental events cause an increase in the behaviors they follow and how other environmental events cause a decrease in the behaviors they follow. This principle of operant learning theory can be successfully applied to educational problems involving easily observable behaviors.

The heart of operant learning theory involves techniques for increasing and decreasing the frequency of targeted behaviors. Behavior will increase in frequency when it is followed by reinforcement. Reinforcement occurs in three forms: Primary reinforcers (e.g., food, water, sex, warmth), which have inherent reinforcing properties; conditioned reinforcers, which acquire their reinforcing properties by being paired with primary reinforcers or with other conditioned reinforcers; and negative reinforcement, which involves the removal of an unpleasant stimulus. Negative reinforcement should rarely be used in the classroom because it involves establishing an unpleasant situation that can have unfortunate side effects. Primary reinforcers can be used, but conditioned reinforcers are the most useful means of increasing desirable classroom behaviors.

There are three techniques for reducing the frequency of a behavior: Extinction is a procedure for reducing the occurrence of a behavior by withholding reinforcement when the behavior occurs. A second technique for reducing the frequency of a behavior is by denying a student access to reinforcers. An example of this technique would be the removal of a student from the classroom for disruptive behavior. The third technique is to administer punishment when an unwanted behavior occurs. Because of the undesirable side effects that sometimes accompany punishment, extinction and denying access to reinforcers are the recommended techniques for reducing the frequency of unwanted classroom behaviors.

Implementing a behavior change program involves a five-step program. The first step entails identifying the general goals of the program and identifying specific target behaviors that comprise the goals. The second step is to design a data-recording system and record preliminary data. The third step is to decide on a behavior change strategy. This involves selecting the techniques that will be used to increase desirable behaviors and/or decrease undesirable behaviors. The fourth step is to communicate the intent and procedures of the program to the students and to implement the program. The fifth step entails evaluating the desired goals.

A common fear about behavioral approaches to instruction is that they will reduce intrinsic motivation. The evidence suggests that this is a danger if rewards are provided for merely participating in educational activities. However, if reinforcement is provided for performance rather than participation, intrinsic motivation will not be affected.

FOR FURTHER STUDY AND APPLICATION

Skinner, B. F. *The technology of teaching*. New York: Appleton-Century-Crofts, 1968.   A wide-ranging discussion of applying operant learning theory to educational problems, by the master himself.

Meacham, M. L., and Wiesen, A. E. *Changing classroom behavior: A manual for precision teaching*. Scranton, Pa.: International Textbook Co., 1969.

Sulzer-Azaroff, B., and Mayer, G. R. *Applying behavior-analysis procedures with children and youth*. New York: Holt, Rinehart and Winston, 1977.   Two sources discussing the basic principles of applying operant learning theory to education.

Sulzer-Azaroff, B., and Reese, E. P. *Applying behavioral analysis: A program for developing professional competence*. New York: Holt, Rinehart and Winston, 1982.   An excellent how-to introduction to applying operant theory.

7

ASSOCIATIVE APPROACHES TO INSTRUCTION: INSTRUCTIONAL DEVELOPMENT

CHAPTER OVERVIEW

Associative learning theory can be used to guide the design of instruction that is to be used in helping students master basic information. The theory is based on five principles, which outline how connections are formed between stimulus events in the environment and the responses made by the learner. These principles describe how connections can be strengthened through practice and weakened through disuse; how previously learned material can influence the acquisition of current material and how material currently being learned can, in turn, influence the retention of material learned earlier; and how a complex task can be decomposed into a set of hierarchically arranged subtasks.

The procedure for applying associative learning theory to an instructional problem involves using a "systems model" of instructional development. This model consists of two phases: the first is concerned with the actual development of an instructional sequence; the second is concerned with evaluating the effectiveness of the instruction, diagnosing problems in the instruction, and revising the sequence to enhance its effectiveness.

The third section of the chapter is concerned with developing instructional materials that will positively transfer to other instructional material. Transfer is the process whereby the material a student is learning now will influence the learning of material encountered later. This section of the chapter will describe procedures for designing instruction that will help rather than hinder future learning.

Linda Holmes teaches half-time at Princeton High School in Princeton, Missouri—a small (population 1,200) farming community in the north-central part of the state, approximately 15 miles from the Iowa-Missouri state line. She went through school in Princeton and attended Northeast Missouri State College, where she graduated with a major in business education. She has also done postgraduate study in distributive education at Warrenburg, Missouri. She has been teaching for 7 years, having previously taught English in a junior high school and business education at the high school level. Princeton High has about 200 students, many of whom live on surrounding farms and ride buses to school in the morning. In addition to her teaching career, Linda Holmes has operated her own retail business for 6 years. The interview began with a question about her teaching activities at Princeton High.

A.   I teach in a program called the Cooperative Occupational Education Program. I generally have about twenty students in the program, and they go to school for half the day and work for half the day. Some of the students go to school in the morning and work in the community in the afternoon, and some work in the morning and go to school in the afternoon. My job is to teach for one hour a day and to coordinate the program for the remaining three hours of the day. Coordination involves finding jobs for students in the career areas they select, keeping tabs on them to make sure they are learning the things they should be learning, and making sure that things are going smoothly in their jobs.

Q.   What kinds of jobs are your students placed in?

A.   All kinds. I have students working as gas station attendants, as bank tellers, as legal secretaries, as dental assistants, as clerks and salespeople in retail stores, and as nurses' aides.

Q.   Is there any relationship between what your students are learning in school and what they are learning in their jobs?

A.   Oh yes, that's a major part of my teaching responsibilities. I work out a training plan for each student that is coordinated with the employer. The training program consists of a number of things that the employer agrees to teach the student, and then I work out a series of class projects that supplement what the students are learning on the job.

Q.   It sounds like you are running a program that is different for each student; one that is completely individualized. Is that correct?

A.   That's right, no two students in my classroom are doing the same thing. I have twenty different students and twenty different curriculums.

Q.   How do you decide what learning goals to emphasize when you have all of those students doing different things?

A.   The process is kind of indefinite, but there are a number of things we go through with each student. The first thing we do is have the student go through the materials we have in the counseling office that describe different occupations. The students pick several they are interested in, and then they do a study on each one to determine demand, training requirements, etc. My goal for each student is to have them really learn about jobs. As a help in doing this, I have some curriculum materials from the University of Missouri that list learning activities and also provide some learning materials. The students and I sit down and go through these materials, and we try to pick out those that are most relevant.

Deciding on goals and picking learning experiences is actually the hardest part of my job. It's much more difficult than when I was teaching business education, because then everybody was learning the same thing. Now, everybody is doing something different.

Q.   I would guess that in most of the jobs you work with, the skills in the job can be thought of as a kind of hierarchy, with simple skills and knowledge forming the foundation for more complex skills. Is that correct?

A.   I think that's true. For example, I have had students who have worked as gas station attendants, and I wanted them to learn many things other than simply learning how to pump gas. I try to teach them a little about the oil industry, how it affects the economy, how the filling station affects the local economy, and how important the owner of the retail station is to the community. In addition, I try to teach them about running a small business. I guess a number of these things could be thought of as simple skills leading up to harder skills.

Q.   Have you ever heard of mastery learning? It involves the idea that the task to be learned should be presented in order from most simple to most complex, and that lower-level skills should be mastered with certainty before the student moves on to more complex skills.

A.   I haven't heard it referred to by that name, but we do have some new curriculum materials that seem to be based on that idea. I haven't learned how to use them yet, but it involves a student taking out a card and taking a pretest; and then doing a task and taking a posttest. If he does not pass the posttest, he goes back and does another task, then he takes another posttest. As soon as he has mastered that, then he goes on to the next project.

Q.   What do you think of that idea?

A.   I think it's a good idea, I really do. Because why go on to learning something else if you haven't mastered the first thing. It seems to me that if you didn't do it that way you would have a bad foundation. You would be pretty shaky when you got up a little higher on the skills.

Q.   Do you think you could do something like that with a course you knew a lot about? Accounting, for example? That is, could you decide where you want your students to be at the end of the year, then get some idea of what skills they are starting out with, and then break down the course into a series of steps to be mastered that move from the simple to the complex?

A.   Sure, I think so. I really think it might be possible to teach each student at his own speed if you were willing to do that. The problem is you have to present each chapter in a subject like bookkeeping. The way they have bookkeeping set up now, they do have more difficult projects for the student that is more advanced. But that's not really getting at the same idea. There is no way you can get all of your students to learn at the same speed. If you could do it, if it were possible to set it up, if you could have a project for the slower student, one for the middle student, one for the faster student, it would be great.

Q.   Some of the students could accelerate and move at their own rate?

A.   Yes. By the end of the school year some students could be learning how to do corporation accounting. Some might never get past personal bookkeeping, but that would be acceptable. If someone would come out with a textbook that would do that, it would be super! I don't know if you could do it in bookkeeping, but you should be able to. I couldn't write the book, but I could teach it if someone would set it up. It doesn't bother me if students are not all working at the same speed. It used to until I got into Cooperative Occupational Education. It bothered me because I wanted everybody to finish the chapter and then go on to the next chapter together. I guess now I think that really isn't the only way.

I believe the more you can get your students to do, the better. I don't think it should be just busy work, doing the same things over and over just to keep busy. I really think students should be challenged. In some cases, however, I think you would have to alter your thinking on children with learning disabilities and that kind of thing. I read something very interesting that made me think— really stop and think. I believe we get out of our students what we expect from them, and if you don't expect them to do anything, they are not going to do it. I read or I heard on the radio that this teacher got her assignment of students for the year and by each name they had written the IQ of the student. She was amazed because she had never had a group of students who all had fairly good IQs. They were not brilliant but above average. She didn't have any extremely slow students or any especially fast ones. She thought, "I'm really going to work these kids this year," and she did. She worked their tails off, and when she finished the year they had accomplished more than they had ever done before. It was only later that she found out the numbers were not IQs but locker numbers. So to me, that means that students will accomplish what you expect them to accomplish. If you don't expect much from them, you won't get much.

Q.   Why do students at Princeton High enroll in your Cooperative Occupational Education Program?

A.   I know some do because they want the money. They need the money. I think most of them want to find out whether they are really interested in a particular occupation, and if nothing else, they learn whether they do or don't like that occupation before they have already become involved in it. That's what I think helps the college-bound students. For instance, one of the girls wanted to major in finance in college, and she worked in a bank. She found that she didn't like working in a bank, and she decided not to major in finance. But I don't know what their major reasons are for enrolling, it's not that simple. I think most of the students just want to learn about an occupation.

Near the end of Chapter 5 it was suggested that different learning theories could provide beneficial approaches to different kinds of educational problems. This chapter describes how associative learning theory can be used to develop valuable approaches to the mastery of basic educational skills.

In the interview, Linda Holmes provided some examples of the process teachers go through when instructing students. Goals and objectives must be formulated, an analysis of the goals must be conducted to determine what component skills make up the overall learning goal, and materials must be selected or designed to achieve those goals. Moreover, as Ms. Holmes suggested, provision should be made to accommodate instruction to the abilities of individual students. The first section of the chapter reviews the principles of associative learning theory, which can provide a valuable basis for approaching issues like those listed above.

ASSOCIATIVE LEARNING THEORY APPROACHES TO THE MASTERY OF BASIC INFORMATION

Critics of traditional approaches to education have often suggested that learning should be easy, and that if it isn't easy, it's the school's fault because the school is doing something to make it difficult. This attitude is contrary to the facts. Although many things *are* easy to learn, in general, they are things we already know a great deal about. For instance, a biologist can easily acquire the gist of a highly technical article on microbiology in a single reading. The average

Spelling Doesn't Have to be Boring

Spelling is one of those basic skills that can be learned only through hard work. But Susan Petreshene (1981), in an article in *Instructor* magazine, makes the point that hard work doesn't have to be boring. She begins by noting that "When it comes to spelling, there's no substitute for practice, and when it comes to practice there's no substitute for variety" (p. 45). Petreshene then goes on to indicate thirty-eight ways to make spelling exercises more interesting. Several of her ideas are presented below.

- In an exercise called *ghost writing,* the child dips a cotton swab into bleach, then uses the swab to write words on black construction paper. As the bleach dries, the words appear, like magic!
- This exercise is called *concentration.* A child selects eight of the week's hardest spelling words. Each of the eight words is written on two slips of paper. The sixteen slips are then shuffled and placed face down on a table. The first contestant turns over a card and says and spells the word. The contestant then chooses a second card, looking for the other card with the same word on it. If the contestant makes a match, he or she continues. If not, the second contestant plays. The winner is the contestant with the most matches.
- *A letter at a time* has a child write, on the first line of a sheet of paper, the first letter of a word. On the second line, the student writes the first and second letters of the word, continuing in this way until the entire word is written. Petreshene notes that this exercise is especially beneficial for the child who has difficulty sequencing letters within words.
- In *alpha bits* each child "writes" one of the list words, using Alpha Bits (a sugar-coated breakfast cereal), then spells the word without looking at it, to a friend. Correctly spelled words may be eaten!

person could not match this performance even after many readings. A great many of the things that children learn in school are not things they know a lot about. They must learn, for example, to distinguish letters from one another and to attach sounds to those letters. To be successful in school, children must have learned to recognize instantly, and know the meaning of, thousands of words. They must learn the symbols for numbers, and they must associate the concept of specific amounts to each of those symbols.

There is no simple way to accomplish this kind of basic learning. It requires hours of study and practice. There is no way, for example, to teach a child the multiplication tables in a single session. Mastery of the tables requires study and practice spread over an extended period of time. But the emphasis on study and practice does not mean that the learning of unfamiliar material need be dull and monotonous. A creative teacher and a considered choice of instructional materials can, in fact, transform an unpleasant chore into an interesting and exciting learning experience, as is demonstrated in the accompanying box.

In addition to developing creative ways to teach basic material, teachers also need to know something about how to analyze, structure, and sequence instructional activities. Associative learning theory can provide some valuable guidelines as to how to do these things. These guidelines are discussed in detail later in the chapter. But first, the principles of associative learning theory need to be outlined in greater detail.

The Principles of Associative Learning Theory

The central assumption of associative learning theory is that learning involves the formation of associative bonds between stimulus and response events. One way to think of this is to imagine that one's mental representation of stimuli and responses consists of an interconnecting network of *neurons* that can be activated as a cohesive unit. When two units are repeatedly activated at the same time, neurons in between the two constellations of neurons become "attached" to each constellation. Thereafter, whenever the neuronal constellation for the stimulus is activated, the activation is passed through the "bond," and the constellation corresponding to the response is activated. Thus a connection forms between the representation for the response event, and activation of one can produce activation of the other. This imaginary process is illustrated in Figure 7-1.

Five basic principles govern the formation and dissolution of associative bonds.

neurons the nerve cells that make up the nervous system

FIGURE 7-1   Operation of an Imaginary Associative Bond

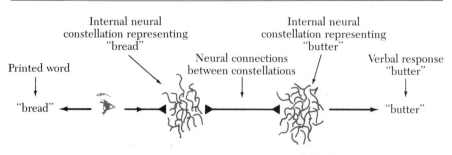

Principle 1: Bonds strengthen with practice

Associative bonds increase in strength as a function of repeated pairings of stimulus and response events (Battig, 1968; Kausler, 1974; Underwood and Keppel, 1962).

This principle means simply that the more times one has experienced a stimulus and response event together, the more likely it is that upon encountering the stimulus event one will be able to provide the response. People know that $8 \times 8 = 64$ because they have experienced the stimulus (8×8) and the response (64) together hundreds, perhaps thousands, of times. The more practice obtained on a skill or item of information, the better it will be learned. The educational implications of this principle are obvious. If a teacher wants a skill or item of information to be well learned, it is important that he or she provide sufficient practice on it.

Principle 2: Bonds weaken with disuse

Associative bonds decrease in strength as a function of disuse (e.g., Nelson, 1971; Tyler, 1934a).

This principle is the converse of the first. If one has learned something and does not use it for a long period of time, it is likely to be forgotten. As an illustration, try to think of the names of the people who sat in front and behind you when you were in the first grade. No doubt you knew this information very well at one point in time. But after many years of disuse, the chances are you will not be able to remember it. The educational implication of the second principle is that the teacher should periodically provide for the review of important skills and information so that they will not be forgotten as a result of disuse.

Principle 3: Previous learning can influence current learning

Acquired associative bonds can influence the learning of subsequent associative bonds. This influence can be positive (facilitative), where prior learning makes subsequent learning easier; neutral, where prior learning has no effect on subsequent learning; or negative (inhibitory), where prior learning interferes with subsequent learning (Ellis, 1965; Osgood, 1949; Underwood, 1957).

Similar Stimuli and Responses Make Learning Easier. Previously acquired associative bonds can make subsequent learning easier when the stimuli and responses in both are similar (Ellis, 1965; Kausler, 1974). As an example, suppose that a class of students were taught that the colors of the American flag are red, white, and blue. Then suppose that at a later stage, the class were taught that similar to the colors of the American flag, the colors of the French flag are also red, white, and blue. The third principle of associative learning theory says that the class who knew the colors of the American flag before they learned the colors of the French flag will learn the French flag colors more easily than a group of students who did not know the colors of the

American flag. The educational implication in this part of the third principle of associative learning is that (1) The similarities between stimulus and response events in those instructional events having similarities should be emphasized so as to promote easier learning, and (2) those instructional events having similarities should be sequenced so as to take advantage of the easier learning that can occur when the events are taught in reasonable proximity to one another.

Dissimilar Stimuli and Response Have Little Effect on Learning. Instructional events that have stimuli and responses that are very dissimilar to one another will have a neutral effect on ease of learning (Battig, 1968; Ellis, 1965). Learning that $8 \times 8 = 64$ has no impact whatsoever on learning that *gateau* is the French word for cake. In this example, the stimuli and responses are so different that learning one item of information does not affect the learning of the second.

Similar Stimuli and Dissimilar Responses Make Learning Difficult. When instructional events have stimuli that are similar but responses that are different, learning one event can inhibit the learning of the second (Slamecka, 1959). Imagine, for example, that a teacher wanted to teach the rules of cricket (a game of British origin that resembles baseball in some respects) to a group of American students and to a group of Chinese students. Chances are that the American students would find the rules more difficult to learn because their knowledge of the rules of baseball would interfere with their learning of the rules of cricket. The games have a number of similarities. Both involve a player who "pitches" ("bowls" in cricket terminology) a ball to a batsman who attempts to strike the ball; and both involve fielders who attempt to get a batter "out" by a variety of means, including catching a struck ball in mid-air. Beyond these similarities, however, there are a great many differences. Cricket has eleven players on a side rather than nine, and a struck ball can travel in any direction and be in play, whereas a struck baseball must be hit to a defined field or it is a "foul" ball. Given these differences, it is highly probable that the American students' knowledge of baseball rules would get in the way of their learning cricket rules. The Chinese students, not knowing anything about baseball, would not have this interfering prior knowledge and would probably learn the rules of cricket more rapidly.

The educational implications of this part of the third principle of associative learning theory are that teachers should make every effort to reduce the potential interfering effects of learning instructional events that have similar stimulus components and dissimilar response components. Two ways this could be done are by emphasizing the differences in stimulus events (rather than their similarities), thereby making the relationship between the learned events more neutral; and by sequencing learning tasks in such a way that events having a potential negative relationship to one another are not taught closely together.

Principle 4: Current learning can influence the retention of previous learning

Acquired associative bonds can affect the *retention* of bonds acquired previously. This effect can be positive, in the sense that current learning can *increase* the chances that previously learned material will be remembered; it can be neutral, in the sense that current learning will have *no effect* on remembering previous learning; or it can be negative, in the sense that current learning can *decrease* the likelihood that previously learned material will be remembered.

Similar Stimuli and Responses Enhance Retention.   When the stimulus and response components of successively learned events are similar, not only is the learning of the second event easier (as specified in the third principle), but in addition, learning the second event will actually enhance the ability to remember the first event (Anderson and Myrow, 1971; Ausubel, Stager, and Gaite, 1968). Returning to the example of the colors of the American and French flags, the fourth principle of associative learning theory says that learning the colors of the French flag after having learned the colors of the American flag will increase the chances of remembering the American flag colors. The educational implications of this principle are the same as for the previous principle: if a teacher wants to enhance the memorability of previously learned information, he or she should emphasize the similarity of the stimulus and response characteristics of previous and current learning, and should sequence the learning events in such a way as to emphasize those similarities.

Dissimilar Stimuli and Responses Do Not Affect Retention.   The second part of the fourth principle indicates that some learning events will have a neutral effect on previously learned information (Anderson and Myrow, 1971). This will happen when the stimulus and response components of current and previous learning are very different.

Similar Stimuli and Different Responses Reduce Retention.   The final part of the fourth principle says that in some cases, current learning can cause a decline in the ability to recall previously learned information (Anderson and Myrow, 1971, Slamecka, 1960, 1962). This will happen when the stimulus components of the two learning events are similar but the responses differ. If one learns the rules of baseball then learns the rules of cricket, the chances are that one's ability to recall the rules of baseball will be worse than it would have been if one had never learned the cricket rules. In educational situations, if teachers want to decrease the likelihood that current learning will reduce the retention of previous learning, they should emphasize the dissimilarities between the stimulus components of the two learning events, and they should sequence the learning events so as to reduce their temporal proximity to one another.

Principle 5: Complex skills can be viewed as hierarchically arranged subskills

Some complex skills can be viewed and taught as a hierarchy so that lower-level skills can be chained together to serve as associative signals (stimuli) for the performance of higher skills (Gagné, 1970).

Many of the skills learned in school consist of subskills that are activated in a chained sequence to produce the complex skill. Reciting the alphabet is an example of a chained skill sequence. For most English-speaking adults, reciting the alphabet is a highly overlearned skill. But try reciting it backward, or compare the ease of determining which letters precede and which follow a given letter (the second task is much easier). These exercises illustrate that for most people, reciting the alphabet represents a chain of skills, in which saying one letter serves as the stimulus for production of the next letter in sequence.

Linda Holmes provided a much more complex example of a series of skills that could be thought of as a hierarchy. When she wanted her students to learn about running a gas station, she divided the task into component parts. Pumping gas was the simplest and lowest skill in the hierarchy; it was followed by more complex skills, such as learning how to run a small business, learning about the role of the filling station in the local economy, and learning about the oil industry in general. When viewed as a whole, learning all these skills may appear an overwhelming task. However, when approached in a systematic, piecemeal manner, the task is much more manageable.

The educational implications of the fifth principle of associative learning are that teachers should be adept at recognizing how skills can be analyzed and broken down into subskills whose learning can be sequenced. They should then teach those skills in such a way that activation of the initial subskill will result in successful performance of the entire complex skill.

THE APPLICATION OF ASSOCIATIVE LEARNING THEORY TO INSTRUCTIONAL DEVELOPMENT

The Systems Model of Developing Instruction

Now that the principles underlying associative learning theory have been introduced, the procedure for applying the theory to instructional development can be outlined. The process that instructional developers go through when developing an instructional sequence, known as the "systems model," (De Cecco, 1964; Barson, 1965) is illustrated in Figure 7-2. Note that the process is divided into two phases. The first phase is concerned with developing an instructional sequence; the second phase involves evaluating the instruction

FIGURE 7-2 The Systems Model of Developing Instruction

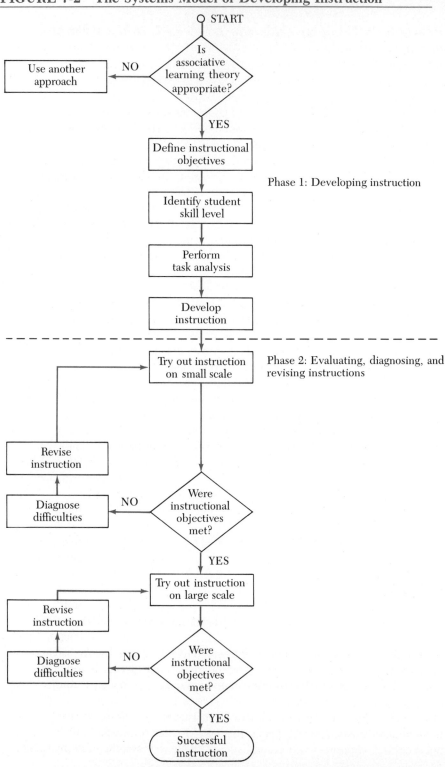

to determine if it does what it is supposed to do, diagnosing difficulties, and revising the materials to eliminate those difficulties. A detailed discussion of the specific steps involved in each of these phases follows.

Phase 1: Developing Instructional Materials

As Figure 7-2 indicates, there are five distinct steps involved in completing the first phase of the systems model:

1. Deciding whether associative learning theory provides an appropriate approach to the problem
2. Defining the complex skill that is the goal of the instruction
3. Identifying the skill level that the student has attained prior to beginning instruction
4. Performing a task analysis, which involves breaking down the complex skill into component subskills and identifying the sequence in which the subskills must be performed.
5. Designing instruction so that subskills are acquired in the appropriate sequence and the acquisition and retention of skills are maximized.

Each of the steps is now discussed in turn.

Deciding whether associative learning theory provides an appropriate approach to the problem

Educational approaches based on associative learning theory are most appropriate when several conditions exist. First, it must be possible to define clearly the terminal skill that will serve as the goal of instruction. The best kind of definition, from the perspective of associative learning theory, is one that specifies what the person will be able to do when they have acquired the skill. For example, if a teacher is concerned with teaching a student the skill of long division, the skill can be defined in terms of the nature of the problems to be solved, the conditions under which the skill will be performed, and the level of performance that will be taken as evidence that the skill has been mastered. A second condition, which is implicit within the first, is that the terminal skill must be objectively measurable. The long division example satisfies this requirement. One could, for instance, say that the skill would be considered mastered when the student correctly solved nine out of ten new long division problems having four digits in the dividend and two in the divisor, using only paper and pencil to solve the problems. Note that the goal is stated in such a way that there can be no question about whether or not the student has satisfied the goal.

Skills that can be clearly defined and objectively measured need to be distinguished from forms of school learning that are more difficult to define and measure. An objective for a high school English class, for example, might

It is easy to tell whether most manual skills have been mastered. It is frequently more difficult to determine whether cognitive skills have been mastered. (© Fredrik D. Bodin/Stock, Boston)

be for the students to read, comprehend, and appreciate Shakespeare's *Hamlet*. This is a very worthy educational goal, but it is one that is difficult to define clearly and measure objectively. The difficulty in part revolves around what is meant by such terms as "comprehend" and "appreciate." If one were to ask ten different English teachers what a student who has comprehended and understood *Hamlet* should be able to do, the chances are they would give ten different answers. Moreover, such terms as "appreciate," "understand," and "comprehend" often refer to internal states that are difficult if not impossible to measure objectively.

A third condition that should be present before a teacher decides to use associative learning theory is that the educational goal must be decomposable into a number of subskills. Again, long division can serve as an example. Long division involves multiplication, subtraction, estimation, and a number of other skills that must be performed in a set sequence in order to solve the problem correctly. These subskills and the sequence in which they are performed can be easily identified and transformed into a series of instructional activities.

In contrast, consider a skill that is not easily decomposable into subskills, such as appreciating *Hamlet*. The components of appreciating *Hamlet* are not at all apparent. Moreover, even if an individual came up with some ideas as to why he or she appreciates *Hamlet*, it is unlikely that those ideas could serve as the basis for developing instructional treatments.

When deciding whether to use associative learning theory as an approach to an educational problem, then, three questions should be asked: (1) Can the educational goal be clearly defined? (2) Can the goal be objectively measured? (3) Can the goal be decomposed into a series of definable subskills? If the answer to all three of these question is yes, then the goal is a good candidate for an approach based on associative learning theory.

Defining the complex skill that is the goal of the instruction

If associative learning theory is to be used successfully, the goal that is the target of instruction should be defined in terms of the behaviors to be performed by the student when demonstrating attainment of the goal. Defined this way, educational goals are known as *behavioral goals* or *behavioral objectives*.

behavioral objectives instructional goals defined in terms of the behaviors the student will perform when demonstrating attainment of the goal

Ralph Tyler (1934b) is generally credited with the concept of behavioral objectives. Tyler was interested in developing a means of communicating goals from one teacher to another so that each teacher would have exactly the same understanding of the goal. This is virtually impossible when goals are defined in such nonobjective terms as "understand," "comprehend," or "appreciate." Teachers would each have their own interpretations of these terms making it unlikely that they would have a similar understanding of the instructional goal. Tyler's insight was that educational goals can be defined in an unequivocal manner if they are stated in terms of student behaviors. Thus rather than using such terms as "knowing," "understanding," and "appreciating," which are subject to a great many interpretations, Tyler suggested using such terms as "identify," "differentiate," "solve," "list," etc., which refer to observable behaviors. Terms that refer to observable behaviors are subject to far fewer interpretations than are terms that refer to subjective internal states.

In his book *Preparing Instructional Objectives*, Robert Mager (1962) thoroughly discussed the procedure for developing behavioral objectives. He has summarized the procedure as follows:

1. A statement of instructional objectives is a collection of words or symbols describing one of your educational intents.
2. An objective will communicate your intent to the degree you have described what the learner will be doing when demonstrating his achievement and how you will know when he is doing it.
3. To describe terminal behavior (what the learner will be doing):
   a. Identify and name the over-all behavior act.
   b. Define the important conditions under which the behavior is to occur (givens, restrictions, or both).
   c. Define the criterion of acceptable performance.
4. Write a separate statement for each objective; the more statements you have, the better chance you have of making clear your intent. (Mager, 1962, p. 53)

Examples of instructional objectives that meet Mager's requirements are listed below:

> To demonstrate his ability to read an assembly blueprint, the student must be able to make the item depicted by the blueprint given him at the time of the examination. The student will be allowed the use of all tools in the shop (Mager, 1962, p. 56).

> The student must be able to reply in grammatically correct French to 95% of the French questions put to him during examination (Mager, 1962, p. 50).

> Given a human skeleton, the student must be able to correctly identify by labeling at least 40 of the following bones; there will be no penalty for guessing (list of bones inserted here) (Mager, 1962, p. 49).

Using guidelines such as the ones described above, teachers should begin by clearly defining each instructional goal. When this step has been accomplished, the teacher can proceed to the next step.

Identifying the skill level that the student has attained prior to beginning instruction

Using associative learning theory to develop an approach to an educational problem involves breaking down a complex skill into component subskills and then developing instruction designed to lead to systematic mastery of each of the subskills. One issue to be addressed in this process is how to identify the point at which the analysis of subskills should be ended. For example, long division can be broken down into such subskills as subtraction and multiplication. But these subskills can be further broken down into such subskills as having the concept of numerical value, being able to label individual numbers, and even being able to differentiate one number from another. The question is, at what level should the analysis of subskills be halted?

Two concepts are important in answering this question: the first is the concept of *target population;* the second is the concept of *intact entering behavior.*

target population the group of students who will be the recipients of instruction

Target Populations.   When a teacher begins the development of an instructional package, he or she does so with a particular group of students in mind. We call the group of students who are to be the recipients of instruction the *target population.*

Target populations can be defined very generally or they can be defined very specifically. If one worked for a publishing company that developed textbooks, the best one could do would be to provide a general definition of the target population. One might, for example, indicate that a particular science text would be most appropriate for sixth graders who have average reading skills, who have had at least some previous exposure to biology, and who have access to certain kinds of laboratory equipment so that they can perform some of the experiments described in the text.

Note that this general definition of the target population provides little guidance as to where to begin an analysis of skills. This means that instruction will begin at a point that is fairly arbitrary. It will be appropriate for some students; but others will already have advanced beyond the chosen instruction point, and still others will be hopelessly lost because the starting point assumes a level of knowledge they do not have.

In contrast, the individual teacher can provide a specific definition of the target population. A sixth-grade teacher in a given school knows the general capabilities and learning histories of the students entering his or her classroom and can specify those characteristics in considerable detail. Having a detailed, specific definition of the target population means that instruction can be tailored to fit student needs accurately, which is not the case when one has only a generally defined target population.

Intact Entering Behaviors.   Once the target population has been defined, members of that population can be tested to determine what skills they have mastered before instruction begins. Skills that a target population has mastered prior to beginning instruction are known as *intact entering behaviors.* Imagine, for example, that one wanted to develop instructional materials to teach long division to a well-defined target population. One knows that such subskills as number identification, estimation, subtraction, and multiplication are all component subskills of the long division skill. One would therefore test members of the target population to determine which of the subskills are intact entering behaviors for most members of the target population. One could then begin the analysis of instruction at the skill level just beyond that of the intact entering behaviors.

In summary, the answer to the question of where to begin the development of instructional materials involves two steps: first, one must define in as great detail as possible the students who are going to be the recipients of instruction (the target population); second, one must test members of the target population to determine what skills they have already mastered (intact entering behaviors).

intact entering behaviors
skills that the target population has mastered prior to beginning instruction

Task analysis: Breaking down the complex skill into component subskills and identifying the sequence in which the subskills must be performed

Once the target population has been defined and the level of intact entering behaviors has been assessed, the next step is to break down the complex instructional goal into component subskills and to establish the order in which those subskills must be performed. The process of breaking down a complex skill into a sequenced series of component subskills is known as *task analysis* (see Gagné, 1962). An example is given in Figure 7.3.

Richard Anderson and Gerald Faust (1975) have suggested that a task analysis

task analysis
the process of breaking a complex skill into component subskills and identifying the sequence in which the subskills must be performed

FIGURE 7-3   An Example of Task Analysis

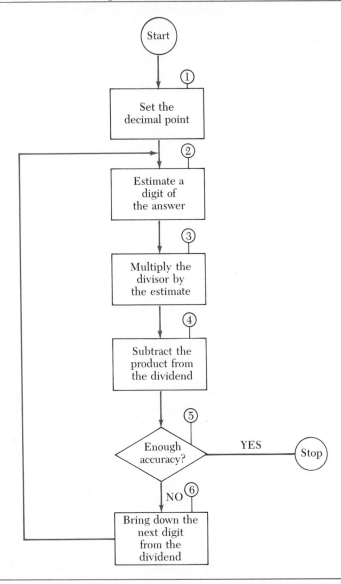

This flow chart includes the major components in a common long-division procedure. The numbers in the circles identify the steps.
(Anderson and Faust, 1975, p. 56)

"provides a blueprint of the things that a student must master if he or she is to reach the objective that has been set" (p. 82). They go on to indicate that a good task analysis should have the following characteristics:

1. It should be complete.
2. It should be presented in the proper amount of detail.
3. It should clearly specify relationships among component skills and concepts.
4. It should identify when and under what circumstances each component skill should be performed.

An example of the use of task analysis is presented in a study by Harold Silberman (1964). Silberman was interested in developing a procedure to teach below average intelligence first graders beginning reading skills. Specifically, he wanted to teach the children to be able to read three-letter words formed by the initial consonants "f," "r," "s," and "m," and the word endings "-an," "-it," "-at," and "-in." Silberman's initial lesson involved the assumption that children would discover the appropriate letter/sound relationships if the words were presented frequently in a variety of contexts. Accordingly, the children were presented with such words as "man," "ran," and "fan," in which the initial consonant changed but the word ending remained the same. Unfortunately, this resulted in attention being given only to the initial consonant, and the children would respond "fan," when presented with the word, "fit." The next attempt involved holding the initial consonant constant while varying word endings, as in the sequence "son," "sit," "sum," and "sat." This procedure did not work either, and Silberman writes that it "resulted in greatly increased error rates, accompanied by the annoying tendency of the children to avoid looking at the words" (1964, p. 2). At this point Silberman decided to put aside intuition and perform a systematic task analysis of the instructional goal.

The task analysis identified two subcomponent skills involved in the task. The first was the sounding out of each of the letter components of the word; the second was the blending together of the sound components to form a word. After this analysis, an instructional approach was developed that consisted of (1) training in sounding out letters, (2) training in blending those letters together to form coherent words, and (3) considerable practice in using the sounding out and the blending skills with words that had not been seen before. Children taught through the use of this instructional approach were successful in reading the majority of the new three-letter words presented to them.

Designing instruction so that subskills are acquired in the appropriate sequence and the acquisition and retention of skills are maximized

In the first section of this chapter, five principles of associative learning theory were presented. For review, they are summarized here as follows:

1. Associative bonds increase in strength as a function of repeated pairings of stimulus and response events.
2. Associative bonds decrease in strength as a function of disuse.

3. Previously learned associative bonds can influence current learning in a positive (facilitative), negative (inhibitory), or neutral manner.
4. Current learning can influence the retention of previously learned associative bonds in a positive (facilitative), negative (inhibitory), or neutral manner.
5. Subskills that are components of a complex skill can be taught as a hierarchy, in which the performance of each lower-level skill serves as a signal for the performance of the next skill in the hierarchy.

These principles can guide the development of an instructional sequence that is designed to maximize acquisition and retention of the instructional materials. For example, ample practice should be provided on each of the skills to be acquired (principle 1), and frequent reviews should be given to ensure that skills are not lost through disuse (principle 2). Care should be taken to point out explicitly the similarities between new skills to be learned and old skills already acquired (principles 3 and 4). The purpose of this last point is twofold: first, to enhance the retention of previously learned skills by emphasizing their relationship to skills currently being acquired; second, to enhance the acquisition of new skills by pointing out similarities to previously acquired skills. Moreover, interference of previous with current learning can be reduced by carefully distinguishing between previously acquired skills and skills currently being learned.

Another feature that should be contained in many instructional sequences is feedback to the student. The reinforcing value of positive teacher comments was discussed in some detail in the previous chapter. But the use of feedback is not limited to oral classroom instruction. Raymond Kulhavy (1977), for example, has written an extensive review of the research literature on providing feedback with written instructional materials. Feedback to students regarding their performance can be provided in programmed instruction sequences, in problem sets, in study and review question sets, and in testing situations. Kulhavy's (1977) review indicated that providing feedback to students enhanced learning in all situations except two: If the material was so difficult that a great deal of guessing occurred, feedback was not beneficial. And if feedback was easily available, students sometimes looked at the feedback before they attempted the questions or problems.

An Example Using Checkbook Balancing.
James Royer and Richard Allan (1978) have provided an example of developing an instructional sequence using the principles of associative learning theory as guidelines. They developed an instructional sequence on checkbook balancing that included the following steps:

Step 1: Pass out sample packets of bank statements, checkbooks, and canceled checks to the class. The canceled checks in the packet should contain a variety of problems such as (1) some of the checks in a given packet are numbered and some are not; (2) several of the checks are misdated; (3) several of the checks are written for amounts different from those recorded in the checkbook; and (4) several of the checks were written on the same date.

After the packets have been passed out, ask the students to sort the checks in order by date, number, or both. When the canceled checks are sorted correctly, ask the students to mix them up and exchange packets. After giving a number of practice exercises in check sorting, proceed to the second step of instruction.

Step 2: Have the students sort a new packet of checks. Then have them check off each canceled check in the checkbook opposite its number or date. In addition, have them check to see if the amount of each canceled check agrees with the amount listed in the checkbook. If it does not, ask them to correct the amount listed in the checkbook and revise the checkbook balance.

After the students have correctly completed their packets, have them exchange packets and practice with a new packet. After several practices, proceed to the third step.

Step 3: Identify for the students the place on the bank statement where the service charge appears, and explain that this charge should be subtracted from the balance listed in the checkbook. Have the students practice this step a number of times with different packets. Go on to the fourth step.

Step 4: Have the students list all of the checks recorded in the checkbook which were not returned with the bank statement. Then have them total these checks and subtract this total from the balance listed in the bank statement. The final step involves comparing the resultant total with the balance listed in the checkbook. The two figures should agree. Have the students exchange packets and go through the steps several times until the skills are well practiced. (Royer and Allan, 1978, pp. 101–102)

The instructional steps listed above illustrate attention to several of the principles of associative learning theory. The considerable practice given to each of the component skills is designed to make sure that they are well learned. In addition, periodic review sessions could be set up to make sure that the skills were not lost through disuse. Moreover, steps could be taken to maximize acquisition and retention by emphasizing similarities and differences between current and previous learning. For example, it is likely that instruction on checkbook balancing would take place as part of a course on home management and business practices. Such a course might include content related to checkbook balancing, such as home budgeting, home accounting, and tax report preparation. All of these activities involve the repeated use of a common set of basic skills such as addition, subtraction, and listing procedures. In this situation, both the acquisition of new skills and the retention of old skills could be enhanced by the teacher explicitly pointing out that a skill learned previously is very similar to the one being learned in the present task.

Pointing out the similarities between previous learning and current learning is one way of maximizing acquisition and retention. But its potential for creating difficulties should also be recognized. For example, although activities such as budgeting, accounting, tax preparation, and checkbook balancing all use a common set of basic skills, *all* of the skills in these activities are not the same. Moreover, the sequence in which the skills are performed is likely to be different for each of the activities. These differences set up a situation where previous learning can interfere with current learning, and where current learning can disrupt the retention of previous learning.

To guard against these potential difficulties a teacher should build in procedures to differentiate between activities that could potentially be confused. There are no set ways to do this. The technique used with the checkbook example was to utilize a memory device called a mnemonic for each of the confusable activities. A *mnemonic* is a sentence, a word, or even a rhyme that helps one remember things. For example, "*i* before *e* except after *c*" helps one's spelling; and "thirty days hath September, April, June and November" helps one remember the number of days in each month. The authors of the instruction noted that checkbook balancing involved the sequential performance of the following four subskills:

1. *Sort* the canceled checks.
2. *Check* off each canceled check in the checkbook.
3. *Subtract* the service charge.
4. *List* the nonreturned checks, *total* them, and subtract the total from the balance shown in the bank statement.

They then constructed the mnemonic "To balance a checkbook, *sorted checks subtract* from the *listed total*" (Royer and Allan, 1978). Note that this mnemonic *encodes* each of the subskills as well as the sequence in which they are performed. A student who memorized a different mnemonic for each of the related complex skills learned in a course should be able to keep the skills distinct from one another even though they may be very similar.

encode to transform a set of stimuli into a meaningful message or code

Phase 2: Evaluating, Diagnosing, and Revising Instruction

When an instructional developer has completed an initial draft of an instructional sequence, he or she is ready to begin the second phase of the development process. This phase involves three activities: (1) evaluating the instructional sequence to determine if it accomplishes what it is supposed to accomplish, (2) diagnosing the source of any instructional failures that might exist, and (3) revising instruction to eliminate the causes of failures. These activities are illustrated in Figure 7-2.

Evaluating an instructional sequence
The basis for evaluating an instructional sequence is contained in the original behavioral objective. An example of an instructional objective given earlier in

this chapter was, "To demonstrate his ability to read an assembly blueprint, the student must be able to make the item depicted by the blueprint given him at the time of the examination. The student will be allowed the use of all tools in the shop" (Mager, 1962, p. 56). To evaluate the effectiveness of the instruction designed to attain this goal, a teacher would hand out blueprints to a class, and see if students could make the designated item. If they could, then the teacher would know that the instruction had been effective. If some of the students could not make the item, the teacher would know that the instructional sequence was not satisfactory, and revisions would have to be made.

Objectives Specify the Standard of Effectiveness.

One thing to note about the instructional objectives with respect to the evaluation of instruction is that the objective specifies the standard of effectiveness. In the blueprints objective, no specific criterion was mentioned, thereby indicating that an effective instructional sequence would bring *all* of the students receiving the instruction up to the specified level of performance. In many cases, however, it may be unreasonable to expect that an instructional sequence will be able to bring every student up to a designated performance level. In these cases, a criterion is established at a less than perfect level. For example, a number of years ago the United States Air Force established a 90/90 criterion for all of their training programs. This criterion says that an instructional program will be considered successful only if 90 percent of the students entering the course master 90 percent of the designated material. If a sequence does not meet this criterion, it is revised and tested again. This cycle continues until the students receiving the instruction attain the desired performance levels.

Failure Is the Fault of the Instruction, Not of the Student.

Another thing to note about the instructional objectives method of evaluating instruction is that success or failure is a characteristic of the instruction, rather than of the student. This is a significant departure from traditional attitudes about schooling, which assume that if instruction is presented by a teacher, book, or some other means, and the student doesn't learn it, it is the student's fault, not the fault of the instruction.

The fact that success or failure resides in the instruction and not in the student means that the development of a successful instructional sequence frequently involves cycles—in which instruction is developed, students are given the instruction and tested, difficulties are diagnosed, revisions are made, and the instruction is tried out again. This cycle of tryout, diagnosis, and revision was graphically illustrated in Figure 7-3.

The tryout and revision method of instructional development is an extraordinarily powerful technique for developing educational materials. The power resides in the fact that nothing less than the performance level specified in the instructional objective is acceptable. This process guarantees that the teacher will end up with materials that work.

Small- and large-scale tryouts of instruction

Figure 7-3 indicated that instruction goes through two tryout cycles. The first is limited in scale and generally involves just a small number of students. The second is larger in scope and involves many more students. However, this is an ideal situation that may not always be met in the real world.

Most instructional sequences contain a great many "bugs" when they are initially developed. Experienced teachers will tell you that it has taken them years to develop a good instructional sequence. Moreover, most will tell you, in moments of candor, that the first time they taught a particular sequence it was pretty bad.

In an ideal situation, a newly developed instructional sequence is tried out with a small number of students. This allows the instructional developer to work on a virtual one-to-one basis with students, which in turn provides an opportunity to question students about points of difficulty. The sources of problems can thus be quickly isolated.

Again, in ideal situations, small-scale tryouts are followed by larger-scale tryouts. Most of the major problems can be identified and eliminated in the small tryout, and the purpose of the larger tryout is to smooth out any remaining problems that might become apparent only after presenting the materials to larger numbers of students.

Ideal situations, in which both small- and large-scale tryouts are feasible, can be found when a group of professional instructional developers are preparing materials for large numbers of people. Examples are publishing companies preparing materials for nationwide use and the military preparing instructional materials for thousands of trainees. Most teachers, however, do not have the luxury of trying out materials in small- and large-scale cycles. One solution to this problem is to select several students in the class to work with intensively regarding the effectiveness of the instruction. The teacher can then get the extensive feedback needed in the early stages of instructional development while at the same time attending to the needs of all of the students.

Diagnosing problems and making revisions

Diagnosing problems in an instructional sequence and then revising to correct for those problems is one of the critical parts of the associative learning theory approach to the development of instruction. The diagnostic-revision process begins after an instructional sequence has been developed and tried out, and it has been determined that students do not meet the performance standard specified in the instructional objectives. The success of the diagnostic-revision process is dependent on being able to determine *why* the instruction didn't work, and then deciding *how* to fix it so it will work.

Diagnosing Faulty Instruction.   Deciding why an instructional sequence didn't work is a matter of carefully examining both the task analysis that was performed early in the instructional development process and the student's

Working closely with a small number of students is the best way to try out a new instructional procedure. (© Frank Siteman/The Picture Cube)

test performance obtained after completion of the instructional sequence. Two factors are generally responsible for the failure of an instructional sequence: (1) an inadequate or incomplete task analysis and (2) poorly developed instruction.

The first step in isolating the cause of instructional failure is to examine carefully the performance records of students while they were receiving instruction and their performance on the test following instruction. This examination will generally reveal a point, prior to which student performance was fine, and after which performance was inadequate. This point should then be examined in the task analysis. It is often the case that instruction has failed because there is a "gap" in the task analysis—that is, a critical linking skill was omitted from the task analysis, resulting in failure to develop an important skill in the instructional sequence. Gaps in task analyses often occur because teachers have overlearned skills to such an extent, they inadvertently omit linking skills that turn out to be critical to a naive learner. For example, Silberman (1964) neglected to include the "blending-sounds-together" skill in his initial instructional sequence designed to teach early reading skills mentioned in the task analysis section of this chapter (pp. 229–231).

If a careful examination of the task analysis does not reveal any gaps or inadequacies, the source of instructional failure is probably in the materials. One benefit of having a complete task analysis and good student performance records is that the place in an instructional sequence that is responsible for failure can generally be pinpointed. Again, the process involves searching student records for a place where prior performance was acceptable but subsequent performance is not. This indicates the point at which revision of the materials should be undertaken.

Revising Materials.   The most frequent cause of instructional failure attributable to the materials themselves is inadequate mastery of subcomponent skills. Whether because of a failure to elicit a previously learned intact skill, a failure to teach a newly learned skill adequately, or insufficient practice that results in the loss of a weakly learned skill, a link is missing in the chain of subskills needed to attain the instructional goal. If the problem is failure to elicit a previously learned skill, then the materials may need to be revised so as to make it clearer that a familiar skill is to be used. If the problem involves the teaching of a new skill, an alternative way of teaching that skill may have to be considered. If the problem seems to involve loss of a weakly learned skill, additional practice may be required to strengthen that skill.

ASSOCIATIVE LEARNING THEORY AND THE TRANSFER OF LEARNING

One goal that the instructional developer—whether a classroom teacher or a developer working on an entire curriculum—should always strive for is to enhance the transfer of learning characteristics of their instructional materials. Enhancing the transfer of learning characteristics means developing materials so that new learning and problem solving can be eased by relating it to relevant prior learning, and so that the retention of previous learning can be enhanced by relating it to current learning (Ellis, 1965).

Transfer of learning can be viewed from a very narrow or a very broad perspective. Some aspects of the topic from the narrow perspective were discussed earlier in this chapter. There, it was indicated that facilitation of current learning and retention of previous learning can be enhanced by emphasizing similarities and differences between current and previous learning tasks. Establishing good conditions for the transfer of learning can, however, be viewed from a much larger context than that provided by emphasizing relationships between tasks in a given instructional sequence. For this larger perspective, some familiarity with theories of the transfer of learning is needed.

Royer (1979) completed an extensive review of theories of the transfer of learning, in which he suggested that there are two basic types of learning transfer theories: one that emphasizes events in the environment outside of the learner and another that emphasizes events occurring within the learner. Given the focus of this chapter on analysis of the stimulus and response events occurring outside of the learner, the discussion here will concentrate on theories emphasizing events external to the learner. In the next chapter, where cognitive approaches to instruction are described, theories of the transfer of learning that emphasize events occurring inside of the learner will be discussed.

The Theory of Identical Elements

Modern theories of learning transfer that emphasize events external to the learner have their historical roots in a theory proposed by Edward Thorndike and Robert Woodworth in 1901. Thorndike and Woodworth proposed that transfer from one task to another occurs only when the two tasks share a set of common stimulus features. This theory, which they called the *theory of identical elements,* states that learning involves associating a response to a set of stimulus features specific to a given task. When two tasks *share* a set of stimulus features, the stage is set for the possibility that a response learned to one task may generalize to the second task. Moreover, the more stimulus features the two tasks share, the greater the likelihood that a response learned to the first task will also be elicited by the second task.

theory of identical elements the theory that skills are transferred from one task to another only when the two tasks share a set of common stimulus features

Building positive transfer features into instruction
Given this theoretical perspective, the process of encouraging positive transfer of learning involves either building in stimulus similarities between instructional tasks or taking advantage of similarities that already exist. Encouraging positive transfer by using either of these techniques works best when a teacher or instructional developer begins with a very broad view of instruction. Far too often both teachers and curriculum developers begin the task of developing an instructional sequence by focusing only on the skills and subskills they are trying to teach. This narrow focus does not encourage taking advantage of previously learned skills, nor does it encourage building in instructional features that will facilitate the acquisition of material to be learned in the future. In contrast, if developers view the instructional goal they are focusing on in the context of potentially related skills that have already been acquired, or will be acquired in the future, they can construct and sequence materials so as to take advantage of the positive transfer of learning.

After a teacher or instructional developer has identified past, current, and future educational goals that are potentially relatable, the next task is to analyze carefully the stimulus features associated with those goals so as to determine the extent of the shared elements. If the overlap is great, facilitative transfer can be enhanced by making sure that the student establishes the connection between the previously learned skill and the skill currently being learned. If the overlap is not very great, the instructional developer or teacher may want to build stimulus features into the two tasks that will make them more similar. As an example, a mathematics instructor teaching his or her students to calculate percentages may want to emphasize that calculating percentages simply involves solving a special kind of long division problem. Moreover, when initial instruction on calculating percentages begins, the teacher may want to set the problems up in the *form* of a familiar long division problem so as to make sure the student recognizes that a previously learned skill is to be employed.

Near and Far Transfer

near transfer the transfer of skills from one school-related event to another

One distinction several authors (e.g., Mayer, 1975; Royer, 1979) have made is between near and far transfer. Royer defined *near transfer* as transfer from one school-learned event to another school-learned event, and he defined *far transfer* as transfer from information learned in school to a real-world (out-of-school) problem or learning situation.

The distinction between near transfer and far transfer is important because it emphasizes the need for school-learned material to be relevant to out-of-school problem solving and learning. As educators, teachers would completely fail if the information they taught their students was relevant only to learning and problem-solving tasks encountered in school. Instead, the information they teach should be relevant to the learning of subsequently encountered in-school tasks (near transfer) *and* to the learning of subsequently encountered out-of-school tasks (far transfer). (See the accompanying box.)

far transfer the transfer of skills from a school-related event to a real-world problem

As Royer (1979) has indicated, theories that emphasize analysis of the stimulus features of tasks (e.g., identical elements theory) are excellent tools for strengthening the near transfer characteristics of school instruction. Generally speaking, educators can identify with considerable precision the goals of instruction. Then, through the process of analyzing the stimulus features of tasks, and developing instruction in accordance with that analysis, the near transfer properties of instruction can be greatly enhanced.

Enhancing far transfer within the framework of theories emphasizing the analysis of stimulus elements is much more difficult. The problem is that it is almost impossible to identify with any precision the range of out-of-school learning or problem situations that might be eased by calling upon a school-learned skill (Royer, 1979). For example, the number of possible real-world problems that might be approached using long division skills must be extraordinarily large. Moreover, the diversity of the kinds of problems is such that even an attempt to classify the problems into several types would be extremely difficult. Thus a teacher or instructional developer would find it very difficult to build specific stimulus features into school-learned tasks that will enhance their transferability to a wide range of out-of-school tasks.

The next chapter discusses another way to approach the problem of developing far transfer characteristics into school instruction. But at this point, a general rule for enhancing far transfer can be provided. *If you want school-learned material to transfer to out-of-school problems, instruction must include numerous instances of the real-world application of the school-learned skill.*

For example, arithmetic problems given to elementary students should include real-world instances of the application of arithmetic skills. If this general rule were followed, then perhaps there would be fewer instances of students who perform well enough to advance through the school system but after graduation cannot manage a checkbook, set up a household budget, or write a convincing letter for a job application.

Minimal Competencies: Concerns About School Skills Transferring to the Outside World

Education, like most human endeavors, is subject to fads, and one of the hottest around nowadays is the assessment of minimal competencies. The problem of students exiting the school system without having acquired such basic skills as the ability to read and write has been around for a long time. In recent years, however, the problem has taken on sharper focus, probably as a result of such instances as the New York City resident who sued the public school system because he had graduated from high school without being able to read. He lost the suit, but the publicity generated by the case fueled concern about the issue.

One common response to the problem is to have students take and pass "minimal competency tests" before they are allowed to graduate from high school. In general, these tests measure performance on minimal-level real-world tasks that call upon skills learned in school. Reading a short newspaper article or a driver's license exam, balancing a checkbook, or completing an income tax form are examples of tasks that might be included in the tests.

The idea behind these tests is that they will force schools to stop the procedure of "social promotions" and instead oblige them to beef up the curriculum in order to prepare students for the tests, which are to be taken in either the eleventh or twelfth grade. As of January 1981, thirty-six states had passed legislation requiring some form of minimal competency testing.

Critics argue that minimal competency testing is nothing more than a fad, and that it will soon pass on to a well-justified early demise. Faddish or not though, the movement has focused attention on the question of whether school-learned skills can be applied to real-world problems and tasks. Unfortunately, the experiences of the past indicate that the answer to this question has not always been positive. Perhaps the minimal competency testing movement will contribute to changing this situation.

There are many things children can learn in school that can be used outside of school. (© Alan Carey)

THE ART AND SCIENCE OF INSTRUCTIONAL DEVELOPMENT

The process of education involves the utilization of both an art and a science. This is certainly true when using associative learning theory as a basis for instructional development. The scientific aspects of this process should be clear at this point, in the step-by-step, systematic approach utilized.

What may not be so obvious are the artistic and creative aspects of the process. Instruction developed by going unimaginatively through each of the developmental steps is likely to be dull and colorless—and probably inefficient. Students completing the instruction may attain the learning goal, but they may do so only because of considerable practice and repetition. In contrast, a creatively developed instructional sequence can be interesting, entertaining, and highly efficient. Thus developing good instructional materials using associative learning theory involves both the disciplined structure and guidance of a science and the creative inspiration and ingenuity of an art.

SUMMARY

Associative learning theory can provide a useful approach to problems involving the acquisition of basic information. Application of the theory is based on five principles: (1) associative bonds strengthen with practice, (2) associative bonds weaken with disuse, (3) information that has been learned before can inhibit or facilitate current learning, (4) current learning can influence the retention of previous learning, and (5) complex skills can be viewed as hierarchically arranged subskills.

The application of associative learning theory to educational problems is guided by the systems model of developing instruction. This model is divided into two phases: the first phase is concerned with developing the instructional sequence; the second phase is concerned with evaluating the sequence, diagnosing problems, and revising the sequence to eliminate the problems.

Each of the two phases can be broken down into steps. The instructional development phase has five steps, the first of which is the decision as to whether associative learning theory can provide a viable approach to an instructional problem. The answer is yes when three conditions are met. The first is that the terminal skill that serves as the goal of instruction must be clearly definable; the second is that the terminal skill must be objectively measurable; the third is that the terminal goal must be decomposable into a number of subskills.

After associative learning theory has been judged a suitable approach to the problem, the next step is to define objectively the terminal skill that is the goal of instruction. This entails defining the skill in terms of the behaviors the student should be able to perform to demonstrate mastery of the skill. The third step in phase 1 is to identify the skill level that the student has attained prior to beginning instruction. This is accomplished by identifying a target population, which is the group of students that the instruction is being developed for, and by measuring the target population's *intact entering behavior*, which is defined as skills that the target population has mastered prior to beginning instruction.

The fourth step in phase 1 is to perform a task analysis, which entails breaking down the complex skill into a set of component subskills, and then identifying the sequence in which the subskills should be performed.

The final step in phase 1 is to design the instructional materials in a manner consistent with the principles of associative learning theory. The purpose of this step is to maximize the acquisition and retention of the materials.

Phase 2 of the instructional development process is directed toward evaluating the instructional sequence, diagnosing problems, and revising materials to eliminate difficulties. This phase is divided into three major activities, the first of which is establishing an evaluation plan. The objectives set at the beginning of the instructional development process provide the basis for evaluating the instructional sequence. If, after instruction, students are performing at the level specified in the objective, the materials are working as they should.

Actual student performance is compared to the performance specified in the objective by conducting small- and large-scale tryouts of instruction, the second activity in phase 2. Ideally, instruction should be cycled through both a small-scale tryout and a large-scale tryout; but reality may dictate that a combination of the two approaches be used.

The final activity in phase 2 is to diagnose problems and make revisions to eliminate those problems. Most problems can be attributed to one of two sources: an inadequate or incomplete task analysis, or a poorly developed instructional sequence. Revision of the materials is directed by the problems identified in the diagnostic process.

A goal that instructional development takes into account is the transfer of learning. The transfer of learning as it relates to associative learning theory is best understood in terms of the theory of identical elements. This theory says that transfer between instructional tasks will be enhanced when the two tasks share a set of common stimulus features. Transfer can be thought of in two ways: near transfer, which is transfer from one in-school instructional task to another, and far transfer, which is transfer from a school-learned task to an out-of-school activity. Both of these kinds of transfer can be enhanced by careful instructional design.

FOR FURTHER STUDY AND APPLICATION

Ellis, H. *The transfer of learning*. New York: Macmillan, 1965. A very readable little book that presents the basics of associative learning theory.

Mager, R. F. *Preparing instructional objectives*. Palo Alto, Calif.: Feron, 1962. A book that provides a step-by-step description of how to write good instructional objectives.

DeCecco, J. P. *Educational technology*. New York: Holt, Rinehart and Winston, 1964.

Gagné, R. M. Military training and principles of learning. *American Psychologist*, 1962, *17*, 83–91. Two perspectives on the application of learning science to educational problems.

Royer, J. M. Theories of the transfer of learning. *Educational Psychologist*, 1979, *14*, 53–69. A review of transfer theories with a specific focus on educational applications.

8

COGNITIVE APPROACHES TO INSTRUCTION: DEVELOPING UNDERSTANDING

CHAPTER OVERVIEW

Much of the material that students are exposed to is outside their immediate realm of experience, and it is sometimes difficult to understand. This chapter is concerned with developing approaches to understanding that are based on cognitive learning theories.

The term "understanding" is used in the chapter in a rather special way. Instead of having its common meaning—an immediate sense of comprehension or of empathy—the term is used to mean the ability to use acquired knowledge in new situations or to acquire additional new information. Thus the critical indicator of whether acquired information has been understood is whether it will *transfer* to previously unencountered situations.

From the perspective of cognitive learning theory, information will be understood (in the sense that it will transfer) when it is integrated into a student's existing knowledge structure. This perspective leads to several techniques for achieving the integration of information into knowledge structure.

All of the techniques begin with the development of cognitive instructional objectives, which focus on making learned information transferable to new situations. Once objectives have been established, a teacher can teach for understanding by activating knowledge that the student already has so that new information can be integrated with it, or the teacher can provide "bridging" information that allows a connection to be made between new information and existing knowledge.

Another important aspect of teaching for understanding is maintaining active cognitive processing in students. The two most important techniques for doing this are giving students instructional objectives and asking them questions while they are receiving instruction.

Sister Mary Ellen Dow grew up and went to school in Chicago, Illinois, where she graduated from Notre Dame High School. She then attended the University of Dayton in Dayton, Ohio, where she graduated with a B.S. degree in elementary education. She also has an M.S. degree in theology from Fordham University in New York City. She taught in a Catholic elementary school in Chicago for 5 years after graduating from college (teaching "everything," she says, in grades 1–5) and then stopped teaching for 6 years to work with young women who were interested in entering her religious community. Recently, Sister Mary Ellen returned to teaching, and she now teaches religion classes at Chaminade-Julienne High School—the only Catholic high school within the city limits of Dayton. The school has around 1,000 students and is coeducational, and about 15 percent of the enrollment is from minority groups. The interview began with a question about the classes and the subjects she teaches:

A.   I have five classes, two freshman and three sophomore. All of them are religion classes, but the freshman classes and the sophomore classes are different. The freshman classes are geared toward the Old Testament, pretty much of a factual approach. The sophomore classes are directed more to the feeling, experiential, level of religion. Not so much toward facts, but more toward relationships—building relationships, human encounters, and how those encounters can transfer into an encounter with God.

Q.   What do you think are the basic differences between teaching in a public school and teaching in a parochial school?

A.   It's hard to say, but I think one of the biggest things is discipline—a sense of discipline based on Christian values in accordance with Christian and Catholic philosophy; our discipline grows from that. We have some problems, but they're not like those they have in some public schools.

Q.   When you have discipline problems in your classroom, how do you approach them? Do you have any kind of standard approach?

A.   I think so, I try to. I've been told, and I think this is true, that I never raise my voice. I do a lot with eyes and voice. I don't believe in making an issue in a classroom if a student is a problem. I'll ask to see him or her after class and then I'll talk to the student. If it continues to be a problem, I rely on parents a good bit. I make it very clear that I will call a student's parents if I continue to have problems.

Q.   Do you think that the system works in part because parents are willing to back up the school and the teachers?

A.   Yes, I think so. That's part of our philosophy, to work closely with parents. A couple of them have told me, "If my kid's not doing well, I want to know. I don't have that kind of money to waste."

Q.   What materials do you use in teaching your religion classes?

A.   We have New Testaments for everyone, and for both the freshman and sophomore classes I use a textbook. The freshman text is new—it's current, with a lot of solid biblical material and great pictures.

Q.   What proportion of the text is historical versus more of a religious nature?

A.   In the freshman book, a lot is historical; it's about 70 percent historical, I would say. The Egyptians, the Hebrews, and a lot of scientific facts that have been found that prove that things written about in the Bible really happened. The sophomore book is based on our relationship with Jesus Christ, and relies heavily on the New Testament. So I'm really enjoying the texts. You see, religion in the past 10–15 years has made such a transition from the old church to the modern church. I grew up with the Baltimore Catechism, which traditionally for Catholics was the only book that was even used to teach religion. And it was question and answer: Who is God? God is dadadada. Why did God make you? God made me dadadada. You got a question and you gave it back.

Q.   Tell me more about the Catechism and the newer approaches.

A.   The Baltimore Catechism is a book that was developed for all age ranges— even high school I believe. The whole approach was, the teacher asked a question and the students gave the answer back from memory. After the Vatican Council II, we swung toward a more modern church, and this involved an attempt to try to talk to the modern child about God, to try to incorporate a little psychology into the teaching of religion.

Q.   It sounds like the old way of teaching was based on the assumption that if you had memorized something it meant you understood it.

A.   I think that's right. If you could repeat it back, it became yours. There is a lot of controversy about how to teach religion today. Many people say, "I was taught with the Catechism, and I made it. Why can't my child be taught with the Catechism?" The other extreme is to make things too experiential. Then students might not learn anything. A child could get out of Catholic high school and not know the ten commandments. I think that's a disservice. There are some things they should know, but they should also know their own relationship with religion. So personally, I try to combine the knowing and the experiential in my own teaching.

Q.   I'm interested in the way you move from the facts of religion to the experiencing of religion. How do you teach that?

A.   I try to bring things home to the students. I try to make things practical for what they know today by pointing out parallels between historical events and teachings in the Bible and their own lives. I also think the mind needs symbols to hang onto, and I do a lot with symbols.

Q.   What do you mean by symbols?

A.   Well, as an example, we were talking about the Holy Spirit in one of our classes, and the Holy Spirit is a mystery. That's one of those things I could talk about for an hour and they would say that they don't understand it. But a symbol for the Holy Spirit in the New Testament is the wind, and I have had quite a bit of success in using the wind as a symbol for the Holy Spirit. Fire is another I have used. Fire warms as one approaches it, just as a person is warmed and enlightened when they approach the Holy Spirit.

Q.   One of the things we talk about in this text is how understanding must entail relating something that is new to something you already know. It sounds as if you might agree with that, given what you just said about symbols.

A.   I do, in terms of my teaching of religion. About 5 percent of the students in my classes are not Catholic, the others have been through eight years of Catholic schools. In the case of the non-Catholics, it's difficult for them to understand things in the same way as the others. For the Catholic students, you have to move them from a child's understanding of religion to an adult's understanding. What I try to do is to take them to a deeper level, to the choice level, to the level where they ask, "What does all this information about God mean to *me*?" It seems to me that they are at a stage where they have facts that haven't been brought to life. I try to bring them to life.

This series of chapters on the application of learning theories to educational problems began with the suggestion that learning theories can provide useful approaches to problems involving observable student behavior, the mastery of basic material, and the understanding of complex information. In the previous two chapters, approaches to problems involving observable behaviors and problems involving the mastery of basic information were discussed. In this chapter, approaches to problems involving understanding are dealt with.

In the interview that began this chapter, Sister Mary Ellen Dow touched upon the key to developing understanding. In discussing her approach to teaching experiential aspects of religion, she indicated that she tries to relate aspects of religion to her students' everyday lives, and that she tries to give them symbols to hang onto. These themes, though worded differently, form the core of this chapter. People understand things by relating them to things they already know, and one encourages understanding by building "bridges" between what the student knows and the new information that one is presenting.

"Understanding" is a deceptively simple term. Most people have an immediate sense of knowing what the term means, and they probably think that a teacher would have little difficulty determining whether a student has acquired understanding. But upon more careful reflection, understanding is more complicated than it might seem at first glance. The chapter begins by exploring this complexity, a process that entails investigating the various meanings of the term "understanding" and deciding on a meaning that is most relevant to education.

THE MEANING OF UNDERSTANDING

How do teachers know when they have a problem with understanding? The question may, at first glance, seem trivial to you. Teachers know they have a problem with understanding when a student is asked, "Do you understand?" and the student responds, "No." Obviously this is one way to determine if something has been understood. But it turns out that understanding has a variety of meanings, and several of the more interesting meanings from an educational point of view are not assessed very well by asking a student directly. Understanding can be viewed in two ways: as a subjective sense of comprehension or empathy, and as a psychological state that enables the individual to perform various tasks. From an educational perspective, the second way of viewing understanding may be more important than the first.

Understanding as a Subjective Sense of Comprehension or Empathy

When students are asked if they understand something, their response is generally based on a subjective sense of comprehension or empathy. For instance, when you read the sentence "Green plants require light to live," you probably have the subjective impression that you know what the sentence means. In contrast, with the sentence "They are eating apples," you probably have a less sure sense of understanding. The sentence could be about people (or other creatures) eating apples, or it could be a statement distinguishing eating apples from other kinds, such as cooking apples.

A second subjective basis for determining understanding is in terms of a shared emotional experience. When a person relates an experience that has made them feel happy or sad, one can, if one has had a similar experience that produced similar emotions, say, "I understand." The subjective sense of understanding in this case is based on a belief that one can imagine the emotional state of the other person and thereby "understand" the feelings being experienced.

These subjective senses of understanding are critical indicators of the extent to which a message has been successfully passed from one individual to another, from an author to a reader, or from any medium to the recipient of that medium. Teachers obviously should be concerned about whether students comprehend what they are saying. They also should be concerned about whether students can successfully comprehend the emotional experiences conveyed in art, literature, and music.

Understanding at a Cognitive Level

There is no question that the subjective sense of understanding that has been discussed thus far is extremely important. However, there is another kind of understanding that is certainly as important to teachers. This form of understanding allows learned material to serve as a problem-solving tool, and it provides a knowledge base that eases the learning of subsequent material (see Bransford and McCarrell, 1974).

Consider learning to compute an average, as an example. A teacher might say to a class, "To compute an average you add together all of the numbers and then divide the sum by the number of numbers contributing to the sum." The teacher might then ask the students if they understand. But note that this question really asks whether the students think they have understood the words in the sentence. At a very different level, *the teacher is interested in knowing whether the students can do something with their understanding.* In this case, the teacher is interested in knowing whether a student can actually compute an average when given a series of numbers. But here again, several levels of complexity can be distinguished. At one level is the situation where the student can successfully complete an averaging problem that is in a form the student has experienced many times before. For instance, the student may have practiced on problems in which a series of numbers are given, along with the direction to compute the average of the numbers. Following instruction and practice, mastery and understanding of the skill could be tested by giving the student a number of problems resembling those given during instruction.

At a level signifying a deeper mastery and understanding of a skill, is the case where the student is expected to apply the averaging skill to a situation that is very different from those encountered during instruction. For example, a student who had repeatedly practiced averaging problems during instruction might be given the task of calculating a household budget, given an income and a list of expenses for an entire year. Successful completion of this task would require that the student compute average monthly expenditures and income, and then translate these values into a budget. Students who can apply a skill or a piece of knowledge to a task that is different from any they have previously encountered are not only demonstrating that they have acquired some information, they are also demonstrating that they have acquired that information at a depth of understanding that allows it to be used as a problem-solving tool (Anderson, 1972).

Let us return now to the original question of how teachers know when they are faced with a problem in understanding. Two kinds of understanding have been discussed: The immediate, subjective sense of understanding can be determined by either questioning students or being sensitive to the nonverbal cues they emit. At a deeper cognitive level, understanding can be assessed by asking students to perform an activity that closely resembles the activity encountered during instruction. And at the deepest level of understanding, students can be asked to apply what they have learned to a situation they have not previously encountered. A student's failure to accomplish either of these tasks would indicate that his or her understanding of the material is not as complete as it might be.

In this chapter, the focus is on *understanding that can be used as a tool* for doing other things. This kind of understanding is by far the most important of

Knowledge of the world around them is one of the most important tools children can possess for further learning. (© Frank Siteman/Stock, Boston)

any that can be provided by a school. Yet, unfortunately, it is probably the kind that receives the least amount of emphasis. The goal of formal education is not to teach things in such a way that children will momentarily understand the instruction; nor is it to teach things that are irrelevant once the student leaves the classroom. However, teaching often seems to be focused on the momentary understanding of formal knowledge that does not transfer to situations outside the classroom.

UNDERSTANDING FROM THE PERSPECTIVE OF COGNITIVE LEARNING THEORY

Before turning to a discussion of how a deep understanding of instruction can be enhanced by using approaches derived from cognitive learning theory, the process of understanding itself needs to be examined in greater detail.

In Chapter 5 of this book it was indicated that theories of learning accept one of two views of the learner. One view sees the learner as a passive recorder of external stimulus events; the other sees the learner as highly active during the process of learning.

If the view that the learner is a passive recorder of stimulus events is accepted, there is really not very much to be said about the understanding process, except that the "understanding" of an event is going to be determined by the number of times the event, or a similar event, has been encountered before. In contrast, the cognitive perspective, which views the learner as an active participant in the learning process, provides a richly detailed view of the process of understanding.

Ausubel's Theory of Meaningful Learning

The discussion of the cognitive view of understanding begins with the views of David Ausubel, one of the pioneers of the cognitive approach to instruction.

Ausubel (1963) drew a sharp distinction between what he called "rote learning" and "meaningful learning." *Rote learning* was the process wherein a learner acquired information that had no inherent meaning. This kind of learning is best exemplified by the common laboratory task of learning lists of nonsense syllables (e.g., FTD, SUV, TZQ, etc.), but it is also characteristic of some school learning activities, such as learning multiplication tables in a way that cannot be meaningfully related to anything the learner already knows. In contrast to the memorization effort required in rote learning, *meaningful learning* occurs much more easily because the information can be related to something the learner already knows. Ausubel (1963) suggested that memory

FIGURE 8-1   Example of a Knowledge Structure Arranged as a Hierarchy

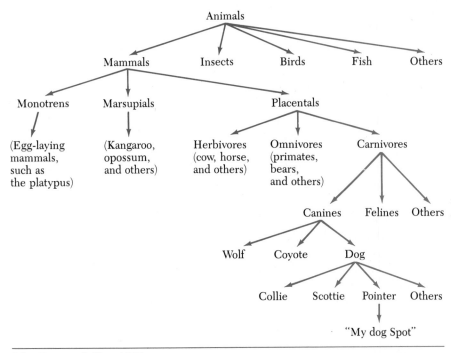

(After Royer and Allan, 1978)

resulting from meaningful learning could be conceptualized as a hierarchical structure, with inclusive abstract concepts forming the top of the hierarchy and the most specific items of information forming the lowermost levels of the hierarchy. For example, Figure 8-1 illustrates the way in which a knowledgeable person might represent their knowledge of animals. At the very top of the hierarchy is the concept "animal," and underneath it are progressively more specialized concepts, until at the very bottom, one finds very specific items of information.

Ausubel's notion was that meaningful learning involves a process in which information is integrated into a previously established *knowledge structure*. The process of "subsuming" new information into an existing knowledge structure was said to be easier than memorizing meaningless material by rote. Moreover, meaningful material that is subsumed into a knowledge structure was said to be "anchored" in that structure, thereby making the information more resistant to forgetting than unanchored, meaningless material.

Ausubel's concept of meaningful learning is adopted in the sections of the book that follow. When the term "meaningful learning" is used, it should be understood as the *process* whereby new information gets integrated into existing knowledge. Meaningful learning results in the *state* of understanding,

knowledge structures the patterns of information which are organized in long-term memory which in turn allows the material that has been understood to be used in new learning situations.

Recent Developments in Cognitive Theory as It Relates to Understanding

With his suggestion that it was necessary to know something about a learner's knowledge before one could know whether meaningful learning was taking place, Ausubel provided a foundation for subsequent developments in cognitive theory. Ausubel's theory assumed, however, that a message was received by the learner, comprehended, and then added to (subsumed into) the learner's existing knowledge structure. Subsequent theoretical efforts have viewed this process as being more dynamic in nature. Learning and understanding are not seen as a process of receiving messages and subsuming the comprehended message into an existing knowledge structure. Instead, *interpretations* of messages are constructed (Jenkins, 1974; Royer, 1977), so that the message that is added to a dynamic knowledge structure is not the same as the message that was received. For an explanation of how this process might work, and an interesting example of the role of metaphors in thought, see the accompanying box.

Understanding involves an interaction among a message, context, and knowledge

Modern cognitive theory suggests that meaningful learning, and hence understanding, is a constructive process involving a message, the context in which the message is received, and the knowledge possessed by the recipient of the message. To illustrate these three factors, consider the following paragraph:

> With the hocked gems financing him our hero bravely defied all scornful laughter that tried to prevent his scheme. Your eyes deceive he had said. An egg, not a table, correctly typifies this unexplored planet. Now three sturdy sisters sought proof. Forging along, sometimes through calm vastness, yet more often through turbulent peaks and valleys, days became weeks as many doubters spread fearful rumors about the edge. At last, from nowhere, welcome winged creatures appeared signifying momentous success. (Dooling and Lachman, 1971, p. 217)

You probably had no trouble *receiving the message*. That is, you probably understood each of the words, and the words are arranged into coherent sentences. But the chances are, nevertheless, that you could not do much with the message after you had received it. That is, you couldn't process the paragraph to the point of understanding it. Now let's add *context*. Imagine that you encountered the paragraph embedded in a story about Christopher Columbus. Now if you reread the paragraph, you should experience a sense of easy comprehension of the material. Providing a context for the paragraph

Michael Reddy's Toolmaker Metaphor: An Alternative View of Understanding

The linguist Michael Reddy (1979) has proposed that the way in which people think about the process of understanding is in error, and he has proposed a different way of thinking about it. Reddy suggests that people's thinking about understanding is shaped by what he calls, the "conduit metaphor." He offers examples such as those that follow as instances of the conduit metaphor in action:

- Try to get your thoughts across better.
- Jane gives away all her best ideas.
- It is very difficult to put this concept into words.
- The sentence is without meaning.
- Everyone must get the concepts in this article into his head by tomorrow or else!
- It is a notion that I didn't catch right away.
- Did you get what I meant?

Reddy suggests that these sentences signal the presence of a metaphor which infers that communication is a process in which a communicator "packages" a message and sends that message via some medium (e.g., print or speech); the recipient of the message receives the package, unpacks it, and "gets" the meaning. Reddy labeled this nonobvious metaphor the "conduit metaphor," to indicate that the nature of the process is viewed as the passing of a package of meaning from sender to receiver through a conduit or communication channel.

The problem with the conduit metaphor, according to Reddy, is that it gives a totally false impression of how the understanding process works. Instead of meaning being packaged, sent, and unpacked, Reddy suggests that meaning has to be *constructed* by the receiver. To explain his position, Reddy invented a new metaphor, which he called the "toolmaker metaphor."

He began his metaphor with the suggestion that communication between individuals was analogous to interactions between people in slightly different environments. This situation could be imagined by thinking of people who live in separate compartments of a huge compound that is shaped like a wagonwheel (see accompanying figure). Reddy asked that his audience imagine that each pie-shaped sector of the wheel is an environment that has much in common with the others—water, trees, plants, rocks, etc.— but none of the environments is exactly like another: one is swampy while another is dry and rocky, the vegetation is different, and so on. At the hub

Box continues on next page

Reddy's Toolmaker World

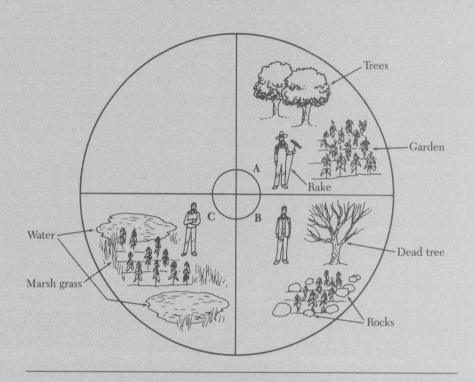

of the wheel is a device that delivers sheets of paper to people in the other environments. This is the only means of communication; the people cannot communicate directly, and they cannot experience each other's environment. Reddy then suggests that one person, say the person living in environment A, discovers how to build a wooden rake to clear dead leaves and other debris away from his cultivated plants, and he decides to share his discovery with the residents of the other environments. He draws the plans for his

has indicated the specific kind of knowledge that should be brought to bear in interpreting it. Finally, you should note that your *knowledge* about Christopher Columbus is critical to constructing a sensible interpretation of the paragraph. If you did not know that Queen Isabella sold her jewels to pay for Columbus's famous voyage, the phrase "with hocked gems financing him" would be meaningless. Likewise, interpretation of the sentence about an egg and a table requires that you know that many sailors during Columbus's time believed that the world was flat instead of round.

rake on a sheet of paper and drops the plans through the slots for delivery to the people in environments B, C, and D. The people living in the other environments receive the sheets and begin to construct what they can from them.

Environment A contains a great many trees, which is why the rake was made of wood and was useful for gathering fallen leaves. The environment in sector B, however, is mostly rock and contains few trees. After finding a piece of wood suitable for a handle the person living in environment B begins to construct a rake head out of stone. The resulting implement is too heavy to be lifted; moreover, he can't imagine any possible use for it. Suddenly, he gets an inspiration. If the stone head is modified so that it consists of only two large prongs, it will be useful for digging stones from the field. Person B makes his new implement and is very happy with the result.

Environment C is wet and swampy, and the person living there cannot see any use for the device invented by person A. However, after some experimenting he devises a hoe, which is very useful for combating the rampant plant growth that threatens his garden.

Reddy continues with his story, but at this point we can see the direction he is taking. Persons B and C live in environments that are similar enough to that of person A to enable them to recognize the general purpose of the rake plans, and each individual has received exactly the same message. However, the *interpretation* of the message differs because of the differing environments. A rake becomes a stone digger and a hoe because these are the only tools that make sense in terms of environments B and C.

Reddy suggests that the nature of the language communication process is more similar to the toolmaker metaphor than it is to the conduit metaphor. We do not *receive* the meaning of a message passed intact along some conduit. Instead, we must *construct* a meaning by interpreting the message in light of our own knowledge. Thus the process of understanding involves an interaction between a received linguistic message, the context in which the message is received, and the knowledge background of the person receiving the message.

The paragraph about Christopher Columbus is somewhat unusual in that it so clearly draws attention to the critical roles of message reception, context, and knowledge in the process of understanding. In most everyday instances of reading or listening, one is not aware of these three factors because the process occurs so effortlessly. At this point, you are such a highly skilled "receiver" of spoken or written English that initial reception of a written or spoken message occurs automatically most of the time. Moreover, most things you read or hear are received in context, so that you know which parts of your knowledge should be brought to bear in interpreting the received message. And finally, you generally have sufficient knowledge about the subject matter of the message that constructing an interpretation is an easy matter.

The exceptions to the above generalization are probably familiar to you. If your mind wanders while you are listening or reading, you won't receive the message. Or if you are reading in a very unfamiliar subject matter area, such as a highly technical field, you may not have the knowledge needed to construct an interpretation of what you are reading.

The problem of representational variability

A logical implication of the constructive process of understanding is that any two individuals who experience and comprehend the same message will have different representations of that message in memory. James Royer and Donald Cunningham (1981) have called this consequence *representational variability*.

representational variability refers to the tendency for individuals who have experienced the same message to have different representations of it in memory

Representational variability occurs because the knowledge base used to construct interpretations of messages differs with every individual. Although many aspects of the knowledge base are similar from individual to individual—just as the features of the different environments in which Michael Reddy's toolmakers lived were similar (see the box that appeared earlier in this chapter)—there are also many things that are unique. This means that for any two individuals the memory representations of a message will be different, even when those two individuals experience the same message at the same time.

The concept of representational variability is important for teachers to keep in mind. It is important first because it focuses a teacher's attention on the uniqueness of each student. Every student has a somewhat different knowledge base, and if teachers are to be at all successful, they must be sensitive to the fact that instruction should be tailored to some extent in accordance with the background knowledge students bring to their classrooms.

A second reason teachers should keep the concept of representational variability in mind is as a reminder to them that the way they have something represented in memory cannot be directly transferred to their students. Many teachers have great appreciation for the lucidity and logical elegance of certain areas of human knowledge. But they make the mistake of trying to transfer the knowledge they possess directly and intact to their students. What they forget is that their representation of knowledge is the product of years of constructive activity between new knowledge and knowledge they already possessed. A student cannot be expected to "ingest" in one fell swoop the product of all those years of mental activity. Like a builder who begins construction of a house with the foundation and puts it together piece by piece, a teacher must begin instruction from the student's existing knowledge base and add to it bit by bit.

The above point is particularly important with young children. Harking back to Chapter 2, one instructional implication from Piagetian theory was that presented information should not be so far from the student's current knowledge state that the student cannot assimilate or accommodate it. With young children, the teacher has the dual problem of knowing not only what the student's knowledge state is but what stage of development the student is in.

The final reason that a teacher should keep the concept of representational variability in mind is that it maintains focus upon what instruction is supposed to accomplish. As has been emphasized in this chapter, successful instruction is not merely a matter of getting information into a student's head. Instead, it is a matter of getting information into a student's head in a *form* in which it will be maximally useful. Let's return to the Christopher Columbus paragraph as an example of the different forms in which knowledge could be presented.

Imagine that two teachers want to have their students understand the Christopher Columbus passage. The first goes about it by systematically explaining what each of the phrases in the passage refers to. "Hocked gems" refers to a queen's jewels that were sold, "the edge" refers to the edge of the world, "three sturdy sisters" refers to three ships, etc. At the end of such instruction, the students would undoubtedly be able to say what the passage is about, and one would be able to say with confidence that the students have a representation of the instruction in their heads.

The second teacher proceeds very differently. This teacher begins the instruction with a history lesson on the events leading up to and encompassing Columbus's historic voyage. As the lesson proceeds, the students are urged to guess about the events to which the passage refers. After instruction, the students in the second teacher's class would be able to interpret the passage, and again one could say that the students have a representation of the information in their heads.

The difference would lie in the form of the memory representation the two teachers have passed along to their students. The first teacher has instructed the students in a manner that is unlikely to result in a memory representation having any enduring benefit. The students have learned enough to satisfy the task at hand, but what they have learned is probably not going to be useful for any other purpose. In contrast, the students in the second teacher's class have acquired information in a form that not only allows them to interpret the passage at hand but may be very useful in interpreting subsequently encountered information.

Teachers frequently have the choice of presenting information in a straightforward, supposedly efficient manner, or in an elaborated manner that may require more time. If teachers keep in mind the fact that representations will vary, depending on the nature of instruction and the student's background knowledge, then perhaps they will ask themselves, What form of presentation for this instruction is going to be most useful to my students in the future? Having done this, they will have taken the first step in developing an instructional approach based on cognitive learning theory.

Teaching and the Facilitation of Understanding

Given the perspective that understanding is an interactive process, what can a teacher do to facilitate the process? A number of specific approaches to the facilitation of understanding are discussed in the next section; but first, here is a very general answer to this question.

Teachers can facilitate understanding in two ways: (1) by increasing the likelihood that students will bring appropriate prior knowledge to bear when receiving instruction, and (2) by providing students with information that will assist the meaningful learning of subsequently presented instruction. Getting students to use beneficial knowledge they already have means embedding instruction in a context that elicits prior knowledge useful in interpreting the instruction. Teaching by analogy is an example of this. When a teacher explains that the movement of electromagnetic radiation through space can be thought of as analogous to the movement of ripples caused by throwing a stone into a pond, he or she is providing a context that elicits prior knowledge useful in interpreting the new message.

Providing knowledge that will be useful later on works in a similar way, except that rather than eliciting information the student already knows to assist in understanding, one teaches students something new that will allow them to interpret subsequently presented new information.

For example, students sometimes have difficulty understanding the concept of the flow of an electrical current through a wire. However, if they are first taught about the structure of atoms, then it is easier for them to understand current flow since the process actually entails the movement of free-floating electrons in the wire.

INSTRUCTIONAL APPROACHES BASED ON COGNITIVE LEARNING THEORY

Developing Instructional Goals from a Cognitive Orientation

Instructional practices based on cognitive learning theory begin in the same place that approaches based on operant and associative learning theories began: with instructional objectives. The reason should be apparent at this point. If teachers are not certain of what they are trying to do, they are unlikely to do much of importance. Instructional objectives form the foundation on which sound instructional approaches are built.

However, there is a significant difference between objectives established for operant and associative learning theory and those written from a cognitive perspective. Operant and associative learning theory objectives focus on the acquisition of behaviors or abilities that are targeted during an instructional period. For instance, an operant learning theory approach might focus on the production of good study behavior, or an associative learning theory approach might be designed to teach a student a particular mathematical skill. In both of these instances, the behavior or skill targeted by the objective has been the focal point during instruction. In contrast, a cognitive learning theory objective focuses on how well information learned during instruction *transfers* to situations that have not been previously encountered.

As indicated earlier, one of the more important forms of understanding from an educational perspective is the acquisition of knowledge in a form that allows it to be used as a tool for problem solving or as a means to ease the acquisition of additional information. Instructional objectives are written in a manner that focuses on the extent to which acquired information transfers to other situations, thus indicating that the goal of instruction is the deep and significant understanding of learned information.

Near transfer, far transfer, and cognitive objectives

The distinction between near and far transfer (e.g., Royer, 1979) was indicated in Chapter 7: near transfer refers to transfer between one school-learned task and another school-learned task; far transfer refers to transfer between a school-learned task and an out-of-school task.

This distinction is relevant in the writing of cognitive instructional objectives. One concern, for example, that a teacher or instructional developer might have, is how to specify tasks to which school-learned material might transfer. The distinction between near and far transfer assists in this process, in that it reminds one that school-learned material can transfer to other school tasks, to out-of-school tasks, or to both of these. As an example, imagine that a high school chemistry class included a section on highly volatile liquids, and that gasoline was one of the liquids being discussed. Near transfer cognitive objectives could be written that assessed the extent to which the students could characterize the properties of a volatile liquid they had not heard of before. The far transfer properties of the instruction could be assessed by asking questions regarding the proper storage container for gasoline or regarding the necessary precautions in situations involving the use of gasoline.

Near transfer and far transfer objectives are not equally appropriate for all information. Some kinds of information can reasonably be expected to apply only to near transfer tasks, other information only to far transfer tasks. Deciding to emphasize either (or both) in an objective is largely a matter of judgment. For example, in teaching very basic subject matter such as beginning reading or simple mathematical skills, the teacher might decide to emphasize near transfer objectives, since these skills are going to serve as the basis for much of the school learning that follows. Alternatively, if the subject matter is highly relevant to out-of-school activities, it makes more sense to emphasize far transfer objectives.

Some skills that are acquired in school transfer naturally to out-of-school activities. (© Mark Antman, The Image Works)

Selecting transfer tasks

The final issue about cognitive objectives is how to select the near and far transfer tasks for inclusion in the objectives. Near transfer poses the easier problem. The teacher begins by examining the curriculum the student will encounter after completing the lesson he or she is designing. Representative instances of tasks that involve the use of the skill being taught are then selected. For example, imagine you are an English teacher who is teaching paragraph structure to a group of ninth graders. You know that next semester's English class will, among other things, be concerned with writing reports on books and plays. You then choose, as a near transfer task, the writing of a report on a recently read book (or perhaps on a recently seen movie), as a check on whether your students have mastered your instruction on paragraph structure.

Far transfer tasks are more difficult to choose because there are so many possibilities. Much of what students learn in school is relevant in some way to out-of-school functioning. The problem is to decide which of the available possibilities is the best choice. As was the case when deciding to emphasize far transfer in an objective, choosing a particular far transfer task is largely a matter of judgment. There are, however, a number of guidelines that can be followed. The first is that the far transfer task should be reasonable. It would make no sense, for example, for a biology teacher to choose as a far transfer task the successful identification of edible mushrooms if his or her school were located in the Mojave Desert. Nor would it make any sense to choose a far transfer task that called for undue expense or that would be difficult to assess. Instead, tasks should be chosen that can be readily assessed in the course of normal school activities. Incidentally, this does not rule out the assessment of far transfer tasks in out-of-school settings. In fact, combining in-school and

The Zoo School: Teaching Skills That Transfer

The John Ball Zoo School is a one-year alternative program for highly motivated sixth graders that is located in a two-room building on the grounds of the Grand Rapids, Michigan, public zoo. The school has the expressed purpose of preparing learners to tackle the problems of life in the twenty-first century.

The school has two classrooms serving fifty-two youngsters from every socioeconomic level in the city. Achievement also varies, with the children ranging from the fourth grade to the twelfth grade in mathematical and verbal ability.

The Zoo School has as its goal the acquisition of eight independent learning skills. They are: reading, writing, research, planning, problem solving, self-discipline, self-evaluation, and presentation. The idea is that mastery of these skills prepares the learner to tackle virtually any problem.

The skills are taught in a three-stage sequence. At the beginning of the year, the students are introduced to each of the skills and presented with a rationale for why they should be mastered. They then work through several projects in a systematic step-by-step fashion. In this stage, instruction is presented to the entire class, and all of the students are involved in the same activity at the same time.

In the second stage, the focus is on more individualized learning. Students are given projects that outline the steps they are to go through, but considerable room is provided for student decisions. This stage also allows for considerable out-of-classroom activity. The zoo, in particular, becomes a setting for learning, and many students pursue topics relating to the adaptation, habitat, food-web, reproduction, and rearing habits of zoo animals.

In the last third of the year, the students work independently of one another on projects that are selected from a number of available options. Each of the projects requires that the students use all eight of the learning skills that are the focus of the program. The culmination of the year is the annual open house, in which the students display and present the projects they have been working on to friends, relatives, and visitors.

The Grand Rapids school system undertook a comprehensive evaluation of the Zoo School in 1979. Students who had passed through the program, and their parents, were virtually unanimous in their praise of the program. They all felt that the school had provided skills that were going to generate benefits for many years to come. (Schlemmer, 1981)

out-of-school instruction is potentially one of the most exciting ideas in educational practice (see the accompanying box).

To summarize this section, educational approaches based on cognitive learning theory begin with instructional objectives, just as do approaches based on operant and associative learning theory. The cognitive learning theory objectives are different, however, in that they emphasize the transfer capabilities of learned information. This emphasis on transfer stems from the perspective that deep and meaningful understanding of learned information enables students to apply what they have learned to other school-learned tasks, and to tasks they encounter outside the school.

Techniques for Achieving the Meaningful Acquisition of Instruction

As indicated earlier, there are two general techniques for enhancing the meaningful acquisition of instructional material. The first involves activating information that the learner already possesses. The second involves teaching students something they do not already know and then using this newly learned information as a learning aid for the targeted instructional material. Each of these techniques is now examined in greater detail.

Enhancing meaningful learning by activating appropriate prior knowledge

This method of enhancing meaningful learning can be illustrated by drawing an analogy between home building and instructional practice. When a contractor builds a home, he begins by laying a foundation and then systematically adding parts to a firm and solid lower structure. Walls are not built before the foundation is laid because they would collapse without support. The roof is not added until after the walls have been built because it needs to be supported by the walls.

Meaningful learning can be thought of in similar terms. If information is to be meaningfully learned, it must be firmly integrated into the existing knowledge structure. Without integration, information can be momentarily learned, but it is likely to be quickly forgotten and is unlikely to be readily transferable to other learning situations.

One way to enhance meaningful learning is by activating the knowledge that students already have so that incoming information can then be integrated into the activated structure. Several ways for doing this are now examined.

Using mnemonics to acquire information

One of the simplest techniques involving the activation of prior knowledge as a learning aid is through the use of mnemonics. A *mnemonic* is a device that assists in the learning of a specific item of information. One of the most thoroughly documented educational uses of mnemonic procedures is a technique called the *keyword method*. The term "keyword method" was coined by Richard Atkinson (1975) to describe a technique of foreign language vocabulary learning that involves associating the foreign language word with a well-known concrete English word, which is called the keyword. The keyword need not have a meaning relationship with the foreign word. It must, however, be similar in sound. For instance, the keyword used by Michael Raugh and Richard Atkinson (1975) to teach the Spanish word for duck (*pato*—pronounced *pot-o*) was "pot." As another example, the keyword for learning the Spanish word for horse (*caballo*—pronounced *cob-eye-yo*) was "eye."

The keyword method divides vocabulary learning into two stages. The first step requires the student to associate the spoken foreign word with the keyword. This association is generally learned quickly because of the sound similarity between the foreign word and the keyword. The second stage requires the subject to form a mental image of the keyword "interacting" with the English translation of the foreign word. For example, the student might form an image of a duck with a pot on its head as an aid in learning the meaning of *pato*. Or the student might imagine a horse with a large eye in the middle of its forehead as an aid in learning the meaning of *caballo*.

The keyword technique has proven to be a remarkably effective way of acquiring foreign language vocabulary, in a variety of settings and with a number of different kinds of students. Atkinson and Raugh (1975) had one group of Stanford University undergraduates study a 120-word Russian vocabulary list using the keyword method while a control group instructed to learn the words in any way they chose studied the same list. At the end of a set period of time, the group using the keyword technique had learned an average of 86 of the 120 words, whereas the control group had learned an average of 55 of the words. In addition, this learning advantage persisted over time. When tested 6 weeks later, the keyword group remembered the meaning of 43 percent of the 120 words, whereas the control group remembered only 28 percent of the words. In another study involving college students, Raugh and Atkinson (1975) reported that a group using the keyword method mastered 88 percent of a 60-word Spanish vocabulary list, whereas a control group studying the list for the same period of time mastered only 28 percent of the list.

The keyword method has also proven to be a very effective means of learning foreign language vocabulary with much younger students. Two studies (Pressley and Levin, 1978; Levin, Pressley, McCormick, Miller, and Shriberg, 1979) have reported experiments that involve teaching elementary-age children the meaning of Spanish words. In every study involving children in this age group, students who learned the words using the keyword method learned the meaning of more words than did students who used their own methods to learn the words. Moreover, the margin of advantage for the keyword students was frequently greater than 2:1.

Thus far, the research reviewed has focused on the *acquisition* of foreign words. Let us now consider evidence that the keyword method also meets the criterion for deep, meaningful learning, in that it produces superior *transfer*. Michael Pressley, Joel Levin, and Gloria Miller (1980) reported several studies in which college students learned the definitions of infrequently used English

keyword method a mnemonic procedure using similar sounds and vivid images to remember novel stimuli, such as foreign languages

acquisition initial learning

words using either the keyword technique or using a technique of the student's own devising. The students then performed a variety of tasks that included identifying when a targeted word was used correctly or incorrectly in a sentence, selecting the appropriate sentence into which a targeted word could be inserted, and constructing a sentence that involved the correct use of a targeted word. In all of these transfer tasks, the groups that learned the words using the keyword technique performed at a level superior to that of the control group.

Using mnemonics represents one of the simplest means of activating prior knowledge as an aid in achieving the meaningful learning of new material. The research reviewed here focuses on the acquisition of vocabulary, but it should be noted that the technique could be used for acquiring a variety of kinds of information, such as technical names or the names of people or places (Lorayne and Lucas, 1974).

Using analogies to facilitate subsequent learning

analogy resemblance between things that are objectively unlike one another

Another way of activating prior knowledge that can then be used to facilitate subsequent learning is through the use of *analogies*. But interestingly enough, despite the intuitive appeal of using analogies to assist the understanding process, there has been relatively little educational research that focuses on the use of analogies. There is, however, one series of studies that used analogies to assist in teaching physics concepts to college freshmen.

Royer and his associates (Royer and Cable, 1975, 1976; Royer and Perkins, 1977) have completed a number of studies that focus on teaching college students the physical properties of metals that make them good conductors of heat and electricity. In the initial study, Royer and Glen Cable (1975) wrote two passages, one of which was concerned with the transfer of electricity through metals. Each of these passages was then rewritten in two forms. One form—called the "concrete" form—was written in easily understandable form that made extensive use of analogies to assist in the understanding of difficult concepts. The other version—called the "abstract" version—was purposely written in a highly abstract style that was supposed to be difficult to understand.

As topics for their passages Royer and Cable chose the conduction of heat and electricity through metals because of the considerable similarities between the two phenomena. Metals are excellent conductors of both heat and electricity because they are crystalline in structure and have a great many free-floating electrons. These properties were explained by analogy in the following way:

> Heat transfer actually involves the transfer of molecular motion. In the case of heat conduction through metals this transfer of motion occurs through a solid substance such as a bar of iron. If we were able to examine a bar of iron through an extremely powerful microscope, we would see that the interior consists of a series of regularly shaped and spaced structural units known as crystal lattices. In order to picture these lattices, imagine a box made of many tinker-toys with smaller boxes inside consisting of other joined tinker-toys. The solid round parts of the tinker-toys would

correspond to the molecules within the crystal lattice. In our bar of iron, which is a good conductor of heat, each of the bonded molecules within the lattice has associated with it several "free floating" electrons. Each crystal lattice then is an orderly array of molecules surrounded by a cloud of electrons that are not attached to any particular molecule, but are free to move at random through the lattice. You can picture this by imagining many tiny particles floating through the series of tinker-toy boxes. (Royer and Cable, 1975)

By using analogies such as the tinker-toy analogy, Royer and Cable hoped to activate prior knowledge that could be used to facilitate the deep understanding of the material being presented in the passages. This deep understanding could then be assessed by presenting the students with related material and seeing if what they had learned previously *eased* the learning of the related material—in short, determining whether the learned material would positively transfer to the learning of additional material.

The results of the experiment supported the prediction that activating knowledge by using an analogy would ease the learning of subsequent related material. Students who read the analogy material prior to reading a second passage learned at least 40 percent more from the second passage than did a group that did not read the analogy material.

The results of the initial Royer and Cable (1975) study have been replicated many times (Royer and Cable, 1976; Royer and Perkins, 1977; Perkins, 1978). In addition, Royer and Marcy Perkins (1977) were able to demonstrate that the meaningful learning produced by using analogies persisted over time. They presented college students either with an initial passage that contained analogies or with a control passage, and they then had the students read a second, transfer passage immediately, after 2 days, or after 1 week. Their results indicated that the positive transfer attributable to using analogies was as strong after 1 week as it was immediately.

Coming up with exactly the right analogy to achieve meaningful learning of conceptually difficult material is a truly creative act. This is especially true since many analogies don't work very well. Describing a living organism, for example, as being like a factory that takes in raw materials and puts out waste products, may capture one attribute of living organisms; but the poor "fit" of the analogy may generate so much confusion as to negate any benefit that might accrue from its use. For example, a discerning student might point out that one of the defining features of factories is that they produce a product. If living organisms are like factories, what "products" do they produce?

Another caution with using analogies to assist in achieving meaningful learning is that the supposedly known part of the analogy must, in fact, be part of the learner's knowledge. If you were told that *Aplysia* (a large sea snail) is a favorite organism of study by neurobiologists because a characteristic of its nervous system is similar to the also favored squid, chances are that you would not be in the least enlightened by the information. Only if you know that squid have very large nerve cells, thereby making them easy to examine and study, would you benefit from being told that *Aplysia* is a favorite organism of study for the same reason. Teachers should be very careful to make sure that the supposedly known part of the analogy is, in fact, part of the learner's knowledge. Otherwise, using the analogy certainly won't help the learner; in fact, it may be worse than nothing in that learners now have two things they do not understand rather than one.

Enhancing Meaningful Learning by Teaching Students Information That Will Ease Subsequent Learning

The previous section discussed techniques for achieving meaningful learning by activating information the student had already learned. This section examines techniques for achieving meaningful learning that involve teaching the student new information that can then be used to ease subsequent learning. Returning to the home-building analogy used earlier, the techniques to be described are analogous to laying a foundation, upon which the rest of the structure can be built.

Advance organizers

advance organizers introductory statements that are presented at a higher level of generality than the new material to be learned

In the early 1960s, David Ausubel (1960, 1963) suggested *advance organizers* as a device for easing the learning of subsequently presented material. Advance organizers are statements that are "presented at a higher level of abstraction, generality, and inclusiveness than the new material to be learned" (Ausubel, Novak, and Hanesion, 1978, p. 171). Ausubel envisioned advance organizers as a bridge between "what the learner already knows and what he needs to know before he can meaningfully learn the task at hand" (Ausubel, Novak, and Hanesion, 1978, p. 172).

Ausubel and his fellow researchers conducted many studies during the 1960s (Ausubel, 1960; Ausubel and Fitzgerald, 1961, 1962; Ausubel and Youssef, 1963; Fitzgerald and Ausubel, 1963) that demonstrated the efficacy of presenting students with advance organizers prior to their engaging in a learning task. A typical study (Ausubel and Youssef, 1963) involved having college students read a passage on Buddhism after reading a "comparative advance organizer" (examining the relation between Buddhism and Christianity) or a control passage. They found that the students who had initially read the organizer passage retained more from the Buddhism passage than did the students who initially read the control passage. In addition to Ausubel's studies, which have shown greater acquisition of subsequently presented material, other studies (Merrill and Stolurow, 1966; Grotelueschen and Sjogren, 1968; Scandura and Wells, 1967) have shown that material preceded by advance organizers is more likely to transfer to remote tasks than material not preceded by advance organizers.

At this point there seems little doubt that advance organizers can improve the learning of subsequent material under certain conditions. Ausubel (Ausubel,

Novak, and Hanesion, 1978) has indicated two of these conditions. First, the material to be presented must involve unitary topics or related sets of ideas. If the ideas to be presented are highly varied, as might be the case, for example, in a college-level survey class (e.g., introductory psychology), then it would not be possible to generate a single advance organizer to encompass all of the ideas. This does not preclude, however, breaking the subject matter into unitary topics and then preparing advance organizers for each topic.

The second condition is that a true advance organizer must take account of the learner's existing knowledge structure. This means that if advance organizers are to serve as a bridge between material to be presented and material the learner already knows, it is essential to know what the learner already knows. Otherwise, a teacher might end up presenting a learner with two things (the advance organizer *and* the target material) that he or she has difficulty in learning, rather than just one (the target material).

Models as a form of concrete advance organizer

Ausubel defined an advance organizer as a statement that was at a higher level of abstraction than the target material to follow. Another kind of advance organizer that has received considerable investigation is the model or concrete advance organizer.

A model or concrete advance organizer is either a statement or a representation that provides a concrete general overview of a system the student is going to study in detail. An example of the use of a model as an advance organizer can be found in Richard Mayer's research on teaching college students a computer programming language (Mayer, 1975, 1976; Mayer and Bromage, 1980). Mayer (1975) presented one group of students with a text that began with a diagram of the working components of a computer. The diagram included an "input window" (described as a ticket window), an "output pad" (described as a pad of message paper), a "memory scoreboard" (described as an eight-space, erasable scoreboard), and a "program list with pointer arrow" (described as a shopping list). The use of such descriptors was designed to make the unfamiliar components more familiar by relating them to information the students already possessed. After the students had become familiar with the model, they received instruction on computer programming that made continued reference to the model. In effect, the student was asked to "role-play" what the computer did with each of the programming statements.

A second group of students in this study was instructed in a more traditional manner. They were given definitions of programming statements and examples of the appropriate use of each of the statements. Following instruction, each of the groups was asked to write a number of short computer programs that varied in type of problem and complexity. A comparison of the performance of the groups revealed that students who had received the model as an advance organizer performed significantly better on the programming transfer task than did students who had received the traditional instruction. The results were subsequently replicated in later studies (Mayer, 1976; Mayer and Bromage, 1980).

Mayer's research on computer programming represents one instance where a model can serve as a highly beneficial advance organizer. In fact, models can be beneficial in any area of study involving a concrete system. Imagine, for example, that you were teaching an automotive repair course. A good strategy would be to begin the course with an overall model of an automobile engine. Moreover, it would probably be beneficial to review the model as the students moved from one system to another. So, for example, if the students had been working on the carburetor and were ready to move to the ignition system, it would probably be worthwhile to present the model of the entire engine again so that they could relate the functioning of the ignition system to the overall operation of the engine. Biology is another example of an area of study that can greatly benefit from concrete advance organizers. Biological models can be presented at many levels. If instruction was targeted at organ systems, an appropriate model might demonstrate the functioning of the organism as a whole. Alternatively, if instruction was focused on intercellular bodies, an appropriate model would focus on cellular functioning.

Models and concrete examples are especially appropriate in teaching young children, given the implications of Piagetian theory. Piaget's point is that abstract concepts must be firmly grounded in a bedrock of concrete instances. A child will be able to learn and understand abstract concepts only by being able to relate them to concrete events.

Techniques for Maintaining Active Cognitive Processing

Thus far, what it means to understand and techniques for enhancing understanding have been discussed. There is another level of problem, however, in the general area of instructing for understanding. This is the problem of how to maintain an appropriate level of cognitive processing and how to focus attention on the instructional content that is believed to be most important (see Royer, Bates, and Konold, 1982).

Giving students instructional objectives

When instructors teach a course, they do not expect the students to master all of the information presented. Instead, they generally have specific goals that they would like the students to attain, and only part of the information presented will be directly relevant to those goals. The material not directly relevant to the goals is presented for its interest value—as examples of the principles or rules described in the goals or as context material that will make the targeted material easier to understand.

However, students sometimes have difficulty in distinguishing between information that is important for them to master and material that is peripheral to the central objectives of instruction. They find themselves mastering examples and context material while failing to attend to the most important information.

The most direct way of dealing with the problem of student uncertainty about what to focus on is to provide students with the instructional objectives for the course. In general, these objectives should be either the same as, or derived from, the objectives that the teacher or instructional developer began with prior to designing the instructional sequence.

There has been a considerable amount of research in the last 10 years on the effects of providing students with instructional objectives. This research began with a study by Ernst Rothkopf and Robert Kaplan (1972) in which college and high school students either read or did not read learning objectives prior to studying a 3,000-word text concerned with systems training at a telephone company. They found, as one might suspect, that students who read the objectives learned more of the material specified in those objectives than did students who had not read the objectives. Much more surprising, however, was the fact that the group that read the objectives also learned more of the material that was not keyed to an objective. This result suggests that providing students with learning objectives has a general beneficial effect in addition to the specific effect of promoting better learning of material identified in the objectives. The results of this study were subsequently replicated and expanded upon (Kaplan, 1976; Kaplan and Rothkopf, 1974; Kaplan and Simmons, 1974; Nassif-Royer, 1977). In addition, a review (Duchastel and Merrill, 1973) of the early research in this area has been provided.

There is little doubt that providing students with learning objectives can have positive effects. There is a danger, however, that teachers should be aware of. Ernst Rothkopf (1968) once suggested that many students operate in accordance with the "law of least effort." That is, they expend only the amount of learning effort that is required to attain instructional goals. Teachers also can be guilty of operating in accordance with the law of least effort, and this is particularly bad when they generate and distribute hastily prepared learning objectives.

It is very easy to generate trivial learning objectives: You simply say that at the end of instruction, students will know such and such facts. The danger with trivial objectives is that they focus attention on trivial, low-level knowledge that has little utility outside the classroom. However, if teachers expend the time and effort required to generate good cognitive objectives, the students will benefit from knowing what aspects of instruction to focus on, and the instructional process as a whole will benefit from a focus on goals that are truly important.

Asking questions during instruction

Another technique for maintaining active cognitive processing is to ask students questions during instruction. One can see when students are looking at a book or watching a teacher. But one cannot see whether they are doing anything in *addition* to gazing at the book or at the teacher. Are they, in fact, processing the information they are receiving? Asking questions is one way of increasing the likelihood that a student is actively attending to instruction. These questions can be embedded in a text the student is reading or they can be asked during oral instruction.

Inserting questions in written material

Research on embedding questions in text is more extensive than is research on asking students questions, so text-embedded questions will be considered first. Several years ago, Richard Anderson and W. Barry Biddle (1975) conducted an extensive review of the research literature on questioning people while they read, and they found research from early in this century (Gates, 1917) that showed increased learning and retention as a function of questioning. In the last fifteen years, there has been a veritable explosion in research on this topic, and Anderson and Biddle's review has been brought up to date with two more recent reviews (Rickards, 1979; Andre, 1979). The bulk of this research can be traced back to a study by Rothkopf (1966), and this experiment will be examined in detail as an exemplar of much of the research that followed.

Rothkopf (1966) had students read a 5,200-word text concerned with oceanography, under several different questioning conditions. Thirty-nine objective, completion-type, questions were generated from this text, and some of the students received these questions *prior to* reading the text. Note that this procedure would allow the students to search for content relevant to answering the questions they had just seen. Other students received a set of five or six questions immediately *after* reading the segment of text in which the answers to the questions could be found. In other words, this group knew they were going to receive questions, but they did not know what the questions were until they had finished reading the relevant segment of text. Two final groups were control groups that read the text after having been instructed to learn as much of the content as they could.

After all the students had read the text, a test was administered that requested two kinds of information. The first was information of the same kind as had been asked for in the questions given either before or after reading the text. The second was information of a kind that had not been asked for in any previous questions. As one might expect, students who had received questions either before or after reading the text performed better on the same questions when they appeared on the test than did students who had not received the questions. Thus questioning students apparently increased the learning of material asked for in the questions. The second major outcome in Rothkopf's study was not nearly as predictable. The students who had received questions *after* reading the relevant text material recalled more of the material not tested in the questions than did any of the other groups. This result suggests that students who knew they were going to encounter questions after reading a segment of text attended to all of the text more carefully than did students in the other groups, thereby improving their performance on material relevant to answering the first set of questions *and* on material that would not be tested until the final posttest. In other words, having questions follow the reading of the text increased the extent to which that text was actively processed by the students.

The beneficial effects associated with embedding questions in text have been replicated many times since Rothkopf's study. For instance, the three review articles mentioned previously (Anderson and Biddle, 1975; Andre, 1979; Rickards, 1979) examined over 100 separate studies, the vast majority of which report results consistent with Rothkopf's original study.

Choosing the right level of inserted questions

Another important concern about embedding questions in text relates to the level at which the questions should be written. Should questions call for specific factual information, or should they be written at a higher level, calling for the application of learned information to instances not encountered in the text? Watts and Anderson (1971) reported a study that addressed this issue. They had high school students read a text about psychologists and their theories under four question-type conditions. Two groups read the passages and then answered questions that asked for low-level factual recall or the selection of an example of a principle that had been seen before. A third group was asked questions that called for applying principles to examples they had not seen before. The final group read the passages without questions. After completing the study phase of the experiment, all the students took a posttest that contained factual and application questions, some of which had been seen before by the question groups and some of which were new. The results of the study were that the students who had received application questions performed better on the test than any of the other groups. The application group not only performed at a higher level on application questions; they also performed at a very high level on the remaining types of questions.

The results of the Watts and Anderson (1971) study seem to indicate that whenever possible, questions embedded in text should assess higher-order knowledge. Andre's (1979) review of subsequent studies, however, provides a cautionary note to this generalization. If higher-level questions prove to be exceptionally difficult, they might produce frustration in the student and result in drastically lower performance.

Asking questions during oral instruction

Is it also true that oral questions can have a positive effect on cognitive processing? The answer to this question seems to be yes, but there is not much research on the topic. Here again the question is whether it is better to ask low-level, factual questions or higher-level questions calling for the application of material.

Winne (1979) has reviewed the research literature on asking oral questions at varying levels, and he has concluded that a compelling case has not been made for the beneficial effects of asking questions at higher cognitive levels. In part, this conclusion is a reflection of the difficulty of doing conclusive research on a very complex problem. One problem, for instance, involves training teachers so that they can consistently formulate higher-level cognitive questions. Most teachers automatically ask lower-level questions, and they must break some well-established habits before they can begin to construct good higher-level questions. Another problem is asking questions at the appropriate level of difficulty. If application questions are extremely easy there is no reason to believe that they will produce effects any different from factual questions. Alternatively, if they are too difficult, they are more likely to be harmful than beneficial.

Even though there is no solid experimental support for asking higher-level questions while teaching, there is ample commonsensical support for doing so. Throughout this chapter the importance of teaching knowledge that will transfer to out-of-school settings has been emphasized. Asking good higher-level questions is one way of moving toward this goal. (See the accompanying box.)

Asking questions is the most important way of determining if students understand. (© Cary Wolinsky/Stock, Boston)

Developing a Theory of Question Asking

Allan Collins, a psychologist at Bolt, Beranek, and Newman, Inc., has been working for several years on a theory of Socratic tutoring. His assumption is that the purpose of education is to teach a variety of knowledge and to teach the skills necessary for applying that knowledge to new problems or situations (Collins, 1977). Collins sees the Socratic teaching method as an ideal way of accomplishing his purposes.

Collins has identified twenty-four rules for question asking that systematically move from probing low-level factual information to very sophisticated questions calling for high-level thinking. Collins's rules for questioning are presented in the accompanying figure, with examples drawn from a lesson on the factors governing rice growing.

Allan Collins's Rules for Question Asking

Rule 1:   Ask about a known case: If (1) it is the start of a dialogue, or (2) there is no other strategy to invoke, then (3) pick a well-known case and ask what the value of the dependent variable is for that case, or (4) ask the student if he knows a case with a particular value of the dependent variable.

Example: Ask the student "Do they grow rice in China?" or "Do you know any place where rice is grown?"

Reason for Use: It brings out any well-known facts the student knows about, such as rice growing in China.

Rule 2:   Ask for any factors: If (1) a student asserts that a case has a particular value of the dependent variable, then (2) ask the student why.

Example: If a student says they grow rice in China, ask why.

Reason for Use: This determines what causal factors or chains the student knows about.

Rule 3:   Ask for intermediate factors: If (1) the student gives as an explanation a factor that is not an immediate cause in the causal chain, then (2) ask for the intermediate steps.

Example: If the student mentions monsoons in China, as a reason for rice growing, ask "Why do monsoons make it possible to grow rice in China?"

Reason for Use: This insures that the student understands the steps in the causal chain, for example, that rice needs to be flooded.

Rule 4:   Ask for prior factors: If (1) the student gives as an explanation a factor on a causal chain in which there are also prior factors, then (2) ask the student for the prior factors.

Example: If the student mentions water as a factor in growing rice, ask him "What do you need to have enough water?"

Reason for Use: Same as Rule 3.

Box continues on next page

278 LEARNING AND INSTRUCTION

Allan Collins's Rules for Question Asking

Rule 5: Form a general rule for an insufficient factor: If (1) the student gives as an explanation one or more factors that are not sufficient, then (2) formulate a general rule asserting that the factor given is sufficient and ask the student if the rule is true.

Example: If the student gives water as the reason they grow rice in China, ask him "Do you think any place with enough water can grow rice?"

Reason for Use: This forces the student to pay attention to other causal factors.

Rule 6: Pick a counterexample for an insufficient factor: If (1) the student gives as an explanation one or more factors that are not sufficient, or (2) agrees to the general rule in Rule 5, then (3) pick a counterexample that has the right value of the factor(s) given, but the wrong value of the dependent variable, and (4) ask what the value of the dependent variable is for that case, or (5) ask why the causal dependence does not hold for that case.

Example: If a student gives water as the reason they grow rice in China or agrees that any place with enough water can grow rice, pick a place like Ireland where there is enough water and ask "Do they grow rice in Ireland?" or "Why don't they grow rice in Ireland?"

Reason for Use: Same as Rule 5.

Rule 7: Form a general rule for an unnecessary factor: If (1) the student gives as an explanation one or more factors that are not necessary, then (2) formulate a general rule asserting that the factor is necessary and ask the student if the rule is true.

Example: If a student says rainfall is a reason for growing rice, ask "Do you think it is necessary to have heavy rainfall in order to grow rice?"

Reason for Use: This forces the student to consider the necessity of a particular factor.

Rule 8: Pick a counterexample for an unnecessary factor: If (1) the student gives as an explanation one or more factors that are not necessary, or (2) the student agrees to the general rule in Rule 7, then (3) pick a counterexample with the wrong value of the factor and the correct value of the dependent variable, and (4) ask the student what the value of the dependent variable is for that case, or (5) ask why the causal dependence does not hold in that case.

Example: If the student gives rainfall as a reason for growing rice, ask "Do you think they can grow rice in Egypt?" or "Why do they grow rice in Egypt when they don't have much rainfall?"

Reason for Use: Same as Rule 7.

Rule 9: Pick a case with an extreme value: If (1) the student is missing a particular factor, then (2) pick a case with an extreme value of that factor and ask why the dependent variable has a particular value in that case.

Example: If the student has not mentioned temperature with respect to rice growing, ask "Why don't they grow rice in Alaska?"

Reason for Use: This forces the student to pay attention to any factor he is ignoring.

Rule 10: Pose a misleading question: If (1) there is a case in which a secondary

Allan Collins's Rules for Question Asking

factor overrides the primary factors, then (2) pose a misleading question to the student, based on the fact that the value of the dependent variable is different from what would be predicted from the primary factors above, or (3) pose a misleading choice as to the dependent variable between two cases in which consideration of the primary factors alone leads to the wrong prediction.

Example: Because the tree cover in the Amazon jungle keeps the temperature down to a high of about 85 degrees, ask the student "Do you think the temperatures in the Amazon jungle reach a 100 degrees?" or "Do you think it gets hotter in the Amazon jungle or Texas?"

Reason for Use: This forces the student to learn about common exceptions, about secondary factors, and about the limitations of general rules.

Rule 11: Specify how the variable depends on a given factor: If (1) the student mentions a factor, but does not specify how the dependent variable varies with that factor, or (2) only partially specifies the relationship, then (3) ask him to specify the relationship more precisely, or (4) suggest a possible relationship to him.

Example: Ask the student "Can you say how temperature depends on latitude?" or "Does average temperature increase linearly the further south you go?"

Reason for Use: This forces the student to specify more precisely the functional relation between the factor in question and the dependent variable.

Rule 12: Probe for a necessary factor: If (1) a student makes a wrong prediction of the dependent variable because he has not identified one or more necessary factors, then (2) tell him he is wrong, and ask him to formulate a hypothesis about another factor that is necessary.

Example: If a student thinks they can grow rice in Ireland because of the heavy rainfall, point out they cannot grow rice there and ask "Can you make a hypothesis about what other factor is necessary for rice growing?"

Reason for Use: This forces the student to use hypothesis formation as a systematic strategy for dealing with unexplained problems.

Rule 13:   Probe for a sufficient factor: If (1) a student makes a wrong prediction of the dependent variable because he treats a factor as necessary when it is not, then (2) tell him he is wrong, and ask him to formulate a hypothesis about another factor that might be sufficient.

Example: If a student thinks they cannot grow rice in Egypt because there is little rain, point out they can grow rice there and ask "Can you think of what other factor makes it possible to grow rice there?"

Reason for Use: Same as Rule 12.

Rule 14: Probe for differences between two cases: If (1) a student cannot think of a factor that could account for different values of the dependent variable between two cases, then (2) ask him to consider what the differences are between the two cases that might account for the difference in the dependent variable.

Example: If a student cannot think of why they can grow rice in China but not in Alaska, ask what the differences are between China and Alaska that might account for the difference in rice growing.

Reason for Use: Same as Rule 12.

Box continues on next page

Allan Collins's Rules for Question Asking

Rule 15:   Request a test of the hypothesis about a factor. If (1) the student has formulated a hypothesis about how the dependent variable is related to a particular factor, then (2) ask him how it could be tested.
Example: Ask the student "If you want to test whether distance from the ocean affects temperature, would you compare the temperature in January for St. Louis with Washington, D.C. or Atlanta?"
Reason for Use: By getting the student to test hypotheses, it forces him to learn to control other factors that might affect the variable.

Rule 16:   Ask for a prediction about an unknown case: If (1) a student has identified all the primary factors that affect the dependent variable, then (2) pick a case that is either hypothetical or unlikely to be known and ask the student to predict the likely value of the variable for that case.
Example: If the student has identified the factors that affect rice growing, then ask "Do you think they can grow rice in Florida?"
Reason for Use: This forces the student to use the factors he has accumulated in a predictive way.

Rule 17:   Ask what are the relevant factors to consider: If (1) the student cannot make a prediction, then (2) ask the student what are the relevant factors to consider.
Example: Ask the student "If you cannot predict whether they grow rice in Florida, what factors do you need to consider?"
Reason for Use: This teaches the student to ask the right questions in trying to make reasonable predictions about new cases.

Rule 18:   Question a prediction made without enough information: If (1) a student makes a prediction as to the value of the dependent variable on the basis of some set of factors, and (2) there is another value consistent with that set of factors, then (3) ask the student why not the other value.
Example: If the student predicts they grow wheat in Nigeria because it is fertile and warm, ask him why not rice.
Reason for Use: This forces the student not to jump to conclusions without enough information.

Rule 19:   Point out irrelevant factors: If (1) the student asks about the value of an irrelevant factor in trying to make a prediction, then (2) point out the factor is irrelevant, or (3) ask whether the irrelevant factor affects the dependent variable.
Example: If the student asks whether Denver or Salt Lake City is further west in trying to decide which has the colder temperature, then point out that longitude does not matter, or ask whether longitude affects temperature.
Reason for Use: This forces the student to learn what is irrelevant, as well as what is relevant, in making any decision.

Rule 20:   Point out an inconsistent prediction: If (1) a student makes a prediction about the dependent variable which is inconsistent with any of the values of the factors discussed, then (2) point out the inconsistency, or (3) ask whether the value of the factor discussed is consistent with his prediction about the dependent variable.
Example: If the student predicts they grow rice in Spain after the dryness of the climate has been discussed, either point out that a dry climate is incompatible

Allan Collins's Rules for Question Asking

with rice growing unless there is irrigation, or ask how he thinks they can grow rice when the climate is so dry.

Reason for Use: This reminds the student to consider all the relevant factors in making a prediction, and insures he understands the relation between the factor and the dependent variable.

Rule 21:   Ask for consideration of a possible value: If (1) there is a value of the dependent variable that has not been considered and which either is consistent with several factors or important to consider a priori, then (2) ask the student to consider that value.

Example: If the student has not considered rice as a possible grain in Nigeria, ask him to consider it.

Reason for Use: This forces the student to actively consider alternatives in making any prediction.

Rule 22:   Test for consistency with a given hypothesis: If (1) a particular value of the dependent variable is being considered, and (2) the values of one or more relevant factors have been discussed, but (3) whether these values are consistent with the particular value of the dependent variable has not been discussed, then (4) pick one or more of the factors that are consistent with the dependent variable and ask if they are consistent, or (5) pick one or more of the factors that are inconsistent with the dependent variable and ask if they are consistent.

Example: If the hot climate and rainfall in Java have been discussed, the student can be asked "Is the heavy rainfall in Java consistent with growing wheat?" or "Is the hot climate and heavy rainfall consistent with growing rice?"

Reason for Use: This tests whether the student understands the functional relations between the various factors and the dependent variable.

Rule 23:   Ask for consideration of relevant factors: If (1) a student makes a wrong prediction in a particular case, or (2) cannot make a prediction, then (3) pick the most relevant factor not discussed and (4) ask the student what the value of that factor is for the particular case.

Example: If the student predicts that the average temperature is very hot in Buenos Aires, ask if he knows what the latitude of Buenos Aires is.

Reason for Use: This forces the student to consider relevant factors in making a prediction, and elicits whether a mistake is due to wrong information about a case, or a mistake about how the dependent variable varies with different factors.

Rule 24:   Trace the consequences of a general rule:* If (1) a student agrees to a general rule such as Rule 5 or Rule 7, then (2) ask if he agrees with the consequences of that rule in a particular case.

* Rule 24 was added after the paper was completed. To the degree there is a grouping of the rules, it would be most appropriately grouped with Rules 5 through 8.

As can be seen in Collins's rule sequence, asking questions at the appropriate level of difficulty can be a highly effective means of imparting information, and it can also help students develop their own ability to think for themselves.

UTILIZING COGNITIVE LEARNING THEORY IN THE CLASSROOM

This chapter began with the question of how to enhance student understanding of instructional material. In this context, "Understanding" has not meant the instantaneous sense of comprehension one gets on hearing or reading something. Rather, the focus has been on understanding as the ability to use acquired knowledge as a tool for problem solving or as a means of easing subsequent learning.

A teacher should begin the effort of achieving significant understanding by formulating objectives that focus on the transfer of learned information to other situations—preferably situations involving the use of the information in real-world settings. Once objectives have been established, plans can be made for presenting instruction so as to enhance the likelihood that it will be understood at a meaningful level. Achieving this level of understanding entails relating the information to knowledge already possessed by the student. As has been indicated, there are two general procedures for doing this. The first involves making an explicit connection between new information and prior knowledge by using mnemonic techniques or analogies. The second procedure involves presenting students with new material that can then serve as a "learning bridge" between instruction and old information. This new material can be in the form of abstract organizers that provide a superstructure for the material to follow, or in the form of concrete organizers that can serve as a model of systems or processes.

The final question a teacher may want to consider is how to direct student attention to important material and how to encourage high levels of student cognitive processing. This can be accomplished by providing students with learning objectives or by questioning students at appropriate times.

SUMMARY

The material in this chapter is concerned with developing instructional approaches to enhance understanding. The term "understanding" has several meanings. Two of these, although important, are *not* the central focus of this chapter. The two are (1) understanding as an immediate sense of comprehension and (2) understanding as an expression of empathy. The focus of the chapter is on understanding in a way that allows learned information to serve as a problem-solving tool or as a base for acquiring information later on. Thus information that has been learned and understood, in the sense that "understood" is being used here, can transfer to new learning situations. Teachers know they have a problem with achieving understanding in their students when the learned information does not transfer to new situations.

The cognitive perspective on understanding can be traced back to David Ausubel, who was one of the first psychologists to view learning as an act involving interaction between the information to be learned and the learner's existing knowledge structure. Ausubel distinguished between what he called "rote learning" and "meaningful learning." Rote learning is the process whereby a learner acquires information that has no inherent meaning. In contrast, meaningful learning involves the acquisition of information by integrating that information into the existing knowledge structure.

Ausubel laid the foundation for current cognitive views of understanding, with his suggestion that meaningful learning involves integrating new information into existing knowledge structure. More recent theories have viewed the process as being somewhat more dynamic than Ausubel envisioned. Recent views suggest that understanding is the result of an interactive process involving the incoming information, the environmental context in which the information is experienced, and the learner's existing knowledge. Without these three elements, the process of meaningful learning will not occur, and the state of cognitive understanding will not be achieved.

A logical implication of the interactionist view of understanding outlined above is that every student will have a somewhat different memory representation for an instructional event that has been meaningfully learned. This is a consequence called representational variability. Teachers should keep the idea of representational variability in mind for three reasons: (1) it focuses a teacher's attention on the uniqueness of each student, (2) it reminds teachers that the information they have in their heads cannot be transferred intact to their students, and (3) it maintains focus on the fact that teachers should try and get information into a student's head in a form that allows the information to be transferred to new learning situations.

Teachers can facilitate the understanding process in two ways: (1) by increasing the likelihood that students will bring appropriate knowledge to bear when receiving instruction, and (2) by providing students with information that will assist the meaningful learning of subsequently presented information.

The procedure for developing instructional approaches to enhancing understanding involves several steps. The first step is to develop cognitive instructional goals, that is, goals that focus on the transfer of learned information to new learning situations. This is in contrast to associative and operant learning goals, which focus on the acquisition of targeted behaviors or skills. Cognitive instructional goals can be written to emphasize near transfer tasks (tasks involving other school-learned material) or far transfer tasks (tasks involving out-of-school activities). If near transfer goals are to be emphasized, the tasks should be representative of instructional tasks students will encounter later in the curriculum. If far transfer goals are stressed, the tasks should be representative of tasks the students might encounter in their everyday activities, and they should not involve undue expense or assessment difficulty.

Having developed the instructional goals, the next step is to choose a technique for enhancing understanding. The first general way is to activate appropriate knowledge that the student already has. There are two ways to do this. The first is to use a mnemonic, which is a mental device used to assist the learning of a specific item of information. The most thoroughly researched use of a mnemonic device is the keyword method, which involves associating a word or concept to be learned with a well-known concrete English word.

A second technique for activating prior knowledge is by using analogies. Analogies relate knowledge the student already has to new knowledge by pointing out similarities between the two. Devising the "right" analogy to teach a particular item of information is a truly creative act. Analogies should be constructed with caution, since inappropriate analogies can be confusing. Another caution is that the part of the analogy that is supposedly known must, in fact, be part of the learner's knowledge. If not, the learner will be faced with two new things to learn rather than one.

The second general way to enhance understanding is to teach the student something new that can then serve as a bridge between existing knowledge and new information. One way to do this is to use advance organizers. Advance organizers are inclusive statements that outline the general content the learner is to be exposed to. After learning the advance organizer, the learner can then integrate the details of instruction into this newly established knowledge structure.

A second bridging technique is to use a model as a form of concrete advance organizer. Models provide a representational overview of the information students are going to study.

In addition to the techniques for enhancing understanding that are described above, there are also a number of techniques that can be used to maintain active cognitive processing in students. These techniques include providing students with instructional objectives, giving students written questions embedded within text materials, and asking students questions during oral instruction. An issue related to embedding questions in text and asking students questions during oral instruction is determining the appropriate level at which to ask the question. In general, it has been found that higher-level questions—those calling for the application of learned material—result in more useful learning than do questions asking for the lower-level recall of factual information.

FOR FURTHER STUDY AND APPLICATION

Ausubel, D. P. *The psychology of meaningful verbal learning.* New York: Grume and Stratton, 1963.   A classic by an instructional psychologist way ahead of his time.

Lorayne, H., and Lucas, J. *The memory book.* New York: Ballantine, 1974.   A fun book devoted to using mnemonic techniques to improve memory.

Anderson, R. C., Spiro, R. J., and Montague, W. E. (Eds.). *Schooling and the acquisition of knowledge.* Hillsdale, N.J.: Erlbaum, 1977.

Lesgold, A. M., Pellegrino, J. W., Fokkema, S. D., and Glaser, R. (Eds.), *Cognitive psychology and instruction.* New York: Plenum Press, 1978.   Two collections of articles that discuss applying cognitive psychology to instruction.

III
SOCIAL FACTORS IN EDUCATION

9

GROUP FACTORS IN CLASSROOMS

CHAPTER OVERVIEW

This chapter and the three that follow discuss social factors that relate to education. This chapter describes the social interaction that occurs as a result of being educated in groups. It examines the ways in which a classroom is a group, as formally defined by psychologists. Some of the important effects that all groups have on their members, such as pressures to conform, norms regarding appropriate behavior, and the determination of power and leadership, are discussed as they pertain to classroom groups. Finally, the chapter considers how groups influence learning, and it examines techniques for using groups in educational settings. Group processes represent an important (and sometimes overlooked) dynamic in classroom situations, and as such they are a key factor in understanding what goes on in learning situations.

"Master teacher" is not a term that can be used lightly; few teachers meet the requirements implicit in its use. However, students and colleagues would readily confer such a title on George Harriston, a high school instructor for almost 30 years. Now teaching English and Latin at James Caldwell High School in West Caldwell, New Jersey, George Harriston has taught a number of generations of students and is in a position to look back at the changes that have taken place during his tenure.

The discussion—a particularly frank and revealing one—began with a question as to how societal and social changes have affected the teaching profession over the past 30 years.

A.   There have been a number of changes. Many of the things that were teacher decisions—about procedures, techniques, and so on—are no longer teacher decisions. Many of them are dictated by the administration, which in turn is being dictated to by the state. Teachers have less freedom of choice in public education, at least in New Jersey, than even 10 years ago.

Q.   Can you give me an example?

A.   We have to submit all final exams for approval before we give them. Such things aren't easy to live with, but one has to. And teachers tend to be the way they have always been: they accept and obey. You don't get many people that protest.

Q.   How about the students? Have they changed?

A.   I think that they devote less time to school these days. Many of our kids work now every day after school and on weekends—and the job comes first. Also, you get the impression that some of the kids aren't really very concerned about what they're learning or doing; the important thing is the grade, and whether their grade-point average will get them into a good college. I think their attention is much more on the performance as it appears on a record than on the performance done out of that old-fashioned saying, "joy of learning."

Q.   Do you think that you're as good a teacher as you were earlier in your career?

A.   That's a good question. I have never had the concern that many of my colleagues have had with their image and how they come across as a bad teacher, a good teacher, an easy teacher, a tough teacher. I have simply taught. My major summation of my teaching is that I have never ever been completely satisfied with what I've done. I have evaluated myself constantly, and sometimes I've been happy with it and sometimes I've not been happy with it. The day that a teacher says "I'm a wonderful teacher and I couldn't be any better," well, that's the day he ought to leave.

I guess I do consider myself a good teacher but I've never been able to go beyond that. I leave it to the people who come to my classes. And they, frankly, have always been much more satisfied with the performance they saw than I have been.

Q.   What would you say to someone who came to you and said that they were thinking of becoming a high school teacher?

A.   I would say that they should think it over carefully. I'm not sure that with all the controls and interference, whether good or bad, by the state and administrators, teaching can ever be the great joy it once was. I'm just so glad I was in it for so many years when it was an absolute joy. I also can no longer countenance bright young people accepting the financial burden of being a teacher. It's unfair; it's criminal. You can love it all you want, but you wake up one morning and you realize that you've grown considerably older and you just can't pick up and go into something else. The rewards financially are still pathetic, and they will always be until the public understands that you are doing more than just playing with children six hours a day. I think the public still feels, "What could be very hard about that kind of job?" I would ask a young person to think very, very carefully, especially if the person wanted to have a family and had certain aspirations—all those wonderful things we associate with the American dream. As a teacher, you're going to have to wait a little longer or maybe never get them. You can't replace wanting to teach though, and teaching can be wonderful.

Q.   You've given me a more pessimistic view than I had anticipated.

A.   Well, see, I don't see it as pessimistic. I see the view as unromantic, but I think there's been too much romanticism in education. I don't think we've always been realistic, and I don't think as teachers we've always seen where things in society are going.

As the interview with George Harriston points up, teaching does not stand in isolation from the rest of the world. Rather, it is closely tied to the policies, attitudes, and mores of society. Teachers cannot ignore the fact that administrators and the state place controls over their teaching; nor can they forget that the salary may not always be sufficient to meet even some basic needs. Rather than being simply a one-to-one, teacher-student activity, teaching is located within the context of a series of social relationships and networks that encompass the state and federal government, the school administrators, other teachers, other students—the permutations and combinations are endless.

THE CLASSROOM AS A GROUP

Consider the amount of time students in school are with other people. They study in groups, go to recess in groups, eat lunch in groups. Almost everything that goes on in the typical school is done either with or in the presence of others. Because the experience of being with other students and teachers in groups has important effects on students' behavior, the study of group processes represents an important part of educational psychology. But before one can understand how groups affect an individual's educational experience, one needs to consider just what is meant, in a formal sense, by the term "group."

Groups: A Formal Definition

Psychologists use four criteria for labeling a collection of people as a group:

1. *Interaction of members.* Perhaps in the most basic sense, a group consists of a collection of people who must interact with one another on a fairly regular basis. It is difficult to envision a group that does not present opportunities for the members to meet at least occasionally. However, it is also possible for group interaction to be relatively transitory, as in the case of a college class that gets together for a reunion every ten years.

2. *Shared goals and values.* A second criterion that may be used to determine whether a collection of people is a group has to do with whether there is a set of goals shared by the members of the group, and shared norms. *Norms,* which refer to behaviors and activities that are acceptable to and expected from group members, can arise either formally—as in the adoption of a constitution or by-laws—or as is more frequently the case, implicitly, as a result of custom. The most important point is that the goals and norms found in a group tend to influence the behavior of the members. Moreover, a member's behavior is influenced whether he or she is physically present or absent from the group. Individuals generally belong to groups because they are engaged in activities that culminate in some common result that all the members desire.

3. *Interdependence of fates.* If group members share particular goals, it is likely that they will be interdependent in terms of how successful they are in reaching the goal. In other words, group members depend on one another for reaching goals related to the group. If the group as a whole succeeds, it will reflect on the individual members; if the group fails, the individual members will suffer. Thus each member of the group is dependent on the actions of the other group members.

4. *Perception of group membership.* The final criterion for determining whether a collection of individuals is a group in a formal sense follows from the first three characteristics. In order for a formal group to exist, the members must perceive that they are indeed part of a group. If they have no perception of being involved in a group, it is unlikely that there will be interaction, that shared goals and values will exist, or that the fate of the individual will rest in part on the actions of others.

norms behaviors and activities that are acceptable and expected for group members

Is the Classroom a Group?

Having suggested four criteria that can be considered necessary for a group to be formally regarded as a group, let us examine the typical classroom to see how well it fits these criteria. It is clear, first of all, that there is interaction among the members of the class. Particularly in an elementary school classroom, the students work together, carry out joint activities, and play in groups. But group interaction exists even in traditional higher-level lecture classes: students talk together before the lecture begins, they study together for exams, they are exposed to the same events (the lectures), and they react in similar ways (e.g., by taking notes). Hence it appears that there is interaction among the members of a class.

It can also be argued that classes share particular goals and norms. The idealist might suggest that students share the basic goal of learning as much as possible from a given class. The more cynical observer might propose that an even more important goal for students is to maximize their grade for a given course. In either case, it is clear that certain goals are common to the members of a class.

It is likely that norms will also develop within a particular classroom. As indicated earlier, norms can be defined as acceptable and expected behaviors and activities within a group. Classes very quickly develop their own norms. In some classes, it is the norm for students to help one another when carrying out some project; in others, students not only do not help one another, they actively compete against their peers. Another aspect of norms in a classroom concerns behavior toward the teacher. In some classes, it might be considered quite reasonable to be friendly and to act positively toward the teacher; in others, however, the norm might be to be relatively hostile and unfriendly, and any attempt to engage the teacher in a friendly interchange might be viewed negatively by the class. Thus it can be argued that classes hold shared goals and norms, and that these goals and norms can have quite a powerful effect on the members of the class.

The third criterion for formal groups involves the interdependence of the group members' fates. Interdependence of fates exists on a number of levels in a classroom. In a very tangible sense, what students in a class personally receive from a teacher is dependent on the other members of the class. For instance, a class that has discipline problems might receive a very different kind of instruction from the teacher than a class in which the students are well-behaved—just in terms of the amount of time the teacher is able to devote to each student. Another example involves the kinds of questions that students ask the teacher. Teachers who have taught the same material many times find that each session is unique because of the different questions asked by the students. Thus the instruction a student receives in a class is partly a function of who his or her fellow students are. Even in lecture classes, in which there is little or no opportunity for teacher-student interchange, there can be fate interdependence. For example, in many classes students are graded along a "curve" relative to one another. If there are a large number of brilliant students in the class, the average student will receive a relatively lower grade than if there were only a few brilliant students.

Classrooms, then, seem to fit the first three criteria of a group. In a classroom there is interaction among the members, shared goals and norms, and interdependence of fates. But what of the final characteristic, that of perception of group membership? Here in fact, it is easiest to argue that a classroom is a formal group. Especially in elementary schools, in which the students stay with the same teacher all day, students are apt to identify themselves as members of a classroom. Even in large lecture classes, in which there can be a sense of anonymity, the students may feel they are part of a specific group. When they see other members of the class in the library, for instance, they may talk of their shared experience in the class. Thus perception of membership seems to exist for members of most classrooms.

Having established that the classroom can indeed be considered a group, let us now turn to some of the theory and research on the effects of group membership. It turns out that groups can have a very powerful effect on their members.

GROUP PROCESSES

Conformity

The old television show "Candid Camera" once did a classic piece on conformity in military situations. The show arranged for a military officer to lecture a set of six new recruits. In reality, five of the recruits were instructed to follow a specific series of rather unusual behaviors during the course of the lecture. At certain points, they all removed their hats, they stood up, they put on their hats, they turned their backs on the lecturer, and ultimately they walked out of the room, as the lecturer droned on.

And what of the sixth recruit, who had no inkling that the others were acting out a script? If you are an astute observer of human behavior, you might suspect that the naive recruit followed the lead of the others. Although looking somewhat bewildered, this is just what he did. When the others stood, he stood; when they took off their hats, he did; he conformed to their behavior, to the point of marching out of the room with them.

This "Candid Camera" sequence is in fact quite similar to a famous experiment carried out by Solomon Asch in the 1950s (Asch, 1958). Asch had groups of six undergraduates enrolled in prestigious Swarthmore College participate in an experiment supposedly about the judgment of perceptual relations. Subjects were shown a card on which a line was drawn, called the standard, and in addition were shown three lines that varied in length. The subjects were told that one of the three lines was the same length as the standard, and it was their task to pick out the line that matched. Since one of the lines clearly matched the standard, it appeared to be a simple task. The experiment began with all subjects (who had been asked to make their judgments aloud) agreeing on the first two trials. But on the third trial, something curious occurred. Each of the first five subjects unanimously agreed that a particular line matched the standard, while the last subject felt quite strongly that another of the lines was obviously the correct one. The question for the last subject became one of deciding what to do—answer with what he was certain was the correct response, or yield to the group's majority opinion.

The subject's dilemma arose from the fact that everyone in the group, other than himself, was a paid confederate of the experimenter. The confederates had been told to answer erroneously and unanimously on a certain percentage of trials, and the purpose of the study was to determine how often the real subject would conform to the group.

The results of this experiment, which proved to be a classic demonstration of conformity, showed that subjects were indeed swayed by group pressure. The average subject conformed to the group on about one-third of the trials. But there were also extreme individual differences. Some of the subjects yielded to the majority on almost every trial, and some were completely independent. Of course, these results tell us little about whether subjects actually changed their opinion (as in true conformity) or, more likely, were merely acting compliant to avoid embarrassment or sanctions from the group. Still, the results show clearly the power of groups over their members.

Conformity in the classroom

Because research has shown that school-age children are even more susceptible to conformity pressures than adults (Allen and Newston, 1972), one might expect that conformity pressures would be common in classrooms, and this is the case. It is the rare student who is able to resist the pressure to avoid

Conformity processes are readily apparent in style of dress. As a result, students may appear to be wearing a "uniform." (© Nancy J. Pierce 1977/Photo Researchers, Inc.)

Conforming to the Minority

While psychologists have spent a good deal of time investigating what it is that makes people conform to pressure from the majority in a group, much less energy has been spent looking at the opposite side of the coin—the processes involved in allowing a minority to remain independent from a majority.

One theory that is useful in explaining how a minority in a classroom can not only remain independent but can even influence and sway the majority has been suggested by the European psychologist Serge Moscovici (Moscovici and Faucheux, 1972). Pointing to historical instances in which single individuals were able to convince the world of the validity of their own point of view through consistent behavior (Freud is one example), he suggests that the critical element in persuading the majority in a group of the accuracy of a minority's point of view is unyielding *consistency*. Because groups tend to form a consensus or norm that takes into account the point of view of all their members, the persistent consistency of a minority may have an inordinate effect on a group attempting to reach agreement.

A dramatic experimental confirmation of this hypothesis was carried out concerning judgments of color. In the experiment (Moscovici and Faucheux, 1972), groups of six subjects—two of whom were actually confederates—

wearing a particular style of clothing that is considered unfashionable by classmates. On a more important level, it can be difficult for a student to express an opinion that is unpopular. For instance, most students would hesitate to suggest publicly that recess be cut short in order that there be more time for an English lesson. A student proposing such a change might expect to experience a good deal of hostility from the other class members.

Why people conform

One reason that people conform to group majorities is that there is evidence showing that groups eventually reject persons holding points of view different from those held by the majority. For instance, Stanley Schachter (1951) formed a series of discussion groups, made up of from eight to ten people, to talk about the case of a juvenile delinquent named Johnny Rocco. The case was described in such a way as to make most participants quite sympathetic to Rocco, and thus discussants tended to recommend lenient treatment. Within each of the discussion groups, however, were three confederates. One confederate was instructed to agree with the majority opinion (which was,

were shown a series of thirty-six slides, all of which were obviously blue. Yet on every trial the two confederates said that the slides were green, a clear error. After several trials on which the minority consistently responded contrary to the majority, the *majority* began to yield. Despite the fact that all the slides were blue, 32 percent of the subjects agreed that at least one slide was green. Overall, 8.42 percent of all responses that were made by the actual subjects agreed with the (erroneous) minority. And the effects of the minority persisted: on a subsequent individual perception test, subjects were more apt to label ambiguous forms as being green than subjects not exposed to the minority feedback.

There are a number of possible reasons why a minority can be effective in influencing the majority. Members of the majority are likely to spend time and energy trying to understand why a minority who are being very persistent hold their particular point of view. The effort involved may make the majority understand the minority's point of view in a different way— and may even make the minority's view more agreeable. A second plausible explanation is that consistent minorities elicit more communication from the majority than inconsistent minorities, and thus have a greater opportunity to persuade the majority of the wisdom of their point of view.

Whatever the reason, it does seem that consistency can sometimes lead to attitude change. Thus there may be hope for teachers who consistently espouse the value of particular behaviors—even if the majority in the class initially hold a very different point of view.

invariably, to suggest giving Rocco another chance). The second confederate, called the "slider," first disagreed with the group but later changed his opinion to match that of the group. The final confederate (the deviant) consistently dissented from the group's majority opinion.

At the end of the discussion, the experimenter informed the group members that it might be necessary to decrease the size of the group in the future. Each subject then was asked to indicate, by a secret ballot, the names of others in the group whom he would like to have remain. As you might guess, the person who was least likely to be included was the deviant; he was chosen significantly fewer times than the other two confederates. In addition, tallies of the number of communications directed to the various group members showed that although initially many attempts were made to change the mind of the deviant confederate, by the end of the session there was little attempt made to communicate with him at all. It thus appears that deviants from majority group opinion tend to be rejected by the members of the group and that, in some senses, acquiescence to the group is a "reasonable" strategy to bring about acceptance.

What can a teacher do about it?

How does a teacher deal with conformity pressures that exist in the classroom? Obviously, it is unreasonable to suggest that students with deviant opinions be encouraged to conform to the group, simply for the sake of being accepted. A more rational strategy is to encourage a change in the norms of the classroom group, in order to bring about an environment that is more accepting of deviance and more tolerant of dissenting opinions. One way to do this is to encourage dissent actively, by producing evidence that historically, people holding deviant opinions have made some of the greatest contributions to society and the world (for example, Copernicus and Freud). Another way, which is likely to be even more successful, is to make explicit the nature of the norms that operate in a classroom and to show the damaging effects they may have on both the majority and the minority. By discussing with the students themselves the norms that exist in a class, it is possible to clarify and identify the types of pressures that exist and ultimately to change the environment to a more accepting one.

Norms

In the 1930s, Bennington College in Vermont could be characterized politically, economically, and socially as having a liberal, almost radical, atmosphere. Yet most of the students came from homes that were upper-class and conservative, and on entering Bennington, they had themselves held conservative attitudes. What was the change that occurred? A study of the students' attitudes suggested that the liberal norms of the school tended to "convert" the conservatives to liberalism. There was strong approval of liberal attitudes by faculty and upperclassmen, as well as relatively great exposure to politically oriented information (Newcomb, 1961).

Norms and academic performance

As can be seen from the Bennington study, and from the research on conformity discussed earlier, norms can be influential in changing attitudes. It turns out that the type of norms that exist in a given group also are related to academic performance. For instance, one study vividly illustrated that particular groups within an English boys' high school held different norms for acceptable behavior (Hargreaves, 1967). The school was divided into five ability groupings, based on scores achieved on examinations that the boys had taken before they entered the school. What is interesting is that even though particular students were shifted from one group to another over the course of their four-year attendance, the behavioral norms within a particular group remained constant.

The boys in the highest-ability group held norms that were consistent with the stated, formal goals of the school. Academic achievement was highly valued, and teachers were held in high esteem. The norms also held that cheating and plagiarism should be punished severely. In addition, the members of this group all endorsed these particular norms.

The second group of boys held different norms. They were less academically committed, and group members who "messed about" in class were highly esteemed. Strict adherence to rules was looked down upon. But in contrast to the highest-ability group, there was less agreement between what the boys actually thought and the norms that influenced their behavior.

The third and fourth groups had norms that diverged the most from the formal goals of the school. Indeed, there was active antagonism toward academic excellence, and in the lowest group, poor performance was actually encouraged. There was a relatively high rate of delinquent behaviors; truancy and lateness to class were valued; and in the lowest-ability group, physical coercion was used against group members who followed the teachers' orders.

It should be noted, however, that in some of the groups, there were subgroups that held different norms from those predominant in the larger groups. For instance, there was a deviant subgroup in the third-lowest group which held norms that were congruent with those in the highest-ability group. They attended school more regularly, listened to the teacher more, and held school work to be important more than the rest of the members of their group. Another point is that the differing norms prevailing in the four groups resulted in very little intergroup interaction, which in turn resulted in the development of stereotyped attitudes of group members toward the members of other groups. For example, the fourth group was seen to be made up of troublemakers, and the highest group was viewed as being snobbish.

Perhaps the most important point to emerge from Hargreaves's study concerns the finding that boys who moved from one ability group to another changed their attitudes and behavior to be congruent with the norms that existed in their new group. It is not surprising that classroom behavior and attitude toward the teachers would change. But it turned out that even academic performance was affected: Boys who were moved from one group to another modified their academic achievement—up or down—to be congruent with the norms of the new group.

The implications of this study for classroom teachers are clear. Individuals will be less motivated to perform at their highest possible level if the norms within their peer group say that academic success is undesirable. Of course, the converse holds: students can be motivated to do their best if their group's norms are congruent with the goals of the school and encourage high academic performance. Thus one way to motivate students to perform at high levels is to encourage the development of norms within a class that are favorable to academic achievement.

Norms and social class

The importance of norms has been shown to be especially great when examining social-class factors. Lower-class and minority group students tend to value academic success less and to have lower expectations about their performance than do middle-class and majority students. However, these values are affected by the group norms prevalent within the school social situation. Thus lower-class students who begin to attend a primarily middle-class school and make friends with middle-class students tend to show increases in achievement and aspirations. On the other hand, middle-class students attending schools with primarily lower-class children may show a corresponding drop in aspiration and achievement. And the greater the proportion of students in a school from a particular group, the greater the likelihood that the individual will form friendships with people from that group and be influenced by the norms of the group. Interestingly, however, the results for middle-class and lower-class students are not entirely symmetrical: it appears that lower-class students are *more* influenced by middle-class students than middle-class students are influenced by lower-class students (Bain and Anderson, 1974; Kandel and Lesser, 1970).

Group Cohesiveness

Perhaps the only pleasant aspect of taking a course from a truly poor teacher is the camaraderie that can grow among the members of the class. Sharing in the misery of boring lectures and inept tests somehow can make the experience more bearable. And in the process, attraction to the other class members can grow substantially.

cohesiveness the degree to which the group members want to belong and be a part of the group

The characteristic that refers to how much individual members are attracted to the group is known as *group cohesiveness*. Cohesiveness can be formally defined as the degree to which the group members want to belong to and be a part of the group. Determining the cohesiveness of a group allows a relatively direct comparison among various groups. In addition, measuring cohesiveness can provide a teacher with some very interesting insights into the patterns of friendship that exist within a class. Sometimes, in fact, quite unexpected findings will emerge.

Measuring cohesiveness

The most direct way of measuring cohesiveness in a class is simply to ask each student who their one or two most preferred partners would be when engaging in a particular activity. The activity could vary, depending on the specific area of greatest interest to the teacher. For instance, each student might be asked which two people he would most like to sit next to on a bus to a field trip visit to a museum. Once these choices are made, it is possible to tabulate the data and find out who are the most popular children (those who are chosen the most) and who are the isolates (those who are not chosen at all).

sociogram a chart that shows the choices made by and toward each individual who has been asked to name preferred partners in a group

It is also useful to illustrate the children's choices graphically in what is known as a *sociogram*—a chart that shows the choices made by and toward each individual in a group. A simplified example is shown in Figure 9-1—a sociogram of five individuals. Each letter represents an individual, and each arrow pointed toward a letter represents a choice of that person by another.

FIGURE 9-1   A Simple Sociogram

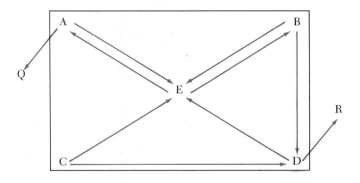

Hence, person E has chosen persons A and B but has been chosen by persons A, B, C, and D. It is clear that person E is quite popular. One can also quickly see from a sociogram who is an isolate, a person not chosen by anyone. In this case, it is person C. By allowing students to choose individuals who are not members of the class, it is also possible to determine roughly the overall level of cohesiveness of the group—by counting the number of times group members are chosen and comparing it to the number of times individuals outside the group are chosen. In Figure 9-1, persons Q and R are the only two chosen from outside the group (compared with eight choices of persons within the group). This suggests that the group is relatively cohesive.

The example chosen is relatively simple, since it involves only a five-student group. Unfortunately, things can get complicated very quickly. Imagine the number of arrows, and the complexity of the sociogram, when a class of, say, twenty-five students is involved. Still, it is possible to construct a sociogram even with this many pupils, and it is well worth the effort for a classroom teacher. Many interesting and unexpected findings can emerge when a sociogram is constructed and examined, and a teacher can learn quite a bit about friendship patterns in the class that may not have been evident previously. In fact, there is research evidence showing that teachers do not always have a good conception of their students' friendship patterns. For example, some studies show that teachers tend to believe that students who relate well to *them* (and to adults in general) are more popular than they actually are with their peers. Moreover, they tend to underestimate the popularity of children who do poorly in school or who have low ability (Barclay, 1966).

Cohesiveness in the classroom

You may wonder why knowledge of group cohesiveness would be important to a teacher. Should teachers really care whether or not the students like their class and enjoy one another, as long as they are learning? The answer is that cohesiveness is in fact quite important, since many studies show that cohesiveness is directly related to the successful functioning of a group. For instance, most research shows that highly cohesive groups have a lower rate of absenteeism among the members. In addition, there is generally more participation in groups that are high in cohesiveness (Cartwright, 1968).

There is also evidence showing that groups that are highly cohesive tend to be more influential over the membership than those that are low in cohesiveness. Conformity also tends to be higher in such groups. One might expect from this finding that the more cohesive a class, the more enthusiastic and energetic its members would be in carrying out their assignments and other classroom activities—and this is so when the norms and goals of the class are related to academic success. But cohesiveness can be a two-edged sword. If the goals of the group are not oriented toward classroom success but instead value nonacademic activities, or—even worse—if the group's goals are anti-academic, then a high rate of cohesiveness in the class can be a real liability to a classroom teacher.

There is one other way in which the degree of cohesiveness of a class can affect the group, and this is related to the personal adjustment of its members. There is some evidence from research on groups in industry that members of high-cohesive groups feel less nervous about their work than do members of low-cohesive groups. In addition, high-cohesive group members seem to feel comparatively more secure and less anxious, and they have higher self-esteem (Cartwright, 1968). Although research done on nonclassroom groups must be generalized very cautiously to educational settings, these findings do suggest that students will perform better in highly cohesive classrooms than in those in which the group is relatively low in cohesiveness.

sociometric index a numerical index that is used to identify differences between people on the basis of social constructs

There is in fact some direct experimental evidence regarding group cohesiveness and classroom performance. In one older study, students were grouped according to their sociometric choices and a *sociometric index* was developed so that classes consisted of people who liked one another (Zeleny, 1939). Not surprisingly, morale tended to rise. These results suggest that if morale is indeed higher in highly cohesive groups, then members of such classes might be expected to learn better and more efficiently than members of groups that are low in cohesiveness. In a test of this hypothesis, a series of three-person groups were formed that varied in cohesiveness, as measured by the stated preferences of the subjects (Shaw and Shaw, 1962). The groups were asked to learn to spell lists of words, with the members working together in their groups. Attitudinal and performance measures were afterward obtained, and both kinds of measures showed that the highly cohesive groups were generally superior. Compared to low-cohesive groups, the members of the high-cohesive groups were more cooperative and friendly, there was more verbal praise for fellow group members, the groups did more planning about how they would approach the problem, and a more democratic type of leadership tended to emerge. In addition, considerably more nontask, social kinds of activity emerged in high-cohesive groups.

However, the most interesting and suggestive results came from the measures of how many words the group members learned to spell. Initially, the high-cohesive groups performed better than the lower-cohesive groups. However, over the course of the experiment, the performances of the high-cohesive groups declined. The reason? The subjects spent more and more time socializing and less time working on the task at hand. Thus high cohesiveness in a classroom might turn out to be something of a mixed blessing.

Suggestions for promoting cohesiveness

Other research tends to support, although not consistently, the hypothesis that groups perform better when they are high in cohesiveness. Hence it seems that cohesiveness might be something that a teacher would want to encourage in the classroom. Unfortunately, there is no ready recipe that will ensure a high level of cohesiveness within a classroom. But there are a number of factors that do appear to enhance the development of cohesiveness, and a teacher might keep the following preconditions of cohesiveness in mind:

1. *Communication.* A number of studies have found that allowing frequent opportunities for the members of a group to communicate with one another leads to increased cohesiveness. For instance, a study by Bovard (1956) showed that teachers who participated in class discussions as members of the discussion group, as opposed to teachers who led the discussion by talking privately to one student at a time, tended to produce more cohesive groups.

2. *Class climate.* Class climate refers to the general social atmosphere of a classroom. A warm, accepting, and pleasant class climate will lead to greater cohesiveness among the students. A teacher should strive to maintain an open relationship with his or her students, one in which the students feel able to communicate their desires and feelings to the teacher. Such a climate is likely to result in increased cohesiveness among the members of the class.

3. *Size of group.* Much research has shown that as group size increases, cohesiveness decreases. Although it is rare that a teacher will have control over the size of his or her class, it may be possible to break a class down into smaller units if it is very large. Doing so may initiate the development of cohesiveness within the subgroups, and ultimately in the class as a whole.

4. *Competition.* When a group is placed in the position of competing against another group, there is usually an increase in cohesiveness—within both groups. Thus, allowing classes to compete against one another should lead to enhanced group cohesiveness. A tournament of games, a spelling bee, or any other situation in which students compete as a class to attain some desirable goal, ought to be quite effective in increasing cohesiveness. (See the box on page 304.)

These four factors constitute the primary ways that cohesiveness can be increased in a classroom situation. But keep in mind the caution mentioned

Promoting Group Cohesiveness

One technique for increasing group cohesiveness was discovered many years ago by psychologist Muzafer Sherif in a classic study (Sherif, Harvey, White, Hood, and Sherif, 1961). The experiment was set in a boys camp in Oklahoma known as Robbers Cove. Not knowing that they were to be participants in a study, two busloads of boys arrived at camp and were sent to separate cabins quite a distance from each other. For the first week of camp, the boys played solely with, and engaged in activities that required a good deal of cooperation with, boys from their own cabin. This cooperation led to the development of a strong sense of group cohesiveness—but only regarding their own cabin mates.

Because cooperation among group members had led to the development of cohesiveness, Sherif reasoned that group competitiveness could lead to intergroup hostility. In order to test this hypothesis, he arranged for a tournament of games between the two cabins. After a sportsmanlike beginning, the tournament degenerated into fighting and name-calling, and it was clear that members of each group felt quite hostile toward members of the other group.

Having demonstrated clearly how group hostility could be produced, the research turned to the question of how cohesiveness could be increased—a cohesiveness that would encompass the camp as a whole. One possibility was to give the boys a chance for pleasant, stress-free interaction. But this proved to be completely ineffective in reducing intergroup conflict: whenever the boys were together, there was immediate fighting and name-calling.

Recalling that cooperation had originally served to unite the boys within their own cabins, Sherif solved the problem by using a similar technique. He devised a series of (bogus) emergencies in which it was necessary for members of *both* cabins to cooperate with one another in order to alleviate the difficulty. For instance, the water in the camp went off, and the boys had to form a bucket brigade to haul water to the camp. Sherif termed the goal for which cooperation was necessary a "superordinate goal," because to be attained, the goal required the active participation of both groups. The use of superordinate goals remains one of the most effective techniques for bringing about cohesiveness in members of hostile groups.

earlier: if the norms of a class are such that academic competence is looked down upon, the increase in cohesiveness will result in greater problems than the teacher had before. For this reason, the teacher ought to have a good idea of what the specific norms and values of a class are before trying to boost group cohesiveness.

CLASSROOM POWER AND LEADERSHIP

Suppose you were asked to be the teacher in a situation in which you were to teach a series of paired words to a learner. You are to read the word pairs aloud to the learner, who is in an adjacent room, and then test him on his recollection of the words. To promote learning, each time the learner makes a mistake, you are to administer an electric shock using a shock generator with a series of switches. The generator is designed to give increasingly severe shocks, starting at 30 volts and going all the way up to 450 volts, in 30-volt increments. The shock switches also have verbal designations, ranging from "slight shock," through "intense shock," to "danger: severe shock," to three ominous red X's at 450 volts. According to the instructions given to you, you are to increase the severity of the shock for each wrong answer.

Would you agree to be the teacher under these circumstances? And if you did agree to teach, how severe a shock would you administer before you stopped?

Answers to these questions are suggested by a series of experiments carried out by Stanley Milgram in the early 1960s (summarized in Milgram, 1974). In the studies, the subject was the teacher, and the point was to determine how severe a shock subjects would administer before they refused to continue with the experiment. The results of the studies suggest first, that you would readily have agreed to be the teacher under such circumstances. Almost none of Milgram's subjects, when informed of the nature of the teaching, refused to participate in the study. The answer to the second question is more unsettling. If you are like the majority of the subjects that were studied, you would give the highest level shock (450 volts) to your student if the experimenter urged you to do so. Fully 60 percent of the subjects continued giving shocks to the highest level. (You may be somewhat relieved to learn that in reality none of the "learners" received any shocks; the learner was a confederate of the experimenter. But the teachers didn't know this, and their behavior toward their students is both startling and revealing.)

Although Milgram was primarily concerned with obedience to the experimenter's authority, the studies are of interest here because of their use of the teacher-student relationship. Milgram chose this particular context because it seemed quite plausible for a teacher to wield such authority over a student. Indeed, teachers are generally expected to be strong, authoritative figures. In this section of the chapter, research is examined that bears on the teacher's special role in the classroom in terms of power and leadership. In this context, the teacher is viewed as a member of the classroom group, but a somewhat special member.

A Typology of Power

Let us begin by examining the types of power that teachers can employ in classrooms (French and Raven, 1959):

1. *Attraction Power*—power that is due to the attractiveness of the teacher, how much the teacher is liked or identified with by his or her students
2. *Reward Power*—power that derives from the teacher's ability to provide rewards (such as grades, extra recess, etc.) for the students
3. *Coercive Power*—power that is based on the teacher's ability to punish the students
4. *Legitimate Power*—power that resides in the students' belief that teachers have the right, simply because of their role or position, to control students' behavior
5. *Expert Power*—power that is based on the students' belief that the teacher knows more and has greater resources with respect to a particular body of knowledge.

It seems likely that students would prefer teachers who use expert or attraction power, rather than teachers who employ legitimate or coercive power, and research bears this out. Coercive power, particularly, has been shown to be an undesirable technique for maintaining leadership. For instance, Kounin (1970) found that teachers who relied on coercive power alone were markedly less effective than teachers who used coercive power but also held attraction power. (Interestingly, these results are congruent with what learning theorists have found: as discussed in Chapter 6, techniques involving punishment are usually less effective than positive reinforcement in modifying behavior.)

Another problem that occurs with the use of both coercive power and reward power is that eventually they can be used up (Guskin and Guskin, 1970). A teacher who uses punishment too frequently may find that students habituate to it and that it no longer has much impact on them. For instance, if a child were frequently not allowed to go out for recess but instead had to stay in the classroom, what would his reaction be? At first he would likely be quite frustrated and angry, but eventually he would learn to adapt to the situation by amusing himself in some way (no doubt in a way that his teacher would not approve!). In a similar fashion, it is possible to use too much reward power. Students in a class in which the teacher gives A's 95 percent of the time will not be particularly motivated to do their best work. The same principle holds true for verbal praise: indiscriminate positive verbal reinforcement will soon lose its effectiveness if the teacher constantly responds to the students' answers with "good!"—regardless of the quality of the answer.

There is also good reason to believe that students' perceptions of what motivates a teacher's use of power will affect how cooperative they are. If the teacher is seen to use power in a benevolent way, for the good of the students, then it is likely that there will be more positive effects than if the teacher is seen as using power for less positive or for selfish reasons. Indeed, there is evidence from research carried out in nonschool settings that individual performance is a function of the perception of the motives of a powerful person. One study, for instance (Komorita, Sheposh, and Braver, 1968), examined the effect of perceiving that a high-power group member intended to use his power benevolently, malevolently, or passively (that is, not use his power). The greatest cooperation and best performance occurred in the benevolent condition; the malevolent condition produced the worst cooperation and lowest performance. Thus the perceived intentions of the high-power individual can affect the performance of low-power individuals.

Leadership in Classrooms

Apart from the formal power that teachers have, what determines how effective they will be as leaders? One approach has been to study stylistic and personality characteristics of the leader in order to learn the specific behaviors that seem to be associated with group effectiveness.

Leadership style

The classic study on leadership style was carried out by Kurt Lewin and his colleagues Ronald Lippitt and Robert White (summarized in White and Lippitt, 1966). The investigators were asking a question that they felt had wide implications for society: What are the effects of autocratic, democratic, and laissez-faire leadership styles? The three styles were experimentally produced in a small-group setting of 11-year-old boys who had joined after-school hobby groups. The groups were led by an adult who behaved in a way that was authoritarian, democratic, or laissez-faire, respectively. Each group experienced all three kinds of leadership.

In the *authoritarian* condition, the leader decided the policy for the group and told the group members exactly how to proceed in their activities, without any consultation with the members themselves. The directives were given piecemeal to make sure that future activities would be uncertain. The autocratic leader was quite subjective in his praise and criticism of the group members, and an attempt was made to have him appear to be relatively impersonal and aloof. In contrast, the *democratic* leader allowed the group members to participate in the making of decisions, and the group determined its own policy. The group leader was not passive, however; he suggested general ways to proceed, and he proposed alternative activities that could be carried out.

The members of the group were able to choose who to work with, and the leader was objective in his praise and criticism of the members. In contrast to both the authoritarian and the democratic group leaders, the *laissez-faire* leader gave the boys complete freedom in planning and carrying out their activities. When asked for comments and suggestions, he responded; but otherwise, he was essentially a nonparticipant.

As you might expect, the style of leadership markedly affected the behavior of group members. Very detailed records were kept of the members' conversations, interactions, and behaviors, and analysis of these results showed that there were quite a few differences according to leadership style. There was almost thirty times more hostility in the autocratic groups than in the democratic groups, and aggression was eight times more frequent in the autocratic than in the democratic groups. The autocratic groups tended to find a scapegoat and blame problems on that one individual, and they liked their leader significantly less than did the other groups. The members of the laissez-faire groups tended to be less task-oriented, and they engaged in more horseplay than the other groups. There was also a larger amount of within-group friction between members.

In terms of productivity of the groups, the results were somewhat less pronounced. There was no significant difference in the number of completed products (such as the number of toy models produced). There was, however, a difference in the quality of products; the democratic groups tended to make things that were of significantly higher quality than the products of the other two types of groups.

The conclusion that can be drawn from this study is that the democratic group leader is the most effective, and that notion has received a good deal of support (Anderson, 1970; Withall, 1951). However, it seems that democratic leaders are not *always* superior to autocratic leaders and that, in fact, there are times when authoritarian leadership results in more success. For instance, McKeachie (1963) suggested that authoritarian teaching techniques may be the most effective when facts and concepts are being taught, even though they are not as successful in promoting positive attitudes. In a sense, it becomes a matter of values: Should teachers be primarily interested in academic learning per se, or ought they to be more concerned with attitudes?

Personality and leadership

Rather than focusing on a leader's style, another approach to classroom leadership has examined personality characteristics of the leader. Indeed, there are more than 1,000 separate studies that have attempted to determine what personality traits are shared by all successful leaders. Unfortunately, the results of this extensive research are not all that useful. In a review of the literature on personality measures, Gibb (1969) found that only a few characteristics appear to be correlated with successful leadership, and these are not particularly informative. Leaders, compared to followers, tend to be more intelligent, taller, more attractive, better adjusted, and more confident. But the traits vary

Research suggests that a democratic style of leadership is most successful in many situations. (© Michal Heron 1981/Woodfin Camp & Assoc.)

so much from one situation to another that there is little consistency, and the correlations that are found are generally low. Indeed, only intelligence is associated consistently with leadership, and even then only when certain kinds of leadership are considered. In addition, if leaders are much more intelligent than their followers, they tend to lose their effectiveness. Thus the search for evidence of a particular set of traits related to leadership has been unsuccessful. It does not appear that successful leaders can be characterized on the basis of personality type.

An interactional model of leadership

An alternative, and much more fruitful, approach to leadership has been concerned not just with characteristics of the leader but with the nature of the situation in which leaders find themselves. The basic premise of the approach is that under certain kinds of situations one kind of leadership style might be most effective, while in other circumstances another leadership style might be most effective. There is thus an *interaction* between leader personality and situational factors.

The major theoretical model of leadership that has simultaneously considered the characteristics of the leader and the situation is known as the *contingency model* of leader effectiveness (Fiedler, 1971, 1978). Although the model is meant to apply primarily to task-oriented work groups, it seems reasonable to assume that the theory is also applicable to classroom situations, particularly where the children work together to accomplish joint goals.

The major variable regarding the leader relates to the attitude that he or she holds toward a person called the "least preferred co-worker" (LPC). LPC's are the individuals whom leaders name as persons with whom they have the greatest difficulty getting along, out of all the people they have ever worked with. The leaders are then asked to rate their LPC's on a series of descriptive scales, which include such adjective pairs as "pleasant-unpleasant," "friendly-unfriendly," and "boring-interesting." It turns out that some leaders rate their LPC's relatively high, finding some good in even those they prefer not to work with. These people are said to be high-LPC leaders. On the other hand, some leaders rate their LPC's quite severely, and these are considered low-LPC leaders.

The second part of the contingency model concerns the situation. The model suggests that there are three characteristics of the situation that need to be considered: (1) the *affective relations* between the leader and members of the group; (2) the amount of *structure* in the task the group is carrying out; and (3) the *power position* of the leader. The affective component, which is the most important, refers to the degree to which the leader is supported by the members and has their loyalty. The structure dimension is related to the degree of clarity or ambiguity inherent in the task. Finally, the third dimension, the leader's power position, is related to the degree of power the leader maintains over the other members of the group. Power, here, is related to how the leader is able to reward, punish, and recommend sanctions against the members of the group.

Fiedler's research has shown that by combining the three characteristics of the situation just discussed, it is possible to order situations in terms of their favorability to the leader. The most favorable situation is one in which leader-member affective relations are positive, the task is highly structured, and the leader power position is strong. The worst situation is one in which the affective relations are poor, the task is unstructured, and the power position is weak. The other combinations fall along a continuum, as shown in Figure 9-2. As can be seen from the figure, the leadership style best suited for each of the combinations forms an inverted U shape on the graph. From the figure it can be seen that high-LPC leaders tend to perform best under conditions of moderate favorability for the leader. In contrast, low-LPC leaders are best under conditions at the two extremes of the leadership favorability continuum: when the conditions are either very good or very poor, low-LPC leaders elicit optimal performance.

The reason that high- and low-LPC leaders differ in their effectiveness has to do with the personality characteristics that are associated with the two leadership styles. High-LPC leaders tend to be permissive, considerate, and sensitive individuals, and this type of person tends to reduce the anxiety of the group members. Thus when the task is moderately unstructured or the power position is weak, the high-LPC can overcome the unfavorable conditions because of his or her positive personal qualities. If the situation is extremely adverse, however, the low-LPC is superior. The low-LPC leader tends to be assertive, very directive and controlling, and he or she is able to hold the group together. But why should the low-LPC leader also do well when the situation is very favorable? The answer is that in very favorable situations, the group is ready to be directed by the leader and is task-oriented. The low-LPC is quite adept at managing such a situation.

A wide variety of evidence supports the contingency model of leadership, and it appears to be the best and most sophisticated model for determining leadership effectiveness. Unfortunately, almost all the available evidence in support of the theory has come from groups in vocational and military settings, as well as from laboratory experiments. Thus one can only speculate about how closely the model approximates leadership in classroom settings. But it seems clear that there are rather strong implications for teachers and students. One might expect that a relatively easy-going, open, and relaxed teacher would be most successful in classes that were relatively organized, structured, and accepting of the teacher's authority. In contrast, a strict, task-oriented disciplinarian might be expected to produce the greatest learning in situations in which the class either was disorganized and questioned the teacher's authority, or was relatively passive and accepting of the teacher's power position. One can see from this that the same teachers will not always be successful; a lot will depend on the particular position in which they find themselves.

FIGURE 9-2   Optimal Leadership Style According to Fiedler's Model

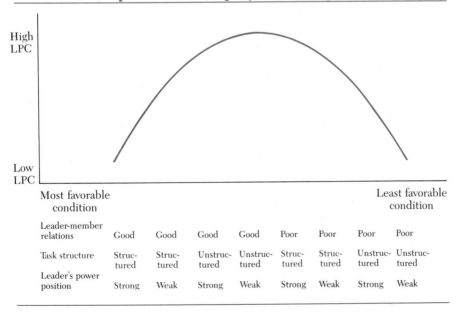

	Most favorable condition							Least favorable condition
Leader-member relations	Good	Good	Good	Good	Poor	Poor	Poor	Poor
Task structure	Structured	Structured	Unstructured	Unstructured	Structured	Structured	Unstructured	Unstructured
Leader's power position	Strong	Weak	Strong	Weak	Strong	Weak	Strong	Weak

LEARNING IN GROUPS

According to one Soviet elementary school manual, the very first thing that a teacher should say to his or her class on the opening day of school is, "Let's see which *row* can sit the straightest." The purpose of this statement is immediately to impart the message that each student is interdependent on and must cooperate with the other members of his or her row. This interdependence becomes the basis for classroom success; rows are rewarded for strong academic performance, and members of a row help one another for the sake of the group's success.

Such Soviet techniques for educating elementary school students, described by psychologist and educator Urie Bronfenbrenner (1962), are in contrast to typical American procedures, in which students work independently and compete with their peers. However, as the Soviet example shows, it is just as feasible—although much less traditional in our own society—to have people learn material cooperatively, working together to attain some joint level of competence. In this section, some of the ways in which groups have been shown to affect individual performance are examined. Some recent innovative group techniques that have actually been employed successfully in classrooms are then discussed.

Effects of Working in Groups

Historically, one of the very first laboratory-type experiments concerning social and group factors examined performance when individuals were alone versus performance in groups. In 1897, Norman Triplett looked at a very mundane motor skill: he observed whether individuals working alone or in pairs turned fishing reels more rapidly. He found that children working alone moved the reels significantly more slowly than children who were competing with a *social facilita-* partner. This effect, which is now called *social facilitation,* has withstood the *tion the prin-* test of time (and much more sophisticated examination). It seems quite clear *ciple that per-* that performance in simple tasks is improved by the mere presence of others. *formance on* And not just motor tasks are affected; on tests of memory and verbal skills, *certain tasks is* people seem to do better when others are present than when they are alone. *improved when* However, later research has modified the findings. It turns out that only *the tasks are* well-learned skills show social facilitation effects. When individuals engage in *conducted in* an unfamiliar or unpracticed task, the presence of others has an inhibitory *the presence of* effect, and performance is lower than when the task is performed alone. Thus *another person* on a test for which they had done a great deal of studying students would probably score higher if they took the test with their classmates than if they took it alone. On the other hand, on a test in which the material was not too familiar or for which they had not spent too much time or effort studying, they might score higher if they took the test alone.

Interacting with others

Although the results of studies on social facilitation effects have implications for student performance, they do not get at the more interesting question of how level of performance is affected by interacting with others. The basic question here is whether groups or individuals perform better. Although this is a complicated question—and one that depends on the nature of the task, the kinds of measures employed, and whether one is looking at the number or quality of the solutions produced (André, Schumer, and Whitaker, 1979)—the best evidence seems to suggest that groups do, in fact, produce a greater number of, and better, solutions to problems than do individuals (Shaw, 1976). Thus, if a group is asked to solve some sort of analytical problem, the group will probably come to a solution that is qualitatively better than the *average* quality of the solutions of the same individual's working alone. There are a number of reasons for the group superiority, including the rejection by the group of individual errors, the greater influence of the most competent group member, the greater interest in the task when it is carried out in the group, and probably most important, the initial increase in the number of ideas that can be examined in the group.

The superiority of group performance is mitigated somewhat when *time* is taken into consideration, however. In terms of efficiency (measured by the number of hours invested in obtaining a solution), individuals are superior to groups. Thus there appears to be something of a trade-off involved in the use of groups. The group may obtain a better solution than the individuals would alone, but it is at the expense of time.

The fact that better *solutions* to problems are obtained from group interaction suggests that there is something about the interaction process itself which leads to different solutions than would be obtained by merely combining the individual responses. If this is the case, it would seem that behaviors occur within the group that would not occur if the members were by themselves. Thus group experience could be expected also to affect how well a particular set of materials is *learned*.

In fact, it does appear that members of groups who jointly attempt to master a lesson can perform at higher levels than those who learn the material on their own. There are some interesting experimental studies that attest to this fact. For instance, one study (Perlmutter and deMontmollin, 1952) examined learning in French Sorbonne students who worked either alone or in groups. The task was to memorize nonsense syllables (three-letter units that have no meaning). Half of the subjects began by working individually within the presence of others and then, after a 15-minute break, worked in a three-person group.

The other subjects first worked in groups, and then worked alone. The results showed the clear superiority of group performance: There was significantly greater learning when the subjects were in groups than when they were working individually. But a further interesting finding emerged: Those subjects who had worked in groups first, and then worked individually, later performed

Although learning in groups has been found to be superior in many respects to learning alone, group learning techniques are not widely employed in schools today. (© Donald Dietz 1980/Stock, Boston)

at significantly higher levels as individuals than those persons who had not had the group experience prior to working alone (although they still performed worse alone than while in the groups). It thus seems that the group experience had an effect on the subsequent individual learning of the subjects.

Other, more naturalistic, studies show the same effect. For instance, one experiment examined the learning of a ghost story called the "War of the Ghosts" by groups of children (Yucer, 1955). The children heard the story in groups of four and then were asked to recall it either alone or with their group. Group performance was best in almost all of the forty groups studied.

What is it about groups that can result in superior learning? No one knows for sure, but researchers suspect that it has something to do with the *interaction processes* that occur when an individual finds himself or herself in a group (Webb, 1982). When a person is part of a group, a number of things occur that don't happen outside of a group. First, the other group members can provide increased motivation and stimulation. Since people usually try to present themselves favorably to others, the group experience may put people on their best behavior. A second factor may be that the group encourages a higher level of thinking—more abstract and contemplative—than that which the individual alone engages in (Sharon and Sharon, 1976). The contributions of others must be understood, synthesized, and evaluated, and this takes cognitive effort. In the end, such effort may result in superior learning of the material being discussed. Finally, there is the simple fact that greater resources are available in a group. If you were attempting to find a solution to a difficult problem, wouldn't you try to bring together as much information and advice as you could? In a similar fashion, the group provides disparate points of view that can enhance the understanding of a problem.

Issues relating to group learning

Since most of the evidence just reviewed seems to suggest that learning in groups can be better than learning alone, a very reasonable question comes to mind: Why is it so rare to find groups employed in classrooms? The answer hinges on a number of interrelated factors. One reason is that while groups may produce better learning, they are generally not as efficient. In other words, it often takes the average group member a longer time to learn material than it would take him or her to learn the same amount of material individually. Another factor that militates against the use of groups in classrooms is that groups can sometimes be relatively distracting and overstimulating, which can lead to a lack of concentration on the part of group members. This depends, of course, on the kinds of norms inherent in the group and in the classroom, but it can make a real difference in group performance. Indeed, it is usually the case that only small groups—of around seven or fewer persons—can successfully be used, because larger groups suffer from communication problems that can lead to difficulties in group performance.

Perhaps the most important reason for the relatively small use of groups is one that is far removed from the actual workings of groups: Group learning is not in line with the predominant American values of competition and individualism. As will be suggested in later chapters, the values that are held by a particular cultural group influence to a great extent what is deemed appropriate by that culture. The dominant value of American classrooms seems to be one of interpersonal competition. David Johnson and Roger Johnson point out that there is a great deal of evidence supporting the following conclusions:

1. Most American students think that schooling is a competitive situation
2. American school children, in general, are more competitive than children from other cultures
3. American children show increasing competitiveness as they go through school
4. Even within America, members of the dominant "Anglo" culture show greater academic competitiveness than blacks or Mexican-Americans and
5. Children in urban settings are more competitive than those raised in rural settings.

(Johnson and Johnson, 1974, p. 217)

But this does not mean necessarily that competition enhances an individual's success in school. There is evidence suggesting that, in fact, competition does

not produce higher achievement. Competitive motivation may produce interference with complex problem-solving processes, because the individual spends
insufficient time dealing with the problem itself and exerts a disproportionate
amount of energy on interpersonal competition. Even the idea that competition
"builds character" seems to be a myth. For instance, in one experiment
(Ogilvie and Tutko, 1971) the effects of competition on personality development
in athletes were studied. Over an 8-year period, no evidence that personality
was enhanced by competition was found, and in fact athletic competition
appeared to hinder development in some areas.

Despite these problems from the effects of competition, outperforming one's
peers still represents the dominant value orientation in America. And one
suspects that the use of cooperative groups in schools is relatively infrequent
because of the normative constraints against them. These constraints are seldom
explicit, but probably they are largely responsible for the fact that group
learning has not enjoyed much popularity in the past, at least in schools in the
United States.

However, the use of groups in schools has an enthusiastic array of supporters,
and a number of techniques have been developed to employ cooperation
among students (Owens and Barnes, 1982). Two major methods of cooperative
learning in groups, which have been developed in recent years, can be
discussed.

The jigsaw technique

Social psychologist Elliott Aronson has developed a method of group learning
that has been used in a number of elementary schools in the United States.
The technique is based on the principles of building a jigsaw puzzle (Lucker,
Rosenfield, Sikes, and Aronson, 1976). As everyone knows, jigsaw puzzles are
constructed by taking various odd-shaped pieces, and putting them together
to form a meaningful whole. In the same way, Aronson and his colleagues
have suggested that students working together in groups can each be given a
relatively small amount of information and then can teach the material to their
group partners. When the information is put together, it forms a coherent
whole, and the group can understand fully the content of the lesson.

As an example, a teacher might want his or her students to learn about the
life of Einstein. One pupil in a six-person group might be given information
about his early childhood and difficulties in school, another might be told
about his university career, another about the development of his famous
theories, and so forth. Each segment of information could be given in a written
paragraph or two, and each student would receive just one segment. The
student would then be required to study the material so that he or she could
teach it to the others. Because the students are told that there will later be a
quiz on Einstein's entire life, the students are motivated to cooperate with
one another in the teaching-learning process. By the time each group member
has taught his or her part of the lesson, the group as a whole has learned the
complete biography of Einstein. But something more has happened: The group

Power to the Pupil: Peer Tutoring

Tutoring, a practice that was common 100 years ago in small, rural, one-room schools, has been resurrected as a modern-day educational innovation in many school systems. Typically, programs are set up in which older children in an elementary school act as tutors on a weekly basis to younger children (the tutees) in other classrooms. In other cases, same-age and same-grade students tutor each other, alternating in the tutor and tutee roles according to who has the greater expertise in a given subject area (Annis, 1983).

While the benefits to the student being tutored are obvious, the tutor sometimes gains as much or more from the tutoring experience as does the tutee. For instance, one study found that by the end of a 2-week period, fifth graders had learned a set of lesson materials better when they were tutoring the material than when they were simply asked to learn the information for themselves (Allen and Feldman, 1973). Apparently, teaching others enhances motivation to learn the lesson content—if for no other reason than to avoid embarrassment. Moreover, having to think about how to present information so that it will be comprehensible to a tutee forces tutors to think about the material in a qualitatively different way than if they had to learn it only for themselves (Cohen, Kulik, and Kulik, 1982).

There are other reasons why tutoring may bring about positive benefits for the tutor. Tutors often form social relationships with their tutees and are cast into the situation of acting as models for their tutees. This new role can lead to more desirable behavior on the part of the tutor, because being a model can make the tutor more cognizant of the negative consequences of antisocial behavior. Additionally, just being allowed to act as a teacher—a position that traditionally is held in high esteem and certainly has a higher status than the student role—can be beneficial for the tutor.

Tutoring is also beneficial because it can lead to a decrease in egocentrism, the pervasive tendency in young children to view the world from their own point of view. Effective tutors quickly learn that it is necessary to take the perspective of their tutees in order to present material in a way that can be understood by them. Presumably the tutor's loss of egocentrism can generalize past the tutoring situation.

Perhaps the most important benefit to arise from tutoring is that it gives the tutor a chance to help someone else. For most students, such a circumstance is an unusual one; they are usually the recipients of help from others. Altruistic behavior is rewarding in and of itself, and tutoring provides an excellent opportunity for the tutor to provide meaningful aid to another person.

members have formed a cooperative, cohesive unit, and they probably also have learned their own part of the lesson in a different (and better) way than if they had not had to teach it.

The latter point is particularly important. It turns out that people who act as teachers tend to learn material in a more thorough way than if they had studied the material alone, without having later to teach it (Allen and Feldman, 1973). The reason? Basically, the superior learning is due to the higher motivational levels that occur when individuals know they must learn material well enough so that they can eventually impart it to someone else. Teachers don't want to be embarrassed while teaching by having to say that they really don't understand the material they're trying to get someone else to learn. (See the box on page 317.)

The jigsaw technique thus has a number of advantageous results. The students may learn more, they become more cooperative with one another, and some research even suggests that their own self-concepts and their general attitudes toward school become more positive.

The STAD technique

A critical reader might be saying at this point, "Sure, the jigsaw technique improves cooperation, but it does so only because the students have to take a quiz at the end of the lesson. Thus cooperation occurs only because the traditional individualistic, competitive orientation is still around." We agree. But there are other techniques for promoting classroom cooperation that do not rely quite so heavily on individual competitiveness. Instead, competitiveness is turned to a positive end, by devising a system in which the performance of each individual helps others to meet their goals. In other words, rewards are structured so that the *group's* performance determines the reward that will be received by the individual group members.

The model that has incorporated a *cooperative reward structure* to the highest degree has been developed at Johns Hopkins University and is known as the student teams–achievement divisions (STAD) technique (Slavin, 1979). The model consists of two basic elements, teams and achievement divisions. Each team has four or five members, and the members are heterogeneous in terms of past achievement levels, race, sex, and ethnic background. The purpose of a team is to provide practice for its members to take individual quizzes, which occur twice a week. During practice sessions for the team, the group members are given worksheets which include material that will be on the quiz. After the quiz, the individual scores are used to produce team scores, and a class newsletter is published once a week which shows the teams that achieved the highest scores. Thus there is competition within the STAD system, but it is competition between the teams. This leads the students to cooperate with their own team members.

The second part of the model, the achievement divisions, was designed, first, to acknowledge the fact that because of differences in basic ability, not all members of the team could be expected to contribute equally to the team effort, and second, to ensure that all team members would work at their highest level of ability. To form divisions, which are independent of teams, the individuals are ranked in ability, on the basis of teacher ratings and past grades. The six highest students are placed in the first division, the next six in the next division, and so on. The divisions are used for no other purpose than to transform quiz scores into team points; there is no interaction among division members. Students' individual quiz scores are computed on the basis of how well they perform *relative to others in their own division*. If they rank first in the division they receive the highest score; if they rank last, they receive the lowest score, and intermediate scores are calculated similarly. The individual scores of all the people on a team are then tallied together to find a team score. What this means is that a low-achieving student who gets a relatively low absolute score on the quiz may contribute the highest score to his team—if the other members of his division scored lower than he did. On the other hand, a team member who scores very high on the quiz may actually contribute a lower score to his team—if within his division he does poorly. There is also a way of changing division membership each week so as to take performance into account.

The results of this complicated system seem to indicate that it is worth the effort to implement and maintain (and it is quite a bit of work!). The use of teams leads to increases in academic achievement, compared with students who practice the material in more traditional, nonteam ways. The reason for this appears to be, basically, that motivation is increased because of team members' encouragement and support for the students' efforts. There are nonacademic gains as well. Studies have shown that the use of integrated teams increases the amount of cross-racial interaction, even at times other than team meetings. In addition, cross-racial attitudes become more positive for students who participate in integrated teams. More generally, it seems that interpersonal attraction and some components of self-concept are increased through the use of the STAD technique.

Both the jigsaw and the STAD methods appear to be quite useful tools for increasing the amount of cooperation that occurs in classrooms. Although they require a good deal of time and effort, they can be effective in increasing academic achievement and enhancing attitudes toward school and self. But even more important, the two methods may lead to a change in values, from a primarily competitive orientation among students to one of cooperation. And this might be the most beneficial effect of all.

Modifying Group Composition: Ability Grouping

It is quite possible that you recall from your elementary school days a feature that was found in almost every classroom: a ranked series of reading groups. Whether labeled groups 1, 2, and 3, or called "Redbirds," "Bluebirds," and "Blackbirds," the groups clearly were organized around the students' reading ability level. The names fooled no one; every student in the class could rank-order the groups from the highest to the lowest.

homogeneous grouping placing students of similar ability or achievement levels together in groups

In forming such groups, the expectation is that *homogeneous grouping* (in which the members share a similar level of ability or achievement) will facilitate teaching and learning, at least when compared to heterogeneous grouping (where there is a range of abilities represented within each group). The rationale for homogeneous grouping is that when similar students are grouped together, the teacher is able to present materials that are most appropriate to the actual level of the students. In addition, students can advance at their own rate, since their peers will be improving at the same speed. It has even been argued that when students are placed in homogeneous groups, those in the lower groups are challenged to move ahead to the next group, and their motivation is thereby increased (Esposito, 1973).

Of course, there are arguments against homogeneous grouping and in favor of heterogeneity, and they appear to be just as valid. The predominant argument is that homogeneous grouping adversely affects the self-concept of the children in the lower groups by making them feel stigmatized and inept. Similarly, the students in the higher groups may develop self-concepts that are falsely inflated. In addition, *heterogeneous grouping* provides students with the opportunity to work with and learn from students who have greater ability. Heterogeneity is also more reflective of the situations people face when they are adults, and it has been argued that schools should prepare students for getting along and working with all sorts of people. Finally, homogeneous grouping can, in actual practice, result in segregation along racial and economic lines, not just by ability.

heterogeneous grouping grouping students so that there is a range of different ability or achievement levels in each group

There are other reasons for expecting better performance in heterogeneous groups than homogeneous ones. Recall that earlier in the chapter it was suggested that groups seem to perform and learn better than individuals partly because the available range of information, abilities, and skills is greater than when a person is alone. Thus heterogeneous groups might result in increased performance for the group as a whole.

Research findings

The most appropriate means of resolving the issue is to examine the data that have been collected on the relative merits of homogeneous versus heterogeneous grouping. Although ability grouping has a long history—dating back to the 1860s, when St. Louis introduced homogeneous grouping in its elementary schools—it was not until 60 years later that any serious evaluations were carried out. And even the more recent research attempts have not provided definitive answers. Think of what is involved in carrying out such a study. First of all, a decision must be made regarding what kind of ability will be used to group the students. Will it be IQ scores, achievement test scores, grades? And how will the heterogeneous groups be made up? Will subjects be randomly assigned to groups, or should each group consist of an equal proportion of high-, medium-, and low-ability pupils? Finally, what assessment criteria will be employed? Grades? Self-concept measures? Sociometric choices? All of these factors must be considered in designing an experiment.

Given the many difficulties involved in research on homogeneous and heterogeneous grouping, it is not surprising that the evidence collected is open to many interpretations. But a number of statements can be made with relative confidence. After reviewing all the existing literature, Esposito (1973) reports the following conclusions about ability grouping:

1. There is little consistent evidence that homogeneous grouping leads to higher performance. In fact, average and below-average students seem to suffer, although some studies show high-ability students gaining scholastically.
2. The effects of homogeneous grouping on attitudes are essentially negative.
3. Homogeneous grouping may act to foster separation among students and thus be undesirable from a social point of view.

The existing literature thus clearly does not support the use of homogeneous ability grouping. Not only are the academic benefits minimal or entirely lacking, but the effects on such social factors as self-concept and attitudes toward school may be negative. The experimental research done on small-group productivity, which shows the superiority of heterogeneous groups, thus seems to be supported.

Still, you are likely to find ability grouping in many schools, particularly *within* the classroom for the teaching of specialized subjects. The negative effects of homogeneous grouping will not be as strong when it is limited to within-classroom grouping for particular subjects. The greatest difficulties occur when children are placed in completely homogeneous classrooms, in which there is little variation in ability for *all* subjects. Perhaps the best outcome of homogeneous grouping occurs when ability grouping is carried to its logical extreme, which is individualized instruction. Each student can then be placed in his or her own "group" and is not tied to the ability of his or her peers. The trade-off here, of course, is that the benefits of heterogeneity are lost.

SUMMARY

Group processes are an important factor in classroom situations, affecting a student's learning and social activities. Classrooms meet the four criteria that are necessary for a collection of individuals to be considered a group in the formal sense: (1) interaction of members, (2) shared goals and values, (3) interdependence of fates, and (4) perception of group membership.

Conformity, in which there is yielding to group opinion, is particularly prevalent in classrooms. One reason that conformity pressures operate is that groups reject persons who hold deviant points of view. Teachers can consider using strategies that actively encourage dissent, and they can clarify the norms regarding conformity.

Norms, which are the behaviors and activities that are acceptable to and expected from group members, also are related to academic performance. Research has shown that students' classroom behavior is affected by the nature of the norms the students hold. The importance of norms is especially great when examining social-class factors, because lower-class and minority group students tend to value and expect academic success less than do middle-class and majority students.

Group cohesiveness refers to the degree to which the members of a group are attracted to the group. Cohesiveness can be illustrated using a sociogram, a graphical display of group members' choices. Cohesiveness leads to successful classroom functioning, greater participation of the group members, and the potential for better academic performance. Cohesiveness can be promoted by increased communication, positive class atmosphere, smaller group size, and between-group competition.

Teachers are powerful figures, wielding one of five kinds of power: attraction power, reward power, coercive power, legitimate power, and expert power. The type of power employed will determine its level of effectiveness and how cooperative the students are.

Studies of leadership effectiveness show that the leader's style affects a group's productivity and social-emotional climate. Although democratic leaders typically are most effective, in some situations autocratic leaders are better. Interactional models of leadership, which take into account the nature of the situation *and* the leader's personality, have proven to be most effective. The contingency model of leadership considers the affective relations between the leader and members of the group, the degree of task structure, and the power position of the leader.

Social facilitation effects show that well-learned skills are performed better in the presence of others than alone. Groups also reach solutions that are better than the average quality of the solutions of the same number of individuals working alone. However, group performance is less efficient. Learning in groups can also exceed solitary learning.

It is likely that groups are used relatively little in schooling because of the importance of the norm of competition. Two group methods that have been used are the jigsaw technique and the student teams–achievement divisions (STAD) technique. Both have shown positive results.

One grouping issue that is controversial concerns the relative merit of homogeneous versus heterogeneous grouping. Although there are logical arguments in favor of both techniques, research evidence provides little support for homogeneous grouping.

FOR FURTHER STUDY AND APPLICATION

Aronson, E., Blaney, N., Stephan, C., Sikes, J., and Snapp, M. *The jigsaw classroom.* Beverly Hills, Calif.: Sage, 1978.

Slavin, R.E. *Using student team learning.* (Rev. ed.) Baltimore, Md.: Center for the Social Organization for Schools, 1980.   These two books provide information for understanding and implementing two major techniques for using groups in the classroom.

Sharon, S., and Sharon, Y. *Small-group teaching.* Englewood Cliffs, N.J.: Educational Technology Publications, 1976.   Other techniques for group teaching and learning are included in this useful publication.

Johnson, D. W., and Johnson, R. *Learning together and alone: Cooperation, competition, and individualization.* Englewood Cliffs, N.J.: Prentice-Hall, 1975.   Gives an evaluation of various means of promoting cooperation and competition in the classroom.

Shaw, M. E. *Group dynamics: The psychology of small-group behavior.* New York: McGraw-Hill, 1976.   Provides a comprehensive overview of the theory and research relating to behavior in groups.

10

UNDERSTANDING AND JUDGING OTHERS: ATTITUDES, EXPECTATIONS AND PERSON PERCEPTION

CHAPTER OVERVIEW

The topic of how individuals view others is an important one. Think back, for instance, to the first day of any of the many classes that you have had over the years. As you waited for the instructor to enter the class, you probably had a number of questions about what he or she was like: Would the instructor be interesting or boring, intelligent or stupid, articulate or bumbling, warm or cold? Would the class be taught well? Would you "relate" to the instructor?

As soon as the teacher arrived, you probably began to try to answer your questions. At the beginning, you probably used the way the instructor looked, was dressed, the way he or she moved to form an opinion. Later, you were likely to use the way he or she behaved toward the class and with individual students, to determine just what kind of person your instructor was.

At the same time that you were engaged in this effort to figure out what your instructor was like, the instructor was probably involved in a similar process regarding *you*. In the mind of the teacher, the students in the class were the unknown quantity, and he or she was probably devoting a good deal of effort to understanding what they were like.

Research indicates that the decision that both you and your instructor reached regarding each other was likely to have a profound effect on your impressions of the course as a whole, and potentially on your performance— and even on your instructor's performance—in the course. This chapter examines the processes involved in determining what other people are like. The explicit goal is to make you aware of the procedures that everyone uses in forming impressions of others, so that you can be a more intelligent critic of the way in which you judge others and, ultimately, be more accurate in the impressions you form. Because so much of what a teacher does is based on such judgments, knowledge of the processes involved in impression formation can have a direct impact on one's effectiveness as a teacher.

Each year, Dallas, Texas, chooses one of its 7,000 schoolteachers to be named "Teacher of the Year." Based on the recommendations of administrators, fellow teachers, and students, the award is a prestigious one and is highly valued.

Recently, Jay Armstrong, a teacher of only 7 years experience, was named Dallas Teacher of the Year. Armstrong is an art teacher at Oliver Wendell Holmes Middle School, a large institution with a predominantly minority student body. The first question posed to Armstrong was an obvious one: What is it that makes you a good teacher?

A.   That's not easy to answer, but I think that it has to do with having a good relationship with the students. I relate well to them. I'm firm and strict, but I'm also very honest. They know that I'm going to be there, being on their side. They know that I'll stand up for them and back them up as long as they're doing the right thing and are doing their best.

Q.   What kinds of students go to your middle school?

A.   We've got a variety of kids. We've got kids whose parents are doctors and lawyers, and then we have a lot who are on welfare. So I've got a mixture in my classes. My method for dealing with this heterogeneity is to relate to each kid individually. I don't group them or label them. I've heard a lot of statements that the kids in my school can't learn—that they can't read, that they can't write. But that hasn't been my experience.

Q.   But isn't it hard to ignore labels, to ignore the kind of low expectations that people often have for the poor, minority kids?

A.   Not really. I think the thing that is most important is the student himself. I can look at a test score and see that a student has a real low IQ or a real high IQ, but it doesn't make any difference. You've got to look at each student as an individual. You can find out a whole lot just by sitting down and talking to the kids. They'll tell you where they need help. I had a student last year who said, "I can't read. I want to know how; I need some help. The kids laugh at me, the teachers laugh at me. Can you help me in any way?" I said I'll do all I can. I'm working with him after school with his reading. It's just that you need to know them as individuals.

Q.   Is it easier to teach art than such subjects as reading and writing? A critic could say that you don't have to deal with the really hard problems in teaching.

A.   I've heard that before, but it doesn't fit the facts. In my art classes, I teach a lot of history, as it relates to art. Every week we have a reading and writing assignment. I give spelling tests. I use a lot of specialized terms, so the kids are getting some language arts, too. We even do some math when it's related to art. So I cover a lot of ground when I am "just" teaching art.

Q.   I'm beginning to see why you were chosen Teacher of the Year—I'm sure your efforts in subjects other than your specialty are unusual. You seem so enthusiastic and encouraged with the kind of results you get. Do you see yourself in 20 years feeling the same way and doing the same things?

A.   I think so. I'm a career teacher—I don't think there is anything else I could do and be happier. For example, I just got back from an overnight field trip for forty-four kids. A lot of them had never been to a motel before. A lot had never been out to eat. It made me feel good to see them do something that they might not be able to do again for a while, or maybe not ever do again. So that's what I mean about loving teaching. It's fulfilling for me to know that I'm giving my time to do something that I really enjoy doing.

Q.   What distinguishes your success from the problems that many teachers experience?

A.   I think in general you have to spend more time and effort to do a good job. Teaching isn't a 9 to 5 job. You can't say that you're not going to grade papers at home, or not going to call the parents, or not going to work with the community, or not going to do any favors for the kids outside of school. I think what makes me a good teacher is that the kids know that I not only want to teach them art, but that I'm there for anything else that I can help them with. I know a lot of teachers who know their own subject matter, but the kids aren't learning because the teacher has the attitude that they're going to learn the subject matter, and that's it—don't talk about anything else. I think you've got to touch kids, you've got to relate to them. You can't say "this is your area, this is my area, and don't come around my space; I'm here only to teach." That's when the kids lose out.

If one analyzes Jay Armstrong's description of a good teacher, much of it can be expressed in terms of understanding what students are like and knowing what their needs are, and then responding to those needs. His interview thus provides a good introduction to the present chapter, which examines how teachers form an understanding of and make judgments about their students.

TEACHER EXPECTATIONS ABOUT STUDENTS

One of the basic tenets of American education is that all students should be treated with equality by their teachers. If a student performs in the same way that a peer does, he or she ought to get the same response from the teacher. Unfortunately, this point of view is somewhat idealistic, given the fact that teachers, no differently from anyone else, respond to their students on a number of levels. It is not just performance per se, divorced from the student's other characteristics, that leads to a teacher's responsiveness; it is a teacher's overall impression of the student.

attitude a tendency to respond to a particular person or thing with a positive or negative orientation

In this section, a number of factors that influence teachers' attitudes toward and about their students are discussed. The concept *attitude* refers to a tendency to respond to an individual with a positive or negative orientation. Attitudes are generally assumed to have three parts, a cognitive component (thought), an affective component (emotion), and a behavioral component. Thus attitudes not only reflect an individual's internal thoughts and emotions but also affect a person's behavior.

Stereotyping by Group Membership

Attitudes can have a profound effect on the educational process when they take the form of *stereotypes*, which are general attitudes toward members of a particular group or class of people. When stereotyping occurs, individual student attributes are ignored and teachers react to characteristics assumed to be present in all group members—whether or not an individual student displays them. Let us first examine three student characteristics that are particularly important in determining teachers' behavior: sex, socioeconomic status, and race.

Sex of student

The sex of a student is taken into account by teachers, even if the teacher is not aware of this fact. Research has shown, for instance, that boys receive significantly more criticism and disapproval than do girls, at least at the elementary school level (Jackson and Lahaderne, 1967). Of course, such findings are somewhat questionable, because most elementary school teachers are female. Thus the apparent preference for females may be caused by the (female) teachers simply being more familiar with girls.

Of greatest consequence for the students is the finding that boys receive lower grades than girls—even when actual achievement is identical. In one experiment (Carter, 1952), the grades of boys and girls in six classrooms were compared to an objective measure of their performance. In contrast to the girls, who were graded quite fairly, the boys received lower grades than their actual achievement warranted.

Do the findings of such studies as these indicate that teachers are intrinsically prejudiced against male students? Although it cannot be said for sure, one mitigating factor suggests that the answer to this question might be no. It is likely that in fact male students *are* more disruptive and less obedient than females, and thus "deserve" a greater degree of reproach than the females. Moreover, if grades awarded by teachers are related to student conduct—and there is evidence that this is the case—then males are going to receive lower grades. Thus teachers may use grades, in part, to reward students for good conduct, and females come out ahead when such use is made of grades (Brophy and Good, 1974).

Socioeconomic status of student

One of the most important factors affecting how teachers perceive and act toward a student is the socioeconomic status (SES) or social class of the student. Although a student's SES is less obvious than his or her sex, teachers quickly determine and use a student's SES to draw a set of inferences. Moreover, these inferences result in differential behavior toward the students.

The general finding to emerge from research on the effects of SES is that teachers hold lower expectations for lower-class students and tend to treat them less positively than they do middle- and upper-class students. For instance, one study (Friedman and Friedman, 1973) observed the amount of verbal and nonverbal reinforcement given to middle- and lower-class children in twenty-four fifth- and sixth-grade classrooms. The results showed that significantly more reinforcement was given the middle-class children, particularly on a nonverbal level.

Questionnaire data also show differences due to SES. In an extensive survey of 212 teachers and their students (Yee, 1968), teachers (and students) in middle-class schools held significantly more positive attitudes than teachers and students in the lower-class schools. On every dimension that was measured, the teachers in the middle-class schools were more positive toward their students: they were more tolerant, warm, trustful, sympathetic, and progressive. In contrast, teachers in the lower-class schools were more blaming, cold, fault-finding, punitive, and traditional.

Experimental studies support the bias in favor of middle-class students. In one such experiment (Miller, McLaughlin, Haddon, and Chanksy, 1968), teachers were shown four bogus case histories of students that were matched in terms of IQ, school grades, and history of behavior problems. The major difference among the reports was that two students had middle-class backgrounds and two had lower-class backgrounds. The teachers were asked to rate the students in terms of their probable future academic success, classroom behavior, and achievement after high school. The results showed that although the students were matched on the presumably most important factors of IQ and grades, the middle-class students were rated higher on ten of twelve scales. For instance, it was predicted that the lower-class students were considerably more likely to have lower grades in the future.

The Consequences of Early Labeling

Imagine a situation in which a teacher assigns kindergarten pupils to tables on the basis of her *guess* of the pupils' intellectual ability. The guess is based on the teacher's first impressions of the student's appearance, use of language, and socioeconomic status. On the basis of the teacher's intuitions about the student, the child is assigned to a seating position, with the best students placed closest to the teacher and the students assumed to have the least ability seated farthest away. If there is an air of unreality to all this, there shouldn't be.

For this is just what occurred in one ghetto classroom. In a fascinating case study, Ray Rist (1970) reports his observations of a group of children beginning from the time they entered kindergarten, up through the second grade. What is particularly disturbing is that the children were placed into one of three ability groups, which corresponded very directly to their socioeconomic status; and having once been assigned to a group, they were almost never shifted.

The children who were seated at the front of the room were labeled fast learners, and they received a greater frequency of interactions from the teacher. Moreover, the nature of teacher-student interactions was generally more positive for the so-called fast learners. In time, students in this group developed feelings of superiority over the remaining students.

The initial assignment of students to a group generally persisted into the first and second grades, relatively independent of how well the students actually performed. Indeed, some of the differences in treatment between the highest and lowest groups increased in magnitude the more schooling the students had. It appeared that the teachers were more concerned with disciplining members of the lower groups, as opposed to teaching them, whereas in the case of the fast learners, teachers were more interested in academic performance. This discrepant treatment produced feelings of failure and frustration in the lower-group children and led to an enhancement of the upper group's feelings of superiority.

Rist's work clearly indicates how teachers' first impressions of students can lead to a likely permanent impact on students' performance, academic success, and—more than likely—their self-concept. Even though this outcome is unintentional from the teacher's point of view, the consequences of labeling children at an early stage in their school career can be profound.

It is clear that teachers' perceptions of and expectations for lower-class students are less positive than they are for upper- and middle-class students. And as will be seen in the chapter that discusses subcultural differences in academic performance (Chapter 12) there are often objective performance differences related to SES. Thus it is possible that one rationale for holding less positive expectations for lower-class students is that, historically, they have performed less well academically.

Before agreeing with such a hypothesis, however, an equally plausible explanation should be considered: It is possible that negative expectations and stereotypes about members of the lower class lead teachers to behave less positively toward lower-class individuals, which in turn results in the expected behavior. Thus instead of poor performance leading to the development of low expectations, it is possible that it is the expectations themselves that lead to the poor performance. This possibility is examined in a later section of this chapter, when teacher expectation effects are discussed.

Race of student

Another frequent research finding is that teachers generally hold more positive attitudes and expectations for white students than they do for black students (Karlins, Coffman, and Walters, 1969). Although such findings must be qualified, since they generally involve looking at white teachers' attitudes, they are still disturbing. What is even more unfortunate is that in many instances even black students who are performing well are held in lower esteem than white students.

Other, more experimental evidence suggests that teachers may behave congruently with their attitudes. In one experiment (Rubovits and Maehr, 1973) sixty-three college-age white subjects acted as teachers to seventh- and eighth-grade students who were either white or black and who were described as gifted or nongifted. In general, the black children were treated less well than the white children. They were given less attention, they received less verbal praise, they were criticized more, and fewer comments were elicited from them. Furthermore, the "gifted" label resulted in different effects according to whether it was applied to a white or black student. When a white student was labeled gifted, that student was called upon more than when labeled nongifted. In contrast, blacks labeled gifted received *less* attention than those labeled nongifted. These results suggest that white teachers may find that the high achievement of a black student disconfirms their expectations about black students in general. To avoid this discrepancy between expectations and reality, the white teachers may simply ignore or discourage the black student's high achievement.

Another experiment shows that even when teachers are making positive comments on a verbal level, their *nonverbal* behavior may differ according to the race of the student they are teaching. An experimental study (Feldman and Donohoe, 1978) had white and black undergraduate subjects teach a lesson to a white or black student. The student was actually a confederate of the experimenter, and he was made to appear quite successful during a test. Because the teachers were told to use the phrase "Right—that's good" whenever the student answered a test item correctly, all the teachers were praising their student frequently. However, secret videotapes of the teacher's nonverbal

Teachers may hold discrepant attitudes about students and may behave differently toward them on the basis of race. (© David S. Strickler/The Picture Cube)

facial expressions, taken while they were verbally praising their student, showed that there was a relationship between race of teacher and race of student in how nonverbally positive the teacher appeared. Both the white teachers *and* the black teachers appeared more facially positive to a student of their own race than to a student of the other race. White teachers looked more pleased with white than black students, and black teachers seemed more pleased with black than white students—although student performance was identical in all cases. Interestingly enough, only white judges could distinguish the differences in nonverbal positiveness of the white teachers, and only black judges could determine the differences in nonverbal positiveness of the black teachers. Still, it is clear that the nonverbal behavior of the teachers was more positive to same-race students. One can only guess at the feelings of confusion that may result when, for example, a black student finds her white teacher being verbally reinforcing but displaying relatively negative nonverbal facial expressions.

In general, then, it can be seen that teachers' attitudes and behavior are affected by the race of their pupil. Members of minority groups are, in general, viewed and treated more negatively than majority group students—although this point has been demonstrated most clearly when non–minority group teachers have been observed.

The Effect of Individual Characteristics

Up to this point, the discussion has focused on how teachers' attitudes and behavior vary as a consequence of their students' membership in a particular group (sex, SES, or race). But in forming impressions, teachers also respond to the individual characteristics of their students. In this section, the major kinds of student characteristics affecting the development of teachers' attitudes are examined.

Physical attractiveness

One of the first things that teachers notice about their students is their physical attractiveness. And although society professes to agree that "beauty is only skin deep," it turns out that in fact many decisions about people are based on their attractiveness.

Even at the time children enter kindergarten, physical attractiveness is taken into account, both by the children's peers and by their teachers. Children at that age are able to distinguish and rate their friends on at least one dimension of physical attractiveness—that of body build—and they express negative feelings for chubby body types (Gellert, Girgus, and Cohen, 1971). Even more important, there is evidence that a child's physical attractiveness is related to his or her popularity. In one experiment (Dion and Berscheid, 1974), a group of younger and older nursery school children were asked to name the classmates whom they especially liked and disliked. In addition, two adult judges rated each child in physical attractiveness.

The results of the study indicated that physical attractiveness did indeed affect the children's ratings, but the effects were dependent on the age and sex of the children. The unattractive boys in both the older and younger groups were liked significantly less than the attractive ones. On the other hand, the ratings of females differed according to their age. In the younger group, the unattractive girls were more popular than the attractive ones. But in the older group, the attractive girls were significantly more popular than the unattractive ones. One explanation for this finding is that the girls may be developing awareness of the social value of being physically attractive.

Of course, the foregoing study relates to children's perceptions of their peers. Are teachers subject to the same kind of biases in favor of physical attractiveness? The answer clearly appears to be yes.

The strongest evidence that teachers are affected by students' physical attractiveness comes from a comprehensive study (Clifford and Walster, 1973). They showed 400 fifth-grade schoolteachers a copy of a student's report card that contained information on the student's grades in reading, language, arithmetic, social studies, science, art, music, and physical education for six grading periods. In addition, there were grades for healthful living, personal development, and work habits and attitudes. Finally—and this is the crucial factor—the teachers were shown a picture of the child. In the corner of the grade report, the experimenters pasted a picture of either an attractive or an unattractive child. All information, other than the picture, was the same on all report cards.

On the basis of the report card, the teachers were asked to judge the student's IQ score, his parents' attitude toward school, his social status among his peers, and the sort of future educational attainment that could be expected from him. Despite the fact that there were no differences in the information about the students that the teachers received, there were strong differences in the teachers' evaluations—on the basis of just the physical attractiveness of the students. The attractive students were judged to have a higher IQ, superior social status, better likelihood of future educational accomplishment, and more interested parents than the unattractive ones.

Physical attractiveness also has been shown to lead to differential interpretations of disruptive behavior (Dion, 1972). Subjects received a description of a mild or severe instance of misbehavior on the part of a 7-year-old and were asked to assess how the child usually behaved. The descriptions included a photograph of a child who was either attractive or unattractive; there were no other differences in the description the subjects received.

When the misbehavior was relatively mild, there was no effect due to the attractiveness of the child. But when the misbehavior was severe, strong differences in the subject's assessments emerged due to the child's attractiveness. When an attractive child had misbehaved severely, the behavior was judged to be just a temporary aberration. For example, an attractive child who threw a rock at a sleeping dog was described in this way by one subject:

> She appears to be a perfectly charming little girl, well-mannered, basically unselfish. It seems that she can adapt well among children her age and make a good impression. . . . She plays well with everyone, but like anyone else, a bad day can occur. Her cruelty . . . need not be taken seriously (Dion, 1972, quoted in Berscheid and Walster, 1974, p. 192).

The same type of incident when attributed to an unattractive girl tended to be thought indicative of an antisocial nature. Thus unattractive girls who had committed a severe transgression were described as chronically misbehaved and likely to be behavior problems. For example, of an unattractive girl who threw a rock at a sleeping dog, one subject wrote:

> I think the child would be quite bratty and would be a problem to teachers . . . she would probably try to pick a fight with other children her own age . . . she would be a brat at home—all in all, she would be a problem (Dion, 1972, quoted in Berscheid and Walster, 1974, p. 192).

It thus appears that the interpretation that is placed on a student's behavior is partly a function of his or her appearance. More generally, it seems as if teachers' impressions and attitudes are affected by the physical attractiveness of their students. Teachers do sometimes act as if beauty were more than skin deep!

Achievement of students

It could well be the case that, at least in the classroom, the smart get smarter and the dumb get dumber. For it appears that students who perform well academically receive more interest and attention from their teachers than those who may need it the most—the children who are doing poorly.

The idea that students who perform well academically are liked more and held in higher esteem by their teachers probably does not strike you as particularly surprising. After all, teachers are supposed to teach, and it is likely that they feel the greatest success at their jobs when their students are doing well. It follows that students who are performing well and are associated with feelings of teacher satisfaction are going to be viewed most favorably by their teacher.

There is a great deal of evidence to support this view. For instance, in one study (Allen and Feldman, 1974) tutors were asked to rate their liking for their students after a short lesson session. Not only were successful pupils liked more, but the teacher enjoyed teaching considerably more when the student did well than when the student was unsuccessful. Perhaps even more important, these attitudes were reflected in the teacher's behavior toward the pupil. An analysis of the teacher's verbal behavior found that the proportion of statements representing positive feelings was much higher when the student was successful than when the student was not successful (Feldman and Allen, 1979). Similarly, the nonverbal behavior of the tutor tended to reflect the performance of the student; there were differences in eye contact, nodding and shaking of the head, and other postural cues, corresponding to the student's performance.

The phenomenon of more positive behavior being accorded to the more successful student is not new. A relatively old study (Horn, 1914) investigated the frequency of students being allowed the opportunity to recite in class. After dividing the students into quartiles based on achievement, Horn found that the pupils at the top of the distribution were allowed to recite about 40 percent more often than those at the bottom of the distribution. Even more interesting, there was an increase in the discrepancy with age. Whereas the differences in recitation rates were generally small for the youngest students, by high school the rates for the top quartile were almost twice as high as for the bottom quartile.

Have times changed? Probably not, for the evidence suggests that even now teachers are more positive toward the students they perceive to be the most able than they are toward the poorer students. For instance, one study (Heller and White, 1975) examined the rate of verbal approval and disapproval emitted by teachers to students in high- and low-ability classes in an inner-city junior high school. They found that, although the approval rate did not vary according to the ability of the students, the disapproval rate was significantly higher for the lower-ability students. The extra disapproval received by the lower-ability

Table 10-1   Response Opportunities Given to High,
Middle, and Low Achievers

	High	Middle	Low
Mean response opportunities	29.9	17.1	10.1
Range of pupil response opportunities	17–35	7–37	1–21
Total number of response opportunities	479	274	162

Adapted from Good, 1970

students was directed primarily at promoting classroom discipline. The data also revealed the interesting fact that the teachers almost never praised either the high- or low-ability pupils for being well-behaved. Given that positive reinforcement is generally more effective than punishment in maintaining desired behavior, it seems as if the teachers may have been using the wrong tactics to promote classroom discipline.

In any case, there are many studies that show more positive behavior toward the high achiever than the low achiever. Some reveal that the poor students do not even have the opportunity to perform well, even when they are trying to. An example of this phenomenon is shown in a study by Thomas Good (1970), who observed first-grade students characterized by their teachers as high, middle, and low achievers for 10 hours each. Looking at a number of classrooms, Good found that the higher the performance of the students, the more opportunities they were given to respond to a question. The mean, range, and total number of response opportunities are shown in Table 10-1. These results suggest that even when a low achiever may be doing well on a particular lesson, there may be less opportunity to display his or her knowledge.

In summary, it appears that teachers' attitudes and behavior are related to how well their students perform in class. But note the kind of chicken-versus-egg argument that can be made here: Are the teacher attitudes and behavior that seem to be related to academic performance a *consequence* of the student's performance, or are such attitudes and behaviors the *cause* of the student's performance? Which comes first? Although the most reasonable explanation at first appears to be that the performance precedes and causes the development of certain attitudes and behaviors, there is a significant body of literature which suggests that teachers who initially hold particular attitudes and expectations about a student, and who act upon their expectations, can actually bring about the expected behavior. The next section of the chapter takes up this issue.

TEACHER EXPECTATION EFFECTS

Suppose at the beginning of a new school year, you were told that the students in your class had taken a test that was described in this way:

All children show hills, plateaus, and valleys in their scholastic progress. A study being conducted at Harvard with the support of the National Science Foundation is interested in those children who show an unusual forward spurt of academic progress. These spurts can and do occur at any level of academic and intellectual functioning. When these spurts occur in children who have not been functioning too well academically, the result is familiarly referred to as "late blooming."

As part of our study we are further validating a test which predicts the likelihood that a child will show an inflection point or "spurt" within the near future. This test which will be administered in your school will allow us to predict which youngsters are most likely to show academic spurt. . . . The development of the test for predicting inflections or "spurts" is not yet such that *every* one of the top 20 percent will show the spurt or "blooming" effect. But the top 20 percent of the children *will* show a more significant inflection or spurt in their learning within the next year or less than will the remaining 80 percent of the children (Rosenthal and Jacobson, 1968, p. 66).

What would your reaction be to the information that some of the students in your class had been identified as "bloomers"? Do you think it would affect your behavior toward the students who had been so designated?

Evidence from one experiment (Rosenthal and Jacobson, 1968) suggests that in fact teachers are affected by such information. In the experiment, teachers were told the five children in the class who would be likely to "bloom" in the coming year, on the basis of the test described above. In reality, however, the information was bogus; the names of the children had simply been picked at random, although the teachers didn't know that. At the end of the school year, the children were administered an intelligence test that was identical to one they had taken a year earlier. According to the authors, the results showed clearly that there were differences in the intellectual growth of the "bloomers," compared with the remaining members of their classes. Those randomly designated as likely to make significant gains did, indeed, improve more than the other students. However, the results were not uniform: The greatest differences were found for students in the earlier grades (grades 1 and 2), with smaller differences for students in grades 3–6.

The study aroused immediate controversy after its publication. The general public was intrigued by the findings, which suggested that teachers' expectations might well be blamed for the performance—good or bad—of their students. On the other hand, serious criticism of the study came from some statisticians, who argued that the differences found by Rosenthal and Jacobson were illusory (Snow, 1969), and a number of efforts at replicating the research were not successful.

Regardless of the validity of the original findings, the phenomenon investigated by Rosenthal and Jacobson has been shown to be quite real. Since the original study, there have been literally dozens of experiments designed to investigate what has come to be called the *teacher expectancy effect*. The effect refers to the phenomenon in which the teacher who holds an expectation about a student transmits the expectation and actually brings about the expected

*teacher-expect-ancy effect
the phenome-non in which a teacher who holds an ex-pectation about a stu-dent transmits the expecta-tion, which brings about the expected behavior*

Student Expectations About Teachers

Just as teachers hold expectations about their students, one might guess that students hold—and act upon—expectations about their teachers. This hypothesis received strong support in a laboratory study (Feldman and Prohaska, 1979).

In the experiment, subjects were recruited to be in a teaching experiment in which they were to be the student. Just prior to participation, a confederate, who supposedly had been in a similar experiment earlier, told the subject either that the teacher was quite effective (positive expectation) or that the teacher was very incompetent (negative expectation). Subjects were then taught the lesson by a teacher, who did not know what kind of expectation the subject held. Three types of data were obtained after the lesson. First, subjects' attitudes toward the lesson and the teacher were measured. Second, tests on the content of the lesson were administered. Finally, the nonverbal behavior of the subjects was examined.

The results of the study showed that subjects' behavior varied quite directly as a result of their expectations about the teacher. Students expecting a good teacher held more positive attitudes about the lesson and the teacher, seemed to learn more, and acted somewhat more positively on a nonverbal level than did subjects expecting a poor teacher. Thus expectations about the teacher clearly affected the students' behavior.

But could a student's expectations be transmitted to the teacher and

behavior. This phenomenon is actually a special case of a broader concept known as the self-fulfilling prophecy, in which a person's expectation is capable of bringing about the expected outcome. For example, physicians have long known that providing patients with placebos (fake, inert drugs) can sometimes "cure" a patient, simply because he or she expects the medicine to work.

The most reasonable explanation for the teacher expectancy effect is that instructors, after forming an initial expectation about a student's ability, transmit their expectations to the student through a complex series of verbal and nonverbal cues that indicate just what their expectations are. These transmitted expectations in turn act to indicate to the student what behavior is appropriate, and the student then acts in accordance with the teacher's expectations.

Forming Expectations

A great deal of research has been carried out in an attempt to document the dynamics of teacher expectation effects, and it is worthwhile to examine just

ultimately affect the teacher's behavior? To answer this question, a second experiment was carried out. In this study, confederates acting as students emitted either positive or negative nonverbal behavior (similar to the nonverbal behavior found to result from positive or negative expectations in the first experiment) toward subjects acting as their teachers. Thus in one condition, the (confederate) student gazed more at, sat closer to, was more directly oriented toward, and leaned closer to the (subject) teacher. In the other condition, the student looked less at, sat further away from, was less directly oriented toward and sat more upright relative to the teacher.

The results of this second experiment clearly indicated that the teachers were affected by the students' behavior. Teachers' attitudes about their own success as well as their ratings of students were more positive when the student was acting nonverbally positive than when the student was acting nonverbally negative. Most important, ratings of the teacher's adequacy by observers were significantly higher when the student was nonverbally positive than when the student was nonverbally negative.

These experiments suggest a cycle: If differential expectations lead to differences in nonverbal behavior (as was demonstrated in the first experiment), and if differential nonverbal behavior leads to differences in teacher adequacy (as was demonstrated in the second experiment), then the initial expectation ultimately can be linked to behavior congruent with the expectation. Thus it does seem that student expectations can lead the teacher to behave in accordance with those expectations. Teachers therefore should be aware that their own behavior may actually be a reflection of their students' expectations.

what is known about how the effect operates. One line of research has investigated the *sources* of the teacher's initial expectations. A number of factors have been identified, most of which were discussed earlier in terms of teachers' impressions and attitudes about their students. Such factors as the sex, SES, ethnic background, and physical attractiveness of a student clearly affect the nature of the teacher's expectations about that student.

But, interestingly, even more subtle factors can affect the teacher's expectations. For instance, knowledge of the academic performance of an older sibling can influence what a teacher expects from a child. Burleigh Seaver (1973) studied the achievement of a group of seventy first graders who had followed a bright or dull older sibling. Seaver found that when the first graders were taught by the *same teacher* as the older sibling, their performance varied according to the intelligence of the older sibling. When they were in a class with a teacher who had not taught an older sibling there was a much weaker relationship between older and younger sibling performance. It therefore appears that the teachers who had taught an older sibling formed an expectation about the younger sibling based on the performance of the older one, and the younger students acted in accordance with that expectation.

Perhaps most disheartening is that even the name of a student affects a teacher's expectations. One study that examined the unusualness of names (Harari, 1973) found that teachers held lower expectations for students with uncommon names.

Probably the most direct source of expectations about student performance is one that is sanctioned by school authorities: the formal grade and test records that are kept by the school. A teacher need only read a student's permanent file to find a complete record of his or her past performance, achievement test scores, and IQ scores. It is hard to imagine how such information could fail to produce a set of expectations about a student's future performance, and research is quite clear in supporting the notion that students' records do indeed affect teachers' expectations. In fact, even when people specifically are warned against the effects of teacher biases, they can still be affected by the contents of psychological reports (Mason, 1973). Thus the permanent records of students can have a powerful effect on a teacher's expectations.

Transmission of Expectations to the Student

Once an expectation about a student is formed, it has to be transmitted to the student in some way if it is to have an effect on his or her performance. According to Rosenthal (1974), there are four basic ways in which teachers' behavior in the classroom can communicate their expectations to the student: the social-emotional *climate* in the classroom, the type of *feedback* the teacher gives the student, the different *input* that occurs when students are given learning materials that differ according to the teacher's expectations, and differing opportunities for student *output* in terms of the frequency of responses allowed.

Social-emotional climate
Teachers seem to create a warmer, more pleasant environment for students for whom they hold high expectations. For instance, one study (Chaiken, Sigler, and Derlega, 1974) found that subjects acting as teachers to a 12-year-old boy who was labeled bright, dull, or was unlabeled tended to act in a significantly more positive way to the student, the higher their expectation. Teachers who thought their student was bright tended to smile and nod their heads more, look at the student more, and lean closer to the student than teachers who thought their pupil was dull. Observations of actual classrooms confirm that teachers are more friendly and interested in students who are thought to be bright (Kester and Letchworth, 1972).

Feedback to students

The kind of verbal (and nonverbal) responses that teachers give to their pupils differs according to their expectations. A review of the literature suggests that teachers tend to give more positive and differentiated verbal feedback to their high-expectation students than to students of whom they expect less. Thus it seems that even when a low-expectation student performs well, the kind of feedback he or she receives is less positive than when a high-expectation student performs well. The converse is true for poor performance; low-expectation students receive proportionally more criticism when they respond incorrectly than do high-expectation students (Cooper, 1979). Basically, then, teachers are verbally more positive to high-expectation than to low-expectation students.

Input to students

Teachers seem to regulate the amount and kind of material they assign to their students according to their expectations about them. It appears that teachers provide fewer learning opportunities to their low-expectation students, and the material that is taught to them is less difficult (Beez, 1970; Cornbleth,

Teachers' expectations can be transmitted through the social-emotional climate of the classroom. (© Alan Carey)

Davis, and Button, 1974). Thus the amount and quality of the materials that low-expectation students receive is lower than it is for students whom teachers regard as having a greater likelihood of success.

Output from students

Teachers who expect a student to perform well tend to elicit a different kind of response from that student than they do from a student of whom they expect poor performance. High-expectation students are interacted with significantly more than low-expectation students and thus are given much greater opportunity to respond in class. In addition, the nature of the interaction that occurs between teacher and student is qualitatively higher for high- than for low-expectation pupils (Gay, 1975).

Student Responses to Teacher Expectations

Given the degree to which teachers' expectations lead to differential behavior, it is not surprising that the students would be affected by it. Student behavior in congruence with teachers' expectations is thus the final link in the teacher expectation phenomenon. The student who receives less positive verbal and nonverbal feedback from the teacher, less clear reinforcement, and less opportunity to respond is much more likely to develop a negative self-concept, to begin working less hard, and ultimately to do more poorly than the student who receives more positive treatment from the teacher. Thus the cycle is complete: The teacher's expectations have led to the expected behavior. What is worse, the student's performance then is considered a confirmation of the initial expectancy, and this leads to maintenance of the expectancy!

The Basic Model

To summarize, the basic sequence of the teacher expectation effect appears to follow this model:

1. The teacher forms differential expectations for student performance;
2. He then begins to treat children differently in accordance with his differential expectations;
3. The children respond differentially to the teacher because they are being treated differently by him;
4. In responding to the teacher, each child tends to exhibit behavior which complements and reinforces the teacher's particular expectations for him;
5. As a result, the general academic performance of some children will be enhanced while that of others will be depressed, with changes being in the direction of teacher expectations;

6. These effects will show up in the achievement tests given at the end of the year, providing support for the "self-fulfilling prophecy" notion.

(Brophy and Good, 1970, pp. 365–366)

What Can the Teacher Do?

The foregoing description of the teacher expectation effect has concentrated on the kinds of things that teachers do to transmit their expectations. This focus is deliberate, because transmission of expectations seems to be the area in which teachers have the most control over the effect. It is unlikely that a teacher can stop the initial formation of an impression or expectation. But since it is so easy to make a mistake in the impression that is formed (as much of this chapter is devoted to pointing out), it seems doubly important for teachers to learn how to avoid the effects of those often ill-founded expectations.

Unfortunately, there is no easy answer regarding ways to avoid expectation effects. However, awareness of those effects is the first step. Teacher training programs might well sensitize teachers to the problem and teach alternate behaviors. Keeping constantly in mind, for instance, that students should receive reinforcement that is directly contingent on performance, and not based on prior expectation, might be a useful step toward decreasing expectation effects. Another strategy that teachers might follow is to communicate high expectations—by setting high, but ultimately attainable, goals for all students. Finally, teachers should recognize the differences that exist between mere impressions and more objective sorts of measures of student behavior, and try to base their feedback to students on evidence that is as firm and objective as possible.

DETERMINING THE CAUSES OF BEHAVIOR

Consider the following scenario. Marian is a student in Sarah Dion's sixth-grade class. Her fellow class members tend to view her in this way:

Marian can do no wrong. Ms. Dion calls on her more, responds more favorably to her comments than to anyone else's, and generally seems to like her a great deal. And Marian takes advantage of this. She is always raising her hand and trying to help Ms. Dion. It's clear that Marian is basically a manipulative person, always trying to curry favor with the teacher.

But now let's view the situation from Marian's point of view. If she were asked, she would probably say something like this:

> I really like Ms. Dion. She's a good teacher. She tries to motivate
> students to do their best, and she's very responsive when someone tries to
> answer questions. Because of her attitude, I try a lot harder than I normally
> would. I'm very grateful for the atmosphere that she's provided.

Quite a different perspective, isn't it? But there's still one party left to be heard from in this situation, and that's the teacher herself. From her we get the following:

> This year, my class is basically a good one. But certain students always
> stand out. This year, it is Marian. She is attractive, works hard, is always
> prepared, and tries very hard. I've really developed a fondness for her, and
> I can't help wishing that more of my students worked as consistently as she
> does.

As you can see, the parties in the above scenario bring differing perspectives to bear on the situation. And although there is probably a kernel of truth in each of their positions, each party is to some extent biased in the way they look at the situation.

This section of the chapter examines some of the underlying processes involved in the formation of impressions about others, which is known as *person perception*. In one sense, perceiving other people is just a special case of perception in general. After all, on the most basic level one begins forming impressions of others by considering shape, size, color, and other overt characteristics—which is much the same process as is involved in forming an impression of, say, a bowl of fruit. But person perception carries the process of perception a number of steps further. First, one makes the assumption when viewing other people that they have the capability of experiencing internal states. Because we can ourselves feel happiness, anger, or fear, we assume that others may be experiencing the same types of emotions in similar ways.

People also tend to be somewhat skeptical when viewing others' behavior. One is aware that other persons are capable of dissimulating their feelings as well as of trying to manipulate or exploit others. Thus when Marian smiles at Ms. Dion, one cannot be sure whether she is really pleased or is simply trying to present herself well. Such problems in interpretation don't arise in one's perception of inanimate objects.

It is thus much more difficult and involved to perceive accurately what other people are like. Indeed, a number of theories have evolved that deal specifically with the problems that arise with person perception and impression formation. These theories examine how the underlying traits, notions, and intentions of a person are determined from examination of that person's overt behavior—a process that is known as *attribution*.

person perception the underlying processes involved in the formation of impressions about others

attribution the processes and methods people use to reach conclusions about what underlies the overt behavior of others

Attribution Processes

Most people act at times like psychologists, and teachers and students are no exception. Everyone is interested in determining and understanding the causes of behavior—which, indeed, is the basic definition of the science of psychology. Attribution theory attempts to make explicit the processes and methods that are used in order to come to conclusions about the factors underlying an individual's overt behavior. Most of one's information about others comes from first observing their behavior and then inferring the presence of various underlying personality traits, motives and intentions (Heider, 1958).

The problem that an individual faces when making attributions is not an easy one, given that others behave not just on the basis of their internal states and dispositions but also in response to external, environmental pressures. Thus one of the first questions one asks when viewing another's behavior is whether the behavior is motivated by environmental influences or is due to internal dispositional influences. For instance, if Marian, in the middle of the semester, tells her teacher that she is doing an excellent job, Ms. Dion, while hardly likely to engage in argument, is probably going to begin an attributional quest to determine whether Marian's behavior is externally motivated (i.e., Marian is only praising her in order to get a higher grade) or internally motivated (i.e., Marian really likes her and is grateful to her). The less likely or plausible the external reasons for a behavior are, the more likely that the behavior will be inferred as representative of an underlying, internal disposition. Thus if Marian makes a special effort to tell Ms. Dion that she liked her class *after* the school year is over (and the grades have been filed), she is more likely to be seen as being truly grateful, given that external pressures are low or absent.

Unfortunately, people are not always as rational in making attributions as the foregoing example implies. Indeed, there are a number of inaccuracies that regularly occur when one is attempting to understand and make attributions regarding others' behavior. Let us examine some of the most frequent pitfalls.

Attribution distortion: Actor versus observer

Returning to the example of Marian, note that she attributes her behavior as being due to the inspiration of Ms. Dion's motivating tutelage—a factor that is *external* to herself. Yet her classmates perceive the causes of Marian's behavior as originating in a factor *internal* to Marian—her manipulativeness.

Although the example is fictional, the principle it illustrates is not. In fact the example illustrates one of the most pervasive forms of attribution distortion. When people are in the role of *observer* they tend to attribute the behavior of others to internal factors—such as ambition or aggression; yet when they are themselves in the role of *actor,* they tend to attribute their own behavior to external factors—such as the actions or attitudes of other people (Jones and Nisbett, 1972). In other words, one tends to see others as the source or origin of their own behavior, while others see the environment as the cause of their behavior.

It is clear how this bias can cause problems in classroom settings. Suppose, for instance, that you are the instructor of an argumentative student who misbehaves in class. To you, it is clear that there is something about the student that makes him argue with you—he is argumentative by nature, or

Combining Traits to Form Opinions of Others

Put yourself in the following situation: Your regular class instructor informs you that the next class is to be taught by a guest lecturer. You receive a biographical description of the lecturer, which includes the statement that people generally consider him to be "a rather warm person, industrious, critical, practical, and determined." If you were asked to rate the instructor, what do you think your overall impression would be?

Now, let's change the description a bit. Suppose the biography says instead that the guest lecturer is "a rather cold person, industrious, critical, practical, and determined." What would your general impression now be?

If you are like most people, your opinion of the lecturer would probably shift quite drastically with the change in wording. Generally, the "warm" lecturer is rated much more positively than the "cold" one. Indeed, this result was found in an actual experiment in which a group of subjects, half of whom were given the warm description and half the cold description, actually heard a lecturer lead a discussion. Although the lecturer's behavior was the same for all subjects, the initial one-word change in the description has a dramatic effect on how the lecturer was viewed (Kelley, 1950).

The above experiment, which has become a classic in the psychological literature, illustrates quite graphically the role of *central traits* in forming general impressions of people. Certain personality traits seem to exert an unusually large influence on one's general impression of a person. Such central traits act to organize one's impression, and they serve as a framework for understanding and interpreting information that one subsequently learns about an individual. Indeed, Solomon Asch, the psychologist who first proposed the notion of central traits (Asch, 1946), suggests that the very meaning of additional descriptive traits is altered after one has come across a central trait. For example, Asch suggests that a hypothetical stimulus person who is described as "warm and determined" is viewed differently from one who is described as "cold and determined"—not just because of the difference between warm and cold, but also because one's understanding of the word "determined" changes, depending on the context in which one encounters it.

It appears, then, that certain traits, such as warm and cold, have a substantial effect on one's impressions of others. These traits tend to provide a structure around which other, less central traits are organized.

Models of Impression Formation: Cognitive Algebra

One drawback of Asch's central trait model of impression formation is that it does not provide us with very concrete information about the process by which a series of adjectives are combined. Some psychologists, using information-processing models similar to those discussed in the chapter on learning theories (Chapter 5), suggest that it is possible to predict in relatively precise ways what one's overall impression of another person will be through the use of mathematical models.

Two major types of models have been suggested: adding and averaging. The adding model suggests that people form impressions of others by simply adding together cognitively the degree of likability of each of a person's traits. For instance, if a student is intelligent, hard-working, and neat, one would simply sum those three traits together, assigning each one a value on, say, a 10-point scale. Thus one might rate intelligent as 9, hard-working as 8, and neat as 4. To use the adding model, one would simply sum the three traits together to find one's overall impression of the person:

$$9 + 8 + 4 = 21$$

But note that by using this model, the greater the number of traits included, the more positive one's impression of the individual will appear to be.

Using the averaging model, one begins in much the same way as with the adding model. However, instead of simply summing the assigned values of the traits, one finds the *average* of the three:

$$\frac{(9 + 8 + 4)}{3} = 7$$

The averaging model has particularly important implications when the impact of additional information is considered. Suppose, for instance, that one finds that the student is also considerate, which one assigns a value of 5. Using the averaging model, one would have the following new equation:

$$\frac{(9 + 8 + 4 + 5)}{4} = 6.5$$

Thus one's impression of the student would actually be less positive than if one hadn't included the additional information. In contrast, the adding model would simply add the new information into the old, and one's impression would become more positive.

Which of the two models—adding or averaging—is best? Most evidence seems to support the averaging model. However, it appears that the process of impression formation actually involves the use of a *weighted* average (Anderson, 1974). The greatest accuracy in predicting an individual's impression comes when one weights the average to take into account both the importance of each individual piece of information and the degree of positivity of the information.

stupid, or just plain nasty. In short, it is something about his personality that is the cause of his behavior. But now let's look at the situation from the point of view of the student. Since actors tend to attribute the cause of their behavior to the environment, it is unlikely that the student himself feels responsible for his argumentativeness; he probably blames it on something outside of himself. Thus *he* may feel that it is something about you that is responsible for his misbehavior. Given that these are vastly differing interpretations of the cause of the misbehavior, it becomes all the more difficult to alleviate the problem. A teacher, therefore, must always be aware of the tendency to label the behavior of others as being caused by internal or dispositional factors, and aware that those being judged will tend to attribute their behavior to someone or something in the environment.

Why is there such a pervasive tendency toward these actor-observer discrepancies in attribution? Edward Jones and Richard Nisbett (1972) suggest that there are two main reasons. The first explanation is mainly perceptual in nature, and it relates to the fact that people are simply less well equipped to focus on their own behavior than on the things going on around them in the environment. We cannot see our own facial expressions or observe how we react in a situation. On the other hand, we can observe another person, and it is that other person's behavior that dominates what we are perceiving. Therefore, we are more likely to consider the other person's internal traits or characteristics to be the primary cause of his or her behavior; the situational determinants of the person's behavior may be overlooked.

A second major cause of the discrepancy between observers and actors concerns the nature of the information that is available to each. Unless we know another person well, we generally do not have much information about how that person has behaved in prior situations. Without this information, the tendency is to assume that the other person's behavior is stable over other situations. Therefore, we make a dispositional attribution to that person. In contrast, when we are determining the cause of our own behavior, we are well aware that in other situations our behavior might be different, and that our present behavior might easily be modified if the situation were different. Consequently, we tend to make situational attributions regarding the cause of our own behavior.

Defensive attribution

While the evidence is clear that people tend to attribute the causes of others' behavior to personal characteristics, traits, and dispositions, and view their own behavior as largely determined by situational factors, this is not the only attributional discrepancy that occurs between actors and observers. One other distortion that is particularly relevant to potential teachers concerns what has been called defensive attribution (Shaver, 1970). According to the notion of *defensive attribution,* we try to protect our self-concept and the view of ourselves as a successful, competent individual when we perceive the causes of others'—as well as our own—behavior. In essence, we try to avoid viewing ourselves in a negative light.

Defensive attribution is of particular importance when a teacher tries to determine the source of a student's performance. If the student is doing poorly, a defensive attribution argument would suggest that the teacher is likely to blame the student—after all, what teacher would want to see himself or herself as the cause of the student's poor performance? On the other hand, teachers might be expected to accept much more readily responsibility for the performance of a successful student.

Clear evidence for the foregoing propositions was found in a study by Linda Beckman (1970). She found that teachers who had taught a lesson to a student who improved over the course of the lesson—and thus was ultimately successful—tended to attribute the student's performance to their good teaching. When the student's performance declined, however, leading to ultimate failure, teachers attributed the performance to the student's lack of ability, not to their teaching.

What is particularly interesting about Beckman's study is that she included another experimental group, which merely observed the students' performance (but did not teach them). In contrast to the attributions made by the teachers, the uninvolved observers tended to rate the *student* as being more responsible when the student was successful, and the *teacher* as being more responsible when the student performed poorly—a complete reversal from the teacher's impressions. Thus it is clear that the degree to which an individual is personally involved in a situation will affect his or her decisions about the causes of another's behavior.

Halo effects

One of the factors that is most basic when one forms an impression of another person relates to the other's general goodness or badness (Osgood, Suci, and Tannenbaum, 1957). This good-bad dimension probably is, in fact, the most important dimension involved in person perception. One result of the importance of this dimension is that most other qualities of the person are deduced from this initial decision. However, there is no guarantee that the individual is, in reality, uniformly good or bad. For instance, just because a teacher is impatient and strict—two qualities that may result in a general negative evaluation—does not mean that he or she is a bad teacher as well.

The *halo effect* refers to the bias in impression formation in which a person who receives an initial positive evaluation is assumed to be uniformly positive on all dimensions. (The opposite phenomenon, in which an initial negative evaluation is made, is sometimes referred to as the negative halo effect. Here, the person is deduced as being uniformly bad on all qualities.) The halo effect is exemplified by the case in which an excellent student turns in a poor paper but is still awarded a high grade by a teacher.

The halo effect is just a special case of what has been called "logical error," in which the individual assumes that when one particular trait is present,

halo effect refers to the bias in impression formation in which a person who receives an initial positive evaluation is assumed to be uniformly positive on all dimensions

Characteristics such as the attractiveness of a student can lead to the development of a halo effect, in which a student is assumed (illogically) to have many other positive qualities. (© Katrina Thomas 1981/Photo Researchers, Inc.)

others must also be found. For instance, if you know that a student is intelligent, it is likely that you will also perceive him or her as being imaginative, clever, active, deliberate, conscientious, and reliable (Bruner, Shapiro, and Tagiuri, 1958). It is not because being intelligent logically implies being imaginative; some of the least imaginative people are highly intelligent. Rather, these inferences are logical errors, and they stem from one's *implicit personality theories*. Every person carries around a set of assumptions about the nature of others, and these assumptions are known as implicit personality theories. Unfortunately, one's theories are not always very sound. Because one's implicit personality theories lack complexity, one tends to fit individuals into a relatively few general categories. When a person seems to fit into one of these categories, one may overlook that certain traits that are a part of one's general category are not present in that person. This phenomenon is an example of logical error.

implicit personality theory a set of assumptions about the nature of other people

Projective biases

One of Sigmund Freud's contributions to the field of psychology was the notion that people sometimes attribute their own feelings and characteristics to others. Freud used the term *projection* to refer to instances in which the individual unwittingly sees his or her own traits in others. For instance, if you are easily angered, you probably feel that most people are easily angered in the same way; or, if you study best with a radio playing, you probably think that most people perform best under similar circumstances. Given a lack of precise

projection the process of attributing one's own feelings and characteristics to others

knowledge about others, one tends to assume similarity between them and oneself. While the assumed similarity bias is strongest when such obvious features as sex, race, or religion match one's own it is powerful enough to occur even in instances in which there are differences in basic demographic characteristics.

There are two major results of the tendency to project one's own characteristics onto individuals about whom one is forming an impression (Freedman, Sears, and Carlsmith, 1978). First, one typically ends up with an inaccurate impression, since one assumes that the target person is more similar to oneself than is actually the case. (Of course, if the individual is indeed very similar to oneself, then one's impression is even more accurate than would otherwise have been the case!)

A second result of the tendency to assume similarity is even more intriguing. In many cases, we distort the other person's characteristics so much that our ratings are better indicators of what our own personality is like than of what the other's personality is like. In other words, our perception of the other person's characteristics really can be based on our impression of our own personality. So in a sense, we may be providing an even better indicator of our own personality than if we were rating ourselves directly. The reason for this rests on the likelihood that when overtly rating our own personality we might try to present ourselves well, in a socially desirable fashion. Thus in the ratings of another—which really represent a judgment about ourselves—we have perhaps the best measure of our own personalities.

The implications of the assumed similarity bias for the classroom teacher are clear, since so much of teaching involves making accurate judgments of others. If teachers tend to project their own personalities onto their students, they are probably getting an inaccurate view.

Leniency effects

One bias that does not have as potentially damaging effects as other biases is the leniency effect (Bruner and Tagiuri, 1954). The *leniency effect* reflects the finding that in the absence of much information about a stimulus person, ratings of that person tend to be more favorable than unfavorable. There appears to be a general propensity toward making positive evaluations rather than negative ones. For instance, examination of how subjects in laboratory experiments rate others reveals that they are almost always on the positive end of the scale being used. In addition, people generally find positive evaluations of others to be more pleasant, they are better able to learn positive evaluations, and when they change their evaluations of another person, it is generally toward a more positive impression (Freedman, Sears, and Carlsmith, 1978).

The leniency effect thus suggests that if everything else is equal, teachers will tend to view their students in a positive rather than negative light. Of course, the key phrase is "if everything else is equal." Classroom teachers, who are in constant close contact with their students, are likely to be much less susceptible to this bias—at least on a long-term basis.

Biases in general

A good deal of space has been spent discussing various types of bias to which teachers are susceptible when they form impressions and make attributions about the causes of others' behavior. This has been done quite deliberately, because one of the ways in which such biases can be reduced is if individuals are aware of the errors they are likely to make when arriving at judgments about others. As mentioned earlier, much of a teacher's responsibilities involve making decisions about the source of a student's problems or determining what the best teaching strategy is for a particular type of student. In order for such decisions to be carried out wisely, it is necessary first to acquire an accurate impression of the student. The types of biases that have been discussed all operate to reduce the teacher's ability to make intelligent, reasonable decisions. It is hoped that by having the potential sources of bias made explicit to them, teachers will be able to deal effectively with such biases and counteract their effects.

SUMMARY

Forming impressions of others is a universal phenomenon that both teachers and students engage in. This chapter examines the processes underlying the formation of attitudes, expectations, and an understanding of others' behavior based on group membership, individual characteristics, and performance.

Three group membership characteristics strongly affect teachers' attitudes towards students: sex, socioeconomic status, and race. Boys generally receive lower grades than girls, even when actual achievement is identical. Teachers also tend to favor middle- and upper-class children, reserving lower expectations and less positive treatment for lower-class students. Finally, teachers generally hold more positive attitudes and expectations toward their white students than toward their black students.

Major characteristics of the individual student also affect impressions. A student's physical attractiveness is a powerful variable that leads to perceptions of greater social and academic skill, both by teachers and by peers. Prior successful academic performance results in higher levels of interpersonal attraction and better treatment from teachers, while low achievers are not as well liked or as well responded to.

Teachers' expectations about the academic success of a pupil affects their behavior toward that pupil and may actually cause the expected behavior to come about. This phenomenon is known as the teacher expectation effect. A number of sources lead to the formation of expectations, including sex, SES, ethnic background, physical attractiveness, older sibling academic performance, student name, and formal records of past academic performance.

Once an initial set of expectations is formed, the expectations are transmitted to the student via the social-emotional climate in the classroom, the type of feedback the teacher gives the student, the different input that occurs when students are given learning materials that differ according to the teacher's expectations, and the differing opportunities for student output in terms of the frequency of responses allowed. Eventually, the student begins to perform in accordance with the teacher's expectations, completing the cycle of expectation transmission.

Person perception refers to the processes involved in the formation of impressions about others, and attribution refers to the way in which the reasons underlying an individual's overt behavior are determined. There are a number of errors that often occur in attribution. One frequent distortion is that individuals acting as observers tend to see internal dispositions or characteristics as the cause of the behavior in others, but see external or situational causes as the source of their own behavior when they are the actor in question. Individuals also engage in defensive attribution, in which they try to view themselves in a favorable way.

Another bias, the halo effect, refers to impression formation in which a person who is initially judged positively is assumed to be uniformly positive on all dimensions. The halo effect derives from implicit personality theory, an individual's assumptions about the nature of others. The projective bias is one in which individuals mistakenly attribute their own feelings and personality characteristics to others. Finally, the leniency effect reflects the finding that in the absence of detailed information, ratings of a person will tend to be more favorable than unfavorable.

All of the biases discussed reduce teachers' ability to make accurate judgments concerning their students. An awareness of the biases can lead to a reduction of the problem.

FOR FURTHER STUDY AND APPLICATION

Brophy, J. E., and Good, T. L. *Teacher-student relationships: Causes and consequences*. New York: Holt, Rinehart and Winston, 1974. A masterful compendium of the factors affecting teacher-student relationships and the development of teacher expectations. Provides some practical strategies for dealing with pupils.

Rosenthal, R., and Jacobson, L. *Pygmalion in the classroom: Teacher expectation and pupils' intellectual development*. New York: Holt, Rinehart and

Winston, 1968.   This is the book that started it all: the results of a large-scale study of teacher expectations. Much esteemed and much maligned.

Shaver, K. G. *An introduction to attribution processes.* Cambridge, Mass.: Winthrop, 1975.

Hastorf, A. H., Schneider, D. J., and Polefka, J. *Person perception.* Reading, Mass.: Addison-Wesley, 1977.   These two books provide an excellent introduction to the areas of attribution and person perception, respectively.

Brophy, J. E., and Evertson, C. M. *Student characteristics and teaching.* New York: Longman, 1981.   Reports in a readable, practical manner the results of a massive study of student effects on teachers.

11

COMMUNICATION PROCESSES IN THE CLASSROOM

CHAPTER OVERVIEW

In this chapter, a number of facets of teacher-student communication in the classroom are examined. First, a model is presented that serves to illustrate the process of classroom communication. The discussion then turns to some of the ways in which an individual's cultural and subcultural backgrounds affect verbal communication in the classroom. Finally, the chapter examines the two major channels along which communication occurs, the verbal and the nonverbal.

Adrienne Taylor is a teacher in the small town of Anadarko, Oklahoma. Teaching eighth-grade English at Anadarko Junior High, Ms. Taylor has classes that are very heterogeneous ethnically. Forty-two percent of her students are Native Americans (Anadarko calls itself the "Indian capital of the world"), 10 percent are black, 38 percent are Caucasian, and 10 percent are representatives of various other groups. At one time, there were even a number of Vietnamese. Such rich heterogeneity is hardly typical in a town with a total population of only 5,300.

The interview began with a question about whether the teaching Ms. Taylor does is influenced by the diverse ethnic background of her students.

A.   It certainly is. Let me give you one small example of the differences in the educational and social backgrounds of the kids. One of the Indian children in my class had really been acting up, and I took him out of class into the hallway, and I gave him the "word." Among the things that I said to him was, "And you'll look me in the eye when I talk to you." At that point, the principal just happened to be walking by. He didn't say anything then, but later he told me that I shouldn't make a male Indian student look me in the eye, because they have been taught not to look women directly in the eye. He told me that I probably was telling him to do something that was against his customs. So there are differences, and although they might sound picayunish to someone who wasn't trying to understand the child's culture at home, they're important. You can get yourself into difficulty; the child may be trying to cooperate but just not be able to do so in the way you want him to.

Q.   Do you notice any other cultural differences that might affect school performance?

A.   One thing is that the Native Americans tend to be extremely generous and noncompetitive, traits that may work against them in the school situation. If you're teaching school, sometimes the lack of what we would commonly call motivation or aggression is a problem scholastically. Some people tend to think of it as a drawback rather than as charming or unselfish.

Q.   I guess it would prevent people from succeeding in the way that our American society generally labels success.

A.   Right. Sometimes I would like my students to work for a better grade or to be more aggressive by speaking up in class. And they just aren't going to do it. It doesn't mean there's anything wrong with that, but at first you get frustrated as a teacher—it's an adjustment. And of course I don't mean that all Indian students are alike; they're not all quiet, they're not all nonaggressive. But the culture in general is more relaxed, more generous, and more family-oriented than you find in other parts of society.

Q.   What's the biggest problem you face as a teacher?

A.   Lack of interest. We have a lot of absenteeism. The kids get behind, and then they have to make up the work. There's just generally a lack of motivation—the kids are just taking things because they have to.

Q.   And how about the most rewarding thing to you about teaching?

A.   I think that moment when the "light comes on" and a kid understands something and you know that they've got it. You don't ever lose the thrill of having a kid figure something out.

Q.   One last, more general question. What are the characteristics of good teaching?

A.   I guess the best teacher is somebody who knows something you need to know and wants to teach it. In other words, you need to know your subject matter first and then you've got to be enthusiastic enough to communicate it. That sounds kind of simplistic, but basically, the kids will learn the way you teach.

As Adrienne Taylor points out, one of the essential parts of teaching is being able to communicate your ideas and understanding about a topic to your students. The ability to communicate clearly and precisely is at the very heart of teaching. Unless a teacher can convey what is being taught in a way that is appropriate for a particular student, learning will be unlikely to occur. And unless the student is able to communicate that learning has in fact occurred, the teacher will not know how to proceed appropriately. Indeed, it can be argued that a chief characteristic of an effective teacher is the ability both to communicate effectively and to understand the meaning of students' communications accurately.

A MODEL OF COMMUNICATION PROCESSES

Consider the following interchange:

MS. BROCHSTEIN: (Thinking to herself): *An equilateral triangle has three straight sides of equal length, has three equal angles, and is a plane, closed, and simple figure. But Michael doesn't understand that. Let me start with something simple.* (Aloud, to Michael): Michael, an equilateral triangle is a figure with three sides. The three sides are all the same length.

MICHAEL: I'm not sure what you mean by "figure."

MS. BROCHSTEIN: You can think of "figure" as just another word for drawing.

MICHAEL: I get it.

This simple interchange, an example of innumerable conversations in innumerable classrooms, provides a clear illustration of communication processes in the classroom. Despite the seeming simplicity of the conversation, the process of communication is complicated and involves a number of stages

FIGURE 11-1   A Model of Teacher-Student Communication Processes

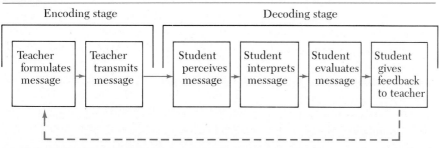

encoder the person who sends a verbal or nonverbal message to another person

relevant to the teacher who sends the message (formally termed the *encoder*) and the student who receives it (the *decoder*). A model of the communication process is presented in Figure 11-1.

Encoding by Teachers

decoder the person who receives a verbal or nonverbal message from another person

As in the example of Ms. Brochstein, who moved from her own understanding of an equilateral triangle to a point closer to what she thought young Michael could understand, teachers do not just think of a concept and then, independent of the student, communicate it. A person who wants to communicate a concept must first translate the concept into a form the listener can understand. This translation process is known as *encoding,* and it consists of two basic parts. First, the message must be encoded according to the characteristics of the listener or listeners to whom the communication is being directed. Second, the message must actually be transmitted (Hurt, Scott, and McCroskey, 1978).

Message formulation

To be effective communicators, teachers must encode messages in ways that take into account the characteristics of their students and the specific situation. John Flavell and his associates (1968) suggest a theoretical process in which the speaker first decides what the nature of the message is to be, mentally using language that is most accurate from his or her own point of view. The next step is to make a judgment about student characteristics that are relevant to the message and the kind of language that would be most appropriate for the student. It is possible, of course, for the new message to be identical to the way the teacher first encoded it internally. (We would expect this to happen if, for instance, the teacher and student were contemporaries and shared the same education and background.) On the other hand, if there are numerous differences between teacher and student, substantial changes may be made in the initial encoding, or an entirely new message may be formulated. In the foregoing example, for instance, Ms. Brochstein changed her initial wording, which used "equal length," to "same length," as well as making other simplifications for young Michael. The important point is that communication competence requires that the teacher take the nature of the student's abilities and developmental level into account to formulate a comprehensible message.

Another important point about the communication model is that it makes a distinction between teacher *linguistic competence* and teacher *communicative competence.* The initial message that a teacher encodes, prior to any consideration of the nature of the student, gives an indication of the teacher's linguistic competence. The teacher is likely to formulate the message initially at a level of linguistic competence that is at or close to his or her greatest ability. Moreover, the message initially will take into account message characteristics (called *referents*) that are most salient to the teacher. Thus, Ms. Brochstein first thinks of an equilateral triangle in formal definitional terms that are familiar to her. This represents her level of linguistic competence.

linguistic competence the ability to generate a verbal message to represent an idea one wants to communicate

However, if she does not recode the message to fit the characteristics of the student, she will not have much success in communicating what an equilateral triangle is. By breaking down the message into components and using a less sophisticated vocabulary, her communicative competence is increased considerably. Linguistic competence and communicative competence, then, may be quite independent of each other.

It should be noted, however, that the characteristics of the listener are not represented merely by the listener's vocabulary level. As indicated in the discussion of cognitive development in Chapter 2, children vary a great deal in the nature of the understanding that is possible for them at a given age. Thus no matter how well stated a concept may be, the child will not be able to understand the message in the same way the teacher does if the child has not attained the necessary cognitive level.

It is also important to note that teachers often do not have the luxury of encoding to a specific child. Rather, they must direct their communications to a particular normative level, a kind of "classroom average" of attainment. In practice, this means that for some children the message may be too sophisticated and for others too elementary. Thus teachers must walk a fine line when they are formulating messages to a class as a whole.

communicative competence the ability to transform a verbal message into a form that will be understood by the decoder

Students cannot understand what they're taught unless teachers communicate with language that takes into account the students' characteristics. (© Norman Hurst/Stock, Boston)

Transmitting the message

Once the nature of the message that the teacher intends to communicate has been encoded, the message must be transmitted to the student. So far, the discussion has been only in terms of verbal language. But verbal language is in fact only one of the ways in which messages can be transmitted. One of the richest sources of information available to a decoder resides in nonverbal channels. Such nonverbal cues as facial expression and eye gaze can provide information about what the teacher intends to communicate (as well as communicating unintended messages). Nonverbal channels of communication are discussed later in the chapter. For now, though, keep in mind that nonverbal channels can provide information as important to the student as does the verbal communication channel.

Decoding by Students

Once the teacher has transmitted the message, the second phase of the communication process begins: decoding by the student. One team of researchers (Hurt, Scott, and McCroskey, 1978) suggests that decoding involves four major phases: (1) perception of the message, (2) interpretation of the message, (3) evaluation of the message, and (4) feedback to the teacher.

Perception of the message

When the teacher transmits the message to the student, the student must first be aware of it on a sensory level. Thus the initial stage in decoding a message is arousal of the sensory mechanisms. In the case of verbal channels, it is typically auditory arousal that occurs; but nonverbal messages require the use of additional senses, particularly the sense of vision.

Interpretation of the message

After the student has perceived the message, he or she must interpret its meaning. This interpretation process is based on prior experience—both with the nature of the message and with the specific teacher. For instance, Michael was unable to interpret the meaning of "figure," which Ms. Brochstein may never have used previously.

One of the important developmental changes relevant to the interpretation phase relates to the student's ability to recognize deficiencies in the communication of the teacher, so that the teacher can be asked to reformulate the message. Young children are unable to make fine distinctions in their interpretation of messages (Glucksberg, Krauss, and Higgins, 1975); they do not easily recognize ambiguous or uninformative messages.

This problem suggests that young children may have difficulty in learning material for two reasons. First, they may not understand the material because it is cognitively too advanced for them. Second (and more important in the present context), the message they receive from the teacher may be inadequately formulated, but the children may not have sufficiently sophisticated interpretative skills to understand that a better formulation of the message might allow them to understand the material. In such cases, they will provide no feedback to the teacher indicating a desire to have the message restated, and thus the concept may ultimately not be learned.

When considering children's interpretation of a teacher's message, it is important to note that the interpretation may be based not just on the literal content of the message but on the *metacommunicative* content. Metacommunication refers to the hidden or underlying content of a message. Thus a teacher who says, "Jonathan, get your hands off Joshua's desk," may actually be communicating, at a metacommunicative level, the message, "I'm very angry with you, Jonathan." Thomas Gordon, author of *Teacher Effectiveness Training* (1974), has suggested that attention to the metacommunicative aspects of a message is essential to effective communication.

metacommunicative content the hidden, or underlying, content of a message

Evaluation of the message

Assuming that the student has interpreted the meaning of the message, the next step in the communication process is for him or her to evaluate the meaning of the message. Here, the student has wide latitude in affecting the nature of the interactive communicative process. For instance, a student might feel that a teacher does not really understand what she is talking about and may decide to ignore the message entirely.

But in practice, teachers are very credible as communicators, primarily because they are generally considered to be high in expertise. Thus students tend to believe their teachers' opinions about the world. However, this credibility may not be so high in relation to topics that the student considers outside the realm of the teacher's expertise. For example, it is likely that a teacher's message about smoking marijuana will not be credible. The students are likely to assume that the teacher has little experience or knowledge in that particular area and will probably disregard the communication.

Feedback from the student

The final part of the communication sequence involves feedback from the student to the teacher. Many times a teacher has no real sense of the success of his or her message until the student indicates either that the message is understood or that it requires reformulation. The feedback indicates whether the student in fact interpreted the message appropriately. For example, Michael explicitly indicated that he had not understood the word "figure," and Ms. Brochstein therefore recoded the message.

Feedback also acts in another, more subtle fashion. Because the feedback leads to successful encoding and decoding, it is reinforcing to both participants in the communication process. In a classroom situation, this can lead to teachers

Communication Networks in the Classroom

The model of communication that has been discussed is based on two-person communications. This model is obviously an oversimplification, particularly when one is discussing the classroom; because it is unfortunately rare for teachers and students to have the luxury of one-to-one communication.

The systems whereby people communicate with one another in many different sorts of patterns and arrangements are known as *communication networks*. The kind of network that is found in a classroom has important implications for the functioning of communication, and it also determines, at least partially, the social-emotional climate that exists in the class.

The Typical Classroom

In the typical classroom, the formal communication network that exists is clear: The teacher is the pivotal individual and is the recipient and the source of almost all communications. Students, in fact, are admonished not to speak to or otherwise communicate with their peers. If one were to represent such a communication network graphically, it would look something like this figure (a class size of four is assumed for purposes of illustration):

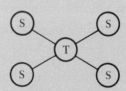

In this diagram, characterized as a wheel, the central figure is obviously the teacher. However, there are many possible variations in a four-student, one-teacher situation. The figure on the next page shows a number of them, but it does not exhaust the possibilities.

There has been a great deal of research comparing the functioning of small groups in relation to their particular type of communication network. Some studies have focused on group productivity; others have examined the satisfaction of group members in relation to the type of network of which they are a part. The two lines of research interestingly yield different sorts of results.

If one is interested in maximizing problem-solving efficiency, the wheel would seem to be the network of choice, as long as the problem is a relatively

Possible Communication Networks in Classrooms

T = Teacher
S = Student

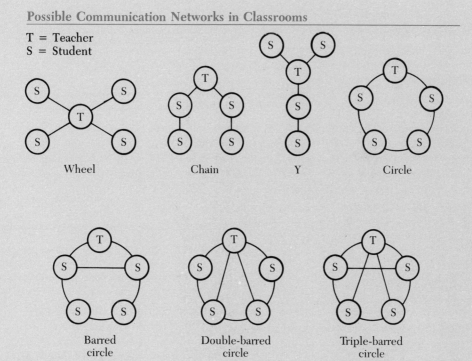

Wheel   Chain   Y   Circle

Barred
circle

Double-barred
circle

Triple-barred
circle

(Adapted from Shaw, 1976, p. 139)

simple one. However, if the task is relatively complex, then decentralized networks are more efficient.

Saturation

Why is there this difference between simple and complex tasks in the optimum communication network? The answer appears to be related to a concept known as saturation (Gilchrist, Shaw, and Walker, 1964). *Saturation* refers to the degree to which a group member is "overloaded" by group demands, and it occurs when an individual receives and must send so many communications that he or she cannot effectively contend with the task. In terms of teaching, saturation is not likely to be a problem with simple tasks, since the teacher's role is largely one of collecting and keeping track of minimal amounts of information. When the task is complex, however, saturation may occur, with the teacher receiving too many communications to be able to exercise control effectively. In this instance, a decentralized network, in which information can be shared more equitably, will result in

Continued on next page

greater efficiency. It should be noted, though, that efficiency is not always a requirement of classroom learning, and even more important, most learning in the classroom does not occur cooperatively. Thus the centralized communication network employed in classrooms should not be too severely faulted.

However, there is one dimension related to communication patterns that has been shown to have direct relevance for typical classroom situations: that of the social-emotional climate. Experiments have consistently shown that the more central the position an individual holds in a network, the greater will be that person's satisfaction. It is not hard to think of reasons why this would be the case. The central person can talk with anyone else and is in an influential and powerful position. Those persons at the periphery can talk with only a few or sometimes with only one person, and their

feeling confident that their teaching has been effective and to students feeling that they have learned in an appropriate manner.

Given that feedback tends to increase the accuracy of communications, it would seem to be a reasonable strategy on the part of the teacher to attempt to promote its use. But unfortunately, this is not always easy to do. It is particularly difficult to provide negative feedback in a way that does not discourage or embarrass a student. Likewise, students frequently find it difficult to provide verbal feedback to a teacher that indicates they have not understood what the teacher is saying, for fear of being embarrassed themselves. Thus negative feedback can be difficult to provide—for both teacher and student. It should be mentioned also that neither is it always easy to administer positive feedback; several studies have shown that positive feedback is sparingly used in actual classroom situations (Brophy and Good, 1974). But teachers should be aware of the facilitative effects of feedback and should make every effort to encourage it in their classrooms.

Once the student has provided feedback to the teacher, the final step in the communication sequence is for the teacher to reformulate the message if necessary—as Ms. Brochstein did by altering her description of "figure" to fit more closely to what Michael would understand. Teachers must reformulate what they have communicated in light of the feedback they have received.

The Student as Communicator

Thus far the model of communication has been discussed as if communications were always initiated by the teacher. Although this is probably most typical of what actually happens in classrooms, there are still a substantial number of

communications can easily get lost in the shuffle. When this logic is applied to the typical classroom, it is reasonable to expect that the teacher, who is at the center of the communication network, will feel considerably more satisfied with the situation than the students, who are all on the periphery of the network.

A solution to these discrepancies in satisfaction may lie in restructuring the typical centrality of the teacher's position. For instance, such innovations as the use of student group-learning techniques (discussed in Chapter 9) can make the students feel part of a more decentralized network, and this in turn can lead to greater feelings of satisfaction. Indeed, probably any technique in which the student's role as a peripheral figure in the communication network is modified toward greater centrality will increase student satisfaction.

instances in which the student is placed in the role of encoder and the teacher is the decoder. In almost all respects, the model so far presented—involving teachers communicating to their students—holds for the opposite sequence, in which students communicate to their teachers. But there is one point that becomes crucial when considering the nature of the feedback that teachers give after a student has formulated a message to them: The feedback must be age-appropriate for the student (analogous to the need for the teacher's message to a student to be appropriate for the student's comprehension level). There is a wide range of possible kinds of feedback that a teacher can give to a student, and the greater the clarity of the feedback, the greater the likelihood that the communicator will recode his or her message in a more useful way.

The importance of the nature of the feedback provided to a communicator was illustrated in a study (Peterson, Danner, and Flavell, 1972) in which 4- and 7-year-old children were asked to describe something to an adult. Three kinds of feedback—all indicating a lack of understanding on the part of the adult—were used. In one kind, the adult expressed puzzlement and lack of understanding through a facial expression, and did not *say* anything that would indicate that the child should reformulate the message. A second kind of feedback, which was also rather inexplicit, was used in which the adult said, "I don't understand, I don't think I can guess that." Finally, the most explicit feedback consisted of the phrases, "Look at it again. What else does it look like? Can you tell me anything else about it?"

The results for the various conditions differed dramatically. Out of twenty-four 4- and twenty-four 7-year-olds, only four 4-year-olds and seven 7-year-olds reformulated the message on receiving the facial expression feedback. Seven 4-year-olds and twenty 7-year-olds recoded the message when the inexplicit verbal feedback was used. However, *all* the subjects reformulated

Power and Solidarity as Expressed Through Language

Part of the power of language lies in the subtleties that can be conveyed through particular word choices. One example is related to the use of personal pronouns in terms of address and the kinds of choices that speakers must make, using a complicated set of criteria.

At one time, English speakers had to choose between the use of *thou* (for familiar people) and *you* (for formal usage). Although this decision is no longer required in English, in many other languages the choice still exists. In German, for instance, a speaker must choose between *du* and *Sie*; in Spanish, between *tu* and *usted*; and in French, between *tu* and *vous*. Each language has its own rules. In French, for example, speakers use *tu* for close friends, family, and children, and *vous* for nonfamily adults. Children use *vous* for all adults except closest family members.

The decision to use *tu* rather than *vous* is based on what has been called the power semantic and the solidarity semantic (Brown and Gilman, 1960). The *power semantic* refers to the power or status relationship between speaker and listener. The more powerful and high-status a person is, the more likely that *vous* will be used; persons in a lower-status role will be

the message when the very explicit request was made. It appears, then, that young children must have feedback that is quite specific; they may be unaware of the meaning of such subtleties as nonverbal requests for feedback or even inexplicit verbal attempts at eliciting feedback.

DIFFERENT WAYS OF COMMUNICATING: THE VERBAL CHANNEL

The model of teacher-student communication that has been described provides a general description of the kinds of processes involved in classroom communication systems. Let us turn now to the specific form by which communications are transmitted. The verbal communication channel is discussed first because it is the most obvious and in many ways the primary form of communication in classrooms. Later, however, the various types of nonverbal channels will be considered because they too play an important role in how teachers and students communicate with one another.

verbal channel the mode of communication that consists of spoken language

The *verbal channel* consists of spoken language, and it is the foremost means of communication in any classroom. Almost all formal teaching operates through

addressed as *tu*. The *solidarity semantic* refers to social distance, which is the degree of shared social experience between individuals. People who are close neighbors, attend the same college, or share membership in a club, are close in solidarity, and they are likely to use the familiar *tu*.

There are historical trends with regard to which of the semantics, power or solidarity, is predominant. Formerly the power semantic was primarily operative, but in recent decades the solidarity semantic has dominated. And due to the rise of egalitarianism, more people in France are today addressed as *tu* than ever before.

English, too, has its examples of the power and solidarity semantics, shown by degrees of formality in forms of address. Close friends use one another's first names, while persons of greater social distance use formal titles and last names. A good example of asymmetry in the use of forms of address is in teacher-student relationships. The traditional form is for the teacher to use the students' first names—Leah and Harry—but for the teacher to be addressed by his or her title and last name—Ms. Vorwerk, Mr. Langdon. The use of a teacher's first name by students is so unusual, in fact, that it can be indicative of a serious breach of discipline. The importance to teachers of both the power semantic and the solidarity semantic is shown by the fact that they will call one another "Mr." and "Ms." when students are present, but generally use one another's first names in private.

the spoken word, and for this reason alone it is of importance to the teachers. But the verbal channel operates in other important ways. It allows the student to respond to questions, and it is directly used in solving problems. For instance, take a student who is asked to memorize this list of words: *fork, fig, sun, cup, chocolate, knife, orange, stars, moon.* Rather than memorize the list by rote, students proficient in language usage will note that there are three eating utensils, three celestial objects, and three food items, and they will use these linguistic categories as an aid to memorization. Thus problem solving is facilitated by competence in the use of the verbal channel.

Perhaps even more important, there are some investigators who argue that the kind of language used determines the nature of an individual's thinking. This argument, which has become known as the Sapir-Whorf hypothesis (named for its two major proponents) bears some careful scrutiny.

The Sapir-Whorf Hypothesis

The *Sapir-Whorf hypothesis* is actually made up of two propositions. The first suggests that language tends to shape the way individuals in a particular culture

Sapir-Whorf hypothesis the proposition that language shapes the way in which individuals of a particular culture understand the world

understand and experience the world. The second and more extreme part of the hypothesis is that language actually determines how an individual thinks about the world. The evidence for the hypothesis rests primarily on differences in vocabulary that exist between different languages (Whorf, 1956). For instance, Eskimos have twenty or thirty words for snow, whereas the English language has only one. In another example, the Hanunoo tribe has ninety-two names for different kinds of rice. But before you get the idea that English suffers from a dearth of vocabulary in comparison to other languages, the Hopi use one word to name all flying things except birds, whereas English speakers can identify insects, butterflies, airplanes, blimps, etc. According to Benjamin Whorf, the availability of multiple linguistic categories enables an individual to make better discriminations than can be made by persons whose language does not have an equal range of linguistic categories. Hence an American would not be as adept at perceiving different kinds of snow as would an Eskimo. This suggests that snow is actually understood differently (and more accurately) by the Eskimo.

Such evidence is not sufficient to confirm the Sapir-Whorf hypothesis, however. One direct alternative explanation is that linguistic categories are produced *because* an individual's culture provides certain experiences and environmental stimuli that are particularly relevant. Thus the Eskimo's need for detailed knowledge about the various types of snow ultimately resulted in the development of many different words corresponding to the different kinds of snow. Most English speakers, on the other hand, have had little need to go beyond awareness that snow can be wet or dry or hard, and appropriate words have therefore not been devised in the English language. Hence rather than language leading to a particular way of explaining the world, certain experiences may have led to the development of particular linguistic categories.

There is even more direct evidence against the Sapir-Whorf hypothesis. Individuals using different languages are quite capable of making the same kinds of perceptual discriminations (Brown and Lenneberg, 1954). There is a difference, however, in the speed with which they are capable of identifying and labeling discriminations in stimuli. Thus speakers of English may have to use the longer phrase, "soft, wet snow that melts quickly," instead of a one-word Eskimo term; but they *can* make the distinction, albeit more slowly and in a more cumbersome fashion.

It does appear, though, that language affects how things are stored in memory and how well they can be retrieved. In one study (Lenneberg and Roberts, 1956), Zuni Indians were asked to identify an orange stimulus, which was shown among other orange and yellow objects. Because there is only one word for both orange and yellow in the Zuni language, it was hypothesized that there would be difficulty in recalling objects in this area of the spectrum. The results showed, as predicted, that monolingual Zuni made the most errors of recall, followed by subjects who spoke both Zuni and English, and a control group of monolingual English speakers made the fewest errors. It appeared that the monolingual Zuni had the ability to make the necessary discriminations initially; the difficulty arose in later *recalling* the distinction.

It thus appears that the original Sapir-Whorf hypothesis was too strongly put. Language does have an effect on the way that objects and events are stored in and retrieved from memory, but it does not appear to affect one's perception or one's basic thinking processes directly.

Subcultural Variations in Use of the Verbal Channel

Subcultural differences in the use of the verbal channel are a conspicuous reminder of how a student's culture may affect his or her school performance. One need only compare the language of children playing on an urban street in a poor section of a city with children on the playground of an exclusive and expensive private school to see the vast differences that exist. The word choice, the accent, the sentence construction, and the grammar will all differ.

The differences that exist in use of the verbal channel among various subcultural groups have been the source of much controversy (Feagans and Farran, 1981). Some researchers have argued that nonstandard forms of language usage represent a clear deficit on the part of subcultural groups—a deficit that ought to be remediated by the teaching of "proper" linguistic usage. Others have suggested that nonstandard forms of English are sophisticated and follow a certain logic, and that their usage fits subcultural environments better than standard English. This section presents two major theories that have been used to explain the use of nonstandard forms of English in particular subcultural groups.

Restricted and elaborated codes

Basil Bernstein (1961a, 1972) has suggested that the complexity of speech varies as a function of social class. He has theorized that lower-class families tend to use a *restricted code,* in contrast to the *elaborated code* used by middle-class families. In a restricted linguistic code, the language tends to be relatively concrete and concerned with physical objects and actions. For instance, a child might be told to "Turn off the TV" or "Don't hit your sister." Users of restricted codes are also likely to ignore the motives and intentions that lie behind the behavior of the person who is being addressed. Rather than saying, "Even though you like to eat candy, it's bad for your teeth, so don't eat it," a user of a restricted code might simply admonish a child to "Stop eating candy." Restricted codes also tend to use social status as a way of rationalizing and controlling behavior. Rather than explaining why homework is a desirable behavior, a mother might tell her child to do her homework, "Because I told you to do it."

Examples of dialogue between a mother and child, cited by Bernstein (1967), illustrate concretely the use of elaborated and restricted codes. The first shows a mother responding in a restricted code:

MOTHER: Put away your blocks.   (Child: Why?)

MOTHER: Put them away.   (Child: Why?)

restricted code language that tends to be relatively concrete and concerned with physical objects and actions

elaborated code language with a relatively sophisticated and explicit expression of meaning and motivation

MOTHER: They mess up the house. (Child: Why?)

MOTHER: I told you to put them away, didn't I?

The second example shows a mother responding in an elaborated code:

MOTHER: Put away your blocks. (Child: Why?)

MOTHER: You have finished playing with them. (Child: Why?)

MOTHER: Because we should learn to put away our toys when we are finished using them. If the toys are left on the floor, the house will look untidy. (Child: Why?)

MOTHER: Now put the blocks away, darling, and don't make such a fuss.

(Bernstein, 1967, p. 236)

As can be seen from these examples, the user of the restricted code tends to respond with direct, concrete, imperative admonitions, whereas the mother using the elaborated code tries to explain and reason with the child. In terms of what can be learned from the situation, the child whose mother employs an elaborate code is in a much better position to learn new information and concepts.

Bernstein has summarized a number of general characteristics of restricted codes. In general, restricted codes show:

1. Short, grammatically simple, often unfinished sentences with a poor syntactical form stressing the active voice.
2. Simple and repetitive use of conjunctions (so, then, because).
3. Little use of subordinate clauses to break down the initial categories of the dominant subject.
4. Inability to hold a formal subject through a speech sequence; thus a dislocated informational content is facilitated.
5. Rigid and limited use of adjectives and adverbs.
6. Infrequent use of impersonal pronouns as subjects of conditional clauses.
7. Frequent use of statements where the reason and conclusion are confounded to produce a categoric statement.
8. A large number of statements and phrases which signal a requirement for the previous speech sequence to be reinforced: "Wouldn't it?" "You see?" "You know?" This process is termed, "sympathetic circularity."
9. Individual selection from a group of idiomatic phrases or sequences will frequently occur.
10. The individual qualification is in the sentence organization: It is a language of implicit meaning.

(Bernstein, 1961a, p. 169)

The elaborated code is essentially the converse of the restrictive code. The range of vocabulary is broader, the grammar is more sophisticated, higher-order concepts are employed, and the meaning that the speaker intends to convey is more explicit. Rather than being oriented to the individual's overt behavior, elaborated language is concerned with underlying motivations and intentions.

The child who uses an elaborated code has a distinct advantage in school over children who employ a restrictive code, primarily because teachers use elaborated codes. According to Bernstein, one of the central responsibilities of the teacher is to show the child using the restricted code how to employ elaborated forms of language. He makes the important point, though, that it is not necessary—and probably is undesirable—to make the child drop restrictive code usage altogether. Doing so would make the child's behavior incongruent with his or her home environment and would thus be inappropriate.

The source of the differences in use of language by middle- and lower-class families may lie in the role that language plays in the home environment. Bernstein suggests that lower-class families are more frequently involved in situations in which physical activity is necessary and there is little importance in determining others' motivation and intent. In addition, lower-class families, in contrast to middle-class ones, have less need to view the world abstractly. However, these are merely speculations on Bernstein's part, and empirical evidence in support of these assertions is lacking.

Indeed, there are those who criticize Bernstein's basic theory. For instance, Bernstein's research has been restricted to British subjects, and some critics argue that there are fundamental differences between British and American middle and lower classes. More important, the question of whether lower-class children use restricted codes out of necessity or out of choice has not been resolved. In other words, it is possible that lower-class children are quite as adept in the use of elaborated codes as middle-class children but simply prefer the use of the restricted code. In fact, evidence for such a position has been obtained (Robinson, 1965). He asked lower- and middle-class boys to write two kinds of letters. One was a formal, business-type letter, and the other was an informal letter. If Bernstein's theory were correct, the lower-class children should have been at a disadvantage in writing the formal letter. However, it turned out that there were significantly fewer differences between the lower- and middle-class children's *formal* letters than between their *informal* ones. What this finding indicates is that the use of restrictive codes in speech may be due more to lower-class members choosing to use restrictive codes rather than to some underlying linguistic (or even more general intellectual) impoverishment. The results of this experiment also suggest that teachers need to be quite adept at choosing appropriate exercises and testing situations for their students in order to maximize performance and get a true indication of their pupils' underlying abilities.

Nonstandard dialects

Until now we have been considering differences that exist in language among different social classes. Another approach to examining subcultural differences

Table 11-1   Examples of Nonstandard English Usage

Variable	Standard English	Black English
Linking verb	He is going.	He goin'.
Possessive marker	John's cousin.	John cousin.
Plural marker	I have five cents.	I got five cents.
Subject expression	John lives in New York.	John he live in New York.
Verb form	I drank the milk.	I drunk the milk.
Past marker	Yesterday he walked home.	Yesterday he walk home.
Verb agreement	He runs home.	He run home.
Future form	I will go home.	I'ma go home.
"If" construction	I asked if he did it.	I ask did he do it.
Negation	I don't have any.	I don't got none.
Indefinite article	I want an apple.	I want a apple.
Pronoun form	We have to do it.	Us got to do it.
	His book	He book.
Preposition	He is over at his friend's house.	He over to his friend house.
	He teaches at Francis Pool.	He teach Francis Pool.
Be	Statement: He is here all the time.	Statement: He be here.
Do	Contradiction: No he isn't.	Contradiction: No, he don't.

(Baratz, 1969)

Reprinted with permission from Baratz, J. C. Teaching reading in an urban Negro school. In J. C. Baratz and R. W. Shay (Eds.), *Teaching Black Children to Read*. Washington, D.C. Center for Applied Linguistics. 1969.

involves the examination of language differences among various racial and ethnic groups. By far the most controversial issue associated with this approach is the concern over what has been termed nonstandard English, or sometimes, black English. Nonstandard English has been found, rather consistently, to be spoken by lower-class, urban blacks.

Some examples of one type of nonstandard English usage can be seen in Table 11-1. As shown in the table, nonstandard English is characterized by such forms as a lack of linking verbs ("he goin'" for "he is going") and the improper use of possessives ("John cousin" for "John's cousin"). Use of such language in a classroom setting can result in difficult problems for the student, because most teachers tend to assume that such linguistic performance is ungrammatical and unsophisticated. However, there is compelling evidence that nonstandard English may, in fact, be quite as complicated and sophisticated as standard English.

The main proponent of the view that nonstandard English follows a logic of its own is William Labov (1973). His evidence is derived from linguistic analyses of interviews carried out with black children in Harlem. He cites as an example of the use of nonstandard English an interview with a black 15-year-old ninth grader who is constantly in trouble with his teachers and does quite poorly academically. When he is asked his views on God and life after death, he responds in this manner:

LABOV: What happens to you after you die? Do you know?

LARRY: Yeah, I know.

LABOV: What?

LARRY: After they put you in the ground, your body turns into ah— bones. . . .

LABOV: What happens to your spirit?

LARRY: Your spirit—soon as you die, your spirit leaves you.

LABOV: And where does this spirit go?

LARRY: Well, it all depends . . .

LABOV: On what?

LARRY: You know, like some people say if you're good . . . your spirit goin' to heaven . . . 'n' if you bad, your spirit goin' to hell. Well, [no]. Your spirit goin' to hell anyway, good or bad.

LABOV: Why?

LARRY: Why? I'll tell you why. 'Cause, you see, doesn' nobody really know that it's a God, y'know, 'cause I mean I have seen black gods, pink gods, white gods, all color gods, and don't nobody know it's really a God. An' when they be sayin' if you good, you goin' t'heaven, tha's [wrong], 'cause you ain't goin' to no heaven, 'cause it ain't no heaven for you to go to.

(Labov, 1973, pp. 36–37)

This is hardly the kind of a dialogue with which most teachers would be pleased. But Labov goes beyond the surface language, which he describes as a classic example of the use of nonstandard English, given such phrases as "don't nobody know," "you ain't goin' to no heaven," "if you bad," and other nontraditional forms of English. Labov suggests that Larry's arguments are quite logical and basically suggest the following thoughts:

1. Everyone has a different idea of what God is like.
2. Therefore nobody really knows that God exists.
3. If there is a heaven, it was made by God.
4. If God doesn't exist, he couldn't have made heaven.
5. Therefore, heaven does not exist.
6. You can't go somewhere that doesn't exist.
7. Therefore, you can't go to heaven. Therefore, you are going to hell.

(Labov, 1973, pp. 36–37)

One may argue, of course, that the interchange between the interviewer and Larry would have been greatly facilitated by the use of standard English initially. However, that is missing Labov's point. If a child can communicate effectively—using whatever means are at his disposal—then that child should be considered competent in his or her use of language, be it standard or nonstandard English.

Other researchers have been less inclined to view nonstandard English in as positive a light as Labov. For instance, one theorist (Baratz, 1969) has suggested that certain phonological discrepancies between standard and nonstandard English may lead to difficulties in learning to read. One example of such differences involves the frequent omission of the last consonant at the end of words, producing homonyms that do not occur in standard English: "past" and "pass," and "going" and "gone" are two such examples. The phonological similarities between such artificial homonyms can produce difficulties when children try to use phonological cues to sound out words they see in print.

Another argument against the use of nonstandard English sets aside the issue of how linguistically sophisticated the language is and argues instead that adults who use nonstandard English suffer a distinct social disadvantage. For instance, the use of nonstandard English provides clues to a speaker's social status that are quite accurately and consistently decoded by listeners. Perhaps of greater consequence is the fact that American schools provide instruction in standard English, and teachers generally attempt to change the language of children who speak in any way different from the predominant culture. Hence the speaker of nonstandard English will be at a disadvantage during the entire course of his or her schooling. Ultimately, the speaker of nonstandard English must compete for jobs in a society in which standard English is predominant—a society which argues that nonstandard English should be discouraged in the speech of children.

In many ways, the question of the relationship between nonstandard English and schooling is a social one. It could be argued (and it has been) that to discourage the use of nonstandard English is to denigrate an important part of a specific subculture's heritage. Moreover, it has been suggested that nonstandard English may, in fact, be a more effective means of communication among subcultural members than standard English. Nonstandard English actually may also have greater application to the immediate environment in which the speaker is living than standard English does (Dillard, 1972). Such views, however, do not reflect the thinking of the majority of educators. Implicit in the proliferation of remedial programs for disadvantaged children is the notion that the use of nonstandard English is a deficit that must be corrected if the child is to function successfully as an adult. At an even more extreme level, some educators have argued that the use of nonstandard English can impede children's basic cognitive development, although there is little evidence for such a view.

DIFFERENT WAYS OF COMMUNICATING: THE NONVERBAL CHANNELS

There is more to communicating than that which meets the ear. So far the focus has been on communications that occur through the spoken word; but there are a host of other channels through which it is possible to encode one's thoughts, feelings, and emotions in ways that other people can understand. Indeed, nonverbal communication can occur unwittingly, even when an individual is intending to hide an emotion that is being experienced.

The term *"nonverbal communication"* refers to the ways in which messages are transmitted without the use of verbal language. There are many different channels through which nonverbal behavior may occur, including facial expressions, eye contact, tone of voice, posture, seating position, the distance between two interacting people, and many others. Despite the diversity of behaviors that can be classified as nonverbal, there are a few types that are of special relevance to educational settings, and the focus will be on these.

nonverbal communication the transmission of messages without the use of verbal language

Facial Expressions

When Lady Macbeth looks at Macbeth and says, "Your face, my thane, is like a book where men may read strange matters," she is expressing a sentiment

Teachers communicate as much—or more—through their nonverbal behavior as they do through verbal channels of communication. (© Elizabeth Crews)

about facial expressions that is shared by most of us: One of the primary ways in which a person makes decisions about what others are experiencing is through their facial expressions.

Research has confirmed that in fact a set of primary emotions are expressed quite clearly through the face—including happiness, anger, sadness, interest, surprise, fear, and disgust/contempt (Ekman, Friesen, and Ellsworth, 1972). Not only is there high agreement among observers in identifying these emotions, but there is also evidence for cross-cultural similarity in the display of some of these emotions. For example, Ekman (1972) found that even primitive natives in New Guinea, who had very little or no contact with Westerners, showed high accuracy in the identification of such emotions as happiness and anger; and they also displayed emotions in ways similar to Westerners. Such findings suggest that at least basic emotions are conveyed in a similar fashion by all humans.

More subtle kinds of feelings can also be revealed through an individual's facial expressions. For instance, the nature of one's feelings toward a person with whom one is interacting can be judged from such behaviors as smiles, frowns, the wrinkling of the forehead, the pouting of the lips, and so on. Smiling is particularly important in this regard. For instance, one experiment (Keith, Tornatzky, and Pettigrew, 1974) analyzed the verbal and nonverbal behavior of successful student teachers, and they found that smiling teachers who were verbally probing tended to be associated with thoughtful and responsive students. In addition, another study (Feldman, 1976) found that college undergraduates acting as teachers tended to be more facially positive to students they liked than to students they disliked—even though student performance was uniformly excellent. Thus a teacher's facial expressions are apt to reflect the kind of feelings held toward the student.

Students, too, may communicate both their emotional state and how much is being understood through their facial expressions. Indeed, young children, who haven't learned much about how to present themselves socially, can sometimes be quite open in their facial displays.

Other studies show that the degree of understanding that children have for material they are being taught is reflected in their facial expressions. For example, in one study (Feldman and Allen, 1979) third-grade children learned two lessons, one of which was easy (on a first-grade level) and one of which was quite difficult (on a sixth-grade level). The students were secretly videotaped while listening to the lesson, and then groups of third-graders, sixth-graders, and adults were asked to judge from the videotapes (without sound) how much the students understood the lesson. The results showed that, overall, third- and sixth-grade observers were able to distinguish when the children were listening to the difficult lesson. Interestingly, though, the adults were not able to make this distinction—a surprising finding, since most of the adult observers were experienced classroom teachers. But apparently the students' facial expressions did reveal their degree of understanding, and these cues could potentially be of use in the classroom.

Hiding feelings

It has been assumed throughout the discussion so far that facial expressions quite directly reflect the emotions or cognitive state that is being experienced by an individual, and that no attempt is being made to hide the emotion to mislead an observer. This is, of course, a simplification, because people do try to manipulate their facial expressions (as well as their other nonverbal behavior) to conform with an impression they intend to give. For instance, by the time students reach the college level, they have usually perfected a facial expression, worn during classtime, that is meant to convey to the instructor something like, "I'm interested in your fascinating lecture, but I'm not so interested that you should call on me."

Just how successful are such student attempts at controlling their natural behavior? Evidence from research examining the nonverbal behaviors that accompany verbal deception shows that facial expression can reveal when a person is being deceptive, particularly when the subjects are younger children. However, the face is not always revealing, because people develop the ability to control their facial expressions better with age (Feldman, Jenkins, and Popoola, 1979).

Students are not the only ones to engage in verbal deception, of course. Consider the case of the teacher who holds the quite reasonable notion that verbal reinforcement is important in promoting learning. But suppose the teacher provides positive feedback when she does not really think it is entirely appropriate. While she is verbally praising the student, will her nonverbal behavior betray her? The answer to the question is yes, according to the results of a study in which teachers were told always to use the phrase "Right— that's good" when their student answered a test item—regardless of whether the item was answered correctly or not (Feldman, 1976). The results showed that the facial behavior of the teachers betrayed when they were not being truthful. Because other research shows that children are capable of decoding nonverbal behavior accurately, praise that the teacher feels is not entirely appropriate probably ought to be avoided, since the teacher's lack of enthusiasm might be revealed nonverbally, potentially leading to confusion and misunderstanding on the part of the student.

Eye Contact

Throughout history, the eyes have been used to gauge the feelings of others, and the notion that the eyes provide "windows to the soul" is just as appropriate today as it was when first stated. There is by now a great deal of scientific evidence showing that, up to a point at least, the more someone looks at one, the better that one thinks they feel. On the other hand, people who avoid eye contact are thought to be nervous, deceptive, uninterested, or guilty. For instance, one study showed that observers assume that couples who maintain a lot of eye contact like each other more than couples who spend less time gazing at each other (Kleinke, Meeker, and LaFong, 1974).

Eye contact serves another important function: One tends to assume (again within certain limits) that the more a person looks at one, the more that person is attracted to one and is exhibiting liking (Knapp, 1978). However, there is one exception to the rule that the greater the eye contact, the more one tends to make attributions of liking. When gazing exceeds a certain level, people tend to interpret it as an act of aggression. For example, when someone stares continuously at an individual, it is usually taken as a sign of hostility, and it is apt to produce tense and nervous feelings. In fact, staring produces general physiological arousal in the person who is being stared at (Strom and Buck, 1979).

There is evidence that eye contact can be useful to the classroom teacher. For instance, eye contact can help to make students more attentive to the teacher. Breed (1971) found that students paid greater attention when they received relatively high levels of gaze than when the teacher looked at them less often. Thus eye contact not only can provide indications of liking to the student but also can act as a motivational technique.

Interpersonal Spacing

Nonverbal behaviors do not always involve use of parts of an individual's body. Also to be considered are such things as a teacher's use of space, which it turns out is related to the nature of the relationship between teacher and student.

In every society, there are implicit norms about what is an appropriate distance to maintain between two interacting people. Anthropologist Edward T. Hall (1966) has classified the norms for middle-class Americans into four "distance zones," which vary according to the intimacy of the relationship between two people:

1. *Intimate distances* extend from direct contact to about 18 inches. This distance zone is reserved for one's most intimate and close relationships.
2. *Casual-personal* distances range from 1½ to 4 feet. Interactions with one's close friends are carried on within this zone.
3. *Social-consultative distances* are those in which most interactions between acquaintances and most formal business encounters occur. These distances range from 4 to 12 feet.
4. *Public distances* extend beyond 12 feet to the limits of being seen and heard. Beyond 12 feet, one can ignore someone one doesn't want to address without seeming to be rude. Most people involved in public lectures and meetings use this distance.

What are the consequences of violating these distances? Discomfort, embarrassment, sometimes even fear. And most times the individual will either attempt to change the distance to be less uncomfortable, or he or she will simply leave the situation (Sommer, 1969).

Classroom Spatial Arrangements

In the traditional classroom, where the teacher sits at the front of the class and the students are in straight rows, a curious phenomenon emerges. Invariably, it is the students sitting in the front and middle of the class who participate the most, while students sitting at the far rear and sides participate the least (Sommer, 1969; Hurt, Scott, and McCroskey, 1978). Since this phenomenon occurs whether the students choose their own seats or the teacher assigns them, it appears to be due to something about the seating position itself. One reason may be that the students in the front and center of the class can maintain eye contact more easily with the teacher, and the teacher is thus more apt to call on them. It is not clear, though, that this is the sole explanation for the phenomenon.

Other research has shown that deliberately moving students into seating locations in which there is typically high participation can increase their class participation. One study (Koneya, 1976), for example, found that most students increased their rates of participation when moved to more central locations in the classroom. However, this was not true for those who rarely spoke in class; even when moved to a "better" location, low verbalizers remained at low participation levels.

Finally, it appears that the structure and use of classroom space can affect how students behave in classrooms. In one study (Weinstein, 1979), the furnishings of a second-to-third-grade open classroom were changed, and dramatic effects occurred. The children's spatial patterns were changed, with the children using parts of the room that had never been used previously. The types and frequencies of various behaviors were also increased. Other research shows that even more dramatic effects occur as a result of changes from traditional to open classrooms. Thus, the physical structure of the classroom environment can affect the students in numerous ways.

Other Nonverbal Behaviors

There are many other sorts of nonverbal behaviors that influence what goes on in educational settings, and researchers are just beginning to scratch the surface. Such areas as gestures, body movements, tone of voice, posture, and even touching behavior are all likely to affect the nature of interpersonal interaction—just as do facial expressions, eye contact, and interpersonal spacing. Since most of the time teachers and students share a common communication code, interactions proceed fairly smoothly. However, in the case of cross- and subcultural interactions, there is the real possibility of communication difficulties. The next section of the chapter examines some of the differences that

Cleanliness Is Next to . . .

Among the more mundane factors that can affect students' impressions of a classroom and a teacher is neatness. In a revealing experiment, Carol Weinstein and Anita Woolfolk (1979) showed college-age and fifth-grade students colored slides of empty elementary school classrooms that varied in terms of whether they were open or traditionally arranged, and in terms of whether they were messy or neat. They hypothesized that students would make inferences about a teacher's personality and degree of interest in his or her class from the apparent care with which the classroom was arranged.

The results of the study supported this reasoning. A messy classroom led to less favorable expectations about the teacher along a number of dimensions, including teacher kindliness, creativity, and organization. Moreover, pupil behavior was expected to be significantly worse when a classroom appeared messy than when it seemed neat. These findings about neatness held, regardless of whether the classroom was arranged in an open or traditional manner.

There was one effect relating to classroom arrangement per se: the college students rated open classroom arrangements more positively than traditional ones. (The elementary school children rated the two types of arrangements the same.) It is possible that the college students felt that teachers in open classrooms—a fairly innovative arrangement—were more creative and less rigid than those in traditional classrooms, where the teachers had not adopted such an innovation.

Perhaps the most important finding of the study was the ease with which the subjects came to a serious negative characterization of a teacher solely on the basis of the degree of messiness of the classroom. As one subject reasoned, "Well the room was so messy, the teacher must not care about her job very much, or maybe she's just lazy." In a time of increasing demands for teacher accountability, it is hardly reassuring to note how readily observers make judgments based on limited (and relatively trivial) information.

have been identified, and then discusses some attempts that have been made toward increasing proficiency in nonverbal communication.

Cultural Differences in Nonverbal Behavior

As a white teacher explains a simple mathematical concept, his black student looks down at the ground. The teacher, sensing that the student does not yet understand the concept, repeats it, using different wording. Still, the only response from the student is a muttered "m-hm"; the student does not look at the teacher's face to indicate comprehension but rather averts his gaze. Finally, the teacher becomes exasperated and, thinking that the student simply is not paying attention, sharply rebukes him.

Unfortunately (particularly for the student), the above example illustrates one of the most frequent types of failure to communicate in classroom settings that are multiracial. As with spoken language, there are important, but sometimes subtle, differences in the ways members of particular cultural and subcultural groups behave nonverbally. These differences can lead to difficulties for both the teacher and the student, and thus an awareness of them is critical for the successful functioning of the multicultural classroom.

Cross-cultural differences

If you ever hold a conversation with a new student from an Arab land, you might be excused for an initial feeling of discomfort when the Arab begins talking to you at a distance of only 1 foot—so close that you can feel his breath as he talks. This discomfort is largely due to the fact that you and the Arab probably adhere to very different norms about distance zones. As mentioned earlier, Americans tend to hold conversations with those who are not close friends at a distance of 4 to 12 feet. In contrast, Arabs feel more comfortable when interacting at a much closer distance. In fact, an Arab might feel quite put off when an American tries to back off so as to maintain a more "reasonable" (to the American) distance.

Such differences in ideas about what is a desirable distance while conversing are not unique to Arabs and Americans. Indeed, there are quite a few variations in perceived optimal spacing. For instance, members of most Mediterranean and South American cultures tend to space themselves more closely than the British, Americans, or Canadians (Montagu, 1971). In addition, members of cultures that desire closer interpersonal spacing also tend to touch one another more often, gesture more, and embrace or kiss more when meeting one another. Interestingly, though, some of these differences seem related to social class. In cultures that are more demonstrative, it appears that such behaviors are more pronounced in members of the lower class than among those of the middle and upper classes (Wolfgang, 1979).

One other area in which there are cross-cultural differences in nonverbal behavior is in the realm of facial expressions. Although, as mentioned earlier, there are similarities in the cross-cultural expression of very basic emotions, there are also many subtle differences. For instance, members of Oriental cultures tend to be much more restrained and reserved facially in the classroom, showing little expressivity in their facial expressions (Ng, 1975). Another example is found in the types of smiles employed in particular cultures. One study (Brannigan and Humphries, 1972), for example, has identified what is called a "wry smile," which consists of raising one corner of the mouth and lowering the other corner. This smile appears to be uniquely British, and members of other cultures have difficulty decoding it.

Subcultural differences in nonverbal behavior

Earlier, the interpretation that a white teacher might give to a black student's averted gaze was mentioned. The teacher is most likely to assume that the student is trying to avoid eye contact because he lacks understanding of what the teacher is saying.

But such an interpretation is probably erroneous, for research has shown that there are substantial differences in the way that whites and blacks listen during conversation. While whites tend to gaze at a speaker quite steadily while conversing, blacks spend considerably less time looking at the speaker (LaFrance and Mayo, 1978). Thus the black speaker's averted gaze is just a normal pattern of conversation. Moreover, there is another factor that might act to mislead a black student's white teacher, and this relates to the finding that black parents tend to teach their children to avoid deliberately looking at adults. The black child is taught that looking an adult in the eye is a sign of disrespect (Byers and Byers, 1972). Recalling the interview with Adrienne Taylor that began this chapter, a similar phenomenon may hold for Native Americans.

Another black-white difference is in the way blacks and whites use *back-channel behaviors,* which are the brief sounds made by listeners to signal a speaker that they are listening. White speakers tend to use head nods, accompanied simultaneously by verbal responses such as "m-hm." In contrast, blacks tend to use *either* the head nod *or* verbal responses. In practice, this means that a black student whose eyes are averted but who makes the sound "m-hm" may in fact be just as attentive as the white student whose subcultural background teaches him to nod and verbally respond at the same time that eye contact is maintained.

This discussion of the differing nonverbal behavioral norms that prevail among various cultures and subcultures should make clear that the opportunities for mutual misinterpretation are many. Teachers must be sensitized to the possibilities of culture divergence in the meaning of particular nonverbal behaviors, and they should attempt to be aware of the effects of a student's cultural background on his or her nonverbal as well as verbal behavior.

Training in Nonverbal Behavior

Given the existing body of knowledge about the kinds of nonverbal behaviors that are seen as reflecting positive feelings and as being reinforcing, it ought to be possible for the classroom teacher to use such behaviors to contribute to better teaching. Unfortunately, though, knowledge of what is happening on the nonverbal level far exceeds the understanding of how to promote the use of effective nonverbal behavior in the classroom.

Probably the major reason that not many effective training techniques have been evolved lies in the fact that nonverbal behaviors do not just occur or not occur (e.g., a person doesn't just smile or not smile); rather, they occur in a particular sequence and with a particular timing (Birdwhistell, 1970). Thus it

Students from different cultural backgrounds may differ in their nonverbal behavior in subtle, yet important, ways. (© Fredrik D. Bodin/Stock, Boston)

is not enough to tell future teachers to maintain eye contact with their students; they must also be instructed on when and how long they should look into their students' eyes. Obviously, this is an enormously complicated undertaking. Birdwhistell gives an example of a group of counselors who were taught that nodding of the head would result in positive effects. Although the counselors did nod their heads more, it turned out that they were doing so not in response to their client but rather at times when they themselves were experiencing anxiety. Thus learning to be effective nonverbally is a tricky undertaking.

On the other hand, there have been some reports of successful training in appropriate nonverbal behavior. For instance, in one study (Kazdin and Klock, 1973), teachers were trained to smile at and touch retarded elementary school age students, and the students increased a great deal in their degree of attentiveness. In another example (Raymond, 1972), a group of prospective science teachers were taught to use nonverbal cues to elicit desired student behavior, and it was found that the teachers' positive nonverbal affect emitted toward their students tended to increase.

The more extensive research that has been done in therapy or counseling situations suggests that the use of appropriate nonverbal behavior can in fact be trained. For example, psychologist Michael Argyle has set up a program called "social skills training," which attempts to ensure competence in interacting with others in such areas as nonverbal expression and presentation of self. Argyle's program consists of first explaining the procedures and rationale and then placing the trainees in role-playing exercises in which they have the opportunity to practice the skills that are being taught. During the role-playing procedure, the trainees are videotaped, and the trainer then provides feedback on the basis of the videotape. The role-playing is then repeated. Eventually, the trainees are asked to try out their new skills in an actual setting, after which they receive still more feedback from the trainer (Argyle & Trower, 1974; Argyle, 1979).

The other side of the coin with regard to the training of nonverbal behavior relates to skill in decoding the nonverbal behavior of others. Here, as with training for the enactment of particular behaviors, there is not much research. One technique that appears to be promising, though, involves asking trainees to make initial judgments about the meaning of a particular nonverbal behavior that has previously been elicited (that is, the experimenter knows beforehand what the actual significance of the behavior is). After the trainee has made the judgment, he or she receives immediate feedback regarding its accuracy. Through such a teaching technique, accuracy in decoding nonverbal behaviors should be improved significantly (Rosenthal, Hall, Archer, DiMatteo, and Rogers, 1979).

In one study (Jecker, Maccoby, and Breitrose, 1965) that attempted to train teachers to be more accurate in their interpretation of nonverbal behaviors relating to student comprehension, the researchers held discussions on the meaning and interpretation of nonverbal cues that were related to student understanding. They identified a number of behaviors that were important indicators, including orienting toward the source of information, brow furrowing and raising, chin rubbing, and the number of times and length of time students spent looking at the source of information. After 6 to 8 hours of training the teachers improved significantly in their ability to identify, on the basis of nonverbal cues, when students were not understanding material.

It thus seems that it *is* possible to train teachers—both to behave nonverbally more positively to their students and to be more sensitive to their students' nonverbal behaviors. Still, such training is at a relatively rudimentary level of development, and it will probably be some time before training relating to nonverbal behavior becomes a standard part of teacher education. In the meantime, just being aware of the importance of nonverbal behaviors in the classroom will help to promote positive educational outcomes.

SUMMARY

Communication is an essential characteristic of good teaching. Communication processes are complicated and involve a number of stages relevant to the teacher who sends a message (called the encoder) and the student who receives it (the decoder).

The encoding process begins with formulation of the message, which must take into account characteristics of the listener (the decoder) and the specific situation, by using language that is appropriate for the listener. In this process, it is important to distinguish between linguistic competence (the ability level of the encoder) and communication competence (which has to do with how well the message is encoded for a particular listener). Once the message has been encoded, it must be transmitted via verbal or nonverbal channels.

The decoding phase of communication consists of perception of the message on a sensory level, interpretation of the message, and evaluation of the message. The decoder then provides feedback to the encoder, who may need to reformulate the message, depending on the decoder's response.

Spoken language has a major role in the communication process. The Sapir-Whorf hypothesis suggests that language tends to shape the way that individuals in a particular culture understand and experience the world and, second, that language may even determine how people think. Although the latter proposition has not been confirmed, language does affect how things are stored in and retrieved from memory.

There are subcultural variations in the use of the verbal channel. One difference is the use of restricted codes by lower-class speakers, in which language is relatively concrete and concerned with physical objects and actions. Middle- and upper-class speakers tend to use elaborated codes, in which the range of vocabulary is broader, the grammar is more sophisticated, higher-order concepts are employed, and language is more abstract. Another approach to subcultural differences is to study the use of nonstandard English. Although some educators have claimed that nonstandard English is grammatically sophisticated, others have argued that it results in social disadvantages for its users.

The nonverbal channels also are part of the communication process in the classroom. Facial expressions provide information about emotions and attitudes, as well as about the degree of comprehension of a student and whether a person is being verbally deceptive. Eye contact and interpersonal spacing are related to interpersonal attraction, as well as student attentiveness. Even the physical arrangement of the classroom affects student behavior; seating position, for instance, is related to student participation. There are also cross- and subcultural differences in nonverbal behavior. Cultural variations in interpersonal spacing and eye contact can lead to difficulties in interpreting nonverbal behavior accurately.

Attempts have been made to increase both the encoding and the decoding skills used in nonverbal behavior. Although there has been some success at training teachers, training programs are at a relatively rudimentary level of development.

FOR FURTHER STUDY AND APPLICATION

Hurt, H. T., Scott, M. D., and McCroskey, J. C. *Communication in the classroom.* Reading, Mass.: Addison-Wesley, 1978. This paperback provides a very useful overview of theoretical and practical approaches to communication in educational settings. Covers both verbal and nonverbal communication channels.

Dickson, W. P. *Children's oral communication skills.* New York: Academic Press, 1981. A collection of technical articles examining recent approaches to children's communication on a verbal level. Although primarily theoretical, it has many good ideas that are potentially useful to teachers.

Brown, R. *A first language: The early stages.* Cambridge, Mass.: Harvard University Press, 1973. This fascinating book gives an overview of the uses and functions of language as it develops.

Wolfgang, A. (Ed.). *Nonverbal behavior: Applications and cultural implications.* New York: Academic Press, 1979.

La France, M., and Mayo, C. *Moving bodies: Nonverbal communication in social relationships.* Monterey, Calif.: Brooks/Cole, 1978.

Leathers, D. *Nonverbal communication systems.* Boston: Allyn and Bacon, 1976. Each of these three books provides an interesting, useful introduction to nonverbal communication processes, both in and out of the classroom.

12

THE CULTURAL CONTEXT OF EDUCATION

CHAPTER OVERVIEW

In a multicultural society such as the United States, the educational system is influenced in many ways by the racial, ethnic, and religious background of the students being taught, because the cultural heritage that students bring to a classroom affects the way in which they can be educated. This chapter examines cross-cultural and subcultural differences in basic psychological processes and then discusses how subcultural membership affects educational aspirations, expectations, and school performance. The goal is to demonstrate that an individual's cultural background has a profound effect—not only on that person's mannerisms and outward appearance but on how he or she perceives, understands, and thinks about the world. Data from cultures very different from the American culture are examined in order to show the range of differences that exist. In addition, differences among the subcultures in American society are discussed. But the chapter begins with a few general comments on culture and education and the various ways of viewing cross- and subcultural differences that have been proposed.

Hartford, Connecticut, a fairly typical New England city of 150,000 people, has a minority population of more than 70 percent. Susan Zarbo, who works in the Martin Luther King, Jr., School in a predominantly black and Hispanic section of the city, teaches a combined second- and third-grade class that is part of Hartford's bilingual education program. The program is designed to accommodate the many students who enter the city's schools speaking little or no English. Ms. Zarbo, who trained as an elementary school teacher at Drew University, has been teaching for four years. The interview began with a question about her students' level of ability in English at the start of the school year.

A.   They ran the whole spectrum of familiarity with English. The median student in my class had minimal speaking ability and next to no reading ability in English.

Q.   How about reading ability in Spanish?

A.   My highest reader in Spanish at the beginning of the year was a second grader reading at first grade, second half level.

Q.   So these children were not very proficient in reading their native language?

A.   On the spoken level, too. They didn't speak proper grammatical Spanish. Constructions were off, verbs weren't good, and their grammar was poor.

Q.   That's interesting. You seem to have the problems that inner-city teachers would have with lower-class native English speakers who don't speak English very well. That sounds enormously complicated. Your students hardly speak English, and they don't speak Spanish well. Where do you begin? Do you start teaching them English, or do you start working on their Spanish to get that proficient?

A.   I don't worry about the English very much, because we have English-as-a-second-language teachers, and my students go out to those teachers daily for an hour. Because of that, I don't have to handle the formal teaching of English. But what I do have to contend with is teaching them first to use their Spanish to communicate in the classroom so they can get their ideas across, and later to communicate in English. Whether they know something in Spanish or English is of no consequence to me, as long as they can communicate some kind of knowledge at the beginning. I start out speaking Spanish to get them comfortable with me, to let them know they can communicate with me. Then I try to scale down the amount of Spanish I use over the course of the year, until at the end of the year I'm using mostly English.

Q.   And are they responding to you in English?

A.   By the end of the year, yes. I've had a great deal of success in conversation with them.

Q.   What about reading?

A. In terms of reading, sorting them out by ability at the beginning of the year is very complicated, in view of the range of their language abilities. I do language dominance testing at the beginning of the year to see whether English or Spanish is their dominant language. According to their degree of proficiency in English, I place them into a reading group. You can't just go by what they did in the past year because you run into a lot of forgetting what they learned before. I also have trouble with previous teachers who exaggerate their students' capabilities for the record.

Q. I'm curious. Do the kinds of lessons you teach reflect anything about the Spanish culture? Do you bring in Spanish heroes and talk about Spanish history?

A. Yes, I do. For instance, we emphasize Christopher Columbus and that he discovered the United States. And we spend a lot of time on the Three King's Day, which is January 6. We do Lincoln's birthday and Washington's birthday as well. I do try to maintain a bicultural outlook; I try to read to them every day and I try to split what I read between American and Hispanic authors.

Q. Do you use reading groups?

A. Yes. In fact, I ended up with nine reading groups this year.

Q. Nine? With how many students?

A. As an average, I had twenty children in the class.

Q. So essentially that was two students to a reading group?

A. My biggest reading group had four children in it. I had numerous "groups" of single children, and that was a problem the whole year; but they were grouped very accurately and they made very nice progress.

Q. Do the children in the bilingual program feel that they're in a remedial program?

A. I think they do sometimes. You try to head that off before it happens. In a lot of cases you can't, particularly if they have friends in the neighborhood who will tell them that they're stupid because they're in the bilingual class. "You can't speak English so you're stupid." That usually involves me sitting down and having a talk with the child. Letting them know that just because they don't speak English doesn't mean that they're stupid, especially when they just came from Puerto Rico the year before.

The difficulties faced by Susan Zarbo are not limited to the fact that her students do not speak English well. Rather, they include the problems inherent in teaching students whose cultural backgrounds are very different from those typically found in American students. These problems are discussed in this chapter.

CULTURE AND EDUCATION

What Is a Culture?

Margaret Mead, the famous anthropologist, has said, "In its broadest sense, education is the cultural process, the way in which each newborn human infant, born with a potentiality for learning greater than that of any other mammal, is transformed into a full member of a specific human society, sharing with the other members of a specific human culture" (Mead, 1942, p. 633). Thus *culture* can be loosely conceived of as a set of behaviors, beliefs, values, and expectations shared by members of a particular society. But although culture is generally thought of in a relatively broad context (for example, Western culture versus Oriental culture), it is also possible to view particular cultures as existing within subgroups of a larger society. When this is done, the smaller groups are known as *subcultures*. For instance, one can speak of certain minority groups within the United States as subcultures: while they share many of the same kinds of behavior and values as the majority culture, they also have distinctive patterns of behavior and attitudes that differ from the majority. The minority may be comprised of members of a certain racial, religious, or ethnic group, or it may be composed of persons sharing similar economic characteristics. Thus blacks, Jews, and Italian-Americans form separate subcultures, as do the lower, middle, and upper classes.

culture a set of behaviors, beliefs, values, and expectations that are shared by members of a particular society

There are substantial numbers of students in the American educational system today who belong to ethnic or racial subcultures, particularly in urban areas. All of the largest cities in the United States have fewer white than nonwhite students. In New York City, for example, almost one-third of the pupils are native Spanish speakers, and of the remaining students, close to half are black. Indeed, this trend is increasing: As white families move from the cities, the number of nonwhites in the schools increases, and at a rate greater than the increase in the total nonwhite population of the city. What makes these demographic trends of more than passing interest to an educator is the fact that the cultural background that a student brings to a classroom has a profound effect on that student's school performance.

Difference Versus Deficit

Before examining some of the specific effects of cultural membership, let us consider the ways in which any differences that are identified can be understood. To begin the discussion—in a somewhat oblique way—let us compare two hypothetical high school athletes. The two share a number of characteristics: they are male, they have participated on a varsity team for two years, and each has about a B-plus average. The major difference between the two athletes is that they excel at different sports: one is a tackle on the football team, the other is a first baseman on the baseball team. The football player is 6 feet 2 inches tall, weighs 210 pounds, and is a great tackle; but he's a relatively slow runner and is not too good at bat when he plays baseball. The baseball player is shorter, lighter, and much quicker, and he hits .350; but he is totally ineffective when he tries to tackle in a football game. Now, who is the better athlete? Or putting it another way, which athlete shows the most deficits? One cannot dispute the fact that the first baseman can hit a baseball better than the football player. But one can dispute whether this represents a deficit in the football player, whether he should be condemned or pitied for his poor hitting ability, and whether remedial help should be offered to the football player to teach him how to hit better.

Obviously, the preceding example is facetious. But it is useful in pointing out an important (and controversial) problem relating to how differences in cross- and subcultural performance are viewed. To take a real example, suppose that one subcultural group scores lower on measures of competitiveness than do members of the dominant culture. Since one of the predominant values of American society is competitiveness, should one say that the low competitive-

Schools must take into account the rich cultural diversity that students bring to the classroom. (© Robert V. Eckert, Jr./EKM-Nepenthe)

ness of the subcultural group represents a deficit? Most people would probably say no. But let us change the example somewhat. Suppose one subcultural group consistently scores lower on tests of language ability than does another group. It is perhaps easier to view the lower scores as representing a deficit. On a logical level, however, there is no difference in the two examples. The important point is that the *value* placed on the difference determines whether or not it is considered a deficit.

Some educational psychologists argue quite strenuously against a deficit orientation when viewing cultural differences. There are two main grounds for this argument. The first, which has just been stated implicitly, is that the differences that have been found do not represent deficits but are merely manifestations of subcultural members' different backgrounds and socialization.

In contrast, another argument rejects the notion that there are fundamental differences among subcultures at all. When differences do appear, it is argued that they are relatively minor; and if major differences are found, it is assumed that they are the result of an inappropriate test or testing situation being employed. For instance, as was mentioned in the discussion on intelligence (in Chapter 3), subjects from different subcultures can be at a disadvantage when taking a test. If a subcultural group does not care how it performs on a given test, performance will suffer relative to subjects who are highly motivated. Even more important, there can be differences in the way the subjects perceive a stimulus presented in a test. The word "cat" can have a very different meaning to a child whose family has one for a pet than to a child whose only experience of cats is through television commercials. Thus when two children from two different cultural groups are asked the same question, one cannot assume that their responses are responses to the same question. The responses may be more a function of the subjects' differing perceptions of the meaning of the question than of differences in the trait being measured—say, intelligence.

In sum, it is important to realize that the differences found among cross- and subcultural groups can be viewed in many different ways and have many different potential causes. Before labeling any difference as a deficit, one should explicitly consider the underlying values that are being brought to bear. Determining the meaning of such differences thus requires caution, sensitivity, and thoughtfulness.

Education in a Multicultural Society: The Case of Bilingualism

There is no better example of how an individual's cultural membership is relevant to school than bilingualism. As was demonstrated in the interview that began this chapter, many children in the United States come to school having learned languages other than English as their first means of communication. Indeed, some of these children speak no English at all. There would be no difficulty with this if schools were geared to use multiple languages as the means of instruction. Until relatively recently, however, English was the only language taught in schools, and the use of a student's proficiency in any language other than English was strongly discouraged.

Imagine the plight in which the bilingual student is thus placed. At school he is punished for speaking his native language, yet at the same time he may be chastised by his family and peer group if he doesn't use his native tongue. For in some ways, language is the primary means of maintaining identification with one's own cultural heritage when immersed in what is viewed as a foreign culture. For instance, William Madsen suggests that:

> From the Anglo viewpoint Spanish is the primary symbol of the "foreignness" of the Mexican-American. For the Latin, Spanish is the primary symbol of loyalty. . . . The Mexican-American who speaks English in a gathering of conservative Latins is mocked and regarded as a traitor. (Madsen, 1964, p. 15)

Thus language provides an important link to an individual's cultural heritage.

Background of bilingual education

The earliest attempts to deal with children who were bilingual or who came to school with English as a second language followed a "cultural assimilation" model. This model suggests that American society resembles the proverbial melting pot, in which individual cultural identities are assimilated into a unique, unified American culture. Operationally, this meant that non-English speakers were discouraged from speaking their native language and were totally immersed in English.

However, in the late 1960s, educators and minority group members began to suggest that the cultural assimilation model ought to be replaced by a "pluralistic society" model, in which American society would be made up of diverse, coequal cultural groups and each culture's features would remain intact. This concept grew in part out of the notion that by forbidding the use of a student's native tongue, teachers were in a sense denigrating the student's cultural heritage and in turn lowering the self-esteem of the student. For instance, some educators began to argue that even the initial step that many teachers made when a non-English speaker entered school—Americanizing the child's name—could result in feelings of resentment on the part of the student. The following comment on a school visit illustrates how such a change can affect a child:

> A girl's name was written on a paper attached to the table in front of her; *Rosie*. I asked, "*Asi es que te llamas Rosie?*" (So your name is Rosie?; literally, "So you call yourself Rosie?") She looked at me very deliberately and said, "*Yo me llamo Rosa*" ("My name is Rosa"; literally, "I call myself Rosa"). And a little boy at the same table with the name "Joe" written on the paper in front of him quickly added "*Y yo me llamo José*" (And my name is José; literally, "And I call myself José"). (Christian, 1976, p. 22)

This distortion of an individual's given name is a rather blatant example of how programs that immerse a student in English can in some senses be quite humiliating. Since a name is so closely associated with a child's identity and

Educating the Newest Immigrants

The United States is once again engaged in the task of absorbing large numbers of immigrants. Not since the early part of the century has the country been required to take in such numbers of newcomers from cultures very different from its own. And no institution has been as closely linked to these newest immigrants as the schools.

The most dramatic case of newcomers arriving in the United States is that of the Indo-Chinese—those who escaped from Cambodia, Vietnam, and Laos in the early 1980s. They have been called the "boat people" because of their perilous escapes in small, makeshift boats from war-ravaged homelands. Many of the Indo-Chinese arrived in this country with little more than the clothes on their backs—and no knowledge of English or of Western culture and customs.

One city that was faced with dealing with a sudden influx of Indo-Chinese was Des Moines, Iowa, in which about 1,100 refugees were resettled. The biggest hurdle faced by the immigrants was that of learning English. Because the immigrants spoke six different languages, the Des Moines schools used an English-as-a-second-language approach in which a speaker's native language is not used. In this approach, the students are first taught a set of basic words that facilitate day-to-day living and then move on to phrases and sentences. Most of their initial schooling is spent learning English, but they also have classes in art, music, and physical education—areas that do not require much language skill. Once their English is proficient, they are placed in regular classes.

There is a great deal of variation in achievement levels among the immigrants. Some have come from very poor backgrounds and have never attended school, even in their native country. Other students are from wealthy, well-educated families, and these children experience fewer difficulties.

Some of the cultural differences are more subtle than simply a lack of language skill. For instance, one Des Moines teacher, Roxanne Reimer, noted that even though students may nod their heads in response to a teacher, it doesn't necessarily mean they really understand what is being said. In her words, "They know they're supposed to understand the teacher. They're nodding their heads because they don't want to be embarrassed" (NEA Reporter, 1981).

self-concept, attempts to change it can have profound implications for the child. And what is particularly notable is that original Spanish names such as Rosa and José are not even difficult to pronounce.

Some problems of bilingualism

One difficulty for the child whose parents do not speak the language taught and used in school is related to problems that occur when the child tries to learn to read and write a language that he or she has not spoken previously. One of the things that is involved in first learning to speak a language is giving meaning to particular sounds and structures while at the same time rejecting and ignoring many other kinds of sounds and structures (Christian, 1976). If upon entering school a child is taught that many things that he has in the past disregarded and ignored are now important, it is not surprising that many children are confused and eventually develop lowered self-concepts as a result.

A concrete example of the difficulties involved in learning to read and write a language that one has not previously spoken is provided by Robert Lado (1957). He notes that the *i* sound in the English word *sit* does not occur in spoken Spanish. Therefore, a native Spanish speaker—because of his prior cultural experience—will have difficulty in distinguishing between *sit* and *seat*, *ship* and *sheep*, *lip* and *leap*, and many other sets. Moreover, he must not only be able to distinguish the sound, but must learn to spell it correctly using *i, y, ie, e, ee, o, u,* or *ui.* This contrasts to Spanish, in which vowel sounds are represented in only one way.

Of course, some of these problems occur any time that an individual attempts to learn a second language. But they are magnified quite a bit for the student who is somehow being given the message that his original language is not appropriate for the society in which he or she lives.

It appears that there are also a number of problems that emerge when children are taught to read and write only English, and never learn to read and write their original spoken language. First, there is an almost inevitable slant in terms of the kinds of textbooks that are used. For example, English texts are unlikely to present some of the great Hispanic themes that go through Spanish literature and history (such as the search for the Fountain of Youth and Don Juan) in the same way that a Spanish text would. The Anglo culture of the United States may be inclined to view such themes as rather frivolous, particularly in the context of the Puritan tradition. A second problem, alluded to earlier, is that children who do not learn to read and write their native language may begin to consider identification with members of the dominant society to be more important than identification with family and friends of their own cultural heritage, and they may make an attempt to assimilate completely into the dominant culture (Christian, 1976).

Some solutions

It thus seems that there are a number of problems inherent in schooling in which a child's first language is simply ignored or downplayed and only English is taught as the appropriate language to be read and written. But this does not *have* to be the case. In countries such as Canada, for instance, which are officially bilingual, children who are raised with a particular language easily learn to read and write both their native and the second language. The reasons

bicultural schooling bilingual programs that teach the cultures of the speakers of both languages of instruction

for this appear to be that the schools are not only *bilingual* but also *bicultural*. They teach the cultural background and traditions of speakers of all the languages that are being taught, and this tends to enhance the self-image of speakers from both the majority and the minority culture. It seems that successful bilingual programs also attempt to bring together language and everyday social relationships. Children use different kinds of language according to the social relationship they have with the person to whom they are communicating, and the nuances of both languages that are being taught must be taken into consideration. It is also important in bilingual-bicultural classrooms to acknowledge and identify the different strategies used by children in learning a different language. Some children tend to rely on rote memorization, while others spend more effort on the structural aspects of language. There thus may be a need for greater diversity in the approaches employed in bilingual classrooms because of the multicultural heritage of the students.

An ultimate test of whether a bilingual-bicultural classroom actually works is how well the students learn *both* languages. Research done on French Canadian schools shows quite unequivocally that such classrooms can be successful. For instance, one study (Swain and Barik, 1976) surveyed Canadian children who initially spoke English. They were enrolled in special French classes beginning with kindergarten; and by the time the pupils reached third grade, there was no difference in IQ scores or in English ability (their native

Bilingual and bicultural classrooms not only provide the opportunity to learn a second language, but also may enable students to increase their general cognitive abilities. (© Cary Wolinsky/Stock, Boston)

language), compared with pupils who had needed little instruction in French. Thus the learning of French in the bilingual program did not result in the students falling behind in their own language, nor was there any effect—beneficial or harmful—on their cognitive development. Their French performance was, of course, much better than peers with little or no training in French, although it still did not match the performance of native French speakers.

There is even some evidence that being bilingual may have positive effects on intelligence. Although employing a limited sample, one survey (Lambert and Peal, 1972) studied the effects of bilingualism in French Canadian schoolchildren and found that children who were bilingual scored significantly higher on verbal and nonverbal tests of intelligence. Why would this be? One explanation is that bilingual children have greater cognitive flexibility. By being able to think in more than one language, there is a greater set of conceptual possibilities to draw upon. And bilingual speakers have the categorizations of more than one language at their disposal. It thus seems that bilingual and bicultural classrooms offer great opportunities for the students involved. These benefits are not just in terms of learning another language per se but possibly may result in heightened cognitive abilities.

CROSS-CULTURAL AND SUBCULTURAL DIFFERENCES IN BASIC PSYCHOLOGICAL PROCESSES

It is not unusual for a member of the Trukese tribe, a small, isolated Micronesian society, to sail a canoe over the open ocean for more than 100 miles. The destination is often only a small dot of land less than a mile across. Yet the Trukese do not use a compass, chronometer, sextant, or any of the other tools on which Westerners rely. Instead, the canoeist uses a dead reckoning process, in which he examines the rising and setting of the stars and the pattern of the waves. The waves are particularly important: the appearance, sound, and even feel of the waves against the boat are considered. The Trukese method of navigation works even when prevailing winds do not allow a direct approach to the island and it is necessary to tack in a different direction. In contrast, the Western sailor plans and charts an entire voyage in advance. Progress is measured in terms of how closely the ship's course conforms to a predetermined plotted path.

While the Westerner can logically describe the procedure that he is using, the Trukese is unable to articulate what he is doing and why he is doing it at any given moment. Moreover, there is a difference in the type of logical processes employed by members of the two groups. The Westerner tends to use a deductive process, beginning from broad, general principles and then deriving details from those principals. In contrast, Trukese logic works in quite a different fashion. The Trukese begins with the details of a problem but does not proceed much beyond the individual facts; principles do not emerge. Yet as the sailing example suggests, both strategies work: members of each group ultimately reach their final destination (Gladwin, 1964).

This comparison of the type of cognitive strategy employed by Westerners and Trukese suggests that even in such basic psychological processes as the way in which an individual thinks there can be profound differences due to culture. This section of the chapter examines some of the major cross- and subcultural differences that have been identified.

Cognitive Style and Culture: Field Dependence

cognitive style the stable perceptual and thinking processes by which individuals within a culture comprehend their world

field dependence a type of cognitive perceptual processing in which events are organized as parts of a whole, undifferentiated from the environment

field independence a type of cognitive perceptual processing in which events are organized on the basis of structural differences and similarities

That all individuals do not think in the same way probably does not come as much of a surprise to you. But what is intriguing about the existing knowledge regarding thinking processes is that there seem to be commonalities in the way in which individuals within particular cultures tend to organize and process information and experience. The term *"cognitive style"* is used to describe these relatively stable ways in which people organize the world. The consistency that exists extends to the perceptual, intellectual, and social domains.

By far the greatest amount of work in the area of cognitive style has been done by Herman Witkin and his associates, and they have tended to focus on differences in people's perceptual cognitive styles (Witkin, Moore, Goodenough, and Cox, 1977). Witkin has identified what he calls field dependence–field independence as a major factor in cognitive functioning. *Field dependence* refers to the degree to which experience is organized as relatively global. Events are perceived and organized as parts of a whole and are not differentiated from the environment in which they are seen. In contrast, *field independence* is manifested by a tendency to structure and analyze experience and to organize the environment into its various parts.

An example of a technique frequently used to measure a person's field dependence (or independence) provides an intuitive feeling for the concept. Figure 12-1 is an example of an item from the embedded figure test. The subject's task is to identify where the figure at the top can be found in the more complex figure below. The ease and speed with which individuals are able to identify the exact location of the simple stimulus varies dramatically from one person to another. Those who are able to find the hidden stimulus rapidly are considered to be relatively field-independent; they are capable of analyzing the parts of the larger stimulus relatively easily and are not confused by the figure as a whole. In contrast, people who are relatively field-dependent have great difficulty in locating the embedded figure, as the overall structure of the complex figure tends to dominate their perception. Cognitive style is of interest—not only in and of itself but because it has been shown to be related to how people approach problem-solving situations. For instance, field-

FIGURE 12-1   Sample Test Used to Determine Field Independence

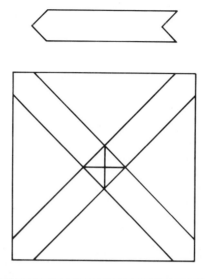

independent people are likely to approach problems by analyzing the component parts of the problem and by imposing structure when it is lacking. In contrast, field-dependent people are more apt to analyze a problem as a whole and are unlikely to consider the individual parts.

Cross-cultural differences

There is good evidence suggesting broad variations among cultures in the predominant cognitive style. Generally, it appears that cultures using child-rearing techniques that encourage independence and the separation of the child from the mother tend to produce individuals who are relatively field-independent. Likewise, the nature of the physical environment in which a person is brought up has been hypothesized to result in differential field dependence (Berry, 1966). If the environment is relatively bleak and undifferentiated and thus requires careful structuring to survive, the ability to be field-independent is enhanced.

Evidence that both child-rearing practices and environmental factors are related to cognitive style comes from a cross-cultural study in which Canadian Eskimos and the Temne (a tribal group found in Sierra Leone, West Africa) were compared (Berry, 1966). The child-rearing practices of the Eskimos are quite nonrestrictive except for a few clear rules, which are enforced firmly and consistently. Thus there is a great deal of freedom given children—which ought to encourage field independence. Likewise, the Eskimo environment is quite harsh and unrelenting. In the winter, both land and ocean appear a uniform white; in the summer (which is quite short), the land is a common shade of gray-brown. In order to hunt for food successfully, it is necessary for the Eskimo to develop great visual acuity. This, too, should lead to field independence.

In contrast to the Eskimos, the child-rearing practices of the Temne are very harsh and restrictive. The mother is dominating, and discipline is severe. The Temne environment also is quite different from that of the Eskimo. It is lush and variegated, and there are great color contrasts. It would not seem that the Temne would be as likely to develop field independence as would the Eskimo.

In fact, the data on field independence of the two groups is in accord with the assumptions mentioned. The Eskimos are quite field-independent, as determined by the embedded figure test and other measures, while the Temne display little in the way of field independence. Keep in mind, of course, that these results cannot determine unequivocally the source of the Eskimo's field independence or the Temne's lack of it. While it is possible that either the child-rearing practices or the spatial environment (or both) determine the degree of field independence displayed by members of the culture (Laosa, 1980), it is also possible that some third factor, as yet unidentified, is responsible. What does appear to be true, however, is that particular cultures engender particular abilities and ways of thinking about the world.

Subcultural differences

Just as differences in cognitive style across cultural groups were found to exist, it is reasonable to expect that there would be subcultural differences in cognitive style related to the type of child rearing that is used in a particular subcultural group. Although there is not as much evidence for subcultural differences as for cross-cultural differences, the evidence that does exist is rather intriguing.

One comparison between subcultural groups (Ramirez and Price-Williams, 1974) suggested that family background is the critical variable in the development of a particular perceptual cognitive style. In this research, a direct comparison was made between Mexican-Americans, blacks, and Anglo-Americans. The three groups were identical in terms of distribution of socioeconomic status and sex. The basic hypothesis guiding the research was that children would tend to be field-independent when raised in subcultures that have a highly organized family structure and friendship patterns, and where such functions as leadership and child care are assigned to specific individuals within the group but are not all the responsibility of one particular person. Such features were suggested to be characteristic of the dominant Anglo culture.

In contrast, subcultures in which there are a great number of shared functions might be expected to produce relatively field-dependent children, since school activities and group identity are important characteristics of each individual. Moreover, the cultural groups with stricter child-rearing practices, greater emphasis on authority and formal ties to the father, and closer emotional ties to the mother were expected to show greater field dependence. These latter patterns are characteristic of the Mexican-American and black subcultures. As hypothesized, the Mexican-American and black children scored significantly higher in field dependence than did the Anglo children.

Implications for teaching

Although such findings of differences in field independence among subcultural groups are interesting in and of themselves, they become particularly important in view of research showing that field independence is related to academic success. Most educational tests of achievement and intelligence tend to be weighted more heavily in the direction of field independence than field dependence. Moreover, it appears that teachers are generally high in field independence, and that they view students with cognitive styles that match their own more favorably than students whose cognitive styles do not match their own. Teachers are also more accurate at predicting their students' performance when the students' cognitive styles are similar to their own (Packer and Bain, 1978). Thus the lower field independence of the Mexican-American and black students (relative to those of Anglo students) can result in less than optimum student-teacher interactions.

One way of overcoming mismatches in teacher-student field independence is to make the teacher explicitly aware of how such differences manifest themselves in cognitive style. Teachers can then adapt their teaching styles to the needs of particular students. For instance, field-dependent individuals have a greater need for external structuring, and teachers could attempt to provide such students with very explicit plans and directions.

Problem Solving and Culture

It was mentioned earlier that the navigational techniques of the Trukese and traditional Western societies are very different. The example is representative of a broad set of findings demonstrating that individuals raised in very diverse cultures approach problem-solving situations in clearly different ways. The "tools" for thinking that a culture provides tend to shape the technique that is used to find solutions in circumstances that necessitate problem solving.

Cross-cultural differences

The best evidence for cultural differences in problem-solving abilities across cultures comes from research on the Piagetian notion of conservation. You will recall from the discussion of development in Chapter 2 that the Swiss psychologist Jean Piaget suggested that the attainment of the ability to conserve (i.e., the understanding that a particular quantity, weight, or volume does not change, regardless of changes in shape or appearance) occurs quite consistently among children in Western cultures around the age of 6 or 7. The attainment of this understanding occurs very reliably and has been demonstrated over and over again.

Although there is far less evidence regarding the ability of non-Westerners to conserve, compared with the massive amounts of data collected on Europeans and Americans, the research that has been carried out is clear in demonstrating cultural differences in the development of conservation abilities. For instance, Patricia Greenfield (1966) administered the classic Piagetian task of describing changes in the amount of liquid poured from one glass to another to members of the Wolof tribe in Senegal, West Africa. Because the glasses are of different shapes, the water rises to different levels in the two glasses. Two samples of Wolofs were used: children who had received a Western-type education and those who had been raised traditionally without any schooling. All the children who had received schooling had attained the ability to conserve by the age of 11 to 13 years, although at age 6 to 7 (when almost all Western children are conserving), only about 45 percent of the schooled Wolofs could conserve. In contrast, the results of the children who had received no education showed that only about 25 percent had attained conservation at age 6 or 7, and by 8 or 9 years of age less than 50 percent were conserving. Indeed, it appeared that children who had not attained conservation by age 9 were not going to do so, for by age 11 to 13 the percentage able to conserve increased just a few points. These data suggest that the traditional Wolof culture does not provide children with the kind of environment that encourages or enhances the development of conservation. It is not that they are inherently incapable of it; that hypothesis is contradicted by the results of the educated Wolof children. Rather, there is apparently something about the traditional culture that causes the difference in conservation skills.

What is the mechanism that inhibits the development of conservation in the Wolofs? Patricia Greenfield and Jerome Bruner (1969) suggest that it may be due to child-rearing practices, which encourage children to be concerned with social relations and to view themselves as members of a group or collectivity. Eventually, children come to look at social factors as the cause of the changes in appearance when the liquid is poured from one beaker to another. For example, many nonconserving Wolof children suggest that the amount of water changes when poured because the *experimenter* is pouring it. This kind of thinking—which is based on the social presence of the experimenter, rather than on any kind of reasoning about the physical nature of the task—is almost never used by Western subjects. Thus it might be—and this is quite speculative—that the Wolof's nonconservation is caused by a reliance on social explanations, as opposed to physical kinds of explanation.

Apart from the evidence of cultural differences in conservation, there are other areas of work on problem solving that demonstrate cross-cultural differences. Some of it can be quite interesting. For example, some investigators have attempted to ascertain how such seemingly straightforward concepts as what is a diagonal are acquired across cultures. One researcher (Olson, 1970) found that Western children are able to construct a diagonal of checkers across a checkerboard by about age 6 and to recognize one at an even earlier age. On the other hand, Kipsigis and Logoli children raised in traditional cultures had much less success. Only 25 percent of 7-year-olds were able to construct a diagonal, and the percentage increased to only about 70 percent for 13-year-olds. Some of the kinds of mistakes made in constructing a diagonal are startling to the person raised in a traditional Western culture (see Figure 12-2).

The research that has been carried out on members of diverse cultures shows, then, that there are major differences in how problems are approached and solved. This does not mean, however, that there are inherent differences in underlying capabilities. Rather, it demonstrates once again that an individual's cultural background has a strong effect on observed performance.

Subcultural differences

Some of the most fascinating research concerned with subcultural differences in problem solving has looked at social-class differences in cognitive abilities. Most of the research has tended to link children's early family experience with the strategies that children eventually develop to deal with new problems.

Psychologists Robert Hess and Virginia Shipman have suggested that perhaps the major influence on a child's problem-solving approach is through mother-child communication systems. They contend that the structure of the social system and family in which a child is raised tend to be related to the language and communication used by the child. Building on the research on restricted language forms, which was discussed in Chapter 11, Hess and Shipman have suggested that language acts to shape thought and cognitive styles in problem-solving situations. According to their hypothesis, the kind of control systems used during mother-child interaction tends to shape the alternatives for action and thought that the child has available. Mothers who use relatively restricted, inexplicit language have children who tend to be rather impulsive and ineffective

FIGURE 12-2   A Model Diagonal and Typical Errors of Reproduction Made by Kenyan Children

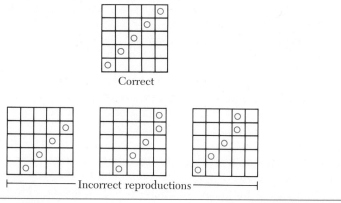

Correct

├─────── Incorrect reproductions ───────┤

(Adapted from Olson, 1970)

in their problem solving, and learning is relatively passive. In contrast, mothers using more elaborate and detailed language take into consideration the particular characteristics of the child being addressed. This results in a more assertive approach to problem solving by the child, in which he or she actively seeks out solutions to problems.

To test out their hypotheses, Hess and Shipman (1970) conducted what has become a classic study. They used 163 black mothers and their 4-year-old children who were characterized as belonging to one of four different social-class groups. After interviewing the mothers twice in their homes, the experiment itself was conducted. The mother was asked to teach three simple tasks to the child. Two of the tasks consisted of sorting toys and blocks, and the third was to copy a series of designs using an etch-a-sketch toy.

As hypothesized, there proved to be many important differences in the kind of language used in teaching the children, related to the family's social class. The middle-class mothers used much greater elaboration, and the kinds of statements they made tended to be more oriented toward the individual characteristics of their children. The middle-class mothers also tended to be much more explicit than the lower-class mothers. For example, here is an illustration of a middle-class mother's instruction:

> "All right, Susan, this board is the place where we put the little toys; first of all you're supposed to learn how to place them according to color. Can you do that? The things that are all the same color you put in one section; in the second section you put another group of colors, and in the third section you put the last group of colors. Can you do that? Or would you like to see me do it first?" (Hess and Shipman, 1970, p. 182)

In contrast, the lower-class mothers tended to be more authoritative, using normative kinds of admonitions ("Do it because I'm your mother and I tell you to do it"). In general, the language used by the lower-class mothers was much less explicit. For example, the following is a transcript of a lower-class mother instructing her child on the same sorting task as in the previous illustration:

> "I've got some chairs and cars, do you want to play the game?" Child does not respond. Mother continues: "O.K., what's this?" Child: "A wagon?" Mother: "Hm?" Child: "A wagon?" Mother: "This is not a wagon. What's this?" (Hess and Shipman, 1970, p. 182)

The lower-class mother has not even told the child what is expected of him, and the child is left to guess the purpose of the task.

In general, the results of the experiment showed that the middle-class children tended to outperform the lower-class children on each of the three tasks. (Interestingly, though, there was no difference in the amount of affection or positive regard shown by the mothers to their children.) It thus appears that the kind of teaching strategy employed by the mother might be critical in developing a particular problem-solving approach. More important, the social class of the family is related to the child's success at problem solving. Thus once again it can be seen that an individual's subcultural membership has an effect on school-related behavior.

Perception and Culture

Visual perception

Even as basic a process as perception can be affected by the culture in which an individual is raised. To understand this, consider the vast differences in the nature of the home environment that exist between various subcultural groups in the United States. For instance, lower-income homes have sometimes been characterized as providing visual stimulation that is relatively dull and uninteresting. Because of a lack of variation in color and shape in the environment, a child may be unable to organize and make sense of his or her world, and may be confused by the range of conflicting stimuli found in other situations (Deutsch, 1963).

If these characterizations of lower-class homes are indeed correct, as some evidence suggests, then the child's lack of opportunity to organize the world visually can result in a decreased capacity to use visual cues in making judgments and solving problems outside the home. This means that the child may be unable to make responses involving visual stimuli as effectively as children from more enriched environments. For example, Ornstein (1978) suggests that a child from a deprived environment might have difficulty in determining what the relevant stimuli are when viewing a picture of a boy riding a bicycle in a parklike setting. To a child who is not familiar with a park such as that shown in the picture, the things that are central to the discrimination process might be the trees, whereas a middle-class child (and a middle-class teacher) might attend more to the bicycle.

Another example of how perception is affected by subcultural membership is illustrated by a classic experiment (Bruner and Goodman, 1947). The researchers were interested in how the value of a stimulus would affect the way in which it was perceived. Subjects in the experiment were shown coins and valueless disks of the same size as the various coins, and the children were asked to estimate the size of each. The results showed that all subjects tended to accentuate and overestimate the size of the more valuable coins as compared with the less valuable ones, while the noncoin disks of a similar size were not overestimated. Most relevant in the present context, the background of the subject was reflected in the size estimations. Poor subjects tended to overestimate the size of the coins significantly more than did rich subjects. Although this study later generated much controversy, the basic hypothesis—that differences in socioeconomic status can affect perception—appears to have been borne out (Tajfel, 1969).

Perceptual Illusions Across Cultures

You might assume that judging the length of a line would be a fairly straightforward process, with little or no variation across cultures. But you would, in fact, be wrong. Research has shown that there are substantial differences in what is perceived visually, according to the culture in which an individual is brought up.

There is no better example of cross-cultural variations in perception than susceptibility to visual illusions. Consider, for instance, the illusion shown in the accompanying figure. If you are like most members of Western cultures, you will probably feel that the line with the arrows pointing toward each other is the longer of the two. However, the lines are identical in length.

The illusion is so strong and compelling that you might think that everyone would be affected in the same way that you are. However, this is not the case. A fascinating line of research carried out in remote regions of southern New Guinea and in India has shown that there are consistently strong variations in susceptibility among various cultural groups (Segall, Campbell, and Herskovits, 1966).

To test susceptibility to the illusion, an instrument was devised in which the non-Western subjects were asked to produce physical estimates of the length of the lines. In comparison to a control group of English subjects, the native groups were *less* susceptible to the illusion. That is, they were more accurate in producing the actual length of the lines than were the Englishmen. This finding has two consequences: first, it dispels the belief that this misconception is common to all human beings. But second, it raises the specter of what has been called the "noble savage" hypothesis: Perhaps the natives do not share the illusion because they have not been "corrupted" by Western civilization and thus are more attuned to nature.

The noble savage explanation would have been at least a possibility had the research stopped there. However, the natives in the study were also examined for susceptibility to other perceptual illusions, and they were found to be *more* susceptible to other illusions than were the control group of English subjects. These results disproved the noble savage hypothesis. Native groups do not simply have greater visual skill.

The explanation for these findings that seems to make the most sense rests on the notion that the experience an individual has in a particular culture tends to affect and modify the way in which objects and events are perceived. Individuals bring a set of learned expectations to bear when they engage in any activity—including judgments about the length of lines. When individuals are shown a particular stimulus, they view it in relationship to prior learning and experiences. Thus a line is not seen as an isolated entity; rather, a person's past experience in a culture lends meaning to that line. The figure being viewed is seen as a representation of some object with which the observer has had prior experience. Of course, this process occurs very rapidly, and the individual is not aware that it is happening.

The preceding hypothesis can be used to provide an explanation for the findings of the differential susceptibility to visual illusions among members of various cultural groups if one assumes that the shapes of the two figures in the illusion evoke past experiences of the observers (Segall, Campbell, and Herskovits, 1966). For instance, experience with rectangles may be especially critical in determining susceptibility to this particular illusion. It is possible that persons who have had much experience with rectangles view each horizontal line as being representative of part of a rectangular box. The top line, in which the arrows point away from each other, may unconsciously be perceived as representing the front edge of a rectangular box extending out in space, away from the viewer and on a plane going out behind the page—making the line seem closer to the viewer. On the other hand, the second line may be perceived as representing the back edge of a rectangular box extending forward from the page—that is, toward the observer—making the line seem further away from the viewer. Because experience has taught that distant objects are actually larger than the image projected on the retina suggests, a viewer of the second line might compensate and assume that the second line is actually longer than the first.

The foregoing explanation suggests that greater experience with rectangles would be the key to susceptibility to the illusion. Certainly Westerners live in a world filled with rectangles, living as they do with rectangular houses, walls at right angles to the ceiling and floors, rectangular furniture, books, and so on. And it turns out that this is especially true in comparison to tribes in which architecture is not based on right angles. Thus one could expect Westerners to show greater susceptibility to the illusion as compared to non-Western groups—which is just what the data show.

Although such explanations for cross-cultural differences in susceptibility make sense, they are of course not the only ones possible. These explanations are complicated and make many assumptions. Moreover, there are surely factors other than living with right angles or in less angular environments that contribute to susceptibility to illusions. It is clear, though, that a person's cultural experiences can affect such basic psychological processes as perception. Even a straightforward task such as gauging the length of a straight line shows the effects of culture.

Educational Implications.   Differences in how stimuli are perceived visually can have important educational implications for both reading and writing among subcultural members. Since reading is partially based on the abilities of discrimination and spatial organization, any deficits in perceptual development can result in difficulty in learning to read. Likewise, writing ability may suffer if perceptual development is incomplete. Children learn to write by using internal representations of letters, and difficulties may occur when perceptual abilities are not strong.

Auditory discrimination

Another factor that might have potential relevance to learning abilities involves auditory discrimination. The child who is raised in a disadvantaged environment—for instance, a crowded ghetto apartment—receives a great tangle of auditory stimuli that cannot easily be shut out. The sounds of other people, television sets, radios, and street noises provide an almost constant din. It now seems established that this high level of auditory activity can result in children not attending to auditory stimuli. Simply put, the children learn to "tune-out" sounds through the process of habituation, discussed in Chapter 5. Because of this inattention to auditory stimuli, the ability to discriminate auditory cues eventually suffers, relative to children raised in environments that are less auditorily stimulating (Deutsch, 1968). By itself, the lack of auditory discriminatory power would not be particularly debilitating, but it turns out that auditory acuity is related not only to pronunciation when reading but to the general level of reading ability (Richardson, 1977).

Another factor relating to auditory discrimination involves the ability to concentrate on tasks. Children living in homes in which there is little if any chance for long, uninterrupted conversation, or in which *any* auditory stimulus is of relatively short duration, will be faced with a difficult problem when they first attend school. Teachers' lessons can be insurmountably long for a child with a short auditory attention span; in fact, even a ten-word sentence may be of a length that presents difficulty to a child without appropriate prior auditory experiences (Lenneberg, 1970). Hence, children who lag in the development of auditory discrimination abilities can be placed at a very real disadvantage in the classroom.

Implications for teaching

The principles of perception that have been discussed suggest a number of teaching strategies. For instance, teachers should try to keep the classroom relatively quiet for certain parts of the day and should attempt to keep movement from being excessive. Teachers should also provide opportunities for students to study alone, without the distraction of classmates. For example, a corner of the classroom could be set aside for students to work quietly, without speaking to others or being spoken to.

Memory and Culture

Alex Haley, in his book *Roots,* describes his emotional meeting with an African *griot,* who recites an oral history of Haley's family.

> The old man sat down, facing me, as the people hurriedly gathered behind him. Then he began to recite for me the ancestral history of the Kinte clan, as it had been passed along orally down across centuries from the forefathers' time. It was not merely conversational, but more as if a scroll were being read; for the still, silent villagers, it was clearly a formal occasion. The griot would speak, bending forward from the waist, his body rigid, his neck cords standing out, his words seeming almost physical objects. After a sentence or two, seeming to go limp, he would lean back, listening to an interpreter's translation. Spilling from the griot's head came an incredibly complex Kinte clan lineage that reached back across many generations: who married whom; then their offspring. It was all just unbelievable. I was struck not only by the profusion of details, but also by the narrative's biblical style, something like: "and so-and-so took as a wife so-and-so, and begat . . . and begat . . . and begat. . . ." He would next name each begat's eventual spouse, or spouses, and their numerous offspring, and so on. To date things the griot linked them to events, such as "in the year of the big water"—a flood—"he slew a water buffalo." To determine the calendar date, you'd have to find out when that particular flood occurred. (Haley, 1974, pp. 577–578)

The *griot* continued for almost two hours, literally spanning hundreds of years of history.

One cannot but be impressed when members of nonliterate cultures are able to remember long lists of events that took place generations before. Indeed, there is a saying among contemporary South American Indians that "When an old man dies, a whole library burns" (Cole and Scribner, 1974). Because living memory is the source of knowledge of the past in oral societies, the use of memory takes on special significance. The extraordinary memory of persons living in nonliterate societies seems to suggest that there are substantial differences in memory *capacity* across cultures. After all, who in our culture could recite long lists of past generations and events? However, it seems that such differences in memory across cultures are more apparent than real.

Cross-cultural differences in memory capacity

Differences in memory capacity are probably due merely to the differential interest placed on various objects and events within a particular culture. For example, Sir Frederick Bartlett (1932) recounts how a Swazi cowherder was able to recall minute details of a cattle sale in which he had been only peripherally involved one year earlier. The cowherder knew the price paid for particular cattle and even the identifying marks. But such feats of memory are most likely due not to a general superiority of the memory of members of a particular culture but rather to the significance and relevance an event has within a given culture. Thus the memory of a sports buff in recalling the winning pitcher in a particular ball game years earlier might be considered extraordinary by the Swazi cowherder.

An excellent illustration of how the relevance of a particular event or item affects what is remembered is provided by an experiment (Deregowski, 1970) investigating the concept of time in members of a tribe in Zambia. He used two groups of subjects: half lived in urban settings, and half in rural villages. The urban sample consisted of primary school students, who were faced with school schedules and relatively rigid requirements for conforming to timetables. In contrast, the subjects living in villages had no clocks or watches, and time was not a relevant consideration. To test for differences in memory, a short story was read to each subject. The story contained eight pieces of information relating to numbers, and four dealt specifically with time. In a recall test, the urban subjects retained the time information significantly better than the rural subjects, whereas there was essentially no difference in recall of the nontime numerical information.

Cross-cultural differences in how things are remembered

It thus appears that there are cultural differences that affect *what* is remembered. But are there also cultural variations in *how* things are remembered? The answer to this question also appears to be affirmative. There is evidence suggesting that there are differences in the way in which various cultural groups are able to recall material that is presented to them, at least in experimental contexts. In one typical study (Cole, Frankel, and Sharp, 1971), Liberian Kpelle tribesmen and a control group of American children were presented with either lists of items or the items themselves. The items were of two types. One condition contained groups of items that were "clusterable," which meant that they fell into reasonably related categories (for example, potato, onion, banana, and orange). In another condition, the words were unclusterable, that is, they were unrelated to one another (e.g., stone, book, shirt). The subjects were then asked to recall the items verbally after their presentation.

The results of the experiment showed that both cultural groups performed better when the words were clusterable. However, the American children tended to cluster their recall by saying words from the same category together, while the Kpelle showed almost no spontaneous clustering. In addition, the Kpelle subjects learned the lists of words at a generally *lower* level of recall than did the Americans. Evidence such as this suggests that there are differences in the way in which memories are stored.

Other research suggests that as the incidence of formal, Western-type education increases, the way in which non-Westerners store items in memory becomes more similar to what is found in Westerners. For instance, when highly educated Liberians are tested in studies similar to those already described, results are remarkably similar to those of well-educated Americans.

The differences that occur in memory performance seem to be due to more experienced and better-educated subjects using any structure that is available in an item list to facilitate their recall. Indeed, they actively search for structure. In contrast, relatively uneducated subjects tend to use no such clustering techniques spontaneously. But if uneducated subjects are specifically instructed to make use of a structuring technique, cultural differences are minimal or do not appear at all (Cole and Scribner, 1974).

The basic conclusion that seems to emerge from the research on memory and culture is that the specific characteristics of a culture (what is important, meaningful, and relevant to its members) determines how well particular items can be recalled and what the structure of memory will be like. Thus once again it is evident that a person's cultural background can affect a very fundamental psychological process.

SUBCULTURAL DIFFERENCES IN AN EDUCATIONAL CONTEXT

Up to this point in the chapter, the discussion has dealt rather generally with how individuals are affected by their culture—that various cultural and subcultural groups differ in the way they perceive, think, and solve problems. However, school performance has not yet been specifically addressed.

This section focuses on the direct effect of subcultural membership on educational outcomes. Before proceeding, though, it would be well to consider the meaning of such terms as "social class" and "race." Although it is likely that you had no difficulty in understanding what was meant, for example, by the term "lower-class mothers," in fact the assessment of an individual's social class is less straightforward than might at first appear, for there is little general agreement over what is meant by social class. Some researchers use a tripartite division—upper, middle, and lower class based on the father's profession. Others use educational attainment as a measure, while still others use occupational prestige scales. Indeed, the overlap of measures is so great that a person categorized as middle-class in one study might be called working-class in another study (Hess, 1970). Thus there are problems in the measurement of an individual's social-class membership.

Even categorizations based on race can present difficulties. Although race refers to a group of people who share a certain set of purely physical characteristics, very often it is difficult to examine race independently of particular cultural and religious characteristics. Moreover race as represented by physical characteristics is constantly changing, as marriages between people with diverse genetic backgrounds bring about changes in appearance. Hence, neither social-class nor racial classifications are simple, and reports of research on subcultures must be viewed cautiously.

Educational Aspirations and Expectations

One of the truisms of American society is that parents feel that their children can aspire to join any profession they please, regardless of who their parents are and from what socioeconomic status they come. Unfortunately, researchers who have examined educational aspirations and expectations have found this to be something of a myth. In fact, the kind of future one envisions for oneself or one's child is very much a function of socioeconomic factors.

There has long been evidence that college education is emphasized much less in lower-class homes than in middle- and upper-class homes, and this is still the case (Hyman, 1953; Sewell and Shah, 1968). Moreover, lower-class families tend to recommend to their children occupations requiring physical labor, whereas middle-class families tend to recommend occupations requiring college degrees. The parental recommendations appear to have an impact on the expectations and aspirations that children develop, as early as the elementary school years. Children from lower-class homes tend to aspire to occupations that are relatively typical of their own social class. In almost all studies, it seems as if lower-class subjects' choices coincide with occupations that are relatively low in prestige.

It would be only a trivial matter that lower-class individuals show lower aspirations and expectations about the future if there were no relationship between expectations and actual achievement. However, this is not the case:

Educational attainment is influenced by parental aspirations and expectations. (© Hazil Hankin/Stock, Boston)

there is a strong association between the nature of an individual's expectations and what ultimately occurs. Lower-class individuals tend to be underrepresented in the higher levels of educational attainment, including college and graduate school. High school dropouts tend to be disproportionately from the lower classes. And even at the nursery school level, children from poor families are underrepresented. Since later success in schooling can be related to early training, children from lower-class families may be at a real disadvantage in schooling.

School Performance

There is one finding that emerges in study after study, independent of the kind of measure of social class that is used: lower-class children do less well in school than middle- and upper-class children. The lower-class child generally has lower grades, lower achievement test scores, lower IQ scores, and lower promotion rates.

The Coleman report: Subcultural differences

Perhaps the most comprehensive survey to date on the educational performance of minority students was that done by James Coleman, a University of Chicago sociologist. The survey, which has become known as the Coleman report, was carried out as a direct response to the concern that there was inequality in educational opportunity among the various subcultural groups in the United States. Indeed, the survey was mandated by Congress in the Civil Rights Act of 1964. The Coleman survey was massive, encompassing 625,000 children, 60,000 teachers, and 400 different schools (Coleman et al., 1966). The final report contained over 500 pages of statistics—enough so that the data can be (and have been) reinterpreted to fit all sorts of contradictory views.

However, one finding about which there is relatively little room for argument is that *the* most important factor in determining how a child performs in school is his or her family background. All the minority groups specifically studied (blacks, Native Americans, Mexican-Americans, and Puerto Ricans) showed significantly lower achievement test scores than the average white pupils— except Oriental Americans, who scored about the same as whites. The discrepancy is evident in the first grade, and it increases during the course of schooling. As Coleman puts it, "Whatever may be the combination of nonschool factors—poverty, community attitudes, low educational levels of parents— which put minority group children at a disadvantage in verbal and nonverbal skills when they enter the first grade, the fact is that the schools have not overcome it" (Coleman et al., 1966, p. 296).

As influential as the Coleman report has been, it is not without its critics. One major problem is that the study looked only at comparisons of ethnic groups and did not specifically examine socioeconomic status *within* ethnic groups. While it can be argued that the ethnic groups that were examined

School Desegregation

There is probably no other topic related to education that has as consistently evoked greater emotion over the past 30 years than that of school desegregation. When viewing the issue over that long a period of time, it is interesting to note that the underlying arguments in favor of desegregation have changed very little.

A major proponent of desegregation at the time of the 1954 Supreme Court case of *Brown* v. *Board of Education* was psychologist Kenneth Clark. Clark had carried out a series of now classic studies about racial preferences in young black children (Clark and Clark, 1947). He used a technique in which a black child was shown a white doll and a black doll and then was told by the examiner, "Give me the doll that looks bad," "Give me the doll that is a nice color," etc. In every case, the children, aged 3 to 7 years, preferred the white dolls over the black ones. From results such as these, Clark testified that black self-esteem was low in segregated schools.

Other arguments also were made against segregation. Psychologist David Krech testified that because blacks were segregated from whites, and placed typically in inferior schools, beliefs on the part of whites that blacks were indeed not only different but also inferior were reinforced. Finally, it was argued that blacks tended to achieve at lower levels than whites and that ending segregation would bring about an increase in black performance (Kluger, 1976).

Partly on the basis of these arguments, the Supreme Court ruled that segregation is "inherently unequal" and that schools should be desegregated

consist largely of people in the lower socioeconomic strata, this is still a serious deficiency in the report. Another problem is Coleman's reliance on measures of verbal abilities, which are more a product of home factors than of schooling. If other forms of measures had been used, the effects of type of school might have emerged as being more important (Dyer, 1968).

An interesting secondary conclusion drawn by the Coleman report was that a very important factor in school achievement was the socioeconomic status of the other pupils in a student's school. It appears that when children from backgrounds that provide limited educational support are placed in an environment with students who have higher educational aspirations, their achievement improves. But the converse does not hold: That is, children who already come to school with high aspirations do *not* decline in their performance when placed in an environment with minority children. This finding argues quite

with "all deliberate speed." Unfortunately, almost 30 years after the original Court decision, it is still too early to say unequivocally whether or not desegregation has been successful. Although one comprehensive review of the literature (Stephan, 1978) found that 29 percent of the studies on desegregation showed significant increases in achievement and only 3 percent of the studies showed a decrease, 67 percent showed either no difference between segregated and desegregated schools or mixed effects due to desegregation.

Still, research has found a number of ways of encouraging the potential benefits of desegregation. A study by the Educational Testing Service shows that outcomes are, to a large extent, under the control of school personnel (Educational Testing Service, 1976). In a 2-year survey of over 200 schools, the investigators were able to identify five variables that are related to positive student racial attitudes:

- The school and teachers provided specific activities that were designed to promote association across races.
- The teachers rated the principal of the school highly.
- The teachers held positive racial attitudes. These attitudes were measured by self-reports of the teachers, as well as being perceived by the students.
- There was general support for desegregation within the community and on the part of parents, students, teachers, and principals.
- There was a general lack of conflict in areas other than race (but also on racial matters).

Thus a supportive environment can make an important difference in determining whether desegregation will be effective.

directly for the use of integration to achieve greater equality in educational opportunity for minority group members.

The Jencks study: Social-class differences

Whereas the Coleman report was most concerned with ethnic minority group differences and schooling, a second major study, focusing on the effects of social class *per se* and completed in 1972, has generated almost as much controversy. Christopher Jencks and his colleagues at Harvard University reanalyzed a number of major sources of data, including the Coleman report and the U.S. Census. In at least one major respect, the Jencks study confirmed Coleman's study: Success in school depends primarily on the family of the student, with all other factors being of lesser importance. But it is not just differences in income that have an effect. As Jencks suggests:

> Cultural attitudes, values, and taste for schooling play an even larger role than aptitude and money. Even if a middle-class child does not enjoy school, he evidently assumes that he will have to stay in school for a long time. Children with working-class parents or lower-class parents evidently assume that if they dislike school they can and should drop out. (Jencks et al., 1972, p. 141)

Thus subcultural attitudes can have an important effect on the ultimate educational attainment and success of a child.

The Lesser study: Ethnic group and social-class differences

Until now, the focus of discussion has been the rather broad differences that exist between the dominant and subcultural groups in the United States. But a few studies have looked at educational performance in specific ethnic groups *and* in different classes simultaneously, and these data provide the most definitive information regarding the nature of subcultural group differences.

A study that has proved to be a classic was carried out by Harvard psychologist Gerald Lesser and his colleagues on a group of Chinese, Jewish, black, and Puerto Rican New York students (Lesser, Fifer, and Clark, 1965; Stodolsky and Lesser, 1967). What is most notable about the study is the care with which the sample of 6- and 7-year-olds was drawn to ensure that there were equal numbers of middle- and lower-class subjects within each ethnic category. Moreover, the materials that were used to test the children were designed to be culture-fair to all ethnic groups. In the materials used, questions were devised that would be familiar to children raised in urban environments. For example, pictures of such objects as buses and police cars were used, instead of pictures of xylophones and giraffes (which are included in one of the most commonly administered picture vocabulary tests). It was reasoned that lower-class children would have greater opportunities for exposure to buses than to xylophones and thus would not be at a disadvantage when compared to middle-class children, who generally have greater experience with books.

Another attempt to provide a fair testing situation was made by the use of test examiners of the same ethnic group as the particular subject. Thus there was a black examiner, a Spanish-speaking Puerto Rican examiner, a Yiddish-speaking Jewish examiner, and three Chinese-speaking examiners (to deal with the eight different Chinese dialects that were found among the subjects). While the use of same–ethnic group testers allowed the children to become more relaxed and made it more likely that they would perform at an optimal level, it also provided the danger that the testers might empathize *too* much with the subjects and thus bias the test administration. To guard against this, the examiners were carefully trained in the administration of the tests. Videotapes were used extensively, allowing each tester to compare himself or herself with the others.

Four separate abilities were examined. The first was verbal ability, which was defined simply as memory for verbal labels. (Most typically, verbal ability is seen as the best predictor of academic success.) The second ability measured was reasoning, which included the ability to devise concepts and to draw inferences and conclusions from the concepts. Number facility, the ability to use numbers in addition, subtraction, multiplication, and division, was the third ability to be tested. And space conceptualization, the ability to visualize and use spatial relations and sizes of objects was the final ability measured.

Lesser's Findings.   The least surprising results to come out of this impressive and ambitious study concern the basic effects of social class and ethnic group. As could be predicted from prior research, both factors had significant effects on the general level of performance. The middle-class children scored significantly higher (within and across all ethnic groups) than did the lower-class children. Moreover, there were strong general ethnic group effects. But even more interesting, the pattern of abilities was different for each of the ethnic groups. For instance, as Figure 12-3 shows, for verbal ability, Jews score highest, blacks second, Chinese third, and Puerto Ricans lowest. But for reasoning ability, the Chinese were first, followed by Jews, blacks, and Puerto Ricans. And these specific *patterns* turned out to be almost unaffected by

FIGURE 12-3   Pattern of Scores for Each Ethnic Group

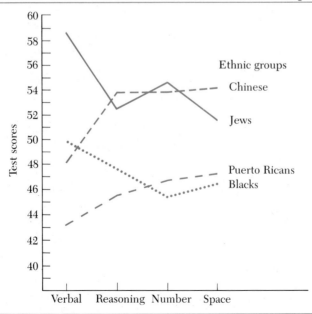

(Stodolsky and Lesser, 1967)

social class. Although performance by high social-class subjects was always superior to that of low social-class subjects, the pattern on the four abilities for a given ethnic group remained almost identical. Hence, social-class differences seemed to affect performance in an absolute sense, but they did not seem to influence which of the four abilities a particular ethnic class member would perform best in.

The results of the Lesser study illustrate the important effect of social class and ethnicity on performance. Lesser draws two major conclusions from this research:

1. The effects of social-class differences appear to be most amenable to change. Within each ethnic group, the lower-class students perform more poorly than the middle-class students; therefore it is reasonable to suggest that differences in performance between lower- and middle-class students are less due to factors relating to basic ability and more due to situational factors relating to environmental poverty. The results also suggest that the most reasonable approach to improving lower-class performance does not involve the school. Rather, one should concentrate on changing family income, housing, and jobs. An advance toward middle-class status could be expected to raise the level of performance of the lower-class children to resemble more closely those of the middle-class, because the lower-class children would then have more of the advantages they had earlier lacked.

2. Ethnic effects, which occur regardless of social class, appear to be of greater relevance to the teacher than social class. Changing social-class status will not make a difference in the pattern of abilities. Because members of various ethnic groups differ in what they can do best, schools ought to take into account a specific child's pattern of abilities in terms of the kind and timing of instruction. Children who have special abilities in, say, verbal skills should have those skills enhanced; children who excel in spatial relations should receive special instruction in that area.

The above reasoning, which Susan Stodolsky and Gerald Lesser (1967) have called the "Equal Opportunity for Maximum Development" argument, presents a somewhat atypical view of the goals that schools ought to have. The argument suggests that schools should provide opportunities for individuals to reach their highest level of development possible, regardless of whether group differences still exist, disappear, or even get larger as a result of schooling. In their words:

> Let us take a specific, if partially hypothetical, case. Our evidence indicates that young Chinese children have their strongest skill in Space Conceptualization and their weakest in Verbal ability. Conversely, young

Jewish children are strongest in Verbal ability and weakest in Space Conceptualization. Following our principle of matching instruction and ability, we incidentally may enhance the initial strengths which each group possesses. For example, through the incidental enhancement of the space-conceptualization skills of the Chinese children, we may produce proportionally more Chinese than Jewish architects and engineers. Conversely, through incidental enhancement of verbal skills of the Jewish children, we may produce proportionally more Jewish than Chinese authors and lawyers. We will not have put members of these two ethnic groups on an "equal footing" for entering a particular occupation. But can we say that we have produced a socially-destructive outcome by starting with the knowledge of differences in ability patterns and adapting our instructional strategies to this knowledge to produce a maximum match for each child, even if this process results in inequality of certain educational and professional attainments? We are willing to accept, then, one possible consequence of arranging instruction to capitalize maximally on distinctive patterns of ability: that, in certain areas of intellectual accomplishment, rather than reducing or bringing toward equality the differences among various groups, we may actually magnify those differences. (Stodolsky and Lesser, 1967, pp. 585–586.)

An Alternative Argument.   The view expressed above is a minority one. The American educational system has been built on the notion that the goal of schooling is to provide equal opportunity for all groups in the society to reach equal levels of achievement. If particular subcultural groups do not achieve at the same levels, the fault is assumed to lie within the schools. It is therefore incumbent on schools to change the manner of instruction to provide all students with identical skills.

This point of view is implicit in much of the judicial and legislative decisions of recent years that mandate integration and busing of students to provide more equal educational opportunities. Beginning with the Supreme Court decision of 1954, in which it was determined that segregated schools were inherently unequal, through the Court decisions of the 1970s, which ordered school systems to attain racial "balance" in each school by busing children, the United States has attempted to bring about equal opportunities for all students. Indeed, many affirmative action programs, in which minority and disadvantaged groups are given special treatment in terms of admissions to college and graduate schools (as well as jobs), have been implemented.

Although the problems relating to cultural factors are great, solutions appear to be growing. As understanding of the psychological processes relating to a student's cultural heritage increases, it should become possible to design schools and classrooms not just to overcome a student's background but to retain it and use it for that student's educational advancement. Indeed, the rich heterogeneity possible in a multicultural society should benefit all its citizens.

SUMMARY

The cultural background that a student brings to a classroom has a profound effect on that student's school performance. Culture, which can be thought of as the behaviors, beliefs, values, and expectations shown by members of a particular society or group, influences ways of thinking, problem solving, perception, and memory. Cultural and subcultural differences can be viewed simply as differences, or they can be viewed as deficits; the label chosen is a function of the values involved.

Bilingualism represents an example of the effects of culture on education. Early attempts to deal with non-English speakers took the form of assimilating them into American society by discouraging use of their native language. More recent models of bilingual education have promoted the use of bicultural classrooms, in which the language and cultural background of all the students is taught to the students in the class.

One important cultural difference involves cognitive style, which refers to the relatively consistent ways in which people organize their perceptual, intellectual, and social world. The style that has been researched most is field dependence–field independence. Field dependence refers to the degree to which experience is organized globally and perceived as parts of a whole. In contrast, field independence is manifested by a tendency to structure and analyze experience and to organize the environment into its parts.

Cultures using reasoning techniques that encourage independence, or those in which the environment requires careful structuring for survival, are more apt to produce field independence in their members. Field independence is related to academic success. Teachers can use their knowledge of a student's cognitive style to meet that student's specific needs.

Research on problem solving and perception shows major differences across cultures. For instance, the ability to conserve liquids does not appear in some African tribes. Even within the United States, there are social-class differences in the kind of language used when mothers teach their children, which in turn are related to the children's problem-solving ability. Visual and auditory discrimination are also different for certain subcultural segments of society and can affect scholastic performance.

Specific characteristics of a culture (what is important, meaningful, and relevant to its members) determines how well particular items can be recalled and what the structure of memory will be like. Memory capacity, per se, does not appear to differ across cultures.

Both educational aspirations and school performance are affected by subcultural membership. Children and parents from lower-class homes tend to hold lower aspirations for future success, both scholastically and occupationally, than middle- and upper-class families. They also tend to perform worse in school, having lower grades, lower achievement test scores, lower IQ scores, and lower promotion rates.

There are also differences in patterns of abilities related to ethnic group membership, and a study by Stodolsky and Lesser argues that these differential abilities should be enhanced. This argument is contrary to the view that students should all rise to equal levels of achievement.

FOR FURTHER STUDY AND APPLICATION

Henderson, R. W., and Bergan, J. R. *The cultural context of childhood.* Columbus, Ohio: Merrill, 1976.   Reviews the data on the impact of culture on child development. A comprehensive and useful guide.

Coleman, J. S., Campbell, E. Q., Hobson, C. J., McPartland, J., Mood, A. M., Weinfeld, F. D., and York, R. L. *Equality of educational opportunity.* (2 vols.) Office of Education, U.S. Department of Health, Education, and Welfare. Washington, D.C.: U.S. Government Printing Office, 1966.

Jencks, C., Smith, M., Acland, H., Bane, M. J., Cohen, D., Gintis, H., Heyns, B., and Michelson, S. *Inequality: A reassessment of the effect of family and schooling in America.* New York: Harper Colophon Books, 1973.   These two books provided the basis for a great deal of debate in the 1970s on the effects of subcultural membership on achievement. Useful to peruse, if only to see just how complicated the issues are.

Tiedt, P. L., and Tiedt, I. M. *Multicultural education: A handbook of activities, information, and resources.* Boston: Allyn and Bacon, 1979.   A very useful handbook for teachers in multicultural classrooms.

IV

SCHOOLS AND TEACHERS

13

PSYCHOLOGICAL PRINCIPLES OF MOTIVATING STUDENTS

CHAPTER OVERVIEW

When one speaks of motivation, one is discussing the factors that drive and orient behavior toward a particular goal—in this case, the goal of academic success and achievement. Three major approaches to motivation are examined. One approach deals with motivation on a broad scale, looking at factors that direct behavior toward the goal of self-actualization and fulfillment. Next, two theories of achievement motivation are described, one dealing with the personality characteristics that affect the choice of achievement goals, and one that is concerned with understanding the reasons for people's successes and failures. All three approaches share the basic notion that to understand what makes people learn and perform well in school, one must be aware of the nature of their underlying motivation toward success in life and toward the academic setting.

In a huge complex resembling more an old college administration building than a high school, Nancy Rosenfelt teaches a class of junior high school students who are labeled educationally handicapped. The school, Holenbeck Junior High, is located in the heart of a poor Hispanic area of Los

Angeles. Trained in Connecticut, Ms. Rosenfelt began teaching a few years ago in this so-called educationally impacted school, knowing that the teacher turnover rate was high and that the school situation was such that teachers were paid an additional stipend for the extra time, energy, and emotion that were required.

The interview began with a question about the kinds of problems that lead a student to be labeled educationally handicapped.

A.   Their problems are very heterogeneous. Very often they're picked out of a classroom of thirty children as being the one student who is not able to work independently; or they're aggressive; or they just don't keep up and are put in the lowest reading and math groups. Some are unable to deal with criticism: If they get a paper back that's not done right, they'll rip it up, swear, and tell you they're not going to work on it.

Q.   Are these children isolated from the rest of the school's population?

A.   No, not all. Although when I first got here, the kids never left my room. But I made some waves, and now they are integrated into physical education, industrial arts classes, and if possible regular math and English classes; whatever they can do.

Q.   When your students are put into "regular" classes, it results in a very heterogeneous grouping for the regular classroom teacher. Does this present problems?

A.   For the majority of the students it works very well. They like the idea of being with other kids, and I think it's probably good for their classmates as well.

Q.   How diverse are students in the school on other dimensions? What's their socioeconomic status, for instance?

A.   They're mostly poor, with parents on welfare. To give you an idea of the magnitude of the poverty, out of about 2,400 students, perhaps just 50 pay for their lunch. The other students are eligible for free meals.

Q.   Because your students have special needs, you probably need to work closely with their families in planning their educational programs. Do you find the parents supportive?

A.   Generally. But often educational issues are lower priority than other problems. School difficulties are minuscule compared to other problems the families may be encountering. They have other children who are in jail. *Two* of my students have witnessed murders, and sometimes they can't come to school because they've been called to court. One parent tried to hide his kid from the court trial, because testifying would have placed the child in the middle of a gang war. Another child had a brother who was hit by a truck, and he had to accompany his mother to the hospital because it's so far away and the brother couldn't be moved. So he wasn't in school fifteen days of the month. You're fighting so many battles, not just in terms of learning handicaps in school. There are divorces, cases of wife beating, girls being assaulted by their fathers. These kids' lives are in turmoil.

Q.   How long can you keep fighting these battles? Are you going to keep at it?

A.   Let me put it this way: During my first year at the school, I said to myself daily, "What am I doing here?" I thought I'd make it through the year and then get another job. And then the kids said to me in June, "Well, it's nice knowing you, miss." I said, "What are you talking about?" And they replied that nobody ever stayed in this school for more than a year. But a funny thing happened. I got three job offers that summer—but then I came back to the same school. Something draws me to the challenge and convinces me that I'm doing something positive, even if it's because I'm the only consistency in their lives.

One of the central questions facing Nancy Rosenfelt is how best to produce motivation in her students; how to encourage them to work their hardest, do their best, become excited by learning, and ultimately, develop an intellectual curiosity about the world that will last a lifetime—especially given the multiple difficulties her students face. This chapter addresses the issue by examining a number of approaches to motivation and a number of specific techniques for motivating students.

WHAT IS MOTIVATION?

In a formal sense, *motivation* refers to the arousal of behaviors oriented toward a particular goal and the direction that behavior will take in order to attain the goal. When studying motivation, educational psychologists are concerned most with the factors associated with students' desire to learn academic skills (or the factors that inhibit such learning). But academic skills are just one set of goals that students can be motivated to attain; others include the goals of self-fulfillment, self-awareness, affiliation, and physical achievement. The concept of motivation is used to explain how behavior is directed and sustained to reach a particular goal.

*motivation
the factors that
impel an indi-
vidual to be-
have in a cer-
tain way*

The Yerkes-Dodson Law

High motivation does not, by itself, always ensure success at attaining a goal, however. While it might seem reasonable that higher arousal would generally

arousal the degree of motivation

Yerkes-Dodson Law the finding that performance on simple tasks generally benefits from greater arousal than is useful for complex tasks

lead to greater achievement, in some cases the quality of performance actually declines as a result of too much *arousal* of motivation.

The critical element in determining the relationship between motivational arousal and performance success relates to the complexity of the task. Performance on simple tasks generally benefits more from higher levels of arousal than does performance on more complex tasks. The reason is that simple tasks, by their nature, generally are limited to only a few alternative approaches; in other words, the solution is obvious and there are limited ways of responding appropriately. Because high levels of arousal tend to increase the probability of responses being made in general, the appropriate response is the one likely to be made, given that there are few reasonable alternative responses. With complex tasks, on the other hand, many responses are possible, and high levels of arousal can lead to erroneous responses being made. Thus, all other things being equal, a complex task is performed better under lower levels of arousal than is a simple task. This principle is known as the *Yerkes-Dodson law*.

Of course, at very high levels of arousal, the quality of performance drops

Motivation to succeed is manifested in many activities that take place during school. (© Rick Smolan/Stock, Boston)

for both complex and simple tasks. The reason? Too high a level of arousal can be distracting and anxiety-producing. Students begin to think more about the implications of their success or failure on the task than of the task itself.

In practical terms, this means that to produce optimum performance, students should be more aroused for simple tests than for complex ones. Unfortunately, this dictum is hard to follow, since people are likely to be more motivated when taking a difficult test than an easy one.

MASLOW'S HIERARCHY OF MOTIVATIONAL NEEDS

Why are some students highly motivated to learn whereas others are not? One approach to this problem has involved the development of a model to explain the way in which human needs are ordered. The clinical psychologist Abraham Maslow (1970) has suggested that before high-order needs—the kinds of needs that are uniquely human and necessary for education—are met, certain primary or basic needs must be satisfied.

Maslow's model can be conceived of as a pyramid, in which the more basic needs are at the bottom and the higher-order needs are at the top (see Figure 13-1). For a particular need to be activated and guide a person's behavior, the more basic needs—those lower down in the pyramid—must be met. The most fundamental needs are physiological; a person must have air, water, food, and sleep before any other needs can become important. The next category of needs are what Maslow calls safety needs. These refer to the desire to be protected from potential danger and to have a safe, secure environment in which to live. Maslow refers to physiological and safety needs as basic, or lower-order, needs.

Once an individual moves beyond the basic needs, he or she can then try to fulfill the higher-order needs (or "metaneeds," in Maslow's terms) of love and belongingness, esteem, and self-actualization. Love and belongingness needs are related to the need to give and receive affection—the desire to be wanted and to be a part of a group or society. After love and belongingness needs are fulfilled, the individual turns to needs for esteem. According to Maslow, one needs to feel a sense of personal self-worth and to think that others share that sense of one's competence and value.

Once these four levels of needs are fulfilled, the individual attempts to satisfy needs for self-actualization, the peak of the model. Self-actualization is not only the hardest need to fulfill, it also represents the most difficult concept of Maslow's hierarchy. Perhaps the best way to explain it is in reference to some of the people that Maslow initially identified as being self-actualized: Abraham Lincoln, Eleanor Roosevelt, and Albert Einstein. But self-actualization is not limited to the famous. Rather, it consists of people realizing their potential—a state in which they know and understand the world and have the

FIGURE 13-1   Maslow's Hierarchy of Motivational Needs

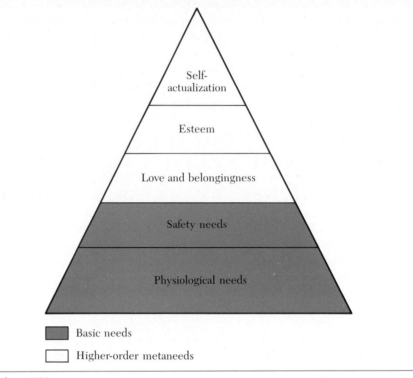

(Maslow, 1970)

ability to use their talents to the greatest extent possible. Thus someone with great talents for teaching might become self-actualized by becoming a teacher; someone with parenting skills and ability could become self-actualized by raising children. The important feature of self-actualization is that people experience a sense of mastery and competence and a sense that their lives are reaching the limits of their ability for productivity.

Implications for Teaching

Maslow's hierarchical model is important because it points out that without satisfaction of the more basic needs, human growth and potential are limited. Thus students from impoverished backgrounds who come to school hungry are not likely to progress beyond the first stage of physiological needs. But besides suggesting the obvious—that children must have their physiological needs attended to before anything else—it suggests that teachers should attempt to provide fulfillment for higher-order needs by enhancing belonging-ness needs and building student self-esteem.

Maslow's theory, which has been incorporated into a general philosophy known as humanistic psychology, also suggests that teachers should strive to facilitate student growth, rather than directing students into particular channels. The teacher ought to be humanistically oriented, supporting and encouraging student performance in general. Basically, Maslow views the teacher as a helper, as opposed to the notion that a teacher is a superior who imparts knowledge.

Maslow's theory is not without its critics. For instance, his particular ordering of needs is not accepted as being universal. Moreover, many psychologists are not comfortable with terms as broad in meaning as "self-actualization." Despite these potential drawbacks, Maslow's concept provides a useful goal for teachers to strive toward when working with their students. Indeed, teachers themselves can find much of what Maslow is arguing a useful guideline for understanding their own needs.

MOTIVATION TO ACHIEVE: THE NEED FOR ACHIEVEMENT

Ms. Vorwerk prided herself on the degree of independence she allowed the students in her tenth-grade English class. Not only could each student choose the particular author and literary form that he or she wanted to study each month, but Ms. Vorwerk had carefully determined the level of difficulty of each author's writings, and her students could take that factor into consideration as well. She was puzzled, however, as to why it was that certain students seemed consistently to choose authors of a particular level of difficulty. For instance, Jonathan Saulman almost always picked an author of moderate difficulty—one that was not too hard and not too easy. (And he usually performed pretty well on such material.) In contrast, Kathy Maxwell was less consistent. Sometimes she picked a very low-level author. And of course she then had an easy time of it and did well, but so did everyone else who chose that author. Sometimes, though, she picked a very difficult author to study. It was almost as though she wanted to be sure that there was a high likelihood that she would fail.

The behavior of Ms. Vorwerk's students is just one example of how individuals strive for different levels of achievement in academic tasks. Indeed, the description of Jonathan and Kathy closely fits what is known about people who have different levels of *need for achievement*. The need for achievement is an enduring learned personality trait that relates to the degree and nature of motivation that will be aroused in striving for achievement-related goals (McClelland, Atkinson, Clark, and Lowell, 1953).

It has been shown that need for achievement is actually composed of two

need for achievement an enduring learned personality trait that underlies the amount of an individual's motivation

separate kinds of motivations: the motivation to achieve success, and the desire to avoid failure (fear of failure). The relative strength of these two motivations determines the kind of tasks that are sought out by people. Individuals who are high in fear of failure, relative to the desire to achieve success, tend to seek out tasks that are either very easy or very difficult. On very easy tasks, they are sure of succeeding; and on very difficult tasks, *everyone* is likely to do poorly, and individual failure will be minimized. It is on tasks of medium difficulty that individuals with high fear of failure are likely to feel most uncomfortable, because they may fail but others may be successful.

In contrast, people who are high in motivation to achieve success but relatively low in fear of failure are likely to prefer tasks that are intermediate in difficulty. In this case, their success will have real meaning, since others will potentially be failing. This line of reasoning also suggests that very easy and very difficult tasks will be avoided by individuals high in motivation for success (Atkinson and Feather, 1966).

This analysis of need for achievement provides a reasonable explanation of the behavior of Ms. Vorwerk's students. Jonathan, who chooses authors of moderate difficulty, probably has a high need for achievement; Kathy, who picks either very easy or very difficult authors, probably has a low need for achievement.

Measuring Need for Achievement

Thematic Ap-perception Test (TAT) a projective test that assesses need for achievement

The measure that is most often used to assess need for achievement is a test called the *Thematic Apperception Test*, or TAT (Atkinson and Raynor, 1974). In the TAT, an individual is shown a series of ambiguous pictures, similar to the one shown in Figure 13-2, and is then asked to write a story about each picture, paying particular attention to such questions as What is happening? Who is the person? What led up to this situation? What is being thought? What is wanted? and What will happen?

Once a story has been written about each picture, a standard scoring system is used to determine the amount of achievement imagery that has been included. For example, an individual who writes a story in which a central concern is comparing his performance to that of his peers on a test the teacher is about to give back would be scored high for achievement imagery. The central assumption is that the story the individual writes is going to be representative of the way in which he or she views the world, and that the concerns the writer attributes to the people in the story are actually his or her own concerns.

After many years of development, the scoring system for TAT's has been shown to be a valid measure of an individual's need for achievement. In addition, other techniques for measuring need for achievement have been developed. For instance, one approach has examined the level of achievement imagery found in children's readers or in folk tales. Using this method, one

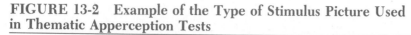

FIGURE 13-2   Example of the Type of Stimulus Picture Used in Thematic Apperception Tests

can assess general levels of achievement imagery for a society or cultural group as a whole.

Outcomes of High Need for Achievement

There is compelling evidence that measures of the need for achievement derived from TAT's and other types of stories are, in fact, closely related to actual achievement. People with a high need for achievement more readily enter into achievement-related situations, their expectations of success are higher, and their persistence on academic tasks is greater than is the case for people with a low need for achievement. Students high in need for achievement are more likely to go to college than persons low in need for achievement; and in college they tend to receive higher grades in classes that are related to their future careers than in other classes (Atkinson and Raynor, 1974).

In addition, David McClelland, a pioneer in work on need for achievement, has found that there is a strong relationship between level of achievement imagery present in children's readers and subsequent economic growth in a

Achievement Values in Children's Reading Books

In a study that illustrates quite clearly that a society's values are reflected in children's education, Richard DeCharms reports on an analysis of imagery found in children's reading books (DeCharms and Moeller, 1962). In their study, they examined reading texts that were widely used in the United States from 1800 through 1960. After gathering a sample of at least four fourth-grade books from each 20-year period, they scored every third page for the degree of achievement imagery and for instances of direct moral teaching.

The results of their analysis showed that there was a fairly steady rise in achievement imagery until about 1890, when there began a decline that lasted up to the end of the sample period. What is particularly interesting is that the changes in achievement imagery closely parallel the number of patents granted in a given period. Because number of patents issued represents a reasonable measure of economic activity, it appears that there is a close relationship between achievement imagery in children's reading books and actual economic activity. Whether the amount of economic activity is caused by reading about achievement as a child, or whether economic activity leads to changes in children's readers, cannot be determined; either sequence is plausible. (Indeed, it is possible that some third, unmeasured factor causes changes in both indexes.)

While the degree of achievement imagery showed a rise and then a decline during the period under consideration, the measure of the amount of direct moral teaching showed no similar variation. Rather, there was a steady decrease over time. In 1810, about 64 percent of the pages in readers contained some moral admonition; in 1950, less than 0.2 percent of pages contained any moral teaching. (An example of moral teaching found in an 1857 McGuffey reader: "A little boy took care of his faithful dog as long as he lived, and never forgot that we must do good to others, if we wish them to do the same to us.")

Although the study did not go beyond the 1950s, it is interesting to speculate what the levels of achievement imagery and moral teaching are now. What do you think those levels would be today, given current cultural and economic conditions in the United States?

given society. In a landmark study, McClelland (1961) measured achievement imagery in children's reading books in twenty-three countries during the 10-year span from 1920 to 1929, and the level of economic success of the country in 1950 (25 years later). He reasoned that those exposed to achievement imagery in their childhood had grown to have an impact on their society over the 25-year period. After correcting for various factors such as wars and natural disasters, McClelland did find a significant relationship between the amount of achievement imagery and the economic prosperity of a country. Thus the type of achievement imagery present in children's readers (which is presumably reflective of the norms and values of the general society) does appear to be related to the future achievement of a society (McClelland, 1961). (See the accompanying box.)

Raising Achievement Motivation

It is reasonable to ask what factors result in some people being high and others low in need for achievement. The best answer seems to be that children who grow up to be high in achievement motivation receive an unusual amount of independence training from their parents. There is a stress on self-reliance, the active encouragement of initiative, and success is valued and rewarded (Winterbottom, 1953; Brown, 1965). In addition, there is evidence showing that fathers' occupations are strongly correlated with the achievement needs of their sons. For instance, sons of fathers who are in professions in which they are independent and have to make decisions tend to be higher in need for achievement than those whose fathers hold routine, dependent jobs, in which there is close supervision.

What makes questions regarding the development of achievement motivation of particular interest is the notion that it might be possible to train people to increase their need for achievement, and for them actually to achieve more subsequently. In fact, a number of training programs have been tried, although the results have been mixed. One reason that such programs have not been universally successful involves the nature of traditional schooling. As McClelland (1969) points out, one way in which a student can be successful is to conform to a teacher's demands and do just what the teacher wants. But since motivation training programs involve teaching independence skills, such programs can be potentially counterproductive.

Still, some achievement motivation training programs have been successful. An example is a 6-week summer program conducted for a group of high school age boys who were identified as underachievers (Kolb, 1965). During the program, the participants were taught the characteristics of a person with a high need for achievement: "He likes and chooses to take personal responsibility for his actions, he takes moderate risks, and he likes and attempts to obtain knowledge of the results of his actions" (Kolb, 1965, p. 785). They were also taught how to score higher on TAT tests, and they were involved in playing a number of simulation games in which they could try to act in ways that were consistent with an achievement-oriented person. The basic strategy, then, was to teach the subjects how those with high achievement scores behaved, and to get them to act that way.

The results of the program were encouraging, particularly for boys from upper-class backgrounds. In a 1½-year follow-up, the grade-point average of the participants improved significantly over that of a control group who had not participated in the program. Thus the program was basically a success. The reason that it worked best with upper-class subjects is not entirely clear, but it may be related to the home environment to which the boys returned at the end of the program. The upper-class homes may have provided more reinforcement for success in school, and thus for these children the message of the program was given greater support.

The important point that can be derived from work on training programs is that it is, in fact, possible to modify the achievement motivation level of students through appropriate intervention. The need for achievement is not an unmodifiable trait; it can be changed and enhanced to produce greater achievement.

UNDERSTANDING SUCCESS AND FAILURE: AN ATTRIBUTIONAL APPROACH TO MOTIVATION

Implicit in the comments of Nancy Rosenfelt at the start of this chapter is her desire to understand and explain the reasons behind her students' performance and achievement-related motivation. This search for causal explanations is at

Students' interpretations of their performance are based on attributions of ability, effort, task difficulty, and luck. (© Elizabeth Crews/Stock, Boston)

Table 13-1 Ability Attributions

Stability	Locus of Control	
	Internal	*External*
Stable	Ability	Task Difficulty
Unstable	Effort	Luck

the heart of a major approach to achievement motivation that is based on attribution theory.

You will recall from earlier chapters that attribution theory is concerned with explaining how individuals make decisions about the underlying causes of behavior. In the case of achievement-related behaviors, attribution theory has been used to determine how students, and teachers observing their performance, understand and interpret the causes of academic success or failure. According to Bernard Weiner, the principal architect of the achievement motivation attributional theory (Weiner, 1979), the way in which one perceives the causes of one's performance is of critical importance, because one's understanding of past achievement can directly influence future achievement-related behavior.

Weiner suggests that four elements are critical both in the interpretation of previous outcomes and in the prediction of future success on a task: ability (*How smart am I?*), effort (*How hard do I try?*), task difficulty (*How hard is the task?*), and luck (*How much of my performance is due to chance?*). Thus people will attempt to explain their past outcomes, as well as their future performance, in terms of their *ability* to perform the task, the degree of *effort* expended, how *difficult* the task was, and the degree to which *luck* was responsible for the outcome. It is also assumed that people explain the causes of others' achievement-related behavior through a consideration of the same four criteria.

One of the interesting things about the four factors identified by Weiner as critical in forming achievement-related attributions is that they fall along two separate dimensions, that of locus of control and stability. The *locus of control* dimension refers to whether individuals see an event as being caused by their own behavior—demonstrating an *internal locus of control*—or as being caused by environmental factors that are independent of themselves—demonstrating an *external locus of control*. Referring back to the four factors identified by Weiner as being related to achievement motivation, it is clear that ability and effort are associated with an internal locus of control, and task difficulty and luck with an external locus of control. The stability dimension also can be used to classify the four perceived causes of success. For any given task, stability, which is related to a factor's invariance over time, is relatively high for ability and task difficulty. In contrast, effort and luck are rather unstable, since they are likely to vary a great deal over time.

internal locus of control the attributional interpretation by individuals that events are caused by their own behavior

external locus of control the attributional interpretation by individuals that events are caused by environmental factors, not their own behavior

Achievement Motivation in Women

One of the curious characteristics of work on achievement motivation is that most of it has been carried out on males. The reason for this is not just a case of neglect of women by male researchers; rather, it turns out that the typical TAT technique just doesn't work all that well for women. The method is unreliable, and results don't correlate with actual achievement as strongly as in the case of males.

Suspecting that the reason for the anomalies in the data for the females might have something to do with cultural stereotypes and norms about female success, Matina Horner (1972) asked a group of male subjects to make up a story about the following situation:

At the end of finals, John finds himself at the top of his medical school.

At the same time, a group of female subjects were asked to compose a story about an identical situation—except that in this case the stimulus sentence described a person named Anne who was at the top of her medical school class.

Horner reasoned that although achievement, success, and competitiveness are highly valued, socially acceptable, and indeed expected for males, things are very different for females. Success in a female may be seen as an unfeminine characteristic—something to be avoided. In fact, Horner suggested that females may have a fear of success, in the same way that males have a need for achievement. The greater the likelihood of success, the greater a woman's fear of losing the approval of others.

To test this theory, the stories that were written about John and Anne were content-analyzed to compare the types of themes that subjects wrote.

If the four factors and two dimensions are considered simultaneously, one comes up with the tabulation shown in Table 13-1. As can be seen, ability is stable and internal; task difficulty is stable and external; effort is unstable and internal; and luck is unstable and external. What is important about this model is that a good deal of research has shown that the locus of control dimension influences people's feelings of pride (in the event of success) and shame (as a result of failure). Pride is increased when one attributes one's success to one's internal qualities (ability and effort) and is decreased when one perceives success to be caused by external circumstances (task difficulty and luck). Similarly, feelings of shame are maximized when failure is explained by internal determinants, and minimized when failure is attributed to external causes.

about. (As with a TAT, it was assumed that the story a subject wrote was actually representative of the subject's true feelings.) Each story was analyzed for the number of references to the following factors: negative consequences of success, future behavior that moved the person into less successful areas, deeming the success as just an atypical happening, and a number of other factors relating to fear of success. The results of this analysis supported the initial hypothesis: Whereas only 9 percent of the males wrote stories about John that had elements of fear of success, over 65 percent of the females wrote such stories.

Horner's work demonstrated quite nicely a possible explanation as to why traditional measures and theories of need for achievement might work better for males. A female, even though she may have a high desire for success, may simultaneously harbor a fear of the very success for which she is striving. Given the ambivalence of her feelings, it is not at all unreasonable to expect that she may act less on her achievement motivations than a comparable male—and may indeed actively avoid competitive situations where she might be highly successful.

Unfortunately, the work on fear of success has not received notable support from subsequent research. One problem with the initial study was that it involved a profession that is perceived as being male-dominated, one where female success is rather atypical. Moreover, when males were asked to write stories about Anne, *their* stories also showed a high degree of negative imagery equivalent to a fear of success. Thus there are difficulties with the concept (Zuckerman and Wheeler, 1975).

Despite these problems, females traditionally have felt that success is somehow not as positive an accomplishment as have males. Although the feminist movement has probably tended to reduce such kinds of thinking about female success in recent years, it is reasonable for classroom teachers to be especially sensitive to issues of achievement motivation—and the ambivalence success may engender—as they relate to female students.

The dimension of stability is closely related to an individual's expectations of success or failure in the future. Attributing performances to stable causes (ability and task difficulty) leads to the expectation of similar performance—be it good or bad—in the future, while unstable causal explanations (effort and luck) result in the expectation that future performance may vary from previous experiences of success and failure.

When all the parts of the model are combined together, specific predictions can be derived for how a student will react to success or failure, depending on whether he or she attributes performance to ability, effort, task difficulty, or luck. Figure 13-3 shows the eight possible outcomes. For example, if a student attributes a successful performance to effort (an internal, unstable

FIGURE 13-3 Affective and Cognitive Reactions in Situations of Success and Failure as a Function of Attributions

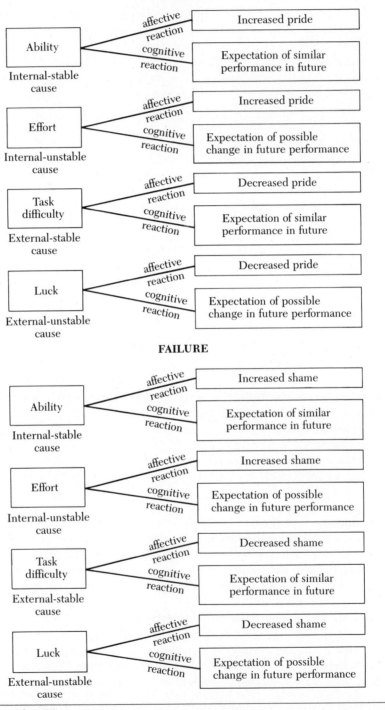

(Afer Bar-Tal, 1978)

cause), he or she might feel increased pride but expect a possible future change. On the other hand, if success is thought to be caused by luck (an external, unstable cause), there is decreased pride as well as an expectation of future changes in performance.

Studies of students' understanding of the reasons behind their own performance are congruent with these predictions (e.g., Weiner and Kukla, 1970; Weiner, Russell, and Lerman, 1979). More important, the expectations that individuals develop as a result of their attributions are reflected in their future performance. For instance, students who tend to think that their success is due to effort are apt to work longer and harder than those who attribute their performance to ability, and people who think that their failure is due to ability tend to spend less time at future tasks (Dweck, 1975).

Weiner (1979) has refined his attributional model by suggesting that the locus of control dimension actually consists of two subdimensions: the locus dimension (which refers to internal or external causes) and a new controllability dimension (which refers to whether the cause can be controlled by the student or is out of his or her control). Although supportive evidence is not as complete as for the earlier model, recent data tend to support the reformulation (Weiner, 1979).

Subcultural Differences

One important point for teachers that comes out of attributional approaches to motivation relates to differences in achievement attribution among various racial, ethnic, and social-class groups. Because different groups can develop different perceptions about the way things in the world fit together, it is not surprising that there are subcultural differences in how achievement-related behaviors are understood and explained. For instance, blacks are less likely than whites to attribute success to internal causes (Katz, 1967). Specifically, black children tend to feel that task difficulty and luck (external causes) are the major explanations for their performance outcomes. In contrast, white children seem to feel that ability and effort (internal causes) are more influential in determining their success (Friend and Neale, 1972).

There also are sex differences in achievement attribution. Consistent with findings showing that women have traditionally been taught to hold lower expectations for success than men, females seem to make attributions that are less adaptive than those of males. For instance, females tend to attribute their unsuccessful performance to low ability, but they do not attribute their successful performance to high ability (Dweck and Bush, 1976). What is maladaptive about such an attribution pattern is that when low ability is thought to be the cause of poor performance, logic dictates that even with future effort, success cannot be attained. Thus females who use such an attributional explanation may be less inclined to expend effort in subsequent tasks.

It seems that certain groups in society hold attributional biases that may hinder their ultimate success on academic tasks. However, it has been found possible to change maladaptive attributions through the use of retraining programs.

Retraining Attributional Patterns

We have seen that individuals have particular attributional styles, in which they have a tendency to attribute their performance to ability, effort, task difficulty, or luck. In some cases, this results in enhanced pride and positive expectations about future success, but in other cases the reverse is true. The crucial question is whether maladaptive attributional patterns can be changed.

A tentative answer to this question was provided by an interesting program designed by Carol Dweck (1975). Dweck identified a group of elementary school children who showed learned helplessness—they were underachievers who tended to attribute their failures to a lack of ability, which meant that they showed very little persistence (because they believed that effort was not particularly important in determining how well they performed). These children were given twenty-five individual attribution retraining sessions, in which they were taught to attribute failure to lack of effort, rather than to low ability. The results showed that after retraining, the students learned to explain failure in terms of insufficient effort; and they subsequently showed greater effort and more successful performance. Thus teaching individuals that it is effort, and not necessarily ability, that determines success can have positive effects on future performance.

Implications for Teaching

For a teacher, the most important point of the attribution model of achievement motivation is that students have characteristic causes to which they attribute their success or failure. Thus some students typically think that their performance is caused by ability, while others might have a tendency to rely on explanations of effort, task difficulty, or luck. While some types of attribution may lead the student to work harder, others may be maladaptive. For instance, students who characteristically attribute failure to low ability are likely to feel displeased with their performance and to expect similar performance in the future. Likewise, attributing success to task difficulty ("I did well because the test was easy") leads to decreased pride in performance.

The attributional analysis of motivation suggests, then, that teachers should try to correct maladaptive attributions, which lead students to perform below their potential. Thus students may benefit by the encouragement of internal explanations (ability and effort) when they perform successfully, and lack-of-effort attributions for unsatisfactory performance. Of course, encouraging unrealistic patterns of attribution ultimately would be detrimental to the student's performance. So care must be taken to foster explanations of achievement that fall within a student's potential. Individualized instruction, in which goals can be set that are within a student's reach, is an effective means of preventing the frustration that results from striving for unreachable levels of achievement (Dweck, 1975).

PROMOTING STUDENT MOTIVATION

Up to this point, the discussion has focused on motivation in terms of individual students and what it is they bring to the classroom in the way of their own unique motivational characteristics. The focus changes now to some general techniques, appropriate for classroom use, that are designed specifically to enhance the motivation of a class to succeed in school. This section discusses a number of current programs that have proven to be successful in leading to increases in student motivation, including an individually guided motivational package, the use of open classrooms, the employment of multiage and multigrade instructional units, and team teaching.

Although each of these strategies is discussed in terms of a complete system, it is quite possible to employ individual techniques or portions from any or all of the programs presented. Indeed, in times or locales where educational resources are scarce, it may be impossible to adopt a totally new educational program—particularly one that requires a great deal of individualization or extra personnel. But it is possible to employ particular aspects of these programs, even in a traditional self-contained classroom.

Individually Guided Motivation Program

Individually Guided Motivation (IGM) is an instructional program that was developed at one of the major government-funded educational research centers in the United States, the Wisconsin Research and Development Center for Cognitive Learning (Klausmeier, Jeter, Quilling and Frayer, 1973; Klausmeier, 1975). The program, which is designed to be implemented in school settings, uses a number of specific procedures to enhance student motivation, including teacher-student individual conferences to set specific goals, tutoring by peers, and small-group conferences that are aimed at developing positive motivational behavior.

One part of the program is a weekly 10- to 15-minute conference between teacher (or other adult) and student. The teacher uses a number of techniques during the conference to encourage the student to do more work than that which was assigned. For instance, if the target behavior were increased motivation to read, the teacher would exhibit positive behaviors and attitudes toward reading; this strategy can facilitate modeling of the teacher. The teacher can help the child to set reasonable goals by helping to choose books at the proper level of difficulty. In addition, the teacher should provide verbal reinforcement for display of desired behaviors relating to reading. Such straightforward techniques have been shown to be effective in producing increases in student motivation.

On the basis of work on the IGM system, Herbert Klausmeier (1975) has suggested the following general principles for teacher behaviors that lead to higher student motivation:

1. *Develop specific objectives for students, and focus their attention.* By providing appropriate materials, student curiosity is aroused. The physical environment can be altered, or new materials can be brought into the classroom. In addition, questions and discussions can be used to get students to attend to the objectives that have been developed.

2. *Use the students' inherent need for achievement.* Most students have some desire to do well in school, and the teacher should try to arouse that need by decreasing fear of failure and increasing self-confidence. This can be done by providing tasks that can be accomplished, and by minimizing the penalties for unsuccessful attempts.

3. *Help students to set realistic goals and to attain them.* When realistic goals are set, the student is more likely to experience success. Such success can increase student motivation because the attainment of goals is very rewarding.

4. *Provide feedback.* When students receive appropriate feedback and have their errors corrected, they are able to improve their performance and can be helped to reach the goals they have set. Clear, precise, and informative feedback is a prerequisite for improvement.

5. *Provide models for student behavior.* Teachers who show that they enjoy a particular subject can serve as a model for students to emulate. However, it is important to display not just a general positive attitude to a subject area but specific behaviors that can be copied and can lead to improved performance.

6. *Provide students with the opportunity to discuss desired behaviors.* Discussion of values ensures that students are aware of them and understand them, and increases the likelihood that they will eventually accept them.

7. *Use positive reinforcement following desirable behavior.* Teachers should reward displays of achievement and motivation.

8. *Stress should be avoided.* Arousal of anxiety can be detrimental to performance and motivation. Thus procedures that increase stress are potentially harmful and should not be employed.

These principles are a useful set of guidelines for appropriate teacher behavior, and they have been shown to be effective. Moreover, they are effective not just on an individual, one-to-one basis but in teaching groups of students or classes as a whole.

Open Classrooms

One school innovation that has sometimes been used as a means to capture intrinsic student motivation, as well as to increase motivation in general, is the open classroom. The open class concept became popular in the United States in the late 1960s, and it grew directly out of innovations in British education that were widely acclaimed in that country. Beginning around World

Open classrooms provide opportunities for students to freely choose activities and materials. (© Bohdan Hrynewych/Stock, Boston)

War II, educators in Britain began to adopt teaching techniques in elementary schools that were considerably more informal than prior methods. Rather than promoting rigid and authoritarian classrooms, teachers were encouraged to provide relaxed, unstructured environments that were student-oriented and in which the emphasis was on individualized instruction.

The definition of open education is somewhat imprecise. Joseph Silberman, an early American proponent of the innovation, has said that open education is "less an approach or method than a set of shared attitudes and convictions about the nature of childhood, learning, and schooling" (Silberman, 1970, p. 208). Specifically, those convictions include the idea—drawn primarily from the work of Piaget—that teachers should be *facilitators* of students' education, in that they should provide children with the materials and equipment necessary to learn independently. Direct instruction by the teacher is considered less effective than allowing students to follow their own direction.

In addition, open education can be thought of as a teaching technique in which the physical space in a classroom is used consciously to promote learning. Various sorts of activities are grouped in different areas and are arranged to be physically appealing and inviting. In some senses, the open classroom is a kind of "department store" of learning materials, in which the students browse and make their choices of what activity to become involved in. In many open schools, the traditional walled-in, rectangular classroom has been replaced by open areas and few interior walls. Children have easy access to other classrooms, as well as to such areas as libraries, instructional media centers, and the like.

At the center of the open education philosophy is the notion that children, when given the opportunity, make the kind of choices that will enable them to be effectively educated. Drawing on Piaget's research, which suggests that children have a natural tendency to manipulate materials in a way that enhances their cognitive abilities, open educators feel that children should follow their own interests. The role of the teacher, in this view, is to answer a student's questions and to provide an open, accepting atmosphere in which the student can guide his or her own education.

If it appears that the teacher's role in open education is minimal, this is an erroneous impression. In fact, a teacher in an open classroom may work much harder than an instructor in a traditional classroom. The reason for this is the factor of individualization. Teachers are not considered primarily as transmitters of knowledge to a set of students. Rather, they must diagnose each student's level of ability and problems individually, and they must motivate the students to take an active role in working with the materials that are developed for them. This individualization can be quite time consuming; but according to proponents of open education, the results are worth the extra time and effort that are necessary. In the view of proponents, students who learn in the more active fashion of open education are apt to learn more and learn it better than those schooled by means of traditional techniques. Moreover, the excitement of learning generated by the open classroom will motivate students to reach their full potential.

Freedom and Motivation

Much of the theory behind the implementation of such classroom arrangements as open education, nongrading, and multiage classrooms rests on the assumption that increased student freedom will lead to increased motivation to learn. The student is thought to be intrinsically motivated, and the removal of some of the constraints associated with traditional classrooms, such as letter grades and assignments for the class as a whole, are assumed to enhance the student's intrinsic motivation. Is such an assumption justified?

The answer appears to be yes. One important source of evidence favoring classroom freedom comes from the work of Richard DeCharms (1968, 1972). He suggests that persons tend to feel either that they are the *origins* of their behavior or that they are the *pawns* of some other person, thing, or event. Origins feel that they have control over their environment and that what happens to them is a result of their own actions. In contrast, pawns feel that the environment is not under their control and that they cannot determine the cause of events. A feeling of mastery over a situation is thus lacking in pawns. DeCharms argues that schools ought to strive to provide an environment in which students will be led to perceive themselves as origins, for this will lead to increased performance and motivation.

To increase a student's perception that he or she is an origin, at least two kinds of classroom freedom can be employed (Maehr, 1974). First, students will tend to perceive themselves as origins when they have freedom from external evaluation. Thus a lack of constant teacher evaluation can enhance feelings of being an origin. Second, freedom to choose among various classroom alternatives and activities promotes the perception of being an origin. Having a choice, then, can be motivating to the student.

It thus appears that procedures that increase student freedom and autonomy can result in higher levels of student motivation. It should be noted that these techniques do not necessarily require major changes in classroom arrangements; they can be implemented through the climate that the teacher creates in the classroom.

On the other hand, open education is not without its critics. The sheer effort required of teachers is one source of dissatisfaction. Moreover, some teachers find it difficult to allow the amount of disorder and nondirective activities that open education requires. This form of education is also not the most efficient for imparting information (although one can argue whether efficiency in learning is an important requirement for education). Finally, not all students react positively to the freedom and unstructured environment of open classrooms.

Perhaps the most reasonable comment regarding the efficacy of open education comes from a careful review and critique that compared 200 students in traditional and open classes (Horowitz, 1979). In a summary of the results, the author concluded:

> At this time, the evidence from evaluation studies of the open classroom's effects on children is not sufficiently consistent to warrant an unqualified endorsement of that approach to teaching as decidedly superior to more traditional methods. But there certainly is enough evidence now to defend the idea that the open classroom should be supported as a viable alternative when teachers and parents are interested in such a program. (Horowitz, 1979, p. 83)

Multiage and Multilevel Techniques

Another instructional technique that can lead to enhanced student motivation is the use of the multiage classroom, which involves placing students of many ages in the same class. This system of teaching is best represented by the one-room school, which, as mentioned in Chapter 2, is still being used in some areas of the United States. The distinctive feature of the one-room school is that a teacher simultaneously provides instruction for children in a wide span of ages and grades. While students in one grade (or adjacent grades) are being taught, the other students work either by themselves or with their peers.

In an age in which instructional technology and techniques are so advanced, one might surmise that students in a one-room school would be at a distinct disadvantage. And in fact, one recent survey of 110 one-room schools in Nebraska found many teachers complaining of the lack of equipment and about having insufficient time to teach everyone in every subject. But they also cited a surprising number of clear motivational advantages to the system, which they felt strongly outweighed the disadvantages. In terms of academic success, many teachers suggested that students in a one-room school can receive more individualized attention and can progress at their own rate. Moreover, children can learn from one another, and quite a bit of informal peer tutoring occurs. In the area of social development and character formation, many teachers commented that the students learn to work and play with children of ages other than their own and that they gain understanding of younger children and learn responsibility for younger children. In sum, there can be clear advantages to multiage systems of schooling (Allen, 1976).

A technique that is related to multiage classrooms is the use of multilevel (or nongraded) systems. In multilevel systems, students are not assigned to any particular grade or level on the basis of their chronological age. Rather, multilevel programs have children working on material that is specific to their own level of achievement for each subject.

The rationale for nongrading programs follows from the obvious fact that children do not always perform at the same level on all subjects. For instance, a child who reads at a fourth-grade level does not automatically perform at a fourth-grade level in arithmetic. In a multilevel system, a child can be grouped appropriately for each subject area. Multilevel systems avoid the frustration of consistently performing poorly at certain tasks, because the material being studied will be appropriate for a student's particular level. This can lead to enhanced interest and motivation.

In the typical multilevel system, children are regrouped within various classrooms during the day to form multiple classes working with different teachers. A form of multilevel instruction can also be accomplished within a self-contained classroom by providing curriculum on multiple levels of difficulty simultaneously.

Most studies of students in multilevel systems have shown that they learn either as well as or better than students in traditional, graded systems. In addition, motivation appears to be enhanced; nongrading results in positive attitudes (Martin and Pavan, 1976). Thus multilevel grouping appears to be a viable technique for increasing student motivation and success.

Team Teaching

Team teaching techniques are designed to promote motivation and academic success through the use of principles of group behavior. In this approach, a group of teachers work together in planning an instructional program. When the students are actually taught, each of the team members teaches his or her own area of interest and expertise. The rationale for this procedure is that the total quality and quantity of resources available to each student is increased, and because the teachers are covering the material of greatest interest to them, their enthusiasm helps to ignite student motivation. Moreover, since members of the team are not only teaching students but "performing" for their colleagues as well, it is possible that they will do a better job of preparing.

Although team teaching is not uncommon, in many cases potentially positive benefits that could come from its implementation have not occurred (Armstrong, 1977). The major reason for this lack of success is that team teaching, as it actually is practiced by teachers in a school, may not be all that different from traditional teaching. For instance, some teachers may view team teaching as primarily an administrative arrangement, in which the goal is to coordinate lesson plans and curriculum with others. When it comes to actually teaching students, teachers' behavior may not be all that different from what they typically do. Obviously, little enhancement of student achievement and performance over traditional teaching techniques can be expected if there is no difference in teacher behavior.

In sum, team teaching seems to be a promising technique for enhancing student motivation and learning, although actual results are far from consistent. But the logical reasons for favoring team teaching are compelling: The possibility of input from diverse individuals into curriculum and instructional decisions

What the Country Can Do: The Report of the National Commission on Excellence in Education

"Our nation is at risk. The educational foundations of our society are presently being eroded by a rising tide of mediocrity. If an unfriendly foreign power had attempted to impose on America the mediocre educational performance that exists today, we might well have viewed it as an act of war."

With statements like these, the National Commission on Excellence in Education blasted the American educational system in the spring of 1983. Composed of a Presidentially appointed panel of educators and laypersons, the Commission issued a stunning indictment of the quality of education in the United States in a report titled, *A Nation at Risk: The Imperative for Educational Reform*. Among the Commission's specific criticisms were:

- Teaching quality is, in general, remarkably low;
- There is a serious shortage of math and science teachers in almost every area of the country;
- Academic standards are lax, with students choosing electives instead of more fundamental—and important—subjects;

should lead to better decisions; the range of teaching abilities and knowledge available to the team, and consequently to the students, is wider with a team teaching approach; team teaching can reduce teacher stress and workload; and finally, because students can be exposed to a diverse set of teaching styles, it is more likely that they will find a teacher with whom they are comfortable and compatible (Shaw, 1976). For all these reasons, team teaching is a technique worth considering.

What the Teacher Can Do

Although the discussion in this section has featured changes in classroom arrangements that can promote student motivation, there are also steps that

- No state has a foreign-language requirement for high school graduation, and just one year of math and one year of science are required for graduation in the majority of states.

Given its very negative image of the state of American education, how did the Commission propose to improve the quality of the system? The basic strategy suggested is a "get tough" policy. The Commission recommended more stringent requirements for high school graduation—including four years of English, three years of math, science, and social studies, and instruction in computer science for every student. It suggested that school days be lengthened and the length of the school year increased and it said that student progress should be measured by frequent achievement tests. Finally, it urged that colleges become more selective by raising their admission standards.

The Commission also pointed to a number of improvements that can be made in the teaching profession itself. Teaching programs in colleges ought to become more selective. And once teachers are in the classroom, the status of education as a profession should be raised. Salaries should be increased and salary increases should be based more on merit and less on time-in-rank.

In the end, the Commission noted, such educational reforms can come only through increased citizen involvement. The changes that were suggested are expensive, requiring new funds to be appropriated by state legislatures. On the other hand, the ultimate cost of doing nothing might be far greater.

teachers in the traditional classroom can take. The following are among the most useful things a teacher can do:

1. *Respect and encourage individual strengths in students.* Students may have a variety of strengths, and their expertise in a particular area should be presented as valuable to them and to their classmates.
2. *Emphasize that learning is a lifelong undertaking* and not something that should take place only during school time.
3. *Reward displays of intrinsic motivation.* Performance and learning that occur because of the students' intrinsic interest in a topic should be encouraged, while working just for extrinsic rewards (such as grades) should not be positively reinforced.
4. *Encourage participation and involvement.* Students should feel that

they affect what goes on in the classroom and have a voice in its affairs.

5. *Make students aware of how much progress they have made* over the course of the school year. Even minor progress can be motivating if it is made apparent to the student.

While the above techniques are not exhaustive, they do provide at least the essentials for enhancing student motivation.

SUMMARY

Motivation refers to the factors that drive and orient behavior toward a particular goal. In the context of education, the typical goal is academic success and achievement. One important aspect of teaching is to arouse motivation in students that is directed toward educational goals.

The relationship between motivational arousal and performance success is related to the complexity of the task and is known as the Yerkes-Dodson law. Performance on simple tasks is best at relatively high levels of arousal, whereas complex tasks require relatively lower levels of arousal for optimum performance.

Maslow has suggested a hierarchical, ordered set of needs to explain different levels of motivation. The five needs are: physiological, safety, love and belongingness, esteem, and self-actualization. A person can move toward higher-order needs only after the more basic needs are fulfilled. The highest level, self-actualization, is reached when individuals realize their potential and experience a sense of mastery and competence.

The need for achievement is a personality trait that relates to the degree and nature of motivation aroused in striving for achievement-related goals. Measured by the Thematic Apperception Test (TAT), need for achievement is made up of a desire to achieve success and a fear of failure. People with a high desire to achieve success and a low fear of failure tend to prefer tasks of moderate difficulty; those with the opposite pattern of motivations prefer either easy or difficult tasks. Need for achievement can be taught, by identifying the characteristics of people high in need for achievement and leading students to adopt those behaviors.

Attribution theory approaches to motivation suggest that people use the factors of ability, effort, task difficulty, and luck to evaluate their academic performance. These factors fall along the dimensions of locus of control (internal or external) and stability (stable or unstable). The particular cause to which success or failure is attributed leads to pride or shame regarding the performance, as well as to expectations of future change or similarity in performance. There are subcultural and sex differences regarding performance attributions that may inhibit successful performance. However, it is possible to retrain maladaptive attributional patterns.

A number of instructional techniques have been developed to increase student motivation and performance. Individually guided motivation (IGM) provides a set of specific procedures employing teacher-student goal-setting conferences, peer tutoring, and small-group meetings. Open education helps students shape their own education by providing them with materials and options for their own decisions. The teacher's role is to provide an open, accepting environment for the student.

Multiage classrooms have students of many ages in the same classroom, where they may receive more individualized instruction and have cross-age peer interaction. Multiage programs enable children to work on their own level for each individual subject. Because children are working at an appropriate difficulty level, frustration is reduced and motivation enhanced. Team teaching, in which a group of teachers plan and instruct students jointly, can enhance the quality and quantity of educational resources available to each student.

FOR FURTHER STUDY AND APPLICATION

Maslow, A. H. *Motivation and personality*. New York: Harper & Row, 1970. A guide to Maslow's theory of motivation, with particular reference to the concept of self-actualization.

McClelland, D. C., and Winter, D. G. *Motivating economic achievement*. New York: Free Press, 1969. Although written in reference to economic success, this book provides many techniques that can be adapted by the classroom teacher.

Weiner, B. *Achievement motivation and academic success*. Morristown, N.J.: General Learning Press, 1974. A sophisticated look at research relating to the use of attribution theory in the understanding of performance attainment and expectations.

Ball, S. (Ed.). *Motivation in education*. New York: Academic Press, 1977. Provides a series of chapters by authorities on topics relating to motivation.

Stephens, L. S. *The teacher's guide to open education*. New York: Holt, Rinehart and Winston, 1974. A very practical guide to organizing a classroom along the lines of open education.

Klausmeier, H. J., Jeter, J., Quilling, M., and Frayer, D. *Individually guided motivation*. Madison: Wisconsin Research and Development Center for Cognitive Learning, 1973. Provides a detailed description of the individually guided motivation program, including specific techniques and activities.

14

PSYCHOLOGICAL PRINCIPLES OF EFFECTIVE INSTRUCTION

CHAPTER OVERVIEW

This chapter discusses what is known about what makes instruction effective. First, the goals of education are examined. Then, in the remainder of the chapter, the three major avenues through which educators can attain those goals—the instructional environment, the physical environment, and the school environment—are analyzed. Teaching need not be a haphazard venture; there are specific techniques and procedures that can be employed to increase the likelihood of success in the classroom.

As Assistant Secretary for Elementary and Secondary Education, and chief administrator of a $5-billion budget, Dr. Vincent E. Reed is one of the most powerful figures in American education today.

One of seventeen children, Dr. Reed began his career as a high school teacher and at various times held the position of counselor, assistant principal, principal, assistant superintendent, and superintendent of schools. He is in a unique position to discuss education in the United States today.

The interview, which took place in Dr. Reed's office near the Capitol, began with a question about what the role of the federal government in education ought to be.

A.   I think the federal government shouldn't have control over what takes place in local school districts along the line of what's taught in the classroom. But I do think the federal government can play several roles. They can play a role by giving technical assistance; they can play a role by doing research from the standpoint of collecting data and programmatic information, and disseminating it; and they can offer initiatives to school districts that are willing to try something new and experimental. Thus the federal government can stand by to fund, reinforce, or support those programs that are presented by school districts to enhance the children of those school districts; or the federal government can go out front and put forward initiatives that school districts can buy into.

Q.   Should it be doing anything else?

A.   I don't think the federal government should play much of a role beyond that. I think that education is basically the responsibility of the parent, and the local school district and the state should be there to reinforce and support that education. I think that the federal government in the past has been too much involved in education by controlling the purse strings, and if you control the purse strings, you control the actions. Basically, then, I think the federal government should stand on the outside as much as possible and lend a helping hand when needed, without any strings attached.

Q.   Are you familiar with the "new" Coleman report, which suggests that private schools are superior to public ones?

A.   Oh yes. I say you should send your child to a private school if you think private schools benefit your child. I don't think that all youngsters fit into public education. Nor do all youngsters thrive in a private education setting. I think private schools play a role in education in this country, and I think they should be recognized and accepted as an important part of education.

Q.   Do you accept Coleman's conclusion that private schools are better?

A.   There are three things that private schools have going for them. Number one: students are there because they want to be there. Number two: private schools can force parental involvement by saying that if you don't become involved, we won't keep your children. Now, I don't know of any educational program in this country that has been successful on a sustained basis that didn't have some kind of parental involvement. So I'm very much concerned and an advocate of parental involvement. Number three: if you don't do what they say, they'll send you back to public school—and the public school has to take you. So I don't knock private schools for their success rate. But if public schools had these same things going for them, they would be more successful too. They would be just as successful as any private school. (And of course not all private schools are successful, even with these things going for them.) I think the report served a purpose, but it didn't tell people the whole truth.

Q.   What advice do you have for prospective teachers?

A.   I think we have to go back and stop misleading our young people into thinking school is fun. School is hard work. You know and I know that studying sometimes can become very laborious and can become very hard, so the youngsters are disillusioned. I'm saying for people who want to be teachers, "Go ahead and bite the bullet, and take the hard road, and prepare yourself to be a teacher."

It used to be that you didn't make much money teaching, but now teachers' salaries, while not quite comparable to those of private industry, have come closer to it than they were 15 or 20 years ago. You can make a heck of a contribution. Years ago, when we were making almost no money at all, and my friends used to tease me about being in public education instead of something that paid more money, I'd think about leaving sometimes. And just when I'd get to the point of saying I'm going to give this thing up and go and do something where I'm going to make more money, some youngster would do something that made me think that education was worthwhile. Some youngster would come up and say, "Thanks, Mr. Reed, for helping me with my work" or "I saw this little girl in the street, wandering around, and, based on the kinds of things you told me, I took her to the nearest policeman." These kinds of things keep you in this business.

I don't think there's any business that gives you greater emotional rewards than teaching. There are other businesses that give you more financial kinds of rewards, but to young people, I say, "Prepare yourself for teaching and don't lock yourself in too tight and specialize. Give yourself a broad and liberal kind of education so you can follow any avenue of teaching. And young people will give you rewards back—rewards that, in the long run, are more lasting than the dollar bill."

Q.   Why don't we have as many people going into education?

A.   I'm disturbed that we can't find teachers, but I do understand. We've got to go back to saying that we don't hire teachers to be policemen; we hire teachers to teach. And those youngsters that disrupt class should be excluded from class. I don't think any youngster has a right to deny other youngsters an education. I think that every time a teacher takes more than 1 percent of his or her time to discipline any youngster, that youngster should be excluded. Because I really believe that discipline is a parental problem and not a school problem. And I think that parents have to be responsible for how their youngsters behave in school, and teachers shouldn't be burdened with disciplinary problems. That's what's driving teachers out of teaching. Most teachers who leave teaching are going out because they say, "I just can't take it any more. I'm fighting all day long." Well, they shouldn't be fighting all day long. They should be able to prepare a lesson, and enjoy their interaction with their students without having to fight students all day long about their disruptive behavior. So I think that we, as educators, have to make sure that teachers don't encounter that.

Everyone can agree with the implicit view of Dr. Reed that without high-quality instruction, students will not learn effectively—or at all. As you will read, teaching does make a difference.

THE GOALS OF EDUCATION

There is hardly a more complex question than What makes instruction effective? The reason for this complexity resides in the fact that one must first determine what one expects and hopes the outcomes of education will be; only then can one evaluate what it is that must be done in order to attain such outcomes.

Among the many goals of education, the following are four of the most important: transmission of a body of knowledge, realization of each student's unique potential, maximization of student self-respect and self-actualization, and the socialization of the norms, mores, and values of society. Each of these bears some elaboration:

1. *Transmission of a body of knowledge.* At the most fundamental level, schooling consists of teachers communicating a set of facts, theories, and means of thinking to their students. Educators must teach subject matter that can be mastered by their students and that has at least potential relevance for their lives beyond the years in which they attend school.

2. *Realization of each student's unique potential.* As noted throughout this book, students are individuals with unique characteristics, needs, and potential. One important goal of education is to ensure that this potential is realized. This view is maintained not just for the good of the individual; it is assumed that society as a whole will benefit from the maximal success of its individual members.

3. *Maximization of self-respect and self-actualization.* Although not the primary goal of American education, the hope that education will lead to self-respect and self-actualization are generally assumed to be a part of the rationale for educating individuals in American society. Schools attempt to provide activities that build character and make students feel that they can make an active contribution to society, even if not in the areas of academics. The nearly universal incidence and promotion of sports activities in the nation's schools provides an example of how educators attempt to provide all students with some vehicle for enhancing and developing self-respect and self-actualization.

4. *Socialization of norms, mores, and values.* One of the least explicit but most important of the goals of education relates to the

socialization of the norms, mores, and values of a given society. Schooling is used to teach children such notions as the importance of equality, individuality, and competition. Although these ideas are usually not taught directly, they are expressed implicitly in the choice of activities, grading practices, and curricular decisions.

Attaining the Goals of Education

Not all of these goals can be met simultaneously, of course, and it may be reasonable to question whether any one person or instructional system can *always* be effective in meeting *all* four goals. Indeed, when one looks at studies of teacher effectiveness, it can be seen that schooling has almost always been considered effective solely on the basis of how much students have learned (the first goal). Still, many of the same things that promote learning outcomes are likely to bring about success in terms of the other goals of education.

In the remainder of the chapter, three major areas of educational impact on students are discussed—teacher behavior, the physical environment, and the structure of the school—and an attempt is then made to identify what strategies are most effective in achieving the goals of education.

THE INSTRUCTIONAL ENVIRONMENT

Although some people have argued that teaching is an art and that teachers are born, not made (Fenstermacher, 1979), work on teacher effectiveness refutes such a point of view. For certain teacher behaviors result, fairly consistently, in better student performance.

What can a teacher do to promote an effective instructional environment? Let us examine two broad areas of teacher behavior that are related to successful teaching; the use of appropriate instructional strategies, and the application of specific management techniques.

Effective Instructional Strategies

Independent of the nature of the subject matter or curriculum that is being taught, there are certain instructional strategies that have been shown to be quite effective in promoting student learning. Among these are the use of reinforcement and criticism, asking questions effectively, and maintaining a clear and enthusiastic verbal style.

Using reinforcement and criticism

It should come as no surprise that the use of reinforcement by teachers is a powerful technique for modifying student behaviors. As discussed in the chapter on operant learning techniques (Chapter 6), appropriate reinforcement can lead to improvements in student deportment and student achievement, and this has been demonstrated in many studies. The key word here is *appropriate;* reinforcement that is not directly contingent upon desired behavior will not result in positive outcomes (Brophy, 1981).

While positive reinforcement on the part of the teacher generally produces higher performance, the relationship between strong teacher criticism and student achievement is generally negative. High amounts of criticism lead to *lower* student success (Rosenshine and Furst, 1971). On the other hand, mild forms of criticism may actually enhance performance. The reason is that mild forms of criticism usually include a directional element—informing students how to carry out some academic task, for example. In this situation, the criticism can clarify what desirable performance is and thus ultimately can serve to increase student achievement. Thus although strong criticism does not seem to facilitate student performance, mild, corrective criticism can be an effective teaching technique.

Asking questions effectively

Although asking students questions seems a fairly straightforward task, it turns out to be a bit more complicated than might at first be thought—as noted in Chapter 8. Teachers may ask for information; or they may ask for an explanation; or the question may require analysis or synthesis of various points of view; or it may require creativity and divergence from material that has already been presented. Even the nature of teacher probing, once a student has responded, can vary.

Although the research findings are complex (Winne, 1979; Dillon, 1982), it does appear that the complexity of questions is particularly important. There is some evidence suggesting that the level of a student's response is related to the nature of the teacher's question. Simple questions tend to elicit simple responses, while more complex questions seem to result in richer student answers. For instance, in one study (Willson, 1973), teachers were trained to ask higher-order questions than those to which they had been accustomed. The results showed that not only did student responses reflect the more sophisticated questions they were being asked, but the teachers themselves began to change the way they were thinking about the material—as indicated by changes in their questioning behavior.

The implication of this finding is that it is important to put some effort into choosing appropriate and challenging questions for students. The level of questions should match the teacher's objectives in order to encourage maximal reflection on the material. Thus if teachers want their students to be capable of synthesizing various facts into a cohesive whole, the level of questions must reflect this goal.

The complexity with which a question is asked is related to the quality of student responses. (© Roger Malloch/Magnum)

Maintaining a clear and enthusiastic verbal style

The clarity and enthusiasm with which a teacher presents material to a class affects student performance. Although it is difficult to operationalize the meaning of "clarity" a number of suggestions can be made based on observations of successful teachers (Rosenshine and Furst, 1971). For instance, teachers should use short, easy-to-understand comments that are direct and specific. The material must, of course, be appropriate for the cognitive level of the students in the class. Additionally, such imprecise words as "some," "many," and "a little" should be avoided for maximal student learning. Finally, each lesson as a whole should have a clear, precise organization to it.

Teacher enthusiasm also is clearly related to student achievement. Teachers who are rated by their students as being involved, vigorous, and interested in their subject matter tend to be the most effective (Solomon, Bezdek, and Rosenberg, 1963). "Enthusiasm" is likely a combination of tone of voice, gestures, and other nonverbal behaviors that indicate genuine teacher involvement in the material and concern that students should learn effectively.

Classroom Management Techniques

Without a sense of organization, classrooms will not provide an atmosphere conducive to the actual process of teaching and learning. Some of the most important decisions that a teacher must make revolve around classroom management techniques concerning the maintenance of discipline, the use of a variety of teaching methods, and the use of classroom time.

Promoting discipline

The maintenance of an orderly classroom environment is of primary importance in effective teaching (Medley, 1977). In the classrooms of effective teachers, there are fewer disruptive pupils and fewer consequent rebukes than in the classrooms of less effective ones.

There are a variety of means by which teachers can promote and maintain discipline in a classroom situation. One thing that appears to be particularly important is for teachers to communicate to pupils that they have the ability to monitor and keep track of events in all parts of the classroom, something that has been termed "withitness" (Kounin, 1970; Irving and Martin, 1982). Moreover, successful teachers make certain that this awareness is communicated to their students. Thus effective teachers are able to prevent small incidents from growing into large ones.

Another factor that differentiates teachers who maintain well-managed classrooms from those who do not is the ability to attend to and encourage different group activities simultaneously. Good teachers are constantly monitoring various groups, and they are able to keep their students involved in appropriate activities. This strategy prevents classrooms from becoming focused on just a small number of students.

Teachers also are more effective when they manage to involve all their students while teaching. Jere Brophy (1979) suggests that successful teachers are better able to deal with individual students even in group meetings. For instance, such teachers may ask questions of one student after another in a fixed, sequential manner, rather than skipping from one to another in an unplanned way. In this way, all students receive an equal opportunity to respond, as well as getting individual attention from the teacher.

Using variety

Teachers who use a variety of materials, teaching devices, and activities are more effective than those who use less diversity in their teaching (Rosenshine and Furst, 1971). This finding implies that a consistent teaching style is less reinforcing to students than one in which the teacher shows flexibility. What is particularly interesting about this phenomenon is that it is not so much the content of the variety that is important in enhancing teaching effectiveness but the idea that the teacher is flexible and actually makes changes in the classroom.

Time on task

One of the most important factors leading to teacher success is something that has been termed *time on task*. Time on task refers to the actual amount of time that is spent on direct teaching activities, and during which students are engaged in learning, in the course of a school day.

It is clear that the greater the amount of time spent on task, the greater the amount of student learning. Interestingly, it seems that students who enter school with the greatest deficits benefit proportionally the most from larger amounts of time spent on task (Stallings, 1976).

Of course, it should not be assumed that having a teacher spend more time on a given topical area will automatically result in greater student learning, regardless of the *quality* of the instruction. For instance, the nature of teacher-student interaction can be a better predictor of student achievement than the amount of time on task (McDonald and Elias, 1976). It is likely that a combination of time allocated to learning, student engaged time, distribution of time across tasks, and appropriateness of task provides the best indicant of student success (Stallings, 1980).

Basically, results of time-on-task studies indicate not only that there are wide variations from classroom to classroom in the amount of time spent on task but that such variations can have meaningful effects on student performance. Generally, the more time spent teaching academic subjects, the higher student performance on those subjects will be.

time on task the actual amount of time that is spent on direct teaching activities, and during which students are engaged in learning

Putting It All Together

The state of the art regarding knowledge of what teachers can do to promote student learning can be summed up by citing five major conclusions about teacher behavior, derived from an exhaustive review of work on teacher effectiveness (Brophy, 1981).

1. Teachers *do* affect student learning. Some teachers bring about more student success than others do, and their success is tied to specific, identifiable teacher behaviors.
2. However, there are no specific behaviors that *always* result in superior student performance. It is overly simplistic to say that a behavior is appropriate regardless of the circumstances.
3. How teachers perceive their role as a teacher is crucial to their success. Teachers who feel that their *instructional* role is primary—as opposed to a more "laissez-faire" role—are more apt to be successful. The reason seems to be attributable to the fact that these instructionally oriented teachers simply spend more time teaching students.
4. Successful teachers are better managers of their students' time.

Learning What Makes Teachers Effective: Some Methodological Considerations

Research on teacher effectiveness is among the most complicated to carry out, and this is one of the reasons that firm generalizations are so difficult to make. For instance, there are enormous methodological problems in exploring the relationship between teacher effectiveness and student outcomes. One problem that researchers encounter relates simply to defining behavior in a way that will enable it to be systematically observed. On what basis, for instance, should teacher nonverbal reinforcement be assessed? On the basis of a teacher's smiling, gesturing, and amount of movement? Or should it be determined on the basis of students' ratings (in which case one would have no real idea of what criteria were involved)?

Related to the difficulty of defining teacher behavior in a given area is the problem of deciding what to measure. If one decides to examine the goal of transmission of a body of knowledge, one has first to determine how student performance is going to be measured. Student performance can be viewed as general, overall achievement; as achievement in a specific subject area; or as achievement in relation to a specific lesson that the investigator has chosen to have a teacher use for a short-term experiment. All these approaches are valid, but they result in different kinds of information with different degrees of generalizability. If one chooses one of the more nebulous goals of education (such as the realization of student potential), the task is even harder.

Finally, much of the research on teacher effectiveness is correlational in nature. This means that a researcher will go into a certain number of classrooms, measure how much a teacher shows a particular behavior, and then measure, say, student performance. However, this does not necessarily

Things run smoothly, there are relatively few disruptions because of nonacademic matters, and the transitions between activities are handled effectively.

5. Finally, teachers are more efficient when they use a strong curricular approach. Students seem to learn more, in less time, when the teacher structures material and presents it directly to the students, rather than using more indirect techniques. In Brophy's words:

The instruction that seems most efficient is the kind in which the teacher works with the whole class (or with small groups in the early grades), presents information in lectures/demonstrations, and then follows up with

mean that the teacher's behavior *caused* the student's performance. It is just as plausible that student performance (as well as possibly the teacher's behavior) was caused by some third, unmeasured factor. Therefore, without well-controlled experimental research, in which there is a comparison group of some kind, it is impossible to make unequivocal statements about the relationship between teacher behavior and student performance. For example, if one wanted to find an unambiguous causal relationship between teacher nonverbal reinforcement and student performance, one possibility would be to train a group of teachers to be nonverbally reinforcing and then compare their students' performance to that of a group of students who were taught by teachers who had been trained to avoid nonverbal reinforcement. If one were lucky, such a study might show a causal relationship. (Even in this case, though, critics might be able to come up with a number of plausible alternative explanations.)

Despite the difficulty of carrying out research on teacher effectiveness, it is possible at this point to draw quite a few firm conclusions. And if you think that the research has not really found much that is not obvious, it is worth noting that a number of behaviors that one might intuitively assume to be associated with student outcomes are not. Consider this:

> The strongest findings may appear to represent mere educational platitudes. Their value can be appreciated, however, only when they are compared to the behavioral characteristics, equally virtuous and 'obvious', which have *not* shown significant or consistent relationships with achievement to date. These variables [include] . . . warmth . . . , flexibility . . . , teacher talk . . . , teacher absence . . . , teacher time spent on class participation . . . , teacher experience, and teacher knowledge of subject area (Rosenshine and Furst, 1971, p. 55).

The body of knowledge about what does and what does *not* make teachers effective is not inconsiderable, and it is continuing to grow.

recitations or practice exercises in which the students get opportunities to make responses and receive corrective feedback. The teacher maintains an academic focus, keeping the students involved in a lesson or engaged in seatwork, monitoring their performance, and providing individualized feedback. The pace is rapid in the sense that the class moves efficiently through the curriculum as a whole (and through the successive objectives of any given lesson), but progress from one objective to the next involves very small, easy steps. Success rates in answering teacher questions during lessons are high (about 75 percent), and success rates on assignments designed to be done independently are very high (approaching 100 percent). (Brophy, 1981, p. 139)

Computers Come to School

In Minnesota students learn everything from physics to the rules of volleyball, and virtually every student in the state, from the elementary to the high school level, has access to a computer. In Falmouth High School on Cape Cod, Massachusetts, a computer is used to keep daily updated attendance records, to produce class lists, and to schedule students into classes (Waring, 1982). An elementary school in Broomfield, Colorado, has placed the library card catalog on a computer, leaving the librarian more free time to work on educational tasks (Malsam, 1982). At Milton Academy in Massachusetts, a computer produces class lists and report cards, and maintains up-to-date student records (Zucker, 1982).

The examples cited above illustrate a phenomenon of growing proportions—the use of computers in the school. The addition of computers to the traditional scholastic curriculum promises to change schooling as we have come to know it.

The Computer Makes Its First Appearance: Early Computer-Based Instruction

Given the burgeoning presence of computers in school settings, it is amazing to realize that as recently as the late 1960s broad-based computerized education was largely a futuristic dream.

In 1969, Richard Atkinson and H. A. Wilson published a book that contained most of the scholarly papers that had been written about using computers for educational purposes. In the introduction to the book, Atkinson and Wilson estimated that in the 1967–1968 school year, several thousand students ranging from elementary-school to university level received a significant portion of their instruction in at least one subject area under computer control. They went on to predict that in coming years the number of students exposed to computer controlled instruction would expand many times.

Computer controlled education at the time Atkinson and Wilson published their book consisted of using the computer system as a kind of highly sophisticated workbook. Students were presented with problems, and after answering them, they were given feedback and then presented with new problems. The computer kept detailed records of student progress and it selected problems at the appropriate level of difficulty, but it did little in the way of actually presenting new instructional material. Instead, it was used as a means of providing practice on material that had been presented by the teacher or in the textbooks.

The workbook-like use of computers is called an individualized drill-and-practice system. Patrick Suppes (1968), in a paper reprinted in the Atkinson and Wilson book, described two other ways in which computers might be used in the classroom. The first, which Suppes called a tutorial system, entailed having the computer take over the main responsibility both for presenting a concept and for developing skill in its use. The second system envisioned by Suppes was something he called a dialogue system. In a dialogue system the student would actually be able to "converse" with the computer in a language understood by both the computer and the student. Suppes (1968) predicted that in the decade following the publication of his paper many students would use individualized drill-and-practice systems in elementary school and that by the time these same students reached high school, tutorial systems would be available on a broad basis. Suppes went on to predict that the children of these children (in approximately 1990) would be widely exposed to dialogue systems.

The predictions of Atkinson, Wilson and Suppes were quite startling when they were made, but they have all come true. And they have come true at a rate exceeding even the wildest expectations of the late 1960s. It is a certainty that the use of computers in the classroom will continue to accelerate and that virtually every student in the United States will soon be affected by computers. For example, a recent survey by the U.S. Department of Education found that about one school in four has a computer available for student use (Zucker, 1982). Arthur Melmed (1982) has also estimated that by 1990 every student in the United States elementary and secondary school system could participate for a moderate cost in a computer enriched educational instructional program consisting of 30 minutes of computer contact per day.

Types of Computers

There are probably hundreds of manufacturers in the country that make computers in an enormous variety of style, function, and design. Basically, however, it is most convenient to classify computers by size. Computers are available in three general sizes—mainframes, minicomputers, and microcomputers (Heinich, Molenda, and Russell, 1982).

Mainframes.   Mainframe computers are very large and fast machines that are widely used for business and scientific computing. Mainframe computers have very large memories that allow the storage of extensive amounts of data and the use of highly complex programs. They can be connected to many terminals in a manner that allows a large number of users simultaneous access to the machine. Because of their size and expense, mainframe

Continued on next page

computers are infrequently used at the elementary and high school level, but they are widely used at the college and university level.

Minicomputers.   Minicomputers are between mainframe and microcomputers in size. The moderate memory capacity of minicomputers allows the use of "high power" computer languages, but they do not provide the enormous amount of number crunching capability of mainframe machines. Minicomputers are widely used at all levels of education for both administrative and instructional purposes. When used for instructional purposes a minicomputer can support several dozen terminals (Heinich et al., 1982).

Microcomputers.   Microcomputers, or personal computers as they are frequently called, are small relatively inexpensive machines suitable for use by one person at a time. Microcomputers use a relatively simple language that can be learned by even very young students. This common language allows the student to communicate with the machine in ways that have profound implications. As Seymour Papert (1980) has written:

> In many schools today, the phrase "computer-aided instruction" means making the computer teach the child. One might say the computer is being used to program the child. In my version, the child programs the computer and, in doing so, both acquires a sense of mastery over a piece of the modern and powerful technology and establishes an intimate contact with some of the deepest ideas from science, from mathematics, and from the art of intellectual model building. (p. 5)

Whereas the simple language is an advantage in terms of providing easy communication with the machine, it is also a disadvantage in that the memory requirements of the simple languages do not leave much capacity for the processing and storage of large amounts of data. This means that microcomputers are ideal systems for use with students one at a time, or for storing small numbers of records, but they are unsuitable in situations in which several students need to interact with the machine simultaneously or in which very large numbers of records need to be processed and stored.

The coming years will undoubtedly see many more microcomputers in classrooms, in part because of a very aggressive marketing policy by microcomputer companies. As one newspaper story put it, "The country's leading personal computer manufacturers are betting that the fastest route to placing a small computer in every American living room is to first get through the school house door" (New York Times, 1982, p. D9). One way in which the companies are pursuing this policy is by lobbying for federal legislation that will allow companies to write off two times the manufacturing cost of the computer if it is donated to an elementary or secondary school (New York Times, 1982). Passage of such legislation would greatly accelerate the use of microcomputers in American classrooms.

Software and Courseware

The machines that do the computing are called, in computer jargon, *computer hardware*. The instructions that direct the computer to do what it does are known as *computer software*. When these instructions have an educational purpose, and when they include instructional materials, they are known as *computer courseware*.

Computer Software.   Computer software (also known as a computer program) directs a computer to do what the user wants it to do. These programs can be commercially produced and available for purchase, as in the case of accounting systems, statistical-analysis packages, computer games,

Continued on next page

Computers are becoming an important part of classroom instruction. (© Elizabeth Crews)

or word-processing systems or they can be written by an individual user for some specially designed purpose. Frequently these specially produced programs can be used by other people, and a number of different clearinghouses have arisen to facilitate the interchange of locally developed software packages (Heinich et al., 1982).

Computer Courseware.   Computer courseware consists of a package of educational materials designed for use with a computer. Courseware could include instructions to the computer as to how materials were to be presented, how student responses were to be processed, and how material should be sequenced depending on the nature of the student response. Courseware could also include the instructional materials themselves: instructional text, graphics and displays, pictures and illustrations, audio components, and animated sequences. Virtually anything of an instructional nature can be presented via computer.

Currently, computer courseware is the biggest bottleneck in the effective use of computers in the classroom. There is simply not enough high quality courseware to fill instructional needs. The problem is not in quantity (there are thousands of instructional programs available) but in quality. One source has estimated that 80 percent of the courseware available is "junk". (Heinich et al., 1982).

There are two reasons for the lack of high quality instructional courseware. First, good courseware is very expensive to produce. One writer has estimated that one hour of quality courseware requires 200 hours and costs $30,000 to produce (Melmed, 1982). The second reason is that there is a lack of people who have the training required to produce good courseware. A courseware designer should have all of the training required of a good curriculum developer, plus a good background in how to translate the instructional material into a form usable by the computer. There are currently few people with this particular combination of training.

It should be noted that the last conclusion—that individualized and discovery approaches are less efficient than direct instruction—is controversial and is disputed by many educators and psychologists. One counterargument is that efficiency, per se, is hardly the most important criterion for teacher success. In addition, while it may be true that academic outcomes in terms of concrete achievement are greater from direct instruction, abstract thinking, creativity, and problem-solving skills may not be enhanced thereby (Peterson, 1979). Thus what is meant by "effective instruction" must be considered when making generalizations about teacher behavior and the instructional environment.

Computers in Education

Administrative Uses.   Many aspects of modern approaches to education require extensive record keeping. Individualized instruction, comprehensive curriculums, evaluation of progress in terms of mastery of instructional objectives, and the evaluation of educational programs all require detailed and thorough records. Computers can handle the tasks involved in keeping these records quickly and efficiently, freeing up the time of teachers and administrators for more important educational tasks. They can be used to keep attendance records, to store student test scores and grades, to schedule students into classes and to produce class rosters, to maintain scores and to calculate statistics useful in assigning grades. In short, the bulk of the administrative paper work educators are involved with can be done faster and more efficiently by computers.

Instructional Uses.   There are two ways in which computers can be used to assist the instructional process. *Computer managed instruction* (CMI) involves using the computer as a highly sophisticated manager of educational progress. The computer can administer diagnostic tests, score the tests, prescribe instructional materials, and keep detailed records of student progress. In CMI, the computer does not actually present instruction. Instead, the computer tests for mastery of instructional content and makes decisions about future instructional steps (Heinich et al., 1982).

Computer assisted instruction (CAI) involves the direct delivery of instruction by the computer in a manner that allows the student and the machine to interact. The computer-presented instruction can be relatively simple, as was the case with the previously described drill-and-practice routines, or it can be highly complex, involving both auditory and visual presentation of instruction and offering several ways for the student to interact with the computer.

THE PHYSICAL ENVIRONMENT

Although one usually thinks of a student's success in school as being caused by such things as teacher effectiveness and the student's intelligence and ability at taking tests, nonhuman factors such as the environmental features of a classroom can have important effects on student performance. In this section, aspects of the physical environment of the classroom that relate to student behavior are discussed.

Classroom Arrangement

The prevailing image of classroom spatial arrangement is a rectangular room with straight rows of desks facing a blackboard. Does it have to be thus? The answer is no; typical classroom shape and arrangement are dictated by tradition. In the early 1900s, it was considered important to have natural light entering over each pupil's left shoulder. In order to meet this goal, rooms were typically long and narrow. Moreover, the rectangular shape and the rows of desks facilitated surveillance by the teacher. Although this pattern met many reasonable needs in the early part of the century, those needs are not so important now, given technological advances in lighting and new construction techniques. Nevertheless, most classrooms remain rectangular (Sommer, 1969).

The spatial arrangement of classrooms would not be particularly noteworthy were it not for the fact that there is considerable evidence showing that room arrangement has an impact on student (and even teacher) performance. For instance, the level of student participation is clearly related to where the student is seated in the traditional classroom arrangement. Students seated in the front rows of the classroom tend to participate more than those in the rear. In addition, students seated centrally tend to verbalize more frequently than those at the sides. This phenomenon is consistent across age of student, type of teacher, and subject matter (Adams and Biddle, 1970). Even participation in college seminars tends to be associated with seating pattern. One study showed that students sitting directly opposite the instructor tended to participate more than those at the instructor's side. Indeed, seats located at the instructor's side were shunned for the most part (Sommer, 1969).

The question that arises from these data is of the chicken-and-egg sort. Do students who sit in the front of the classroom do better *because* they are sitting in the front, or do students who would do better anyway choose to sit in front? Although one can't be certain, there is some evidence that spatial location, per se, can actually contribute to better performance. Students who are *assigned* to particular locations tend to be affected by the position in which they find themselves. For instance, one study (Schwebel and Cherlin, 1972) examined the relationship between assigned seats and student behavior in kindergarten through fifth grade. The results showed that students who had been assigned to seats in the first few rows spent more time on "appropriate" activities than those in the back rows. Moreover, the front-row students tended to be more attentive.

In an interesting modification, students were then assigned to new seats in completely random fashion. The results of this switch showed that students who were moved closer to the front had the largest increase in time spent working appropriately, and they also showed the greatest decrease in the amount of time spent on nontask activities. Even more startling were changes in the ratings of students made by their teachers. Students who had moved closer to the front received more positive ratings for likability and attentiveness, while those who had moved toward the rear of the classroom were given lower ratings than before.

Why should student performance be affected by seating location? One reasonable hypothesis is that teachers may spend more time communicating and interacting with the students seated closest to them. Moreover, there may be greater eye contact with students seated closer to the front, and these students can more easily be provided with positive reinforcement (in the form of head nods, smiles, and the like) than can those further back in the classroom.

This reasoning argues that teachers should make a concerted effort to circulate within a classroom while teaching, rather than standing consistently in a front and center position. Alternatively, a teacher might consider changing student seating patterns from time to time in order to equalize the positive effects of sitting close to the teacher.

Density and Crowding in Classrooms

As one observer pointed out about classrooms, "Nowhere else are large groups of individuals packed so closely together for so many hours, yet expected to perform at peak efficiency on difficult learning tasks and to interact harmoniously" (Weinstein, 1979, p. 585). Yet little is known as yet about the effects of *density*, which refers to the objective number of people in a given setting, and *crowding*, which refers to the subjective experience of too many individuals in a given space, on the behavior of teachers and students. It is known, though, that density and crowding produce significant decrements in the performance of complex tasks—at least in laboratory studies. For instance, increases in group size, decreases in room size, and decreases in interpersonal distance all lead to lower achievement on complex tasks (Paulus, Annis, Seta, Schkade, and Matthews, 1976). In addition, there is evidence that individuals' liking for a task is also affected by changes in density. Thus at least in terms of complex tasks, density has an effect on individual performance and attitudes.

density effect the effect of the number of people in a given setting

crowding effect the effect due to the subjective experience that there are too many individuals in a given space

It also seems clear that social behavior is affected by density and crowding. When density becomes too high, students tend to show less social play and a higher level of solitary activity. There is also some evidence that aggressive behaviors increase in younger students when there is greater density, although this may be due to the fact that under conditions of crowding there is greater competition for toys and other desirable objects (Weinstein, 1979).

Finally, reports of college students indicate that their ratings of satisfaction with a class are at least partially dependent on the density of the class. For example, one study examined the responses of students in thirty-two different classes, all of which met in the same classroom. Although the average class size was 13, the number of students varied from 5 to 22. The results showed that students in the larger classes were more dissatisfied with the room, room size, and ventilation than students in the smaller classes—even though the

Classroom crowding may result in poorer scholastic performance. (© Michael Weisbrot/ Stock, Boston)

room was the same in all cases (Sommer and Becker, 1971). Thus density and crowding are clearly factors that affect student behavior and attitudes.

Privacy

One environmental feature that is all but ignored in typical classrooms is the provision for student privacy. Looking back on your school career, try to recall what opportunities you had to be truly alone. In most schools, restrooms provide almost the only possibility of privacy—and then only in the most limited sense.

Despite the pervasive lack of privacy for students, little is known about its effects on education. Most work has consisted of examining the effects of installing small cubicles in classes with special populations of students, including the mentally retarded, the brain-damaged, and hyperactive children. The only research that has been done on normal populations is that comparing traditional schools with open schools, in which there are no self-contained classrooms. Interestingly, student ratings indicate that open schools yield twice as much adequate area for studying alone as traditional schools (Brunetti, 1972).

It does seem important to provide areas in which students can be alone for at least part of the school day. Many adults choose to study in the isolated nooks and crannies of libraries, and it is possible that providing spaces where students can work or play by themselves could be an effective strategy for enhancing student performance.

Noise

Associated with the lack of privacy ordinarily found in classrooms is a relatively high level of noise. Except when a test is being given, classrooms typically are fairly noisy places, depending on the strictness of the teacher and the kind of activity in which the students are engaged.

Common sense dictates that the level of noise in an environment is likely to affect the level of performance, and the results of laboratory studies tend to confirm that high levels of noise can in fact reduce achievement (Gulian, 1974). However, most knowledge about noise and achievement come from one-time, laboratory-type studies, in which students are placed in isolated chambers and hear noise that is electrically amplified to various levels. These studies hardly approximate actual classroom conditions, in which it may be possible for students to adapt to high levels of noise over a period of time.

One can be more confident of results of studies that examine noise level in actual classroom settings. Here results show that reactions to noise are dependent on whether the noise is short or long-term in nature (Weinstein, 1979). Studies of short-term exposure to high levels of noise tend to show essentially no effects. However, when the evidence looking at long-term exposure to noise is examined, the results suggest that extreme levels of noise may indeed lead to performance decrements. For example, one study examined reading scores of students in a school that had an elevated railroad on one side. Students in the classrooms closest to the railroad had significantly lower reading scores than did students who were in classes on the opposite side of the building (Bronzaft and McCarthy, 1975). Thus high, intermittent levels of noise (trains went by for 30 seconds about every 4.5 minutes) had an adverse effect on student performance. Interestingly, after the classrooms closest to the trains were outfitted with sound-reducing material, achievement levels rose significantly (Goldman, 1982).

Still, it is possible that children exposed to regular, high levels of noise can eventually learn to filter out the sounds. The danger here is that such a filtering process can become indiscriminate, and even sounds that ought to be heard (such as the teacher's voice) may be ignored. It thus seems important to limit high levels of noise in classroom settings.

Size of Class

There has been a good deal of research on the effect of class size on student achievement, and the evidence is clear: smaller class sizes are associated with greater academic achievement.

It is not hard to think of reasons why smaller classes would lead to greater achievement: the fewer students present the more attention they are able to receive from the teacher. In addition, lessons and instructional materials can be more readily individualized in a smaller classroom. Probably equally important, students in smaller classes have more opportunity to participate during discussions. They can voice their opinions more, and the teacher is able to respond to their questions and comments in greater detail.

The relative lack of student participation in large classes was demonstrated in an early study (Dawe, 1934) that examined the number and length of comments made in kindergarten classes that ranged in size from 15 to 46. Students in larger classes were less likely to participate, and those that did were likely to make shorter comments. Moreover, the *total* amount of discussion was lower in larger classes than in smaller ones. More recent work (Thana, 1969) has confirmed that there is an inverse relationship between class size and participation at the college level. (It was also found that the average number of questions asked in large, 50-minute lecture classes was only 2.3 questions per class.) Larger classes, then, can be expected to produce less class participation than smaller ones.

But is class size also associated with actual student achievement? The answer is affirmative. In an analysis of some eighty studies (involving about 900,000 students, all told), Gene Glass and Mary Lee Smith (1978; Glass, Cohen, Smith, and Filby, 1982) found that 60 percent of the comparisons that were made between smaller versus larger classes favored small classes. When integrated graphically (see Figure 14-1), these studies show a clear relationship between class size and achievement. This relationship is especially pronounced for classes that are smaller than 20, but it is still important for classes containing 20 to 40 pupils. (Keep in mind, though, that these data are collapsed across

FIGURE 14-1   Relationship Between Achievement and Class Size

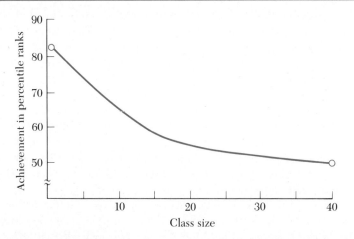

(Glass and Smith, 1978, p. vi)

many situations, and the addition—or subtraction—of one or two pupils is not necessarily going to have a significant effect on actual class achievement.)

Extrapolating from their findings, Glass and Smith predict that if a "typical" student in a "typical" class of 40 received an achievement score at the 50th percentile, that pupil would have scored at the 55th percentile if he or she had been in a class of 20 pupils. If class size had been 10, he or she would have scored at the 65th percentile; and had class size been 5, the score would likely have been at the 74th percentile. Obviously, such differences are important and argue strongly in favor of smaller classes.

Some educators have made the argument that because achievement differences in class size are relatively small when just the larger class sizes are considered, class size can be increased from 20 to 40 students "without noticeable effect on achievement" (Educational Research Service, 1980). Whether a 5-point difference in achievement score percentile due to class size (the predicted difference between the two class sizes) is "noticeable" is arguable, of course, and depends on one's perspective. Parents and teachers are apt to view the difference as quite significant, whereas administrators and school boards intent on cutting costs are likely to judge it as negligible.

THE OVERALL SCHOOL ENVIRONMENT

Teachers operate within a social network that extends well beyond the classroom. They are an intrinsic part of a school system, which in turn is located within a community, state, and federal system. In this part of the chapter, a number of factors are discussed that relate to the overall school environment, factors that in turn affect the success of the classroom teacher and the student.

Size of School

It was seen earlier that smaller *class* size is most beneficial for student achievement. Is *school* size similarly related to student performance?

The answer to that question is not simple, but one comprehensive attempt has been made at investigating it. In a classic study, Roger Barker and Paul Gump (1964) examined how school size relates to students' participation in extracurricular activities. One might reason that larger schools would offer a greater number, as well as a greater variety, of extracurricular activities than smaller schools. To check the accuracy of this hypothesis, Barker and Gump examined a sample of high schools that ranged in size from 35 to 2,287 students. The schools were homogeneous in most respects other than size: They were

Teachers Take a Test

One approach to determining the effectiveness of teachers is to assess their knowledge of subject matter content. In many states today, newly graduated teachers must take a minimum competency test to receive state certification. The test typically consists of a set of multiple-choice items designed to assess teachers' competence in their specific areas of specialization. The tests are designed to ensure that teachers fulfill at least minimum standards before they are assigned a class. In some cases, such tests are also used with more experienced teachers to aid in the determination of salaries.

The rationale behind certifying teachers via test scores is the assumption that teachers ought to have a set of at least minimal academic competencies if they are to be successful teachers. Some educators go further, however, and suggest that higher scores on teacher examinations may be associated with more effective classroom teaching (Haefele, 1980). However, this association has not been demonstrated: research has not shown that greater teacher knowledge is necessarily related to higher classroom effectiveness.

The tests have further been criticized on the grounds that they discriminate against minority group teachers. In many states, a larger proportion of minority group members than majority group members fail, and some observers have suggested that the use of test scores can unreasonably exclude competent minority group members from the teaching profession.

Despite these criticisms, the tests are becoming a fact of life for many new teachers. Ten states now require minimum competency testing of some sort, and at least seven more are contemplating their use (Northern, 1980). Many states employ the National Teacher Examination, a standardized test developed by the Educational Testing Service (the organization that compiles the Scholastic Aptitude Test). Other states have opted for their own customized tests, feeling that the test ought to reflect the unique requirements of the particular locality.

The logic that teachers ought to have basic competence in their subject specializations is unassailable. But whether paper-and-pencil tests are the appropriate means for assessing minimum competency is an open question.

all located in eastern Kansas, were similar along economic, social, cultural, and political lines, and were controlled by the same education authority.

The results of the study proved to be contrary to the original hypothesis. Although there were more activities in an absolute sense in the large schools than in the small ones, the difference between the largest and smallest school was 5 to 1 in number of activities but 20 to 1 in size of student body. Thus proportionally, there were more activities in the small schools than in the large ones. Even more striking, there was little difference in the variety of activities available in large compared with small schools. Despite small size, then, the small high schools seemed to offer similar opportunities for participation in extracurricular activities. Because of this fact, each student had a greater chance to participate in such activities. Indeed, students in small schools participated in twice as many activities as did students in large schools, and the activities tended to be of greater variety.

Differences were also found in the positions held by students in small compared with large schools. In relatively small schools, a higher percentage of students tended to hold positions of leadership and high status than was the case in large schools. Consequently, there tended to be differences in the nature of satisfaction derived from the two settings. While students from larger schools received greater satisfaction from "dealing with vicarious enjoyment" and "learning about their school's persons and affairs," students in small schools received greater satisfaction "relating to the development of competence, to being challenged, to engaging in important actions, to being involved in group activities, and to achieving moral and cultural values" (Barker and Gump, 1964, p. 197).

Lest you think that small schools held the complete advantage, there was one area in which the small schools were less favorably viewed. Although there were more opportunities to participate in the small school, these opportunities were perceived to some degree as pressure to participate. Students felt obligated to contribute to school affairs and felt that their peers expected them to participate. But even this mild disadvantage was in part positive, because the perceived pressure meant that fewer students were left out of extracurricular activities. This in turn seemed to lead to a lower dropout rate in small schools than in large ones.

Thus at least in terms of extracurricular activities, small schools had an advantage. What such data do not tell us is whether there is also an *academic* advantage to small schools. Do students actually learn more in small schools or large ones? Strangely enough, no one has examined this question. However, one might hypothesize that, as with class size, "small is better" in this respect, too.

The Administrative Environment

The administrative environment of a school has been shown to affect both student achievement and teacher behavior. Why should the administrative organization of a school have an effect on what students are able to learn, since student-administrator contact is typically infrequent? The answer is that the effect is an indirect one, mediated by the nature of the relationship between *teacher* and administrator.

Decision making

There is a clear relationship between the nature of the administrative decision-making processes in a school and the predominant type of teaching style

(McDonald, 1976). For instance, the degree of centralization of decision making leads to specific kinds of teaching behaviors. In schools in which decisions are centralized with the administration (i.e., the administrators tended to make decisions unilaterally), there is a greater degree of teaching the class as a whole, rather than teaching in smaller groups. In addition, there is a lower amount of student independent work assigned. Because teaching the class as a whole, as opposed to in small groups, is related to student learning, it can be seen that the administrative structure of the school can have an effect (although it is an indirect one) on student performance.

If you are wondering why centralized decision making tends to lead to teaching the class as a whole, there is a reasonable explanation. A centralized decision-making system may be indicative of an administrator who values strong authority and order, and the administrator, in turn, may reward teachers who have orderly classes—as manifested in such teaching practices as teaching the class as a whole.

A related administrative factor that has an effect on student outcomes may be the administrator-to-teacher ratio (Centra and Potter, 1980). If there is a large number of administrators, relative to the number of teachers in a school, decisions are more apt to be made by administrators than by teachers. Teachers then may be more dissatisfied than in schools in which they have, or share in, decision-making power. Unhappy teachers may not be as effective as those who are more satisfied, resulting in decrements in student performance.

Administrative leadership style

The nature of the leadership style of an administration also has an impact on the general effectiveness of a school (Shoemaker and Fraser, 1981). Most effective are relatively assertive administrators who are oriented toward the achievement of the students in the school. There is a commitment to the development of basic skills in the students, and affective considerations are of less interest to such an administrator. Once again, the effects on students are indirect, resulting from teacher reactions to the administrator's behavior.

Time in School

One would not encounter much disagreement by arguing that 12 years spent in school is going to result in more student learning than 6 years. But when one considers finer gradations (for example, 190 versus 180 days of schooling per year), the issue becomes somewhat less clear-cut.

One of the most convincing demonstrations that even small differences in the quantity of schooling have a potent effect on student achievement was carried out by David Wiley (1976). Using data derived from the Coleman survey (Coleman et al., 1966), Wiley asked some very precise questions about the effects of quantity of schooling. He derived four separate measures: (1) the number of days per year in a school district; (2) the number of hours per day

What the Public Thinks About Today's Schools

Throughout this textbook, research and data derived from educational psychologists and educators have been cited. But what about the views of lay persons, the citizens who pay the taxes? What do they think about the current state of education?

Answers to this question came from a national survey carried out by the Gallup Poll and the Charles F. Kettering Foundation (Fiske, 1979). Based on a sample of 1,514 adults interviewed in 1979, the results reveal that only 8 percent of those polled would give public schools a grade of A on their overall performance. This figure is down from 18 percent 5 years earlier. In addition, those giving a C, D, or failing grade to schools constituted almost half (42 percent) of the total. Fifty-one percent also said that schools had become worse since their own childhood.

In contrast, parents with children currently enrolled in public schools were more favorable toward education, with almost half awarding a grade of A or B. Thus it seems that knowledge of what actually is happening in schools may lead to more positive assessments.

Examining the public's perceptions of the specific problems faced in schools, a lack of discipline was cited by almost twice as many people (24 percent) as the next most frequently cited problems—the use of drugs (13 percent), poor curriculum and poor standards (11 percent), and the difficulty in getting good teachers (10 percent). Lack of discipline has historically been one of the most frequently cited problems, and it appears to the pollsters that "either the public schools have found no way to deal effectively with this problem or the public's perception has not caught up with measures that are being tried" (Fiske, 1979).

One remedy for the perceived decline in quality of education—a remedy that meets the approval of most of those polled—is the imposition of minimum competency tests for teachers. Eighty-five percent of the respondents felt that teachers should be tested before they are hired, to ensure that they meet minimum standards (Fiske, 1979).

that a school was in session; (3) the average daily attendance, defined as the average percentage of pupils attending a school during the school year; and (4) the number of hours per year a school was in session. It should be noted that each of these measures is conceptually quite different. For instance, a 10 percent increase in the number of hours of schooling per day (from, say, 5.0 to 5.5 hours/day) might well have a less positive effect than a 10 percent

Table 14-1   Predicted Effects of Changes in Quantity of Schooling

Variable	Initial Value	Changed Value	Percent Change	Percentage Increase in Achievement		
				Verbal	Reading	Math
Days per year	180 days	190 days	5.55	+ 8.33	+16.42	+8.33
Hours per day	5.0 hrs.	5.5 hrs.	10.00	+14.67	+28.67	+14.83
Average days attended	88%	95%	7.95	+11.75	+23.00	+11.83
Hours per year	871 hrs.	1083 hrs.	24.34	+33.58	+65.50	+33.92

(Adapted from Wiley, 1976, p. 260)

increase in the number of days of schooling per year (from, say, 180 to 198). The reason is that students might well be tired after 5 hours of school, and an extra half hour may simply increase their fatigue and have no positive—and potentially a negative—effect on their cumulative learning. In contrast, an extra 18 days of school might more readily be expected to produce positive gains.

The results of the study—based on a very complicated statistical analysis— were clear and unequivocal. Each of the four measures of quantity of schooling can be expected to produce increments in student achievement if they are increased. Table 14-1 shows what the practical effects of increases in each of the measures would be on three kinds of student achievement (verbal ability, reading comprehension, and mathematics achievement). As can be seen from the table, an increase in school year length from 180 to 190 days (a 5.5 percent increase) is predicted to produce increases in achievement ranging from 8.33 percent to 16.42 percent. Changes in the other variables could be expected to bring about equivalent, and sometimes larger, increases in achievement. In all cases, the percentage increases in achievement are predicted to be larger than the percentage increase in quantity of schooling.

The results of the Wiley study are compelling and suggest quite clearly that increases in the quantity of schooling ought to lead to reasonable—and meaningful—increases in student achievement. Although these are only predictions, based on correlational data, they do indicate the value of increased time spent in school. Moreover, they are quite consistent with the findings of "time-on-task" studies, which show that greater amounts of time spent on a given task result in increased student performance.

Public Versus Private Schooling

One of the more controversial questions about the effectiveness of schools concerns whether public or private schools are more effective. The issue hits at two conflicting goals of American society: the right of individuals to choose the kind of education they feel is appropriate (individualism) versus the importance of providing all children with an effective, free education (egalitarianism). The conflict comes about because if private schools are, in fact, found to be superior, those children who cannot afford a private education are going to be given, by default, an inferior (public) schooling.

The major study to examine this question is an enormous project examining 58,728 high school students in more than 1,000 public, parochial, and other private schools in the United States (Coleman, 1981). Based on reading and math score results, the study suggests that students in private schools learn more than those in public schools, regardless of student socioeconomic background. In the words of the report, "when family background factors that predict achievement are controlled, students in both Catholic and other private schools are shown to achieve at a higher level than students in public schools" (Coleman, 1981).

What could be the source of the achievement differentials—if this report is indeed correct? As Dr. Reed suggests in the interview at the beginning of this chapter, one major difference may be that the private schools have a safer and more disciplined environment than the public schools. In public schools, it is

Are private schools more effective than public ones? Recent research raises this possibility. (© Harvey Stein)

much more difficult to suspend or expel students who are discipline problems, and the continued presence of children who misbehave can lead to disruptions in the education of the other children. In addition, the report argues that teachers in public schools are less able to impose rigorous academic demands than those in private schools.

As you might imagine, the contention that public schools are inferior to private schools was quick to draw the fire of critics. In public statements educational psychologist and statistician Lee Chronbach suggested that it was a mistake to base conclusions about the relative effectiveness of high schools on reading and math scores, which are primarily related to the effectiveness of schooling in the lower grades. Coleman's data may have little appropriateness in assessing high schools.

An even more telling criticism involves possible differences between families who choose to send their children to private schools, compared with those who send their children to public schools. It is not unreasonable to expect that families who are highly motivated regarding academic achievement would be the ones most apt to enroll their children in private schools. If private school populations are made up of more highly motivated students than public schools, it is unreasonable to conclude that higher test scores are due to the *schools*. Rather, the initial motivational differences in the *pupils* would be the most likely source of differences.

Such criticisms are reasonable. However, to sociologist James Coleman, author of the study, the important point is that there *is* an objective difference in test scores between public and private school students, and educators should be doing things to increase the level of public school scores relative to those of the private schools.

THE GOALS OF EDUCATION, REVISITED

This chapter began with a discussion of the basic functions and goals of education in American society. However, almost all the work that has been done on the effectiveness of various teacher and school practices has been oriented toward the first goal: the transmission of a body of knowledge. Hence studies of effectiveness are almost invariably measured in terms of how much students have *learned*.

Until educational researchers begin to study what it is that brings about success in the remaining goals—the realization of each student's potential, the maximization of self-respect and self-actualization, and the socialization of norms, mores, and values—knowledge of what makes schooling effective will be incomplete. In the meantime, quite a bit is known, and this knowledge can provide the foundation for a more complete understanding of the processes involved in effective education.

SUMMARY

This chapter began with the statement that "teaching does make a difference." Effective teaching can be related to one of four main goals of education: the transmission of a body of knowledge, realization of each student's unique potential, maximization of self-respect and self-actualization, and the socialization of the norms, mores, and values of society.

The instructional environment produced by particular teacher behaviors can have a direct and positive effect on student performance, although no behavior *always* results in student success. Teachers who use positive reinforcement and criticism, ask questions effectively, and maintain a clear and enthusiastic verbal style produce greater student achievement. Moreover, classroom management techniques such as maintaining discipline, using variety, and spending greater time on task are related to student success.

The physical environment of a classroom is also related to student performance. For instance, the arrangement of the classroom affects student participation: students who sit closer to the front tend to be more responsive than those sitting toward the back and sides. Higher levels of density and crowding lead to decrements in performance and more negative attitudes. A lack of privacy and long-term exposure to noise can also have adverse effects on school performance. It is also clear that smaller class sizes are associated with greater academic achievement.

A recent addition to many schools is the computer, and its use in education is growing rapidly. There are three general types of computers: mainframes (very large and fast machines), minicomputers (mid-size machines that can support several dozen users simultaneously), and microcomputers (used by a single user at a time). Computer software provides instructions for the computer. When software is designed for instructional use, it is called courseware. Computers are now being used administratively, as sophisticated managers of educational progress in a process called computer managed instruction, and for the direct delivery of instruction, which is termed computer assisted instruction.

The school environment, taken as a whole, can have a profound effect on teachers and students. Among the factors that have been shown to be important are school size, the school administrative environment, time spent in school, and whether the school is publicly or privately funded. Smaller schools provide more opportunities for involvement in extracurricular activities, resulting in more positive attitudes. The administrative organization of a school has an impact on how teachers organize their classes and thus indirectly affects student performance. Predictions suggest that increases in time spent in school would lead to increases in student achievement. Finally, there is evidence that private schools are more successful than public schools, although the evidence is highly controversial.

FOR FURTHER STUDY AND APPLICATION

Centra, J. A., and Potter, D. A. School and teacher effects: An interrelational model. *Review of Educational Research*, 1980, 2, 273–292.   Presents a comprehensive survey of how schools and teachers affect student performance. Not an easy article, but it provides the most recent overview regarding what the research literature deems important.

Gilstrap, P. L., and Martin, W. R. *Current strategies for teachers: A resource for personalizing instruction.* Pacific Palisades, Calif.: Goodyear, 1975. Provides a set of practical activities that classroom teachers can use to make instruction more individualized.

McDonald, F. J., and Elias, P. *Executive summary report: Beginning teacher evaluation study, Phase II.* Princeton, N.J.: Educational Testing Service, 1976.   What distinguishes effective from ineffective teachers? Some answers emerge from this large-scale study of beginning teachers.

EDUCATIONAL MEASUREMENT

THE PURPOSES OF EDUCATIONAL MEASUREMENT

THE TWO BASIC TYPES OF MEASUREMENT:
NORM-REFERENCED AND CRITERION-REFERENCED

RELIABILITY AND VALIDITY

SUMMARY

15

EDUCATIONAL MEASUREMENT: BASIC PRINCIPLES FOR THE CLASSROOM TEACHER

CHAPTER OVERVIEW

If the average person were to list the activities that are important to quality education, testing and measurement would probably not be on the list. But the professional educator surely recognizes that good educational measurement is an important component of quality education. Ann Hansen provides many examples of why this is so, and that view is reinforced in this chapter.

The chapter begins with a discussion of the purposes of testing. First the section talks about the direct instructional impact of testing. For example, tests enhance student learning by providing teachers with objective feedback about the effectiveness of their instruction. The second general purpose of testing is to facilitate administrative decisions. An example would be using test information to help in placing a student at the appropriate instructional level. The final general purpose of testing is to assist in the guidance process. Tests, for example, can help identify students who would benefit from a special program, and they can help diagnose learning difficulties.

Educational tests generally are of two types. Tests that provide information about how a student performs relative to other students who have taken the test are called norm-referenced tests. The second kind of test determines whether a student has attained mastery of a specific instructional content. These are called criterion-referenced tests. These two types of tests have a number of similarities, but they also differ from each other in several ways.

In order for an educational test to be useful, it must have two critical characteristics: the test must be reliable, and it must be valid. *Reliability* refers to the degree to which a test is consistent in measurement—that is, whether it tends to provide similar scores if repeatedly administered. *Validity* is the extent to which a test measures the characteristic that it was designed to measure. If it does not, it is useless for the purpose for which it was designed.

Ann Hansen teaches sixth grade at Longfellow School in Berkeley, California. Berkeley's school system is divided into schools that cover grades K–3, 4–6, 7–9, and 10–12. Longfellow School is a grades 4–6 school that has about 600 students, down from the 1,200 of several years ago. This decline is partly a function of a declining population of school-age children; but another source of the decline is a growing private school enrollment. The student population of Berkeley schools is extraordinarily heterogeneous. Desegregation has been a school district policy for a number of years, and approximately half of the children in Berkeley ride buses to school. About 50 percent of the students in Longfellow School are black, the remaining half being white, Hispanic, and Asian. Socioeconomically, Longfellow runs the gamut of students—from well-to-do families living in the Berkeley Hills to poor black and immigrant children from the lowlands.

Ms. Hansen, who in her spare time serves as the mayor of Pinole, California, has been teaching for 20 years—7 years in a parochial school in Minnesota, and 13 years in the public system in Berkeley. The interview began with a request for information about her educational background.

A. I went to parochial school through the eighth grade and then went to a public high school. After graduation I entered a convent, and after a number of years working in a hospital I began teaching. When I went into teaching, I had one year of college—no teaching certificate—I went right into a sixth-grade classroom. I began taking courses in the evenings, on weekends, and during the summer at the College of St. Benedict in St. Joseph, Minnesota. It took me 22 years to get my degree doing it that way.

Q. That sounds like the hard way to do it.

A. It is the hard way, but there is also an advantage to it. When you are teaching and going to school at the same time, you get to put what you are learning into practice right away.

Q. What kind of information is passed along to you about a student coming into your class?

A. We get cards that the student's previous teacher has filled out. The cards indicate the level of reading that a student is at, their level of math, and if they happen to be in a gifted program or if they have any disabilities of any kind. When you look at the cards, you realize that many of the judgments that teachers make are subjective.

Q. Does the card contain test scores?

A. Yes. Usually scores from the California Test of Basic Skills.

Q. How often do your students take tests like the CTBS?

A. At least every year. Sometimes twice a year.

Q. Are these test scores useful to you? Do you as a teacher get anything out of them that will help you be a better teacher?

A. Sometimes I find them helpful. But I find that the tests I administer at the beginning of the year for diagnostic purposes and placement are more useful than scores on the standardized tests. I do administer standardized tests; but when I administer the tests, I have some kind of feeling of what the students are doing. I can see if a student is just going through the test marking answers at random. I know that the test for that student is going to be as invalid as anything can be and I'm going to have to find some other way of assessing his abilities. That's one kind of thing I lose when I get scores from a previous teacher. I don't know what the child was doing when he or she took the test.

Q. Say you wanted to evaluate a particular student and you had your choice of getting the subjective impressions of a former teacher or getting a complete record of test scores, which would you take?

A. You're really putting me on the spot. If it was one of the teachers on my teaching team, I would take the subjective judgment. In that kind of situation I almost always don't pay too much attention to the test scores because I know those teachers. I know what they expect from their students, I know what their standards are, and I know that I can trust their judgment. That doesn't mean that I'll blindly accept it, but it will certainly have a bearing on my assessment of that child's abilities.

Q. What about teachers you don't know?

A. That's very hard. I guess then I would tend to favor the tests because sometimes you have to be very careful about accepting recommendations from teachers you don't know.

Q. If you were talking to a group of beginning teachers about using standardized test scores, what would you tell them?

A. Number one, with a standardized test you have to know what the conditions of administration were. Secondly, they should never believe that a test is the absolute last word. Never. Because it can depend on whether the kid had a headache that day, whether his mom chewed him out before he came to school, whether he had breakfast that morning, whether he had failed in the past week—there's so much it depends on. I would say you need a couple of tests bearing out the same things before you can depend on them. You can have very large variations between test scores, but if you have a couple that are similar they are more dependable.

Q. We have been talking about using standardized tests, how about teacher-made tests? How do you go about making up your tests?

A. Well, first of all you have to take a look at what you have been trying to teach, at what your objectives in teaching have been. Essentially what you are doing is checking to see whether you have gotten across what you started out to do.

Q. So you use your tests both as a means of assessing the performance of your students and as a means of assessing your own performance?

A. You're always assessing your own performance because if you're not getting something across, you've got to change your methods. Like this past year I had just a terrible time. I was teaching the lower math group and I had just a terrible time getting equivalent fractions across to those kids. They had a block—there was just no way that I could penetrate it. What I finally had to do was go to something else that presupposed that they had equivalent fractions, and when they saw the need for it, we got past it. But you see, I would not know that I was failing unless they proved to me that they really didn't know it, by taking some kind of test. You have to test what you are teaching.

Q. OK, when you sit down to construct a test you start out with a goal or objective, then what do you do?

A. Well, then you have to look at your method of teaching—how did I go about teaching this? You can't throw a curve at the kids and present material in an entirely different way unless it is something you really want them to think through. If it's something that's really mixed up, for instance a mathematical formula or something, you can't present it in such a different way that they are not going to recognize it. There are some things you give them and you make them think it through, and if you've taught them to think then you can do that. But in general, you have to present things in a recognizable way. If I have taught a child saying, "Turn the fraction upside down," and then on a test I throw the word "invert" at him, he's going to fail.

Q. Another kind of test you mentioned was diagnostic and placement tests; what are those used for?

A. It is a policy in our school that anyone who is below a particular percentile in math or reading must take an individually administered diagnostic and placement test. I also sometimes give a word-opposite test and an oral reading test. It is terribly important that you get your students placed at a comfortable instructional level because if you don't get them placed properly, they can waste half a year.

Q. Are all of your students at comparable levels?

A.   Goodness no! I have a boy I retained last year in the sixth grade who is reading at the second-grade level. There was another girl I taught last year who was at the second-grade level. She went to seventh grade, not because we thought she should, but she had come in the middle of the year and I had not been able to work with her. She was ultimately too mature—a very large girl who was already so streetwise that it would have been detrimental to the sixth grade class to have her there another year. Another problem is with non-English-speaking children. Somehow or another we have to get something across to them. But I would say that out of the thirty kids I had last year there were about twelve that were not reading higher than the fourth grade, about eight others who were at second- and third-grade levels, and the rest from the fourth on up to the ninth, tenth, and twelfth grades.

EDUCATIONAL MEASUREMENT

Next to the preparation and presentation of instruction, teachers spend more time preparing, administering, and interpreting tests than they do in any other teaching activity. Ann Hansen's remarks provide evidence for this point. She mentions the administration and interpretation of commercially prepared achievement tests, placement, and diagnostic tests, as well as the preparation and grading of teacher-made tests for use in her own classroom. As she indicates, not all of these tests are designed in such a way as to be maximally useful to the classroom teacher. The California Test of Basic Skills (CTBS), for example, is a commercial achievement test that assesses achievement in a number of subject matter areas. As Ms. Hansen rightly points out, teachers should be very cautious about making important educational decisions based solely on scores from such tests as the CTBS. She is also correct in maintaining that the judgments of a teacher that are based on considerable interaction with a student are frequently more accurate than a single test score. Despite these limitations, however, commercial achievement tests do have an important role to play in education and this role will be examined later in the chapter.

Ms. Hansen also mentions her use of diagnostic and placement tests. Diagnostic tests are used to help identify the source of problems for those students having learning difficulties. Placement tests are used to assist in identifying the appropriate level to begin instruction. Needless to say, both kinds of tests are of great use to a classroom teacher.

The final kind of test Ms. Hansen mentioned was the teacher-made test designed to assess student learning. This undoubtedly is the kind of test that teachers are most involved with. Yet, unfortunately, teachers sometimes construct their tests in a slapdash manner, seemingly acting as if any item constructed in any manner will suffice to measure student learning. All teachers should be concerned with avoiding this pitfall and with developing quality tests of their own.

THE PURPOSES OF EDUCATIONAL MEASUREMENT

The most appropriate place to begin a discussion of educational measurement is with the purposes of measurement. The division into instructional, administrative, and guidance functions that follows was originally proposed by Findley (1963).

The Instructional Functions of Tests

Tests may directly affect the instructional process by improving the teacher's effectiveness and by enhancing student learning.

Tests provide feedback to the teacher

Tests give teachers information about whether they are attaining their teaching goals. Without specific, objective, information about goal attainment, teachers can waste considerable time in ineffective activity.

Tests provide feedback to students

Students, as well as teachers, need to know how they are doing. Tests provide students with objective feedback, and tests can identify specific content areas that are giving the student trouble.

Students learn from tests

Good tests can provide students with a valuable learning experience. This is particularly true of tests that require students to transfer the knowledge they have acquired to new situations. As indicated in the chapter on cognitive learning, test questions of this type can often bring about valuable learning outcomes.

Tests can motivate learning

Research over the years has demonstrated that students learn more when they expect to be tested than when they do not expect to be tested. Many years ago, for example, White (1932) found that students expecting a final exam in a course performed much better than students in the same classes who did not expect to take the final. This general result has periodically been replicated (e.g., Feldhusen, 1964; Williams and Ware, 1976).

Tests encourage teachers to clarify their goals

As frequently noted in this book, quality education rests on a firm foundation of well-defined goals. The process of deciding what they are going to test can help teachers to sharpen and clarify their goals.

Tests provide both students and teachers with feedback on how they are doing. (© Peter Vandermark/Stock, Boston)

The Administrative Functions of Tests

In addition to their direct instructional impact, tests can also have an indirect impact, when they are used for a variety of administrative purposes.

Tests can facilitate placement decisions

As pointed out in the interview, improperly placed children can waste valuable months interacting with instructional materials and procedures that are too difficult or too easy. Proper placement is a critically important educational decision, and test scores can facilitate the decision process.

Tests can provide feedback on school performance

Educational goals are as important to school administrators as they are to classroom teachers. These goals take the form of expectations about the performance levels that should be attained by schools and districts. Tests can provide administrators with information about how well these goals are being attained.

Tests can provide evaluative information

A considerable amount of innovation and development of new programs goes on in most schools. These innovations frequently require decisions as to whether they are more beneficial than the programs they replace, and tests can contribute valuable information to this evaluative process.

Predicting College Performance— Are Entrance Exams Merely a Roll of the Dice?

A study by Alan Nairn (Nairn, 1980), an associate of Ralph Nader, claims that a college entrance exam (the Scholastic Aptitude Test) developed by the Educational Testing Service is useless for the purpose of predicting future college performance. This claim is summed up in Nairn's charge that "for 88% of the [college] applicants . . . an SAT score will predict their [college] grade rank no more accurately than a pair of dice." In order to evaluate Nairn's claim, and to gain a better understanding of the use of tests for predictive purposes, one needs to understand more about the prediction of future performance from a test score.

Let's start out with a hypothetical example. Assume you were a person who liked to make an occasional bet and that a friend approached you with the following proposition. You would flip a coin 100 times, and both you and he would predict the number of times that heads would come up. For every head that you missed it by, you would pay him a dollar, and for every head he missed it by, he would pay you a dollar. With a little thought you should be able to see that what is important in a situation like the coin-flip bet is to *minimize error*. That is, it is unlikely that you will be able to predict *exactly* the number of heads that will appear, so what you want to do is miss the number of heads that come up by as small a margin as possible. With the coin-flip example, it should be obvious how you would do this. Assuming a fair coin, there is a 50 percent probability that a head will appear on any given flip. This means that you will minimize the error in your prediction by always predicting that 50 heads will appear in any 100 tosses.

Now let's make another assumption. Assume that you carefully weighed the coin that was to be used, and you discovered that it was about 5 percent heavier on the heads side than on the tails side. Using your mathematical wizardry, you calculate that this means that heads should come up 55 percent of the time rather than the 50 percent one would normally predict. Hence you now predict that heads will come up 55 times in any given 100 coin flips. You would be surprised if heads came up exactly 55 times, but your prediction of 55 should have a smaller margin of error than if you predicted heads coming up 50 times.

The concept of minimizing error can now be transferred to the situation of predicting college performance. Imagine that you were given the task of predicting the grade-point average (GPA) of 100 entering college freshmen.

If you knew nothing at all about the students, the best possible prediction you could make would be to pick the average GPA actually attained by students in general as the *predicted GPA for each of the 100 students*. This prediction would minimize the amount of error associated with all of your predictions. Again, it would be surprising if there were more than a few students for whom your prediction was exactly right. But using the average grade-point average as the estimated score for each student is the best possible prediction that can be made in this situation, in the sense that it minimizes the amount of error. *The critical question involved in using test scores for predictive purposes is whether the error in prediction can be reduced even further if one has knowledge of the test score.*

Let's return to the situation of predicting the grade-point average of 100 entering freshmen to see how this would work. Imagine that all 100 of the students had taken the SAT exam. Imagine further that you had read the research literature and you knew that there was a moderate relationship between scores on the SAT exam and grade-point averages attained several years later (the correlation is about .41; Educational Testing Service, 1980). You can use this information to improve the predictions that you would otherwise make. For example, if a person had an above-average score on the SAT exam, you might predict that that person would attain an above-average grade-point average. Moreover, if that person's SAT score was *considerably* above average, you might predict a higher grade-point average for him or her than you would for a person whose SAT score was only slightly above average. Note that instead of predicting the same grade-point average for everyone, as you did with no additional knowledge, now, knowing their SAT scores, you can make a different prediction for each individual. In fact, using an equation for predicting performance from an SAT score, you can make a very specific prediction about the performance level each person will attain.

Having made a specific prediction for each person, one must again realize that one is rarely going to be exactly right. As a matter of fact, if one had many people with the same *predicted* grade-point average one would later find that about half of those attained *actual* grade-point averages above the ones predicted, and about half attained averages below the ones predicted. This is a virtual certainty, since the predicted grade-point average is actually an estimate of the average grade-point average attained by students who achieved a particular SAT score. This again is the principle of the minimization of error in operation. If one wants to minimize the error in a prediction, one predicts the average value. The difference between knowing SAT's and not knowing SAT's is that with knowledge of the scores one can make different predictions for each individual. Without an additional knowledge, one would have to make the same prediction for everyone.

Continued on next page

Return now to Nairn's (1980) claim that test scores "predict . . . no more accurately than a pair of dice." In effect, he is arguing that one can predict as well without any additional information as one can knowing SAT scores. To anyone familiar with the statistics of prediction, this is nonsense. The fact that there is a significant correlation between SAT scores and subsequent grade-point averages means that predictions can definitely be made more precisely when one has knowledge of the scores than they could be in the absence of those scores. The predictions will be a long way from exact, but less error will occur than would otherwise be the case.

Since the appearance of Nairn's study, two other studies have appeared examining the validity of such tests as the SAT. The first, by the prestigious National Academy of Science, concluded that ability tests, "on the whole . . . are useful in predicting an individual's academic or work performance, and they can predict equally well for members of minority groups as for whites" (Holden, 1982, p. 950). The second study, by Robert Kaplan (1982) directly addresses the Nairn study. Kaplan concludes that the SAT is a good predictor of college success and that abandoning testing for college entrance purposes is likely to make the process more unfair than it is now.

Tests can contribute to selection decisions

Many educational programs are not available to all students who would like to be admitted. Examples are special programs emphasizing science, mathematics, or the performing arts, and admission to colleges or universities. Tests such as the Scholastic Aptitude Test (SAT) can frequently contribute to the quality of the selections made in admission decisions. When used for this purpose, the tests are predicting how well students are likely to do if admitted. (But see the accompanying box for a controversy about this use of tests.)

Tests can be useful in accreditation, mastery, or certification decisions

Tests frequently contribute to, and sometimes are the sole basis for, accreditation, mastery, and certification decisions. The driver's license exam is the most common example of a test used for this purpose. Other examples include the tests of General Educational Development (GED tests) to obtain high school credit by examination, the College Level Examination Program (CLEP) to obtain college credits by examination, and state board examinations for the licensing of physicians, teachers, lawyers, and psychologists.

Standardized tests are frequently used in the college admission process. (© Arthur Grace/Stock, Boston)

The Guidance Function of Tests

Tests can contribute to the diagnostic process

Tests can sometimes contribute valuable information to decisions regarding individual aptitudes, abilities, and progress. As noted in Chapter 3, not all students are going to be equally responsive to the same instructional approach. Diagnostic tests can frequently provide information that is useful in matching students and programs. In addition, tests can sometimes identify problems being experienced by students who are not making satisfactory academic progress. This information can then be used to design remedial experiences to bring the student up to the appropriate level.

It should be apparent, then, that educational measurement is an important component of the educational process. In fact, one leading expert (Popham, 1981) has written that about 50 percent of the problems that educators encounter involve test construction, test use, or test interpretation. There is obviously an enormous amount of testing going on in education and an enormous number of tests being used. What may not be so obvious is that not all of these tests are of the same type. The next section describes the two categories into which virtually all educational tests can be classified.

THE TWO BASIC TYPES OF MEASUREMENT: NORM-REFERENCED AND CRITERION-REFERENCED

When students are given tests, it is not always the same kind of information that is wanted. Sometimes one wants to know how a student has performed relative to other students. For instance, many schools place students in educational tracks that differ in instructional pace. Students who score very high relative to their peers may be placed in a track where instruction proceeds at a very rapid pace. Students who score lower may be placed in a track where the pace of instruction is somewhat slower. Tests that provide information on the relative performance of students are called *norm-referenced tests*.

norm-refer-enced tests tests that pro-vide informa-tion on the relative per-formance of students

At other times one wants to identify exactly what knowledge or skills the student has mastered. This kind of information might be useful, for example, if one were evaluating the worth of a particular curriculum and wanted to know what the students had learned. Tests that provide information about what content has been mastered are called *criterion-referenced tests*.

criterion-refer-enced tests tests which provide infor-mation about what content has been mas-tered

In a review of advances in testing methodology, Hambleton (1980) outlined a number of areas of comparison between norm-referenced tests and criterion-referenced tests. Two of Hambleton's points of comparison are used to organize the discussion of norm-referenced and criterion-referenced tests.

Norm-Referenced Tests

Information provided

Norm-referenced tests are specifically constructed to provide information that can be used to compare the relative performance of examinees. The term "norm-referenced" refers to the fact that the test has been taken by a (usually) large number of examinees, who constitute the norm group. Thereafter, the performance of any given examinee can be indexed in terms of the "norms" provided by the norm group.

The norming process

Let's examine this process in greater detail. Imagine that a social studies test has been developed for the commercial market for use with fourth, fifth, and sixth graders. The items have been developed—through a procedure that is described in detail later in this chapter—and the test is now ready for a norming study. The first step is to select the norming sample or *norm group*. When selecting the norming sample, several considerations need to be kept in mind. First, whenever a test is constructed, one has in mind a *target population*—that is, the total group for whom the test would be appropriate. The purpose of the norming study is to collect data that will allow construction of norms that are appropriate for use with the entire target population.

target popula-tion the total group for whom a test would be ap-propriate

Assume that the target population for the social studies test is every fourth, fifth, and sixth grader in the United States. In order for the norms to be appropriate for use with the entire target population, the norm group must be a *representative sample* of the target population. A representative sample of a target population is a smaller group that contains subgroups in the same proportion that they appear in the target population. If 30 percent of the target population is from large urban centers, 30 percent of the norm group should be from cities. If 45 percent of the target population is from West of the Mississippi, then 45 percent of the norm group should come from there. If the target population is 19 percent black and 5 percent Hispanic, those minority groups should be represented in the same proportions in the norm group.

representative sample   a sample from the target population that contains subgroups of examinees in the proportion in which they appear in the target population

Once the norm group has been selected, the test is administered to the group. Norming studies typically involve very large numbers of students; as many as 10,000 students might constitute the norm group. The next step is to establish normative scores from the data collected.

Assume that the test consisted of 100 multiple-choice items and that it was administered to 3,000 students in each of the three grades defining the target population at the beginning of an academic year. Assume further that the distributions plotted in Figure 15-1 depict the data collected. These data contain all the information needed to construct test norms.

Several things should be noted in Figure 15-1. First, the data distributions for all three grades are *normal*, that is, the curves are bell-shaped. These symmetrical distributions are typical of those found when norm-referenced tests are administered to large numbers of students. Second, note that grades 4, 5, and 6 differ in terms of average performance. The average fourth grader in this hypothetical norming study answered 40 of the 100 questions correctly, for fifth graders the average was 50, for sixth graders it was 60.

FIGURE 15-1   Hypothetical Data Distributions for Fourth, Fifth, and Sixth Graders Taking the Same Norm-Referenced Social Studies Test

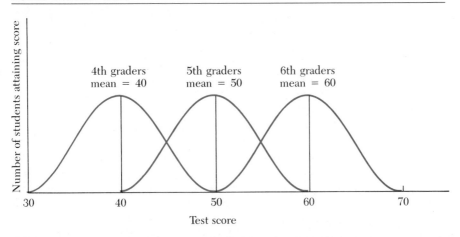

Developing normative scores

*grade equiva-
lent scores
scores derived
from norm-ref-
erenced test
performance
that indicate
relative stu-
dent perform-
ance in grade-
level units*

The different performance levels achieved by the different grades are used to establish *grade equivalent scores*—one of the possible types of normative scores. For example, any student who took the test and scored 40 would have a grade equivalent score of 4.0, indicating that 40 was the average score achieved by a beginning-of-the-year fourth grader. Thus a sixth grader who took the test and achieved a score of 40 would be judged to be performing at a level equivalent to that of an average fourth grader in the first month of school.

Grade equivalent scores are a good example of normative scores because of their obviously comparative nature. By itself, a student's performance (40 correct, for example) is relatively meaningless. The student's performance becomes meaningful only when it is transformed into a comparative score—in this case a score that indicates the student's performance was at the same level as the average performance of beginning fourth graders.

*percentile
scores
derived from
norm-refer-
enced test per-
formance indi-
cating the
percentage of
people achiev-
ing scores
above or below
a particular
point*

Another score commonly used with norm-referenced tests is the *percentile*. A percentile score indicates the percentage of people achieving scores at or below a particular point. If you hear that someone has scored at the 81st percentile on a test, it means that 81 percent of the people taking the test received that score or a lower score. Percentiles for all of the students who took the hypothetical test could be computed for the scores reported in Figure 15-1. Percentiles would be calculated separately for each grade taking the test and are computed by dividing the total number of students taking the test into the number scoring at or below a particular point. So, for example, if 3,000 fourth graders took the test and 2,500 scored 50 or lower, a score of 50 is equivalent to the 83rd percentile. As was the case with grade equivalent scores, the comparative nature of percentile scores should be apparent. The scores have meaning only relative to the other students who have taken the test.

Grade equivalent scores and percentile scores are among the most common means of reporting performance on norm-referenced tests. However, a number of other interpretations can also be derived from norm-referenced tests. Appendix B provides a description of these other types of scores.

A caution regarding grade equivalent scores

Before leaving this section, we would like to add a cautionary note regarding the use and interpretation of grade equivalent scores. Grade equivalent scores have been widely used because they seem so simple. If beginning-of-the-year fifth-grade students have a grade equivalent score of 4.0, they are a year behind in educational progress. If they have a grade equivalent score of 6.0, they are a year ahead in progress. Unfortunately, this simplicity is illusory, and grade equivalent scores can easily be misused and misinterpreted. W. James Popham (1981) has written about several problems with grade equivalent scores that can lead to their misuse and misinterpretation.

The first problem is that test publishers do not have the financial resources to do an across-the-board testing of the target population. Instead, they usually test several grades and extrapolate from the average performance levels of the different grades. The extrapolations are then used to *estimate* the performance of untested populations. For example, in the hypothetical data presented in Figure 15-1, students beginning their fourth-grade year achieved an average score of 40, and students beginning their fifth-grade year achieved an average score of 50. On the basis of these two data points, and on the assumption that the school year is 10 months long, one could estimate the average performance of fourth graders 2 months into the school year as 42, 6 months into the year as 46, and 8 months into the year as 48. But this estimation process would be based on several very shaky assumptions. One assumption is that the content being tested is studied consistently from month to month and year to year. A second assumption is that a student's progress in the content area being tested is constant over time. A third assumption is that the test actually samples everything that is being taught in that subject area at all of the grade levels for which the test is designed. These assumptions are virtually never entirely valid, and the consequence is that estimated grade equivalent scores may seriously underestimate or overestimate actual performance.

A second problem with grade equivalent scores is that the scores do not precisely indicate how a student performed relative to other students taking the test. For example, it is entirely possible that a beginning-of-the-year fifth-grade student could take a test battery and get a math grade equivalent score of 5.5 and a reading grade equivalent score of 5.7, yet score at the 70th percentile on the math test and at the 60th percentile on the reading test.

A final problem with grade equivalent scores is that teachers sometimes mistakenly use them for placement purposes. If a third grader gets a grade equivalent score of 5.0 on a reading test, it does not mean that the third grader should be reading fifth-grade-level material. It means only that the score is an estimate of what the performance of average beginning fifth graders would be if they had taken the test.

For the reasons mentioned above, grade equivalent scores, despite their appealing simplicity, should be used and interpreted with great caution. Percentiles and several other of the standard scores discussed in Appendix B are much more useful for interpretative purposes than are grade equivalent scores.

Test development

The development of a norm-referenced test begins with a *blueprint* for the test that describes the content to be examined and the relative emphasis to be given to each content area. For example, in developing a reading test for use with junior high school students, the test developers might decide to measure general vocabulary, reading comprehension with narrative text, and reading comprehension with social science and natural science text. They then might decide to devote 40 percent of the items to assessing vocabulary, 20 percent of the items to assessing the comprehension of narrative text, and 40 percent of the items to assessing the comprehension of scientific text. The remaining decision relates to the total number of items on the test. This decision is influenced by the time available for testing and by the requirement that a sufficient number of items be included on the test to ensure score stability.

Having developed the test blueprint, the next step is to generate the test items. Test developers typically generate many more items than will ultimately be used on a test. The items are then tried out on examinees from the target population; items that prove to have certain desirable properties are retained for inclusion in the test, and the remaining items are discarded.

Items that are selected for inclusion in a norm-referenced test have two desirable statistical properties: an appropriate difficulty index and an appropriate discrimination index.

Difficulty Indexes.   A *difficulty index* is the proportion of people who get a particular item correct. Norm-referenced tests are constructed entirely of items that have a difficulty index of around .5 (the range is typically from .3 to .7). That is, approximately half of the examinees get each of the items correct. The necessity for constructing a norm-referenced test with items having a difficulty index of around .5 is illustrated in Figure 15-2.

The first curve in the figure illustrates the distribution of data that would result if a test were constructed entirely of items that had a difficulty index of around .2 (20 percent of the examinees get the item correct). The second curve illustrates the distribution resulting from a test consisting of items having a difficulty index of around .5; and the third curve illustrates the distribution resulting from a test consisting of items having a difficulty index of around .8.

Keeping in mind that the goal of a norm-referenced test is to provide comparative information about the performance of examinees, the problem with tests consisting of items having difficulty indexes of .2 and .8 becomes

FIGURE 15-2   Test Score Distributions that Would Result if Tests Were Constructed Entirely of Items Having Difficulty Indices of .2, .5, or .8

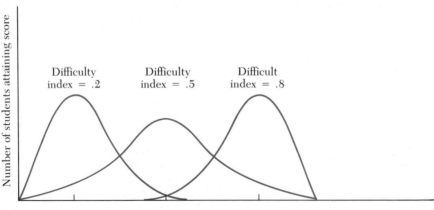

Test score on a 100-item test

clear. In both cases, the scores of the examinees are bunched together at one end of the scale. It is very difficult to make clear-cut comparisons between examinees because there is so little difference in the way most of them have performed on the test. In contrast, the test consisting of items having a difficulty index of .5 provides a distribution that is normal and that is broadly spread across the entire scale. This makes comparisons among examinees clearer and more meaningful.

Discrimination Indexes.   The second important statistical property of good norm-referenced test items is an appropriate discrimination index. A *discrimination index* is essentially the correlation between overall test performance and performance on a particular item. If this index is positive, it means that individuals who scored high on the overall test tended to get the item correct, whereas individuals who scored low tended to get the item wrong. A negative index would mean that individuals who scored low on the test tended to get the item correct, whereas individuals who scored high tended to get the item wrong. Needless to say, there is likely to be something wrong with an item having a negative discrimination index. A negative index would mean that the item was most likely to be answered correctly by those who knew the least! It is commonly the case that items included in norm-referenced tests have at least a moderate positive discrimination index, that is, .3 or above (Thorndike and Hagen, 1969).

discrimination index   the statistical association between performance on a test item and performance on the entire test

Summary

The process of developing a norm-referenced test involves (1) constructing a test blueprint that maps out the content to be covered and the relative emphasis to be given to each topic, (2) constructing test items based on the content description contained in the blueprint, (3) trying out the test items on examinees from the target population, (4) computing difficulty and discrimination indexes for each of the potential test items, (5) discarding items having inappropriate indexes, (6) constructing the actual test form or forms from the items having appropriate indexes, in accordance with the content specifications contained in the blueprint, and (7) administering the test to representative samples of the target population and deriving test norms.

Criterion-Referenced Tests

The basic purpose of a criterion-referenced test is to assess an examinee's performance on prespecified educational objectives. If one thinks of norm-referenced tests as asking the question, "How much does this examinee *know in comparison to other examinees?*" then one might think of criterion-referenced tests as asking, "Has this examinee *mastered this particular content?*"

Information provided

The scores from a criterion-referenced test report on the skills or areas of knowledge that the learner has supposedly mastered. The skills or knowledge areas are specified in educational objectives, and the test is constructed to determine if the objective has been attained. Given the intimate tie between objectives and measurement, criterion-referenced tests are ideal instruments for assessing educational progress.

Test development

The development of a criterion-referenced test begins at the same place as does development of a norm-referenced test—with a test blueprint. But the blueprint for a criterion-referenced test is more elaborate than the one developed for a norm-referenced test. One starts the same way. General content areas are identified, and decisions are made about the emphasis to be given to each area. However, whereas one would start out with a very broad content area for a norm-referenced test (such as high school level biology), a criterion-referenced test typically focuses on a more precisely defined content domain. Cellular reproduction, for example, might be an appropriate chunk for treatment in a criterion-referenced test.

domain specification a procedure that specifies the content to be assessed by a set of test items for a criterion-referenced test

Domain specification

Once the criterion-referenced test developer has mapped out the content specifications for the test, the next step is to develop *domain specifications* or expanded objectives for the test. A well-written domain specification is designed to define clearly and unambiguously the content specified by the objective. Examples of domain specifications are presented in Figures 15-3 and 15-4.

FIGURE 15-3   Example of Domain Specification for a Criterion-Referenced Test: I

Objective

1. Given a number line with the end points labeled 0 and 1 as fractions with the same denominator, the student will be able to find the name of a point on the line.

Sample Item and Directions

Read the problem carefully and choose the best answer. Place the letter beside your answer on the answer sheet next to the number of the problem.

Find the numeral that correctly replaces the pointer in the number line above.

(a) 3   (b) $1\frac{3}{5}$ (c) $\frac{3}{5}$ (d) $\frac{1}{5}$

Content Section

1. The student is given a number line with the end points labeled zero and one, using rational numbers with the same denominator.
2. The divisions on the line shall be equally spaced.
3. The number of divisions on the line will be a multiple of the given denominator.
4. A pointer is used to identify the unknown point on the line.

Response Section

1. There is one correct and three incorrect responses.
2. The responses are given in ascending or descending order.
3. The distractors shall include
   (a) The numeral that represents the ordinal position of the point in question.
   (b) The numeral that represents the length of each division on the number line.
   (c) The numeral that is one more than the correct response.

FIGURE 15-4   Example of Domain Specification for a Criterion-Referenced Test: II

Objective

Student is able to write checks for specified amounts, and record and balance the transactions on check registers.

Level

Senior High School

Sample Directions for Performance

You have a new checking account at a bank. The checks and register have just arrived in the mail. With the checks it is now possible to pay a few bills which require payment. The checking account was opened with a deposit of $525.90. The bills to be paid are:

(1) Bank Plastics, Inc.	$ 75.40
(2) Martha's Gas Co.	$ 12.30
(3) Mortimer J. Snerd	$275.00
(4) Undermountain Utilities	$ 27.53

You should pay these bills by writing checks and recording and balancing each transaction in the check register. The checks need not be mailed; just give them to the proctor along with the register when you are finished.

   You have fifteen minutes to complete the task.

Content/Behavior Domain

1. The examinee will be asked to write at least three and *not* more than five checks.

2. The beginning balance will be given as an amount between $100.00 and $999.99.
3. The checking account will be "new," i.e., there will be *no* checks already on the register.
4. The examinee will give the completed checks and the register to the proctor when finished.
5. There is *no* restriction on the subtraction problems involved, i.e., the examinee will be expected to borrow (as a subtraction procedure), subtract cents and dollars, and keep the decimal point where it belongs.
6. The checks would be written to fictitious companies or individuals.
7. The examinee will *not* be asked to overdraw on the account.

Performance Aids and Environment

1. The examinee will be given a check register form with no previous entries.
2. The examinee will be given double the amount of blank checks which are needed to pay the bills. (This is in case certain checks must be voided.)
3. A pen is necessary.
4. The checks should be authentic checks.
5. The checks should be seriated (prenumbered).
6. Check registers which use stubs should *not* be used.
7. The environment should be a quiet, unhurried one.
8. The workspace should be adequate.
9. Calculators are *not* allowed.
10. A blank piece of paper is allowed.

Popham (1978) has suggested four steps for preparing domain specifications. The first step is to prepare a general description of an objective. The purpose of this description is to convey a general sense of the objective. The second step is to prepare a sample test item that assesses the objective. The sample test item indicates the desired format for subsequently prepared test items, and it clarifies the content targeted by the objective. The third step, which is generally the most difficult, is to describe in specific terms the content or behaviors to be assessed. On occasion, this section also describes what the objective does *not* include in order to define the objective more specifically. The final step in the process is to describe the manner in which the examinee is expected to respond to the test question. This could be a description of the response alternatives available to the examinee (as in Figure 15-3) or it could be a description of the activities to be engaged in by the examinee while demonstrating mastery of the objective (as in Figure 15-4).

After the objectives have been developed, they are reviewed by a group of content experts to make sure they specify the content they are supposed to. Following the review, test items are developed in accordance with the guidelines specified in the domain specification. These items are then reviewed to make sure they measure the content indicated in the domain specification and to make sure they do not contain ethnic, racial, or sexual bias and are free of stereotyping of any kind. The items are then tried out, and any that exhibit flaws are discarded. The remaining items are used to construct the test.

Setting performance standards

After the test has been assembled, the next step is to determine what performance level the student must attain in order to be judged a master. A typical criterion-referenced test might be constructed from ten or more separate objectives (generally from the same area, e.g., biology), with each objective being assessed by at least two, but more often four or more, separate test items. The setting of performance standards entails determining how many items a student has to answer correctly in order to be judged a master of the content specified in the objective. Popham (1981) has reviewed five techniques for setting standards, along with several considerations that should accompany standard setting. The most important thing to be aware of when setting standards, according to Popham, is that all techniques rely on human judgment. This means that it is critical that judgments be expert and informed rather than arbitrary.

The Informed Judgment Model.   The standard-setting models that Popham (1981) reviewed differ in terms of where judgment enters the standard-setting process and whether the model is almost totally judgmental or has quantitative features. An example of a primarily judgmental model is the *informed judgment model*. This model has decision makers consider the importance of a mastery/nonmastery decision, and any special situations that might be involved, as a first step in the standard setting process. For example, if the consequence of being judged a nonmaster is repeating a 2-week instructional sequence, standard setters might be inclined to adopt a stringent standard for mastery. Alternatively, if being judged a nonmaster means having to remain in high school for an additional year, the criterion for mastery might be at a lower level (see the accompanying box).

informed-judgment model   a procedure for designating appropriate mastery-level standards on a criterion-referenced test based on the judgment of experts

Considerations of special situations operate in a similar way. If the test has been newly instituted, it might be prudent and fair to have an initially lower standard for mastery than will be in force at a later date, when students are thoroughly familiar with the testing procedures.

The second step in the informed judgment model is the clarification of competencies. The typical way of completing this step is carefully to examine the tests and items used in the test package to determine if they assess the skills or knowledge they are supposed to assess. The success of this step can be verified by having standard setters sort through items and separate those that measure the targeted competencies from those that are unrelated to the targeted competencies.

The next step involves considering test performance data relevant to standard setting, and it involves collecting input from groups who might be affected by

Criterion-Referenced Tests: Kinds of Classification Errors

One of the decisions that has to be made when setting standards for a criterion-referenced test is how to balance off the classification errors that are going to occur in the testing process. A standard-setting technique called the *contrasting groups model* (Popham, 1981) can serve to illustrate this problem.

The Contrasting Groups Model entails having judges select one group of students who, in their judgment, are certain to be masters of the content to be assessed, and a second group of students who are judged to be certain nonmasters of the content. Imagine that this procedure was carried out, and that a 10-item test was then administered to both groups of students. The accompanying figure presents the hypothetical distributions of scores on the test for both groups.

Note that in the figure, the score distributions for the two groups intersect at the point corresponding to 7 out of 10 correct. Looking at the accompanying table, one can see that if a score of 7 out of 10 correct was used as the cutoff score, approximately 20 percent of the examinees judged to be masters would fall below the cutoff score (would be classified as nonmasters), and approximately 20 percent of the examinees judged to be nonmasters would fall above the cutoff score and would be classified as masters. One can think of these two kinds of people (masters classified as nonmasters and nonmasters classified as masters) as representing *classification errors*. The actual cutoff score can then be established, based on an evaluation of the seriousness of each of the kinds of error. For example, the decision might be made that by far the most serious kind of error is to hold back someone who is in fact a master. If so, the cutoff score could be set at 4; then only 3 percent of those people judged to be masters would be classified as nonmasters. It should be noted, however, that the consequence of this decision is that 70 percent of those people judged to be nonmasters are now erroneously classified as masters. On the other hand, the decision might be that the more serious error is to classify someone erroneously as a master when he or she has not in fact mastered the skills. The consequence of this decision might be to set the cutoff score at 9, thereby classifying only 2 percent of those examinees who are nonmasters as masters. This would, of course, increase the proportion of people who actually are masters but are classified as nonmasters to 55 percent.

Distribution of Test Scores on a Criterion-Referenced Test

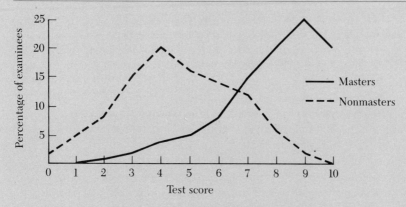

Test score	Percentage of masters	Percentage of nonmasters	Cutoff score	False failures	False passes
10	20	0	10	80	0
9	25	2	9	55	2
8	20	6	8	35	8
7	15	12	7	20	20
6	8	14	6	12	34
5	5	16	5	7	50
4	4	20	4	3	70
3	2	15	3	1	85
2	1	8	2	0	93
1	0	5	1	0	98
0	0	2	0	0	100

(Hambleton, 1980)

In an ideal world, test constructors and educators would not be faced with balancing off these two kinds of errors because tests would have nonoverlapping distributions. That is, there would be a clear demarcation point between the score distributions for masters and nonmasters. The real world, however, is far from ideal. Judges—even the most expert and knowledgeable ones—make errors in classifying students as masters or nonmasters. Students score differently on tests, depending on their physical state and their motivational level, and test items are not perfect indicators of student knowledge. All of these factors mean that there is going to be a certain amount of error in any assessment process and that the prudent decision is to give careful consideration to the consequences of the different kinds of classification errors.

the standard-setting decision. Popham (1981) recommends that data be collected from uninstructed groups, just instructed groups, and previously instructed groups to provide a data base for decision making. For example, if the test determined whether a student had mastered the minimal competencies required for graduation from high school, data might be collected from elementary and junior high school students who would be unlikely to have mastered many of the skills, from high school seniors at whom the test is targeted, and from adults who graduated from high school several years ago. These data could be considered along with input from such interested groups as current high school seniors, persons who graduated from high school several years ago, teachers, administrators, and parents of children who will be taking the test in the future (Popham, 1981).

The final step in the model is to set the actual performance standards. These standards are set after carefully considering the performance data from the tested groups and the preference data from the interested parties.

Nedelsky's method a quantitative method of setting standards for a multiple-choice test by identifying the number of obviously incorrect responses for each test item

Nedelsky's Method.   In 1954, Leo Nedelsky suggested a method of standard setting that can serve as an example of a model containing quantitative features. Nedelsky's (1954) method is designed to be used with multiple-choice tests. However, William Angoff (1971) has contributed an adaptation of Nedelsky's method that can be used with any kind of test. The first step in the Nedelsky method is to appoint one or more judges who are thoroughly familiar with both the content to be assessed and the average student's mastery of that content. Typically, the judges would be teachers or school administrators.

After the judges have been appointed, each judge is asked to make judgments about the items in the mastery test. These judgments involve identifying the distractors (incorrect choices) in a multiple-choice item that, in their judgment, a minimally competent student would recognize as being incorrect. The remaining items, that is, those that the judges determine could not be recognized as incorrect by minimally competent students, are then converted into correct-by-guessing probabilities. For example, imagine that a test item consisted of a multiple-choice question with four response alternatives. Imagine further that the judges decided that two of the distractors could be eliminated by a minimally competent student. This leaves two responses, the correct response and one distractor. Hence the correct-by-guessing probability is one in two, or .5. Or, as other examples demonstrate, if one alternative were eliminated, there would be three responses remaining, yielding a guessing probability of .33, and if three responses were eliminated only the correct response would remain, leaving a guessing probability of 1.0.

After the guessing probabilities have been determined for each test item, they are added together, and the resultant total becomes the score that a student must achieve in order to be judged minimally competent. For example, imagine that a 10-item test yielded guessing probabilities of .25, .5, .5, .33, 1.0, .25, .33, .25, .25, and .33. These probabilities sum to 4, meaning that a student would have to get at least four items correct to be judged minimally competent.

Summary

Criterion-referenced tests provide information about whether students have mastered a well-specified content domain. The development of a criterion-referenced test begins with identification of the content area that is to be assessed by the test. This step is followed by the development of domain specifications that clearly delineate the content to be tested and the manner of testing. After a tryout of the items, the test is constructed and standards of performance are set. The standard-setting methods can be largely judgmental, or they can include both judgmental and quantitative procedures.

RELIABILITY AND VALIDITY

Up to this point, the purposes of educational measurement and the two major types of educational tests have been discussed. We now move on to a consideration of the two essential qualities of any test: *It must be reliable and it must be valid.*

reliability a property of a test representing the degree to which test performance is consistent

Test Reliability

A test is reliable when it yields similar scores or decisions on repeated administrations, that is, when it is *consistent*. Consistency is an absolutely essential quality for any educational test. For that matter, it is an absolutely essential quality for any measurement process. If you step on a scale and weigh 170 pounds, then step off and step on again and weigh 150 pounds, you conclude that the scale is inconsistent; it is unreliable. Moreover, it is worthless as a measuring device. Given the extreme variability in measurement from one time to the next, you would have no way of knowing whether either weight was even close to being accurate.

The same is true of educational tests. If a student is tested on day 1 and then again on day 2, and very different scores are obtained on the two days, the test is probably worthless. The chances of anything happening within a 24-hour period to alter the student's competency significantly is small. Thus the test must be unreliable. In the pages that follow test reliability is examined in greater detail. Since test reliability is somewhat different for norm-referenced and criterion-referenced tests, the two types of tests are discussed separately.

Reliability and norm-referenced tests

The classic way of conceptualizing reliability with norm-referenced tests is to imagine that the same test was administered on two successive days. It is unlikely that even in this imagined situation the scores for each individual would be identical on the two days. For example, physical states and motivational levels could vary from one test occasion to the next, and given the fallibility of human memory, a student might be able to remember a bit of important information for one test that he or she could not remember for the other test. These factors mean that it is a virtual impossibility to construct tests that yield exactly the same scores on different occasions.

The problem is actually even more difficult than this imagined situation would suggest because only on very rare occasions would one want to administer exactly the same test twice. Instead, if an assessment of the same information on more than one occasion was needed, alternate forms of a test would be used. *Alternate forms* of a test would be two versions that contain different items while attempting to measure the same content.

Methods of Assessing Reliability.   Given the difficulty of constructing tests that yield exactly the same scores, the problem becomes one of determining if the tests yield scores of sufficient similarity to meet the standards required of good educational tests. The standard way of determining whether norm-referenced tests have adequate reliability is by calculating a correlation coefficient for the scores collected on the two occasions. A *correlation coefficient* is an index of the extent to which two events are related (see Appendix A for detailed discussion). If the tests administered on the two occasions yielded exactly the same score for each examinee, the resultant correlation between the scores collected on the first occasion and those collected on the second occasion would be 1.0. For reasons stated previously, one knows that test scores are not likely to be identical, so it becomes a matter of establishing how similar they are.

A test yielding highly similar scores (a highly reliable test) would preserve *approximately the same ordering of scores*, and this, in turn, would yield a high correlation coefficient. That is, if the test was reliable, an individual who received the highest score relative to other examinees on one test occasion should be at the top, or at least very near the top, on the second occasion. Likewise, an individual scoring at about the average of a group of examinees on the first test should be in about the same location on the second. If this is not the case, that is, if many individuals drastically change their position from one test occasion to the next, the resulting correlation coefficient would be low, and the test would be considered unreliable.

The situation described above, in which two forms of a test are administered on separate occasions, is called the *test-retest method* of determining reliability, and the correlation coefficient that is calculated to provide an index of the reliability of the test is called a *reliability coefficient*. Quality educational tests should have a reliability coefficient of .90 or better (indicating that the test provides highly consistent measurement), and educators who purchase educational tests should examine the literature accompanying the test to make sure the reliability coefficient is at least this high before buying the test.

correlation coefficient an index of the extent to which two events are related

test-retest method a method of assessing the reliability of test performance by administering two forms of a test at different times

reliability coefficient the correlation coefficient that represents the reliability of a given test

The test-retest technique for determining test reliability is a convenient way of explaining what test reliability means, but it is not the only technique for determining reliability. Another commonly used technique is the *split-half method for determining reliability*.

The split-half method involves only a single administration of a test, but the test is then split in half and treated as if two tests were being administered. As an example, imagine that one had a test consisting of 100 items. One split-half technique would be to divide the test at the midpoint and to treat the score on the first 50 items and the score on the second 50 items as separate test scores for the purpose of calculating a reliability coefficient.

The split-half technique of dividing a test at the midpoint is not used very often because of factors that can differentially affect performance on the first and second half of a test. Fatigue, for example, could contribute to lowering a score on the second half of a test. Time may also come into play. Some students may not get to the last few items on a test because of time press .re. For these reasons, a much more frequently used split-half technique is to divide a test on the basis of odd- and even-numbered items. This technique again splits a test in two for the purpose of computing a reliability coefficient, but it has the advantage of equalizing factors that could differentially lower performance on separate halves of the test.

Correlation coefficients are most meaningful when they are calculated from data having a broad distribution of scores. As described previously, the test development process used with norm-referenced tests is designed to yield broad score distributions (i.e, selected items have difficulty indexes of around .5). For this reason, reliability coefficients are an ideal means of indexing the reliability of norm-referenced tests. Criterion-referenced tests, on the other hand, are not designed to yield broad distributions of data. Therefore, a different procedure is needed for describing the reliability of the tests.

split-half method a method of assessing the reliability of a test by calculating the correlation coefficient between test performance on two halves of the same test

Reliability and criterion-referenced tests

Criterion-referenced tests are designed for different purposes than is the case for norm-referenced tests. The purposes are to assess the extent of examinee knowledge in particular content areas and to make mastery or nonmastery decisions based on examinee performance (Hambleton, 1980). The reliability coefficient technique for indexing test reliability does not provide useful information for determining the reliability of conclusions about whether either of these purposes has been fulfilled. A reliability coefficient indicates the extent to which an examinees' score places a student in the same relative position (relative to other examinees taking the test) on two different occasions. With criterion-referenced tests, one is not interested in relative position. Rather, one is interested in whether students should be classified as masters or nonmasters of a knowledge domain. This means that the reliability issue for criterion-referenced tests is whether or not the test is *consistent in classification* on two separate occasions.

Methods of assessing reliability

Figure 15-5 illustrates the consistency-of-classification approach to determining the reliability of a criterion-referenced test. The hypothetical data in the figure are from two alternate test forms (administered on successive days) of a criterion-referenced test designed to decide whether students are masters or nonmasters of a knowledge area. The figure depicts a four-cell configuration in which one axis records the mastery/nonmastery decision made on day 1 (with test form 1) and the second axis records the decision data from day 2 (with test form 2). Note that if the test were perfectly consistent (i.e., perfectly reliable), all of the examinees would fall in cells 1 and 4: that is, nonmaster day 1/nonmaster day 2 and master day 1/master day 2. The number of examinees in the other two cells represent the degree of inconsistency in the test. An index of the reliability of the test depicted in Figure 15-5 can be calculated by determining the proportion of people falling in cells 1 and 4: 16 percent in cell 1 and 66 percent in cell 4. If these two values are added together a consistency index of .82 is obtained. That is 82 percent of the examinees have been consistently classified on the two occasions. In actual use, this consistency index should be corrected for chance (Swaminathan, Hambleton, and Algina, 1974), but as presented here it provides a reasonable means of determining the reliability of criterion-referenced tests designed for mastery/nonmastery decisions.

Other approaches to determining the reliability of criterion-referenced tests

FIGURE 15-5   Percentage of Masters and Nonmasters as a Function of Selecting Different Cutoff Scores

Day 1 \ Day 2	Nonmaster	Master	Marginal Proportion
Nonmaster	.16	.04	.20
Master	.14	.66	.80
Marginal Proportion	.30	.70	

are highly technical and mathematical in nature. They include a technique for establishing the reliability of domain score estimates (e.g., Hambleton, Swaminathan, and Algina, 1976; Millman, 1974) and a procedure, analogous to a split-half technique, in which the reliability of a criterion-referenced test is assessed from a single test administration (Subkoviak, 1976). Two works (Berk, 1980; Hambleton et al., 1978) provide in-depth reviews of a number of these techniques.

Test Validity

As noted in the previous section, the first essential attribute of an educational test is reliability—that is, the test must provide consistent measurement. The second essential attribute is that a test must *measure what it is supposed to measure*. This attribute is called *test validity*.

It is important to understand the relationship between reliability and validity. A test can be reliable without being valid, but the converse is not true. Assume that one decided that the circumference of the skull is a measure of intelligence. With a little care one could devise a highly reliable measurement technique that would have a very small margin of error. But the fact is that circumference of the skull has nothing to do with intelligence. One would have a highly reliable measurement technique that was not valid; it would not be measuring what it was supposed to measure. In contrast, *if a test is unreliable, it cannot be valid*. If a test gives a high score to an individual on one occasion and a low score on the next, or if it judges an examinee to be a master the first time but not the second, there is no way the test can be measuring what it is supposed to measure.

There are a number of different kinds of validity (Cronbach, 1971), but three are most important for our purposes: content validity, construct validity, and criterion validity.

test validity the attribute of a test indicating that the test measures what it is supposed to measure

Content validity

Most educational tests are designed to measure student knowledge in a particular content area. The extent to which a test measures the content it is supposed to is known as *content validity*.

Content validity is determined by examining the content specifications for a test, and the items that have been generated, to see if there is a match between the two. If independent judges decide that the items contained in a test actually measure the content supposedly being measured, then the test is said to have content validity.

Content validity is defined the same way, and is determined the same way, for both norm-referenced and criterion-referenced tests. With both types of tests, a test is content valid when the items contained in the test assess the content identified in the design specifications for the test.

content validity a type of test validity indicating whether a test measures the content it is supposed to measure

Construct validity

construct va-
lidity the ex-
tent to which
test scores
make theoreti-
cal sense in the
context of ad-
ditional infor-
mation

Construct validity refers to whether scores from a test are theoretically consistent with other measures or observations. Understanding of this type of validity entails familiarity with psychological constructs.

Psychology is a science concerned to a large extent with events that cannot be directly observed. Learning, for example, cannot be seen. One can see only *changes in behavior* and one posits that those changes are attributable to an unobservable internal event that is called learning. Thus learning is a psychological construct. *Psychological constructs* (also frequently called theoretical constructs) are things that cannot be seen directly, but one invents them to make sense out of things that can be seen. Personality is another common psychological construct. People differ in mood, temperament, and manner of interacting with other people. The construct "personality" has been invented to account for the variability in these characteristics. Knowledge is another psychological construct, and this one goes to the heart of what construct validity means in educational testing. When people can tell about things they have experienced before, one says they have knowledge. This thing cannot be directly seen, but the construct "knowledge" has been invented to account for the behaviors that can be seen.

Much of the purpose of education is to impart knowledge to students, and much of the objective of educational measurement is to determine if that purpose is being attained. To be confident that a test is accomplishing its objective one needs to be sure that the scores derived from the test behave in a manner that is theoretically consistent with the construct on which the test is based. This is what construct validity is all about.

As an example, let's imagine that a norm-referenced test has been developed in the area of high school chemistry. The assumption on which the test is based is that students acquire knowledge of chemistry through exposure to instruction and that an estimate of the extent of that knowledge can be obtained by having students answer test questions. Any analysis of the construct "knowledge of chemistry" is going to suggest that it is not something that is sitting isolated in a student's head, cut off from all other kinds of knowledge. One would expect knowledge of chemistry to be related, for example, to knowledge of other areas of science such as biology or physics. Moreover, one would expect that a person who knew a great deal of chemistry would also be likely to know some mathematics and would in fact probably do quite well on an aptitude test, such as an IQ test. These expectations are not *strong* expectations, in the sense that one would anticipate a very high relationship between scores on the chemistry test and scores on the other tests. But a sense of what the construct "knowledge of chemistry" means does lead to the expectation that an individual who scores high on the chemistry test will tend to score above average on these other measures, and that a person who scores low on the chemistry test will tend to score below average on the other measures. If these expectations are fulfilled, one has added to the construct validity of the test. However, if they are not borne out—for example, if there

Individuals with much knowledge in one subject-matter area are also likely to have knowledge in related areas. (© Jean-Claude Ljeune/Stock, Boston)

tends to be a negative relationship between chemistry scores and the other scores, such that high scores on the one tend to be associated with low scores on the others and vice versa, then one would have serious doubts about whether the test was measuring the construct "knowledge of chemistry." This in turn would lead to serious doubts about whether the test was measuring what it was supposed to measure.

Criterion validity

Criterion validity refers to whether a test successfully *predicts what it is supposed to predict*. This use of educational tests was discussed in the section concerned with using tests to make predictions (p. 502), and the familiar Scholastic Aptitude Test was cited as an example of an educational test designed almost exclusively for predictive purposes.

criterion valid-ity the extent to which a test score is useful as a predictive device

When designing a test for predictive purposes, one begins with the thing that one wants to predict, which is termed the *criterion*. Let's say one wants to predict college success, and that the index of college success one has chosen is grade-point average. Grade-point average then becomes the criterion that one is trying to predict with the test.

After the test has been developed, it is administered to a group of college students. Their grade-point averages are then obtained and a correlation coefficient for the two sets of data is computed. The correlation coefficient then becomes an index of the criterion validity of the test, and it provides an index of how accurately the test would predict the grade-point averages of students who took the test before entering college. If the correlation coefficient is sufficiently high, one can say that there is evidence that the test has criterion validity and that the test provides useful predictive information regarding future college performance. This predictive utility could be verified in subsequent research that would involve testing students before entering college, and then correlating the test score with their grade-point averages after they had been in college for three or four years. If, however, the initial correlation coefficient between test performances and grade-point average is low or negligible, one has to go back to the drawing board.

Correlation coefficients computed from test scores and criterion measures do not have to reach a set value before they can be taken as evidence for the criterion validity of the test. Certainly, the coefficients should be well above the level where they might be a chance occurrence, but there is no specific cutoff point for criterion validity. However, values below .35 or so do not add very much to the predictions that can be made without the use of the tests.

SUMMARY

Educational tests can be used for three general purposes. In the *instructional function,* tests can provide feedback to teachers and to students, they can be a source of direct student learning, they can motivate student learning, and they can encourage teachers to clarify their instructional goals.

The second general purpose of tests is the administrative function. When used for administrative purposes, tests can facilitate placement decisions, they can provide feedback on the performance of an entire school or district, they can provide information relevant to evaluating new programs, they can contribute to selecting candidates for admission to programs, and predicting future college performance, and they can be useful for accreditation, mastery, and certification decisions.

The third general purpose of tests is to serve a guidance function. This function entails using tests to diagnose learning difficulties and to provide information useful for matching students with special programs.

There are two types of educational tests. The first provides information about how a student performs in comparison to other students who have taken the test. This type of test is called a *norm-referenced* test because a student's performance is defined in terms of group norms. The second type of test judges whether a student has mastered a particular instructional content. This type of test is called a criterion-referenced test because a student's performance is evaluated in terms of a criterion or standard for mastery.

The basis for comparison in a norm-referenced test are norms that are gathered by administering the test to a representative sample of the target population. The total group for whom the test is designed is the target population, and a representative sample would be a subset of that population that had the same characteristics as the total population.

Several different normative scores are commonly used with norm-referenced tests. A grade equivalent score is the average score for students at a particular grade level. For example, if beginning-of-the-year fourth graders achieve a raw score of 40 on a test, then a score of 40 is equal to a grade equivalent score of 4.0. A second normative score is the percentile. A percentile score indicates the percentage of people achieving scores on a test at or below a particular point.

Grade equivalent scores should be used and interpreted with caution because of several problems with the scores. The first problem is that the scores are frequently based on estimates of how students should perform rather than on actual data. The second problem is that the scores are not precise indicators of how well one student performed relative to others who have taken the test. A third problem is that teachers sometimes mistakenly use grade equivalent scores for placement purposes.

The development of a norm-referenced test begins with a blueprint for the test, which describes the content to be examined and the relative emphasis to be given to each content area. The next step is to write test items, which are then tried out on students from the target population. Items that have a difficulty index of about .5 (meaning that about half of the students got the item correct and half got it wrong) and a discrimination index of .3 or above (meaning that those who got the item correct tended to do well on the test as a whole) are candidates for inclusion in the final version of the test.

A criterion-referenced test measures whether or not a student has mastered a particular content. Development of a criterion-referenced test begins with a blueprint that is more elaborate than that developed for a norm-referenced test. The next step is to develop a domain specification for the test. A domain specification clearly and unambiguously defines the content to be assessed on the test. After items have been tried out and selected for inclusion in the test, the next step is to set performance standards. There are several techniques for doing this, and they vary in terms of whether they are primarily judgmental or also include quantitative features. An example of the primarily judgmental approach is the informed judgment model. An example of an approach containing quantitative features is Nedelsky's method.

The two critical characteristics of a test are that it must be reliable, indicating that it is consistent in measurement, and it must be *valid*, indicating that it measures what it is supposed to measure. The reliability of a norm-referenced test can be determined by correlating the scores obtained—either by administering the test twice (the test-retest method) or by splitting the test into two parts and calculating the score for each part (called the split-half method).

The reliability of a criterion-referenced test is determined by establishing its consistency of classification—that is, the consistency with which the test classifies students as masters or nonmasters on two successive test administrations.

If a test is reliable, it may or may not be valid. However, a test that is not reliable cannot be valid. There are three kinds of test validity. If a test has content validity, it means that the test measures the content it is supposed to measure. If a test has construct validity, it means that scores from the test are theoretically consistent with other scores or observations. If a test has criterion validity, it means that the test predicts what it is supposed to predict.

FOR FURTHER STUDY AND APPLICATION

Popham, W. J. *Modern educational measurement.* Englewood Cliffs, N.J.: Prentice-Hall, 1981. Covers norm-referenced and criterion-referenced measurement with great clarity, and despite the subject matter, the writing is excellent and occasionally even humorous.

Cronbach, L. J. Test validation. In R. C. Thorndike (Ed.), *Educational measurement* (2nd ed.). Washington, D.C.: American Council on Education, 1971. An excellent presentation of the concepts and procedures involved in test validity.

Berk, R. (Ed.). *Criterion-referenced testing: State of the art.* Baltimore: Johns Hopkins University Press, 1980.

Hambleton, R. K. Advances in criterion-referenced testing methodology. In C. R. Reynolds and T. B. Gutkin (Eds.), *Handbook of school psychology.* New York: Wiley, 1980. Two up-to-date sources on criterion-referenced measurement.

Lyman, H. B. *Test scores and what they mean.* Englewood Cliffs, N.J.: Prentice-Hall, 1963. A good primer on interpreting test scores.

16

DEVELOPING TEACHER-MADE TESTS

CHAPTER OVERVIEW

Whereas the previous chapter discussed the basic principles that underlie educational measurement, this chapter discusses the steps that should be followed when developing and scoring teacher-made tests.

The initial step that teachers must take when developing a test is to decide what they want to measure. The chapter begins with a description of a classification system for learning outcomes that is very useful in formulating the decision about what should be measured.

The second step in the test development process is to lay out a blueprint of the test. The second section of the chapter describes how to develop tables of specification that can serve as test blueprints.

After a decision has been made about what the test should measure, and a blueprint has been developed that describes the content of the test, the next step is to develop the items for the test. Three general types of items that a test might contain are described. The first type is simple-form objective items. Within this type are short-answer questions, true-false questions, and matching questions. The second general type of item is the multiple-choice question; and the final type is the essay question. The chapter presents guidelines for developing and scoring each of these question forms, and discusses the advantages and disadvantages of tests that use each of the forms.

Dr. Gerald Helmstadter is professor of educational psychology at Arizona State University. He received his B.A. degree in mathematics from Iowa State University, and at the time planned to go into teaching at the high school level. However, an opportunity to obtain his M.A. degree at Iowa State came up, and after finishing his degree, he went on to the University of Minnesota, where he obtained his Ph.D. degree with a specialty in psychological measurement. After graduating from Minnesota, Professor Helmstadter worked at Educational Testing Service and taught at Colorado State University. He has been teaching at Arizona State University for over 20 years.

Professor Helmstadter is a well-known expert in the area of educational and psychological measurement. He is the author of two books on the subject and numerous journal articles. He has also served as vice president of the American Educational Research Association for the Division of Measurement and Research Methodology. In 1981, Professor Helmstadter served on a statewide task force—consisting of educators, business leaders, parents, and state politicians charged with making recommendations concerning the appropriate test to use in implementing a new law that mandated yearly achievement testing for every student enrolled in Arizona public schools, grades 1–12. We began the interview by asking Professor Helmstadter to give his evaluation of the average teacher-made test:

A.   I would have to say that they are not very good.

Q.   Is that because teachers don't have the training they need to construct good tests, or is it because they simply don't spend the amount of time required to develop good tests?

A.   I think it is primarily a lack of training. Since I have been teaching, I have seen the amount of time that prospective teachers devote to studying measurement steadily decline. Given the critical role that measurement plays in quality education, I think all teachers should have at least one course in measurement.

Q.   What is the role of testing in education? Is it primarily a means of evaluating students?

A.   Not at all. Testing has many purposes, and evaluation is probably not even the most important. Tests give feedback to both teachers and students, they provide information about the effectiveness of programs, and perhaps most importantly, they signal students as to what content it is important for them to learn.

Q.   Would students learn anything in school without tests?

A.   Oh, they would learn a great deal. But I'm not sure that the information they would learn would be the academic information that schools are supposed to be teaching.

Q.   As you know, Bloom's taxonomy of educational objectives is a classification system that divides knowledge into categories that range from the very simple to the very complex. Do you think knowing about Bloom's taxonomy is useful to teachers when they are constructing their own tests?

A.   Yes. I think it focuses attention on the fact that knowledge exists at various levels, and this alone is likely to cut down on the extent to which teachers write test items that focus only on low-level factual knowledge.

Q.   What about tables of specification, which lay out the content to be tested and the manner of testing that content? Is this something that teachers should do when preparing tests?

A.   Absolutely! Preparing a table of specifications is the single best way to ensure that teacher-made tests measure what they are supposed to measure. Whenever I teach a measurement course, I strongly emphasize that teachers should start with a table of specifications.

Q.   Let's talk for a moment about various types of questions. What do you think of simple-form question types like fill-in-the-blank, true-false, and matching questions?

A.   I think they have a lot to recommend them. However, it is true that some people claim that simple-form questions cannot assess higher-level knowledge. I would agree that this is generally true of tests that use this type of item, but this does not reflect a general limitation of the item type. If a test developer really spends the time and ingenuity needed, simple-form items can measure any knowledge level. The real advantage of simple-form items, especially for teachers, is that they require less time to prepare than good multiple-choice items.

Q.   What about the measurement characteristics of multiple-choice questions? Do they make good test items?

A.   Yes, indeed. A good multiple-choice test can measure just about any educational outcome that I can think of. The only exception that comes to mind is the ability to organize arguments and express oneself verbally. For those kind of outcomes you would need to use essay items.

Q.   What do you think of essay tests?

A.   I don't have anything against essay tests that are done right. The problem is that they rarely are done right. To do it right, you should start out with a table of specifications indicating what your test should measure, you should devise a scoring scheme that assigns points for various aspects of the answer, and you should write a model answer. If you do all of those things, the chances are the essay test will be OK. Most teachers, however, don't do this. They devote little time to the test development process, and the result is tests with two major problems. The first, and probably most serious, problem is that the tests do not adequately assess the entire range of content that they should assess. In short, the tests lack content validity. The second problem is that tests that have been hastily constructed are difficult to score reliably. And as you know, unreliable tests make for bad measurement.

The previous chapter dealt with the general principles of educational measurement. This chapter brings the discussion down to the level of the individual classroom and discusses procedures that teachers can use when developing their own tests.

In the interview we asked Professor Helmstadter to give his evaluation of the average teacher-made test. His opinion matches ours. In general, they are not very good. Items are constructed poorly, assessment is focused on the memorization of facts, and the reliability and validity of the tests are probably not very good. It's no wonder that a great many students claim that tests don't measure what they know. They are probably right!

We also asked Professor Helmstadter about the two likely culprits behind poor test development. The first is that teachers simply do not know how to prepare tests. This chapter is designed to remedy that situation to some extent. The chapter will not substitute for a course in educational measurement, but it should at least provide some familiarity with the procedures that teachers should carry out to develop good tests.

The second reason that many teacher-made tests are poor is that a large number of teachers are unwilling to spend the time required to develop good tests. It's not easy. Developing good tests requires a fair amount of work, and even teachers who work very hard at teaching seem to have the attitude that their time could be more beneficially spent developing instruction rather than assessing it. This belief is likely to be erroneous, however. When one tries something different, one needs feedback to determine how one is doing. One's subjective impressions can provide part of this feedback; but sometimes impressions are faulty, and frequently they cannot tell one what one needs to know. Good test data can be a valuable addition to teachers' subjective impressions about the effect of their instruction, and teachers who invest part of their effort in developing measurement techniques will find that the time they have spent was well worth it.

STARTING OUT: DECIDING WHAT INFORMATION TO MEASURE

The starting place in developing good educational measurement is to decide what kind of information you want to measure. Sometimes the goal of instruction is the mastery of low-level information that must initially be memorized. Given such a goal, good assessment might merely involve seeing whether students can recall or recognize what they have heard or read. Other times the goal of instruction might be acquisition of concepts or principles, and the assessment of this kind of learning might involve the determination of whether students can classify unfamiliar instances of a concept, or whether they can apply a rule or a principle in situations they have not previously encountered. At a still higher level the goal of instruction might be to teach students to synthesize separate bits of information into a new rule or principle. Assessment of this goal might entail presenting the students with the pieces of information and seeing if they can derive the rule.

Bloom's Taxonomy of Educational Objectives in the Cognitive Domain

Benjamin Bloom and his colleagues (Bloom et al., 1956) have developed a classification system that is very useful in helping teachers determine the kind of information they want to measure. Bloom's *Taxonomy of Educational Objectives* divides cognitive learning outcomes into six levels. The levels move from the most simple cognitive learning to the most complex.

Knowledge (Level I)

The simplest accomplishment described by Bloom is the *knowledge of some-thing*. This could be the knowledge of specific terms or facts, as illustrated by being asked, "What is the smallest unit of matter?" or "What is the most populated state in the United States?"; or it could entail asking for the recall of a particular rule or generalization, as when a student is asked, "What are the principal characteristics of living organisms?"

knowledge the simplest level of educational achievements, according to Bloom, charac-terized by knowing of specific facts following in-struction

Educational accomplishment at the knowledge level is the simplest level of attainment, but it is by no means the least important. In fact, as was evident in the earlier chapters on learning, knowledge-level information forms the foundation for the higher-level learning that follows.

Testing information at the knowledge level generally involves asking students to reproduce or recognize information in virtually the same form in which it was presented. Examples of items testing information at the knowledge level are presented later in the chapter. One thing to keep in mind about knowledge-level objectives (and about objectives at other levels for that matter) is that the cognitive level tested by a question cannot be determined by merely looking at the item. As an instance, the question about naming the characteristics of living organisms is a knowledge-level item *if* at some point in the instructional process the student has been told what the characteristics are. However, if students *have not been told* what the characteristics are but instead must discern the characteristics for themselves from other, lower-order information that has been presented, a much higher level of attainment is being assessed.

Comprehension (Level II)

comprehension
the second
level of educa-
tional achieve-
ment, accord-
ing to Bloom,
characterized
by translating
instructional
information
into a mean-
ingful form

Assessing knowledge at the comprehension level entails determining if students have *understood* the instruction they have received. As discussed in Chapter 8, which dealt with the applications of cognitive learning theory, understanding has a number of different meanings. Bloom's second level in the cognitive taxonomy represents the most primitive level of understanding. In terms of cognitive learning theory, one might say that a student who has comprehended instruction at Bloom's second level has *translated* that information into a form that captures the meaning of the instruction. The student who has attained the comprehension level in Bloom's taxonomy can respond correctly to questions that are in a form different from that experienced during instruction. For instance, Anderson (1972) has advocated that one way to determine if students have understood the instruction they have been receiving is to develop tests that use paraphrases of the instruction they originally received. The idea is that if the students have comprehended the instruction, they should be able to handle paraphrased and original material with equal ease. However, if they have learned the material only at the knowledge level (i.e., have memorized it), they will not be able to respond to paraphrased material.

Application (Level III)

application
the third level
of knowledge,
according to
Bloom, charac-
terized by
transferring
instructional
information to
new situations

If students have mastered instruction at the application level they will be able to transfer what they have learned to particular and concrete situations they have not previously encountered. Bloom's application level is similar to the concept of near transfer, which was introduced in Chapter 8. Students who have attained this level can use the principles and rules acquired during instruction to solve problems and answer questions that they have not encountered before but that are similar in some sense to those encountered during instruction.

As originally formulated, Bloom's application level would not include the ability to perform transfer activities as they were described in Chapter 8. However, extending Bloom's system to encompass far transfer involves only a minor adjustment of his original taxonomy, and teachers who are concerned about both near transfer and far transfer should definitely write application questions at both levels.

Analysis (Level IV)

analysis the
fourth level of
knowledge, ac-
cording to
Bloom, charac-
terized by the
ability to break
a communica-
tion into its
constituent
parts

According to Bloom, *analysis* entails the ability to break a communication into its constituent parts so that the separate parts can be analyzed independently. This is the first level in Bloom's system that involves what one might think of as a truly "higher-order" intellectual skill. Breaking complex events and phenomena into smaller components is an essential part of understanding them, and it clearly involves a student's reasoning and thinking abilities.

In Bloom's taxonomy, analysis could occur at several levels. It could occur at the level of *elements*, which would involve breaking a complex event into its divisible parts, thereby allowing one to understand the event more clearly.

It could occur at the level of *relationships*, which would involve isolating how the elements in a complex event relate to one another. Or it could occur at the level of *organizational principles*, which would entail an analysis of the overall principles governing a complex event. As an example of these three levels, to understand how the human body functions one would need to study the individual organs (the elements), the manner in which those organs interact with one another (the relationships), and the principles governing the overall functioning of the body (the organizational principles).

Synthesis (Level V)

The previous level involved breaking down an event to study its parts. *Synthesis involves putting elements together to create something new or unique.* One example of the process of synthesis is quality writing. Writing a business letter, a report, a story, or a book involves putting various elements together in a manner that clearly communicates the writer's intent to the reader. When this process is done well, the writer has truly created something unique.

synthesis the fifth level of knowledge, according to Bloom, characterized by putting elements together to create something new or unique

Synthesis should be understood as the creation of something that for a given person is unique. This means that if a student puts several different elements together in a manner new to him or her in order to solve a problem, the student is demonstrating the ability to synthesize—even though the approach he or she has hit upon happens to be the standard approach to solving the problem.

The teacher who is interested in writing test items at the synthesis level can create questions at varying levels of difficulty. The most difficult would be those where students are given minimal help in constructing their answers. For example, students in a biology class might be asked to write an essay entitled "how the human body functions." At a somewhat easier level would be the assignment to write an essay on how the human body functions, keeping in mind the operations of, and the interactions between, the major bodily systems (e.g., cardiovascular, digestive, nervous, masculature, etc.).

Evaluation (Level VI)

The final level in Bloom's taxonomy is the evaluation level. *Evaluation* is the process of making informed judgments about events. Informed judgments are judgments made in accordance with either internal or external criteria. As an instance of evaluating in terms of some internal criterion, imagine asking a group of students to evaluate an argument favoring capital punishment in terms of the logical consistency of the argument. The rules of logical consistency in this example provide a means whereby the overall quality of the argument can be evaluated.

evaluation the sixth level of knowledge, according to Bloom, characterized by making informed judgments about events

Evaluating via external criteria involves assessing a creative product in terms of the highest known standards in a field. Judging, for example, whether a new playwright has attained the stature of a well-known elder, or whether a new band has attained the creative standard set by the Beatles, are examples of the use of external criteria.

Evaluations, by their nature, are not going to command universal agreement. Quite frequently a student's evaluation of a given event is going to differ from that reached by a teacher. For this reason, it is important to examine an evaluation in terms of the criteria and the process that produced it. It is entirely possible to admire the process leading up to an evaluation without agreeing with the conclusion.

LAYING OUT THE BLUEPRINT FOR THE TEST

After a teacher has made some general decisions about the level of knowledge to be assessed by a test, the next step is to develop a "blueprint" that will guide the construction of the test. This blueprint specifies the areas being assessed, the extent of coverage to be given to each area, and the level of knowledge being assessed.

Tables of Specification

table of specification   a blueprint used in test development to specify content, knowledge levels to be assessed, type of test item, and relative emphasis to be given each topic

One of the most common ways of developing a blueprint for a test is to construct a table of specifications. A *table of specifications* describes features of the to-be-constructed test—such as the content or skills to be assessed, the knowledge levels to be assessed, the type of test items to be constructed, and the relative emphasis to be given to each topic. Several different forms of tables of specification are described below, but they are presented purely for the purpose of illustration. Every teacher-designed test is different, and every test should have its own unique table of specifications.

Tables containing only two dimensions

The simplest kind of table of specifications is one that contains only two features, as in Table 16-1, which describes two types of items that are to be

Table 16-1   Table of Specifications Containing a Type of Problem Dimension and an Arithmetic-Skills Dimension

| | Arithmetic Skills | | | |
Type of Problem	Adding Fractions	Subtracting Fractions	Multiplying Fractions	Total
Number problems	15%(4)	20%(5)	40%(10)	75%(19)
Word problems	10%(3)	10%(3)	5%(1)	25%(7)
	25%(7)	30%(8)	45%(11)	100%(26)

Table 16-2   Table of Specifications Containing a Content Dimension and a Knowledge-Level Dimension

Content Areas	Knowledge Level of Items			
	Knowledge	Comprehension	Application	Total
Identification of compounds	10%(5)	15%(8)	15%(8)	40%(21)
Identification of elements	10%(5)	15%(8)	10%(5)	35%(18)
Identification of mixtures	10%(5)	10%(5)	5%(3)	25%(13)
	30%(15)	40%(21)	30%(16)	100%(52)

used to assess the several different arithmetic skills. The first number in the table refers to the percentage of emphasis to be given to each skill and question type. The second number (in parentheses) is the actual number of items to be constructed. This number was generated by assuming that the teacher wanted a test of about 25 items then multiplying the percentage by the total number of items and rounding off the result (e.g., $15\% \times 25 = 3.75 = 4$).

The table of specifications contained in Table 16-1 lists several content areas and two types of problems for assessing knowledge in those content areas. A table of this kind makes sense if all of the questions are to be written at the same knowledge level (e.g., the comprehension level). A somewhat different table would be called for if the teacher wanted to write questions at several different knowledge levels. Table 16-2 contains a table in which each content area is assessed at several knowledge levels. The number of items in the table is based on the assumption that the teacher wants a test containing approximately 50 items.

Tables containing more than two dimensions

On occasion a teacher might want to develop a table of specifications containing more than two dimensions. Table 16-3 contains a table of specifications, for a psychology of learning course, that contains three dimensions.

To this point, what we have done is outline the procedure for describing the content to be assessed by a test, and for deciding the number and type of questions to be written to assess the content. This procedure should not be confused with the *grading* of a test. For example, the teacher who constructs a test from the table of specifications presented in Table 16-3 may decide that application questions should be weighted more heavily than knowledge and comprehension questions, and that short-answer questions should be weighted more heavily than multiple-choice and true-false questions. Given these decisions, the teacher could grade the questions in such a way that heavily weighted questions count for twice as much as do weighted questions.

Table 16-3   Table of Specifications Consisting of Knowledge-Level, Content-Area, and Question-Type Dimensions

| Content Question | | Knowledge Level | | | |
Area	Type	Knowl-edge	Compre-hension	Appli-cation	Total
History of learning	Multiple-choice	2%	4%	10%	16%
	True-false	0	2	0	
	Short-answer	2	2	2	2
					6
					24%
Learning theories	Multiple-choice	2	5	8	15
	True-false	2	3	0	5
	Short-answer	4	0	0	4
					24%
Classical conditioning	Multiple-choice	2	8	10	20
	True-false	2	0	0	2
	Short-answer	4	0	0	4
					26%
Operant Conditioning	Multiple-choice	2	4	10	16
	True-false	2	4	0	6
	Short-answer	2	2	0	4
					26%
		26%	34%	40%	100%

CONSTRUCTING TEST ITEMS

This section describes how to construct test items. The first part describes how to write objective test items; the second, how to write essay test items.

Objective Test Items: Simple Forms

objective test items   test items that can be scored without subjective evaluations of performance

Objective test items derive their name from the fact that judgment does not enter into the scoring process. Students either get the item right or they get it wrong. There is no such thing as being "partially" right or wrong. Moreover, it is immediately obvious if the answer is correct or incorrect.

Simple-form objective test items include short-answer questions, true-false questions, and matching questions. These question types are called simple-form because the information they test is generally at the knowledge level (Level I) of Bloom's taxonomy.

short-answer item   a test item requiring only a word, phrase, number, or symbol in response to a question or a blank to be filled in

Short-answer items

Short-answer questions require the learner to supply a word, a phrase, a number, or a symbol in response to a question or a blank to be filled in.

Table 16-4   Sample Short-Answer Items

Knowledge of Terminology
Lines on a weather map which join points of the same barometric pressure are called
(isobars).
Knowledge of Facts
A member of the United States Senate is elected to a term of (6) years.
Knowledge of Principles
If the temperature of a gas is held constant while the pressure applied to it is increased,
what will happen to its volume? (It will decrease.)
Knowledge of Method or Procedure
What device is used to detect whether an electric charge is positive or negative?
(electroscope)
Simple Interpretations of Data
How many syllables are there in the word Argentina? (4)
If an airplane flying northeast made a 180 degree turn, what direction would it be
heading? (southwest)
Ability to Solve Numerical Problems
Milk sells for $.26 a quart and $.88 a gallon. How many cents would you save on each
quart of milk if you bought it by the gallon? (4)
Skill in Manipulating Mathematical Symbols
If $\frac{X}{6} = \frac{4}{9-1}$, then $X =$ (3)
Ability to Complete and Balance Chemical Equations
_____ Mg + (2)HCL → (MgCl$_2$ + H$_2$)

(Gronlund 1977, pp. 150–151)

Examples of short-answer questions that illustrate a variety of uses are presented
in Table 16-4.

The last three examples in Table 16-4 represent exceptions to the general
rule that short-answer questions can measure only relatively simple learning
outcomes. As these examples illustrate, short-answer questions testing mathematical and scientific content can often test higher-level information.

Suggestions for Constructing Short-Answer Items.   Gronlund (1977) has
developed the following set of rules for constructing short-answer items:

> 1. *The item should be worded so that the required answer is both
>   brief and definite.* Answers that are longer than a simple phrase
>   can sometimes produce problems. Hence it is a good idea to restrict
>   answers to a word, phrase, number, or symbol. Answers should
>   also be definite. This means that there should not be more than
>   one plausible answer to a question. Teachers should ask themselves
>   whether there are any other plausible answers that might fit in the
>   blank. If so, the item should be changed so that all other answers
>   become implausible.

2. *Direct statements from textbooks should not serve as the basis for short-answer items.* Statements frequently have a different meaning in the content of a textbook discussion than they do if taken out of context. For instance, in a textbook discussion of the human brain one might encounter a statement such as, "The human cerebral cortex contains ten thousand million neurons." In context this is a perfectly sensible and informative statement. But note what happens if the statement is made into a short-answer item,

The human cerebral cortex contains _____."

This question is hopelessly indefinite. It could be fixed, though, by changing it to read,

How many neurons are there in the human cerebral cortex? _____

3. *A direct question is generally more desirable than an incomplete statement.* The basis for this rule is that one is generally more specific when asking direct questions than when constructing items containing a blank to be filled in. As an example, consider the following two items:

Animals that are warm-blooded, bear their young alive, and suckle their young are called _____.

What do we call the class of animals that are warm-blooded, bear their young alive, and suckle their young? _____

The first question could be answered with any number of responses—such as "dogs," "cats," "humans," etc. In contrast, the second question is much more specific. There is no inherent reason that completion items cannot be made as definite as direct questions. However, it is generally the case that more care is taken when specific questions are formulated than when completion items are formulated.

4. *When the answer is to be expressed in numerical units, indicate the type of answer wanted.* This rule is most applicable to the situation where a unit of measure is the desired answer. As an example, consider the following question:

If a town were 10 kilometers away, how far away would it be? _____(miles)

By specifying the desired unit for the answer, teachers protect themselves from the smart-aleck student who fills in the blank with "394,000 inches" (a correct answer).

5. *Blanks for answers should be of equal length and in a column to the right of questions.* The reason for keeping the lengths of the blanks equal is probably apparent. If allowed to vary, they become clues as to the length of the desired answer. The reason for placing the answers in a column to the right of questions is purely pragmatic. It makes the answers easier to score.

Advantages and Disadvantages of Short-Answer Items.   Short-answer items have two major advantages. The first is that the items are easy to construct. With a fair amount of attention to possible pitfalls, virtually any teacher can construct a first-class set of short-answer items in a brief period of time. The second advantage to short-answer items is that students have to *supply* the answers to the items. Other kinds of test items provide the opportunity for the student to get the answer correct by guessing, and the likelihood of being correct by guessing is considerably lessened when students have to generate the answer themselves.

The major limitation of short-answer items is their inability to measure complex learning outcomes. The exceptions to this rule, as mentioned earlier, are in the areas of mathematics and science, where it is possible to construct items that require the learner to do more than merely recall memorized facts and terms. Another, lesser problem is in the scoring of items. As careful as one may be in constructing short-answer items, there always seem to be one or two students who come up with plausible answers other than the one intended. For example, in response to the question about the class of animals that are warm-blooded, bear their young alive, and suckle their young, a student might respond, "placentals." Now placentals are a major subclass of the class mammals, so the answer is not entirely wrong. But it is not entirely right either, and this presents some difficulties in scoring.

The ability to construct quality tests should be a skill every teacher has. (© Elizabeth Crews)

True-false items

There are probably few readers of this book who are not familiar with true-false questions, but there are several variations of this general form of question that readers may not be familiar with. Since not all of these types of questions employ the terms "true" and "false," some authors have used the more general description "*alternative-selection items*" (Payne, 1968), or "*alternative-response items*" (Gronlund, 1977).

The general form of alternative-selection items consists of a declarative statement that the student is asked to mark with one of two response options. The options can be true or false, right or wrong, correct or incorrect, fact or opinion, agree or disagree, or any other two-choice alternative that is appropriate (see Table 16-5 for examples).

alternative-selection item a test item consisting of a declarative statement that the student is asked to mark with one or two response options

Suggestions for Constructing True-False Items.
Gronlund (1977) has provided the following suggestions for writing true-false items:

1. *Avoid broad general statements if they are to be judged true or false.* The problem with broad general statements is that one can usually find an exception to them. For example, the statement "United States senators are elected to a 6-year term of office" is true enough, but senators are not *always* elected, nor is the term *always* 6 years. Exceptions to both of these generalizations occur upon the death or resignation of a senator.
2. *Avoid trivial statements.* The problem opposite to that of making statements too broad and general, is to make trivial statements. Trivial statements can occur when attempting to develop statements that are *always* true or false. For example, the statement "George

Table 16-5   Sample Alternative-Selection Items

True	False	The green coloring material in a plant leaf is called chlorophyll.
<u>Yes</u>	No	Is 51% of 38 more than 19?
Fact	<u>Opinion</u>	The first amendment to the Constitution of the United States is the most important amendment.
Yes	<u>No</u>	Leaves are essential BECAUSE they shade the parts of a trunk of the tree.

The next example asks the student to judge a statement as true or false, and also to judge if the converse of the statement is true or false.

True	False	Converse True Converse <u>False</u> All trees are plants.

The next example asks the student to judge whether a statement is true or false, and if false, to change the underlined word to make it true.

True	<u>False</u>	(<u>electrons</u>) Particles of negative electricity are called <u>neutrons</u>.

Washington is called the father of our country" is unequivocally true, but it is not a very important item of information to test for.

3. *Avoid the use of negative statements and especially double negatives.* Students sometimes overlook the negative words in a negative statement and thereby get an answer wrong that they should have gotten right. If negative words are used, the negative words should be underlined to draw attention to them. Double negatives should be avoided because they are very difficult to understand. Consider the statement "No mammal can survive unless it has food" as compared to "Mammals require food to survive."

4. *Avoid long, complex sentences.* The problem with using long complex sentences as true-false items is that they tend to measure reading comprehension and memory as much as they do the knowledge one is trying to test. Compare the following items:

    I. The central assumption in Piagetian theory is that children pass through increasingly complex developmental stages that begin with an infant's acquisition of sensorimotor skills, move to a young child's acquisition of concepts like quantity, then progress to an adolescent's ability to think concretely, and finally end up with an adult's ability to think abstractly about the world around him.

    II. Piaget's theory indicates that a newborn infant passes through four increasingly complex developmental stages on the way to adulthood.

Item II tests approximately the same information as item I and is much easier to follow.

5. *Avoid including two ideas in one statement, unless cause-effect relations are being measured.* The difficulty with true-false items containing more than one idea is that the teacher cannot be sure about the basis the students will use to make their responses. Moreover, it is entirely possible to get an item correct using erroneous information. Look at the following items:

    I. Planaria cannot learn because they do not have a central nervous system.

    II. Trees can manufacture food because they have an extensive root system.

Planaria are primitive worms that can, in fact, learn. Moreover, they *do* have a central nervous system. So item I is false because both main ideas are false. On the other hand, item II illustrates that it is possible to construct an item in which both ideas are true but the relationship is false. The problem with the above items is that three things are being measured: the truth or falsity of the two ideas, and the truth or falsity of the relationship between them. With all of this complexity, it is entirely possible that someone could get an item correct for the wrong reason. A student might, for example, mark item II false because he believes that trees can't manufacture food.

6. *If opinion is used, attribute it to some source, unless the ability to identify opinion is being measured.* Students can rightly be expected to judge the truth or falsity of fact, but it is unfair to expect them to judge opinion. Examine the following items:

    I. The United States' involvement in the war in Vietnam was a serious mistake.

    II. Many liberal politicians believe that the United States' involvement in the war in Vietnam was a serious mistake.

There is really no basis for judging whether item I is true or false. However, item II might test a legitimate learning outcome.

7. *Make true statements and false statements approximately equal in length.* Many teachers inadvertently write longer true statements than false statements. This happens because true statements frequently contain qualifiers (e.g., "most of the time," "frequently," etc.) necessary to satisfy truth conditions and because true statements have to be worded very precisely. The differing length problem can be avoided by adding qualifiers to false statements and by being careful to word them as precisely as true statements are worded.

8. *Make the number of true statements and false statements approximately equal.* The most important reason for this recommendation is fairly obvious; it prevents the test-wise student from "psyching out" the test. Another reason, however, is that students display differing response biases when they are not certain of an answer. That is, some students respond "true" most of the time when they don't know the answer, and others respond "false" most of the time. If the number of true and false items are approximately balanced, neither "true"-biased nor "false"-biased students will be penalized. Incidentally, it is not a good idea always to have *exactly* the same number of true and false items. The student who figures out that there are an equal number of true and false items can use this information as a clue as to how to respond.

Advantages and Disadvantages of True-False Items.   Two advantages are commonly attributed to true-false items. The first is that tests consisting of true-false items are easy to construct. The second is that a wide sampling of course material can be efficiently assessed using the technique (Ebel, 1972; Gronlund, 1977). These advantages may not hold, however. Gronlund (1977), for example, indicates that although construction of bad true-false tests is easy, the construction of good true-false tests may be as time consuming as is the construction of other types of tests. Good true-false tests require careful and painstaking construction. True statements should be obviously true, and false statements should be plausible but false. Teachers who construct their tests by taking statements from a text and changing about half of them to make

Table 16-6   Sample Matching Exercise

Directions: On the line to the left of each description, write the letter beside a President's name that best fits the description. Each President may be used once, more than once, or not at all.

Description	President
_____ 1. President when World War II started.	a. J. Adams
_____ 2. Second President of the United States.	b. A. Jackson
_____ 3. President who abolished slavery.	c. T. Jefferson
_____ 4. President who wrote the Declaration of Independence.	d. F. D. Roosevelt
	e. H. Truman
_____ 5. President whose nickname was "Old Hickory."	f. G. Washington
_____ 6. President whose son also became President of the United States.	g. W. Wilson
	h. A. Lincoln

them false may find test construction easy, but the resultant test will leave a lot to be desired as a measuring instrument.

One disadvantage of true-false items is that some content is not reducible to factual statements. This is particularly true of higher-level conceptual knowledge in some content areas. A second disadvantage is that true-false items are most amenable to the assessment of knowledge-level information. Constructing true-false tests to measure higher-order knowledge is difficult, but it can be done.

Matching items

Most matching exercises consist of two parallel columns of words, symbols, or phrases. The student's task is to match the items in one column with items in the second column.

Table 16-6 illustrates several characteristics of a good matching exercise. First, there are more Presidents listed than there are descriptions. Second, each President can be used (and in one case is used) with more than one description. Both of these features reduce the likelihood of guessing a correct match.

Constructing Matching Items.   The following are some suggested guidelines for developing good matching items (Gronlund, 1977):

1. *Use only homogeneous material in a single matching exercise.* Mixing material from several areas leads to confusion in matching exercises. For instance, imagine that Table 16-6 contained descriptions and names of *famous Americans* ranging from George Washington to Will Rogers to John Wayne to Lee Oswald. Writing descriptions that apply uniquely to each member in such a variable list is more difficult than if one is working with a homogeneous list. Moreover, considerable variety in a matching list suggests a lack of clarity about what one is trying to measure.

2. *Include an unequal number of responses and premises, and instruct students that responses may be used once, more than once, or not at all.* The purpose of this recommendation is to reduce the chances of the student getting a match correct through a process of elimination. With an equal number of descriptions and responses, and with each response being used only once, a student's chances of guessing a correct match by selecting from the items remaining after answering those he or she knows are greatly increased. By presenting more responses than descriptions, and by allowing the possibility that a response may be used more than once, teachers are more likely to avoid this problem.

3. *Keep the list of items to be matched brief, and place the shorter responses on the right.* Long matching exercises are very time consuming and tedious, particularly when responses can be used more than once. Imagine, for example, a matching exercise consisting of twenty descriptions and twenty-five responses. The student would have to scan the entire list of responses for each description. This kind of task would be unduly demanding. If a teacher needed to assess this many descriptions, he or she would do better to separate them into two exercises.

   Placing all of the responses on the right side of the page makes it more convenient for the student, since he or she can read a description and then quickly scan the entire list of responses for the correct match.

4. *Arrange the list of responses in logical order.* This is a recommendation designed to make test taking easier for the student. If the responses are a list of terms or names, arranging them in alphabetical order can ease the task for the student. This allows students who think they know an answer to go directly to the place in the list where it should be. If the responses are numbers or dates, placing them in numerical order has the same advantage.

5. *Indicate in the directions the basis for matching the responses and descriptions.* The basis for most matching exercises is apparent after reading through the descriptions and responses. However, the teacher can save the student some time by stating the basis for matching, rather than making the student reason it out for himself or herself.

6. *Place all of the items for a matching exercise on the same page.* Having to flip back and forth between pages when completing a matching exercise makes things unnecessarily difficult for the student. Placing all of the descriptions and responses on the same page makes for easy and efficient test taking.

Advantages and Disadvantages of Matching Items.   Matching exercises are fairly easy to construct, although as with true-false items, it is much easier to construct bad items than good ones. Another advantage is that a large amount of information can be assessed quickly and efficiently. Care must be taken here, however, not to try to test too much information with a single exercise. It is easy to fall into the trap of including too many items in a single exercise or trying to test several areas at once, thereby disrupting the homogeneity of the exercise.

The disadvantages of matching items is the same as for all simple-form test items: it is difficult to assess learning outcomes above the knowledge level.

Objective Test Items: Multiple-Choice Forms

The simple-form objective test items considered thus far suffer from the common limitation that they can (in general) measure learning outcomes only at the knowledge level. In this section, guidelines are discussed for writing multiple-choice items that can be used to assess learning outcomes at levels of complexity above the knowledge level.

A multiple-choice item consists of an item stem and several alternative responses. The stem can be one of two types: a direct question that can be answered from the set of response alternatives or an incomplete statement that can be completed from the response set. Multiple-choice item forms are by far the most flexible of the objective item forms. They can easily assess learning at the knowledge, comprehension, and application levels, and with some ingenuity they can be written to assess knowledge at the analysis and synthesis levels. Examples of items testing learning at several of these levels are presented in Table 16-7. In examining the items, however, you should remember that the level of learning assessed by an item is definable only in the context of the instruction a student has received. For example, the first item in the "Application Level" section of the table appears virtually identical in form to knowledge-level items. However, the item is at the application level if the student has not encountered the material in the item during instruction.

As is evident from Table 16-7, multiple-choice items can be written to assess learning at many levels. However, the effort involved in producing good items increases as the level of learning increases. Producing good knowledge-level items is easy relative to the effort required to produce good synthesis-level items.

Writing multiple-choice items

The following are some suggestions for writing good multiple-choice items (Gronlund, 1977; Payne, 1968):

1. *Stems that ask a direct question are preferable to stems that are incomplete statements.* This is not a hard-and-fast rule because clearly there are a great many excellent incomplete stem items.

However, there is a tendency to state direct questions more precisely than incomplete statements, and this is the reason for direct questions being preferable.

2. *Stems should specify a singular problem, and they should be stated in a clear and explicit manner.* Compare the following items:

    I. Theodore Roosevelt was
- a. the inventor of one of the first machine guns.
- b. the writer of several best-selling novels.
- c. a winner of the Nobel peace prize.
- d. a very talented and respected painter.

    II. In addition to his accomplishments as a politician, Theodore Roosevelt achieved recognition in which of the following ways?
- a. He invented one of the first machine guns.
- b. He wrote several best-selling novels.
- c. He won the Nobel peace prize.
- d. He was a very talented and respected painter.

The problem with item I is that the item stem does not narrow down the very large number of potential response areas. The students themselves must do the narrowing. By contrast, item II narrows the response possibilities in a way that allows students to begin searching memory *before* examining the response set.

3. *An item stem should be restricted in content to the specific material being assessed. Irrelevant material should be excluded.* There is no point in including information in an item stem that is incidental to the question being asked. Doing so simply adds to reading time and increases the chance that the item will be misunderstood.

Table 16-7   Sample Multiple-Choice Questions Testing Learning at Various Levels

Knowledge-Level Items
Which of the following parts of the eye is the name for the structure that contains the visual receptors and several layers of neurons that conduct impulses to the brain?

- a. Lens
- b. Iris
- c. Retina
- d. Cornea

Which American general accepted the surrender of the Japanese at the end of World War II?

- a. Eisenhower
- b. Patton
- c. MacArthur
- d. Marshall

What is the name of the largest city in the United States?

a. Los Angeles
b. Chicago
c. New York
d. Cleveland

Comprehension-Level Items

Another way to describe learning is as a process whereby

a. a given stimulus always elicits a particular behavior.
b. behavior undergoes a change as a result of reinforcement.
c. behavior undergoes a relatively permanent change as a function of experience.
d. events occurring in the environment are perceived and acted on.

Severe psychopathology is characterized by which of the following states?

a. Extreme attacks of anxiety and fear that occur at a predictable point in a cycle.
b. A stiffening of the limbs and joints accompanied by an inability to interact with other people.
c. A distortion of reality accompanied by an inability to cope with the surrounding world.
d. Hearing noises that threaten the individual or his or her family with bodily harm.

Application-Level Items

Which of the following things is *alive*?

a. a rock
b. a river
c. a tree
d. a teddy bear

If it were possible to devise a cheap way to split water into its constituent elements, this would be an enormously important energy development because

a. the carbon that would be separated from the water is an excellent fuel.
b. the oxygen that would be separated from the water could be used to burn fuel more efficiently.
c. the hydrogen that would be separated from the water is an excellent fuel.
d. the hydrogen-dioxide that would be released by the separation process is an excellent fuel.

Analysis-Level Items

Living organisms, large businesses, and countries are systems that all share which of the following features?

a. hierarchical structuring, one-way communication channels, specialization of function.
b. input-output functions, interlocking structural units, internal defense systems.
c. elemental units, hierarchical structuring, interdependence of structural units.
d. internal defense systems, elemental units, interlocking structural units.

If you had two fruits, three vegetables, and one starch in a bag, which of the following items would your bag contain?

a. one apple, two carrots, two potatoes, and one orange.
b. one pear, one apple, one potato, two oranges, and one carrot.
c. two ears of corn, one carrot, one potato, one orange, and one pear.
d. one pear, two ears of corn, two carrots, and one potato.

Compare the following items:

   I. Alaska, which was one of the last two states to join the union, also is
     a. the largest agricultural state.
     b. the largest meat-producing state.
     c. the largest state in land area.
     d. the largest state in population.

   II. Alaska has which of the following characteristics?
     a. It produces more agricultural products than any other state.
     b. It produces more meat products than any other state.
     c. It is the largest state in terms of land area.
     d. It is the largest state in terms of population.

The information in item I about when Alaska joined the union is totally irrelevant to the information being assessed. Item II is much more direct. One might argue, however, that the additional content serves to provide a hint to the student who has difficulty identifying the material being tested. If this is the purpose of the superfluous content, it should be done much more directly. For example, the item stem might read, "The state of Alaska has which of the following characteristics?"

4. *Negatively stated items should be used very infrequently.* Students sometimes overlook the "not," "no," "least," etc., that characterize negatively stated items. Moreover, most negatively stated items test relatively insignificant learning outcomes. By and large, teachers are not primarily interested in whether students know the *least important* means of doing something, or which of several items *do not* belong to a particular category. Instead, they are interested in determining if students know the *most important* means or the things that *do* belong to a category. Almost all multiple-choice items can be stated in the more desirable positive form.

5. *Items written at the application, analysis, and synthesis levels should contain terms familiar to the students.* By definition, items written at the application level and above are novel to the student. However, the novelty should reside in a new application, a new analysis, or synthesis of material. It *should not* reside in new elements of the problem. For instance, it is perfectly fair to take a principle that the student has just learned and ask which of several familiar instances represents a previously unencountered example of the principle. However, it is unreasonable to ask a student to select the correct application of a principle from a set of instances that are completely unfamiliar to him or her. Likewise, it is unfair to ask a student to analyze a statement containing largely unfamiliar elements or to engage in an act of synthesis when he or she knows little about the components of the task.

Items written at the application level and above ideally require the student to view familiar material from a novel perspective. Answering them correctly requires that the student make a creative response to the problem. And constructing the items requires a creative act on the part of the teacher.

6. *All of the distractors should be plausible.* The purpose of a multiple-choice item is to assess student learning, not to assess test-taking skill. When an item includes one or more implausible distractors test-wise students can alter their guessing strategy so that even when they know nothing about the information being tested, their scores would make it appear that they have learned something. Consider the following item as an example:

I. Leon Czologosz achieved recognition in which of the following ways?
   a. He was the first man to fly an airplane nonstop across the United States.
   b. He was the fourteenth President of the United States.
   c. He was the man who assassinated President William McKinley.
   d. He made the first discovery of gold in Alaska that lead to the Alaskan gold rush.

Even students who don't have the faintest idea who Leon Czologosz is should be able to eliminate alternative (b) and thereby improve their guessing to above chance levels.

7. *Distractors should be of the same approximate length.* Many teachers tend to write correct alternatives that are longer than incorrect alternatives. The student who detects this pattern can greatly improve his or her performance above where it should be. If a teacher finds it very difficult to write distractors of approximately the same length, the next best thing is to vary the length of the distractors in an unsystematic way. In other words, some of the time one or two of the distractors are shorter or longer than the others, but this pattern has no relation to the correctness of the distractor.

8. *Response alternatives such as "none of the above" or "all of the above" should be used with caution.* The basic problem with using "none of the above" or "all of the above" as response alternatives is that students can get the item correct with only partial knowledge. Examine the following item:

I. Which of the animals listed below is a member of the *canine* family?
   a. Dog
   b. Fox
   c. Wolf
   d. All of the above

The student who knows that two of the animals in the above list are canines automatically knows that the correct answer is (d). Thus an item supposedly designed to make a student pay attention to all of the items can be answered on the basis of examining only two of them. The following format is a better alternative:

I. Which of the animals below is a member of the *canine* family?

Yes   No   Dog
Yes   No   Fox
Yes   No   Wolf
Yes   *No*   Bear

By converting the item to a yes-no response format, one requires that the student make a judgment about each of the distractors. "None of the above" items can be transformed into the same kind of format by including a negative in the item stem.

9. *The position of the correct alternative should vary.* Overuse of one or two of the available distractor positions for the correct answer can serve as a distinctive cue to the observant student. This is a recommendation that has been systematically violated in this chapter. The correct answer to all of the multiple-choice example items except the last one is in the third position. Did you notice?

Advantages and Disadvantages of Multiple-Choice Items.

By now the advantages of multiple-choice items should be obvious. With careful construction, learning outcomes at almost all of Bloom's levels can be assessed in a straightforward and objective manner. A second advantage of multiple-choice items, in comparison to simple-form objective items such as true-false or short-answer, is that the pattern of responding can sometimes tell the teacher something about misconceptions students have. That is, if teachers choose their distractors carefully, they can use the *errors* the students make to determine where to improve their teaching. For example, if the majority of students who make an error make the same error, that may tell teachers that they need to devote more time during instruction to distinguishing between the content contained in the error and the content contained in the correct alternative.

The primary limitation of multiple-choice items is that they restrict the assessment of learning outcomes to carefully specified situations. Sometimes teachers want to know whether a student can marshal and organize facts in support of a particular point of view. They cannot determine this outcome with a multiple-choice item (or with any objective item) because all of the elements relevant to solving a problem or answering a question are presented to the student in the item.

A similar limitation is that teachers cannot detect truly creative performance with multiple-choice items. Multiple-choice items contain the elements that the test constructor thinks are relevant to the knowledge being assessed. By

Essay tests are particularly useful for measuring high-level learning outcomes. (EKM-Nepenthe)

providing students with those elements the teacher cannot detect the student who can make a truly creative contribution to a request for demonstration of the mastery of a particular learning outcome.

Essay Tests

Essay tests can measure some of the learning outcomes that cannot be measured with an objectively scored test. One can, for example, examine the degree to which a student can organize information into a coherent framework supporting a point of view. One can also, on occasion, recognize the student who puts things together in a unique and creative manner. Finally, one can measure high-level learning outcomes, such as evaluation and synthesis, which are very difficult to measure with objectively scored tests.

The positive features of essay tests are not acquired without cost. As is indicated later, essay tests have a number of disadvantages, particularly those related to the scoring of the tests. But before considering the advantages and disadvantages of essay tests in greater detail, we need to define more clearly what an essay test is and how essay items are written. We begin by defining the two basic types of essay items: extended-response questions and restricted-response questions.

Extended-response essay questions

extended-re-sponse ques-tion an essay question in which the stu-dent has vir-tually unlim-ited freedom in formulating the answer to a question

The extended-response essay question gives the student virtually unlimited freedom in formulating the answer to a question (Mehrens and Lehman, 1975; Popham, 1981). Consider the following question:

> Describe what you think are the most important factors in quality education. Your answer should be about 300–400 words long (2–3 pages).

In answering this question, students can select those aspects that they think are most important to quality education, they can organize the factors in any manner they choose, and they have complete freedom in expressing the answer.

Extended-response essay questions are ideally suited for measuring learning outcomes at the synthesis and evaluation levels. They allow for the creative integration of ideas, the selection of pertinent details, and the expression of an approach to problem solving. These are obviously important learning outcomes that cannot be measured with any other type of test item (Gronlund, 1977).

The primary problem with extended-response essay questions is that they are difficult to score. The nature of the question ensures that every student will choose a different set of features and a different manner of organizing those features into a coherent answer. This makes it very difficult to score the answers in a fair and reliable manner. Later in this section, we will consider recommendations to maximize the reliability of scoring.

Restricted-response essay questions

restricted-re-sponse ques-tion an essay question that limits the pos-sible answers by placing re-strictions on the form of the answer

A restricted-response essay question limits the possible answers by placing restrictions on the form of the answer. Consider the following question:

> Good teacher education has been suggested as one of the most important factors in quality education. Select three features that you think a good teacher education program should have. Your answer should be limited to 150 words in length (1½ pages).

As you can see, this question is similar to the previous example; but it gives the student the particular factor to write about, and it indicates the number of features that are to be discussed.

Restricted-response questions have the advantage of being easier to write than extended-response questions (Gronlund, 1977), and they can be scored with greater reliability (Gronlund, 1977; Mehrens and Lehman, 1975). Their primary disadvantage is that by restricting the possible responses to a question, they also restrict the possibility of measuring a student's ability to draw together and evaluate diverse bits of knowledge.

Writing essay questions

As was the case with objective item forms, a number of authors have provided guidelines for writing essay questions (*e.g.*, Gronlund, 1977; Mehrens and Lehman, 1975; Popham, 1981). The following are some of their suggestions:

1. *Use essay tests only when the intent is to measure complex learning outcomes.* Essay questions should not be used to determine if a student knows a fact, comprehends a rule, or can apply a principle. These are learning outcomes that can be measured perfectly adequately with objective items. Essay items should only be used to measure more complex outcomes.

2. *Decide on the learning outcome that you want to measure, and then write the question to measure that outcome.* Tables of specification are as important with essay questions as they are with objective questions. If before writing the questions a teacher decides what he or she wants to measure, the questions are going to be more sharply focused and easier to score than they would otherwise be.

3. *Phrase questions so that the student's task is clear.* When students read an essay question, they should know with certainty what they are supposed to do. Teachers can check on the clarity of their essay questions by preparing model answers and by asking knowledgeable colleagues about how they would answer the question.

4. *Use several questions requiring relatively short answers, rather than one or two questions requiring long answers.* There are two reasons for this suggestion. The first is that using several short questions allows a teacher to sample a larger amount of material than would be possible with one or two longer questions. This is one way of reducing the content validity problem that Professor Helmstadter talked about in the interview. The second reason is that short-answer questions are easier to score reliably than are long-answer questions.

5. *Do not use optional questions.* Optional questions present several problems. First, different students will answer different questions, and this eliminates the opportunity for truly comparative evaluation. Second, students will naturally select the questions that they feel most knowledgeable about. This allows the possibility that students could be totally ignorant of a good portion of the content being assessed, yet still get an excellent grade because they have avoided their weakest areas.

6. *Develop a scoring system.* A scoring system could involve writing a model answer and assigning scores according to a standard, or it could involve developing a scoring key that assigns points for inclusion of elements in the answer. In either case, the scoring system should be developed before the test is administered. Developing the scoring system beforehand improves scoring reliability for the test.

Scoring essay questions

Essay questions can be scored using either an *analytic* or a *holistic* approach (Mehrens and Lehman, 1975; Popham, 1981). The analytic approach typically involves developing a model answer and then breaking the answer down into specific points. Other attributes of the answer such as organization, quality of expression, and clarity of writing can also be assigned points. A student's score is then based on the number of points contained in the answer.

Holistic scoring, as the name implies, involves rendering a judgment about the essay as a whole. These judgments should be made with "standards" or "anchor points" in mind. For example, a teacher could either prepare or select answers that were excellent, average, and poor in quality. Subsequent answers could then be compared to these anchor points and assigned a score based on the closest fit.

In addition to attending to the general methods of scoring essays, teachers should also follow specific guidelines when scoring:

1. *Score all of the students' answers to one question before scoring answers to the next question.* The problem with scoring a student's entire exam at once is that the quality of the answer to one question can influence the scorer's evaluation of the next answer. A student who does very well or very poorly on one question may be unfairly rewarded or penalized on the next. Scoring all the answers to one question before starting on answers to the next question reduces this sort of carryover.

2. *Score the answers without knowing the identity of the writer.* Even the most careful teachers can be influenced by their personal attitudes toward a student. Hiding the identity of the writer reduces the likelihood that the teacher's biases can affect a student's score.

3. *If possible, have at least two people score each answer.* This guideline is basically a check on the reliability of scoring. If two readers vary widely in their evaluation of answers, there is something seriously wrong with the scoring system. Moreover, it is possible for one reader to miss a particularly important aspect of an answer that a second reader would catch. If it is not possible to have the answers read by two readers, the same reader should read and score at least a subset of the answers on two different occasions. The score for the first reading should not, of course, be available during the second reading.

4. *Give the students feedback on their answers.* In addition to their evaluative function, essay examinations can also be a valuable learning experience. Their value as a learning experience, however, depends to a great extent on the quality and nature of the feedback that is provided to the student. Detailed comments about both the strengths and shortcomings of an answer are informative to a student and can serve as a strong motivating influence. One has only to remember how disappointing it was to have an essay exam returned with only a grade at the top to recognize the importance of providing feedback on essay answers.

5. *Read each answer twice before assigning a score.* Important content is sometimes missed when a score is assigned after a single reading of an answer. Reading each answer twice reduces this kind of scoring error.

Scoring and grading—two separate activities

Evaluating essay exams involves two activities that can, and should, be separated (Helmstadter, personal communication). The first activity is scoring the answer. As indicated, scoring involves forming a judgment about the degree to which a student's answer matches a model answer or determining where, on a continuum of "knowledge of the topic," a holistic judgment of an answer falls.

Separate from the judgment about scoring an answer is the judgment about what value to assign to a particular score—that is, deciding what grade should be attached to the score. The grading possibilities are almost infinite. One teacher might decide to grade on a three-point system of A, C, and F. Another teacher might take essentially the same distribution of scores and assign grades of A, AB, B, BC, C, CD, D, and F. The grades a teacher assigns depend on many factors, some of which are specific to a given classroom. This means that it is very difficult to make general recommendations about grading exams.

However, not separating scoring and grading can contribute to problems in the overall reliability of a test. If teachers have a distribution of grades in mind when scoring a test, their scoring can be influenced by the imagined distribution. In contrast, separating the two activities of scoring and grading allows a teacher to score answers with unbiased precision.

Advantages and disadvantages of essay tests

We have already alluded to most of the strengths and weaknesses of essay tests. They have several advantages, the first being that teachers can assess complex learning outcomes that are very difficult to assess with other test forms. Moreover, essay tests provide the opportunity for students to demonstrate their ability to synthesize, evaluate, organize, and create. When these are the kinds of outcomes that a teacher wants to assess, there is no substitute for essay tests.

The second advantage for essay tests is that they demonstrate a student's ability to write. Considerable concern has been voiced in recent years about declining writing skills. Essay tests encourage the development of competent writing.

A third advantage for essay tests is that, per unit of time, essay tests are easier to prepare than objective tests (Mehrens and Lehman, 1975). This is not to say that good essay tests are *easy* to prepare. They are not. But a good essay test can generally be developed faster than a good objective test. It should be noted, however, that the preparation-time advantage for essay tests is definitely lost when scoring time is considered.

The final advantage for essay tests is that they can provide a good learning experience. Essays provide the opportunity for students to demonstrate their ability to think, organize, and solve problems. When good feedback is provided, the test can sharpen a student's abilities in these areas.

The most serious disadvantage of essay tests is the problem of reliably scoring the tests. Many studies over the years have demonstrated the problem of scorer reliability (Popham, 1981). Recall the discussion in the previous chapter, where it was indicated that a test that was unreliable could not be valid. Hence a test that cannot be reliably scored is worthless as an assessment instrument. Scoring reliability can be increased by following the guidelines presented in this chapter. But the problem remains a serious one.

A related problem is that a student's fluency of expression can sometimes color a grader's overall evaluation of an answer. An extreme example of this problem (cited by Mehrens and Lehman, 1975) is the case of a student who had excellent writing skills taking an essay exam on a novel he had never read. By stringing together a series of well-written (but basically meaningless) generalities, the student received an A on a topic he knew nothing about. This problem is the basis for the recommendation that if quality of expression is to be considered in grading, it should be separated from the basic content of the answer.

The final disadvantage of essay tests is the time required for scoring. In order to do a good scoring job, teachers should prepare scoring keys and/or model answers; they should read each answer twice, at different times; and they should provide detailed feedback to the student. To do all of this involves a large time commitment; one that, unfortunately, only the most conscientious teachers are willing to make.

GRADING AND EVALUATION

Is Grading Necessary?

Grading is, by its nature, a subjective process, and this makes a good many teachers uncomfortable. They recognize that their own standards of grading are not based on hard-and-fast principles, and they know that standards vary from teacher to teacher. This means that a teacher's basis for assigning grades may vary from year to year, and it means that the same performance may earn different grades from different teachers. Given the lack of firm rules and principles for assigning grades, it is reasonable to ask, Are grades necessary?

The answer to this question is no, grades are not necessary, but there is strong reason to believe that they are desirable. Moreover, although grading may not be necessary, evaluation—the process involved in deriving grades— is an absolutely essential component of an effective educational system.

evaluation the process of deciding whether a particular educational experience has had an impact

Evaluation

Educational evaluation is the process of deciding whether a particular educational experience has had an impact. Evaluation can occur at many levels.

Entire school systems can be evaluated, for example, by comparing the average student performance of the school system with the average school performance of a comparable system, or by comparing the average student performance of a system with national norms. Schools can be evaluated in the same way; and teacher performance can be evaluated through comparisons with other teachers or through comparisons with absolute standards. Finally, student progress can be evaluated through formal tests and through subjective teacher assessments of progress. Evaluation at each of these levels is essential to quality education.

Evaluation can also serve several purposes. Mackay (1975) has called these purposes preparative, formative, and summative evaluation (see Scriven, 1967). *Preparative evaluation* involves determining the attributes possessed by a learner prior to instruction. This purpose of evaluation is essentially equivalent to determining a student's entering behavior, as discussed in Chapter 7. *Formative evaluation* is the process of evaluating the ongoing progress of instruction for the purpose of providing feedback to students and teachers about instructional effectiveness. Ongoing evaluation allows teachers to change ineffective approaches to teaching while instruction is still continuing. *Sum-*

preparative evaluation determination of the attributes possessed by a learner prior to instruction

formative evaluation evaluation of the ongoing progress of instruction for the purpose of providing feedback to students and teachers

Evaluation of student work is an essential part of effective education. (© David S. Strickler/The Picture Cube)

mative evaluation determines whether the objectives of instruction have been attained when instruction has ended. Summative evaluation provides information regarding the worth of an entire instructional sequence.

The Desirability of Grades

If one accepts as a given that evaluation is essential to quality education, it means that the only question remaining is whether to share the evaluative information with the student. There are several reasons to believe that providing students with evaluative feedback is desirable. The first is that virtually all people seek positive recognition of their efforts. Informing students that they have done a good job is an important means of helping them to develop a positive self-concept. A second reason is that there is evidence that students learn more when they receive evaluative feedback than when they do not. For example, a study conducted at Ohio State University (Hales, Bain, and Rand, 1971) compared the performance of students in graded courses with their performance in courses in which they exercised a pass–no credit option. In courses both within a major field and outside of a major field, students performed more poorly when taking pass–no credit courses than they did when taking graded courses. A third reason for providing students with evaluative feedback is that it conveys information about student progress to parents. There is no more potent force in the movement for quality education than concerned and involved parents. If parents are to be an informed force for quality education, they need feedback regarding their children's progress.

Various Forms of Grading

If providing feedback regarding student progress is seen as desirable, there remains a choice as to the form of the feedback. There are two choices: norm-referenced or criterion-referenced indicators of progress.

Norm-referenced grading

norm-referenced grading a grading system that assigns grades to students according to how they perform relative to other students in the evaluation group

As indicated in the previous chapter, norm-referenced measurement entails indexing the performance of a student in comparison to the performance of a norm group. Norm-referenced grading works on the same principle. A student is assigned a grade depending on how he or she performs relative to the performance of other students in the evaluation group. So, for example, students performing at the top 10 percent of the class could be assigned A's, those performing in the next 20 percent B's, etc.

Norm-referenced grading is appropriate when teachers and school officials decide that feedback regarding student performance should indicate where a given student's performance falls relative to the performance of classmates. The disadvantage of a norm-referenced grading system is that it does not give an indication of what the student has learned. It tells whether a student is doing well or poorly relative to classmates, but it says nothing about the specific skills being acquired.

Criterion-referenced grading

As indicated in the previous chapter, criterion-referenced measurement is designed to establish whether students have mastered specific skills. Criterion-referenced grading has a related purpose, in that it gives feedback on the specific skills that a student has mastered. Such feedback would most commonly take the form of a check list of specific educational objectives and a space for recording the date on which an objective was mastered. This procedure allows a student's progress to be charted in terms of the specific skills being attained and the rate of progress.

criterion-referenced grading a grading system that assigns grades to students according to their levels of mastery of given course objectives

Criterion-referenced grading is most appropriate when school officials and parents decide that student progress should be indexed in terms of specific skills being mastered. The disadvantage of a criterion-referenced system is that it provides little feedback about whether a student's progress is rapid, slow, or about average.

Combining grading systems

As the foregoing discussion indicates, both norm-referenced and criterion-referenced grading systems have strengths and weaknesses. One way to benefit from the strengths of the systems while avoiding their weaknesses is to combine the two approaches. For example, check lists of objectives could be developed that allow the teacher to chart a student's progress in terms of objectives mastered. In addition, each report card could contain an indication of the progress of the class as a whole in terms of objectives mastered. This would allow students and teachers to determine what skills had been mastered, and also to determine how a particular student's progress compares to that of other students.

SUMMARY

The quality of most teacher-made tests is probably quite low, and there are two likely reasons why this is so. The first is that most teachers do not have the training required to develop good tests; the second is that many teachers do not devote the time that good test development requires.

The first step in developing a test is to decide what information to measure. Bloom's *Taxonomy of Educational Objectives in the Cognitive Domain* is useful in helping to decide what information to measure.

Bloom divides cognitive learning into six levels that range from simple to complex. At the first, and lowermost, level is knowledge which is knowing a fact, principle, rule, or similar entity. Knowledge is tested by asking students to reproduce or recognize information in virtually the same form in which it was experienced.

The second level in Bloom's taxonomy is comprehension. Comprehension occurs when students understand the instruction they have received, and it is measured by having students respond to questions that are in a different form from the instruction they received.

Bloom's third level is application, which is the ability to transfer learned information to situations that have not previously been encountered. Application can be measured by presenting students with new situations or problems and determining if they can apply the appropriate information needed to solve the problem.

The fourth level is analysis, which involves the ability to break a communication into its constituent parts so that the parts can be analyzed independently. Analytic ability can be measured by presenting students with a complex event and seeing if they can successfully break it down and analyze the parts.

Bloom's fifth level is synthesis, which involves the ability to join elements or components together in a manner that creates something unique. Synthesis can be measured by asking students to take components or items of knowledge and combine them in such a way that a unique product or argument is created.

The final, and most complex, learning activity in Bloom's taxonomy is evaluation. Evaluation is the ability to make informed judgments about events. It can be measured by asking students to evaluate—using some criteria—an argument, a work of art, or any other event that can be judged in an informed manner.

After a teacher has decided what he or she wants to measure, the next step is to develop a blueprint for the test. One of the most common ways to do this is to construct a *table of specifications*. A table of specification describes the features of a to-be-constructed test—such as the content or skills to be assessed, the cognitive level to be assessed, the type of test items to be constructed, and the relative emphasis to be given to each topic. Tables can be constructed in a simple form that utilizes only two dimensions, or they can be more complicated, using more than two dimensions.

After a blueprint has been developed, the next step is to write test items. There are three basic types of test items: (1) simple-form items, which include short-answer items, true-false items, and matching items; (2) multiple-choice items; and (3) essay items.

Short-answer items, the first type of simple-form item, require the examinee to supply a word, a phrase, a number, or a symbol in response to a question or a blank to be filled in. Suggestions for constructing short-answer items are (1) the item should be worded so that the required answer is both brief and definite; (2) direct statements from textbooks should not serve as the basis for short-answer items; (3) a direct question is generally more desirable than an incomplete statement; (4) when the answer is to be expressed in numerical units, indicate the type of answer wanted; and (5) blanks for answers should be of equal length and in a column to the right of questions.

Short-answer items have two advantages. First, the items are easy to construct; second, the students have to supply answers rather than just recognize them. This latter feature reduces the likelihood of a student getting an answer correct by guessing. The major limitation of short-answer items is that they cannot be used to measure complex learning. The exceptions to this rule are in the areas of science and mathematics, where short-answer items can be used to measure complex learning outcomes.

True-false items—or as they are more generally called, alternative-selection items—require that the student classify a declarative statement into one of two response categories (generally true or false). Suggestions for writing true-false items are (1) avoid broad general statements if they are to be judged true or false; (2) avoid trivial statements; (3) avoid the use of negative statements and especially double negatives; (4) avoid long, complex sentences; (5) avoid including two ideas in one statement, unless cause-effect relations are being measured; (6) if opinion is used, attribute it to some source, unless the ability to identify opinion is being measured; (7) true statements and false statements should be approximately equal in length; and (8) the number of true statements and false statements should be approximately equal.

Carefully constructed true-false tests have two advantages. First, the items are easy to construct; second, a great deal of course material can be efficiently tested. The disadvantages of true-false items are that some types of course content are not reducible to factual statements, and that true-false items are most useful for measuring lower-level learning outcomes.

Matching items consist of two parallel columns of words, symbols, or phrases in which the items in one column are to be matched with items in the second column. Suggestions for constructing matching exercises are (1) use only homogeneous material in a single matching exercise; (2) include an unequal number of responses and premises, and instruct students that responses may be used once, more than once, or not at all; (3) keep the list of items to be matched brief, and place the shorter responses on the right; (4) arrange the list of responses in logical order; (5) indicate in the directions the basis for matching the responses and descriptions; and (6) place all of the items for a matching exercise on the same page.

Matching exercises have the advantages of being easy to construct and of being able to measure quickly and efficiently a large amount of information. Their disadvantage is that they cannot easily measure complex learning outcomes.

Multiple-choice items are complex forms that consist of an item stem and several alternative responses, one of which the student is to choose as the correct response. Suggestions for writing multiple-choice items are (1) stems that ask a direct question are preferable to stems that are incomplete statements; (2) stems should specify a singular problem, and they should be stated in a clear and explicit manner; (3) an item stem should be restricted in content to the specific material being assessed, irrelevant material should be excluded; (4) negatively stated items should be used very infrequently; (5) items written at the application, analysis, and synthesis levels should contain terms familiar to the students; (6) all of the distractors should be plausible; (7) distractors should be of the same approximate length; (8) response alternatives such as "none of the above" or "all of the above" should be used with caution; and (9) the position of the correct alternative should vary.

Multiple-choice items have the advantage of being able to measure learning outcomes at almost all of Bloom's levels, and the pattern of errors that students make can be used to diagnose teaching weaknesses. The disadvantages of multiple-choice items are that they restrict the assessment of learning outcomes to carefully specified situations and they cannot detect truly creative performance.

Essay tests can be used to measure the degree to which students can organize information into a coherent framework, and they are especially useful in measuring complex learning outcomes. There are two types of essay questions: extended-response questions, which give students considerable freedom in formulating answers, and restricted-response questions, which place restrictions on the form of the answer. Suggestions for writing essay questions are (1) use essay tests only when the intent is to measure complex learning outcomes; (2) decide on the learning outcome that you want to measure, and then write the question to measure that outcome; (3) phrase questions so that the student's task is clear; (4) use several questions requiring relatively short answers, rather than one or two questions requiring long answers; (5) do not use optional questions; and (6) develop a scoring system.

Essay questions can be scored in an analytic or a holistic manner. Analytic scoring involves developing a model answer and then breaking the answer down into elements that can be assigned points. Holistic scoring involves forming a judgment about the answer as a whole. Suggestions for scoring essay questions are (1) score all of the students' answers to one question before scoring answers to the next question; (2) score the answers without knowing the identity of the writer; (3) if possible, have at least two people score each answer; (4) give the students feedback on their answers; and (5) read each answer twice before assigning a score. Note that scoring and grading should be separate activities.

Essay tests have several advantages: they can assess complex learning outcomes, they can assess a student's ability to write, they are reasonably easy to prepare, and they can provide a valuable learning experience. Essay tests have the disadvantages of being difficult to score reliably, of the scorer being influenced by the verbal fluency of the writer, and of requiring considerable scoring time.

Grading is not a necessary part of quality education, but evaluation is. Evaluation can be preparative, formative, or summative. Grades may not be necessary, but they are desirable because they signal recognition of good performance, encourage learning, and convey information to parents regarding student performance. Grading can be either norm-referenced, criterion-referenced, or a combination of the two.

FOR FURTHER STUDY AND APPLICATION

Bloom, B. S., et al. (Eds.). *Taxonomy of educational objectives in the cognitive domain: The classification of educational goals*. New York: McKay, 1956.   The "bible" of educational objectives.

Gronlund, N. E. *Constructing achievement tests*. (2nd ed.) Englewood Cliffs, N.J.: Prentice-Hall, 1977.

Payne, D. A. *The specification and measurement of learning outcomes*. Waltham, Mass.: Blaisdell, 1968.   Two excellent sources on the development of teacher-made tests.

Appendix A
STATISTICS

Statistics is a mathematical tool that assists in interpreting and making decisions about large amounts of data. In this appendix we discuss statistics that can be used to describe the central tendencies of a data set, statistics that can be used to describe the variability of a data set, statistics that can be used to describe whether two data sets are related to one another, and statistics that can be used to determine if two data sets differ from each other.

MEASURES OF CENTRAL TENDENCY

Imagine that a teacher administered a test to twenty-three students, and they achieved the following scores:

Sally—72	Tim—59	Mike—90	Diane—78
Mark—85	Jill—83	Rich—69	Pat—86
Jim—58	Pam—96	Linda—72	Harry—89
Bill—78	Terry—78	Kent—80	Bob—90
Carol—92	Lance—49	Liz—69	Sheila—73
Judy—86	Ricky—85	Roger—83	

As presented here, the scores are merely a jumble of numbers. One can, however, begin to make some sense out of the scores by arranging them in order from highest to lowest. This sort of arrangement, called a *frequency distribution*, is shown in Table A-1.

Arranging the scores in a frequency distribution allows one to interpret the set visually. For example, one can easily see what the high and low scores are, and one can get a sense of where the middle score in the distribution is. Sometimes, however, one wants a more precise indication of where the central score in a distribution is. In addition, if one has very large amounts of data, arranging scores into a frequency distribution is laborious and time consuming. In these cases one can utilize statistical measures of central tendency.

The Mean

The most useful measure of central tendency is the *mean* (or average). The mean is simply the sum of all of the scores in a distribution divided by the number of scores contributing to the sum. The calculation of the mean of a distribution can be described with the following formula:

$$\text{Mean} = \frac{\Sigma X_i}{N}$$

where: Σ = sum the numbers following the symbol
X_i = a symbol representing all of the scores in a distribution
N = the number of scores in a distribution.

Table A-1   Frequency Distribution

Score	Number of People Attaining Score
96	1
92	1
90	2
89	1
86	2
85	2
83	2
80	1
78	3
73	1
72	2
69	2
59	1
58	1
49	1
Σ = 1800	23

Using this formula with the foregoing distribution of scores one can see that

$$\text{Mean} = \frac{\Sigma X_i}{N} = \frac{1,800}{23} = 78.26$$

Thus the mean provides a numerical index of where in the distribution of scores the average score lies.

In general, the mean is an accurate and stable indicator of the central tendency of a distribution of scores. However, it is not perfect. One problem is that the mean is very sensitive to extreme scores, particularly when relatively few scores are involved. For instance, if two very low scores, say 4 and 6 are added to the distribution of scores, the mean changes considerably:

$$\text{Mean} = \frac{\Sigma X}{N} = \frac{1,810}{25} = 72.4$$

Because of its sensitivity to extreme scores, the mean can sometimes create a false impression when it is used as a measure of central tendency.

The Median

A second important measure of central tendency is the median. The *median* is the point, in a distribution of scores, that divides the distribution exactly in half. Consider, for example, the following distribution of scores: 22, 20, 19, 15, 14, 12, and 11. The score that exactly divides the distribution in half is 15. In the earlier distribution, there were twenty-three scores. Thus in that distribution the twelfth score divides the distribution in half (there are eleven scores above it and eleven below). The twelfth score in the distribution is 80; therefore 80 is the median.

One advantage of the median is that, unlike the mean, it is insensitive to extreme scores. The addition of scores 4 and 6 to the distribution would not change the median more than would the addition of scores 60 and 70. The reason is that the median divides a distribution of scores exactly in half; the magnitude of the scores in the distribution is of no consequence.

Whereas the insensitivity of the median to extreme scores is an advantage in some cases, in others it is a disadvantage. There are times when a measure of central tendency should reflect extreme scores, and in those cases the median is not an ideal statistic.

The Mode

The final measure of central tendency is the mode. The *mode* of a distribution is the score that appears most frequently in the distribution. In most large distributions of scores, the most frequently appearing score will appear near the center of the distribution; hence the mode can serve as a measure of central tendency. But in general, the mode is not a frequently used measure of central tendency. The reasons are that some distributions have more than one mode (as an exercise, imagine what the distribution would look like that was based on the heights of all adults in the United States). These distributions are called *bimodal* (two modes) or even *trimodal* (three modes).

A second limitation of the mode as a measure of central tendency is that it is completely insensitive to scores other than the one that appears most frequently. This means that in most cases the mode will be insensitive to the vast majority of scores in the distribution.

A Comparison of Measures of Central Tendency

In a normal distribution of scores such as the one in Figure A-1, the mean, the median, and the mode fall at exactly the same point. In other words, in a normal distribution the mean score will also be the score that divides the distribution exactly in half and it will be the most frequently appearing score.

The differences among measures of central tendency appear when distributions are not normal. Figure A-2, for example, contains positively and negatively skewed distributions. Note that each of the three measures of central tendency falls at a different point in the distribution when the distributions are skewed.

MEASURES OF VARIABILITY

In addition to wanting to know what the central tendency of a distribution is, one frequently wants to know something about the variability of a distribution. *Variability* is a term that refers to the spread of scores in a distribution. Figure A-3, for example, illustrates two sets of scores that have identical measures of central tendency, but the spread of scores in the distributions is very different.

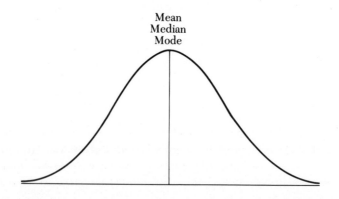

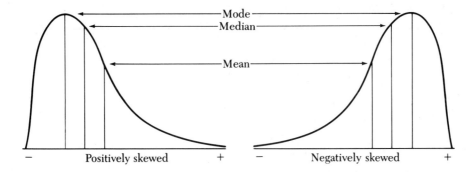

Positively skewed   +   −   Negatively skewed   +

Measures of variability provide a means of communicating information about the spread of scores in a distribution.

The Range

The simplest index of variability is the *range*. The range is calculated by subtracting the lowest score in a distribution from the highest score in the distribution, as indicated by the following formula:

Range $= X_h - X_l$

Where X_h = highest score in distribution
X_l = lowest score in distribution

The simplicity of calculating the range is about its only virtue. The problem with the range is that it is calculated using only two scores. This means, for example, that one could have a bunched up distribution—such as the one depicted on the right side of Figure A-3—and yet have one lone score either very high or very low that would radically change the range, thereby ignoring the variability associated with the vast number of scores in the distribution.

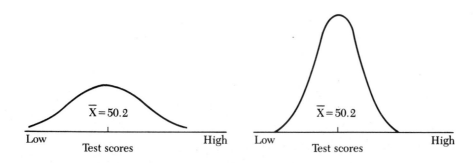

Low   High   Low   High
Test scores   Test scores

The Standard Deviation

Statisticians have invented a far more sensitive measure of variability than the range, called the *standard deviation*. Conceptually, the standard deviation bears some relationship to the mean, in the sense that it indicates something about how distant the *average* score in a distribution is from the center of the distribution. Thus the mean indicates what the average of a distribution of scores is, and the standard deviation tells us *how far the typical score deviates from the mean.* To get a sense of this concept, look again at the two distributions in Figure A-3. Note that the scores in the left distribution are spread out more than are the scores in the right distribution. This means that a measure conveying information about the spread of the scores should be larger for the left distribution than for the right. The standard deviation satisfies this requirement by indicating how distant a typical score is from the center of the distribution.

Standard deviations are calculated by first calculating *deviation scores*. A deviation score is simply a score minus the mean of the distribution, as is illustrated by the following formula:

$$x = X - \overline{X}$$

Where: $x =$ deviation score
$X =$ raw score (the actual score for a student)
$\overline{X} =$ mean of distribution

Subtracting the mean from each score results in a set of deviation scores that are approximately evenly divided into plus and minus scores. Moreover, if these scores are added together the sum will be zero. The next step in calculating a standard deviation is to square each deviation score, thereby eliminating the negative scores. These squared scores are then added together and divided by the number of scores contributing to the sum. The final step is to calculate the square root of the result. The following is the formula for these steps:

$$\text{Standard deviation} = \sqrt{\frac{\Sigma x^2}{n}}$$

Where: $\Sigma x^2 =$ the sum of the squared deviation scores

$n =$ the number of deviation scores

The standard deviation is an excellent index of the variability within a distribution because it is not particularly sensitive to extreme scores, and it is based on the entire set of scores within the distribution. Moreover, as is discussed in Appendix B, the standard deviation serves as the basis for developing standard scores, which in turn serve as the means for reporting the results of many educationala tests.

MEASURES OF RELATIONSHIP

Many educational questions involve the extent to which two scores or variables are related. For example, is performance on an IQ test related to academic achievement? Or, as another example, is performance on a reading readiness test related to reading achievement measured a year later? Questions such as these are frequently asked because they enable teachers to design individualized educational experiences. In this section we describe techniques for providing either graphic or numerical indexes of the extent to which two variables are related.

Graphic Representations of Relationship

Imagine that one wanted to determine the answer to the question regarding the relationship between scores on a reading readiness test and scores on a test of reading proficiency administered a year later. One of the easiest ways to get a sense of the degree to which two variables are related is to construct a *scatterplot graph*. A scatterplot graph illustrating the relationship between reading readiness and reading proficiency is presented in Figure A-4. The figure was drawn by placing reading readiness scores on the X axis of the graph and reading proficiency scores on the Y axis. An individual's score on the two tests is then represented by a dot where the two scores intersect. For example, students who scored low on both tests would have their scores represented by dots in the lower left-hand corner of the graph. In contrast, students who scored high on both tests would have their scores represented by dots in the upper right-hand corner of the graph.

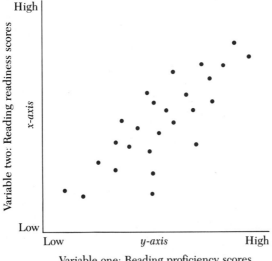

Note that the general slope of the distribution of dots in Figure A-4 is from the lower left-hand corner to the upper right-hand corner of the graph. This indicates that students who received low scores on the first test would have a strong tendency to receive low scores on the second test; that students who received average scores on the first test would have a strong tendency to receive average scores on the second test; and that students who received high scores on the first test would have a strong tendency to receive high scores on the second test. This, in turn, indicates that there is a strong *positive relationship* between the scores on the two tests.

In Figure A-5 a different pattern of relationship is illustrated. Note that the slope of the dots goes from the upper left-hand corner to the lower right-hand corner of the graph. This means that a student who scored low on the first test tended to score high on the second test, and a student who scored high on the first test had a strong tendency to score low on the second test. Therefore, Figure A-5 indicates that there is a strong *negative relationship* between the scores on the two tests.

Figure A-6 illustrates yet another pattern. Note that the dots are distributed evenly around the graph and that there is no discernible slope. This means that there is *no relationship* between scores on the two tests; a low score on one test has equal likelihood of being associated with a low, medium, or high score on the second test.

Scatterplot graphs are an excellent means of providing a concrete indication of the degree of relationship between two variables. They do have several limitations however. First, if a large number of scores are involved, constructing a scatterplot is very tedious and time consuming. Second, on many occasions one is interested in getting a much more precise index of the degree of relationship between two variables than can be obtained from examining a

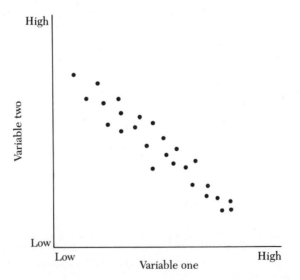

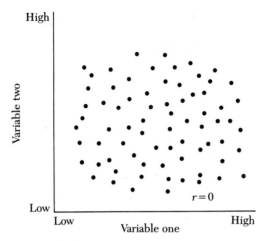

scatterplot. In situations involving large amounts of data, or where a precise index of relationship is needed, the correlation coefficient should be used rather than scatterplot graphs.

Correlation Coefficients

A *correlation coefficient* is a number that indicates the extent to which two variables are related. It ranges in value from +1.0 to −1.0. A correlation coefficient of +1.0 would indicate that two variables have a perfect positive relationship. That is, the person who has the highest score on test 1 will have the highest score on test 2, the person who has the second highest score on test 1 will have the second highest score on test 2, and so on, with the person who received the lowest score on test 1 also receiving the lowest score on test 2.

A correlation coefficient of −1.0 would indicate that there is a perfect negative relationship between two variables. That is, a person who received the highest score on test 1 would receive the lowest score on test 2, the person who received the second highest score on test 1 would receive the second lowest score on test 2, and so on.

Correlation coefficients around zero indicate that there is no relationship between two variables. For example, if a correlation coefficient were calculated using the data in Figure A-6, the coefficient would be somewhere around zero.

Correlation coefficients that range between 0 and −1 or +1 indicate varying degrees of relationship between two variables. For example, a coefficient of −.2 or +.2 would indicate that there is a slight relationship between two variables. If the correlation were around +.5 or −.5, it would indicate that there is a moderate relationship between the variables, and if the correlation were .8 or above, it would indicate that there is a strong relationship between the variables.

The most popular means of calculating correlation coefficients is known as the Pearson product-moment correlation coefficient (represented by the symbol r), after the English statistician Karl Pearson. The formula for calculating r is as follows:

$$rxy = \frac{\Sigma XY - \dfrac{(\Sigma X)(\Sigma Y)}{N}}{\sqrt{\left(\Sigma X^2 - \dfrac{(\Sigma X)^2}{N}\right)\left(\Sigma Y^2 - \dfrac{(\Sigma Y)^2}{N}\right)}}$$

Where:

rxy = the correlation between variables x and y

ΣXY = the sum of the cross products X times Y

$\dfrac{(\Sigma X)(\Sigma Y)}{N}$ = the sum of X times the sum of Y, divided by the number of pairs of scores

$\left(\Sigma X^2 - \dfrac{(\Sigma X)^2}{N}\right)$ = the sum of each squared X score minus the sum of the X scores squared, divided by the number of X scores

$\left(\Sigma Y^2 - \dfrac{(\Sigma Y)^2}{N}\right)$ = the sum of each squared Y score minus the sum of the Y scores squared, divided by the number of Y scores

As an example of using this formula, assume that ten students took two tests and attained the scores listed in Table A-2. The formula for calculating a correlation coefficient can then be used as follows:

$$rxy = \frac{618 - \dfrac{(78)(61)}{10}}{\sqrt{\left(760 - \dfrac{(78)^2}{10}\right)\left(533 - \dfrac{(61)^2}{10}\right)}}$$

$$= \frac{14.2}{156.2}$$

$$= .91$$

As can be seen by the value of the above correlation coefficient, there is a strong positive relationship between the scores on test x and the scores on test y.

The correlation coefficient is used in many instances requiring a measure of the relationship between two variables. For example, as indicated in Chapter 15, educational tests must be both reliable and valid. The reliability and the validity of tests are frequently reported in terms of correlation coefficients. Many indexes of reliability are simply correlation coefficients in which the performance of students on one half of a test is correlated with their performance

Table A-2

Student	Test x	Test y	x^2	y^2	XY
1	8	3	64	9	24
2	2	1	4	1	2
3	8	6	64	36	48
4	5	3	25	9	15
5	15	14	225	196	210
6	11	12	121	144	132
7	13	9	169	81	117
8	6	4	36	16	24
9	4	4	16	16	16
10	6	5	36	25	30
N = 10 Σ	78	61	760	533	618

on the other half. Indexes of validity also frequently involve correlation coefficients. One example is when performance on a test (e.g., the SAT) is correlated with a subsequent measure (e.g., college GPA) as a means of establishing the validity of the test.

INFERENTIAL STATISTICS

Many important decisions in education hinge on the question of whether or not two things are different. For example, a decision about purchasing a new basal reading series for the entire school district might depend on whether students learn to read faster using the old series or the new series. In this case, the question is whether the performance of students using the old series is different from that of students using the new series. At first one might think that questions about differences are simple. After all, it should be easy enough to tell when two things differ. But the truth is, determining whether things are different—or rather whether the difference is real or just due to chance— is not always easy, as we will now proceed to illustrate.

Suppose you had two coins, each of which you flipped 100 times. One coin came up heads 62 times, the other came up heads 46 times. Are the coins different? The problem is that it is difficult to tell. You know that heads should appear about half the time, but what you don't know is whether 62 and 46 are "real" departures from what might be expected, or whether they are merely slight deviations from the expected values.

Questions such as the one just posed revolve around how "probable" certain events are. For example, it would not surprise one at all if heads were to appear 51 times out of 100 flips. However, if heads were to appear 80 times, out of 100, one might be suspicious that something was amiss; and if 90 heads appeared in 100 flips, one might be strongly suspicious of the fairness of the coin. Put another way, given a fair coin, 51 heads in 100 flips is a very probable event, whereas 90 heads is a very improbable event. In fact, it is possible to determine exactly its probability: 90 or more heads will occur by chance only one time in 2 million trials of 100 flips of a fair coin. It could be that a trial resulting in 90 heads is that one-in-2-million event. But it is much more likely that in this case heads and tails are not equally likely on any given flip of the coin—that is, that either the coin or the flip is not fair.

Inferential statistics approaches the question of whether things are truly different in a manner that is conceptually similar to the above example. If the question involves whether students learn more from a new basal reading series than they do from the old basal series, inferential statistics indicate how likely it is that a difference in performance between students using the new series and students using the old series is attributable to chance. By agreed-upon convention, if a particular numerical advantage of the new basal group over the old basal group would occur by chance only 1 time in 20, the difference is said to be *significant*. That is, the difference probably exists because the new series is truly better than the old series, rather than the difference being a chance event. Alternatively, if the difference would occur by chance at frequencies greater than 1 in 20, the decision is that the difference between the new series and the old is not large enough to rule out the possibility of chance.

There are many different kinds of inferential statistics, and they can be found in any introductory level statistics book. The thing that they all have in common is that decisions about whether things are different are based on considerations about how probable various differences are.

Appendix B
INTERPRETING NORM-REFERENCED TEST SCORES

The number of correct answers that a student achieves on a test, whether it be a teacher-made test or a standardized commercial test, is a relatively meaningless piece of data. Say, for example, that a student gets a score of 39 on a test. Without additional information one has no idea whether the student did well or poorly.

The first thing one can do to begin to make sense out of a test score is to compare it with the total possible score. For example, knowing that the test on which the student scored 39 contained 50 items provides some idea of how the student performed. But only some idea. A score of 39 out of 50 seems to indicate good performance; but it might represent very poor performance if the test was very easy and nearly everyone scored in the 40s.

RANKING SCORES

A much better sense of what a particular score means can be obtained by ranking all of the scores from highest to lowest. Imagine that the entire class of twenty students took the test on which our student scored 39, and the following are the ranked scores for the class:

45	39	36	31
44	38	36	30
44	37	35	28
42	37	34	26
41	36	34	24

As can be seen, the top score in the class was 45 and the lowest score was 24. The student who scored 39 received the sixth-highest score in the class, reflecting well above average performance.

Ranking scores is a reasonable way of determining what a score means when the total number of scores is small and when more precise information about a person's performance is not needed. However, when the set of scores is large and when more precise information is needed than can be gathered by looking at a rank-ordered set of scores, other techniques should be used.

PERCENTILE RANKS

One of the simplest and most useful procedures for transmitting information about what a score means is to report a score as a percentile rank. A *percentile rank* indicates the percentage of students who have achieved scores lower than the score of interest. For example, there are 15 scores (including the score of 39) below the student who received 39 on the test. Thus the student's percentile rank is

15 (the number of scores below 39) ÷ 20 (total number of scores) = .75 × 100 = 75.

This number tells us that 75 percent of the students in the class scored 39 or lower on the test. As another example, a student who scored 30 would have a percentile rank of 20 (4 ÷ 20 = .20 × 100 = 20). A percentile rank of 20 indicates that 20 percent of the students received a score of 30 or less.

Another commonly used means of conveying information about test scores is to describe a score in terms of *quartiles*. Quartiles are the scores in a distribution that correspond to percentile ranks of 25, 50, and 75. So if someone says that a particular score falls below the first quartile he or she means that the score falls somewhere between the percentile ranks of 0 and 25. Likewise, a score falling between the first and second quartile would lie somewhere between the percentile ranks of 25 and 50.

Percentile ranks are an excellent means of conveying information about what a test score means when the test is designed to provide a comparison among individuals taking the test (i.e., when the test is a norm-referenced test). The percentile rank indicates how an individual has performed relative to all of the other students taking the test. However, percentile ranks are not useful in conveying information about test performance when the test is designed to assess the mastery of educational objectives. Criterion-referenced tests are examples of this latter kind of test, and typically there are large numbers of students achieving the same "score," thereby making a comparative statistic such as percentile rank relatively meaningless.

STANDARD SCORES

Another common means of reporting test scores is to use one of the varieties of standard scores. There are several kinds of standard scores, all of which are based on standard deviations. Standard deviations are, as was indicated in Appendix A, a measure of the variability of a distribution of scores.

Z Scores

A Z score is a score that indicates, in standard deviation units, how far a score is above or below the mean of its distribution. The formula for a Z score is:

$$Z = \frac{X - \overline{X}}{S}$$

where X = a raw score

$\overline{X}$ = the mean of the distribution

S = the standard deviation of the distribution

Imagine, for example, that one had given a 100-item test to a large class and one calculated the mean as being 58 and the standard deviation as being 13 for the distribution. Now imagine that one wanted to find the Z scores for students who received scores of 29 and 82 on the test. Using the formula one can see that:

$$Z = \frac{29 - 58}{13}$$

$$= \frac{-29}{13}$$

$$= -2.23$$

and

$$Z = \frac{82 - 58}{13}$$

$$= \frac{24}{13}$$

$$= 1.85$$

Thus, a score of 29 corresponds to a Z score of -2.23 and a score of 82 corresponds to a Z score of 1.85. With the first Z score, the negative sign indicates that the person scored 2.23 standard deviation units *below* the mean; the second Z score indicates that the person scored 1.85 standard deviation units *above* the mean.

Scores that are reported in standard deviation units have a number of positive attributes. First, the algebraic sign of the score indicates whether the score is above or below the mean. Second, if one can assume that the test scores are distributed in approximation to a normal curve, as many test scores are, one can easily convert a score from standard deviation units to an approximate percentile rank. Figure A-7 illustrates how this is done. The figure illustrates the relationship between a normal curve and several different ways of reporting test scores. Note first that the curve is divided into symmetrical segments defined by standard deviation units. As you can see, the mean of the curve has a standard deviation unit of 0, and on either side of the mean are $+1$ and -1, $+2$ and -2, and so on.

Looking further down Figure A-7, one can see three lines that are labeled, cumulative percentages, rounded, and percentile equivalents. These lines indicate the percentile ranks corresponding to particular points on a normal distribution of scores. As you can see, a Z score of 0 corresponds to the 50th percentile, a Z score of $+1$ corresponds to the 84th percentile, and so on. If one wanted to know the percentile rank of the students who earned Z scores of -2.23 and 1.85, one could see from Figure A-7 that a Z score of -2.23 corresponds to a percentile rank of approximately 1.8, and a Z score of 1.85 corresponds to a percentile rank of approximately 96.

Another advantage of reporting scores in the form of Z scores is that if one knows a student's Z score as well as the mean and the standard deviation of the distribution of scores, it is relatively easy to determine a student's *raw score*. The formula for calculating a raw score knowing a Z score and mean and standard deviation is:

$$\text{raw score} = Z \times SD + \overline{X}$$

where Z = a student's Z score

SD = the standard deviation of a distribution of scores

$\overline{X}$ = the mean of a distribution of scores

In the example cited, one of the students had a Z score of -2.23, the other a Z score of 1.85, and both scores were from a distribution of scores having a mean of 58 and a standard deviation of 13. Thus (with rounding)

$$\text{raw score} = -2.23 \times 13 + 58$$
$$= -29 + 58$$
$$= 29$$

and

$$\text{raw score} = 1.85 \times 13 + 58$$
$$= 24 + 58$$
$$= 82$$

T Scores

A second kind of standard score is a *T* score. A *T* score is simply a Z score multiplied by 10 to get rid of decimals and added to 50 to get rid of negative

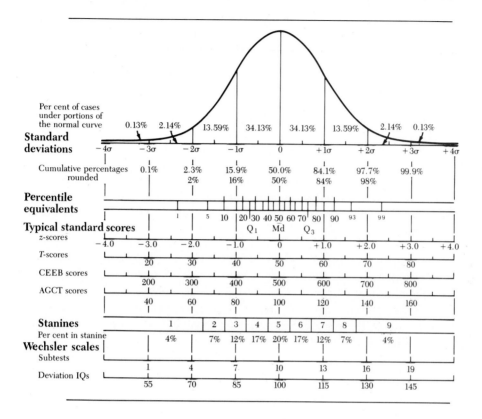

numbers. Thus, the formula for a *T* score is:

$$T = 50 + 10\ Z$$

This conversion process results in a distribution of scores with a mean of 50 (corresponding to a Z of 0) and a standard deviation of 10. The relationship of *T* scores to other ways of reporting scores can be seen in Figure A-7. *T* scores are sometimes used in place of Z scores because they do not involve the use of decimals and negative numbers.

Stanines

Stanines are based on standard deviations. A stanine scale takes a distribution of scores and breaks it into nine segments, which are based on standard deviation units. These segments are of equal length except for the two extremes, stanines 1 and 9. Figure A-7 shows the relationship of the stanine distribution to other types of scores. With the exception of stanines 1 and 9, the other stanine units are 0.5 standard deviation units apart. Stanine 5, as can be seen in Figure A-7, begins 0.25 standard deviation units on either side of the mean. Stanine 6 then covers the area from +0.25 to +0.75 standard deviation units, and stanine 4 covers the area from −0.25 to −0.75. The other stanines are formed by moving out in 0.5 standard deviation units from the mean.

Other qualities possessed by stanine scores are that they have specific relationships with percentiles. These relationships are illustrated in Figure A-7. One can see that the stanines contain differing percentages of scores, with stanine 5 containing 20 percent of the scores, stanines 4 and 6 each containing 17 percent, stanines 3 and 7 containing 12%, stanines 2 and 7 containing 7 percent and stanines 1 and 9 containing 4 percent. In addition, the stanine distribution has a specific relation to percentile ranks. As Figure A-7 illustrates, scores in stanine 1 correspond to percentile rank scores up to 4, scores in stanine 2 consist of percentile rank scores from 4 to 11, and so on all the way up to scores in stanine 9, which consist of percentile rank scores of 96 or better.

Some educators prefer to report test scores as stanines rather than in other forms because stanines provide general information about a student's level of performance without providing specific information that can serve as the basis for potentially harmful comparisons among individual students.

Grade Equivalents

Grade equivalent scores were discussed in Chapter 15 in some detail, so they are mentioned only briefly here. Grade equivalent scores are established by having a target population of students (see Chapter 15 for a discussion of target populations) take a test. Imagine, for example, that groups of beginning-of-the-year fourth, fifth, and sixth graders took the same test and received mean scores, respectively, of 40, 50, and 60. Forty then becomes the raw score corresponding to a grade equivalent of 4.0, 50 becomes the raw score corresponding to a grade equivalent of 5.0, and 60 becomes the raw score corresponding to a grade equivalent of 6.0. Thus regardless of a student's actual grade level in school, his or her performance can be indexed in terms of the average performance attained by students at various grade levels.

Grade equivalent scores have the advantage of apparent simplicity and ease of understanding. However, they also have serious disadvantages, which are described in detail in Chapter 15.

Other Standard Scores

Figure A-7 displays a number of other standard score scales that educators frequently have to deal with. For example, the CEEB scores, better known as Scholastic Aptitude Test (SAT) scores, have a mean of 500 and a standard deviation of 100. AGCT scores are scores from the Army General Classification Test, which is also published in a civilian version.

At the bottom of Figure A-7 you will find the scales for the Wechsler intelligence tests. As can be seen, the general IQ tests have a mean of 100 and a standard deviation of 15. The subtests have a mean of 10 and a standard deviation of 3.

REFERENCES

Adams, R. S., and Biddle, B. J. *Realities of teaching: Explanations with video tape.* New York: Holt, Rinehart and Winston, 1970.

Adamson, W. C., and Adamson, K. K. *A handbook for specific learning disabilities.* New York: Gardner Press, 1979.

Allen, V. L. (Ed.). *Children as teachers: Theory and research on tutoring.* New York: Academic Press, 1976.

Allen, V. L., and Feldman, R. S. Learning through tutoring: Low-achieving children as tutors. *Journal of Experimental Education,* 1973, *42,* 1–5.

Allen, V. L., and Feldman, R. S. Tutor attribution and attitude as a function of tutee performance. *Journal of Applied Social Psychology,* 1974, *4,* 311–320.

Allen, V. L., and Newtson, D. Development of conformity and independence. *Journal of Personality and Social Psychology,* 1972, *22,* 18–30.

Anderson, G. Effects of classroom social climate on individual learning. *American Educational Research Journal,* 1970, *7,* 135–152.

Anderson, N. H. Cognitive algebra integration theory applied to social attribution. In L. Berkowitz (Ed.), *Advances in experimental social psychology,* Vol. 7. New York: Academic Press, 1974. Pp. 1–101.

Anderson, R. C. How to construct achievement tests to assess comprehension. *Review of Educational Research,* 1972, *42,* 145–170.

Anderson, R. C. Schema-directed processes in language comprehension. In A. Lesgold, J. Pelligreno, S. Fokkema, and R. Glaser (Eds.), *Cognitive psychology and instruction.* New York: Plenum Press, 1977.

Anderson, R. C., and Myrow, D. L. Retroactive inhibition of meaningful discourse. *Journal of Educational Psychology,* 1971, *62,* 81–94.

Anderson, R. C., and Biddle, W. B. On asking people questions about what they are reading. In G. Bower (Ed.), *Psychology of learning and motivation,* Vol. 9. New York: Academic Press, 1975.

Anderson, R. C., and Faust, G. W. *Educational psychology: The science of instruction and learning.* Dodd, Mead: New York, 1975.

Anderson, R. C., Spiro, R. J., and Montague, W. E. (Eds.). *Schooling and the acquisition of knowledge.* Hillsdale, N.J.: Erlbaum, 1977.

Andre, T. Does answering higher-level questions while reading facilitate productive learning? *Review of Educational Research,* 1979, *49,* 280–318.

Andre, T., Schumer, H., and Whitaker, P. Group discussion and individual creativity. *Journal of General Psychology,* 1979, *100,* 111–123.

Angoff, W. H. Scales, norms, and equivalent scores. In R. L. Thorndike (Ed.), *Educational measurement.* Washington, D.C.: American Council on Education, 1971.

Annis, L. The processes and effects of peer tutoring. Paper presented at the *AERA Annual Meeting,* 1983.

Applewhite, P. B. Nonlocal nature of habituation in a rotifer and protozoan. *Nature,* 1968, *217,* 287–288.

Argyle, M. New development in the analysis of social skill. In A. Wolfgang (Ed.), *Nonverbal behavior.* New York: Academic Press, 1979.

Argyle, M., and Trower, P. Explorations in the treatment of personality disorders and neuroses by social training. *British Journal of Medical Psychology,* 1974, *47,* 63–72.

Armstrong, D. G. Team teaching and academic achievement. *Review of Educational Research,* 1977, *47,* 65–86.

Aronson, E., Blaney, N., Stephan, C., Sikes, J., and Snapp, M. *The jigsaw classroom.* Beverly Hills, Calif.: Sage, 1978.

Asch, S. E. Forming impressions of personality. *Journal of Abnormal and Social Psychology,* 1946, *41,* 258–290.

Asch, S. E. Effects of group pressure upon modification and distortion of judgements. In E. E. Maccoby, T. M. Newcomb, and E. L. Hartley (Eds.), *Readings in social psychology.* (3rd ed.) New York: Holt, Rinehart and Winston, 1958. Pp. 174–183.

Atkinson, J. W., and Raynor, J. O. *Motivation and achievement.* Washington, D.C.: Winston, 1974.

Atkinson, R. C. Mnemotechnics in second-language learning. *American Psychologist,* 1975, *30,* 821–828.

Atkinson, R. C., and Raugh, M. R. An application of the mnemonic keyword method to the acquisition of a Russian vocabulary. *Journal of Experimental Psychology: Human Learning and Memory,* 1975, *104,* 126–133.

Atkinson, R. C. and Wilson, H. A. (Eds.). *Computer assisted instruction.* New York: Academic Press, 1969.

Ausubel, D. P. The use of advance organizers in the learning and retention of meaningful verbal material. *Journal of Educational Psychology,* 1960, *51,* 267–272.

Ausubel, D. P. *The psychology of meaningful verbal learning.* New York: Grune and Stratton, 1963.

Ausubel, D. P., and Fitzgerald, D. The role of discriminability in meaningful verbal learning and retention. *Journal of Educational Psychology,* 1961, *52,* 266–274.

Ausubel, D. P., and Fitzgerald, D. Organizer, general background, and antecedent learning variables in sequential learning. *Journal of Educational Psychology,* 1962, *53,* 243–249.

Ausubel, D. P., and Youssef, M. Role of discriminability in meaningful parallel learning. *Journal of Educational Psychology,* 1963, *54,* 331–336.

Ausubel, D. P., Novak, J. D., and Hanesian, H. *Educational psychology: A cognitive view.* (2nd ed.) New York: Holt, Rinehart and Winston, 1978.

Ausubel, D. P., Stager, M., and Gaite, A. J. H. Retroactive facilitation in meaningful verbal learning. *Journal of Educational Psychology,* 1968, *59,* 250–255.

Bain, R. K., and Anderson, J. G. School context and peer influences on educational plans of adolescents. *Review of Educational Research,* 1974, *44,* 429–445.

Ball, S. (Ed.). *Motivation in education.* New York: Academic Press, 1977.

Baltes, P. B., and Schaie, K. W. Aging and IQ: The myth of the twilight years. *Psychology Today,* 1974, *40,* 35–38.

Bandura, A. *Social learning theory.* Englewood Cliffs, N.J.: Prentice-Hall, 1977.

Bandura, A., and MacDonald, F. J. Influence of social reinforcement and the behavior of models in shaping children's moral judgements. *Journal of Abnormal and Social Psychology,* 1963, *67,* 274–281.

Bandura, A., Ross, D., and Ross, S. Transmission of aggression through imitation of aggressive models. *Journal of Abnormal and Social Psychology,* 1961, *63,* 575–582.

Baratz, J. C. Teaching reading in an urban Negro school. In J. C. Baratz and R. W. Shay (Eds.), *Teaching black children to read.* Washington, D.C.: Center for Applied Linguistics, 1969.

Barclay, J. R. Variability in sociometric scores and teachers' ratings as related to teacher age and sex. *Journal of School Psychology,* 1966, *5,* 52–59.

Barik, Henri C., and Swain, Merrill. A longitudinal study of bilingual and cognitive development. *International Journal of Psychology,* 1976, *11* (4), 251–263.

Barker, R. G., and Gump, P. V. *Big school, small school*. Palo Alto: Stanford University Press, 1964.

Baroff, G. S. *Mental retardation: Nature, cause, and management*. New York: Halsted, 1974.

Barson, J. *A procedural and cost analysis study of media in instructional systems development*. Final report, Grant No. OE-3-16-030, 1965.

Bar-Tal, Daniel. Attributional analysis of achievement-related behavior. *Review of Educational Research*, Spring 1978, *48*, 259–271.

Bartlett, F. C. *Remembering: A study in experimental and social psychology*. London: Cambridge University Press, 1932.

Bates, J. A. Extrinsic reward and intrinsic motivation: A review with implications for the classroom. *Review of Educational Research*, 1979, *49*, 557–576.

Battig, W. F. Paired-associate learning. In T. R. Dixon and D. L. Horton (Eds.), *Verbal behavior and general behavioral theory*. Englewood Cliffs, N.J.: Prentice-Hall, 1968.

Beckman, L. J. Effects of students' performance on teachers' and observers' attributions of causality. *Journal of Educational Psychology*, 1970, *61*, 76–82.

Beez, W. Influence of biased reports on teacher behavior and pupil performance. In M. W. Miles and W. W. Charters, Jr. (Eds.), *Learning in social settings*. Boston: Allyn and Bacon, 1970.

Benoit, R. B., and Mayer, G. R. Timeout: Guidelines for its selection and use. *Personnel and Guidance Journal*, 1975, *53*, 501–506.

Berg, I., and McGuire, R. Are mothers of school-phobic adolescents overprotective? *British Journal of Psychiatry*, 1974, *124*, 10–13.

Berk, R. (Eds.). *Criterion-referenced testing: State of the art*. Baltimore: Johns Hopkins University Press, 1980.

Bernstein, B. Social class and linguistic development: A theory of social learning. In A. H. Halsey, J. Floud, and C. A. Anderson (Eds.), *Education, economy, and society*. Glencoe, Ill.: Free Press, 1961. Pp. 288–314. (a)

Bernstein, B. Social structure, language, and learning. *Educational Research*, 1961, *3*, 163–176. (b)

Bernstein, B. Social structure and learning. In A. H. Passow, M. Goldberg, and A. T. Tannenbaum (Eds.), *Education of the disadvantaged*. New York: Holt, Rinehart and Winston, 1967. Pp. 225–244.

Bernstein, B. A socio-linguistic approach to socialization with some references to educability. In J. J. Guwperz and D. Hymes (Eds.), *Directions in sociolinguistics*. New York: Holt, Rinehart and Winston, 1972.

Berry, J. W. Temme and Eskimo perceptual skills. *International Journal of Psychology*, 1966, *1*, 207–229.

Berscheid, E. and Walster, E. Physical attractiveness. In L. Berkowitz (Ed.), *Advances in experimental social psychology*. New York: Academic Press, 1974.

Bigge, M. L. *Learning theories for teachers*. (3rd ed.) New York: Harper and Row, 1976.

Birch, J. W. *Mainstreaming*. Reston, Va.: Council for Exceptional Children, 1975.

Birdwhistell, R. L. *Kinesics and context*. Philadelphia: University of Pennsylvania Press, 1970.

Block, J. H. (Ed.). *Mastery learning: Theory and practice*. New York: Holt, Rinehart and Winston, 1971.

Bloom, B. S. et al. (Eds.). *Taxonomy of educational objectives in the cognitive domain: The classification of educational goals*. New York: McKay, 1956.

Bloom, L. *Language development: Form and function in emerging grammars*. Cambridge, Mass: 1970.

Bloomberg, M. (Ed.). *Creativity: Theory and*

research. New Haven, Conn: College and University Press, 1973.

Boring, E. G. *A history of experimental psychology.* (2nd ed.) New York: Appleton-Century-Crofts, 1950.

Boston Globe. Good old days discipline, February 1, 1981.

Bovard, E. Interaction and attraction to the group. *Human Relations,* 1956, *9,* 481–489.

Bower, E. M. The emotionally handicapped child and the school. In H. W. Harshman (Ed.), *Educating the emotionally disturbed.* New York: Crowell, 1969.

Braine, M. D. S. The ontogeny of English phrase structure: The first phase. *Language,* 1963, *39,* 1–13.

Brannigan, C. R., and Humphries, D. A. Human non-verbal behavior, a means of communication. In N. Blurton Jones (Ed.), *Ethological studies of child behavior.* London: Cambridge University Press, 1972.

Bransford, J. D., and McCarrell, N. S. A sketch of a cognitive approach to comprehension: Some thoughts about understanding what it means to comprehend. In W. B. Weimer and D. S. Palermo (Eds.), *Cognition and the symbolic processes.* Hillsdale, N.J.: Erlbaum, 1974.

Breed, G. *Nonverbal behavior and teaching effectiveness.* Vermillion: University of South Dakota, 1971.

Bremner, J. G. Egocentric versus allocentric spatial coding in nine-month-old infants: Factors influencing the choice of a code. *Developmental Psychology,* 1978, *14,* 346–355.

Bronfenbrenner, U. Soviet studies of personality development and socialization. In R. Bauer (Ed.), *Some views of Soviet psychology.* Washington, D.C.: American Psychological Association, 1962.

Bronzaft, A. L., and McCarthy, D. P. The effect of elevated train noise on reading ability. *Environment and Behavior,* 1975, *7,* 517–527.

Brophy, J. E. and Evertson, C. M. *Student characteristics and teaching.* New York: Longman, 1981.

Brophy, J., and Good, T. Teachers' communication of differential expectations for children's classroom performance: Some behavioral data. *Journal of Educational Psychology,* 1970, *61,* 365–374.

Brophy, J., and Good, T. L. *Teacher-student relationships: Causes and consequences.* New York: Holt, Rinehart and Winston, 1974.

Brophy, J. Teacher behavior and its effects. *Journal of Educational Psychology,* 1979, *71,* 733–750.

Brophy, J. Advances in teacher effectiveness research. In H. F. Clarizio, R. C. Craig, and W. A. Mehrens (Eds.), *Contemporary issues in educational psychology.* (4th ed.) Boston: Allyn and Bacon, 1981.

Brophy, J. Teacher praise: A functional analysis. *Review of Educational Research,* 1981, *51,* 5–32.

Brown, R., and Lenneberg, E. H. A study of language and cognition. *Journal of Abnormal and Social Psychology,* 1954, 454–462.

Brown, R., and Gilman, A. The pronouns of power and solidarity. In T. A. Sebeok (Ed.), *Style in language.* Cambridge, Mass.: MIT Press, 1960, 253–276.

Brown, R., and Fraser, C. The acquisition of syntax. In C. N. Cofer and B. Musgrave (Eds.), *Verbal behavior and learning: Problems and processes.* New York: McGraw-Hill, 1963, 158–201.

Brown, R. *Social psychology.* New York: Free Press, 1965.

Brown, R. *A first language: The early stages.* Cambridge, Mass.: Harvard University Press, 1973.

Bruner, J. S., and Goodman, C. C. Value and need as organizing factors in perception.

Journal of Abnormal and Social Psychology, 1947, *42*, 33–44.

Bruner, J. S., and Tagiuri, R. The perception of people. In G. Lindzey (Ed.), *Handbook of social psychology*, Vol. 2. Reading, Mass.: Addison-Wesley, 1954.

Bruner, J. S., Shapiro, D., and Tagiuri, R. The meaning of traits in isolation and in combination. In R. Tagiuri and L. Petrullo (Eds.), *Person perception and interpersonal behavior*. Stanford, Calif.: Stanford University Press, 1958. Pp. 277–288.

Bruner, J. S. On cognitive growth: II. In J. S. Bruner, R. R. Olven, and P. M. Greenfield, *Studies in cognitive growth*. New York: Wiley, 1966.

Brunetti, F. A. Noise, distraction, and privacy in conventional and open school environments. *Proceedings of the ERDA conference*. Los Angeles: University of California, 1972.

Buros, O. K. (Ed.). *Tests in print: II.* Highland Park, N.J.: Gryphom Press, 1974.

Butterfield, E. C., Wambold, C., and Belmont, J. M. On the theory and practice of improving short-term memory. *American Journal of Mental Deficiency*, 1973, 77, 654–669.

Byers, P., and Byers, H. Nonverbal communication and the education of children. In C. B. Cazden, V. P. John, and D. Hynes (Eds.), *Functions of language in the classroom*. New York: Teachers College Press, 1972.

Callahan, C. M. *Developing creativity in the gifted and talented.* Reston, Va.: Council for Exceptional Children, 1978.

Campbell, D. T., and Stanley, J. C. *Experimental and quasi-experimental designs for research.* Chicago: Rand McNally, 1966.

Carter, R. How invalid are marks assigned by teachers? *Journal of Educational Psychology*, 1952, *43*, 218–228.

Cartwright, D. The nature of group cohesiveness. In D. Cartwright and A. Zander (Eds.), *Group dynamics: Research and theory.* New York: Harper and Row, 1968.

Centra, J. A., and Porter, D. A. School and teacher effects: An interrelational model. *Review of Educational Research*, 1980, *50*, 273–291.

Chaiken, A. L., Sigler, E., and Derlega, V. J. Nonverbal mediators of teacher expectancy effects. *Journal of Personality and Social Psychology*, 1974, *30*, 144–149.

Chomsky, C. *The acquisition of syntax in children from five to ten.* Cambridge, Mass.: MIT Press, 1969.

Chomsky, N. *Language and mind.* New York: Harcourt Brace Jovanovich, 1968.

Christian, C. C., Jr. Social and psychological implications of bilingual literacy. In A. Simoes, Jr. (Ed.), *The bilingual child.* New York: Academic Press, 1976. Pp. 17–40.

Clark, H. H., and Clark, E. V. *Psychology and language.* New York: Harcourt Brace Jovanovich, 1977.

Clark, K. B., and Clark, M. P. Racial identification and preference in Negro children. In T. M. Newcomb and E. L. Hartley (Eds.), *Readings in social psychology.* New York: Holt, 1947.

Clifford, M. M., and Walster, E. The effect of physical attractiveness on teacher expectation. *Sociology of Education*, 1973, *46*, 248–258.

Cohen, H. L., and Filipczak, J. *A new learning environment.* San Francisco: Jossey-Bass, 1971.

Cohen, L. B. *Concept acquisition in the human infant.* Institute for Child Behavior and Development, University of Illinois at Urbana-Champaign, 1977.

Cohen, P. A., Kulik, J. A., and Kulik, C. C. Educational outcomes of tutoring: A meta-analysis of findings. *American Educational Research Journal*, 1982, *19*, 237–248.

Cole, M., Frankel, F., and Sharp, D. W. The development of free recall learning in children. *Developmental Psychology*, 1971, *4*, 109–123.

Cole, M., and Scribner, S. *Culture and thought.* New York: Wiley, 1974.

Coleman, J. S., Campbell, E. Q., Hobson, C. J., McPartland, J., Mood, S. M., Weinfeld, F. D., and York, R. L. *Equality of educational opportunity* (2 vols.) Office of Education, U.S. Department of Health, Education, and Welfare. Washington, D.C.: U.S. Government Printing Office, 1966.

Coleman, J. *Achievement in high school: Public and private schools compared.* Washington, D.C.: National Center for Education Statistics, 1981.

Collins, A. Processes in acquiring knowledge. In R. C. Anderson, R. J. Spiro, and W. E. Montague (Eds.), *Schooling and the acquisition of knowledge.* Hillsdale, N.J.: Erlbaum, 1977.

Collins, A. M., and Loftus, E. F. A spreading-activation theory of semantic processing. *Psychological Review*, 1975, *82*, 407–428.

Cook, W. J., and Wollershein, J. P. The effect of labeling of special education students and the perception of contact versus noncontact peers. *Journal of Special Education*, 1976, *10*, 187–198.

Cooper, H. M. Pygmalion grows up: A model for teacher expectation communication and performance influence. *Review of Educational Research*, 1979, *49*, 389–410.

Cornbleth, C., Davis, O. L., and Button, C. Expectations for pupil achievement and teacher-pupil interaction. *Social Education*, 1974, *38*, 54–58.

Cratty, B. J., and Martin, M. M. *Perceptual motor efficiency in children.* Philadelphia: Lea and Febiger, 1969.

Cronbach, L. J. Test validation. In R. L. Thorndike (Ed.), *Educational measurement* (2nd ed.). Washington, D.C.: American Council on Education, 1971.

Cronbach, L. J., and Snow, R. E. *Aptitudes and instructional methods.* New York: Irvington Publishers, 1977.

Davidman, L. Learning style: The myth, the panacea, the wisdom. *Phi Delta Kappan*, 1981, *62*, 641–644.

Dawe, H. C. The influence of size of kindergarten group on performance. *Child Development*, 1934, *5*, 295–303.

DeBono, E. *Thinking course for juniors.* Blandford Forum, Dorset, England: Direct Education Services, 1974.

DeCecco, J. P. *Educational technology.* New York: Holt, Rinehart and Winston, 1964.

DeCharms, R., and Moeller, G. H. Values expressed in American children's readers, 1800–1950. *Journal of Abnormal and Social Psychology*, 1962, *64*, 136–142.

DeCharms, R. *Personal causation.* New York: Academic Press, 1968.

DeCharms, R. Personal-causation training in schools. *Journal of Applied Social Psychology*, 1972, *2*, 95–113.

Deregowski, J. B. Effect of cultural value of time upon recall. *British Journal of Social and Clinical Psychology*, 1970, *9*, 37–41.

Deutsch, M. The disadvantaged child and the learning process. In A. H. Passow (Ed.), *Education in depressed areas.* New York: Teachers College Press, 1963.

Deutsch, M. Environment and perception. In M. Deutsch, I. Katz, and A. R. Jensen (Eds.), *Social class, race, and psychological development.* New York: Holt, Rinehart and Winston, 1968. Pp. 58–85.

Dickson, W. P. *Children's oral communication skills.* New York: Academic Press, 1981.

Diener, C. I., and Dweck, C. S. An analysis of learned helplessness: Continuous changes in performance, strategy, and achievement cognitions following failure. *Journal of Personality and Social Psychology*, 1978, *36*, 451–462.

Dillard, J. L. *Black English: Its history and usage in the United States*. New York: Random House, 1972.

Dillon, J. T. Cognitive correspondence between question/statement and response. *American Educational Research Journal*, 1982, *19*, 540–551.

Dion, K. K. Physical attractiveness and evaluations of children's transgressions. *Journal of Personality and Social Psychology*, 1972, *24*, 207–213.

Dion, K. K., and Berscheid, E. Physical attractiveness and social perception of peers of preschool children. Reported in Berscheid, E. and Walster, E., Physical attractiveness. In L. Berkowitz (Ed.), *Advances in experimental social psychology*, Vol. 7. New York: Academic Press, 1974.

Domino, G. Interactive effects of achievement orientation and teaching style on academic achievement. *Journal of Educational Psychology*, 1971, *62*, 427–431.

Domino, G. Aptitude by treatment interaction effects in college instruction. Paper presented at the annual meeting of the American Psychological Association, 1974.

Dooling, D. J., and Lachman, R. Effects of comprehension on retention of prose. *Journal of Experimental Psychology*, 1971, *88*, 216–222.

Dowaliby, F. J., and Schumer, H. Teacher-centered versus student-centered mode of college classroom instruction as related to manifest anxiety. *Journal of Educational Psychology*, 1973, *64*, 125–132.

Duchastel, P. C., and Merrill, P. F. The effects of behavioral objectives on learning: A review of empirical studies. *Review of Educational Research*, 1973, *43*, 53–70.

Dunn, L. M. Special education for the mildly retarded—Is much of it justifiable? *Exceptional Child*, 1968, *35*, 5–22.

Dunn, R., Dunn, K., and Price, G. E. *Learning style inventory*. Lawrence, Kans.: Price Systems, 1979. (a)

Dunn, R., Dunn, K. and Price, G. E. *LSI manual*. Lawrence, Kans: Price Systems, 1979. (b)

Dunphy, D. C. The social structure of urban adolescent peer groups. *Sociometry*, 1963, *26*, 230–246.

DuPont, H. (Ed.). *Educating emotionally disturbed children*. New York: Holt, Rinehart and Winston, 1969.

Dweck, C. S. The role of expectations and attributions in the alleviation of learned helplessness. *Journal of Personality and Social Psychology*, 1975, *31*, 674–685.

Dweck, C. S., and Bush, E. S. Sex differences in learned helplessness: I. Differential debilitation with peers and adult evaluators. *Developmental Psychology*, 1976, *12*, 147–156.

Dyer, H. S. School factors and equal educational opportunity. *Harvard Educational Review*, 1968, 38–56.

Ebel, R. L. *Essentials of educational measurement*. Englewood Cliffs, N.J.: Prentice-Hall, 1972.

Educational Research Service. Class size research: A critique of recent meta-analyses. *Phi Delta Kappan*, 1980, 239–241.

Educational Testing Service. *Conditions and processes of effective desegregation*. Princeton, N.J.: Educational Testing Service, 1976.

Educational Testing Service. *Test use and validity: A response to changes in the Nader/Nairn report on ETS*. Princeton, N.J.: Educational Testing Service, 1980.

Ekman, P. Universals and cultural differences in facial expressions of emotion. In J. K. Cole (Ed.), *Nebraska symposium on motivation*, Vol. 19. Lincoln: University of Nebraska Press, 1972.

Ekman, P., Friesen, W. V., and Ellsworth, P.

Emotion in the human face. New York: Pergamon, 1972.

Ekstrom, R. B. *Experimental studies of homogeneous grouping: A review of the literature.* Princeton, N.J.: Educational Testing Service, 1959.

Elkind, D., and Weiner, I. B. *Development of the child.* New York: Wiley, 1978.

Ellis, H. *The transfer of learning.* New York: Macmillan, 1965.

Erikson, E. H. *Childhood and society.* (2nd ed.) New York: Norton, 1963.

Esposito, D. Homogeneous and heterogeneous ability grouping: Principal findings and implications for evaluating and designing more effective educational environments. *Review of Educational Research*, 1973, *43*, 163–179.

Eysenck, H. J., and Kamin, L. *The intelligence controversy.* New York: Wiley, 1981.

Fancher, R. E. *Pioneers of psychology.* New York: Norton, 1979.

Fantz, R. L. The origin of form perception. *Scientific American*, 1961, *204*, 66–72.

Fantz, R. L. Visual experience in infants: Decreased attention to familiar patterns relative to novel ones. *Science*, 1964, 668–670.

Feagans, L. and Farran, D. C. *The language of children reared in poverty.* New York: Academic Press, 1981.

Feldhusen, J. F. Student perceptions of frequent quizzes and postmortem discussions of tests. *Journal of Educational Measurement*, 1964, *1*, 51–54.

Feldhusen, J. F., DiVesta, F. J., Thornburg, H. D., Levin, J. R., and Ringness, T. A. Careers in educational psychology. *Educational Psychologist*, 1976, *12*, 83–90.

Feldhusen, J. F. Two views of the development of educational psychology. *Educational Psychologist*, 1978, *12*, 297–304.

Feldman, R. S., and Allen, V. L. Develop-

mental trends in decoding of nonverbal behavior. Paper presented at the annual meeting of the Eastern Psychological Association, Philadelphia, April 1974.

Feldman, R. S. Nonverbal disclosure of teacher deception and interpersonal affect. *Journal of Educational Psychology*, 1976, *68*, 807–816.

Feldman, R. S., and Allen, V. L. Student success and tutor verbal and nonverbal behavior. *Journal of Educational Research*, 1979, *72*, 142–149.

Feldman, R. S., and Donohoe, L. F. Nonverbal communication of affect in interracial dyads. *Journal of Educational Psychology*, 1978, *70*, 979–987.

Feldman, R. S., Jenkins, L., and Popoola, O. Detection of deception in adults and children via facial expressions. *Child Development*, 1979, *50*, 350–355.

Feldman, R. S., and Prohaska, T. The student as Pygmalion: Effect of student expectation on the teacher. *Journal of Educational Psychology*, 1979, *4*, 485–493.

Fenstermacher, G. A philosophical consideration of recent research on teacher effectiveness. In L. Shulman (Ed.), *Review of research in education*, Vol. 6. Itasca, Ill.: Peacock, 1979.

Fiedler, F. E. Validation and extension of the contingency model of leadership effectiveness: A review of empirical findings. *Psychological Bulletin*, 1971, *76*, 128–148.

Fiedler, F. E. The contingency model and the dynamics of the leadership process. In L. Berkowitz (Ed.), *Advances in experimental social psychology*, Vol. 11. New York: Academic Press, 1978. Pp. 59–112.

Findley, W. G. Purpose of school testing programs and their efficient development. In W. G. Findley (Ed.), *Sixty-second yearbook of the National Society for the Study of Education, Part II.* Chicago: University of Chicago Press, 1963.

Findley, W. G., and Bryon, M. W. *Ability grouping: 1970. Status, impact, and alternatives.* Athens, Ga.: Center for Educational Improvement, 1971.

Fishbein, H. D. *Evaluation, development, and children's learning.* Pacific Palisades, Calif.: Goodyear, 1976.

Fiske, E. B. Public school prestige is low and getting lower. *New York Times*, August 26, 1979, sec. 4, p. 24.

Fitzgerald, D., and Ausubel, D. P. Cognitive versus affective factors in the learning and retention of controversial material. *Journal of Educational Psychology*, 1963, *54*, 73–84.

Flavell, J. H., Botkin, P. T., Fry, C. K., Wright, J. C., and Jarvis, P. E. *The development of role-taking and communication skills in children.* Huntington, N.Y.: Frieger, 1968.

Freedman, J. L., Sears, D. O., and Carlsmith, J. M. *Social psychology.* (3rd ed.) Englewood Cliffs, N.J.: Prentice-Hall, 1978.

French, J. R. P., Jr., and Raven, B. The bases of social power. In D. Cartwright (Ed.), *Studies in social power.* Ann Arbor, Mich.: Institute for Social Research, 1959. Pp. 150–167.

Freud, S. Formulations regarding the two principles in mental functioning. In *Collected papers,* Vol. 4. Translated by J. Riviere. London: Hogarth, 1934. (a)

Freud, S. The relation of the poet to daydreaming. In *Collected papers,* Vol. 4. Translated by J. Riviere. London: Hogarth, 1934. (b)

Friedman, H., and Friedman, P. Frequency and types of teacher reinforcement given to lower- and middle-class students. Paper presented at the annual meeting of the American Educational Research Association, New Orleans, 1973.

Frymier, J. The Annehurst system: Built on the recognition that people are different. *Phi Delta Kappan*, 1980, *61*, 682–684.

Gagné, R. M. Military training and principles of learning. *American Psychologist*, 1962, *17*, 83–91.

Gagné, R. M. (Ed.). *Learning and individual differences.* Columbus, Ohio: Merrill, 1967.

Gagné, R. M. *The conditions of learning.* (2nd ed.) New York: Holt, Rinehart and Winston, 1970.

Garvey, C. *Play.* Cambridge, Mass.: Harvard University Press, 1977.

Gates, A. I. Recitation as a factor in memorizing. *Archives of Psychology*, 1917, *6*, 1–104.

Gay, G. Teachers' achievement expectations of and classroom interactions with ethnically different students. *Contemporary Education*, 1975, *46*, 166–172.

Gellert, E., Girgus, J. S., and Cohen, J. Children's awareness of their bodily appearance: A developmental study of factors associated with body percept. *Genetic Psychology Monographs*, 1971, *84*, 109–174.

Gelman, D. Just how the sexes differ. *Newsweek*, 1981, 72–83.

Getzels, J. W., and Jackson, P. W. *Creativity and intelligence.* New York: Wiley, 1962

Gibb, C. A. Leadership. In G. Lindzey and E. Aronsen (Eds.), *The handbook of social psychology,* Vol. 4. (2nd ed.) Reading, Mass.: Addison-Wesley, 1969.

Gilchrist, J. C., Shaw, M. E., and Walker, L. C. Some effects of unequal distribution of information in a wheel group structure. *Journal of Abnormal and Social Psychology*, 1964, *49*, 554–556.

Gilstrap, P. L., and Martin, W. R. *Current strategies for teachers: A resource book for personalizing instruction.* Pacific Palisades, Calif.: Goodyear, 1975.

Ginsburg, H., and Opper, S. *Piaget's theory of intellectual development: An introduction.* Englewood Cliffs, N.J.: Prentice-Hall, 1969.

Gladwin, T. Culture and logical process. In W. Goodenough (Ed.), *Explorations in cultural anthropology: Essays in honour of George Peter Murdoch.* New York: McGraw-Hill, 1964.

Glass, G. V., and Smith, M. L. *Meta-analysis of research on class size and achievement.* Boulder: Laboratory of Educational Research, University of Colorado, 1978.

Glass, G. V., Cahen, L. S., Smith, M. L., and Filby, N. N. *School class size: Research and policy.* Beverly Hills, Calif.: Sage, 1982.

Glucksberg, S., Krauss, R., and Higgins, E. T. The development of referential communication skills. In F. D. Horowitz (Ed.), *Review of child development research,* Vol. 4. New York: Russell Sage, 1975. Pp. 305–345.

Golann, S. E. Psychological study of creativity. *Psychological Bulletin,* 1963, *60,* 548–565.

Goldman, A. L. Scores rise at school after nearby subway is quieted. *New York Times.* April, 1982, B4.

Goleman, D. 1,528 little geniuses and how they grew. *Psychology Today,* 1980, *13,* 28–53.

Good, T. Which pupils do teachers call on? *Elementary School Journal,* 1970, *70,* 190–198.

Gordon, T. *Teacher effectiveness training.* New York: Peter H. Wyden, 1974.

Greene, D., and Lepper, M. R. How to turn play into work. *Psychology Today,* 1974, *8,* 49–54.

Greenfield, P. M. On culture and conversation. In J. S. Bruner, R. R. Olver, and P. M. Greenfield (Eds.), *Studies in cognitive growth.* New York: Wiley, 1966.

Greenfield, P. M., and Bruner, J. S. Culture and cognitive growth. In D. A. Goslin (Ed.), *Handbook of socialization theory and research.* New York: Rand-McNally, 1969.

Grinder, R. E. What 200 years tell us about professional priorities in educational psychology. *Educational Psychologist,* 1978, *12,* 284–289.

Gronlund, N. E. *Constructing achievement tests.* (2nd ed.) Englewood Cliffs, N.J.: Prentice-Hall, 1977.

Grotelueschen, A., and Sjogren, D. D. Effects of differentially structured introductory materials and learning tasks on learning and transfer. *American Educational Research Journal,* 1968, *5,* 191–202.

Guilford, J. P. A psychometric approach to creativity. In H. H. Anderson (Ed.), *Creativity in childhood and adolescence.* Palo Alto, Calif.: Science and Behavior Books, 1965.

Guilford, J. P. *The nature of human intelligence.* New York: McGraw-Hill, 1967.

Guilford, J. P. The structure of intelligence. In D. K. White (Ed.), *Handbook of measurement and assessment in behavioral sciences.* Reading, Mass.: Addison-Wesley, 1968.

Gulian, E. Psychological consequences of exposure to noise: Facts and explanations. In U.S. Environmental Protection Agency, *Proceedings of the International Congress on Noise as a Public Health Problem.* Washington, D.C.: U.S. Government Printing Office, 1974.

Guskin, A. E., and Guskin, S. L. *A social psychology of education.* Reading, Mass.: Addison-Wesley, 1970.

Guskin, J. T. The social perception of language variation: Black and white teachers' attitudes toward speakers from different racial and social class backgrounds. *Dissertation Abstracts International,* February 1971, *31* (8-A), 3954.

Guthrie, E. R. *The psychology of learning.* New York: Harper, 1952.

Haefele, D. L. How to evaluate thee, teacher—Let me count the ways. *Phi Delta Kappan,* 1980, *61,* 349–352.

Hales, L. W., Bain, P. T., and Rand, L. P. An investigation of some aspects of the pass-fail grading system. Paper presented at the annual meeting of the American Educational Research Association, New York, 1971.

Haley, A. *Roots.* Garden City, N.Y.: Doubleday, 1974.

Hall, E. T. *The hidden dimension.* Garden City, N.Y.: Doubleday, 1966.

Hambleton, R. K. Advances in criterion-referenced testing methodology. In C. R. Reynolds and T. B. Gutkin (Eds.), *Handbook of school psychology.* New York: Wiley, 1982.

Hambleton, R. K., Swaminathan, H., and Algina, J. Some contributions to the theory and practice of criterion-referenced testing. In D. N. M. de Gruijter and L. J. T. van der Kemp (Eds.), *Advances in psychological and educational measurement.* New York: Wiley, 1976.

Hambleton, R. K., Swaminathan, H., Algina, J., and Coulson, D. B. Criterion-referenced testing and measurement: A review of technical issues and developments. *Review of Educational Research,* 1978, *48,* 1–47.

Harari, H. Specialist: Name can hinder child. *Minneapolis Star,* June 2, 1973.

Hargreaves, D. H. *Social relations in a secondary school.* New York: Humanities Press, 1967.

Harns, L. S. Status cues in speech: Extra-race and extra-region identification. *Lingua,* 1963, *12,* 300–306.

Hartshorne, H., and May, M. A. *Studies in deceit.* New York: Macmillan, 1928.

Hartup, W. W. Peer interaction and social organization. In P. H. Mussen (Ed.), *Manual of child psychology.* New York: Wiley, 1970. Pp. 361–456.

Heider, F. *The psychology of interpersonal relations.* New York: Wiley, 1958.

Hastorf, A. H., Schneider, D. J., and Polefka, J. *Person perception.* Reading, Mass.: Addison-Wesley, 1977.

Heinich, R., Molenda, M., and Russell, J. D. *Instructional media and the new technologies of instruction.* New York: John Wiley, 1982.

Heller, M. S., and White, M. A. Rates of teacher verbal approval and disapproval to higher and lower ability classes. *Journal of Educational Psychology,* 1975, *67* (6), 796–800.

Hersh, R. H., Paolitto, D. P., and Reimer, J. *Promoting moral growth.* New York: Longmans, 1979.

Hess, E. H. Effects of meprobamate on imprinting in waterfowl. *Annals of the New York Academy of Sciences,* 1957, *67,* 724–733.

Hess, R. Social class and ethnic influences on socialization. In P. Mussen (Ed.), *Carmichael's manual of child psychology,* Vol. 2. New York: Wiley, 1970. Pp. 457–558.

Hess, R. D., and Shipman, V. C. Early experiences and the socialization of cognitive modes in children. In M. W. Miles and W. W. Charters, Jr. (Eds.), *Learning in social settings.* Boston: Allyn and Bacon, 1970.

Hewett, F. M., and Forness, S. R. *Education of exceptional learners.* Boston: Allyn and Bacon, 1974.

Hilgard, E. R. Creativity and problem solving. In H. H. Anderson (Ed.), *Creativity and its cultivation.* New York: Harper, 1959.

Hill, W. F. *Learning.* (3rd ed.) New York: Harper & Row, 1977.

Holden, C. NAS backs cautious use of ability tests. *Science,* 1982, 215, 950.

Holt, J. *How children fail.* New York: Pitman, 1964.

Holt, J. *How children learn.* New York: Pitman, 1967.

Hopkins, K. D., and Stanley, J. C. *Educational*

and psychological measurement and evaluation. (6th ed.) Englewood Cliffs, N. J.: Prentice-Hall, 1981.

Horn, E. *Distribution of opportunity for participation among the various pupils in the classroom recitations.* New York: Teachers College, Columbia University, 1914.

Horner, M. Toward an understanding of achievement-related conflicts in women. *Journal of Social Issues,* 1972, *28,* 157–175.

Horowitz, R. A. Psychological effects of the "open classroom." *Review of Educational Research,* 1979, *49,* 71–86.

Hull, C. L. *Principles of behavior.* New York: Appleton-Century-Crofts, 1943.

Hunt, E. B. What kind of computer is man? *Cognitive Psychology,* 1971, *2,* 57–98.

Hunt, E. B. Mechanics of verbal ability. *Psychological Review,* 1978, *85,* 109–130.

Hurt, H. T., Scott, M. D., and McCroskey, J. G. *Communication in the classroom.* Reading, Mass.: Addison-Wesley, 1978.

Hutt, M. L., and Gibby, R. G. *The mentally retarded child: Development, training, and education.* (4th ed.) Boston: Allyn and Bacon, 1979.

Hyman, H. H. The value systems of different classes. In R. Bendix and S. Lipset (Eds.), *Class, status, and power.* Glencoe, Ill.: Free Press, 1953, 426–442.

Irving, O., and Martin, J. Withitness: The confusing variable. *American Educational Research Journal,* 1982, *19,* 313–319.

Jackson, P., and Lahaderne, H. Inequalities of teacher-pupil contacts. *Psychology in the Schools,* 1967, *4,* 204–211.

Jecker, J. D., Maccoby, N., and Breitrose, H. S. Improving accuracy in interpreting non-verbal cues of comprehension. *Psychology in the Schools,* 1965, *2,* 239–244.

Jencks, C., Smith, M., Acland, H., Bane, M. J., Cohen, D., Gintis, H., Heyns, B., and

Michelson, S. *Inequality: A reassessment of the effect of family and schooling in America.* New York: Harper, Colophon Books, 1972.

Jenkins, J. J. Remember that old theory of memory? Well, forget it! *American Psychologist,* 1974, *29,* 785–795.

Jensen, A. How much can we boost IQ and scholastic achievement? *Harvard Educational Review,* 1969, *39,* 1–123.

Jensen, A. A theory of primary and secondary familial mental retardation. In N. R. Ellis (Ed.), *International review of research in mental retardation,* Vol. 4. New York: Academic Press, 1970

Johnson, D. W., and Johnson, R. T. Instructional goal structure: Cooperative, competitive, or individualistic. *Review of Educational Research,* 1974, *44,* 213–240.

Johnson, D. W., and Johnson, R. *Learning together and alone: Cooperation, competition and individualization.* Englewood Cliffs, N.J.: Prentice-Hall, 1975.

Jones, E. E., and Nisbett, R. E. The actor and the observer: Divergent perception of the causes of behavior. In E. E. Jones et al. (Eds.), *Attributions: Perceiving the causes of behavior.* Morristown, N.J.: General Learning Press, 1972.

Jones, H. E. Adolescence in our society. In J. Seidman (Ed.), *The adolescent: A book of readings.* (Rev. ed.) New York: Holt, Rinehart and Winston, 1960.

Kamin, L. J. *The science and politics of IQ.* New York: Wiley, 1974.

Kandel, D., and Lesser, G. S. School, family, and peer influences on educational plans of adolescents in the United States and Denmark. *Sociology of Education,* 1970, *43,* 270–287.

Kaplan, R. Effects of grouping and response characteristics of instructional objectives on learning from prose. *Journal of Educational Psychology,* 1976, *68,* 424–430.

Kaplan, R., and Rothkopf, E. Z. Instructional objectives as directions to learners: Effect of passage length and amount of objective relevant content. *Journal of Educational Psychology*, 1974, *66*, 448–456.

Kaplan, R., and Simmons, F. G. Effects of instructional objectives used as orienting stimuli or as summary: Review upon prose learning. *Journal of Educational Psychology*, 1974, *66*, 614–622.

Kaplan, R. Nader's raid on the testing industry: Is it in the best interest of the consumer? *American Psychologist*, 1982, *37*, 15–23.

Karlins, M., Coffman, T., and Walters, G. On the fading of social stereotypes: Studies in three generations of college students. *Journal of Personaltiy and Social Psychology*, 1969, *31*, 1–16.

Katz, I. The socialization of achievement motivation in minority group children. In D. Levine (Ed.), *Nebraska symposium on motivation*. Lincoln: University of Nebraska Press, 1967. Pp. 133–191.

Kausler, D. H. *Psychology of verbal learning and memory*. New York: Academic Press, 1974.

Kazdin, A. E., and Klock, J. The effect of nonverbal teacher approval on student attentive behavior. *Journal of Applied Behavioral Analysis*, 1973, *6*, 643–654.

Keasey, C. B. Social participation as a factor in the moral development of preadolescents. *Developmental Psychology*, 1971, *5*, 216–220.

Keith, T. L., Tornatzky, L. G., and Pettigrew, L. E. An analysis of verbal and nonverbal classroom teaching behaviors. *Journal of Experimental Education*, 1974, *42*, 30–38.

Kelley, H. H. The warm-cold variable in first impressions of persons. *Journal of Personality*, 1950, *18*, 431–439.

Kester, S., and Letchworth, G. Communication of teacher expectations and their effects on achievement and attitudes of secondary school students. *Journal of Educational Research*, 1972, *66*, 51–55.

Kirk, S. A. *Educating exceptional children.* Boston: Houghton Mifflin, 1972.

Klausmeier, H. J. *Learning and human abilities: Educational Psychology.* (4th ed.). New York: Harper & Row, 1975.

Klausmeier, H. J., Jeter, J., Quilling, M., and Frayer, D. *Individually guided motivation.* Madison: Wisconsin Research and Development Center for Cognitive Learning, 1973.

Kleinke, C. L., Meeker, F. B., and LaFong, C. Effects of gaze, touch, and use of name on evaluation of "engaged" couples. *Journal of Research in Personality*, 1974, *7*, 368–373.

Kluger, R. *Simple justice.* New York: Knopf, 1976.

Knapp, M. L. *Nonverbal communication in human interaction.* (2nd ed.). New York: Holt, Rinehart and Winston, 1978.

Knowlton, M. P. The Elder Hostel philosophy. *Alternative Higher Education*, 1980, *5*, 65–70.

Kohlberg, L. The development of children's orientations towards a moral order: Sequence in the development of moral thought. *Vita Humana*, 1963, *6*, 11–33.

Kohlberg, L. Stage and sequence: The cognitive-developmental approach to socialization. In D. A. Goslin (Ed.), *Handbook of socialization theory and research*. Chicago: Rand McNally, 1969. Pp. 397–401.

Kohlberg, L. Moral stages and moralization: The cognitive-developmental approach. In T. Lickona (Ed.), *Moral development and behavior: Theory, research, and social issues.* New York: Holt, Rinehart and Winston, 1976.

Kolb, D. Achievement motivation training for underachieving high school boys. *Journal of Personality and Social Psychology*, 1965, *2*, 783–792.

Kolesnick, W. B. *Learning: Educational applications.* Boston: Allyn and Bacon, 1979.

Komorita, S. S., Sheposh, J. P., and Braver, S. L. Power, the use of power, and cooperative choice in a two-person game. *Journal of Personality and Social Psychology,* 1968, *8,* 134–142.

Koneya, M. Location and interaction in row-and-column seating arrangements. *Environment and Behavior,* 1976, *8,* 265–282.

Kounin, J. *Discipline and group management in classrooms.* New York: Holt, Rinehart and Winston, 1970.

Kuhn, T. S. *The structure of scientific revolutions.* (2nd ed.) Chicago: University of Chicago Press, 1970.

Kulhavy, R. W. Feedback in written instruction. *Review of Educational Research,* 1977, *47,* 211–232

Labov, W. The logic of nonstandard English. In N. Keddie (Ed.), *Tinker, tailor . . . The myth of cultural deprivation.* Harmondsworth, England: Penguin Education, 1973. Pp. 21–66.

Lado, R. *Linguistics across cultures.* Ann Arbor: University of Michigan Press, 1957.

LaFrance, M., and Mayo, C. *Moving bodies: Nonverbal communication in social relationships.* Monterey, Calif.: Brooks/Cole, 1978.

Lake, A., Rainey, J., and Papsdorf, J. D. Biofeedback and rational-emotive therapy in the management of migraine headaches. *Journal of Applied Behavior Analysis,* 1979, *12,* 127–140.

Lambert, W. E., and Peal, E. The relation of bilingualism to intelligence. In A. S. Dil (Ed.), *Language, psychology, and culture.* Stanford, Calif.: Stanford University Press, 1972.

Laosa, L. M. Maternal teaching strategies and cognitive styles in Chicano families. *Journal of Educational Psychology,* 1982, *72,* no. 1, 12–18.

Lassers, E., Nordan, R., and Bladholm, S. Steps in the return to school of children with school phobia. *American Journal of Psychiatry,* 1973, *130,* 265–268.

Leathers, D. *Nonverbal communications systems.* Boston: Allyn and Bacon, 1976.

Lee, C. L. Social encounters of infants: The beginnings of popularity. Paper presented at the annual meeting of the International Society for the Study of Behavioral Development, Ann Arbor, Mich., 1973.

Lefrancois, G. R. *Of children.* Belmont, Calif.: Wadsworth, 1973.

Lenneberg, E. H. *Biological foundations of language.* New York: John Wiley, 1967.

Lenneberg, E. H. Speech as a motor skill with special reference to nonaphasic disorders. In *Cognitive development in children: Five monographs of the Society for Research in Child Development.* Chicago: Society for Research in Child Development, 1970.

Lenneberg, E. H., and Roberts, J. The language of experience: A study in methodology. Memoir 13. *International Journal of American Linguistics,* 1956, *22.*

Lepper, M. R., and Greene, D. Turning play into work: Effects of adult surveillance and extrinsic motivation. *Journal of Personality and Social Psychology,* 1975, *31,* 479–486.

Lerner, R. M. *Concepts and theories of human development.* Reading, Mass.: Addison-Wesley, 1976.

Lesgold, A. M., Pellegrino, J. W., Fokkema, S. D., and Glaser, R. (Eds.), *Cognitive psychology and instruction.* New York: Plenum Press, 1978.

Lesser, G. S., Fifer, G., and Clark, D. H. Mental abilities of children from different social-class and cultural groups. *Monographs of the Society for Research in Child Development,* 1968, *30* (4).

Levin, J. R., Pressley, M., McCormick, C. B., Miller, G. E., and Shriberg, L. K. Assessing the classroom potential of the keyword method. *Journal of Educational Psychology*, 1979, *71*, 583–594.

Levine, F. M., and Fasnacht, G. Token rewards may lead to token learning. *American Psychologist*, 1974, *29*, 816–820.

Lewis, M., Goldberg, S., and Campbell, H. A developmental study of information processing within the first three years of life. Response decrement to a redundant signal. *Monographs of the Society for Research in Child Development*, 1969, *34* (9).

Lorayne, H. and Lucas, J. *The memory book.* New York: Ballantine, 1974.

Lorenz, K. The companion in the bird's world. *Auk*, 1937, *54*, 245–273.

Lorenz, K. *On aggression.* Translated by M. K. Wilson. New York: Bantam Books, 1967.

Lucker, G. W., Rosenfield, D., Sikes, J., and Aronson, E. Performance in the interdependent classroom: A field study. *American Educational Research Journal*, 1976, *13*, 115–123.

Lyman, H. B. *Test scores and what they mean.* Englewood Cliffs, N.J.: Prentice-Hall, 1963.

Maccoby, E. E., and Jacklin, C. N. *The psychology of sex differences.* Stanford, Calif.: Stanford University Press, 1974.

Mackay, L. D. The role of measurement and evaluation in science courses. In P. L. Gardner (Ed.), *The structure of science education.* Hawthorne, Victoria, Australia: Longman, Australia, 1975.

MacKinnon, D. W. Personality and the realization of creative potential. *American Psychologist*, 1965, *20*, 273–281.

Madsen, W. *The Mexican Americans of South Texas.* New York: Holt, Rinehart and Winston, 1964.

Maehr, M. L. *Sociocultural origins of achievement.* Belmont, Calif.: Wadsworth, 1974.

Maeroff, Gene I. The unfavored gifted few. *New York Times Magazine*, August 21, 1977.

Mager, R. F. *Preparing instructional objectives.* Palo Alto, Calif.: Feron, 1962.

Malsam, M. The computer replaces the card catalog in one Colorado elementary school. *Phi Delta Kappan*, January, 1982, 321.

Markle, S. M. *Good frames and bad: A grammar of frame writing.* New York: Wiley, 1966.

Martin, L. S., and Pavan, B. N. Current research on open space, nongrading, vertical grouping, and team teaching. *Phi Delta Kappan*, 1976, *57*, 310–315.

Masland, R. L., Sarason, S. B., and Gladwyn, T. *Mental subnormality.* New York: Basic Books, 1958.

Maslow, A. Some educational implications of humanistic psychologies. *Harvard Educational Review*, 1968, *38*, 685–696.

Maslow, A. *Motivation and personality.* (2nd ed.) New York: Harper and Row, 1970.

Mason, E. J. Teachers' observations and expectations of boys and girls as influenced by biased psychological reports and knowledge of the effects of bias. *Journal of Educational Psychology*, 1973, *65*, 238–243.

Matarazzo, J. D. *Wechsler's measurement and appraisal of adult intellegence.* (5th ed.) Baltimore: Williams and Wilkins, 1972.

Mayer, R. E. Information processing variables in learning to solve problems. *Review of Educational Research*, 1975, *45*, 525–541. (a)

Mayer, R. E. Different problem solving competencies established in learning computer programming with and without meaningful models. *Journal of Educational Psychology*, 1975, *67*, 725–734. (b)

Mayer, R. E. Some conditions of meaningful learning of computer programming: Advance organizers and subject control of frame sequencing. *Journal of Educational Psychology*, 1976, *68*, 143–150.

Mayer, R. E., and Bromage, B. K. Different recall protocols for technical texts due to advance organizers. *Journal of Educational Psychology*, 1980, *72*, 209–225.

McClelland, D. C. *The achieving society*. New York: Free Press, 1961.

McClelland, D. C. The role of educational technology in developing achievement motivation. *Educational Technology*, 1969, *9*, 7–16.

McClelland, D. C., Atkinson, J. W., Clark, R. A., and Lowell, E. L. *The achievement motive*. New York: Appleton-Century-Crofts, 1953.

McClelland, D. C., and Winter, D. G. *Motivating economic achievement*. New York: Free Press, 1969.

McConnell, F. Children with hearing disabilities. In L. M. Dunn (Ed.), *Exceptional children in the schools*. New York: Holt, Rinehart and Winston, 1973.

McDaniel, T. R. Exploring alternatives to punishment: The key to effective discipline. *Phi Delta Kappan*, 1980, *61*, 455–459.

McDonald, F. J. *Executive summary report: Beginning teacher evaluation study, Phase II*. Princeton, N.J.: Educational Testing Service, 1976.

Mead, M. Our educational emphases in primitive perspective. *American Journal of Sociology*, 1942–1943, *48*, 633–639.

Meacham, M. L., and Wiesen, A. E. *Changing classroom behavior: A manual for precision teaching*. Scranton, Pa.: International Textbook Co., 1970.

Medley, D. *Teacher competence and teacher effectiveness: A review of process-product research*. Washington, D.C.: American Association of Colleges for Teacher Education, 1977.

Mehrens, W. A., and Lehman, I. J. *Measurement and evaluation in education and psychology*. New York: Holt, Rinehart and Winston, 1975.

Melmed, A. S. Information technology for U.S. schools. *Phi Delta Kappan*, January, 1982, 308–311.

Mercer, J., and Lewis, J. F. *System of multicultural pluralistic assessment: Conceptual and technical manual*. Riverside, Calif.: Institute for Pluralistic Assessment Research and Training, 1978.

Merrill, M. D., and Stolurow, L. M. Hierarchical preview versus problem oriented review in learning an imaginary science. *American Educational Research Journal*, 1966, *3*, 251–261.

Meyerson, L., Ken, N., and Michael, J. L. Behavior modification in rehabilitation. In S. W. Bijou and D. M. Baer (Eds.), *Child development: Readings in experimental analysis*. New York: Appleton-Century-Crofts, 1967.

Milgram, S. *Obedience to authority: An experimental view*. New York: Harper, Colophon, 1974.

Miller, C., McLaughlin, J., Haddon, J., and Chansky, N. Socio-economic class and teacher bias. *Psychological Reports*, 1968, *23*, 806.

Millman, J. Criterion-referenced measurement. In W. J. Popham (Ed.), *Evaluation in education: Current applications*. Berkeley, Calif.: McCutchan Publishing, 1974.

Montagu, A. *Touching: The human significance of the skin*. New York: Columbia University Press, 1971.

Moscovici, S., and Faucheux, C. Social influence, conformity bias, and the study of active minorities. In L. Berkowitz (Ed.), *Advances in experimental social psychology*, Vol. 6. New York: Academic Press, 1972. Pp. 150–202.

Moustakas, C. E. The frequency and intensity of negative attitudes expressed in play therapy. *Journal of Genetic Psychology*, 1955, *86*, 309–325.

Mueller, E., and Lucas, T. A developmental analysis of peer interaction among toddlers. In M. Lewis and L. A. Rosenblum (Eds.),

Friendship and peer relations. New York: Wiley, 1975.

Nairn, A. and Associates. *The reign of ETS: The corporation that makes up minds.* Washington, D.C., 1980.

Nassif-Royer, P. Effects of specificity and position of written instructional objectives on learning from lecture. *Journal of Educational Psychology,* 1977, *69,* 40–45.

NAEP Information Yearbook, (1974)

NAEP Newsletter, (1977)

NEA Reporter. Educating the newest Americans. April–May, 1981, 6–7.

Nedelsky, L. Absolute grading standards for objective tests. *Educational and Psychological Measurement,* 1954, *14,* 3–19.

Neill, A. S. *Summerhill: A radical approach to education.* New York: Hart Publishing, 1960.

Nelson, T. O. Savings and forgetting from long-term memory. *Journal of Verbal Learning and Verbal Behavior,* 1971, *10,* 568–576.

New York Times. Computers: Focus on schools. November 23, 1982.

Newcomb, T. M. *The acquaintance process.* New York: Holt, Rinehart and Winston, 1961.

Newsweek. Minnesota leads the way. November 22, 1982, 116.

Ng, C. A. The educational background of the adult Chinese student. *TESL Talk,* 1975, *6,* 36–40.

Northern, E. F. The trend toward competency testing of teachers. *Phi Delta Kappan,* 1980, *61,* 359.

Nuttall, E. V. System of multi-pluralistic assessment: Test review. *Journal of Educational Measurement,* 1979, *16,* 285–290.

Oden, M. H. The fulfillment of promise: Forty-year follow-up of Terman gifted group. *Ge-netic Psychology Monographs,* 1968, *7,* 3–93.

Offer, D., and Sabshin, M. *Normality: Theoretical and clinical concepts of mental health.* (Rev. ed.) New York: Basic Books, 1974.

Ogilvie, B. C., and Tutko, T. A. Sport: If you want to build character, try something else. *Psychology Today,* 1971, *5,* 63–69.

Olson, D. R. *Cognitive development: The child's acquisition of diagonality.* New York: Academic Press, 1970.

Ornstein, A. C. *Education and social inquiry.* Itasca, Ill.: Peacock, 1978.

Osgood, C. E. The similarity paradox in human learning: A resolution. *Psychological Review,* 1949, *56,* 132–143.

Osgood, C. E., Suci, G. J., and Tannenbaum, P. H. *The measurement of meaning.* Urbana: University of Illinois Press, 1957.

Overmier, J. B., and Seligman, M. E. P. Effects of inescapable shock upon subsequent escape and avoidance responding. *Journal of Comparative and Psychological Psychology,* 1967, *63,* 28–33.

Owens, L., and Barnes, J. The relationships between cooperative, competitive, and individualized learning preferences and students' perceptions of classroom learning atmosphere. *American Educational Research Journal,* 1982, *19,* 182–200.

Packer, J., and Bain, J. D. Cognitive style and teacher-student compatibility. *Journal of Educational Psychology,* 1978, *70,* 864–871.

Papert, S. *Mindstorms.* New York: Basic Books, 1980.

Parnes, S. J., Noller, R. B., and Biondi, A. M. *Guide to creative action.* New York: Scribner, 1977.

Paulus, P. B., Annis, A. B., Seta, J. J., Schkade, J. K., and Matthews, R. W. Density does affect task performance. *Jour-*

nal of Personality and Social Psychology, 1976, 34, 248–253.

Payne, D. A. The specification and measurement of learning outcomes. Waltham, Mass.: Blaisdell, 1968.

Perkins, M. R. Measures of cognitive structure: Do they really assess learning at the level of comprehension? Ph.D. dissertation, University of Massachusetts, 1978.

Perlmutter, H. V., and de Montmollin, G. Group learning of nonsense syllables. Journal of Abnormal and Social Psychology, 1952, 47, 762–769.

Peterson, C. L., Danner, F. W., and Flavell, J. H. Developmental changes in children's response to three indications of communicative failure. Child Development, 1972, 43, 1463–1468.

Peterson, P. Direct instruction: Effective for what and for whom? Educational Leadership, 1979, 37, 46–48.

Piaget, J. The moral judgement of the child. London: Kegan Paul, 1932.

Piaget, J., and Inhelder, B. The growth of logical thinking from childhood to adolescence. Translated by A. Parsons and S. Seagrin. New York: Basic Books, 1958.

Popham, W. J. Criterion-referenced measurement. Englewood Cliffs, N.J.: Prentice-Hall, 1978.

Popham, W. J. Modern educational measurement. Englewood Cliffs, N.J.: Prentice-Hall, 1981.

Pressley, M., and Levin, J. R. Developmental constraints associated with children's use of the keyword method of foreign language vocabulary learning. Journal of Experimental Child Psychology, 1978, 26, 359–372.

Pressley, M., Levin, J. R., and Miller, G. E. How does the keyword method affect vocabulary comprehension and usage? Working paper No. 278. Wisconsin Research and Development Center for Individualized Schooling, March 1980.

Quay, H. C., Morse, W. C., and Cutler, R. L. Personality patterns of pupils in special classes for the emotionally disturbed. Exceptional Children, 1966, 33, 297–301.

Rawatsch, D. G. Implanting the computer in the classroom: Minnesota's successful statewide program. Phi Delta Kappan, February, 1981, 453–454.

Raymond, A. D. The acquisition of nonverbal behaviors by preservice science teachers and their application during student teaching. Dissertation Abstracts International, 1972, 32, 3846A.

Raugh, M. R., and Atkinson, R. C. A mnemonic method for learning a second-language vocabulary. Journal of Educational Psychology, 1975, 67, 1–16.

Reddy, M. The conduit metaphor: A case of frame conflict in our language about language. In A. Ortony (Ed.), Metaphor and thought. New York: Cambridge University Press, 1979.

Rickards, J. P. Adjunct postquestions in text: A critical review of methods and processes. Review of Educational Research, 1979, 49, 181–196.

Riesen, A. H. Arrested vision. Scientific American, 1950, 183, 16–19.

Rist, R. C. Student social class and teacher expectations: The self-fulfilling prophecy in ghetto education. Harvard Educational Review, 1970, 40, 411–451.

Robinson, W. P. The elaborated code in working class language. Language and Speech, 1965, 8, 243–252.

Rogers, C. R. Toward a modern approach to values. Journal of Abnormal and Social Psychology, 1964, 68, 160–167.

Rosenshine, B., and Furst, N. Research in teacher performance criteria. In B. O. Smith (Ed.), Research in teacher education: A symposium. Englewood Cliffs, N.J.: Prentice-Hall, 1971.

Rosenthal, R., and Jacobson, L. *Pygmalion in the classroom: Teacher expectation and pupils' intellectual development.* New York: Holt, Rinehart and Winston, 1968.

Rosenthal, R. *On the social psychology of the self-fulfilling prophecy: Further evidence for Pygmalion effects and their mediating mechanisms.* New York: MSS Modular Publications, 1974.

Rosenthal, R., Hall, J. A., Archer, D., DiMatteo, M. R., and Rogers, P. L. Measuring sensitivity to nonverbal communication: The PONS test. In A. Wolfgang (Ed.), *Nonverbal behavior.* New York: Academic Press, 1979.

Rothkopf, E. Z. Learning from written instructive material: An exploration of the control of inspection behavior by test-like events. *American Educational Research Journal,* 1966, *3,* 241–249.

Rothkopf, E. Z. Two scientific approaches to the management of instruction. In R. M. Gagné and W. J. Gephant (Eds.), *Learning research and school subjects.* Itasca, Ill.: Peacock, 1968.

Rothkopf, E. Z. The concept of mathemagenic activities. *Review of Educational Research,* 1970, *40,* 325–336.

Rothkopf, E. Z., and Kaplan, R. Exploration of the effect of density and specificity of instructional objectives on learning from text. *Journal of Educational Psychology,* 1972, *63,* 295–302.

Royer, J. M. Remembering: Constructive or reconstructive? In R. C. Anderson, R. J. Spiro, and W. E. Montague (Eds.), *Schooling and the acquisition of knowledge.* Hillsdale, N.J.: Erlbaum, 1977.

Royer, J. M. Theories of the transfer of learning. *Educational Psychologist,* 1979, *14,* 53–69.

Royer, J. M., and Allan, R. G. *Psychology of learning: Educational applications.* New York: Wiley, 1978.

Royer, J. M., and Cable, G. W. Facilitated learning in connected discourse. *Journal of Educational Psychology,* 1975, *67,* 116–123.

Royer, J. M., and Cable, G. W. Illustrations, analogies, and facilitative transfer in prose learning. *Journal of Educational Psychology,* 1976, *68,* 205–209.

Royer, J. M., and Cunningham, D. J. On the theory and measurement of reading comprehension. *Contemporary Educational Psychology,* 1981, *6,* 187–216.

Royer, J. M., and Perkins, M. R. Facilitative transfer in prose learning over an extended time period. *Journal of Reading Behavior,* 1977, *9,* 185–188.

Royer, J. M., Bates, J. A., and Konold, C. E. Learning from text: Methods of affecting reader intent. In A. H. Urquhart and J. C. Alderson (Eds.), *Reading in a second language.* London: Longman, 1983.

Rubovits, P., and Maehr, M. Pygmalion black and white. *Journal of Personality and Social Psychology,* 1973, *25,* 210–218.

Scandura, J. M., and Wells, J. N. Advance organizers in learning abstract mathematics. *American Educational Research Journal,* 1967, *4,* 295–301.

Scarr-Salapatek, S. Race, social class, and IQ. *Science,* 1971, *174,* 1285–1295.

Scarr-Salapatek, S., and Weinberg, R. A. When black children grow up in white homes. *Psychology Today,* 1975, *9,* 80–82.

Schachter, S. Deviation, rejection, and communication. *Journal of Abnormal and Social Psychology,* 1951, *46,* 190–207.

Schaie, K. W., and Parham, J. A. Cohort-sequential analysis of adult intellectual development. *Developmental Psychology,* 1977, *13,* 649–653.

Schank, R. C., and Abelson, R. P. *Scripts, plans, goals, and understanding.* Hillsdale, N.J.: Erlbaum, 1977.

Schlemmer, P. The Zoo-School: Evaluation of an alternative. *Phi Delta Kappan*, April, 1981, *62*, 558–560.

Schlesinger, I. M. Production of utterances and language acquisition. In D. I. Slobin (Ed.), *The autogenesis of grammar.* New York: Academic Press, 1971. Pp. 63–101.

Schoar, K. Behaviorist to help labor reduce dole roles. *Psychological Monitor*, June, 1976, *7*, 6.

Schwebel, A. I., and Cherlin, D. L. Physical and social distancing in teacher-pupil relationships. *Journal of Educational Psychology*, 1972, *63*, 543–550.

Scriven, M. The methodology of evaluation. In R. Tyler, R. Gagné, and M. Scriven (Eds.), *Perspectives on curriculum evaluation.* AERA Monograph Series on Curriculum Evaluation, No. 1. Chicago: Rand McNally, 1967.

Sears, R. R., Maccoby, E. E., and Lewin, H. *Patterns of child rearing.* Evanston, Ill.: Row, Peterson, 1957.

Seaver, W. B. Effects of naturally induced teacher expectancies. *Journal of Personality and Social Psychology*, 1973, *28*, 333–342.

Segall, M. H., Campbell, D. T., and Herskovits, M. J. *The influence of culture on visual perception.* Indianapolis: Bobbs-Merrill, 1966.

Seligman, M. E. P., and Maier, S. F. Failure to escape traumatic shock. *Journal of Experimental Psychology*, 1967, *74*, 1–9.

Seligman, M. E. P., Maier, S. F., and Solomon, R. L. Unpredictable and uncontrollable aversive events. In F. R. Bush (Ed.), *Aversive conditioning and learning.* New York: Academic Press, 1971.

Selman, R. L. Stages of role taking and moral judgement as guides to social intervention. In T. Lickona (Ed.), *Man and morality.* New York: Holt, 1974.

Sewell, W. H., and Shah, V. P. Social class, parental encouragement, and educational aspirations. *American Journal of Sociology*, 1968, *73*, 559–572.

Sharon, S., and Sharon, Y. *Small-group teaching.* Englewood Cliffs, N.J.: Educational Technology Publications, 1976.

Shaver, K. G. *An introduction to attribution processes.* Cambridge, Mass.: Winthrop, 1975.

Shaver, K. G. Defensive attribution: Effects of severity and relevance on the responsibility assigned for an accident. *Journal of Personality and Social Psychology*, 1970, *14*, 101–113.

Shaw, M. E., and Shaw, L. M. Some effects of sociometric grouping upon learning in a second grade classroom. *Journal of Social Psychology*, 1962, *57*, 453–458.

Shaw, M. E. *Group dynamics: The psychology of small group behavior.* New York: McGraw-Hill, 1976.

Sheppard, W. C., and Willoughby, R. H. *Child behavior: Learning and development.* Chicago: Rand McNally, 1975.

Sherif, M., Harvey, O., White, B., Hood, W., and Sherif, C. *Intergroup conflict and cooperation: The robbers cave experiment.* Norman: Institute of Group Relations, University of Oklahoma, 1961.

Shiffrin, R. M., and Atkinson, R. C. Storage and retrieval processes in long-term memory. *Psychological Review*, 1969, *76*, 179–193.

Shoemaker, J., and Fraser, H. W. What principals can do: Some implications of effective schooling. *Phi Delta Kappan*, 1981, *63*, 178–182.

Sidman, M. Avoidance conditioning with brief shock and no exteroceptive warning signal. *Science*, 1953, *118*, 157–158. (a)

Sidman, M. Two temporal parameters of the maintenance of avoidance behavior by the white rat. *Journal of Comparative and Physiological Psychology*, 1953, *46*, 253–261. (b)

Silberman, C. E. *Crisis in the classroom: The remaking of American education.* New York: Random House, 1970.

Silberman, H. F. *Experimental analysis of a beginning reading skill.* Santa Monica, Calif.: Systems Development Corporation, 1964.

Simon, S. B., Howe, L. W., and Kirschenbaum, H. *Values clarification: A handbook of practical strategies for teachers and students.* New York: Hart, 1972.

Skinner, B. F. *Verbal behavior.* New York: Appleton-Century-Crofts, 1957.

Skinner, B. F. *The technology of teaching.* New York: Appleton-Century-Crofts, 1968.

Skinner, B. F. *About behaviorism.* New York: Random House, 1974.

Slamecka, N. J. Studies of retention of connected discourse. *American Journal of Psychology,* 1959, *72,* 409–416.

Slamecka, N. J. Retroactive inhibition of connected discourse as a function of practice level. *Journal of Experimental Psychology,* 1960, *59,* 104–108.

Slamecka, N. J. Retention of connected discourse as a function of duration of interpolated learning. *Journal of Experimental Psychology,* 1962, *63,* 480–486.

Slavin, R. E. Student teams and achievement divisions. Paper presented at the annual meeting of the American Educational Research Association, San Francisco, 1979.

Slavin, R. E. *Using student team learning.* (Rev. ed.) Baltimore, Md.: Center for the Social Organization for Schools, 1980.

Slobin, D. I. Cognitive prerequisites for the development of grammar. In C. A. Ferguson (Ed.), *Studies of child language development.* New York: Holt, 1973.

Smith, S. L. School refusal with anxiety: A review of sixty-three cases. *Canadian Psychiatric Association Journal,* 1970,*15,* 257–264.

Snelbecker, G. E. *Learning theory, instruc-tional theory, and psychoeducational design.* New York: McGraw-Hill, 1974.

Snow, R. Unfinished Pygmalion. *Contemporary Psychology,* 1969, *14,* 197–199.

Solomon, D., Bezdek, W. E., and Rosenberg, L. *Teaching styles and learning.* Chicago: Center for the Study of Liberal Education for Adults, 1963.

Solomon, R. L., and Wynne, L. C. Traumatic avoidance learning: Acquisition in normal dogs. *Psychological Monographs,* 1953, *67* (354).

Sommer, R. *Personal space.* Englewood Cliffs, N.J.: Prentice-Hall, 1969.

Sommer, R., and Becker, F. D. Room density and user satisfaction. *Environment and Behavior,* 1971, *3,* 412–417.

Spalding, D. A. Instinct, with original observations on young animals. *Macmillan's Magazine,* 1873, *27,* 282–293.

Sperling, M. School phobias: Classification, dynamics, and treatment. *Psychoanalytic Study of the Child,* 1967, *22,* 375–401.

Sperry, L. (Ed.). *Learning performance and individual differences.* Glenview, Ill.: Scott, Foresman, 1972.

Spiro, R. J. Remembering information from text: Theoretical and empirical issues concerning the state of schema reconstruction hypothesis. In R. C. Anderson, R. J. Spiro, and W. E. Montague (Eds.), *Schooling and the acquisition of knowledge.* Hillsdale, N.J.: Erlbaum, 1977.

Stallings, J. A. How instructional processes relate to child outcomes in a national study of Follow Through. *Journal of Teacher Education,* 1976, *27,* 43–47.

Stallings, J. A. Allocated academic learning time revisited, or beyond time on task. *Educational Research,* 1980, *9,* 11–16.

Stanley, J. C. On educating the gifted. *Educational Researcher,* 1980, *9,* 8–12.

Stephan, W. G. School desegregation: An evaluation of predictions made in *Brown* v. *Board of Education. Psychological Bulletin,* 1978, *85,* 217–238.

Stephens, L. S. *The teacher's guide to open education.* New York: Holt, Rinehart and Winston, 1974.

Sternberg, R. J. *Intelligence, information processing, and analogical reasoning: The componential analysis of human abilities.* Hillsdale, N.J.: Erlbaum, 1977.

Stodolsky, S. S., and Lesser, G. Learning patterns in the disadvantaged. *Harvard Educational Review,* 1967, 37 (4), 546–593.

Strom, J. C., and Buck, R. W. Staring and participants' sex: Physiological and subjective reactions. *Personality and Social Psychology Bulletin,* 1979, *5,* 114–117.

Strommen, E. A., McKinney, J. P., and Fitzgerald, H. E. *Developmental psychology: The school-aged child.* Homewood, Ill.: Dorsey, 1977.

Student learning styles: Diagnosing and prescribing programs. Reston, Va.: National Association of Secondary School Principals, 1979.

Subkoviak, M. Estimating reliability from a single administration of a criterion-referenced test. *Journal of Educational Measurement,* 1976, *13,* 265–275.

Sulzer-Azaroff, B., and Mayer, G. R. *Applying behavior-analysis procedures with children and youth.* New York: Holt, Rinehart and Winston, 1977.

Sulzer-Azaroff, B., and Reese, E. P. *Applying behavioral analysis: A program for developing professional competence.* New York: Holt, Rinehart and Winston, 1982.

Suppes, P. Computer technology and the future of education. *Phi Delta Kappan,* April, 1968.

Swain, M., and Barik, H. C. Bilingual education for the English Canadian: Recent developments. In A. Simoes, Jr. (Ed.), *The bilingual child.* New York: Academic Press, 1976. Pp. 92–111.

Swaminathan, H., Hambleton, R. K., and Algina, J. Reliability of criterion-referenced tests: A decision-theoretic formulation. *Journal of Educational Measurement,* 1974, *11,* 263–268.

Tajfel, H. Social and cultural factors in perception. In G. Lindzey and E. Aronson (Eds.), *The handbook of social psychology,* Vol. 3. Reading, Mass.: Addison-Wesley, 1969.

Terman, L. M., and Oden, M. H. *The gifted child grows up.* Stanford, Calif.: Stanford University Press, 1947.

Thomas, D. R., Becker, W. C., and Armstrong, M. Production and elimination of disruptive behavior by systematically varying teacher's behavior. *Journal of Applied Behavior Analysis,* 1968, *1,* 35–45.

Thorndike, E. L. Animal intelligence: An experimental study of the associative processes in animals. *Psychological Review,* 1898, Monograph Supplement.

Thorndike, E. L., and Woodworth, R. S. The influence of improvement in one mental function upon the efficiency of other functions. *Psychological Review,* 1901, *8,* 247–261.

Thorndike, R. L., and Hagen, E. *Measurement and evaluation in psychology and education.* (3rd ed.) New York: John Wiley, 1969.

Torrance, E. P. Current research on the nature of creative talent. *Journal of Counseling Psychology,* 1959, *6,* 309–316.

Torrance, E. P. Factors affecting creative thinking in children: An interim research report. *Merrill-Palmer Quarterly of Behavior and Development,* 1961, *7,* 171–180.

Torrance, E. P. Sociodrama as a creative problem solving approach to studying the future. *Journal of Creative Behavior,* 1975, *9,* 182–195.

Torrance, E. P. Five models for constructing

creativity instructional materials. *Creative Child and Adult Quarterly*, 1978, *3*, 8–14.

Torres, S. (Ed.). *A primer on individualized education programs for handicapped children*. Reston, Va.: Foundation for Exceptional Children, 1977.

Turnbull, A. P., and Schulz, J. B. *Mainstreaming handicapped students: A guide for the classroom teacher*. Boston: Allyn and Bacon, 1979.

Tyler, R. W. Permanence of learning. *Journal of Higher Education*, 1934, *4*, 203–204. (a)

Tyler, R. W. *Constructing achievement tests*. Columbus: Ohio State University, 1934. (b)

Ullmann, L. P., and Krasner, L. *A psychological approach to abnormal behavior*. Englewood Cliffs, New Jersey: Prentice-Hall, 1969.

Underwood, B. J. Interference and forgetting. *Psychological Review*, 1957, *64*, 49–60.

Underwood, B. J., and Keppel, G. One-trial learning? *Journal of Verbal Learning and Verbal Behavior*, 1962, *1*, 1–13.

Van Riper, C. *Speech correction: Principles and methods*. Englewood Cliffs, N.J.: Prentice-Hall, 1972.

Waring, M. G. Personalizing the high school—via computer. *Phi Delta Kappan*, February, 1981, 455.

Watts, G. H., and Anderson, R. C. Effects of three types of inserted questions on learning from prose. *Journal of Educational Psychology*, 1971, *62*, 387–394.

Webb, N. M. Group composition, group interaction, and achievement in cooperative small groups. *Journal of Educational Psychology*, 1982, *74* (4), 475–484.

Weiner, B., and Rukla, A. An attributional analysis of achievement motivation. *Journal of Personality and Social Psychology*, 1970, *15*, 1–20.

Weiner, B. A Theory of motivation for some classroom experiences. *Journal of Educational Psychology*, 1979, *71*, 3–25.

Weiner, B., Russell, D., and Lerman, D. The cognitism-emotion process in achievement-related contexts. *Journal of Personality and Social Psychology*, 1979, *37*, 1211–1220.

Weinstein, C. S. The physical environment of the school: A review of the research. *Review of Educational Research*, 1979, *49*, 577–610.

Weinstein, C. S., and Woolfolk, A. The physical environment as a source of students' expectations about teaching. Paper presented at the annual meeting of the American Educational Research Association, 1979.

Weiss, M., and Burke, A. A five- to ten-year follow-up of hospitalized school phobic children and adolescents. *American Journal of Orthopsychiatry*, 1970, *40*, 672–676.

Weitzman, L. J., Eifler, D., Hokada, E., and Ross, C. Sex role socialization in picture books for preschool children. *American Journal of Sociology*, 1972, *77*, 1125–1150.

Wender, P. H., and Eisenberg, L. Minimal brain dysfunction in children. In S. Arieti (Ed.), *American handbook of psychiatry*, Vol. 2. (2nd ed.) New York: Basic Books, 1974.

Wessells, M. G. *Cognitive psychology*. New York: Harper & Row, 1982.

Wetherford, M. J., and Cohen, L. B. Developmental changes in infant visual preferences for novelty and familiarity. *Child Development*, 1973, *44*, 416–424.

White, G. D., Nielson, G., and Johnson, S. M. Timeout duration and the suppression of deviant behavior in children. *Journal of Applied Behavior Analysis*, 1972, *5*, 111–120.

White, H. B. Testing as an aid to learning. *Educational Administration and Supervision*, 1932, *18*, 41–46.

White, R., and Lippitt, R. *Autocracy and democracy*. New York: Harper, 1960.

White, S. W. Evidence for a hierarchial arrangement of learning processes. In L. Lipsitt and C. C. Spiker (Eds.), *Advances in child development and behavior*, Vol. 2. New York: Academic Press, 1965.

Whorf, B. L. *Language, thought, and reality*. New York: Wiley, 1956.

Wiley, D. E. Another hour, another day: Quantity of schooling, a potent path for policy. In W. H. Sewell, R. M. Hansen, and D. L. Featherman (Eds.), *Schooling and achievement in American society*. New York: Academic Press, 1976.

Williams, R. G., and Ware, J. E. Validity of student ratings of instruction under different incentive conditions. *Journal of Educational Psychology*, 1976, *68*, 48–56.

Willson, J. A. Changes in mean level of thinking in grades 1–8 through use of an interaction analysis system based on Bloom's taxonomy. *Journal of Educational Research*, 1973, *66*, 423–429.

Winne, P. H. Experiments relating teacher's use of higher cognitive questions to student achievement. *Review of Educational Research*, 1979, *49*, 13–50.

Winterbottom, M. R. The relation of childhood training in independence to achievement motivation. Ph. D. dissertation, University of Michigan, 1953.

Withall, J. The development of a climate index. *Journal of Educational Research*, 1951, *45*, 93–99.

Witkin, H. A., Moore, C. A., Goodenough, D. R., and Cox, P. W. Field-dependent and field-independent cognitive styles and their educational implications. *Review of Educational Research*, 1977, *47*, 1–64.

Wittrock, M. C. Learning as a generative process. *Educational Psychologist*, 1974, *11*, 87–95.

Wolf, M. M., Risley, T. R., and Mees, H. L. Application of operant conditioning procedures to the behavior problems of an autistic child. *Behavior Research and Therapy*, 1964, *1*, 305–312.

Wolfgang, A. (Ed.). *Nonverbal behavior: Applications and cultural implications* New York: Academic Press, 1979.

Wright, H. F. *Recording and analyzing child behavior*. New York: Harper & Row, 1967.

Yee, A. Interpersonal attitudes of teachers and disadvantaged pupils. *Journal of Human Resources*, 1968, *3*, 327–345.

Yucker, H. E. Group atmosphere and memory. *Journal of Abnormal and Social Psychology*, 1955, *51*, 17–23.

Zeleny, L. D. Characteristics of group leaders. *Sociology and Social Research*, 1939, *24*, 140–149.

Zimmerman, J., and Ferster, C. B. Intermittent punishment of S^Δ responding in matching-to-sample. *Journal of the Experimental Analysis of Behavior*, 1963, *6*, 349–356.

Zimmerman, J., and Boydan, N. T. Punishment of S responding of humans in conditional matching-to-sample by timeout. *Journal of the Experimental Analysis of Behavior*, 1963, *6*, 589–597.

Zucker, A. A. The computer in the school: A case study. *Phi Delta Kappan*, January, 1982, 317–319.

Zukerman, M., and Wheeler, L. To dispel fantasy about the fantasy-based measure of fear of success. *Psychological Bulletin*, 1975, *82*, 932–946.

NAME INDEX

ABOUT THE AUTHORS

James M. Royer and Robert S. Feldman are active researchers in their respective areas: classroom instruction and learning, and social and cultural factors relating to education. They both teach educational psychology at the University of Massachusetts, where Royer is Professor, and Feldman is Associate Professor, of Psychology and Education. In 1983 Professor Royer also served as Acting Chair of the Department of Psychology.

A Note on the Type

The text of this book is set in CALEDONIA, a Linotype face designed by W. A. Dwiggins. It belongs to the family of printing types called "modern face" by printers—a term used to mark the change in style of type-letters that occurred about 1800. Caledonia borders on the general design of Scotch Modern, but is more freely drawn than that letter.

This book was composed by Monotype Composition Company, Baltimore, Md., printed and bound by R. R. Donnelley & Sons Co., Crawfordsville, Indiana.

Cover design by Marsha Cohen.
Text design by Karin Kincheloe.